PowerShell Advanced Cookbook

Enhance your scripting skills and master PowerShell with 90+ advanced recipes

Morten Elmstrøm Hansen

www.bpbonline.com

First Edition 2024

Copyright © BPB Publications, India

ISBN: 978-93-55516-732

To View Complete
BPB Publications Catalogue
Scan the QR Code:

Dedicated to

*My beloved wife **Janni**, my sons **Theo-Maximillian** and*
***Milo-Matthæus**, my family, my in-laws,*
my friends and my colleagues at Energi Danmark

About the Author

Morten Elmstrøm Hansen is a dedicated IT professional and entrepreneur. For the past eight years he has been working at Energi Danmark, one of Denmark's leading energy companies. He plays a central role in the IT operations department where he leverages his expertise in PowerShell development, DevOps and server administration to monitor, optimize and automate essential processes, ensuring operational continuity. Morten is proficient in containerization and kubernetes as well as cloud technologies and he utilizes his skills to be the forefront for larger projects involving such cutting-edge technologies.

His professional qualifications include a certification in PowerShell Administration, an AP degree in IT technology and additional courses in digital marketing. Morten also holds a mix of several other technical and commercial educations such as a business college education that provides a solid foundation in commerce and administration, with a focus on economics, sales, communication and IT. Furthermore, he has a higher technical education that combines technical and scientific subjects with general academics. Additionally, he pursued a higher preparatory examination focusing on mathematics and psychology, further preparing him for his academic and professional pursuits in technology.

In addition to his role in IT, Morten co-owns and serves as the part time CFO of a family cleaning business. He also owns and manages an online store, where he applies his skills in digital marketing, IT and economics. His diverse roles demonstrate his ability to navigate and excel in multiple fields, from IT management and development to business operations.

On a personal note, Morten is a devoted family man, living with his wife and two youngest children, on the outskirts of one of Denmark's largest cities.

About the Reviewers

❖ **Lasse Hein Olesen** is an IT Service Engineer, working within the MES and automation field, with an expertise in troubleshooting and problem solving. He is passionate about anything IT related and is always interested in learning something new and finding new challenges. He actually learned PowerShell from Morten, the author of this book. It is his first time being a technical reviewer. He's currently focusing on advancing his PowerShell skills and expanding/building up his homelab. He is hoping to explore DevOps and Kubernetes in the near future.

❖ **Tibor Soós** is a freelance PowerShell developer and trainer, having over 25 years of extensive experience in automating Windows, Active Directory, Exchange, Azure AD, Jira Service Desk and various Identity and Access Management systems like Saviynt, CyberArk, SecZetta. He has contributed his expertise to industry-leading enterprises, showcasing a deep understanding of PowerShell as a former MVP and the author of a Hungarian-language PowerShell book.

Tibor is committed to empowering IT professionals with his wealth of knowledge and his enterprise-grade productivity modules, offering guidance and best practices to enhance their scripting and automation capabilities.

Acknowledgement

My deepest gratitude and heartfelt appreciation to my wife Janni Elmstrøm Hansen and our two boys Theo-Maximillian and Milo-Matthæus. Without you and your continuous love and support, this book would never have become a reality. Even during moments of doubt and harsh times, you are always there to pick me up and make sure I follow my heart and my dreams. You will always be the love of my life and the soul of my being.

I am also deeply grateful for the never-ending love and support from my family: My dad Johnny, my mom Lene, my brother Mads, and my sister Julie and for my wife's family. Without you I would not be the person I am today. You have always picked me up, held me when needed and supported me, especially through the tough times in life.

I would also like to thank and acknowledge all my close friends in life and all my colleagues at Energi Danmark. Thank you for your invaluable support and for always believing in me. You have all been instrumental in my personal and professional development throughout the years, and you have taught and given me more than I could have ever asked for.

Additionally I would like to extend my sincerest appreciation to the reviewers of this book, Lasse Hein Olesen and Tibor Soós. Your input and attention to detail have been invaluable in creating this book and i am deeply grateful for your dedication and support.

Finally, I would like to thank BPB Publications for this incredible opportunity and for all the help and support throughout the journey of making this book become a reality.

Preface

PowerShell is a powerful scripting language, automation framework and command-line shell developed by Microsoft that is built on the .NET framework. It is an essential tool because it allows system administrators and developers to automate and optimize complex administrative tasks across multiple systems efficiently. PowerShell's deep integration with Windows and other Microsoft products makes it an invaluable tool for administrating, managing and optimizing Windows environments.

This book is intended for developers and system administrators with a novice or intermediate understanding of PowerShell who are looking to advance their skills. It is also beneficial for experienced professionals seeking to enhance their existing PowerShell capabilities.

Designed as a cookbook, this book enables readers to expand and build upon their current PowerShell knowledge and skillset. Topics covered in detail include creating PowerShell unit tests using Pester, managing and administrating Azure and AWS cloud services, remote script execution, Active Directory management, PowerShell desired state configuration and more. Each chapter includes recipes that delves into the topics, accompanied by code examples and walkthroughs. After reading this book, readers should have gained knowledge and skills that enables them to build better and more advanced scripts and applications while also understanding key principles of automation and optimization. This will also enable the readers to streamline processes and enhance administrative tasks more efficiently using PowerShell.

Chapter 1: Introduction to Advanced PowerShell Concepts – Explores advanced PowerShell concepts, scripting best practices, and the configuration and setup of the Visual Studio Code **Integrated Development Environment (IDE)**. The chapter also makes a short introduction to the different PowerShell versions available and furthermore, it introduces PowerShell providers which are used to facilitate and provide access to data across different data stores.

Chapter 2: Advanced PowerShell Functions – Delves into advanced PowerShell functions and covers a detailed explanation of its structure and capabilities, including dynamic parameters, parameter sets and lifecycle events. It also covers key elements such as the CmdletBinding attribute, parameter validation and output formatting. Furthermore, it explains how to implement handling for pipeline input and the ShouldProcess capability. The chapter also introduces object-oriented PowerShell concepts in the form of PowerShell classes. It offers a step-by-step guide to constructing classes with properties and methods.

Chapter 3: Flow Control and Looping – Is about using different methods for controlling and optimizing the flow of script execution. It introduces the reader to conditional statements using comparison and logical operators. It deeply covers advanced looping techniques such as nested loops, labelled breaks and continue statements, the use of retry logic in loops and the use of pipeline processing and also the Foreach-Object loop for iterating collections. Additionally, it explains how to utilize the switch statement to handle multiple conditions and it delves into using script blocks for dynamic and flexible flow control in terms of callbacks and event handlers. Furthermore, the chapter introduces the reader to multi-threading in the forms of parallel processing using PowerShell jobs and non-sequential processing using the Foreach-Objects parallel parameter.

Chapter 4: Error Handling – Dives deep into error handling in PowerShell and introduces the reader to topics such as handling different types of errors, implementing error handling blocks in advanced scenarios and how to use the ErrorAction preference variable and the ErrorAction parameter. It also showcase how to create custom error classes for enhanced error reporting and how to handle errors in background jobs.

Chapter 5: Scripting Techniques – Focuses on a range of different scripting techniques that are common among different programming languages but with a focus on such techniques tailored specifically for PowerShell. The chapter covers topics such as script parameters, parameter validation, string manipulation and formatting techniques and scripting for cross-platform compatibility. Additionally, it introduces the reader to PowerShell execution policies and script signing for enhancing script security. Furthermore, the chapter dives deeper into the creation of PowerShell modules and repositories which are essential for organizing and distributing PowerShell code efficiently.

Chapter 6: Remote Script Execution: PowerShell Remote Management – Guides the reader through setting up, configuring, and securely managing remote PowerShell sessions using PowerShell remoting and Windows remote management. It explains how to use session configurations to restrict and grant privileges and permissions for specific users and groups on remote hosts. The chapter also provides a more in-depth insight into securing and authenticating remote sessions using credentials, encrypted XML files, the Windows credential manager and also how to configure secure and encrypted certificate-based authentication.

Chapter 7: Testing with Pester – Introduces the reader to the Pester PowerShell testing framework. The chapter will guide the reader through setting up the Pester framework and it dives into Pesters structure and components. The chapter covers how to create unit tests for PowerShell functions, how to group and organize tests and how to mock dependencies. Furthermore, the chapter will provide strategies for testing infrastructure components and also how to implement code coverage analysis in tests.

Chapter 8: Working with XML and JSON – Presents a detailed introduction to XML and JSON that are used for representing and structuring data in formats that are both human readable and easy for scripts and applications to interpret. While the main focus is targeted at XML, the reader will learn how to read and write XML files using cmdlets, the XML accelerator and by using .NET classes, but the reader will also learn how to read and write JSON files and how to convert between JSON and PowerShell objects. It also dives into querying and extracting data from XML files using XPath expressions and how to serialize and deserialize PowerShell objects using CliXml.

Chapter 9: Active Directory Management - Delves into the essentials of managing and automating Active Directory tasks using PowerShell. This chapter introduces the ActiveDirectory module which is an essential tool in PowerShell for interacting with AD environments. The reader will learn how to manage AD users and groups efficiently. The chapter also introduces techniques for performing bulk operations, which are crucial in larger organizations where managing numerous accounts manually is impractical. Furthermore, it explores how to query and filter AD objects effectively, using PowerShell's filtering capabilities to streamline administrative Active Directory tasks.

Chapter 10: Managing Azure with PowerShell – Examens Azure cloud services management using the Azure command line interface (AzureCLI) and PowerShell. This chapter covers working with and managing Azure virtual machines, storage accounts, blobs, and file shares. It also dives deeper into Azure EntraID and focuses on the creation and management of users, groups, and resource access permissions. Additionally, it provides insight into automating resource provisioning and management focusing on creating service principals that are used for programmatically connecting to Azure using scripts and also how to create scripts that are used for configuration and automatic provisioning of Azure resources.

Chapter 11: Managing AWS with PowerShell – Walks through AWS cloud services management and introduces the AWS tools for PowerShell. It describes how to install and configure these tools and also how to configure credentials for accessing AWS programmatically. The chapter dives deeper into AWS **identity** and **access management (IAM)** showcasing how to manage IAM users and groups and how to create and manage access keys, permissions, and policies. Furthermore, the chapter not only describes how to create and manage EC2 instances, key pairs and security groups but also how to manage S3 buckets and how to upload and download objects to such buckets.

Chapter 12: Microsoft 365 Applications Management – Showcases how to install and use specific application modules that focus on different aspects of Microsoft 365 applications management. The chapter covers management of SharePoint online, Exchange online and Microsoft Teams using PowerShell. Additionally, it introduces the Microsoft Graph API and the Microsoft Graph PowerShell SDK module describing installation, configuration, and authentication. Furthermore, the chapter gives an overview of how to manage Entra ID users and licenses using PowerShell and the modules.

Chapter 13: Desired State Configuration – Provides an extensive insight into desired state configuration with PowerShell and outlines how to write and apply meta configurations from a centralized management server to remote nodes and DSC configurations on remote target nodes. This includes configuring local configuration managers, creating DSC configurations for managing infrastructure and using public resource modules. The chapter also describes how to remove resources and configurations and how to handle failed configurations.

Chapter 14: Managing Windows Components – Is about using PowerShell to manage different Windows server and workstation components. The chapter covers how to create, manage, and delete windows services, how to start and manage processes, how to manage and configure network settings and how to initialize, partition and format disks. It also dives deeper into firewall rules and the Windows task scheduler.

Chapter 15: SAPIEN PowerShell Studio IDE – Explores the advanced PowerShell IDE created by SAPIEN Technologies. This IDE takes PowerShell scripting to a new level and enables you to not only create advanced scripts from templates but also to easily create and compile sophisticated GUI applications, Windows services, and packaged executables from your PowerShell scripts. This chapter introduces the IDE and demonstrates how to use it to create GUI applications and Windows Services. Furthermore, it depicts how to compile scripts into executables and how to create MSI installers for executables using the packager and installer managers. It also peeks into more applications created by SAPIEN Technologies such as the PowerShell module manager and the VersionRecall versioning and backup tool.

Code Bundle and Coloured Images

Please follow the link to download the
Code Bundle and the *Coloured Images* of the book:

https://rebrand.ly/q7m2itb

The code bundle for the book is also hosted on GitHub at
https://github.com/bpbpublications/PowerShell-Advanced-Cookbook.
In case there's an update to the code, it will be updated on the existing GitHub repository.

We have code bundles from our rich catalogue of books and videos available at
https://github.com/bpbpublications. Check them out!

Errata

We take immense pride in our work at BPB Publications and follow best practices to ensure the accuracy of our content to provide with an indulging reading experience to our subscribers. Our readers are our mirrors, and we use their inputs to reflect and improve upon human errors, if any, that may have occurred during the publishing processes involved. To let us maintain the quality and help us reach out to any readers who might be having difficulties due to any unforeseen errors, please write to us at :

errata@bpbonline.com

Your support, suggestions and feedbacks are highly appreciated by the BPB Publications' Family.

Did you know that BPB offers eBook versions of every book published, with PDF and ePub files available? You can upgrade to the eBook version at www.bpbonline. com and as a print book customer, you are entitled to a discount on the eBook copy. Get in touch with us at :

business@bpbonline.com for more details.

At **www.bpbonline.com**, you can also read a collection of free technical articles, sign up for a range of free newsletters, and receive exclusive discounts and offers on BPB books and eBooks.

Piracy

If you come across any illegal copies of our works in any form on the internet, we would be grateful if you would provide us with the location address or website name. Please contact us at **business@bpbonline.com** with a link to the material.

If you are interested in becoming an author

If there is a topic that you have expertise in, and you are interested in either writing or contributing to a book, please visit **www.bpbonline.com**. We have worked with thousands of developers and tech professionals, just like you, to help them share their insights with the global tech community. You can make a general application, apply for a specific hot topic that we are recruiting an author for, or submit your own idea.

Reviews

Please leave a review. Once you have read and used this book, why not leave a review on the site that you purchased it from? Potential readers can then see and use your unbiased opinion to make purchase decisions. We at BPB can understand what you think about our products, and our authors can see your feedback on their book. Thank you!

For more information about BPB, please visit **www.bpbonline.com**.

Join our book's Discord space

Join the book's Discord Workspace for Latest updates, Offers, Tech happenings around the world, New Release and Sessions with the Authors:

https://discord.bpbonline.com

Table of Contents

CHAPTER 1
Introduction to Advanced PowerShell Concepts

Introduction

This chapter of the book introduces you to the concepts of advanced PowerShell and advanced scripting best practices. It will also cover the basics of setting up the **integrated development environment (IDE)** used in this book. We are primarily using the Visual Studio Code IDE with PowerShell extension, but another more advanced PowerShell specific IDE will also be introduced and will be covered more in detail in another chapter. In this chapter we will also look at the different newer PowerShell versions like PowerShell 5, PowerShell 7, and PowerShell Core. Lastly this chapter will make an introduction to the different PowerShell providers that can be used to navigate and leverage the different data stores such as the filesystem, registry, certificate, environment and so on. Most of the code and examples in this book can be used in the different mentioned versions of PowerShell, but some examples might need a specific version like PowerShell 5 or PowerShell 7. In our examples we are (primarily) using PowerShell 7 unless else is specified. If a specific PowerShell version is needed for a specific code example or recipe, it will be mentioned in detail regarding that specific context. Unless else is mentioned specifically, the recipes and examples in this book are created in Windows 10 (And should also be applicable in Windows 8 and Windows 11).

Structure

The chapter covers the following topics:

- Introduction to advanced PowerShell concepts
- PowerShell scripting best practices
- PowerShell integrated development environment
    - **Recipe 1:** Install and set up Visual Studio Code with PowerShell Extension
- Advanced Sapien PowerShell Studio IDE
- PowerShell versions
- PowerShell providers
    - **Recipe 2:** Use providers to access data stores

Objectives

After this chapter you will know more about advanced concepts of PowerShell and know more about what is needed to leverage its full potential to automate complex tasks, managing different systems, streamline administrative processes and build better and more advanced scripts. You will have learnt about common best scripting practices that makes sure your scripts are reliable and efficient and that you keep a certain standard when creating scripts. You will be introduced to different IDE´s and how to setup the VS Code IDE, which is used in this book, and how to utilize this to write scripts and run PowerShell commands directly in the IDE. You will also have been introduced to the more advanced PowerShell IDE, Sapien PowerShell studio, about which we will cover in more detail in a later chapter. Furthermore, you will have been introduced to different PowerShell versions, and learnt how they differ and what the use cases are for these versions. Lastly, you will also have learnt about the PowerShell providers and how to utilize these to access and work with the data in different data stores such as the Windows Registry, the filesystem, certificate stores and more.

Introduction to advanced PowerShell concepts

Advanced PowerShell involves the use of powerful features and techniques that extends beyond the main usage of the PowerShell scripting language. These concepts are for more experienced and expert users who would want to use the full potential of PowerShell for tasks like automation, managing systems and greatly improving scripts. Some of the key aspects of advanced PowerShell are to build modular scripts instead of building simple scripts. The case of breaking down a script into modular and reusable components makes it much more maintainable. This can be broken down to practically defining advanced functions, creating modules, and organizing your scripts into several files to make them more manageable. This will also make it a lot easier to promote code reuse and help in collaboration between different developers.

An example would be if you have created a function in a script that could be reused in other scripts, then instead of having to copy-paste the function into these, you would either create a file containing that function, or even better, to make it more advanced you would create a module and add the function to that module instead for re-usability. Then you would only have to install that specific module on your systems and import it, so you would be able to use that function in every scope and context whenever you need it just by calling it, since it would then already be imported into that scope or context. This is the same principle as with built-in modules and `cmdlet`s that are available to you when you open a new PowerShell session, here it is only your own custom function that are available and can be reused whenever needed, without having to copy-paste or importing it from a specific file every time you would have to use that function. Additionally, you would only have to update and make changes to the function in one place, the module, instead of having to handle multiple copies of a file, in different script paths, where the function file might have been copied too, and then must update the function in each of these files. Just by utilizing this method you would already have begun to make optimizations to your scripts and making use of advanced concepts.

Another necessary aspect of advanced PowerShell is the use of error handling and managing exceptions. Basic PowerShell scripts often lack extensive error handling which is crucial to building a robust script. Implementing advanced error handling mechanisms into scripts greatly improves the reliability and resilience of the script. This includes the use of try-catch blocks to catch and handle exceptions, logging errors for troubleshooting purposes, and displaying user-friendly error messages. Pipeline processing, **object-oriented programming (OOP)**, PowerShell remoting, Classes, workflows, jobs, **desired state configuration (DSC)** and integrating and interacting with other technologies and systems are other fundamental concepts when it comes to advanced PowerShell. This book will cover the various advanced features and concepts that PowerShell offers and when combining the different knowledge from these advanced concepts, you will be able to create more advanced scripts and even write programs using PowerShell, that can be used to greatly optimize and automate not only your scripting and development tasks, but also improve and streamline a lot of your current scripts that you may already have to use in your daily work.

PowerShell scripting best practices

To make sure your scripts and your programs are reliable and efficient it is always a good idea to follow some best practices. Even though best practices are exactly that, *best practices*, meaning they are not resolute and different people have different opinions on what these are, there are still a lot of commonalities between them. These are the following practices I consider to be essential to write powerful and optimal scripts and programs:

- **Use readable and self-documenting code**: Your code should be easy to read and should be understandable. You should use meaningful names for variables, functions, classes, and other elements. You should provide clear comments to explain important details and more complex logic. It is also a good idea to document your scripts with details about its purpose and more specific usage instructions, especially if they should be shared with others.

- **Break your scripts down into reusable functions and modules**: This improves the organization of the code, encourages code reuse and in general simplifies the overall maintenance of your scripts. Each function and class must have a clear purpose and must be designed to perform specific tasks.

- **Gracefully handle errors**: This means to implement proper error handling in your scripts. You should use try-catch-finally blocks to catch and handle exceptions, log errors for troubleshooting purposes and return descriptive error messages to the users. Implementing effective error handling will significantly improve the reliability and resilience of your scripts.

- **Validate input parameters to ensure the stability and security of your scripts**: You should use parameter validation to make sure that constraints are set on input values, especially from users. This can prevent unexpected behavior and script failures and ensures that input values are provided as the correct data types.

- **Use pipeline processing to streamline the processing of data:** Make sure to use `cmdlet`'s and functions that supports pipeline input and output to use filtering and sorting of the data. This also reduces the use of complex loops since this will be handled by the pipeline processor instead.

- **Test and debug your scripts, in different scenarios and environments**: Make use of the built-in functionalities for testing and debugging, like using breakpoints and making unit tests for your functions and classes. This makes it a lot easier to catch issues early in the process and makes your scripts more reliable. You should set up different test scenarios and make extensive testing in different environments.

- **Use a main function**: It is not required in PowerShell like it is in some other programming languages, it would still be a good idea to use a main function in your code. This gives a clear starting point and better control of the flow in your scripts. It also helps you to avoid polluting the global scope and makes it generally more readable. A lot of PowerShell developers do not use a main function in their scripts, but personally I prefer this method, especially when creating Windows services with PowerShell, where the services main loop is an encapsulated function inside the script itself, making it impossible for the function to call the running service script itself from inside that function, at least without a lot of issues and errors, using a main function would solve this. For simple and smaller scripts, adopting the use of a main function might not make much sense and can be omitted. It is generally up to the user to decide whether to use a main function, but as with the Windows PowerShell service, in some cases it is unavoidable and should then be implemented as a default best practice to follow.

- **Performance optimize your scripts**: Especially when dealing with larger sets of data. Here techniques like parallel processing, caching, and optimizing your loops can greatly improve the performance and minimize execution time. If you are using PowerShell 7, implement the use of the *-parallel* switch when using **For Each-Object**. Go through your code and figure out if and where you can optimize the code, can you replace loops with piping something instead and so on.

- **Versioning control**: Another valuable practice is to implement the use of a versioning control system, like GIT. This makes it a lot easier to work together with other developers but also gives you a history of the changes in your scripts and makes it easier to roll back to a previous version if needed. It is also a great method for having backups of your scripts and their different versions.

By following these or at least some of these best practices, you should be able to create scripts that are much more reliable and efficient. And as you are getting better and more experienced in your coding you will eventually adopt your own best practices for your own specific needs. Through this book, we will investigate several topics and recipes that will incorporate these practices for creating efficient and advanced scripts and using techniques that are based on these practices used in different scenarios.

PowerShell integrated development environment

An **integrated development environment** (IDE) is an invaluable tool when it comes to writing advanced and powerful PowerShell scripts, and in software development in general. Without the benefits of the advanced capabilities these tools offer, it could be quite cumbersome to write efficient scripts and programs. An IDE provides a centralized workspace for coding that combines a code editor with debugging capabilities and other essential functionalities into a single program. Some features of an IDE include the ability to highlight syntax, code completion, formatting, line numbering and most of them also provides an integrated terminal or console so you can run commands directly from the IDE without having to use and switch to external tools. These are just the most basic features that an IDE includes, each has its own strengths and weaknesses, it all depends on the preferences of the individual user. Some IDE´s can be used for multiple languages like the Visual Studio Code editor and other IDE´s are meant for more specific languages like the Sapien PowerShell studio which is built solely for PowerShell.

The Visual Studio Code editor is a more lightweight and versatile editor that is free to use both privately and commercially. This editor can also be used on both Windows, Linux, and Mac, but its strength comes in all the extensions that are publicly available, which supports almost every language that you can think of. This makes it a valid choice for scripting and programming purposes, also for PowerShell with the VS Code PowerShell extension. As the writing of this, note that the VS Code PowerShell extension only works for PowerShell version 5.1 or higher. If you want a more advanced and PowerShell specific IDE, the professional-grade Sapien PowerShell studio is recommended. Not only does it offer advanced features for PowerShell script development, like a fully featured PowerShell editor and debugger, but it also includes a GUI designer, features for creating Windows services and packaging capabilities like creating MSI installers and more.

These are just two PowerShell capable IDE´s and again, it all depends on your personal preferences and use cases. For even advanced scripts the VS Code is a more than competent solution, but if you really want to utilize all features and make advanced and powerful scripts and programs, you should go with a specialized tool like the Sapien PowerShell studio. Other valid PowerShell capable IDE´s on the market are PowerGUI, Atom, sublime text and PowerShell Plus. Each with its own strengths and weaknesses. Some of them are specific for PowerShell and others are PowerShell capable with packages and extensions, like the VS Code. Microsoft even has its own PowerShell IDE, the ISE which is a Windows integrated host application for Windows PowerShell. I will not go in much detail about the ISE, since it is no longer in active feature development from Microsoft, but it continues to be officially supported for security and high-priority service fixes though, and there are currently no plans to remove it from Windows. Still Microsoft states that users looking for ISE replacements should use the VS code with PowerShell extensions. The recipes in this book will primarily be created with the use of the VS Code with PowerShell extension, unless it is stated for a specific recipe or chapter. In a later chapter we will dive deeper into the advanced Sapien PowerShell studio and see some of the more advanced features it has to offer. You might already use an IDE that is capable with PowerShell and have the experience using it, then the next recipe might not be for you, and you can skip ahead in the chapter, but for more novice and intermediate users, it would be a good idea to make an introduction to VS Code in this book and explore some of the features it has to offer. For more advanced users, you should look into the Sapien PowerShell studio, which is as mentioned, a professional grade PowerShell IDE and tool that you will find invaluable once you start using it.

Recipe 1: Install and set up Visual Studio Code with PowerShell Extension

In this book we are primarily using the Visual Studio code with PowerShell extension for creating the recipes. As mentioned earlier this is free to use both personally and commercially and is powerful enough to cover a lot of advanced tasks. Throughout this book, we will refer to this editor as VS Code.

There are several downloadable versions. One for user specific installation, one for system wide (all users) installation, a .zip file for stand-alone and a basic CLI version of VS code. They are all supported for different OS architectures like x64, x86 and Arm64. Select and download the version that suits your needs. Installing the user version is recommended, unless you are on a shared computer, and other users should have the tool available, then use the system installer.

1. Download VS Code from the following link **https://code.visualstudio.com/ Download** as shown in *Figure 1.1*:

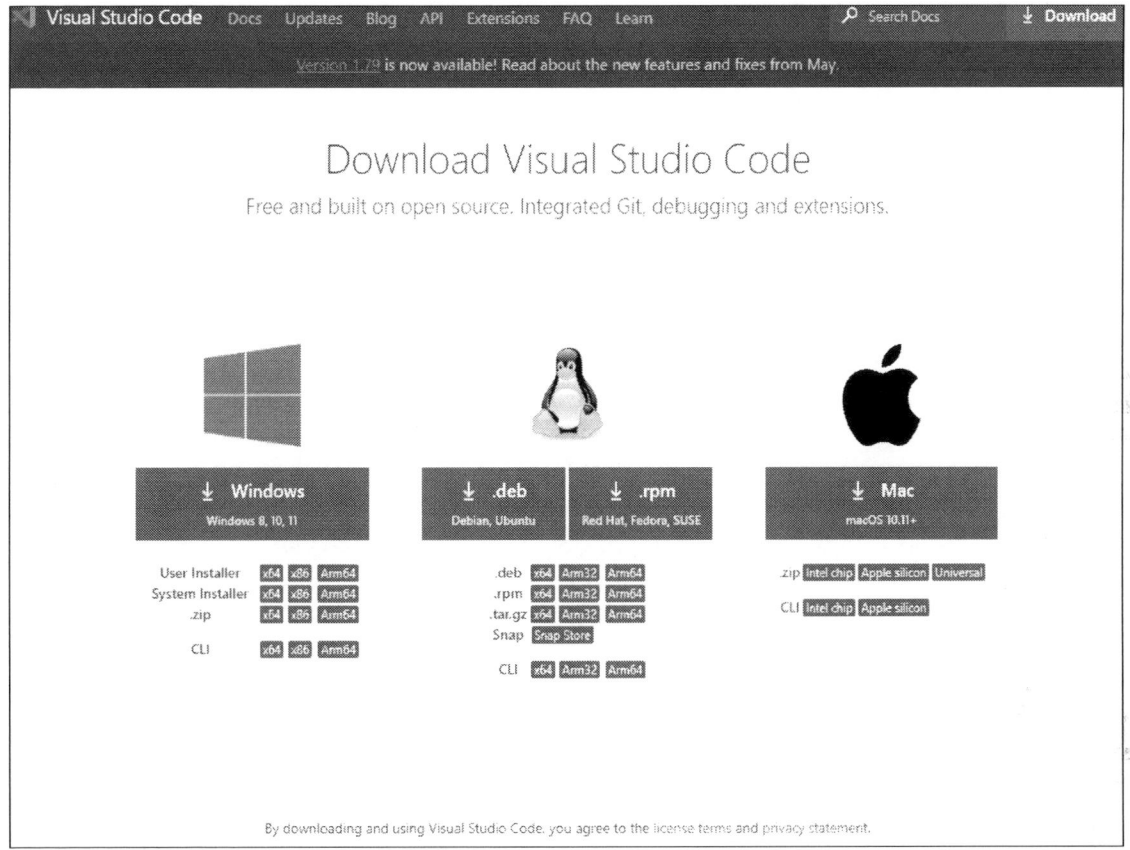

Figure 1.1: Download VSCode

2. After the download has completed, run the installer to initiate the setup process.

3. Read and then **Accept the License Agreement**. Click **Next**.

4. Select the installation destination location and click **Next.** This will take up at least 400 MB of space on the disk.

5. You can then select a start menu folder, uncheck the box if you do not want to create this. Click **Next**.

6. On the select additional tasks page, you can choose to: Create a desktop icon, Add **Open with Code** action to Windows Explorer file context menu. Then add **Open with Code** action to Windows Explorer directory context menu, register Code as an editor for supported file types and Add to PATH (requires shell restart).

Keeping at least the pre-checked settings as is, is recommended, but this is all to your preferences. Click **Next**.

7. On the **Ready to Install** page, check that all settings are set to your preferences. Click **Install**. Once the installation has completed, continue to the next step for launching the application and setting up the PowerShell extension.

Launch application and install PowerShell extension

You can lunch the VS Code Editor by clicking on the desktop shortcut (if you selected this during setup) or you can find the editor by clicking on your start menu and then type **vscode** in the search field, click on the Visual Studio Code application. Once you have opened VS Code, it is recommended you pin this to your taskbar for easy access. Right click on the VS Code taskbar icon and click on **Pin to Taskbar**. Now you will see the welcome page with a **Start**, **Recent** and **Walkthroughs** section. At the top bar we have the File bar, at the bottom we have the status and side bars. And on the left side we have the Activity bar. For a more in-depth explanation on the VS Code User interface, read the docs at: **https://code.visualstudio.com/docs/getstarted/userinterface.** For now, what we are most interested in is the **Activity** bar, more specific the **Extensions** tab (as shown in *Figure 1.2*):

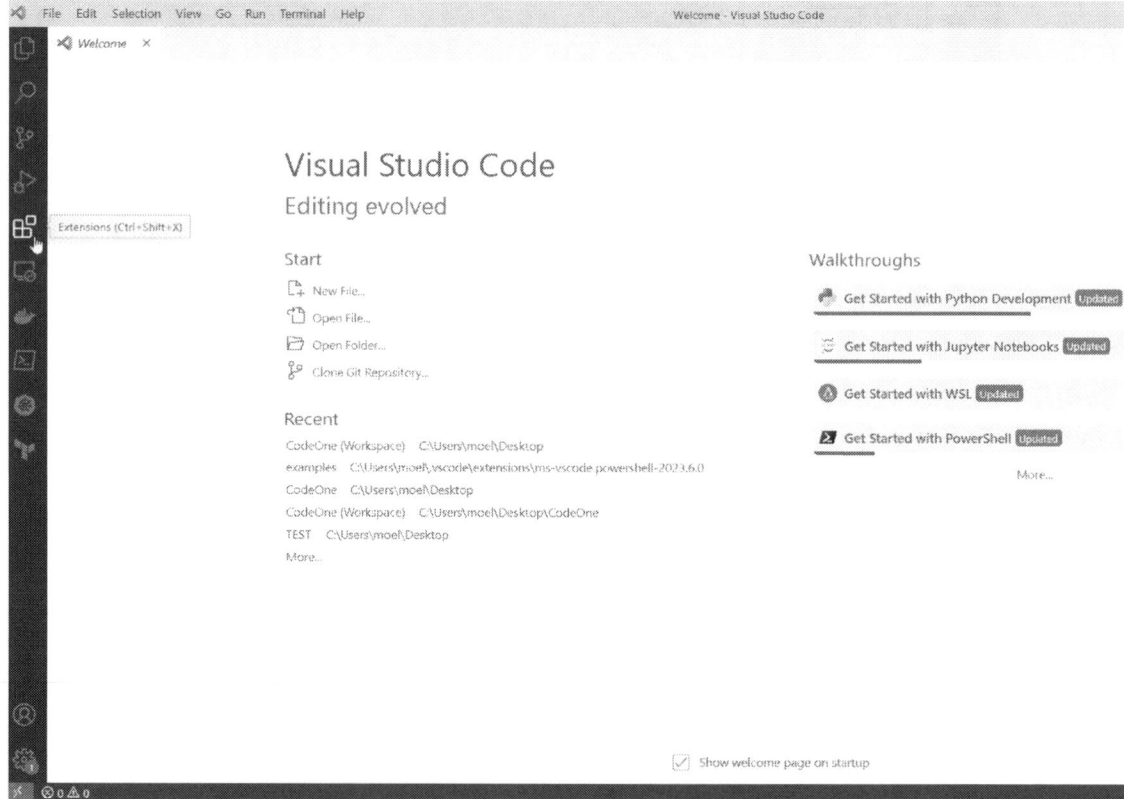

Figure 1.2: *VS Code welcome page and Extensions tab*

You can open the extensions tab, either by clicking on it or by using the specific extensions tab shortcut Windows: *Ctrl + Shift + X*, the shortcut might differ on different systems. In the extensions tab, you will see a search field, where you can search for specific extensions to VS Code. We are of course interested in a PowerShell extension. Type *PowerShell* in the search field. You will get a lot of different extensions for PowerShell, since the extensions are not only available from trusted sources like Microsoft, but also from the VS Code community in general. What we are interested in here, is the official PowerShell extension from Microsoft. We can distinguish the trusted extension from the non-trusted ones, by looking for the *owner verification symbol* (a little blue star with a little approval symbol inside). Click on the extension to get a detailed view with information about and how to use the specific extension, as shown in *Figure 1.3*:

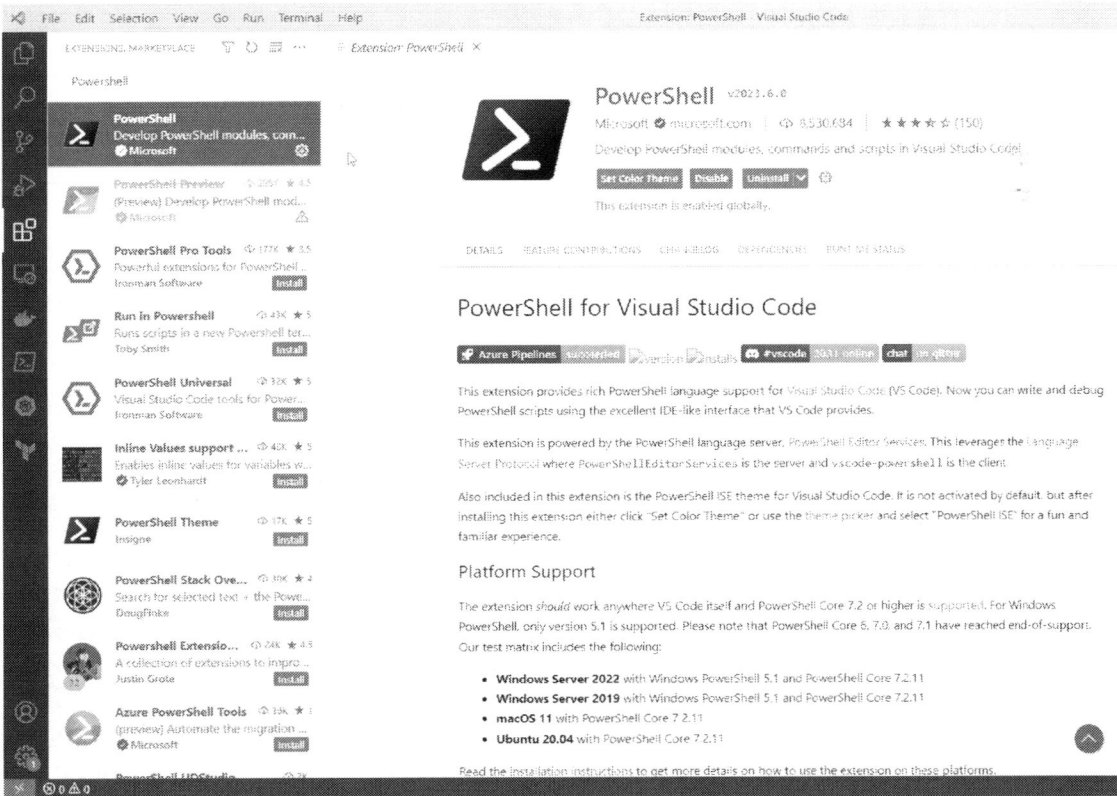

Figure 1.3: *The Microsoft verified VS Code PowerShell extension*

Click on the **Install** button in the detailed view to install the extension into VS Code, this should only take a couple of seconds and when it is successfully installed, that is basically it. Your VS Code is now ready for creating PowerShell scripts. What you might also like about VS Code is the use of workspaces. A workspace in VS Code is a collection of one, or in some cases more, folders that you are opening in the VS Code window, then you will have easy access to all files in that or these folders and their respective subfolders and you will be able to open each file in a new tab by selecting it. To make use of the workspace experience by opening multiple folders in different locations at a time, you simply just open the first folder, and then add another folder to the workspace, you can then save the workspace for easily loading this saved structure again later. *Figure 1.4* shows two different folders, containing files, opened (and saved) in a workspace. The top icon in the activity bar is the explorer icon which is used to open folders when none are opened yet, or to view the opened folders and workspaces. Note that VS Code tells us it is PowerShell (.ps1) files by showing a little PowerShell icon to the left of the filenames, which is another nice feature so you can distinguish between the different types of files:

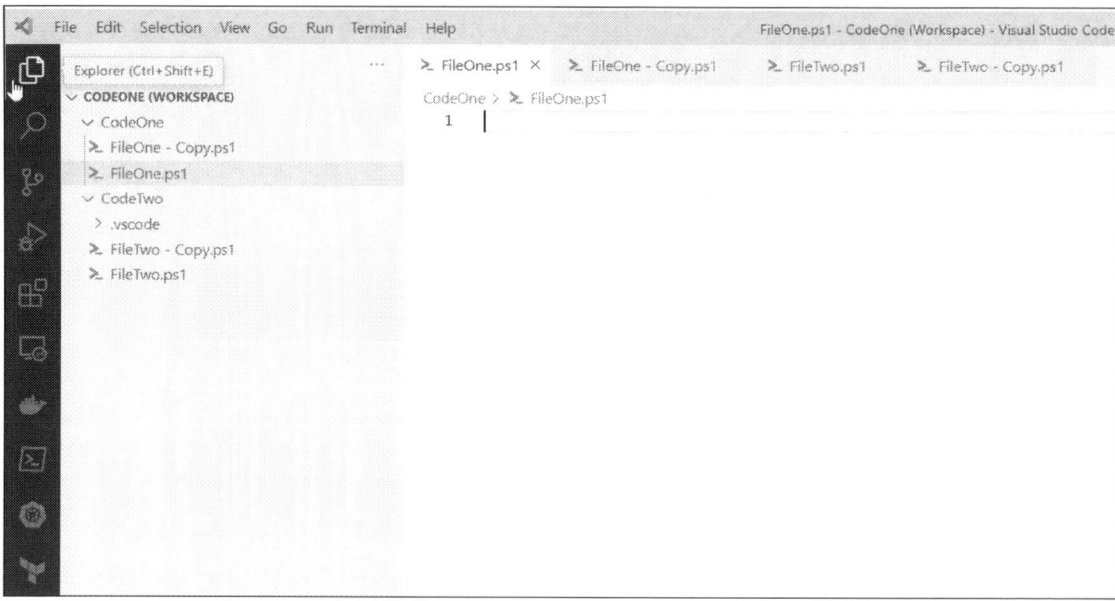

Figure 1.4: Explorer in the activity bar, and opened workspace with two folders containing files

One more thing to note about VS Code is the built-in terminal. You can have more than one terminal opened at the same time making it easy to run commands or scripts in different folders at the same time without changing directories. *Figure 1.5* shows multiple open terminals in different paths. Also note the split-image view for both the code editor windows and the terminals, this makes it a lot easier to edit and run multiple scripts and commands at the same time:

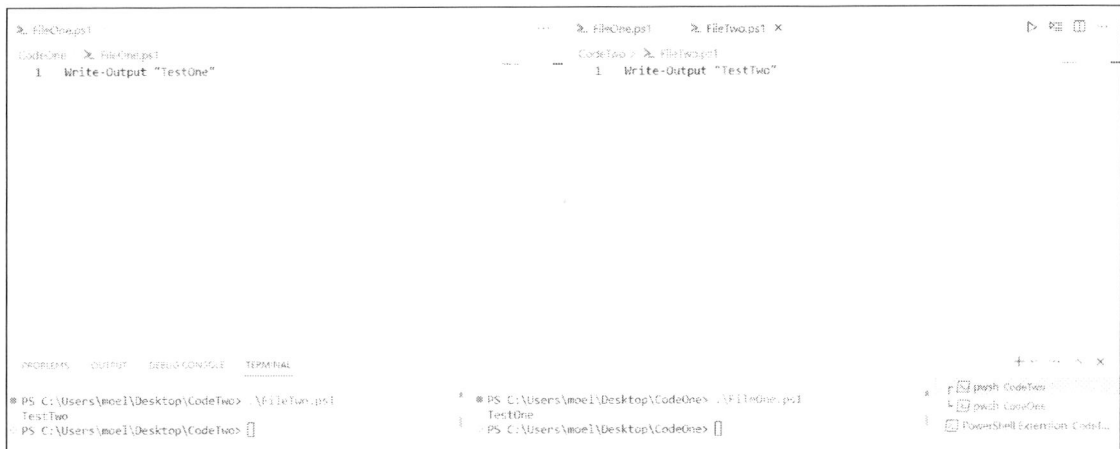

Figure 1.5: Multiple terminals and multiple code editor windows

Of course, VS Code has a lot more to offer but let us not go into any more details in this book about the different features and settings that you can utilize and change. There is also a vast sea of extensions for almost every language and feature you can think of. If you want an extension that works with Docker, install the Docker extension. Do you want to connect to your Kubernetes cluster, install a Kubernetes extension. Want to connect to your Azure subscription, no problem, just install an Azure extension. If you can name it, someone most definitely has made an extension for it.

Features and usage of the VS Code PowerShell extension

We will now investigate the code editor with the PowerShell extension installed and how to create scripts and use the advantages this editor provides. Some of the features of this extension is the PowerShell syntax highlighting, Intellisense and code snippets, it also offers a lot more like debugging, integration with Pester test framework and integration with **PSScriptAnalyzer**. **PSScriptAnalyzer** is a PowerShell module that provides a source code checker for PowerShell modules and scripts so basically it has rule sets that verify the quality of PowerShell code based on PowerShell best practices. The **PSScriptAnalyzer** module is included by default in the VS Code PowerShell extension and automatically performs analysis on the scripts you edit in VS Code. To learn more about all the features and integrations the extension provides refer to the official PowerShell extension documentation: **https://code.visualstudio.com/docs/languages/powershell**. Let us get started using the editor to see its functions in action. Start by creating a .ps1 file and open the file into VS Code. If you start typing the name of a **cmdlet** like **Get-Module** you can see the IntelliSense in action and that it shows you all the **cmdlets** and functions that contains the input you provided, like in *Figure 1.6*. It even shows you extended information when you highlight a cmdlet or function:

Figure 1.6: Intellisense in action for cmdlet´s and functions

If you get more options to choose from, you can use the *up* and *down* arrows to scroll through them and then use the **tab** button to select and let the IntelliSense complete the insertion of the **cmdlet** or function. Another useful component is the Code action feature, this feature lets you easily encase a selected command with a predefined code snippet like **if**, **class**, **function**, and **try/catch** block and so on. Whenever you highlight something in the editor like the *Write-Output* sample in *Figure 1.7* you will see a little yellow lightbulb and when you click on it you will get a code action dropdown where you have options to surround the highlighted text with one of the predefined snippets. In *Figure 1.7* you can also see the output after surrounding the **Write-Output** command with an **if** snippet:

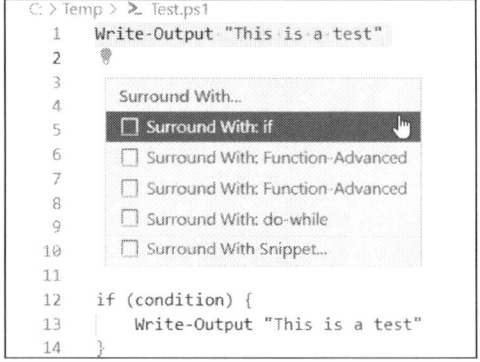

Figure 1.7: Code action snippet feature

You can see that the syntax is highlighted which greatly improves the readability and context of the code, this does not have an impact on the code itself but is strictly for helping the developer to easily distinguish between the different types of elements. Besides the code action feature another feature that is invaluable is the *code snippets*, with this you can easily create elements like **functions, classes, if´s** and **switch** statements and so on. Just start typing the name of the element you want to create, and the code snippet will give you the relevant choices. In *Figure 1.8* we can see that just by typing **func** we get all the available snippets with that name like **function** and **advanced function**. Like with the code action feature, here you just scroll through them with the **up** and **down** arrows, and you can select a specific snippet, it also provides you with more detailed information about the selected snippet:

Figure 1.8: Code snippets in VS Code

As previously mentioned, VS Code offers debugging and Script analysis capabilities for PowerShell code. The first thing we will look at is the **PSScriptAnalyzer**, this is enabled by default in the editor. All code in your script that does not conform to the best practice rules that Script analyzer is based upon, will be underlined with a yellow wave-line. First, I would like to say that the rules the best practices are based upon, is from the Microsoft

PowerShell team and the PowerShell community. What it does is that it gives you guidelines when you have something in your code that does not conform to the best practices ruleset, this could be if you have variables in your script that are assigned but never used, or if you have named a function in a non-traditional manner, like not in the *verb-noun* convention that is generally used in PowerShell **cmdlet**´s naming conventions. But this is not all that the **PSScriptAnalyzer** has to offer, it also checks the code for syntax errors and ensures that your code can be executed without any issues, it checks the formatting of the code for any inconsistencies like indentation, spacing and line breaks, furthermore it also checks the code for security vulnerabilities and alerts you about insecure code that could lead to security breaches and vulnerabilities in your script, so this is also a powerful tool to have in your IDE. In *Figure 1.9* you can see examples of how the **PSScriptAnalyzer** highlights the different issues. Here warnings are just that, warnings. Your code will still function if you do not fix these, but alerts like with syntax errors, the code will not run but returns the error until the issue is fixed. In *Figure 1.9* you can also see that not only are the issues and warnings underlined, but in the *Problems* pane each alert and warning are mentioned with more information and even line numbers, so it is much easier to find and fix these:

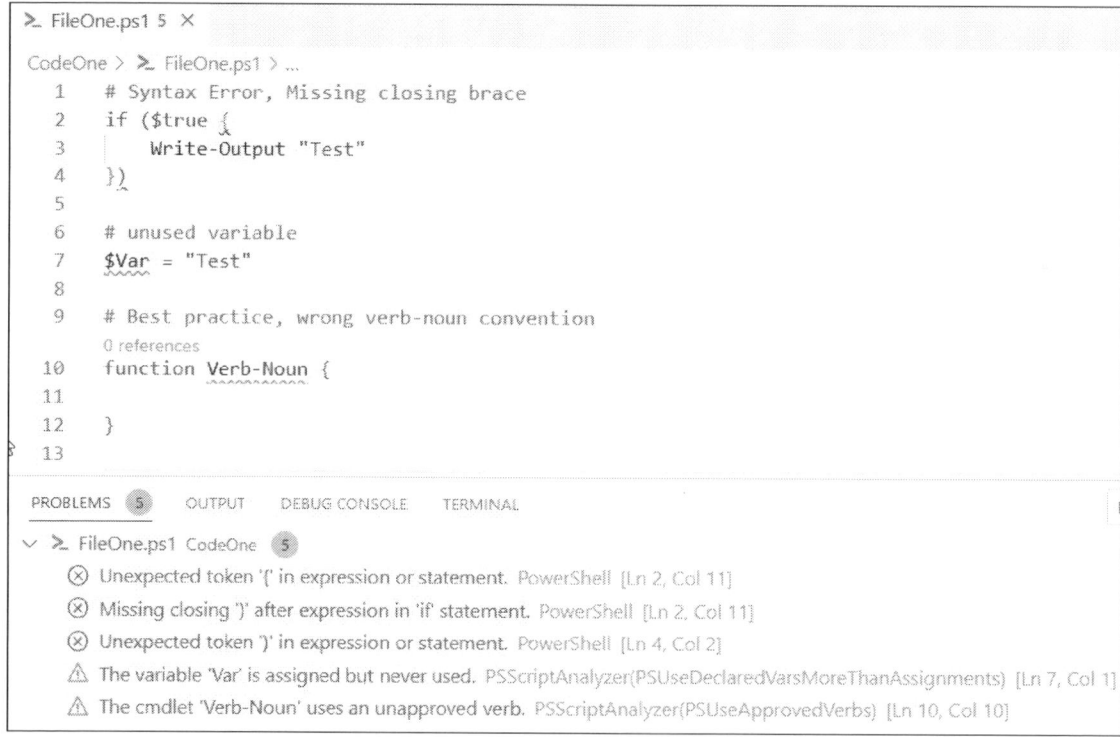

Figure 1.9: Issues and warnings highlighted by PSScriptAnalyzer

The last thing we will cover in this chapter about VS Code is the debugger. We will not go into much detail since it is too big of a subject for this chapter, so let us just cover the basics. The debugger lets you debug your PowerShell scripts directly in the VS Code editor and it contains all the default debugging features like breakpoints, you can set breakpoints which allows you to pause at certain steps in the process and then navigate through the code line by line and get a better understanding of the flow. You can inspect variables at certain steps so you can compare and check if these contain the expected values. This makes it easier to identify potential problems, bugs, and incorrect values. The VS Code debugging console makes it easy to debug and follow the flow of the code. *Figure 1.10* shows the debugging of a *DebugTest. ps1* script (This script comes as an example script with VS Code, to open the example scripts in VS Code use *ctrl + shift + p* to open the commands search bar and search for *PowerShell examples folder*). Here you can see the flow of the code stopped at the Breakpoint on line 7. In the **variables** pane on the left, you can see the current *variables* and their values, and in the **call stack** pane you can see the progress of the script and how it was started and what elements it has traversed, in our case it started the script call in an interactive session then the **<scriptblock>** which in this case indicates that it was invoked as a script. We then see that it traversed into the **Do-Work** function and is now currently stopped at the Breakpoint on line 7 in the **Write-Item** function. The debugger is an invaluable and powerful tool when you learn to master it.

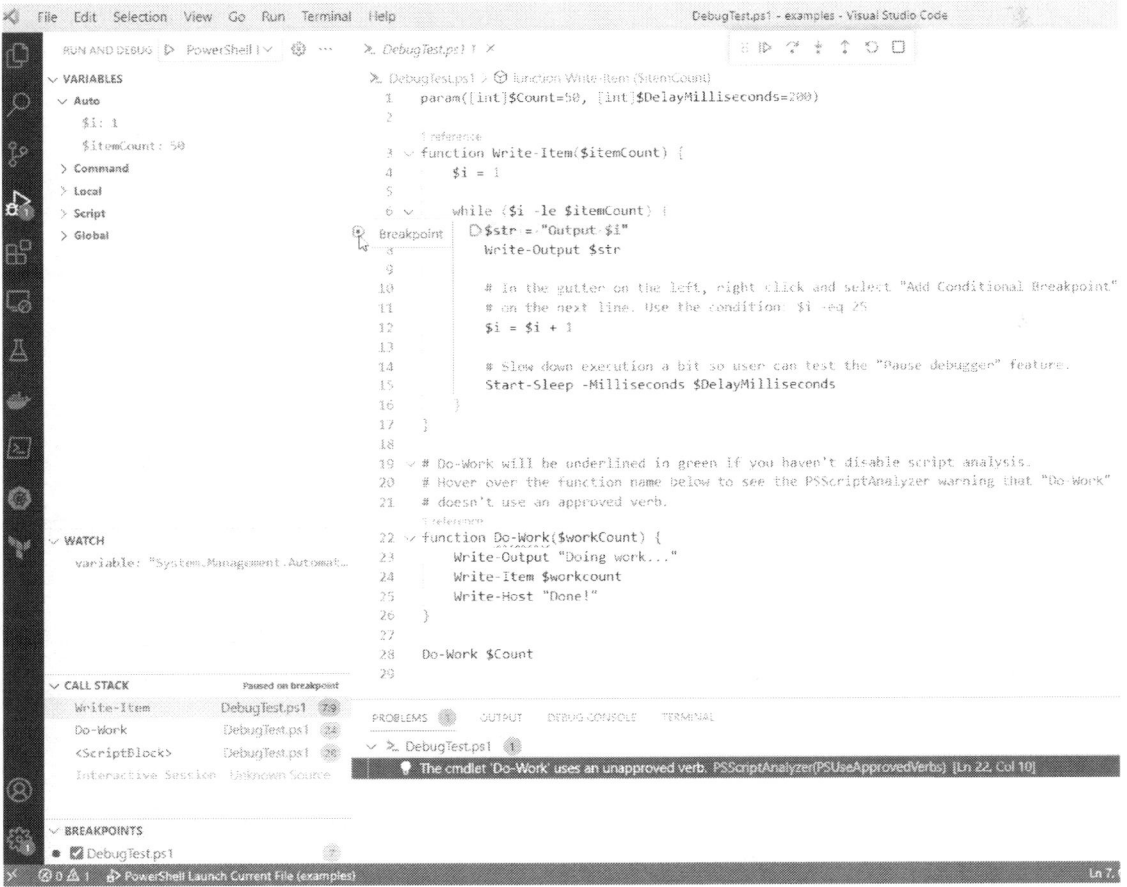

Figure 1.10: *Debugging console stopped at Breakpoint*

By utilizing and combining the features in this chapter, you should be able to make strong scripts quickly and easily with the VS Code editor and be able to analyze and debug them. By using code snippets and actions you can save a lot of time by not having to code these from the start every time you need a new element. With the **PSScriptAnalyzer** you can quickly see syntax and parsing errors and warnings and update your code to conform to the best practices and make sure they are not missing anything that would prevent them from executing. With the debugger you can easily dig deeper into the process and flow of the scripts and make sure all variables and expressions return the expected values in each of their steps, if something should behave in an unexpected manner.

Advanced Sapien PowerShell studio IDE

This is a more advanced and professional grade IDE that not only utilizes the features from other great IDE´s like VS Code, but also incorporates a lot of its own advanced features such as the ability to easily create GUI PowerShell applications with a drag-n-drop approach, create Windows Services from PowerShell scripts, **Executables** (**.exe**) from script files, MSI installers for executables and windows services and much more. So, if you really want to make powerful PowerShell scripts and applications, this would be an ideal IDE to choose. We have dedicated a chapter in this book to go into more detail about this tool, I just wanted to make a brief introduction to this in *Chapter 15, SAPIEN PowerShell Studio IDE* I will go into more detail about what it has to offer and can do and show recipes for creating GUI forms, windows services, and installers for these and about the other advanced features this tool offers.

PowerShell versions

There are not that many different PowerShell versions that still should be used today. On older servers and desktop OS like Windows 8 and Windows server 2012 or earlier you might still find versions like 2, 3 and 4 but in 2016 PowerShell 5 was introduced for Windows 10 and Windows Server 2016. Version 5.1 was soon released after, as an update to version 5, that included a lot of bug fixes and improvements, so when speaking of PowerShell version 5 today, in most cases it would be the 5.1 version which is also referred to as *Windows PowerShell*.

PowerShell 5 is not cross platform, and it is the last major version that is available and build only for Windows and Windows server OS. It is built on the .NET framework and is by default included in Windows 10, Windows 11, and Windows Server 2016. In 2018 PowerShell version 6 was released and it is the first version that was built on .NET Core framework and was made cross-platform, so it is not limited to Windows but also works on other platforms like Linux and Mac. PowerShell 6 is also referred to as PowerShell Core and would be the foundation for all future releases to ensure consistency and cross platform support in all new versions of PowerShell. In 2020 PowerShell version 7 was released and this is the replacement for version 6/core and comes with new features and improvements and have better performance than previous versions. This is now the foundation for current and newer releases, though Microsoft has no plans yet to deprecate version 5.1 so this is still a viable version when only using Windows and versions 5 and 7 can coexist on the same platform without one being a replacement for the other. Some modules, features, and **cmdlet´s** are still only supported by Windows platforms even in the newer versions, but Microsoft have made great effort to mitigate this as much as possible to deliver a unified experience between the different platforms.

As this book is being written the newest release is PowerShell 7.4.2 and when it comes to selecting a version to use, the choice should be between PowerShell 5.1 and PowerShell 7 depending on your requirements. You should only use earlier versions for legacy system support and for script compatability, where scripts have been originally written for and tested with earlier versions of PowerShell. If you are only working on windows and do not need to write cross platform scripts 5.1 is a viable choice, but if you would like to benefit from the new features like **foreach-parallel** or the concise error view and make scripts that works on different platforms, so why not make the transition to version 7 now. PowerShell 7 comes with experimental features that can be listed and enabled with the **Get-ExperimentalFeature** cmdlet and furthermore it offers backwards compatibility with Windows PowerShell modules that can be used to create a *proxy* session, known as **WinPsCompatSession**, between PowerShell 7 and Windows PowerShell so older modules can be imported and its **cmdlet´s** can be executed. In summary, PowerShell 5 is the Windows only version. PowerShell 6 or core was the interim version that later evolved to PowerShell 7 which is now the current cross platform version of PowerShell.

PowerShell providers

A PowerShell provider, also referred to as a PSProvider, is a feature or component in PowerShell that enables you to access different data stores such as the filesystem, Windows Registry, the certificate stores, and environment variables. The PSProvider acts like an interface between PowerShell and the underlying data store where the data is structured in a tree like manner like you would see in a regular directory structure. PSProviders are represented like drive letters and can be accessed as if you were accessing a normal drive letter like the *C:* drive. PowerShell comes with built-in providers but also works with third-party providers that lets you interact with custom data sources such as databases, active directory, cloud storage, API´s and more all in a consistent manner. You can even create your own custom providers. To view all currently available Providers, use the **Get-PSProvider cmdlet**. This outputs the **name**, **capabilities** and **drives** of each available provider as you can see in *Figure 1.11.*

```
● PS C:\Temp> Get-PSProvider

   Name                  Capabilities                              Drives
   ----                  ------------                              ------
   Registry              ShouldProcess                             {HKLM, HKCU}
   Alias                 ShouldProcess                             {Alias}
   Environment           ShouldProcess                             {Env}
   FileSystem            Filter, ShouldProcess, Credentials        {C, Temp, J, N…}
   Function              ShouldProcess                             {Function}
   Variable              ShouldProcess                             {Variable}
   Certificate           ShouldProcess                             {Cert}
   WSMan                 Credentials                               {WSMan}
```

Figure 1.11: *Get-PSProvider cmdlet and output*

```
PS C:\Temp\Superhero> Get-PSProvider
Name                    Capabilities              Drives

----                    ------------              ------

Registry                ShouldProcess             {HKLM, HKCU}

Alias                   ShouldProcess             {Alias}

Environment             ShouldProcess             {Env}

FileSystem              Filter, ShouldProcess, Creden… {C, Temp, J, N…}

Function                ShouldProcess             {Function}

Variable                ShouldProcess             {Variable}

Certificate             ShouldProcess             {Cert}
```

The names in the **Name** attribute are quite self-explanatory, the capabilities attribute tells us which capabilities the elements in the drive have, like with the **ShouldProcess** that are included in most of them, tells us that we can use the -**WhatIf** and -**Confirm** switch parameters on the data in the drive. The **Drives** attribute is the specific drive letter that can be used to access each respective provider. Accessing a provider with its drive letter is like working in any other directory so you can use the **Get-ChildItem** and other relevant cmdlet´s to access and work with the data in the providers.

Recipe 2: Use providers to access data stores

Using providers offers a lot of benefits when working with different data sources where some of the notables are that it has a unified interface, meaning that whatever data store you need to access you can always use the same cmdlets and functions for accessing and working with the data. It has a simplified way to navigate through the tree like data structure just like you would navigate any other directory structure. It integrates with the pipeline so the output from a provider can be piped into another process. One more key benefit to notice is the cross-platform support that lets you create scripts that uses providers on one operating system and then seamlessly run it on another platform. Keep in mind though that some providers are platform specific, like the registry, certificate and WSMan provider, these only work on Windows.

Working with the filesystem provider

You should already know the filesystem provider, as you are using it often without even noticing it. Whenever you are using a **cmdlet** like the **Get-ChildItem** or **Set-Location** with a drive letter or path, you are using the filesystem provider for that specific drive. In *Figure 1.12* we are using the **Set-Location** to switch the current working directory to **C:\Temp** then back again to the **C:** drive. We are then using the **Get-ChildItem** cmdlet to return the content of **C:\Temp** and lastly, we are piping the content returned by **Get-ChildItem C:\Temp** to a **ForEach-Object** loop where we are outputting the name property of each item in the **C:\Temp** directory.

```
⊛ PS C:\> Set-Location C:\Temp
⊛ PS C:\Temp> Set-Location C:\
⊛ PS C:\> Get-ChildItem C:\Temp


    Directory: C:\Temp


Mode                 LastWriteTime         Length Name
----                 -------------         ------ ----
d----        22-06-2023     19:40                 Test
d----        22-06-2023     19:40                 Test (2)
-a---        22-06-2023     19:40              0 Test (1).txt
-a---        22-06-2023     19:40              0 Test (2).txt
-a---        24-06-2023     11:03             10 Test.ps1

⊛ PS C:\> Get-ChildItem C:\Temp | ForEach-Object { Write-Output $_.Name }
Test
Test (2)
Test (1).txt
Test (2).txt
Test.ps1_
```

Figure 1.12: Working with the filesystem provider

Accessing drive letters like **C:** and **D:** is very basic when working with providers. You must already have used this provider a lot when working with directories and drives, you properly did not know it, but you do now. The interesting thing about PSProviders is when you are using it to access data stores that in other contexts might be difficult to access otherwise, like the Windows Registry or the certificate stores. Using the respective providers makes this easy and you can do it in the same way as when we accessed the directory using the filesystem provider.

Working with the registry provider

The Windows Registry is a database containing the configurations of the Windows operating system. It is structured in a hierarchic manner that consist of keys and subkeys, these contains the configuration values or properties. Using the Registry provider makes it easier to manage and update registry keys. The registry is divided into several root keys like **HKEY_CURRENT_USER** and **HKEY_LOCAL_MACHINE** and others, but these are the significant ones. The **HKEY_CURRENT_USER** or **HKCU** are settings specific for the current user, and the **HKEY_LOCAL_MACHINE** or **HKLM** are settings that affects the entire system and all users. For users, these *entries* are divided into so called hives, where each user specific settings are stored into its own hive which then is loaded when the user logs into the system.

Note: Tampering with the Windows Registry can have serious consequences and you can end up damaging the entire operating system if you do not know what you are doing. Always be careful and make a backup of the registry before making any changes.

To access a hive or registry path, we simply use **Get-ChildItem** with the registry drive we want. In *Figure 1.13* we are accessing the **HKEY_CURRENT_USER\SOFTWARE** key using the **HKCU:** drive. This path contains software related configurations for the current user. We can see all the current user's software keys and their properties in the abbreviated output shown in *Figure 1.13*:

```
● PS C:\> Get-ChildItem HKCU:\SOFTWARE\

    Hive: HKEY_CURRENT_USER\SOFTWARE

Name                              Property
----                              --------
7-Zip                             Lang : -
aa51b2b3-6ec1-5b89-bcc4-2b0b1e    InstallLocation : C:\Users\moel\AppData\Local\Programs\Lens
949d84                            KeepShortcuts   : true
                                  ShortcutName    : Lens
Adobe
AMD
Artweaver Free
ATI
Bare Metal Software
BugSplat
```

Figure 1.13: Output from HKCU:\SOFTWARE registry key

If we traverse further down a level to the **HKCU:\SOFTWARE**

\7-Zip key we can get all the settings specific for the 7-Zip software key as shown in Figure 1.14:

```
● PS C:\> Get-ChildItem HKCU:\SOFTWARE\7-Zip\

    Hive: HKEY_CURRENT_USER\SOFTWARE\7-Zip

Name              Property
----              --------
Compression       ShowPassword   : 0
                  Level          : 5
                  Archiver       : zip
                  EncryptHeaders : 0
                  ArcHistory     : {67, 0, 58, 0…}
Extraction        SplitDest    : 0
                  PathHistory  : {67, 0, 58, 0…}
FM                CopyHistory     : {67, 0, 58, 0…}
                  FolderShortcuts : {}
                  FolderHistory   : {67, 0, 58, 0…}
                  PanelPath0      : C:\Users\moel\Downloads\
                  FlatViewArc0    : 0
                  PanelPath1      :
                  FlatViewArc1    : 0
                  ListMode        : 771
                  Position        : {191, 0, 0, 0…}
                  Panels          : {1, 0, 0, 0…}
```

Figure 1.14: Output from HKCU:\SOFTWARE\7-Zip registry key

So, what can we use this for? Let us say that you create a program that should be installed into **C:\Program Files** and you need to keep the settings for your program somewhere that not only can be specific for each user but also have specific settings for all users, then the registry would be an ideal place to set these. You can then set shared or system specific settings in the **HKLM:\SOFTWARE** key and each user could have their own settings to your program saved in their respective hives at **HKCU:\SOFTWARE**:

```
# Create a new TestKey under HKCU:\Software

New-Item -Path "HKCU:\Software\TestKey"

# Create a new SubTestKey under HKCU:\Software\TestKey

New-Item -Path "HKCU:\Software\TestKey\SubTestKey"

# Set test properties for TestKey

Set-ItemProperty -Path "HKCU:\Software\TestKey" -Name "Value1" -Value
"TestValue1"

Set-ItemProperty -Path "HKCU:\Software\TestKey" -Name "Value2" -Value
"TestValue2"

Set-ItemProperty -Path "HKCU:\Software\TestKey" -Name "Value3" -Value
"TestValue3"

# Set test properties for SubTestKey

Set-ItemProperty -Path "HKCU:\Software\TestKey\SubTestKey" -Name
"SubValue1" -Value "SubTestValue1"

Set-ItemProperty -Path "HKCU:\Software\TestKey\SubTestKey" -Name
"SubValue2" -Value "SubTestValue2"

Set-ItemProperty -Path "HKCU:\Software\TestKey\SubTestKey" -Name
"SubValue3" -Value "SubTestValue3"
```

In this code we are using the **New-Item** cmdlet to create a new key called **TestKey** under **HKCU:\SOFTWARE** and under that we create a **SubTestKey.** With **Set-ItemProperty** we are creating 3 properties with values for both **TestKey** and **SubTestKey**. In *Figure 1.15* we use the **Get-Item** to return the keys and their properties (Instead of **Get-ChildItem**, which would return all *child's*, we use the **Get-Item** to get the items of the exact key we specify). The **TestKey** has been created in **HKCU:\SOFTWARE** with the properties and their values and the **SubTestKey** has been created in **HKCU:\SOFTWARE\TestKey** with its properties and their values:

```
* PS C:\> Get-Item HKCU:\SOFTWARE\TestKey

      Hive: HKEY_CURRENT_USER\SOFTWARE

  Name                            Property
  ~~~~                            ~~~~~~~~~
  TestKey                         Value2 : TestValue2
                                  Value3 : TestValue3
                                  Value1 : TestValue1

* PS C:\> Get-Item HKCU:\SOFTWARE\TestKey\SubTestKey

      Hive: HKEY_CURRENT_USER\SOFTWARE\TestKey

  Name                            Property
  ~~~~                            ~~~~~~~~~
  SubTestKey                      SubValue1 : SubTestValue1
                                  SubValue2 : SubTestValue2
                                  SubValue3 : SubTestValue3
```

Figure 1.15: Use Get-Item to return the registry key´s and their properties

To get a specific value we would use the **Get-ItemProperty** as shown in *Figure 1.16*. We can see that not only is the value returned, but also more information about the property like the provider, the drive, and the paths relevant to the property. To get a specific property value, we save it to a variable and then call the variable with the name of the property (in dot notation):

```
* PS C:\> Get-ItemProperty HKCU:\SOFTWARE\TestKey -Name Value1

  Value1        : TestValue1
  PSPath        : Microsoft.PowerShell.Core\Registry::HKEY_CURRENT_USER\SOFTWARE\TestKey
  PSParentPath  : Microsoft.PowerShell.Core\Registry::HKEY_CURRENT_USER\SOFTWARE
  PSChildName   : TestKey
  PSDrive       : HKCU
  PSProvider    : Microsoft.PowerShell.Core\Registry


* PS C:\> $Value1 = Get-ItemProperty HKCU:\SOFTWARE\TestKey -Name Value1
* PS C:\> $Value1.Value1
  TestValue1
```

Figure 1.16: Using Get-ItemProperty to get the value of a registry key property

We can now access the registry, we can create new keys and properties with values, and we can return specific properties and their values using the registry provider with its drive. In *Figure 1.17* you can see how simple it is to remove a key with **Remove-Item** and to remove a keys property with **Remove-ItemProperty**:

```
● PS C:\> Remove-Item -Path HKCU:\SOFTWARE\TestKey\SubTestKey\
● PS C:\> Get-Item -Path HKCU:\SOFTWARE\TestKey\SubTestKey\
  Get-Item: Cannot find path 'HKCU:\SOFTWARE\TestKey\SubTestKey\' because it does not exist.
● PS C:\> Remove-ItemProperty HKCU:\SOFTWARE\TestKey\ -Name Value1
● PS C:\> Get-Item -Path HKCU:\SOFTWARE\TestKey


    Hive: HKEY_CURRENT_USER\SOFTWARE

Name                            Property
----                            --------
TestKey                         Value2 : TestValue2
                                Value3 : TestValue3
```

Figure 1.17: *Remove registry keys and registry key properties*

With these few **cmdlet´s** and the registry provider you will be able to do almost anything within the registry, which is a powerful thing, so again I cannot stress enough how careful you should be when working with the Registry. One last thing to note is that in the examples above we only worked within the current user hive which we have access to, since we are the current user. You cannot work in another user's hive, but you can make changes and work in the local machine hive, this would require elevated privileges though and only work when you are running your editor, terminal, or shell as an administrator.

Working with the certificate provider

Certificates are an important part of many aspects of IT, they can be used as identity verification, for authentication, code signing, TLS encryption and more. The specific details about each type of certificate are out of the scope of this book, but with the certificate provider we can easily access the certificate stores for the local machine and current user a lot like we did with the Registry. It is quite self-explanatory that the local machine store is for all users and the current user store is, you guessed it, only for you the current user.

Certificate stores are the repositories or databases if you will, for storing certificates on the system and can be used both by the operating system itself but also by different applications and the web browsers on your system. They are built in a tree like manner and consists of different sub-stores or folders, where the most used are the ones called the trusted root store, the personal store and the intermediate store, but there are also stores for other purposes. What we will be working with here is the personal store where we will access the stores certificates using the certificate provider, and like with the Registry we are able to both create view and remove certificates using the provider with relevant **cmdlet´s**. In *Figure 1.18* we use **Get-ChildItem** to access the **CurrentUser** certificate store where we can see the different store folders:

```
● PS C:\> Get-ChildItem Cert:\CurrentUser

  Name  :  My

  Name  :  TrustedPublisher

  Name  :  REQUEST

  Name  :  CA

  Name  :  SmartCardRoot

  Name  :  ADDRESSBOOK

  Name  :  ClientAuthIssuer

  Name  :  Trust

  Name  :  Local NonRemovable Certificates

  Name  :  Root

  Name  :  ACRS

  Name  :  AuthRoot

  Name  :  TrustedPeople

  Name  :  UserDS

  Name  :  Disallowed
```

Figure 1.18: *The CurrentUser certificate store*

If you are familiar with the Windows Management Console and certificate view, you will notice that the names do not match the ones returned by the provider and the Management console, but the folder named **My** are the personal certificate folder and the **Root** are the Trusted Root folder. So, to dive deeper we can use **Get-ChildItem** to return the items in the different folders. In *Figure 1.19* we access the **My** or personal store for the current user and view all the certificates in this store. Notice the output might be shortened if your certificates subject names (Canonical Names) are too long, so we pipe our command to **Format-Table** with the **AutoSize** parameter:

```
● PS C:\> Get-ChildItem Cert:\CurrentUser\My\ | format-Table -AutoSize

    PSParentPath: Microsoft.PowerShell.Security\Certificate::CurrentUser\My

Thumbprint                                Subject                                          EnhancedKeyUsageList
----------                                -------                                          --------------------
EB2C8069FA1A89832CC477704EA5AE0DD717CDA4  CN=c8bd5485-634b-4e6f-bf9a-4f542d1225d6  Client Authentication
A9C40EC98176C324C20AFB9DAA1E2D595AB7B584  CN=client1.contoso.com                  {Client Authentication, Server Authentication}
1CB0697754C8F1A15CF4FCDFDBE1A6F1977DA3B5  CN=TestCert-CurrentUser                 {Client Authentication, Server Authentication}
031A4BDC80F25709AC6FE747E9FF2536AEF9CF6C  CN=TestCert                             {Client Authentication, Server Authentication}
```

Figure 1.19: *Output of the current user personal certificate store*

To select and work with a specific certificate there are a few ways to go. First, we could access it with its **index** since the output are in fact an array. We could add the specific certificate **thumbprint** to the drive path and use **Get-Item** on this path or we could pipe the **Get-ChildItem** command to **Where-Object** and match the common name we are looking for with the certificates **subject** attribute or the **FriendlyName** attribute if we know it has a value assigned to this attribute. *Figure 1.20* shows these methods for returning a specific certificate:

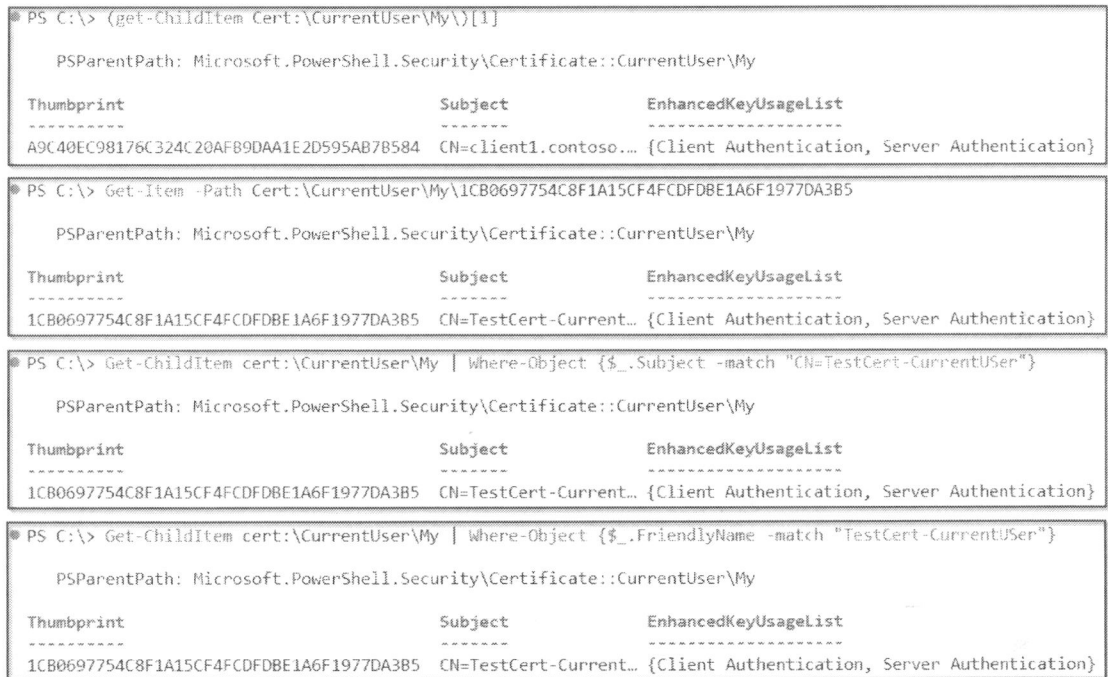

Figure 1.20: *Different methods for returning a specific certificate*

We could save the output in a variable and then pipe the variable to **Select-Object** * to get all the certificates properties like expiry date (**NotAfter** property), serial number and so on. and we would even get the **PSDrive** and **PSProvider** properties for the certificate, as shown in *Figure 1.21*:

```
● PS C:\> $Cert = (Get-ChildItem Cert:\CurrentUser\My\)[1]
● PS C:\> $Cert | Select-Object *

  PSPath                    : Microsoft.PowerShell.Security\Certificate::CurrentUser\My\A9C40EC98176C324C20AFB9DAA1E2D595AB7B584
  PSParentPath              : Microsoft.PowerShell.Security\Certificate::CurrentUser\My
  PSChildName               : A9C40EC98176C324C20AFB9DAA1E2D595AB7B584
  PSDrive                   : Cert
  PSProvider                : Microsoft.PowerShell.Security\Certificate
  PSIsContainer             : False
  EnhancedKeyUsageList      : {Client Authentication (1.3.6.1.5.5.7.3.2), Server Authentication (1.3.6.1.5.5.7.3.1)}
  DnsNameList               : {client1.contoso.com}
  SendAsTrustedIssuer       : False
  EnrollmentPolicyEndPoint  : Microsoft.CertificateServices.Commands.EnrollmentEndPointProperty
  EnrollmentServerEndPoint  : Microsoft.CertificateServices.Commands.EnrollmentEndPointProperty
  PolicyId                  :
  Archived                  : False
  Extensions                : {System.Security.Cryptography.Oid, System.Security.Cryptography.Oid, System.Security.Cryptography.Oid,
                              stem.Security.Cryptography.Oid…}
  FriendlyName              : client1.contoso.com
  HasPrivateKey             : True
  PrivateKey                : System.Security.Cryptography.RSACng
  IssuerName                : System.Security.Cryptography.X509Certificates.X500DistinguishedName
  NotAfter                  : 22-05-2024 13:21:33
  NotBefore                 : 22-05-2023 13:11:33
  PublicKey                 : System.Security.Cryptography.X509Certificates.PublicKey
  RawData                   : {48, 130, 4, 109…}
  RawDataMemory             : System.ReadOnlyMemory<Byte>[1137]
  SerialNumber              : 2D0000000A8CDDF05CEF52DF9B00000000000A
  SignatureAlgorithm        : System.Security.Cryptography.Oid
  SubjectName               : System.Security.Cryptography.X509Certificates.X500DistinguishedName
  Thumbprint                : A9C40EC98176C324C20AFB9DAA1E2D595AB7B584
  Version                   : 3
  Handle                    : 2253743018192
  Issuer                    : CN=Contoso-RCA
  Subject                   : CN=client1.contoso.com
  SerialNumberBytes         : System.ReadOnlyMemory<Byte>[19]
```

Figure 1.21: All the certificates' properties

When we have selected a certificate and assigned it to a variable, we can remove it from the store with the **Remove-Item cmdlet** shown in *Figure 1.22*:

```
● PS C:\> $Cert | Remove-Item
● PS C:\> Get-ChildItem Cert:\CurrentUser\My\

    PSParentPath: Microsoft.PowerShell.Security\Certificate::CurrentUser\My

  Thumbprint                               Subject                EnhancedKeyUsageList
  ----------                               -------                --------------------
  EB2C8069FA1A89832CC477704EA5AE0DD717CDA4 CN=c8bd5485-634b-4e… Client Authentication
  1CB0697754C8F1A15CF4FCDFDBE1A6F1977DA3B5 CN=TestCert-Current… {Client Authentication, Server Authentication}
  031A4BDC80F25709AC6FE747E9FF2536AEF9CF6C CN=TestCert            {Client Authentication, Server Authentication}
```

Figure 1.22: Remove a certificate from the current user personal store

We can import a certificate with the **Import-Certificate** and **Import-PfxCertificate cmdlet´s** and even create a new self-signed certificate into the certificate store. In *Figure 1.23* we use the **New-SelfSignedCertificate** to create a new certificate in the current user personal store. Notice here, that we have called it the same as the one we just deleted but it is not the same certificate, the thumbprint has changed. A certificate thumbprint is not a secret but a unique identifier that is derived from all the certificate properties and since the creation date, serial number and so on., are not the same as the previous certificates, the thumbprint will always be different and unique for each certificate:

```
● PS C:\> $Name = "TestCert-CurrentUser"
● PS C:\> New-SelfSignedCertificate -Subject $Name -DnsName "CN=$Name" -FriendlyName $Name -CertStoreLocation Cert:\CurrentUser\my

    PSParentPath: Microsoft.PowerShell.Security\Certificate::CurrentUser\my

Thumbprint                                Subject                 EnhancedKeyUsageList
----------                                -------                 --------------------
3ADFC39CE251B8580C9E5DE141635F2AF9F2BB44  CN=TestCert-Current…    {Client Authentication, Server Authentication}
```

Figure 1.23: Create a new self-signed certificate into the current user personal store

As we have learnt in this recipe, we can use PSProviders to access the different data stores offered by the system and easily add, modify, and delete data in the stores in a consistent manner, whether it is working with files and folders in the filesystem, certificates in the certificate stores or keys and properties inside the registry. We have barely scratched the surface, but this should give you the basic understanding of how to work with these providers and you can use this to make even more powerful scripts and programs that lets you interact with almost any types of data you can think of. As mentioned earlier there are several other third-party providers that let you work with data in systems such as active directory, databases, cloud providers, API's and more and you can even create your own custom providers to incorporate your own type of custom data.

Conclusion

In this chapter we have been introduced to concepts of advanced PowerShell and we have learned about common best practices for making consistent, reliable, and powerful PowerShell scripts. We have learnt about PowerShell IDE's and we have walked through a recipe for setting up Visual Studio Code IDE with PowerShell extension and learnt about its key features that will help you setting up a consistent and optimized PowerShell scripting environment. Then we have been briefly introduced to a more advanced and professional grade PowerShell Specific IDE, the Sapien PowerShell studio and have looked at some of the features it offers. In a later chapter we will go in-depth and learn more about this Powerful tool and learn how to utilize its even more advanced features such as creating PowerShell GUI forms, and PowerShell Windows Services. We learnt about specific PowerShell versions and how they differ and what version to use depending on your requirements. Are you only working in Windows, or do your scripts have to be cross-platform. Lastly, we have dived into PowerShell Providers and covered a more in-depth recipe about what these are and how they can be used to access various data in different data stores, such as working with the Windows Registry and with certificates in the certificate stores, even though we barely scratched the surface about this topic, you should have a better understanding about them and know how to utilize these in your scripts.

The next chapter delves into advanced PowerShell functions and covers a detailed explanation of its structure and capabilities, including dynamic parameters, parameter sets and lifecycle events. It also covers key elements such as the CmdletBinding attribute, parameter validation and output formatting. Furthermore, it explains how to implement handling for pipeline input and the ShouldProcess capability. The chapter also introduces object-oriented PowerShell concepts in the form of PowerShell classes. It offers a step-by-step guide to constructing classes with properties and methods.

Join our book's Discord space

Join the book's Discord Workspace for Latest updates, Offers, Tech happenings around the world, New Release and Sessions with the Authors:

https://discord.bpbonline.com

CHAPTER 2
Advanced PowerShell Functions

Introduction

In this chapter you will be introduced to and learn about the differences and how to make advanced PowerShell functions that utilizes and incorporates function features like parameter sets and parameter attributes, implementing lifecycle events and more. You will learn to create functions that handles pipeline input and how to incorporate security measures in functions for simulating command executions and prompting users for confirmation before execution. You will also get an insight into object-oriented programming concepts and learn to create PowerShell classes that utilizes properties and methods for creating complex objects. The objective in this chapter is to first create a *simple* advanced function, then as the chapter progresses, we add more advanced features to the function and as we incorporate these features, we see how we can progress the function or create new useful advanced functions, at the end you will be able to create advanced functions for a multitude of purposes. Later in the chapter you will also be introduced to PowerShell classes. Classes are fundamental when it comes to Object-oriented programming, and it would take a whole book to cover this in detail, but in this chapter, we will cover the fundamentals about these classes and learn how to create classes in PowerShell and then take advantages of them in you PowerShell scripts. You will learn how to add and use class properties and methods and how to instantiate multiple instances from the same class. By utilizing and incorporating both advanced PowerShell functions and classes into your scripts, will make them more powerful and versatile and at the end you should be able to make professional grade scripts with advanced functions and classes.

Structure

The chapter covers the following topics:

- Advanced functions.
    - o CmdletBinding attribute
    - o Parameter attributes
    - o **Recipe 3**: Create an advanced function
- Output formatting
- Dynamic parameters
    - o **Recipe 4**: Adding dynamic parameters
- Parameter sets
    - o **Recipe 5**: Adding parameter sets
- Lifecycle events
    - o **Recipe 6**: Implementing lifecycle Begin, Process, and End events
- Support for handling pipeline input
    - o **Recipe 7**: Implementing support for pipeline input
- Support for ShouldProcess
    - o **Recipe 8**: Implementing Support for ShouldProcess
- Object-oriented programming concepts and benefits
    - o **Recipe 9**: Creating a class with properties and methods

Objectives

In this chapter, you will learn how to create advanced PowerShell functions and learn about the different advanced features that can be used inside a function. The `CmdletBinding` attribute, function parameters and parameter attributes and how to add validation to these parameters is also a skill we will be gaining. We will start by creating an advanced function and as this chapter progresses, we will incorporate more advanced features to this function, like dynamic parameters and parameter sets. Then we will add lifecycle events in the form of Begin, Process and End blocks. Additionally learning how to make a function accept pipeline input and how to add security measures in the form of process simulations and user confirmation prompts will be explored in this chapter.

At the end of the chapter, we will take an object-oriented approach and learn how to create PowerShell classes that create instances with properties and methods. When you are done with this chapter you should be able to create advanced functions and classes that can be utilized in scripts and programs to make them even stronger and better, by incorporating functions that solves complex repeatable tasks and classes that make instances of advanced objects.

Advanced functions

A function is a set of instructions encapsulated in a code block, that performs a specific task that can be reused multiple times throughout your code or scripts. You define it once, then call it whenever it is needed. It can be without parameters if it performs a static task that does not require specific input, or it can be parameterized and receive input in the form of arguments that can be processed inside the function. It can have no return value (in other languages usually referred to as **void**) or it can return a value when it has finished its process execution. A function has its own scope, so variables are isolated from the global scope and other scopes, this avoids variable naming conflicts between scopes. It is not bound only to its local scope though, so you can interact with variables in the global scope by specifying this inside the function if needed. A function is declared with the **function** keyword and a descriptive name using the verb-noun naming convention, then followed by curly braces to create the code block. This is basically how you create the simplest form of a function, but it can also take arguments, then you would, in the simple form, just need to add parenthesis before the code block and inside these you would add the parameters. To call the function you would type the name of the function wherever needed, if it takes arguments, you simply add the parameters by providing the arguments to the function call.

> **Note: Usually in books like this you would see examples using the "Hello World" approach. Personally, I think this is outdated so in some of the examples and recipes I have decided to work with superheroes instead. I think this is a good approach since it can be developed upon as we progress through the book. All superhero names in this book are borrowed from the public domain and is not in any way protected by copyright or trademark.**

Figure 2.1 shows the simplest form of a function. It takes no arguments and does not return anything. It just does its work whenever it is called:

```
1   function Comet {
2       "Comet is Flying" | Out-File -FilePath C:\Temp\Superhero\Comet.txt | Out-Null
3   }
4
5   Comet
```

Figure 2.1: *Simple function without arguments and return statement*

You might wonder why the string in this function is piped to **Out-File** and then to **Out-Null** instead of just using the string by itself? In PowerShell whenever a command or expression is called and is not specifically captured in a variable or redirected, PowerShell would automatically send the output to the console, this behavior also applies for functions. PowerShell then assumes that the last command or expression must be returned from the function. This might be convenient when working with PowerShell interactively, because it automatically shows you the output on screen when calling a function with this behavior, but it can also be confusing if you are expecting the function to return a value for using this outside the function, without it being sent to the console. To accommodate this, PowerShell has a built-in *return* statement. By using the **return** statement, you can specify the command or expression that should be returned from the function, without it being sent to console and displayed on the screen. As you can see it is not a requirement to use the return statement and specify what a function should return, it is considered a best practice though to always use the return statement unless you specifically want the command or expression sent to the console. Back to why **Out-File** and **Out-Null** is used in the example, if you did not already guess it? If the string was declared without being further processed, the function would see it as the *last expression* and consider this to be what should be returned from the function, if this was the case, it would not be a **void** function, a function without a return statement which is what we wanted to show with this example. By piping it to **Out-File** and then to **Out-Null** it is ensured that:

- We can confirm it did some work by having it create a file that contains the string with **Out-File.**

- Made sure it did not return anything by piping it to **Out-Null.**

This might have been overkill for such a simple example, but due to PowerShell's way of handling *the last expression* we would make sure that it really was a **void** function and that it could still be shown it did something. You can see that the function is called by its name, without it returning anything. What we want is a file in **C:\Temp\Superhero called Comet.txt** containing the string which is what we got as shown in *Figure 2.2*. This was solely to demonstrate the simplest use of the simplest function that does not take any arguments and has no return statement:

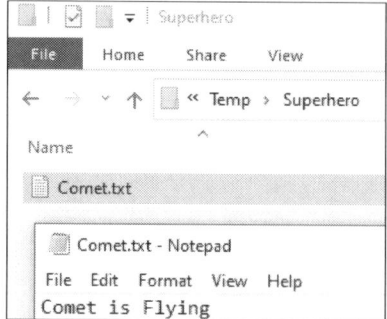

Figure 2.2: Output from simple function with no parameters and no return statement

In *Figure 2.3* we take it a step further and declare two parameters inside the function, the **Name** and the **Ability** parameters, we also still make sure it does not return anything with **Out-Null**. We can now call the function by providing arguments for the parameters and then create different superheroes with different names and abilities from the same function. Already this function is more versatile than the one we created before and we went from an almost total static function to a more dynamic function just by adding a few parameters, it is still just a very simple function though and not at all an advanced function yet:

```
1    function SuperHero ($Name, $Ability) {
2        "$Name is $Ability" | Out-File -FilePath C:\Temp\Superhero\Supeheroes.txt -Append | Out-Null
3    }
4
5    SuperHero -Name "Green Giant" -Ability "Smashing"
6    SuperHero -Name "Lightning Girl" -Ability "Creating thunder"
```

Figure 2.3: Simple function with parameters

As you can see, we call the function a few times with different arguments, thus creating different superheroes. The expected output is shown in *Figure 2.4*:

```
Superheroes.txt - Notepad

File   Edit   Format   View   Help
Green Giant is Smashing
Lightning Girl is Creating thunder
```

Figure 2.4: Output from simple function with parameters but no return statement

The last example of a simple function is shown in *Figure 2.5*. Here we add a return statement to return the expression. The workaround that suppressed the returning of the expression has been removed, so now it is just a simple string that replaces the parameter variables with the arguments provided to the function and then return the string whenever the function is called. As you see in the example, we can now call the function directly and get the returned output shown directly in the console or it can be assigned to a variable and then this variable can be called whenever needed, to use the value it was assigned from the function:

```
14    function Heroes ($Name, $Ability) {
15        return "$Name is $Ability"
16    }
17
18    Heroes -Name "Green Giant" -Ability "Smashing"
19    $AHero = Heroes -Name "Lightning Girl" -Ability "Creating thunder"
20    $AHero
```

```
PROBLEMS    OUTPUT    DEBUG CONSOLE    TERMINAL


PS C:\Temp\Superhero>
Green Giant is Smashing
Lightning Girl is Creating thunder
```

Figure 2.5: Simple function with parameters and return statement

The functions in these examples are just very simple forms of functions in PowerShell, but they are still very usable in many cases, but these functions just show a small bit of what you can do with them so if you would want a more sophisticated function that provides additional features, you should use an advanced function. What defines an advanced function? An advanced function in PowerShell is more sophisticated than a regular function and provides more features such as parameter attributes, pipeline handling, verbose and debug parameters, error handling and a lot more. These features make an advanced function even more versatile than a regular function and will help you to build even more professional and robust scripts. As soon as you incorporate advanced features into a function, you can call it advanced, but in general you must at least incorporate the **CmdletBinding** attribute.

CmdletBinding attribute

The **CmdletBinding** attribute is used to declare that a function should act like an advanced cmdlet and it incorporates advanced features such as the common parameters like **Verbose**, **Debug**, **ErrorAction** and **ErrorVariable** and also enables pipeline support, support for **shouldProcess**, paging and more. It is not mandatory to incorporate the **CmdletBinding** attribute to call a function advanced, but you could take a simple function, declare the **CmdletBinding** attribute in it, and then the function becomes advanced, without adding any more components to it like parameters and pipeline support, it would be an advanced function because you incorporated the advanced features of the **CmdletBinding** attribute. During this chapter, we will investigate these features and how they are utilized in a function. The first step to declare a function as advanced is simply by adding the **CmdletBinding** attribute and a **param()** block to the start of the function.

```
function Show-CmdletBinding {
    [CmdletBinding()]
    param()
}
```

The **cmdletbinding** attribute has its own set of optional parameters that includes **DefaultParameterSetName** To set the default parameter set when the function has multiple parameter sets. This will be used when no parameter sets are specified when the function is invoked. The **SupportsShouldProcess** enables the use of the **-What-If** and **-Confirm** parameters. The -**What-If** is used to simulate the operation of the function, without making any changes and the **-Confirm** is used to prompt the user for confirmation, before making any changes. The **-ConfirmImpact** Is used to define the risk level when using the **-Confirm** parameter. The valid values are none, low, medium and high. **PositionalBinding** is used to enable the use of positional parameters instead of using named parameters. There are a few more optional parameters like **HelpURI**, **SupportsPaging** and **SupportsTransactions**. You would set the parameters like shown here:

```
function Show-CmdletBinding {
    [CmdletBinding(DefaultParameterSetName="SetOne",
    SupportsShouldProcess=$true,
    ConfirmImpact="High",
    PositionalBinding=$false,
    HelpURI="Https://Comet.Can.Fly.com",
    SupportsPaging=$false,
    SupportsTransactions=$false)]
    param()
}
```

The verbose and debug parameters are used for managing verbose and debug output inside the function, you can then specify additional output in the function that will be sent to the console when it is called with the **-Verbose** and/or **-Debug** switches. The **ErrorAction** parameter lets you specify how errors should be handled in the function, the same way you use the **ErrorActionPreference** variable inside a script. It also allows the same parameter values such as **SilentlyContinue**, **Stop**, **Continue**, **Inquire,** and **Ignore**. The **ErrorVariable** allows you to specify a variable where you can store the error messages that the function generates while executing its commands, this variable can then later be accessed, and you can view or process the saved error messages.

```
function Show-Verbose {
    [CmdletBinding()]
    param()
    Write-Verbose "This only displays when -Verbose switch is set"
    Write-Debug "This only displays when -Debug switch is set"
}
$Errors = @()
Show-Verbose -Verbose -Debug -ErrorAction Stop -ErrorVariable Errors
```

> **Note: The -ErrorVariable variable is added as an argument without $ to the parameter. Also note that it overrides the variable content. To add errors to the variable instead of overriding it, use a plus sign in front of the variable name: -ErrorVariable +Errors.**

By adding the **CmdletBinding** attribute and the **param()** block to your function you have already made it advanced and incorporated several features that can be utilized as such. Even though not all functions have parameters, a **function** is usually created with flexibility in mind and usually have at least a few, this of course depends on its specific functionality and what it is used for. If your function does not take any parameters you still include the (empty) **param()** block.

Parameter attributes

Parameter attributes are used for adding specific attributes to the function's parameters like positioning, mandatory and **parametersetname**. Usually, parameters are named and must be specified when calling a function, by its parameter name. With positioning you can specify at what index a specific parameter should be available. It ensures that you do not need to type the name of the parameter when calling the function. If you add a parameter like **Name** to your function and sets its position attribute to **0** then the first argument you provide to the function without specifying its parameter name, will be declared as the **-Name** parameter. By assigning positions to multiple parameters, you can call a function and provide the arguments in a specific order without specifying the parameter names. Adding parameters to a function requires a parameter block, also called **param** block. Inside this **param** block you would define the different parameters and their attributes.

```
function Show-Params {

    [CmdletBinding()]

    param (

        [Parameter(Position = 0)]

        $Name,

        [Parameter(Position = 1)]

        $Age

    )

    # Code goes here

}
```

Another common attribute is the **mandatory** attribute. This indicates whether a parameter is mandatory and must be provided when the function is called, this is indicated by setting the property of the **mandatory** attribute to **$true**. If the attribute property is set to **$false** or omitted, then the parameter is considered optional and does not need to be provided when the function is called:

```
function Show-Params {

    [CmdletBinding()]

    param (

        [Parameter(Mandatory = $true)]

        $Name,

        [Parameter(Mandatory = $false)]

        $Age,

        $Ability

    )

    # Code goes here

}
```

With parameter sets you can divide different parameters into groups, then you can **bind** specific parameters to these groups. When a specific parameter is used when invoking the function, it would trigger a specific subset of code depending on which parameter set it belongs to. An example would be when you use the **Get-Process** cmdlet, you can call it using either the **-Name** or the **-Id parameter** or even omit calling it with any arguments at all. When calling this cmdlet with the **-Name** parameter, the inside logic for finding the specific process is different when invoking the cmdlet using the **-Id** parameter. Without going into many details about the different process logic, one uses a string to search through the Name properties and the other uses an integer to search through the Id properties, of all the processes on the system, then returns the found process, if any. Omitting arguments entirely will use another parameter set and return all processes, this is also the default parameter set for this cmdlet. Notice that the default parameter set, in the **Get-Process** cmdlet omits using any parameters, so when you call the cmdlet without any parameters, it still invokes the logical process for that parameter set. Below you can see how you could define different and default parameter sets.

```
function Show-Params {
        [CmdletBinding(DefaultParameterSetName = "SetOne")]
        param (
                [Parameter(ParameterSetName = "SetOne")]
                $Name,
                [Parameter(ParameterSetName = "SetOne")]
                $Age,
                [Parameter(ParameterSetName = "SetTwo")]
                $Ability
        )
        # Code goes here

}
```

Parameter validation lets you validate the arguments provided to your parameters, if the validation criteria of the parameters are not met, then invoking the function would result in an error. There are different types of validation, where the most common one is the data type validation, this ensures that the provided argument is of the correct data type. If your parameter must be of the string type, setting the data type validation to **string** would enforce this and it would result in an invalid argument if any other data type was provided. You can also validate a range and make sure that the parameter value is within this range, this could be integers between 1 and 10. You can make validation to whether an argument is null or empty and validate sets like saying an argument should be called either A, B or C or it is not valid for that argument. You can use regular expressions, enumerators and even script blocks for validating parameters.

```
function Show-Params {
        [CmdletBinding()]
```

```
    param (
            [ValidateNotNullOrEmpty()]
            [String]$Name,
            [ValidateRange(0, 120)]
            [Int]$Age,
            [ValidateSet("Flying", "Unlimited Power", "LaserEyes")]
            [String]$Ability
    )
    # Code goes here
}
```

With the use of the **CmdletBinding** attribute and parameter attributes you have the building blocks for creating an advanced function. In the next recipe we will create an advanced function by using these attributes and its features and as we progress through this chapter, we will be adding more complex features to this function and create other advanced functions.

Recipe 3: Create an advanced function

We now have the first building blocks for creating an advanced function. As previously stated, as soon as you add the **CmdletBinding** attribute you have made a function advanced, but a function with only a **CmdletBinding** attribute and the features it provides will not do much, unless you of course are only interested in it being able to write some verbose or debug output. We need to add something more. Parameters might be a good idea. It depends on what your function should do, it is not a requirement that a function have parameters and takes arguments, if it just need to do some static work that does not require any input, then parameters are not needed, but your function will be more versatile if you add parameters and can change certain conditions depending on different input provided. Let us create an advanced function. For this function, let us keep using the superhero theme and create something relevant. Let us pretend, *we are creating a simple game with superheroes. They should have names, abilities, and strength. The first thing we need is to create a function that lets us create different superheroes by providing a few arguments. The function should return a superhero object so we can update and change their properties when needed.* We create the function **Add-SuperHero**. Notice the use of **Add** instead of a word like **create**. This is an approved **verb** for PowerShell commands, which is not a requirement but a best practice that also keep the **PSScriptAnalyzer** satisfied.

```
function Add-SuperHero {
    [CmdletBinding()]
    param (
            [Parameter(Position=0,Mandatory=$true)]
            [ValidateNotNullOrEmpty()]
            [String]$Name,
```

```
        [Parameter(Position=1)]
        [ValidateSet("Flying","Indestructible","LaserEyes")]
        [String[]]$Abilities = "None",
        [Parameter(Position=2,Mandatory=$false)]
        [ValidateRange(0,100)]
        [Int]$Powers = 10
    )
    $Object = [PSCustomObject]@{
        Abilities = $Abilities
        Name = $Name
        Powers = $Powers
    }
    return $Object
}
```

Let us break the function down and go through what is happening:

1. We add the [**CmdletBinding()**] attribute. We are not yet using any of its features, but you should not create an advanced function without it.

2. We add the param block, that lets us define parameters with attributes.

3. The first parameter we add is [**String**]**$Name**. By setting the specific type, we make it a requirement that arguments for this parameter must be of the type **String**. If we try to provide arguments of another type, the function will throw an error.

4. For the [**String**]**$Name** parameter we add the **Position** and **Mandatory** attribute by specifying these inside a square bracket where we use the parameter attribute to declare it. We set the **Position** to index 0, meaning that all arguments set as the first argument when invoking the function, will be set as the **$Name** parameter, unless the arguments are provided with named parameters like -**Name** when invoking the function. The **Mandatory** attribute is set to **$true** meaning that setting an argument for this parameter is not optional, and the function will throw an error if an argument for the **$Name** parameter is omitted.

5. The [**ValidateNotNullOrEmpty()**] attribute is quite self-explanatory. If an argument provided for the **$Name** parameter is **$Null** value or an empty string, the function will throw an error.

6. We add the [**String[]**]**$Abilities**=**"None"** parameter to the function. Notice that instead of type **String** we have declared it as **String[].** It will not only accept a single string but an array of strings. Also notice the =**"None"** value. This means that the default value for the parameter will be set to the string **None** if no arguments are provided.

7. We set the **Position** of the **$Abilities** parameter to **1.** Which is the next index in line. We do not set the **Mandatory** attribute, since we have provided the parameter with a default value, it will always have a value, and does not need to be provided one. By setting a default parameter value, you make the **Mandatory** attribute becomes irrelevant for this parameter.

8. For the **$Abilities** parameter we use a validation **set** by specifying **[ValidateSet()]** and add the strings in an array that must be used as valid arguments. If a string argument provided for this parameter is not in the validate set, the function will throw an error.

9. The last parameter is **$Powers**. We declare this as an integer type: **[int]**. Every other type we add as an argument to this parameter will result in an error.

10. We set the **Position** attribute for this parameter to the next index in line, 2. We also specify the **Mandatory** attribute and set the value to **$false**. Since this is the default value of the **Mandatory** attribute, this is unnecessary and can be omitted, the result would be the same. It is just added here as an example.

11. After defining all the parameters, we now want our function to do some work for us. Since we stated that the function should: **Return a superhero object** we simply would gather our parameters into a combined object that defines our superheroes and then return this object so we can save it in a variable. We use the built-in type **PSCustomObject**. This is a type that lets us create an object with custom properties. Instead of having to create a custom class object, this is an easy way to structure our data. We can instantiate the **PSCustomObject** type either by using the **New-Object** cmdlet with at type of **PSCustomObject** and then add the properties as a **Hashtable** like this:

```
$Object = New-Object -Type PSCustomObject -Property @{
    "Abilities" = $Abilities
    "Name" = $Name
    "Powers" = $Powers
}
```

Or we could use the accelerator as we have done in our function: **[PSCustom Object]@{}** the principle is the same, but using the accelerator is faster and more readable and it saves us some code. We create our custom object and save it in the **$Object** variable.

12. The last thing we do is returning our **$Object**, so that it can be saved in a variable when the function is invoked. You could just return the **PSCustomObject** directly without saving it in a variable inside the function before returning it, but for readability purposes it is preferred to always save the object in a placeholder, in this case the **$Object** variable, and then specifically return it, it makes it easier to see what the function is returning.

To sum it all up, we have created an advanced function. It is not a complex function, but it uses advanced features. We start by declaring the **CmdletBinding** attribute. We add parameters with different attributes. Some are mandatory, some not. We validate data in different ways, which makes sure if we are getting the datatypes and values we want, or else we would be notified by the returned error. We combine the input parameter values into a single object with properties and then we return that object. This is an advanced function, no matter the simplicity, and we are using a few different attributes for our parameters. One thing we have not used yet, even though we declared it, is the **CmdletBinding** attribute. As mentioned earlier it is not a *must* to add the **CmdletBinding** attribute to advanced functions, but in most cases, it should be considered a best practice to always add it since it essentially elevates the function to operate like a cmdlet, thereby enabling the features that are also typically associated with cmdlets. We incorporate a simple feature from it into our function, we add verbose output, so it ends up looking like this:

```powershell
function Add-Superhero {
    [CmdletBinding()]
    param (
            [Parameter(Position=0,Mandatory=$true)]
            [ValidateNotNullOrEmpty()]
            [String]$Name,
            [Parameter(Position=1)]
            [ValidateSet("Flying","Indestructable","LaserEyes")]
            [String[]]$Abilities = "None",
            [Parameter(Position=2,Mandatory=$false)]
            [ValidateRange(0,100)]
            [Int]$Powers = 10
              )
    $Object = [PSCustomObject]@{
        Abilities = $Abilities
        Name = $Name
        Powers = $Powers
    }
    Write-Verbose "Created Superhero with the name: $Name"
    Write-Verbose "$Name was given the following abilities: $Abilities"
    Write-Verbose "$Name has a power of: $Powers"
    return $Object
}
```

Let us create a superhero with our function. Let us create **Comet** for now, a mid-tier powered superhero with the ability to **fly** and shoot **lasers** from his eyes. We invoke our function with these arguments and save it as the **$Comet** variable, we also set the **-Verbose** switch to get the verbose output, shown in *Figure 2.6*:

```
PS C:\Temp\Superhero> $Comet = Add-Superhero -Name Comet -Power 43 -Abilities Flying,LaserEyes -Verbose
VERBOSE: Created Superhero with the name: Comet
VERBOSE: Comet was given the following abilities: Flying LaserEyes
VERBOSE: Comet has a power of 43
PS C:\Temp\Superhero> $Comet

Abilities              Name  Powers
---------              ----  ------
{Flying, LaserEyes} Comet       43

PS C:\Temp\Superhero> $Comet.Name
Comet
PS C:\Temp\Superhero> $Comet.Abilities
Flying
LaserEyes
PS C:\Temp\Superhero> $Comet.Powers
43
```

Figure 2.6: Invoking the Add-Superhero function and its output

Our superhero is created as expected and we see the verbose output telling us that he was created with the name **Comet** and that he was given the abilities **flying** and **laser eyes** and has a power of **43**. If we call our **$Comet** variable, we can see that it was saved as an Object with these properties. Not only can we see the properties using dot notation, but we can also change them if our superhero at some point should get stronger and adapt more abilities, shown in *Figure 2.7*.

```
PS C:\Temp\Superhero> $Comet.Powers = 50
PS C:\Temp\Superhero> $Comet.Abilities += "Indestructable"
PS C:\Temp\Superhero> $Comet

Abilities                             Name   Powers
---------                             ----   ------
{Flying, LaserEyes, Indestructable} Comet       50
```

Figure 2.7: Adding abilities and increasing the power of the superhero

Our advanced function is a starting point for creating superheroes of all kinds, though we have limited ourselves to a few abilities and max power with our parameter validations, we can easily create a lot of superheroes, and we can of course update our parameters to accommodate for a lot more abilities and greater power if needed. In *Figure 2.8* we create a few different superheroes and as you can see, we can add the arguments to our function not only by using the named parameters but also using our positioned attributes we added to the parameters in the function. Note that **Black Catman** does not have any abilities, since we did not provide any arguments for the **Abilities** parameter, it uses the default **None** that we specified. We also created some intentionally with invalid arguments so you can see the validation attribute errors that it returned when no valid arguments are provided:

```
● PS C:\Temp\Superhero> Add-Superhero -Name "Miss Fury" -Abilities Indestructable -Powers 55

  Abilities          Name      Powers
  ---------          ----      ------
  {Indestructable} Miss Fury       55

● PS C:\Temp\Superhero> Add-Superhero "Black Catman" -Powers 15

  Abilities Name          Powers
  --------- ----          ------
  {None}    Black Catman      15

● PS C:\Temp\Superhero> Add-Superhero "Flying man" Flying 25

  Abilities Name     .Powers
  --------- ----      ------
  {Flying}  Flying man      25

● PS C:\Temp\Superhero> Add-Superhero "" Flying 5
  Add-Superhero: Cannot validate argument on parameter 'Name'. The argument is null or empty. Provide
   an argument that is not null or empty, and then try the command again.
● PS C:\Temp\Superhero> Add-Superhero "Dancer" Dancing 5
  Add-Superhero: Cannot validate argument on parameter 'Abilities'. The argument "Dancing" does not b
  elong to the set "Flying,Indestructable,LaserEyes" specified by the ValidateSet attribute. Supply a
  n argument that is in the set and then try the command again.
```

Figure 2.8: *Testing parameter and validation attributes*

We have created an advanced function that uses the **CmdletBinding** attribute and some parameter attributes like Positioning, the **Mandatory** attribute, setting default parameter values and different Validation methods. We use the **PSCustomObject** accelerator to return a superhero object with its properties and we incorporated some verbose output, that tells us more about the function process. With this advanced function and the few features and attributes we incorporated, we can make powerful and dynamic objects with properties whenever we invoke our function.

In the following topics and recipes in this chapter we will incorporate more advanced features into our function to make it even more dynamic and versatile.

Output formatting

When a function has finished its process execution and you need to return the data it collected or created, it can be output and returned in different formats. You might just want to write a simple string containing your data to the console or return and save it to a variable for later use. But your data might be more complex than that, and you need to work with it in another function or other types of expressions, then a simple string output might not be enough. Advanced functions are usually meant to perform more complex tasks and the data it should return, if it returns any, are also usually more complex. Inside the **Add-Superhero** function, the parameter values are stored in a **PSCustomObject**. This object is then returned as output from the function and can be assigned to a variable. Using a custom object enables us to not only use the data but also to modify the data values inside the variable object. This meets the requirements in terms of an object where the data inside can be manipulated. If the output data was not properly formatted and returned as a string containing the values, it would be more difficult to use the function output, as input for other functions and expressions. Not only that but it would also be more difficult to modify the values inside. If we decided to return the output from the **Add-Superhero** function as a string instead of a custom object, it could look like this:

```
$Object = "Name=Comet;Abilities=Flying,LaserEyes;Power=43"
Return $Object
```

Not only is the output as a string harder to read, but it is also very static and more difficult to modify when we need to update a value inside it. We would have to use some string manipulation and replacement techniques and we might even need to create another function that we could use to manage this. So why did we choose to return our output as a **PSCustomObject** in the first place? We could also have used a more complex data type instead of a string, like an array or a **Hashtable**. We can see that an array would not be the optimal type for our output, but it might still be a lot better than using a string. At least we could use indexing for finding a specific value, it could be the *Name* property value, if we are consistent in the placement of the different properties, this could work. We could even accommodate for the multi valued **Abilities** property by also using an array for this property. The array approach could look something like this:

```
$Object = @("Comet", @("Flying","LaserEyes"), 43)
```

Not pretty, but still better than the string approach. If our index 0 always is the **Name** property, index 1 is always **Abilities** and index 2 is always the **Power** property then we could call the values using indexing like shown in *Figure 2.9*:

```
● PS C:\Temp\Superhero> $Object = @("Comet", @("Flying","LaserEyes"), 43)
● PS C:\Temp\Superhero> $Object
  Comet
  Flying
  LaserEyes
  43
● PS C:\Temp\Superhero> $Object[0]
  Comet
● PS C:\Temp\Superhero> $Object[1]
  Flying
  LaserEyes
● PS C:\Temp\Superhero> $Object[2]
  43
```

Figure 2.9: Calling values in array object

What if we try to update a value in the array? Let us give Comet another ability, **indestructible**, and upgrade his **Power** to 50:

```
PS C:\Temp\Superhero> $Object[1] += "Indestructable"
PS C:\Temp\Superhero> $Object[2] = 50
PS C:\Temp\Superhero> $Object[1]
Flying
LaserEyes
Indestructable
PS C:\Temp\Superhero> $Object[2]
50
```

Figure 2.10: *Changing property values in array object*

We are still able to add and update the property values inside our array, but we need to know the exact index location for a specific property, this is not optimal. If we had 30 properties, then it could be quite difficult to remember the specific index for each of them and it would be much more prone to errors. If we had a **Power** property at index 27 and a **Level** property at index 28 then you by accident added 10 levels to the superhero instead of increasing its power with 10, because you increased at index 28 instead of 27, you would end up with unwanted behavior and a superhero that is to high level for its current state. The next would be to try a **Hashtable**. This would be much more like our **PSCustomObject** since we are using a **Hashtable** in our **PSCustomObject** accelerator. Let us compare them:

```
$Object1 = [PSCustomObject]@{
    "Abilities" = $Abilities
    "Name" = $Name
    "Powers" = $Powers
}
$Object2 = @{
    "Abilities" = $Abilities
    "Name" = $Name
    "Powers" = $Powers
}
```

They are almost identical, so what makes them different from each other?

A **Hashtable** is an unordered collection of data consisting of key/value pairs. They are suitable when you need to find values based on specific keys whereas a **PSCustomObject** is an ordered object that represents its data in properties and values. This is more suitable for structured and organized data similar to an object-oriented approach and it is also better suited when data needs to be transformed or filtered. A **Hashtable** has more built-in methods that can be used to **add, remove, find keys, find values** and so on, and properties like **count, keys** and **values** that can be used to make it easier working with a **Hashtable**. A **PSCustomObject** does not have all these methods and properties, instead it adds each property as a **NoteProperty** in its object, but it only contains a few default methods like **Get-Type** and **ToString**. By using the **Get-Member** cmdlet we can see the methods and properties for both of these types, as shown in *Figure 2.11*:

```
⊛ PS C:\Temp\Superhero> $Object1 | Get-Member

    TypeName: System.Management.Automation.PSCustomObject

  Name          MemberType    Definition
  ----          ----------    ----------
  Equals        Method        bool Equals(System.Object obj)
  GetHashCode   Method        int GetHashCode()
  GetType       Method        type GetType()
  ToString      Method        string ToString()
  Abilities     NoteProperty  object Abilities=null
  Name          NoteProperty  object Name=null
  Powers        NoteProperty  object Powers=null

⊛ PS C:\Temp\Superhero> $Object2 | Get-Member

    TypeName: System.Collections.Hashtable

  Name            MemberType            Definition
  ----            ----------            ----------
  Add             Method                void Add(System.Object key, System.Object value),
  Clear           Method                void Clear(), void IDictionary.Clear()
  Clone           Method                System.Object Clone(), System.Object ICloneable.(
  Contains        Method                bool Contains(System.Object key), bool IDictiona
  ContainsKey     Method                bool ContainsKey(System.Object key)
  ContainsValue   Method                bool ContainsValue(System.Object value)
  CopyTo          Method                void CopyTo(array array, int arrayIndex), void I(
  Equals          Method                bool Equals(System.Object obj)
  GetEnumerator   Method                System.Collections.IDictionaryEnumerator GetEnume
  GetHashCode     Method                int GetHashCode()
  GetObjectData   Method                void GetObjectData(System.Runtime.Serialization.!
  GetType         Method                type GetType()
  OnDeserialization Method              void OnDeserialization(System.Object sender), vo:
  Remove          Method                void Remove(System.Object key), void IDictionary
  ToString        Method                string ToString()
  Item            ParameterizedProperty System.Object Item(System.Object key) {get;set;}
  Count           Property              int Count {get;}
  IsFixedSize     Property              bool IsFixedSize {get;}
  IsReadOnly      Property              bool IsReadOnly {get;}
  IsSynchronized  Property              bool IsSynchronized {get;}
  Keys            Property              System.Collections.ICollection Keys {get;}
  SyncRoot        Property              System.Object SyncRoot {get;}
  Values          Property              System.Collections.ICollection Values {get;}
```

Figure 2.11: Member comparison between PSCustomObject and Hashtable

So why are we using the **PSCustomObject** instead of a **Hashtable**? It depends on what you want to do with the data at a later time. Do you need to manipulate, transform, or filter it in a certain way? Or do you just need the data to be stored in an object where you can easily access it when needed? Regarding our function, it was actually a calculated choice when choosing the **PSCustomObject** over the **Hashtable**. We should be thinking ahead and wonder if the data objects with all our superheroes, might need to be exported in a structured manner later. With the **PSCustomObject** all the objects can be stored in an array, and then that array can be exported to a CSV file. We would not be able to do this with the data in a structured and ordered manner if it was stored in a **Hashtable**. Look at *Figure 2.12*. We have created an array containing 3 **PSCustomObject** objects and an array containing **3 Hashtable** objects. This corresponds to creating three superheroes with the **Add-Superhero** function where, as it is now, they are returned as **PSCustomObject**´s and then three that are returned as **Hashtable** objects and then saved in an array correspondingly to its returned data type.

```
 8    $PSCustomObjectArray = @(
 9    [PSCustomObject]@{"Abilities" = "Flying"; "Name" = "Comet"; "Powers" = 43},
10    [PSCustomObject]@{"Abilities" = "Flying"; "Name" = "Omega"; "Powers" = 34},
11    [PSCustomObject]@{"Abilities" = "Flying"; "Name" = "Beta"; "Powers" = 50}
12    )
13
14    $HashtableArray = @(
15    @{"Abilities" = "Flying"; "Name" = "Comet"; "Powers" = 43},
16    @{"Abilities" = "Flying"; "Name" = "Omega"; "Powers" = 34},
17    @{"Abilities" = "Flying"; "Name" = "Beta"; "Powers" = 50}
18    )
```

```
OUTPUT    DEBUG CONSOLE    TERMINAL

● PS C:\Temp\Superhero> $PSCustomObjectArray

Abilities Name    Powers
--------- ----    ------
Flying    Comet       43
Flying    Omega       34
Flying    Beta        50

● PS C:\Temp\Superhero> $HashtableArray

Name                     Value
----                     -----
Powers                   43
Abilities                Flying
Name                     Comet
Powers                   34
Abilities                Flying
Name                     Omega
Powers                   50
Abilities                Flying
Name                     Beta
```

Figure 2.12: Arrays with PSCustomObject and Hashtable data types

In the output you can see that the **PSCustomObject** array contains an ordered and structured set of data divided into the different properties whereas the **Hashtable** array consists of unstructured data in key/value pairs. If we export the two sets of data to a **.csv** file, in the **PSCustomObject** file it would have kept the ordered structure, whereas the order in the **Hashtable** data file is random:

```
● PS C:\Temp\Superhero> $PSCustomObjectArray | Export-Csv PSCustomObject.csv
● PS C:\Temp\Superhero> $HashtableArray | Export-Csv Hashtable.csv
○ PS C:\Temp\Superhero> []
```

```
PSCustomObject.csv - Notepad        │  Hashtable.csv - Notepad

File  Edit  Format  View  Help      │  File  Edit  Format  View  Help
"Abilities","Name","Powers"         │  "Powers","Abilities","Name"
"Flying","Comet","43"               │  "43","Flying","Comet"
"Flying","Omega","34"               │  "34","Flying","Omega"
"Flying","Beta","50"                │  "50","Flying","Beta"
```

Figure 2.13: Hashtable and PSCustomObject data sets output to CSV files

Not only will the ordered structured data be better suited if we loop over the data set, but it would also spare us the use of enumerators that we would need if we looped over the **Hashtable** data. It is also better suited for being sent through the pipeline to other cmdlet´s.

As you can see, the way you format your output data matters, it of course depends on how you are going to use that data. If we only needed to use the superheroes created with the **Add-Superhero** function in a simple way, like adding powers or removing abilities inside the code itself, without ever having to loop over it or sending it through the pipeline to other cmdlet´s, then a **Hashtable** would have been enough. Thinking about how you are going to use specific data later is a good idea and then format the output accordingly. In our case we optimized it for later use, both for exporting it and for possibly manipulating it later or using it in other cmdlet´s and functions in a structured manner by using the **PSCustomObject**.

Dynamic parameters

Dynamic parameters are parameters that are based on certain conditions or criteria. They are not a part of the functions main parameter set or sets but are dynamically created when certain criteria or conditions are met. They can be added or removed depending on certain user input, parameter values or other dynamic factors. If we consider the **Add-Superhero** function and its parameters: If we were to add a specific ability to a superhero that would require further properties to be defined, we could add these additional properties using dynamic parameters. It could be that whenever a superhero is given the flying ability, properties such as **Height** and **Speed** might also need to be defined to indicate how high and how fast the superhero can fly. Such properties might not be relevant for superheroes without the flying ability, so if this specific ability is not specified as an argument value for the abilities parameter, the dynamic parameters will not be triggered, and the additional properties are never defined for that superhero. We can conclude that **Flying** is the *trigger* property value for the dynamic parameter. So basically, the dynamic parameters are based on the condition that the flying ability is specified as an argument for the abilities parameter when the **Add-Superhero** function is invoked. If the flying ability is specified as an argument for the abilities parameter, the **Height** and **Speed** parameters becomes mandatory and you must specify their values, if not you will be prompted to provide the arguments just as you would with any other mandatory parameter. To add dynamic parameters to a function, use the **DynamicParam** script block within the function.

It was mentioned that whenever the dynamic parameters are not triggered the respective **Height** and **Speed** properties would never be defined. That is not entirely true in our case, because we add them on purpose. This is to ensure that all superheroes have these specific properties defined by default. This makes it less error prone. If we try to use a superheroes dynamic property or if we later decided to give a superhero a new ability that would require one or more of these properties and the property is not already defined, it could then result in an error. We prevent this by pre-defining these additional properties as **Null** values.

When the *trigger* property value is defined as an argument to the abilities parameter, and arguments are provided for the additional dynamic parameters, the new object properties will be populated with the correct data type and values. In *Figure 2.14.* We call the **Add-Superhero** function after we have added the **DynamicParam** block and create a superhero both with and without the flying ability. We pipe the commands to **Get-Member** to view the available methods and properties for these new superheroes:

```
PS C:\Temp\Superhero> add-Superhero -Name "Walking Man" -Powers 80 | gm

    TypeName: System.Management.Automation.PSCustomObject

Name           MemberType   Definition
----           ----------   ----------
Equals         Method       bool Equals(System.Object obj)
GetHashCode    Method       int GetHashCode()
GetType        Method       type GetType()
ToString       Method       string ToString()
Abilities      NoteProperty string[] Abilities=System.String[]
FlyingHeight   NoteProperty object FlyingHeight=null
FlyingSpeed    NoteProperty object FlyingSpeed=null
Name           NoteProperty string Name=Walking Man
Powers         NoteProperty int Powers=80

PS C:\Temp\Superhero> add-Superhero -Name "Flying Man" -Abilities Flying -Powers 80 -FlyingHeight 100 -FlyingSpeed 32 | gm

    TypeName: System.Management.Automation.PSCustomObject

Name           MemberType   Definition
----           ----------   ----------
Equals         Method       bool Equals(System.Object obj)
GetHashCode    Method       int GetHashCode()
GetType        Method       type GetType()
ToString       Method       string ToString()
Abilities      NoteProperty string[] Abilities=System.String[]
FlyingHeight   NoteProperty int FlyingHeight=100
FlyingSpeed    NoteProperty int FlyingSpeed=32
Name           NoteProperty string Name=Flying Man
Powers         NoteProperty int Powers=80
```

Figure 2.14: *Methods and properties of a superhero with and a superhero without the flying ability*

As shown, the new properties exist whether the superhero has the flying ability property, but they are only properly populated once the flying ability is added, and the new properties become mandatory due to the dynamic parameters.

Recipe 4: Adding dynamic parameters

Let us see how we add the dynamic parameters for **FlyingHeight** and **FlyingSpeed** to our **Add-Superhero** function, whenever an argument for the **Abilities** parameter contains the **Flying** ability. We use the **DynamicParam** script block inside our function, this is specifically created for defining dynamic parameters that can be added dynamically during the execution of a function.

- We declare the dynamic parameters script block, by using the keyword **DynamicParam**.

- Inside the **DynamicParam** block, the variable **$DynamicParams** is declared. This is the placeholder for the collection of dynamic parameters inside the

DynamicParam block. For the value of this variable, we create a new object from the **RuntimeDefinedParameterDictionary** class. This class is designed for storing collections of dynamic parameters that are defined at runtime.

- The **if** block is used to check if the **$Abilities** variable contains the **Flying** value. If it does, it proceeds to create the dynamic parameters for the **FlyingHeight** and **FlyingSpeed** properties. If not, it continues without running the **if** block and no additional dynamic parameters are created.

- For each dynamic parameter we add, we create an object from the **ParameterAttribute** class. Here we define the attributes for each parameter like **ParameterSetName**, **Position** and the **Mandatory** attribute and their values. Notice the use of **__AllParameterSets** which is a special parameter set name that lets you add the parameter to all parameter sets inside the function.

- An attribute collection is then created for each parameter, that holds the parameter attributes and the **ParameterAttribute** object is then added to this collection. It is created from the class **Collection[System.Attribute]**.

- The last object we create is a **RuntimeDefinedParameter**. In this we define the parameter name, **FlyingHeight**, the type of the parameter **[int]** and then we add the parameter attribute collection that contains the parameters attributes and their values.

- The last thing we do is then adding the **RuntimeDefinedParameter** object to the **$DynamicParams** variable we created in the beginning. We specify the key as the parameter name and the value as the **RuntimeDefinedParameter** object that contains our collection of the parameter and its attributes.

- When we have created all our dynamic parameters, and added them to the **$DynamicParams** dictionary variable, we then return this variable back to the function:

```
DynamicParam {

    $DynamicParams = New-Object System.Management.Automation.
RuntimeDefinedParameterDictionary

    if ($Abilities -contains "Flying") {

        $FlyingHeightAttr = New-Object System.Management.Automation.
ParameterAttribute

        $FlyingHeightAttr.ParameterSetName = "__AllParameterSets"

        $FlyingHeightAttr.Position = 3

        $FlyingHeightAttr.Mandatory = $true

        $FlyingHeightColl = New-Object System.Collections.
ObjectModel.Collection[System.Attribute]

        $FlyingHeightColl.Add($FlyingHeightAttr)
```

```
        $FlyingHeightParam = New-Object System.Management.
Automation.RuntimeDefinedParameter("FlyingHeight", [int],
$FlyingHeightColl)

        $DynamicParams.Add("FlyingHeight", $FlyingHeightParam)

        $FlyingSpeedAttr = New-Object System.Management.Automation.
ParameterAttribute

        $FlyingSpeedAttr.ParameterSetName = "__AllParameterSets"

        $FlyingSpeedAttr.Position = 4

        $FlyingSpeedAttr.Mandatory = $true

        $FlyingSpeedColl = New-Object System.Collections.
ObjectModel.Collection[System.Attribute]

        $FlyingSpeedColl.Add($FlyingSpeedAttr)

        $FlyingSpeedParam = New-Object System.Management.Automation.
RuntimeDefinedParameter("FlyingSpeed", [int], $FlyingSpeedColl)

        $DynamicParams.Add("FlyingSpeed", $FlyingSpeedParam)

    }

    return $DynamicParams

}
```

In a function, the **DynamicParam** block is executed before the rest of the function so that the dynamically created parameters are available to the function at its runtime. We add the **DynamicParam** block to our **Add-Superhero** function:

```
function Add-Superhero {
    [CmdletBinding()]
    param (
        [Parameter(Position = 0, Mandatory = $true)]
        [ValidateNotNullOrEmpty()]
        [String]$Name,
        [Parameter(Position = 1)]
        [ValidateSet("Flying", "Indestructible", "LaserEyes")]
        [String[]]$Abilities = "None",
        [Parameter(Position = 2, Mandatory = $false)]
        [ValidateRange(0, 100)]
        [Int]$Powers = 10
    )
    DynamicParam {
```

```
        $DynamicParams = New-Object System.Management.Automation.
RuntimeDefinedParameterDictionary
        if ($Abilities -contains "Flying") {
            $FlyingHeightAttr = New-Object System.Management.Automation.
ParameterAttribute
            $FlyingHeightAttr.ParameterSetName = "__AllParameterSets"
            $FlyingHeightAttr.Position = 3
            $FlyingHeightAttr.Mandatory = $true
            $FlyingHeightColl = New-Object System.Collections.ObjectModel.
Collection[System.Attribute]
            $FlyingHeightColl.Add($FlyingHeightAttr)
            $FlyingHeightParam = New-Object System.Management.Automation.
RuntimeDefinedParameter("FlyingHeight", [int], $FlyingHeightColl)
            $DynamicParams.Add("FlyingHeight", $FlyingHeightParam)
            $FlyingSpeedAttr = New-Object System.Management.Automation.
ParameterAttribute
            $FlyingSpeedAttr.ParameterSetName = "__AllParameterSets"
            $FlyingSpeedAttr.Position = 4
            $FlyingSpeedAttr.Mandatory = $true
            $FlyingSpeedColl = New-Object System.Collections.ObjectModel.
Collection[System.Attribute]
            $FlyingSpeedColl.Add($FlyingSpeedAttr)
            $FlyingSpeedParam = New-Object System.Management.Automation.
RuntimeDefinedParameter("FlyingSpeed", [int], $FlyingSpeedColl)
            $DynamicParams.Add("FlyingSpeed", $FlyingSpeedParam)
        }
        return $DynamicParams
    }
    Process {
        $Object = [PSCustomObject]@{
            Abilities = $Abilities
            Name = $Name
            Powers = $Powers
            FlyingHeight = $PSBoundParameters["FlyingHeight"]
            FlyingSpeed = $PSBoundParameters["FlyingSpeed"]
        }
```

```
        Write-Verbose "Created Superhero with the name: $Name"

        Write-Verbose "$Name was given the following abilities: $Abilities"

        Write-Verbose "$Name has a power of: $Powers"

        if ($Object.FlyingHeight) {

            Write-Verbose "$Name can fly at a height of $($Object.
FlyingHeight) meters."

        }

        if ($Object.FlyingSpeed) {

            Write-Verbose "$Name can fly at a speed of $($Object.
FlyingSpeed) km/h."

        }

        return $Object

    }

}
```

Note that we have added our additional code inside a **Process** block. We have also added verbose output to the two new dynamic functions, the **if** condition for each of these ensures that they are only used when the dynamic parameters exist and contain a value, or else whenever you invoke the function with verbose output, they would be written to console with **Null** values, resulting in wrong an obscure output. Also, note the use of the **$PSBoundParameters** variable. This is an automatic PowerShell Hashtable variable that contains the parameters that are passed to a script or a function. It only includes the values of parameters that were specifically provided by the caller, so it does not include the ones that have been left at their default values. In this case, this variable contains the values for the dynamic parameters that were provided, and we use this to reference these values within the function.

In *Figure 2.15* we create two new superheroes from our updated function. **Walking Man** with no abilities and **Flying Man** with the ability to fly. Here you can see the dynamic parameters are added as soon as **Flying Man** is given the **Flying** ability. The parameters are not added to the function call, so you can see that you will be prompted to provide these if they are not supplied, just like any other mandatory parameter would behave if no arguments were supplied to them. When you know of these dynamic parameters before calling a function, you could add them as any other parameters to the function call as soon as you had specified the **Flying** argument to the **Abilities** parameter:

```
● PS C:\Temp\Superhero> $WalkingMan = Add-Superhero -Name "Walking Man" -Powers 80 -Verbose
  VERBOSE: Created Superhero with the name: Walking Man
  VERBOSE: Walking Man was given the following abilities: None
  VERBOSE: Walking Man has a power of: 80
● PS C:\Temp\Superhero> $WalkingMan

  Abilities    : {None}
  Name         : Walking Man
  Powers       : 80
  FlyingHeight :
  FlyingSpeed  :


● PS C:\Temp\Superhero> $FlyingMan = Add-Superhero -Name "Flying Man" -Abilities Flying -Powers 80 -Verbose

  cmdlet Add-Superhero at command pipeline position 1
  Supply values for the following parameters:
  FlyingHeight: 1000
  FlyingSpeed: 750
  VERBOSE: Created Superhero with the name: Flying Man
  VERBOSE: Flying Man was given the following abilities: Flying
  VERBOSE: Flying Man has a power of: 80
  VERBOSE: Flying Man can fly at a height of 1000 meters.
  VERBOSE: Flying Man can fly at a speed of 750 km/h.
● PS C:\Temp\Superhero> $FlyingMan

  Abilities    : {Flying}
  Name         : Flying Man
  Powers       : 80
  FlyingHeight : 1000
  FlyingSpeed  : 750
```

Figure 2.15: Creating superheroes with the use of dynamic parameters

Parameter sets

We briefly mentioned parameter sets in the parameter attribute topic. With parameter sets we can define and run specific code depending on what parameters are used when a function is called. Using one parameter would trigger a specific subset of code depending on the parameter set it belongs to. As an example, we mentioned the use of either the **-Name** or **-Id** parameter when using the **Get-Process** cmdlet. If you call **Get-Process** with the **Name** parameter, it will search for a process with the name that is provided as an argument. This will use one parameter set with that specific code logic, where in this case it is searching for a string. With the **Id** parameter it will search through all process **id´s** for one matching the integer argument value that is provided to the **Id** parameter, which is a different parameter set whit that specific code logic. When multiple parameter sets are defined in a function (or cmdlet) the provided parameter values are used to determine which parameter set it should use. If the parameters match one set, no parameters from other sets can be used and if no parameters match a set at all, the function will either use the default set, if applicable or throw an error. By using parameter sets you can make your function more flexible, and you can better organize the parameters that are used in specific scenarios, it allows the users to only provide the necessary parameters for a specific set. It also prevents the use of invalid parameter combinations and potential conflicts when invoking a function that contain parameter sets.

Recipe 5: Adding parameter sets

So how can we introduce the use of parameter sets into the **Add-Superhero** function. As it is now, we can only create heroes with basic functionality like giving them a **name**, adding a few **abilities**, and granting them some **power**. Come to think of it, **strength** might be a better word for defining this property. Moving forward the **Powers** parameter will be changed to **Strength**, since the word *power* might lead to think it has something to do with abilities. What we will do is to introduce an **Alignment** property which will enable us to specify if a superhero should be a **Hero**, **Villain** or of **Neutral** alignment. The alignment property will not be created as a parameter so you cannot specify this directly when you invoke the function. Instead, we will introduce the **HeroAbilities** and **VillainAbilities** parameters, each one will define its own parameter set. Each alignment has a set of specific abilities that the other cannot possess, and by granting alignment specific abilities to a superhero, they will per definition, and due to the parameter sets, become of that specific alignment. We will keep the shared **Abilities** parameter so that all superheroes still can be granted general and shared abilities in combination with the alignment abilities.

What if a superhero is created without using any of the **HeroAbilities** or **VillainAbilities** parameters? Then the default parameter set is used, and the superheroes alignment will be defined as *Neutral*. To make it a little more complex, we will also introduce the **Luck** and **Greed** properties and create parameters for these. Unlike the alignment properties, **Luck** and **Greed** are given to all superheroes. To define parameters that will be used independently of a specific parameter set, we could either add the parameter to all parameter sets, or instead use the **__AllParameterSets** property when specifying the parameter set name, in the parameters attribute. Since the **Luck** and **Greed** properties are mandatory for all superheroes, how do they align within the context of parameter sets? When creating superheroes, we expect **Heroes** to be less greedy and luckier than villains. And vice versa, **Villains** are expected to be more greedy and less lucky than heroes. Neutral superheroes will be a bit more of both by default. We will handle these properties within the parameter sets code logic. So how does this work? Let us implement the parameter set logic into the **Add-Superheroes** function.

In the first part we add and define our new parameters and we are then setting the **ParameterSetName** attribute for each of them.

- **__AllParameterSets:** These are parameters that are used for all parameter sets.

- **Neutral:** Is the default parameter set and will only be invoked if neither of the **HeroAbilities** or **VillainAbilities** parameters are used.

- **Hero:** Is the parameter set that is used if the **HeroAbilities** parameter is defined.

- **Villain:** Is the parameter set that is used if the **VillainAbilities** parameter is defined.

```
function Add-Superhero {
```

```
    [CmdletBinding(DefaultParameterSetName = "Neutral")]
    param (
        [Parameter(Position = 0, Mandatory = $true, ParameterSetName
= "__AllParameterSets")]
        [ValidateNotNullOrEmpty()]
        [String]$Name,
        [Parameter(Position = 1, ParameterSetName = "Hero")]
        [ValidateSet("Force Field Generation", "Telepathy",
"Healing", "Precognition", "Super Speed")]
        [String[]]$HeroAbilities,
        [Parameter(Position = 1, ParameterSetName = "Villain")]
        [ValidateSet("Energy Drain", "Pyrokinesis", "Darkness
Manipulation", "Necromancy", "Mind Control")]
        [String[]]$VillainAbilities,
        [Parameter(Position = 2, ParameterSetName = "__AllParameterSets")]
        [ValidateSet("Flying", "Invulnerability", "Super Strength")]
        [String[]]$Abilities = "",
        [Parameter(Position = 3, Mandatory = $false,
ParameterSetName = "__AllParameterSets")]
        [ValidateRange(0, 100)]
        [Int]$Strength = 10,
        [Parameter(ParameterSetName = "__AllParameterSets")]
        [ValidateRange(0, 50)]
        [int]$Luck = 5,
        [Parameter(ParameterSetName = "__AllParameterSets")]
        [ValidateRange(0, 50)]
        [int]$Greed = 5
    )
# Abbreviated...
```

The next step is to implement the process logic for each parameter set. We use the predefined variable **$PSCmdlet** to check which parameter set has been chosen. This is a PowerShell variable that provides information about the function or cmdlet that is currently being invoked. With this we can access different properties and methods that provides relevant information about the function process, such as the **$PSCmdlet.ParameterSetName** property. This property will contain the name of the specific parameter set that the function has been invoked with, it is of course depending on the parameters used for that function call. What we will do in our parameter set logic is that when the parameter set for a **Hero** is used, we combine the values from the **HeroAbilities** parameter with the values from the normal **Abilities** parameter and save these in a new variable called **$AllAbilities,** we then assign this combination of abilities into the **Abilities** property that we use in our output object, we also do not need to create new properties for the **Villain** and **Hero** abilities properties for our superhero and can keep all abilities in one property. We also specify that a **Hero** should have more **Luck** and less **Greed** than a villain. Vice versa we do the same with the parameter set for the **Villain**, but we then combine the **VillainAbilities** with the normal abilities instead. As a villain you get less **Luck** and more **Greed** than a **Hero**. If you are **Neutral** aligned, then you would only get the normal abilities, but you will get a small increase in both **Luck** and **Greed**. To create this logic, we simply add an **if-else** block and check if the **$PSCmdlet.ParameterSetName** property is equal to **Hero** or **Villain**, if none of these matches, then the only parameter set left, is the neutral one. The logic would look like this:

```
if ($PSCmdlet.ParameterSetName -eq "Hero"){
    $Alignment = "Hero"
    $AllAbilities = $Abilities + $HeroAbilities
    $Luck += 5
    $Greed -= 5
}
elseif ($PSCmdlet.ParameterSetName -eq "Villain") {
    $Alignment = "Villain"
    $AllAbilities = $Abilities + $VillainAbilities
    $Luck -= 5
    $Greed += 5
}
else{
    $Alignment = "Neutral"
    $AllAbilities = $Abilities
    $Luck +=2
    $Greed += 2
}
```

Info: You can also use a switch statement to create this kind of code logic.

The last thing we need to update is our **$PSCustomObject,** we change the declaration of the **Abilities** property from the **$Abilities** variable to the **$AllAbilities** variable, which now combines the alignment abilities with the normal abilities. We add the **Alignment** property, update the old **Powers** property to the more Suitable **Strength** property, and we add the **Luck** and **Greed** properties:

```
$Object = [PSCustomObject]@{
    Abilities = $AllAbilities
```

```
    Alignment = $Alignment
    Name = $Name
    Strength = $Strength
    Luck = $Luck
    Greed = $Greed
    FlyingHeight = $PSBoundParameters["FlyingHeight"]
    FlyingSpeed = $PSBoundParameters["FlyingSpeed"]
}
```

Our function now looks like this. Note that some code has been abbreviated:

```
function Add-Superhero {
    [CmdletBinding(DefaultParameterSetName = "Neutral")]
    param (
        [Parameter(Position = 0, Mandatory = $true, ParameterSetName = "__
AllParameterSets")]
        [ValidateNotNullOrEmpty()]
        [String]$Name,
        [Parameter(Position = 1, ParameterSetName = "Hero")]
        [ValidateSet("Force Field Generation", "Telepathy", "Healing",
"Precognition", "Super Speed")]
        [String[]]$HeroAbilities,
        [Parameter(Position = 1, ParameterSetName = "Villain")]
        [ValidateSet("Energy Drain", "Pyrokinesis", "Darkness
Manipulation", "Necromancy", "Mind Control")]
        [String[]]$VillainAbilities,
        [Parameter(Position = 2, ParameterSetName = "__AllParameterSets")]
        [ValidateSet("Flying", "Invulnerability", "Super Strength")]
        [String[]]$Abilities = "",
        [Parameter(Position = 3, Mandatory = $false, ParameterSetName =
"__AllParameterSets")]
        [ValidateRange(0, 100)]
        [Int]$Strength = 10,
        [Parameter(ParameterSetName = "__AllParameterSets")]
        [ValidateRange(0, 50)]
        [int]$Luck = 5,
        [Parameter(ParameterSetName = "__AllParameterSets")]
        [ValidateRange(0, 50)]
        [int]$Greed = 5
    )
```

```powershell
    DynamicParam {… # Abbreviated
    }
    Process {
        if ($PSCmdlet.ParameterSetName -eq "Hero"){
            $Alignment = "Hero"
            $AllAbilities = $Abilities + $HeroAbilities
            $Luck += 5
            $Greed -= 5
        }
        elseif ($PSCmdlet.ParameterSetName -eq "Villain") {
            $Alignment = "Villain"
            $AllAbilities = $Abilities + $VillainAbilities
            $Luck -= 5
            $Greed += 5
        }
        else{
            $Alignment = "Neutral"
            $AllAbilities = $Abilities
            $Luck +=2
            $Greed += 2
        }
        $Object = [PSCustomObject]@{
            Abilities = $AllAbilities
            Alignment = $Alignment
            Name = $Name
            Strength = $Strength
            Luck = $Luck
            Greed = $Greed
            FlyingHeight = $PSBoundParameters["FlyingHeight"]
            FlyingSpeed = $PSBoundParameters["FlyingSpeed"]
        }
        Write-Verbose "Created Superhero with the name: $Name"
        Write-Verbose "$Name is a $Alignment"
        Write-Verbose "$Name was given the following abilities: $AllAbilities"
        Write-Verbose "$Name has a strength of: $Strength, Luck of: $Luck
and Greed of: $Greed"
        if ($Object.FlyingHeight) {… # Abbreviated
```

```
        }
        if ($Object.FlyingSpeed) {… # Abbreviated
        }
        return $Object
    }
}
```

Figure 2.16 shows the effect of the parameter sets when creating different heroes using the **VillainAbilities** and **HeroAbilities** parameters respectively. You can also see that when none of these are specified, the superhero gets a neutral alignment. Also notice the added or subtracted values for the **Luck** and **Greed** property values respectively depending on the superhero's alignments:

```
※ PS C:\Temp\Superhero> Add-Superhero -Name "Evilin" -VillainAbilities "Necromancy","Energy Drain" -Abilities "Invulnerability" -Verbose
VERBOSE: Created Superhero with the name: Evilin
VERBOSE: Evilin is a Villain
VERBOSE: Evilin was given the following abilities: Invulnerability Necromancy Energy Drain
VERBOSE: Evilin has a strength of: 10, Luck of: 0 and Greed of: 10

Abilities    : {Invulnerability, Necromancy, Energy Drain}
Alignment    : Villain
Name         : Evilin
Strength     : 10
Luck         : 0
Greed        : 10
FlyingHeight :
FlyingSpeed  :


※ PS C:\Temp\Superhero> Add-Superhero -Name "Amazing Man" -HeroAbilities "Healing",'Super Speed' -Abilities "Invulnerability","Flying" -Verbose

cmdlet Add-Superhero at command pipeline position 1
Supply values for the following parameters:
FlyingHeight: 5000
FlyingSpeed: 1330
VERBOSE: Created Superhero with the name: Amazing Man
VERBOSE: Amazing Man is a Hero
VERBOSE: Amazing Man was given the following abilities: Invulnerability Flying Healing Super Speed
VERBOSE: Amazing Man has a strength of: 10, Luck of: 10 and Greed of: 0
VERBOSE: Amazing Man can fly at a height of 5000 meters.
VERBOSE: Amazing Man can fly at a speed of 1330 km/h.

Abilities    : {Invulnerability, Flying, Healing, Super Speed}
Alignment    : Hero
Name         : Amazing Man
Strength     : 10
Luck         : 10
Greed        : 0
FlyingHeight : 5000
FlyingSpeed  : 1330


※ PS C:\Temp\Superhero> Add-Superhero -Name "Blue Ghost" -Abilities "Super Strength" -Luck 25 -Greed 25 -Verbose
VERBOSE: Created Superhero with the name: Blue Ghost
VERBOSE: Blue Ghost is a Neutral
VERBOSE: Blue Ghost was given the following abilities: Super Strength
VERBOSE: Blue Ghost has a strength of: 10, Luck of: 27 and Greed of: 27

Abilities    : {Super Strength}
Alignment    : Neutral
Name         : Blue Ghost
Strength     : 10
Luck         : 27
Greed        : 27
FlyingHeight :
FlyingSpeed  :
```

Figure 2.16: Using parameter sets to create different superheroes depending on the different abilities parameters

Lifecycle events

Lifecycle events can be described as different stages in the execution of a function and is used to structure the flow of operations and perform different operations at these stages inside the function. The three main lifecycle events are **Begin**, **Process** and **End**, but there is another event that could also be defined as a function lifecycle event, the **DynamicParam** block. The **Begin** event, or block is the first event in the function execution process, and this block is only processed once. Usually, this event is used for pre-processing or initializations such as establishing connections to databases, servers, API´s and more. You can also use this event to process variables or other objects that are used throughout the rest of the function execution. The **Process** event, or block is where the function's main operations are executed, this is where we would place the core logic of the function. The **Process** block is not only executed one time like the **Begin** or **End** block´s, but once for each input object that is passed to the function, which is relevant especially when the function is built for receiving pipeline input. The **End** event, or block is also only processed once, after every execution in the process block has finished processing. It is used for cleanup operations like closing connections and for outputting or returning process data results. It is not mandatory to use all three events at the same time, you can omit each block if needed, usually it is only the process block that is required for some operations, but as we saw with the first version of our **Add-Superhero** function it is not a requirement. We added it in a later version though, without it being utilized. If your function must receive and handle pipeline input, the process event then becomes mandatory, or the function will not be able to process all objects sent through the pipeline unless you specifically create loops for this, but that would defeat the entire purpose of the process block in such a scenario. More about this later in this chapter. For now, we add the lifecycle event blocks to our **Add-Superhero** function to create flow control and prepare it for being able to receive and handle pipeline input.

Recipe 6: Implementing lifecycle Begin, Process, and End events

In the case of our **Add-Superhero** function it might not currently be the best use case for implementing the lifecycle events, since it only creates one superhero at a time and then returns a single superhero object. This does not sound like an optimal solution, returning only one superhero and then saving it to its own variable. What if we have 100 superheroes? Then it would require having 100 variables in the global scope, not optimal. Let us use this as a case for optimizing our function. Instead of returning one single superhero object, we would have it return an object that could contain multiple superhero objects, that way we will not have to create one superhero at a time and assign each one to its own variable, the output from our updated function would be an object containing all the superheroes created in that function execution process, so only one variable would be needed for containing all superheroes in a single collection. If we then later decide to create additional superheroes, we could then take that new returned object and add it to our current variable containing all superheroes, thus keeping all superheroes always contained in one object in one variable. A very simple but powerful update.

- We add a **Begin** block after the **DynamicParam** block.

- In the **Begin** block, we simply declare a new variable **$Superheroes** and assign it an empty **Hashtable**. We use this for storing our superhero objects within the function.

- Earlier we already added the **Process** block. It did nothing for us, other than specifying that it contained the main logic of our function, so it had no specific value then, other than provide some structure to our code.

- In the **Process** block, we replace the **return $Object** expression with **$Superheroes[$Name] = $Object**. So instead of returning the superhero **$Object** as soon as it is created, we now add the object to our declared **Hashtable** instead. We use the name of the superhero as the **key** since we assume that all superheroes are created with a unique name.

- We create the **End** block.

- Instead of returning the single superhero object from the function, we return the **Hashtable** object that contains our collection of superheroes that the function creates. The object we return from the function, is returned in the End block.

```
function Add-Superhero {
    [CmdletBinding(DefaultParameterSetName = "Neutral")]
    param (... # Abbreviated
    )
    DynamicParam {... # Abbreviated
    }
    Begin{
        $Superheroes = @{}
    }
    Process {
        if ($PSCmdlet.ParameterSetName -eq "Hero"){... # Abbreviated
        }
        elseif ($PSCmdlet.ParameterSetName -eq "Villain") {... # Abbreviated
        }
        else{... # Abbreviated
        }
        $Object = [PSCustomObject]@{... # Abbreviated
        }
```

```
        $Superheroes[$Name] = $Object

        Write-Verbose "Created Superhero with the name: $Name"

        Write-Verbose "$Name is a $Alignment"

        Write-Verbose "$Name was given the following abilities:
$AllAbilities"

        Write-Verbose "$Name has a strength of: $Strength, Luck of:
$Luck and Greed of: $Greed`r`n"

        if ($Object.FlyingHeight) {... # Abbreviated

        }

        if ($Object.FlyingSpeed) {... # Abbreviated

        }

    }

    End{

        return $Superheroes

    }

}
```

This is still a very simple example that shows the usage of the lifecycle events, but at least it is an upgrade and we have prepared our function for handling multiple input objects instead of it just being able to handle one at a time the last bit is missing though, we will get back to this soon. For now, let us create some new superheroes:

```
▣ PS C:\Temp\Superheroes> $Superheroes = @{}
▣ PS C:\Temp\Superheroes> $Superheroes += (Add-Superhero -Name "Captain Battle" -Abilities "Invulnerability" -HeroAbilities "Super Speed" -Verbose)
  VERBOSE: Created Superhero with the name: Captain Battle
  VERBOSE: Captain Battle is a Hero
  VERBOSE: Captain Battle was given the following abilities: Invulnerability Super Speed
  VERBOSE: Captain Battle has a strength of: 10, Luck of: 10 and Greed of: 0

▣ PS C:\Temp\Superheroes> $Superheroes += (Add-Superhero -Name "Red Rube" -VillainAbilities "Pyrokinesis" -Verbose)
  VERBOSE: Created Superhero with the name: Red Rube
  VERBOSE: Red Rube is a Villain
  VERBOSE: Red Rube was given the following abilities:  Pyrokinesis
  VERBOSE: Red Rube has a strength of: 10, Luck of: 0 and Greed of: 10

▣ PS C:\Temp\Superheroes> $Superheroes += (Add-Superhero -Name "Moon Girl" -Abilities "Flying" -FlyingHeight 384400000 -FlyingSpeed 5000 -Verbose)
  VERBOSE: Created Superhero with the name: Moon Girl
  VERBOSE: Moon Girl is a Neutral
  VERBOSE: Moon Girl was given the following abilities: Flying
  VERBOSE: Moon Girl has a strength of: 10, Luck of: 7 and Greed of: 7

  VERBOSE: Moon Girl can fly at a height of 384400000 meters.
  VERBOSE: Moon Girl can fly at a speed of 5000 km/h.
▣ PS C:\Temp\Superheroes> $Superheroes

Name                    Value
----                    -----
Captain Battle          @{Abilities=System.Object[]; Alignment=Hero; Name=Captain Battle; Strength=10; Luck=10; Greed=0; FlyingHeight=; FlyingSpeed=}
Red Rube                @{Abilities=System.Object[]; Alignment=Villain; Name=Red Rube; Strength=10; Luck=0; Greed=10; FlyingHeight=; FlyingSpeed=}
Moon Girl               @{Abilities=System.String[]; Alignment=Neutral; Name=Moon Girl; Strength=10; Luck=7; Greed=7; FlyingHeight=384400000; FlyingSpeed=5000}
```

Figure 2.17: *Creating superheroes saved in one object*

In *Figure 2.17* we start by declaring a new variable, **$Superheroes**, as an empty **Hashtable**. This is used for storing all the superheroes we create within the global scope. Since we know that our function now returns a **Hashtable** object containing superheroes, we can append the output of each function call to the **$Superheroes** variable, we do this simply by using the addition assignment operator **+=**. As you can see the function is called inside parentheses, this is not strictly necessary but it makes the code more readable. If you look closely, you can see that the **Abilities** property type is different for the superheroes. Moon Girl's **Abilities** property type is a string array and not an object array. Both the abilities and the alignment parameters take a string array as an argument. For hero and villain alignments, the alignment parameter value is combined with the abilities parameter value into the **$AllAbilities** variable. When you combine two string arrays you get an object array in return. Moon Girl is of neutral alignment and no specific alignment abilities are added. So, in this case the **$AllAbilities** is just equal to the abilities string array value without being combined with additional abilities, keeping this type as a string array. *Figure 2.18* shows how we can call each individual superhero in our new **$Superhero** object, view the different properties and even change and update the properties. All stored inside **one** variable within the global scope, a collection of superhero objects:

```
PS C:\Temp\Superheroes> $Superheroes."Moon Girl"

Abilities    : {Flying}
Alignment    : Neutral
Name         : Moon Girl
Strength     : 10
Luck         : 7
Greed        : 7
FlyingHeight : 384400000
FlyingSpeed  : 5000


PS C:\Temp\Superheroes> $Superheroes."Moon Girl".Strength
10
PS C:\Temp\Superheroes> $Superheroes."Moon Girl".Strength = 25
PS C:\Temp\Superheroes> $Superheroes."Moon Girl"

Abilities    : {Flying}
Alignment    : Neutral
Name         : Moon Girl
Strength     : 25
Luck         : 7
Greed        : 7
FlyingHeight : 384400000
FlyingSpeed  : 5000
```

Figure 2.18. Retrieving superheroes and update their properties from collection of superheroes

We use our **Begin** block to initialize and declare our collection variable that stores all superhero objects that are created in the **Process** block. We simply update our **Process** block from returning a single superhero object, to append each object created in the process block, to the collection object we instantiated in the begin block. When all iterations of the process block are completed, the **End** block simply returns our entire collection of superheroes. It might be a little wrong to state that we can return an entire collection of superheroes, since our function only still is able to create one superhero at a time, we have not provided proper logic for using the **Process** block's ability to iterate over an object and individually process each item in that object. Let us implement some more logic and update our function to handle pipeline input, so we can benefit more from these lifecycle events.

Support for handling pipeline input

The pipeline is an important and useful part of PowerShell, and it is one of the features that sets it apart from other script and programming languages. The pipeline allows the output from commands to be **piped** to other commands, and it can be chained multiple times with different commands. Pipeline input can be added to a function in two ways. Either **by value** or **by property name.** For a function or cmdlet to be able to accept pipeline input, it must contain a parameter that accepts that input, either by its value, referred to as **ByValue** or by its property name, referred to as **ByPropertyName**. If a parameter accepts input **ByValue** it is the entire object that is passed from one command to another, the receiving command can then perform operations on that object. This object is bound to a parameter that accepts the pipeline input and it is set by using the **ValueFromPipeline** parameter attribute. When a parameter accepts pipeline input **ByPropertyName** then it is only that specific property that is extracted from the source object and is then passed through the pipeline to the receiving command. This is bound to a parameter by using the **ValueFromPipelineByPropertyName** attribute. You can bind multiple parameters by their property names in the same function.

Since we created our **Add-Superhero** function and added features like parameter sets, parameter validation and mandatory attributes we complicated the use of handling pipeline input. Our function does not receive an entire object so receiving pipeline input **ByValue** would be difficult unless we add a specific parameter for this, and then handles the entire input object. In our case, we could do that, and then create a parameter that receives an entire object containing the properties for our superhero, but we should also then add code logic to handle this object specifically. Furthermore, if we keep the current parameters while adding an additional parameter for such an object, then our mandatory parameters would **break** the use of pipelining the object to the function, unless arguments are additionally provided for these manually. Then what about using **ByPropertyName** in our function parameters? We could set all our parameters in our function to receive pipeline input by their property names, but there are a few caveats in the way our function is currently created.

We have added a lot of different features to our function for the purpose of learning, but did we really look that far ahead and plan for further additions? What would be the problems with implementing pipeline handling in our current function? First the parameter sets we added might interfere even though pipelines can use parameter sets, so this should not be an issue. We also added parameters with validation, this is not an issue either if the arguments provided through the pipeline are valid. We also added the dynamic parameters and the function should be able to handle this. So, what might be the issue with our function and pipeline input? It is a combination of all these features and how they are used in our function, in its current state that could cause an issue. Handling pipeline input would work, if the input object contains the correct named properties, with the correct data type, so this should not be that much of an issue. But what if our input data comes from another data source such as a database or a CSV file, then the datatypes would not match those of some of the current function parameters. The different abilities parameters would be single strings containing all abilities and not string arrays. Not only are they set to handle string arrays, but they are also set to only validate a few specific abilities. So, if we have a `.csv` file containing the data for the superheroes we want to create, this type of file does not have an out of the box method for storing arrays or data types other than strings for that matter, so if the data was imported from the CSV file, and we tried to pipe the imported object to our function, it would fail, even though the property names matches the ones in the function. Let us assume we have a hero with the two hero abilities **Telepathy** and **Healing**. First of all, these abilities would have to be stored in the CSV file within the same column. But then we would need to have some sort of separator between them, and keep in mind that this separator must not be the same as the CSV delimiter. They would then count as a single string object, so we would later be able to split them up and create a string array from them before sending them to the function. Here we would have the same issue for all the abilities parameters, but from personal experience I have noticed that an object, that are formatted as the correct type, with the correct values, could be handled differently in the pipeline when it comes to the parameter validation sets. Even though it works with a string array while invoking the function manually, the array object is handled a bit differently so the validation set might see the piped object as invalid. We have a few caveats in our function, so how do we solve this? We could just create a function filter that handles and parses the input object from the CSV file, but even if we created an object containing all the correct property names, the validation set might still see the input arguments as invalid. Another thing seen when testing this with our current function was that the parameter set also, in some cases, did not work properly when trying to handle the pipeline input, even with a proper formatted input object. So even if a function filter was used and this filter piped the CSV input through that filter first, before piping it to our function, we might still not get the behavior we wanted, if the validation does not fail, the parameter set might instead, ending up with all neutral superheroes, since the default parameter set would be used. A function wrapper could be created and used that does the same as the filter, but what differs from a filter and a wrapper is that the wrapper function would properly parse and format our input object, but then it would call the **Add-Superhero** function directly from the wrapper function, making it irrelevant to add pipeline handling in the function, this would then just need to be added to the wrapper function instead. A lot of things to consider. Do we use a filter, and still change something in the function to handle potential issues or do we use a wrapper function for the **Add-Superhero** function, keeping it as is or do we update the function itself and make it more relevant and dynamic? There are a few ways that we can solve the issues now that we have decided to add pipeline handling to our function. It might be the right time to do some remodeling.

Recipe 7: Implementing support for pipeline input

So how do we implement the different types of pipeline handling? In the first example we create a function that handles pipeline input **ByValue**:

```
function Add-ValueFromPipeline {
    [CmdletBinding()]
    param (
        [Parameter(ValueFromPipeline)]
        [PSObject]$Obj
    )
    process{
        Write-Output "$($Obj.Name) is $($Obj.Age) years old"
    }
}
```

The **ValueFromPipeline** attribute is set for the parameter, and we use **PsObject** as the type to ensure that the parameter can handle different data types as input. By setting the **ValueFromPipeline** attribute we enable the function to handle pipeline input and states that it should be **ByValue**. In the process block we create the code logic, in this case a simple console output command that writes the **Name** and **Age** property from the input object. These specific properties must of course exist within the object that is piped to the function. The process block ensures that the command iterates over every object inside the input object.

Figure 2.19 shows the output when piping an array of objects to the **Add-ValueFromPipeline** function:

```
27    $Data = @(
28        [PSCustomObject]@{Name="Comet";Age=43},
29        [PSCustomObject]@{Name="Blue Ghost";Age=207},
30        [PSCustomObject]@{Name="Evilin";Age=33}
31    )
32
33    $Data | Add-ValueFromPipeline

OUTPUT    DEBUG CONSOLE    TERMINAL

● PS C:\Temp\Superhero> . 'C:\Temp\Superhero\2.6_PipelineExamples.ps1'
Comet is 43 years old
Blue Ghost is 207 years old
Evilin is 33 years old
```

Figure 2.19: *Output from piping data to the Add-ValueFromPipeline function*

In the next example we create a function that handles pipeline input **ByPropertyName**.

```
function Add-ValueFromPipelineByPropertyName {
```

```
[CmdletBinding()]
param (
    [Parameter(ValueFromPipelineByPropertyName)]
    [String]$Name,
    [Parameter(ValueFromPipelineByPropertyName)]
    [Int]$Age
)
process{
    Write-Output "$($Name) is $($Age) years old"
}
}
```

In this function we define each parameter, **Name** and **Age** and specify each parameter attribute to handle **ValueFromPipelineByPropertyName**, this attribute needs to be set for each parameter within the function that should handle pipeline input. In the process block we simply use the parameters directly and output the command to the console. *Figure 2.20* shows the output of piping an array of objects to the **Add-ValueFromPipelineByPropertyName** function:

```
27    $Data = @(
28        [PSCustomObject]@{Name="Comet";Age=43},
29        [PSCustomObject]@{Name="Blue Ghost";Age=207},
30        [PSCustomObject]@{Name="Evilin";Age=33}
31    )
32
33    $Data | Add-ValueFromPipelineByPropertyName

OUTPUT    DEBUG CONSOLE    TERMINAL

PS C:\Temp\Superhero> . 'C:\Temp\Superhero\2.6_PipelineExamples.ps1'
Comet is 43 years old
Blue Ghost is 207 years old
Evilin is 33 years old
```

Figure 2.20: *Output from piping data to the Add-ValueFromPipelineByPropertyName function*

Now that we have learned how to implement pipeline handling in a function, how can we use this knowledge to update the Add-Superhero function? The reason for implementing pipeline input handling into the **Add-superheroes** function is so that we dynamically can create multiple superheroes from a data set such as a database or a CSV file. We need to make some changes. First , we simplify the function. It has been used to show how to use parameter sets, dynamic parameters, parameter attributes and validations and also how to add lifecycle events. You can see that the lifecycle events, especially the **Process** block is essential for processing objects piped to the function, so this will not be removed. But we will remove the parameter sets. A superheroes alignment should not be bound specifically to the abilities, even a villain can obtain hero powers and vice versa, and the logic for adding or subtracting **luck** and **greed** points could be handled within the main code logic by implementing a switch statement, so this could handle everything that are specific for each alignment. Heroes and villains should not be bound by specific powers. The validate set´s for abilities are also removed. We should be able to choose between a multitude of abilities for each superhero, not just from a set of a few predefined ones. The dynamic parameters are also removed, since we, for now do not need to have special properties depends on specific abilities. We are removing a lot, but the outcome should end up being almost the same, with the difference that we are able to create a lot of superheroes at once and the function can handle pipeline input. This is how the function will end up look like:

```
function Add-Superhero {
    [CmdletBinding()]
    param (
        [Parameter(Position = 0, ValueFromPipelineByPropertyName)]
        [ValidateNotNullOrEmpty()]
        [String]$Name,
        [Parameter(Position = 1, ValueFromPipelineByPropertyName)]
        [ValidateSet("Hero", "Villain", "Neutral")]
        [String]$Alignment,
        [Parameter(Position = 2, ValueFromPipelineByPropertyName)]
        [String[]]$Abilities,
        [Parameter(Position = 3, ValueFromPipelineByPropertyName)]
        [ValidateRange(0, 100)]
        [Int]$Strength = 10,
        [Parameter(Position = 4, ValueFromPipelineByPropertyName)]
        [ValidateRange(0, 100)]
        [Int]$Armor = 10,
        [Parameter(Position = 5, ValueFromPipelineByPropertyName)]
        [ValidateRange(0, 50)]
        [int]$Luck = 5,
        [Parameter(Position = 6, ValueFromPipelineByPropertyName)]
        [ValidateRange(0, 50)]
        [int]$Greed = 5
    )
    Begin{
        $Superheroes = @{}
    }
    Process {
```

```
        switch ($Alignment) {
            "Hero" { $Luck += 5
                     $Greed -= 5 }
            "Villain" { $Luck -= 5
                        $Greed += 5 }
            Default { $Luck += 3
                      $Greed += 3 }
        }
        $Object = [PSCustomObject]@{
            Abilities = $Abilities -split ","
            Alignment = $Alignment
            Name = $Name
            Strength = $Strength
            Armor = $Armor
            Luck = $Luck
            Greed = $Greed
        }
        $Superheroes[$Name] = $Object
        Write-Verbose "Created Superhero with the name: $Name"
        Write-Verbose "$Name is a $Alignment"
        Write-Verbose "$Name was given the following abilities: $Abilities"
        Write-Verbose "$Name has a strength of: $Strength, Armor of:
$Armor, Luck of: $Luck and Greed of: $Greed`r`n"
    }
    End{
        return $Superheroes
    }
}
```

The **VillainAbilities** and the **HeroAbilities** parameters have been removed and also the validation set for the **Abilities** parameter. We have added the **Alignment** parameter with a validation set, unlike as with abilities, the possible alignments are now limited. A parameter for **Armor** has also been added, but we could add several properties to a superhero such as **Level**, **Weaknesses**, **Weapons** and so on, but let us keep it simple for now. In the process block we have added a simple switch statement to handle specific alignment properties, like adding some luck and subtracting greed if you are a hero and vice versa for villains, also a default has been added to the switch block, this is for neutral superheroes and other types that could be added later that are not of a specific alignment type. The **PSCustomObject** in the process block have also been updated to accommodate the changes. Some have been removed, and as you can see, we have added **-split,** methods to the abilities properties. This is for making sure that when multiple abilities have been added, they will be saved as an array object, instead of a string. By using comma **,** as a separator, we need to make sure that all abilities string variables that are sent to the function are using this to separate the abilities in the string, so it becomes an array of strings instead. This is useful in a **.csv** file that use the **;** (or other character besides a comma) as delimiter. We could then add all abilities in the abilities column divided by a comma and make sure that this is parsed or formatted correctly by our function. This would be defined as a dependency. If another separator is used inside the string in the **.csv** file, then the abilities properties will not be split correctly before being added to the output object. This also applies to data from a database or from any other external data source. Make sure the string containing the abilities in the **.csv** file are separated by a comma. We could add a parameter to the function so that another separator could be used instead and just keep the comma as a default, this would be an easy addition, but for now we assume that all input data are formatted correctly in our data sources. *Figure 2.21* shows a CSV file with superheroes data. Notice the **.csv** delimiter is **;** and the abilities separator is **,**:

```
HeroMap.csv - Notepad

File  Edit  Format  View  Help
Name;Alignment;Abilities;Strength;Armor;Luck;Greed
Comet;Hero;Flying,Super Strength,Invulnerability;80;90;40;5
Blue Ghost;Neutral;Telepathy,Invulnerability;45;70;20;13
Evilin;Villain;Necromancy,Mind Control;35;40;10;26
```

Figure 2.21: Superheroes data in CSV file

We import the **.csv** data and save it to a variable **$Data**. We pipe the **$Data** variable into our **Add-Superheroes** function and save the output in the **$Heroes** variable. *Figure 2.22* shows the following output:

```
● PS C:\Temp\Superhero> $Data = Import-Csv .\HeroMap.csv -Delimiter ";"
● PS C:\Temp\Superhero> $Heroes = $Data | Add-Superhero -Verbose
 VERBOSE: Created Superhero with the name: Comet
 VERBOSE: Comet is a Hero
 VERBOSE: Comet was given the following abilities: Flying,Super Strength,Invulnerability
 VERBOSE: Comet has a strength of: 80, Armor of: 90, Luck of: 45 and Greed of: 0

 VERBOSE: Created Superhero with the name: Blue Ghost
 VERBOSE: Blue Ghost is a Neutral
 VERBOSE: Blue Ghost was given the following abilities: Telepathy,Invulnerability
 VERBOSE: Blue Ghost has a strength of: 45, Armor of: 70, Luck of: 23 and Greed of: 16

 VERBOSE: Created Superhero with the name: Evilin
 VERBOSE: Evilin is a Villain
 VERBOSE: Evilin was given the following abilities: Necromancy,Mind Control
 VERBOSE: Evilin has a strength of: 35, Armor of: 40, Luck of: 5 and Greed of: 31

● PS C:\Temp\Superhero> $Heroes


Name                    Value
----                    -----
Comet                   @{Abilities=System.String[]; Alignment=Hero; Name=Comet; Strength=80; Armor=90; Luck=45; Greed=0}
Evilin                  @{Abilities=System.String[]; Alignment=Villain; Name=Evilin; Strength=35; Armor=40; Luck=5; Greed=31}
Blue Ghost              @{Abilities=System.String[]; Alignment=Neutral; Name=Blue Ghost; Strength=45; Armor=70; Luck=23; Greed=16}
```

Figure 2.22: Output after piping CSV data into the Add-Superheroes function

As you can see our superheroes are successfully created as expected and they are all stored in one object, now saved inside the **$Heroes** variable. As before we can now call our superheroes inside this function and add new ones as we see fit, update current superheroes properties and so on.

The pipeline is a powerful tool in PowerShell, even though we have simplified our function and removed some advanced features the result is almost the same as it was before, with the difference that we can now take large datasets and create superheroes from such data by piping the dataset objects directly into our function and all superheroes are returned as a single object. We can still invoke our function **manually** and use it to create single superheroes when needed. These single superhero objects would be easy to add to the current object containing all superheroes. We could easily use data from other data sources such as a database table if they are formatted correctly and then pipe this data to our function for creating a lot of superheroes at once.

Support for ShouldProcess

The **ShouldProcess** feature in PowerShell is a feature that enables you to incorporate security measures to your functions and cmdlets, by enabling both confirmation prompts and command simulations. You enable the **ShouldProcess** feature by adding the **SupportsShouldProcess** argument to the **CmdletBinding** attribute, this will add the **-WhatIf** and **-Confirm** switch parameters to the function. The **confirm** parameter lets you prompt the user for confirmation before any operations that could be dangerous are executed inside the function, and lets the user decide whether to proceed with the execution. The **whatif** parameter adds the ability to simulate the execution of operations inside the function before any changes are made. Let us say that you add a command that would delete one or more files within a folder, before the command is executed and the files are deleted, you can then simulate what will happen when you invoke the function, by setting the **-WhatIf** switch parameter. You will then be able to see exactly what action will be performed and which files are going to be deleted before the actual execution. This is quite useful especially if you have selected multiple files by using a wildcard or selected a lot of files and are not sure exactly which onces are going to be deleted. Adding the **-Confirm** parameter will enable a confirmation prompt for any potentially dangerous action that you have specified in the function. *Figure 2.23* shows the **shouldProcess** feature using **whatif** and **confirm** on an operation that would remove all items inside a folder:

```
● PS C:\Temp> Get-ChildItem | Remove-Item -WhatIf -Confirm

Confirm
The item at Microsoft.PowerShell.Core\FileSystem::C:\Temp\Superhero has children and the Recurse
parameter was not specified. If you continue, all children will be removed with the item. Are you sure
you want to continue?
[Y] Yes  [A] Yes to All  [N] No  [L] No to All  [S] Suspend  [?] Help (default is "Y"): A
What if: Performing the operation "Remove Directory" on target "C:\Temp\Superhero".
What if: Performing the operation "Remove Directory" on target "C:\Temp\Test".
What if: Performing the operation "Remove Directory" on target "C:\Temp\Test (2)".
What if: Performing the operation "Remove File" on target "C:\Temp\Date.txt".
What if: Performing the operation "Remove File" on target "C:\Temp\DateThree.txt".
What if: Performing the operation "Remove File" on target "C:\Temp\DateTwo.txt".
What if: Performing the operation "Remove File" on target "C:\Temp\Test (1).txt".
What if: Performing the operation "Remove File" on target "C:\Temp\Test (2).txt".
What if: Performing the operation "Remove File" on target "C:\Temp\Test.ps1".
```

Figure 2.23: Simulation and confirmation of Remove-Item process in a directory

We use the **Get-ChildItem** cmdlet to return all the items within a folder and then pipe the output to **Remove-Item,** a destructive command that would delete all files and folders in the selected directory. By invoking the cmdlet with the **WhatIf** and **Confirm** parameters we ensure that, first: we get prompted to confirm all dangerous actions and is asked if we want to continue or not, and second: we are only performing a simulation that tells us what will happen when the operation is executed without any security measures enabled. This would delete files and directories in the **C:**Temp folder. In this case it is of course redundant to use these two parameters together, since we only confirmed the impact on a simulation run. If we ran the command without the simulation, we would still need to confirm it, so we have the option of aborting the execution, if it was somehow started by mistake. Some functions and **cmdlets**, such as the **Remove-Item** cmdlet would not run without confirmation even if we did not specify the **Confirm** parameter upon execution, unless we specifically disabled confirmation, which we can do by setting the confirm switch to false: **-Confirm:false**. This is due to a parameter that is set within **CmdletBinding** attribute called the **ConfirmImpact**. With this parameter we could specify different levels of impact a function or cmdlet would have on data when using the **Confirm** switch, and make sure it always prompts the user for confirmation. In case of the **Remove-Item** cmdlet, the impact is set to **High** by default. There are four levels for the **ConfirmImpact** parameter:

- **None:** The operation has no impact on data and does not require confirmation.

- **Low:** The operation has a low impact on data and typically requires minimal confirmation.

- **Medium:** The operation has a moderate impact on data and generally requires confirmation.

- **High:** The operation has a high impact on data and typically requires explicit confirmation from the user.

The method used for the **SupportsShouldProcess** is **$PSCmdlet.ShouldProcess()**. You add this method in your process, and it checks if an operation in its block should be simulated, confirmed and/or processed. When this method is called it checks for the **WhatIf** and **Confirm** parameters and automatically processes these if they are true. If the **WhatIf** parameter is set, or true, the command is simulated, and it outputs a description of the changes that would happen. If the **Confirm** parameter is set, or true, the execution of the command will pause and prompts the user for confirmation, depending on the **ConfirmImpact** that is set in the **CmdletBinding** attribute. The **$PSCmdlet. ShouldProcess()** method takes a few arguments that can be used to customize the output message when the method is invoked, these are not named per se, but positioned inside the method, so we call these overloads. *Figure 2.24* shows different overloads used in the **$PSCmdlet.ShouldProcess()** method, and the respective output for each of these overloads.

```
52      # $PSCmdlet.ShouldProcess("Target")
53      if ($PSCmdlet.ShouldProcess($File)) {
54          Remove-Item -Path $File
55      }
56      # $PSCmdlet.ShouldProcess("Target", "Action")
57      if ($PSCmdlet.ShouldProcess($File, "Remove")) {
58          Remove-Item -Path $File
59      }
60      # $PSCmdlet.ShouldProcess("Message", "Target", "Action")
61      if ($PSCmdlet.ShouldProcess("RemoveMessage", $File, "Remove")) {
62          Remove-Item -Path $File
63      }
```

```
OUTPUT     DEBUG CONSOLE     TERMINAL

● PS C:\Temp\Superhero> Remove-File Test.ps1 -WhatIf
What if: Performing the operation "Remove-File" on target "Test.ps1".
What if: Performing the operation "Remove" on target "Test.ps1".
What if: RemoveMessage
```

Figure 2.24: $PSCmdlet.ShouldProcess() method overloads and their respective output

The first example use one parameter or overload. We call this **target** since it can be used to define the **Target** object that we are working on such as a file, a directory and so on. In this case we use the **$File** variable which is a filename. The output message shows the default message including the function or cmdlet name that was invoked, and the specific file name we stated in the **Target** overload parameter. The next example use two overload parameters which we define as **Target** and **Action**. The target is the same as before, but the **action** overload enables us to override the function/cmdlet name to give it a more specific action description. The third example use three overload parameters, let us call the third one **Message**, even though you provide the two other parameters, this overload overrides the entire message with the text in this overload parameter as you can see in the last example in the figure.

Note: In PowerShell, the comparison $Variable -eq $true is equivalent to simply evaluating $Variable. This is because PowerShell treats the values $true and $false as boolean values, and the -eq operator checks for equality in a type-sensitive manner. If $Variable is already a boolean value (either $true or $false), then $Variable -eq $true is essentially checking if the boolean value is equal to $true, which is redundant. The result will be the same as just evaluating $Variable. In code examples in this book, where condition variables is booleans the redundant boolean value might have been removed. $Variable -eq $true will be stated as $Variable.

Recipe 8: Implementing support for ShouldProcess

As we can see implementing support for **shouldProcess** to a function or cmdlet can be quite beneficial when working on potential destructive operations. This integrate the option of simulating what will happen and what will be changed and also enables the confirmation prompt, so you have a chance to cancel before anything is executed. Like with the examples in *Figure 2.24*, this is often used when working with functions and cmdlets that would delete files and folders, but it could be implemented in everything that is in some way destructive, like deleting keys from the registry, deleting certificates from the certificate stores and and so on. So how can we incorporate this into our superhero **game** script? Creating superheroes with our **Add-Superheroes** function is not destructive, so how can this be utilized here? Who is not to say that we at some point might need to delete certain superheroes from our **game**, or more precise, from our **$Heroes** object containing all the superheroes. In that case we do not want to delete some by mistake. Let us create a **Remove-Superhero** function where we implement the **shouldProcess** feature so we can simulate and confirm the deletion of characters before executing it for real, making sure that we do not delete the wrong superheroes by mistake. Let us define the function.

1. We need the **shouldProcess** features so we enable these by adding the **SupportsShouldProcess** parameter to our **CmdletBinding** attribute. We also want to make sure the confirmation has a **High** impact. We set this in the **ConfirmImpact** parameter in the **CmdletBinding** attribute.

2. A known parameter is needed from the **$Heroes** object so we can specify which superhero or superheroes to remove. The **Name** parameter here is obvious since this is considered a unique key for each superhero. We also want to remove multiple superheroes at a time and be able to pipeline containing names of superheroes that we want to remove, so we create a **Name** parameter as a string array and enable the support for pipeline input **ByValue**.

3. Since it is not given that the global variable containing to the superheroes is named **$Heroes** we should also add a parameter we can use to explicitly specify the name of the superheroes input object. We add a parameter, **HeroesVariable** that is optional and defaults to the name **Heroes**.

4. Before doing anything else, it is a good idea to check that the global variable we assign to the **HeroesVariable** parameter, exists in the global scope. We use the **Get-Variable** cmdlet within an **if** block to check if the variable exists. If not, we throw an error and exits the function before processing any other commands.

5. Since we are working directly with a global scoped object, we need a method for referencing this inside our function, then making the changes directly to it. We can use the **Get-Variable** cmdlet for this, this also takes a scope argument so we can specify a variable from the global scope, it also has a **ValueOnly** switch so we can get the value from the variable, the value is the **Hashtable** containing our superheroes. We assign the global value to a local value inside our function. Note that the global variable is referenced and not copied when using the equals: = assignment operator with the **Get-Variable** cmdlet, so we can work on the object directly in the global scope from within our functions local scope. This is added inside the functions **Begin** block, since we only need to assign it once, at the beginning of the function.

6. We add a variable called **$Changes = $false**. This is simply used as a switch inside the function, that will be set to **$true** if any changes have been made. We use this later in the **End** block to write different verbose output messages depending on if any changes have been made in the process or not.

7. In the process block we add the code logic. Remember that we also enabled pipeline input, so the process block iterates over each object when sent through the pipeline. The first thing we do is to check that the provided superhero name that we want to remove exists in our **Heroes** object. We can simply do this by calling the **ContainsKey** method on our superhero name inside an **if** block. If a name does not exist, we use the **Return** keyword to iterate to the next object in the process.

8. If the superhero name exists in our superheroes object, the process continues to the next **elseif** statement. This is where we enable the simulation and confirmation by using the **$PSCmdlet.ShouldProcess** method. Inside the block where we have stated this method, we can now add our code logic to remove the superhero from our superhero object. The **Hashtable** contains a built-in method for this, **Remove()**, so we use this method on our superhero object to remove the superhero item with **$Name** inside the global object. Whenever our function is invoked with the **-WhatIf** and/or **-Confirm** parameter, the **$PSCmdlet.ShouldProcess** method and PowerShell will automatically do the work for us and simulate and/or prompt for confirmation before executing the **Remove** command. If the **WhatIf** parameter is not set, then the command will be executed, and the superhero item is removed from the object.

9. We add some verbose output statements for the different commands, so that we can visually check what is happening if needed by enabling the **-Verbose** switch parameter, when invoking our function.

10. In the **End** block we write different verbose output depending on if any changes have been made or not, by checking if the **$Changes** variable has changed from **$false** to **$true**. This gives us a little kind of report at the end:

```powershell
function Remove-Superhero {
    [CmdletBinding(SupportsShouldProcess, ConfirmImpact = "High")]
    param (
        [Parameter(Position = 0, Mandatory = $true,
ValueFromPipeline)]
        [ValidateNotNullOrEmpty()]
        [String[]]$Name,
        [Parameter(Position = 1)]
        [String]$HeroesVariable = "Heroes"
    )
    Begin {
        if (-not (Get-Variable -Name $HeroesVariable -Scope Global
-ErrorAction SilentlyContinue)) {
            throw "Global variable '$HeroesVariable' not found."
        }
        $Heroes = Get-Variable -Name $HeroesVariable -Scope Global
-ValueOnly
        $Changes = $false
    }
    Process {
        if (-not $Heroes.ContainsKey("$Name")) {
            Write-Verbose "$HeroesVariable does not contain a
Superhero name: $Name"
            Return
        }
        elseif ($PSCmdlet.ShouldProcess("$Name")) {
            $Heroes.Remove("$Name")
            Write-Verbose "Superhero: $Name removed"
            $Changes = $true
        }
    }
    End {
```

```
        if ($Changes)  {
            Write-Verbose "Removed Superheroes from and updated the
global variable: $HeroesVariable"
        }
        else{
            Write-Verbose "No changes where made to the global
variable: $HeroesVariable"
        }
    }
}
```

First, we invoke our **Remove-Superhero** function with the **-WhatIf** parameter and try to remove the superhero called **Evilin**. *Figure 2.25* shows the output, and we can see that it only performs the simulation, and it is not actually doing anything, the verbose output also confirms this:

```
● PS C:\Temp\Superhero> $heroes

Name                         Value
----                         -----
Comet                        @{Abilities=System.String[]; Alignment=Hero; Name=Comet; Strength=80; Armor=90; Luck=45; Greed=0}
Evilin                       @{Abilities=System.String[]; Alignment=Villain; Name=Evilin; Strength=35; Armor=40; Luck=5; Greed=31}
Blue Ghost                   @{Abilities=System.String[]; Alignment=Neutral; Name=Blue Ghost; Strength=45; Armor=70; Luck=23; Greed=16}

● PS C:\Temp\Superhero> Remove-Superhero -Name Evilin -HeroesVariable Heroes -Verbose -WhatIf
What if: Performing the operation "Remove-Superhero" on target "Evilin".
VERBOSE: No changes where made to the global variable: Heroes
```

Figure 2.25: Output from Remove-Superhero when invoked with the -WhatIf parameter

In *Figure 2.26* we invoke the function without the **-WhatIf** parameter but with the **-Confirm** parameter instead. We are now getting prompted to confirm this action, and when confirmed, the command is executed, and **Evilin** is removed from the global superheroes object. The verbose output also confirms that changes has been made:

```
● PS C:\Temp\Superhero> Remove-Superhero -Name Evilin -HeroesVariable Heroes -Verbose -Confirm

Confirm
Are you sure you want to perform this action?
Performing the operation "Remove-Superhero" on target "Evilin".
[Y] Yes  [A] Yes to All  [N] No  [L] No to All  [S] Suspend  [?] Help (default is "Y"): Y
VERBOSE: Superhero: Evilin removed
VERBOSE: Removed Superheroes from and updated the global variable: Heroes
● PS C:\Temp\Superhero> $heroes

Name                         Value
----                         -----
Comet                        @{Abilities=System.String[]; Alignment=Hero; Name=Comet; Strength=80; Armor=90; Luck=45; Greed=0}
Blue Ghost                   @{Abilities=System.String[]; Alignment=Neutral; Name=Blue Ghost; Strength=45; Armor=70; Luck=23; Greed=16}
```

Figure 2.26: Output from Remove-Superhero when invoked with the -confirm parameter

Since we set the **ConfirmImpact** to **High** in the **CmdletBinding** attribute, the confirm parameter is redundant, since the High impact will result in the command to always prompt for confirmation. On the other hand, if we had set the **ConfirmImpact** to **None** we would not have been asked for confirmation, unless we specifically set the **-Confirm** parameter when the function was invoked.

Figure 2.27 shows the output when a string array is piped to the function with several superhero names. The only thing we specify is the verbose parameter, to make sure we get some output stating that changes has been made. As you can see, we are still getting prompted to confirm the actions, due to the **High** impact.

We have some options. We choose *Yes [Y]* and is prompted for each operation, choosing to remove a superhero one by one. As you can see, all superheroes are removed from the superheroes object:

```
 PS C:\Temp\Superhero> "Comet","Blue Ghost" | Remove-Superhero -Verbose

 Confirm
 Are you sure you want to perform this action?
 Performing the operation "Remove-Superhero" on target "Comet".
 [Y] Yes  [A] Yes to All  [N] No  [L] No to All  [S] Suspend  [?] Help (default is "Y"): Y
 VERBOSE: Superhero: Comet removed

 Confirm
 Are you sure you want to perform this action?
 Performing the operation "Remove-Superhero" on target "Blue Ghost".
 [Y] Yes  [A] Yes to All  [N] No  [L] No to All  [S] Suspend  [?] Help (default is "Y"): Y
 VERBOSE: Superhero: Blue Ghost removed
 VERBOSE: Removed Superheroes from and updated the global variable: Heroes
 PS C:\Temp\Superhero> $heroes
 PS C:\Temp\Superhero> $heroes.count
  0
```

Figure 2.27: Piping multiple superheroes to the Remove-Superhero function, without specifying any additional parameters than verbose.

We can now implement **security features** that promotes safer scripting practices that gives users the opportunity to test, review and confirm actions before executing anything potentially destructive.

Object-oriented programming concepts and benefits

Object-oriented Programming (OOP) is a concept or a model if you will, that is based upon self-sustainable objects that consists of properties and methods, also known as classes. Classes are structured blueprints that are used to create individual instances of objects with defined properties and methods. What are the differences between a function and a class? A function is a reusable self-contained block of code that is designed to perform a specific task or encapsulate a series of operations. A function can be called multiple times for performing the task or operation when needed. It can also accept input parameters and output results. Unlike a class, a function is not associated with specific instances or objects, and they do not contain or retain properties the same way as a class does and their state are not maintained between function calls. If we look at our **Add-Superhero** function, it is designed to take input arguments. These arguments are then processed and then a result is returned from the function, so consider this a static reusable operation. Its function is completed, and nothing is maintained or saved, it just does the work it was designed to do. When we create an object from a class, we create an instance of that class. This instance has its own set of properties and methods derived from the class it was instantiated from. The state of the properties and methods in an instance are maintained if the instance is instantiated, usually saved as a variable or in a collection holding multiple instances. This might sound like what our output from our **Add-Superhero** function did, but our output from the function is a collection of **PSCustomObjects** and not instances derived from a specific class. Another difference is that our superhero objects only contain properties. So, what are methods and properties when we talk about class objects? Consider properties like data states, or better yet, *Something that it (the instance) is or something it has.*

Let us be more specific and consider the case of a superhero. A superhero has an alignment, it is a hero or a villain. A superhero has abilities, a superhero has 15 luck points and so on. These are examples of states of the data in a superhero instance, these are properties. Consider methods like behaviors, like *Something it can do*, like a superhero can fly, a superhero can shoot laser from the eyes, a superhero can punch with the power of 45 Strength points and so on. So, properties can be considered what it is, and methods what it can do. A class has more features than functions, like inheritance where you can create a class that inherits properties and methods from another class (usually referred to as base or parent class). You can create a new class that extends or modifies the properties and methods from an already existing class. This promotes a lot of flexibility in the terms of code reusability and modularity in your code. A class also have other features like encapsulation, polymorphism, and abstractions. Since this is a chapter about advanced PowerShell functions such features will not be covered. We will stick to the more basics regarding PowerShell classes. What is relevant with this section is that we can extend far beyond the capabilities of our current semi dynamic superhero objects we create with our **Add-Superhero** function. By using another approach to create superheroes and introduce object-oriented programming capabilities into our PowerShell scripts, and by utilizing classes to create instances of superheroes that not only can store and change their properties but also by implementing behavior using methods, that can make them do things such as flying, use their powers, leveling up and so forth. Leveling up, we did not provide the superheroes with any **Level** property. Of course, a game character like a superhero should have levels and be able to level up, why did we not add this to our function earlier? Let us take a new approach to creating superhero objects by creating a class where we can instantiate superheroes that not only contain properties but are also able to do something with their powers and abilities.

Recipe 9: Creating a class with properties and methods

To create a class in PowerShell we simply use the **class** keyword then followed by the name of the class and this is of course followed by a script block:

```
class NewSuperhero {

}
```

Notice that we did not use the **Verb-Noun** convention in the class name, PowerShell syntax rules states that a class should follow the same naming convention as variables. The first thing we do when creating our class is to declare its properties. It is not mandatory to declare the class properties, we could add certain properties later to an instantiated instance of the class, but since we are creating a blueprint for a superhero we will declare all known properties inside the class, or it defeats some of its purpose. By declaring the properties, we define them and their specific datatypes and this is used by PowerShell to create the properties within the objects and are also used to enforce their datatypes:

```
class NewSuperhero {
    [String] $Name
    [String] $Alignment
    [String[]] $Abilities
    [Int] $Strength
    [Int] $Armor
    [Int] $Luck
    [Int] $Greed
    [Int] $Level
}
```

The next step is to create a class **constructor**. This allows us to specify values for the properties whenever we create a new instance of that class, much like creating parameters in a function. The **parameters** in the constructor must correspond to the properties we initiated before:

```
class NewSuperhero {
    [String] $Name
    [String] $Alignment
    [String[]] $Abilities
    [Int] $Strength
    [Int] $Armor
    [Int] $Luck
```

```
[Int] $Greed
[Int] $Level
NewSuperhero(
            [String]$Name,
            [String]$Alignment,
            [String[]]$Abilities,
            [Int]$Strength,
            [Int]$Armor,
            [Int]$Luck,
            [Int]$Greed,
            [Int]$Level
            ) {
        $this.Name = $Name
        $this.Alignment = $Alignment
        $this.Abilities = $Abilities
        $this.Strength = $Strength
        $this.Armor = $Armor
        $this.Luck = $Luck
        $this.Greed = $Greed
        $this.Level = $Level
    }
}
```

It is getting a little more complicated now but let us walk through it. The constructor method is initialized with the same name as the class itself, in this case **NewSuperhero().** In the constructor we add parameters corresponding to our declared properties and their data types. By adding the parameters to the constructor method, we can add corresponding arguments when we instantiate an instance from the class. If we omitted these, we would still have declared the properties for the class instance, but we would have a class constructor that takes no arguments. We essentially add parameters to the constructor, so our class takes arguments. Unlike a function we cannot give our constructor parameters default values, so we would need to specify arguments for each parameter whenever instantiating an object from a class with parameters, this is a minor issue in my opinion. The last and most complicated thing in the constructor is the constructor code block. As you can see, we have introduced a new keyword **$this**. This keyword is an essential part of a class in object-oriented programming. Other languages might use words like **self** (Python) or other names, but the meaning is the same in classes in general. It is used when an instance of an object needs to refer to parameters or properties within itself, so if we had a method inside the class that would need to access the **$Armor** property when it has been instantiated as an object, inside that method, we would have to reference it by using **$this.Armor** instead of just **$Armor.** It is called a self-reference. Inside the constructor block we declare self-referencing variables and set the values to the corresponding parameters. We have created a class that can create superhero objects almost like our **Add-Superhero** function.

How do we instantiate an object from a class? In PowerShell there are multiple ways to instantiate a class. The two most commonly used methods are using the **new** static method. This method is more consistent with object-oriented programming conventions, as it calls a static method named **new** on the class. Note that this method is only available in PowerShell 5 or later versions. The other method is using the **New-Object** cmdlet, this is a more generic cmdlet that can be used to instantiate various types of objects. This also works in earlier versions of PowerShell. In most cases, these methods are interchangeable, and you can use either depending on your preference or the specific requirements of your code. *Figure 2.28* shows the use of both methods for instantiating superhero objects:

```
⊕ PS C:\Temp\Superhero> $Comet = [Superhero]::new("Comet", "Hero", @("Flying", "Invulnerability"),75,80,15,5,1)
⊕ PS C:\Temp\Superhero> $Evilin = New-Object NewSuperhero -ArgumentList "Evilin", "Villain", @("Flying", "Invulnerability"), 60, 45, 2, 20, 1
⊕ PS C:\Temp\Superhero> $Comet

Name        : Comet
Alignment   : Hero
Abilities   : {Flying, Invulnerability}
Strength    : 75
Armor       : 80
Luck        : 15
Greed       : 5
Level       : 1


⊕ PS C:\Temp\Superhero> $Evilin

Name        : Evilin
Alignment   : Villain
Abilities   : {Flying, Invulnerability}
Strength    : 60
Armor       : 45
Luck        : 2
Greed       : 20
Level       : 1
```

Figure 2.28: Instantiating objects from our NewSuperheroes class with "new" static method and with New-Object cmdlet

Now we have superheroes with properties, much like before. There are some few things still missing like, the points added or subtracted from different properties depending on the alignment type. We are not writing anything verbose either, like we did in the function. We are not capable of piping multiple superheroes to the class, and we cannot create default property values if some arguments are not provided as parameters. As mentioned, the class constructor parameters do not support this. What can we do to accommodate these missing features? Let us take one issue at a time and start with how we could handle some sort of default property values.

To do this we would still need to specify all the arguments when instantiating a class object, but what if we said that some arguments could be either **$Null** or **empty strings**.

In *Figure 2.29* we instantiate a superhero object with some arguments set as either empty strings or **$Null** values. We can see that the property values for our Comet object is now set to 0 where we provided an empty string or **$Null** as arguments, so the class can be made to handle this:

```
PS C:\Temp\Superhero> $Comet = [NewSuperhero]::new("Comet", "Hero", @("Flying", "Invulnerability"),75,80,"",$null,$null)
PS C:\Temp\Superhero> $Comet


Name      : Comet
Alignment : Hero
Abilities : {Flying, Invulnerability}
Strength  : 75
Armor     : 80
Luck      : 0
Greed     : 0
Level     : 0
```

Figure 2.29: Instantiation of a class with empty string or $null as arguments

Knowing this, we can simply create a method in our class that is called inside the constructor at instance initialization, that will provide these default values if they are **0**. We use the switch statement here to check the specific property values and set defaults if they are **0**, we also check if no alignments are chosen and set it to neutral as default if the property is an empty string at initialization. We create the **AddDefaultPropertyValues** method, our first class method, and call it in the constructor with **$this.AddDefaultPropertyValues()**. Note some code has been abbreviated. This method and the constructor calling the method, should be added to the current class code:

```
class NewSuperhero {
    [String] $Name
    … # Abbreviated
    NewSuperhero(… # Abbreviated
            ) {… # Abbreviated
        $this.Greed = $Greed
        $this.Level = $Level
        $this.AddDefaultPropertyValues()
    }
    [void] AddDefaultPropertyValues() {
        switch ($null) {
            { $this.Strength -eq 0} { $this.Strength = 10 }
            { $this.Armor -eq 0} { $this.Armor = 10 }
            { $this.Luck -eq 0} { $this.Luck = 5 }
            { $this.Greed -eq 0} { $this.Greed = 5 }
            { $this.Level -eq 0} { $this.Level = 1}
            { $this.Alignment -eq ""} { $this.Alignment = "Neutral"}
```

```
        }
    }
}
```

Figure 2.30 shows the new Comet object when using empty strings or **$Null** valued arguments, when instantiating an instance from the class, after the **AddDefaultProperty Values()** method is added:

```
* PS C:\Temp\Superhero> $Comet = [NewSuperhero]::new("Comet", $null, @("Flying", "Invulnerability"),75,80,"",$null,$null)
* PS C:\Temp\Superhero> $Comet

    Name      : Comet
    Alignment : Neutral
    Abilities : {Flying, Invulnerability}
    Strength  : 75
    Armor     : 80
    Luck      : 5
    Greed     : 5
    Level     : 1
```

Figure 2.30: *Object default properties when instantiated with empty strings and $Null valued arguments*

We can create another class method to adjust the superheroes behavior, the luck and greed points, depending on the superhero's alignment. We create this in the same way as we did before with the **AddDefaultPropertyValues** method, and we also call this in our constructor:

```
class NewSuperhero {
    [String] $Name
    … # Abbreviated
    NewSuperhero(… # Abbreviated
             ) {
        … # Abbreviated
        $this.Greed = $Greed
        $this.Level = $Level
        $this.AddDefaultPropertyValues()
        $this.AdjustBehavior()
    }
    [void] AddDefaultPropertyValues() {… # Abbreviated
    }
    [void] AdjustBehavior() {
        switch ($this.Alignment) {
            "Hero" {
                $this.Luck += 5
```

```
                    $this.Greed -= 5
            }
            "Villain" {
                    $this.Luck -= 5
                    $this.Greed += 5
            }
            Default {
                    $this.Luck += 3
                    $this.Greed += 3
            }
        }
    }
}
```

Now when a superhero is created from the class, the behavior is **adjusted** depending on the alignment. We use a switch statement to check if a superhero is a **Hero** and add **5** luck and subtract **5** greed. If the superhero is a **villain**, we subtract **5** luck and add 5 greed and finally we default to adding 3 luck and greed for any other alignments. *Figure 2.31* shows that we have been granted some luck and greed according to our alignment which defaulted to neutral since the argument for this parameter was set to **$Null**:

```
● PS C:\Temp\Superhero> $Comet = [NewSuperhero]::new("Comet", $null, @("Flying", "Invulnerability"),75,80,"",$null,$null)
● PS C:\Temp\Superhero> $Comet

  Name       : Comet
  Alignment  : Neutral
  Abilities  : {Flying, Invulnerability}
  Strength   : 75
  Armor      : 80
  Luck       : 8
  Greed      : 8
  Level      : 1
```

Figure 2.31: Object after adding the AdjustBehavior method to the class

Now we are just missing being able to handle pipeline input and create multiple superhero objects from our CSV file. A class do not handle pipeline input, so what can we do instead? The simplest would be to use a **wrapper** function. We have not covered the topic of a wrapper function, we only briefly mentioned it earlier, but it is essentially a function that acts as an intermediary between functions and expressions. It **wraps** the functionality of our class inside the wrapper function where we can then add additional logic or create modifications to our class behavior, not to the class itself. In this case it would handle the importing of the **.csv** file, then we would loop through the **.csv** data and use our class to create superhero instances. Like with the **Add-Superhero** function, we can **save** all our superheroes in a single Hashtable object, return this collection of superheroes, and get the same behavior as with our function, with the difference that we now have instances of our **NewSuperhero** class for each superhero, instead of **PSCustomObject´s**. Our wrapper function could look like this:

```
function Wrapper-CsvImport {
    [CmdletBinding()]
    param (
        [Parameter(Position=0,Mandatory=$true)]
        [String]$InputPath,
        [String]$Delimiter = ";"
    )
    $Superheroes = @{}
    $CsvFile = Import-Csv -Path $InputPath -Delimiter $Delimiter
    foreach ($Item in $CsvFile){
            $Superheroes[$Item.Name] = [NewSuperhero]::new(
        $Item.Name,
        $Item.Alignment,
        $Item.Abilities -split ",",
        $Item.Strength,
        $Item.Armor,
        $Item.Luck,
        $Item.Greed,
        $Item.Level)
    }
    Return $Superheroes
}
```

If we use the same .**csv** file as we did in *Figure 2.21* with a slight modification, we add the **Level** property, we can call our wrapper function and assign it to a variable that will now contain our superhero collection of instances from our **NewSuperhero** class. *Figure 2.32* shows how we call our wrapper function and assign the returned output to the **$Heroes** variable. All values in our collection are now instances of the **NewSuperhero** class, and like before we can call the individual instances and not only read and change the properties but also invoke the class methods within. We have not added methods yet, that are not used other than by the constructor, so let us add some and see the potential of a class instance and how it really differs from a function:

```
● PS C:\Temp\Superhero> $Heroes = Wrapper-CsvImport -InputPath .\HeroMap.csv
● PS C:\Temp\Superhero> $Heroes

  Name                        Value
  ----                        -----
  Blue Ghost                  NewSuperhero
  Evilin                      NewSuperhero
  Comet                       NewSuperhero

● PS C:\Temp\Superhero> $Heroes.Evilin

  Name      : Evilin
  Alignment : Villain
  Abilities : {Necromancy,Mind Control}
  Strength  : 10
  Armor     : 40
  Luck      : 5
  Greed     : 31
  Level     : 1


● PS C:\Temp\Superhero> $Heroes.Evilin.Level = 2
● PS C:\Temp\Superhero> $Heroes.Evilin

  Name      : Evilin
  Alignment : Villain
  Abilities : {Necromancy,Mind Control}
  Strength  : 10
  Armor     : 40
  Luck      : 5
  Greed     : 31
  Level     : 2
```

Figure 2.32: *Using wrapper function to instantiate multiple NewSuperhero instances saved in a collection*

Now we have the same functionality as our **Add-Superhero** function and even more when we start creating methods for our class, so our superheroes can get **behavior**, they can start to do things. Let us add a few new methods to the class:

```
class NewSuperhero {… # Abbreviated
    [bool] $Flying
    NewSuperhero(… # Abbreviated
            ) {
        $this.Name = $Name
        … # Abbreviated
        $this.AddDefaultPropertyValues()
        $this.AdjustBehavior()
        $this.Flying = $false
    }
    [void] AddDefaultPropertyValues() {
        … # Abbreviated
    }
    [void] AdjustBehavior() {
        … # Abbreviated }
```

```
}
[void] LevelUp() {
    $this.Level ++
}
[void] LevelDown() {
    $this.Level --
}
[void] Fly() {
    if ("Flying" -in $this.Abilities){
        if ($this.Flying) {
            Write-Host "Superhero $($this.name) is already flying"
        }
        else{
            Write-Host "Superhero $($this.name) starts to fly"
            $this.Flying = $true
        }
    }
    else{
        Write-Host "Superhero $($this.Name) does not have the ability to fly"
    }
}
[Bool] IsFlying() {
    if ("Flying" -in $this.Abilities){
        if ($this.Flying){
            Write-Host "Superhero $($this.name) is flying"
        }
        else{
            Write-Host "Superhero $($this.name) is not flying"
                }
            }
    else{
        Write-Host "Superhero $($this.Name) does not have the ability to fly"
            }
    return $this.Flying
}
[void] StopFlying() {
    if ("Flying" -in $this.Abilities){
        if ($this.Flying){
            Write-Host "Superhero $($this.name) stops flying"
```

```
                    $this.Flying = $false
            }
            else{
                Write-Host "Superhero $($this.name) is not flying"
            }
        }
        else{
            Write-Host "Superhero $($this.Name) does not have the ability to fly"
        }
    }
}
```

Note the abbreviated code and the newly added methods:

- **LevelUp()**
- **LevelDown()**
- **Fly()**
- **IsFlying()**
- **StopFlying()**

Also note that we have added a new property **[Bool]$Flying** and initialized this in our constructor and set a default value: **$this.Flying = $false**. Since it is not a parameter we can set, we do not include it as a constructor parameter. In our class we can set and use this property to state and check if a superhero is flying if it has the ability to do so.

The **LevelUp** and **LevelDown** methods are simple and adds or subtracts 1 **Level** point from the superhero when called. We do this by adding (**++**) or subtracting (**--**) 1 integer from the **$this.Level** property.

With the different flying methods, we can now get the superheroes to do something (if they can fly). All three methods are almost the same with a few differences. They all start by checking if the superhero can fly, if not it simply states this by outputting this to the console. Notice the use of the **Write-Host** which is generally not recommended to use for writing output, but in class methods, no objects get sent to the console except those mentioned in return statements, so we only add this for being visually able to see that something happens when we invoke the methods, since this does not create an object but writes directly to the console. In the **Fly()** method we check if the superhero is already flying, and if it is, we output this to the console, if **not,** we make it fly, outputting this to console and update the new **$this.Flying** property by setting it to **$true**. The **IsFlying()** method is then used to check if a superhero, with the flying ability, is flying or not and simply writes this to console, but it also returns the value of the **$this.Flying** property, so this state can be assigned and used in other variables and statements if needed. The **StopFlying()** method does the opposite of the **Fly()** method, checks if a superhero is already flying or not, if it is, then it sets the **$this.Flying** property to **$false** and lands the superhero, also writing this to console. *Figure 2.33* shows what happens when we invoke the different methods:

```
● PS C:\Temp\Superhero> $Heroes = Wrapper-CsvImport -InputPath .\HeroMap.csv
● PS C:\Temp\Superhero> $Heroes.Evilin.fly()
  Superhero Evilin does not have the ability to fly
● PS C:\Temp\Superhero> $Heroes.Comet.fly()
  Superhero Comet starts to fly
● PS C:\Temp\Superhero> $Heroes.Comet.IsFlying()
  Superhero Comet is flying
  True
● PS C:\Temp\Superhero> $Heroes.Comet.StopFlying()
  Superhero Comet stops flying
● PS C:\Temp\Superhero> $Heroes.Comet.IsFlying()
  Superhero Comet is not flying
  False
● PS C:\Temp\Superhero> $Heroes.Comet.LevelUp()
● PS C:\Temp\Superhero> $Heroes.Comet.Level
  2
● PS C:\Temp\Superhero> $Heroes.Comet.LevelUp()
● PS C:\Temp\Superhero> $Heroes.Comet.Level
  3
● PS C:\Temp\Superhero> $Heroes.Comet.LevelDown()
● PS C:\Temp\Superhero> $Heroes.Comet.Level
  2
```

Figure 2.33: Invoking the different methods in our superhero class in an instantiated instance

You can see that with a few methods we can now make our superhero do something. Leveling up, leveling down, fly, stop flying and check if a superhero is flying or not. With what we have learned we can begin incorporating methods and properties that can make our superhero do almost anything we want, and, in the end, we can use these superheroes in complex scenarios. We can make classes and/or functions that can have Villains and heroes battling each other, we can have our superheroes exploring vast lands and gain Levels and obtain new Abilities and so on, whatever we can think of, almost everything is possible.

A class is a powerful thing in programming and as you can see, we have gone from an advanced function that can create **simple** superhero objects with properties, to implementing an object-oriented approach to our scripting, instantiating objects from classes that not only **is** something but can **do** something. We could utilize this knowledge to make complex and powerful scripts for a lot of different scenarios.

Since we have abbreviated code in the previous class examples, the entire class is shown below:

```
class NewSuperhero {
    [String] $Name
    [String] $Alignment
    [String[]] $Abilities
    [Int] $Strength
    [Int] $Armor
    [Int] $Luck
    [Int] $Greed
    [Int] $Level
```

```
[bool] $Flying
NewSuperhero(
          [String]$Name,
          [String]$Alignment,
          [String[]]$Abilities,
          [Int]$Strength,
          [Int]$Armor,
          [Int]$Luck,
          [Int]$Greed,
          [Int]$Level
          ) {
    $this.Name = $Name
    $this.Alignment = $Alignment
    $this.Abilities = $Abilities
    $this.Strength = $Strength
    $this.Armor = $Armor
    $this.Luck = $Luck
    $this.Greed = $Greed
    $this.Level = $Level
    $this.AddDefaultPropertyValues()
    $this.AdjustBehavior()
    $this.Flying = $false
}
[void] AddDefaultPropertyValues() {
    switch ($null) {
        { $this.Strength -eq 0} { $this.Strength = 10 }
        { $this.Armor -eq 0} { $this.Armor = 10 }
        { $this.Luck -eq 0} { $this.Luck = 5 }
        { $this.Greed -eq 0} { $this.Greed = 5 }
        { $this.Level -eq 0} { $this.Level = 1}
        { $this.Alignment -eq ""} { $this.Alignment = "Neutral"}
    }
}
[void] AdjustBehavior() {
    switch ($this.Alignment) {
        "Hero" {
            $this.Luck += 5
            $this.Greed -= 5
        }
```

```powershell
            "Villain" {
                $this.Luck -= 5
                $this.Greed += 5
            }
            Default {
                $this.Luck += 3
                $this.Greed += 3
            }
        }
    }
    [void] LevelUp() {
        $this.Level ++
    }
    [void] LevelDown() {
        $this.Level --
    }
    [void] Fly() {
        if ("Flying" -in $this.Abilities){
            if ($this.Flying){
                Write-Host "Superhero $($this.name) is already flying"
            }
            else{
                Write-Host "Superhero $($this.name) starts to fly"
                $this.Flying = $true
            }
        }
        else{
            Write-Host "Superhero $($this.Name) does not have the ability to fly"
        }
    }
    [Bool] IsFlying() {
        if ("Flying" -in $this.Abilities){
            if ($this.Flying){
                Write-Host "Superhero $($this.name) is flying"
            }
            else{
                Write-Host "Superhero $($this.name) is not flying"
            }
        }
        else{
```

```
                Write-Host "Superhero $($this.Name) does not have the ability to fly"
                    }
        return $this.Flying
    }
    [void] StopFlying() {
        if ("Flying" -in $this.Abilities){
            if ($this.Flying){
                Write-Host "Superhero $($this.name) stops flying"
                $this.Flying = $false
            }
            else{
                Write-Host "Superhero $($this.name) is not flying"
                        }
        }
        else{
            Write-Host "Superhero $($this.Name) does not have the ability to fly"
        }
    }
}
}
```

Conclusion

As we have progressed through this chapter you have learned about and how to create advanced functions and how to incorporate different advanced features such as parameters and their attributes, dynamic parameters, parameter sets, lifecycle events, support for handling pipeline input and security measures with the **shouldProcess** feature. With what you have learned you should be able to create advanced functions for complex scenarios and be able to incorporate these into your scripts for handling all kinds of different tasks and processes. You have also learned the basic concepts of object-oriented programming and how to utilize these concepts in PowerShell by creating classes that can be used to initialize instances of complex objects that consists of properties and methods.

The next chapter is about using different methods for controlling and optimizing the flow of script execution. It introduces the reader to conditional statements using comparison and logical operators. It deeply covers advanced looping techniques such as nested loops, labelled breaks and continue statements, the use of retry logic in loops and the use of pipeline processing and also the Foreach-Object loop for iterating collections. Besides that, it explains how to utilize the switch statement to handle multiple conditions and it delves into using script blocks for dynamic and flexible flow control in terms of callbacks and event handlers. Furthermore, the chapter introduces the reader to multi-threading in the forms of parallel processing using PowerShell jobs and non-sequential processing using the Foreach-Objects parallel parameter.

CHAPTER 3
Flow Control and Looping

Introduction

Simple scripts usually have a simple code flow that starts from the top of the script, tasks and operations are then performed sequentially and the script ends when it has reached the bottom and executed the last statement. There is nothing wrong with this kind of flow and for simpler scripts this is usually enough to get a job done. It of course depends on the requirements and complexity of the tasks and operations that the script needs to be able to perform. For more complex scripts and programs such as GUI applications or other kind of scripts where users needs to be able to interact during execution, it is not enough that the code is executed sequentially and then the script or application stops when it has executed the last statement. It is essential that you are able to control the code flow of such scripts and applications and that you are able to jump between the different parts of the code and execute it in a non-sequential manner. Another thing that is very important, is the performance and reliability. Some tasks can take a long to time to execute, especially if you are reading sequentially through large datasets. Then it becomes essential to have methods for optimizing the performance and significantly improve the time it takes to read through such data. In this chapter, we are going to dive into different methods for controlling the flow of the code using conditional statements, switch statements, loops and more. We are also going to see how code blocks can be used for different kinds of tasks such as filters, callbacks and as event handlers. Furthermore, we going to see how PowerShell jobs and the ForEach-Object's parallel" parameter can be used for non-sequential and parallel processing.

Structure

The chapter covers the following topics:

- Conditional statements with comparison and logical operators
  - **Recipe 10**: Create advanced conditional statements using comparison and logical operators
- Advanced looping techniques.
  - Nested loops
  - Break and labelled break statement
  - Continue and labelled continue statement
  - **Recipe 11**: Use labelled breaks and continue statements
  - **Recipe 12**: Usage of while and Do-While loops
  - **Recipe 13**: Use retry logic in loops
  - **Recipe 14**: Use pipeline processing and ForEach-Object to iterate collections
- Switch statements for complex scenarios
  - **Recipe 15**: Utilize the switch statement to handle multiple conditions
- Script blocks for dynamic and flexible flow control
  - **Recipe 16**: Script blocks as filters for the Where-Object cmdlet and ForEach-Object loop.
  - **Recipe 17**: Script blocks as callback for cmdlet´s and functions
  - **Recipe 18**: Script blocks as event handlers
- Multi-threading and parallel processing with PowerShell jobs
  - **Recipe 19**: Use PowerShell jobs and parallel processing for improving performance
  - **Recipe 20**: Use the ForEach-Object -Parallel parameter for non-sequential processing

Objectives

This chapter will describe how to implement code flow logic into scripts and applications using advanced looping techniques such as nested loops, labelled breaks and labelled continue statements, conditional statements and using switch statements and script blocks for dynamic flow control. We will investigate multithreading and parallel processing with PowerShell jobs, use the **ForEach-Object** with the parallel parameter for non-sequential processing, for performance optimizing constructs in your scripts and applications. The key to a valuable script and application is to implement a proper logic and control flow operation, making sure they are dynamic and can handle all kinds of different challenges and tasks, depending on both internal and external aspects and making sure their constructs are utilizing the systems resources optimal for better overall performance. The objective of this chapter is to explore and explain different methods for controlling the code execution flow and also how to optimize the performance and reliability with parallel processing. Such methods enable the creation of much more dynamic, flexible and optimized scripts and applications and will in general help enhance the general functionality and reliability

Conditional statements with comparison and logical operators

Conditional statements are a crucial part of programming in general. They are used to make decisions based on different conditions and are used in code constructs like **if/elseif/else**, **switch** statements and loops. A conditional statement always evaluates to either **$true** or **$false**. Comparison operators are used for comparing values in expressions and evaluates whether the expression is either returned as **true** or **false**. There are also logical operators that are used to evaluate or combine expressions, like the **-and** and **-or** operators. Using comparison and logical operators in combination allows you to make complex evaluations of expressions and decision-making logic, with different statements.

Some of the most common PowerShell comparison and logical operators are shown in *Table 3.1*:

Operator	Description	Example
-eq	Equal to	$A -eq $B
-ne	Not equal to	$A -ne $B
-gt	Greater than	$A -gt $B
-lt	Less than	$A -lt $B
-ge	Greater than or equal to	$A -ge $B
-le	Less than or equal to	$A -le $B
-like	Wildcard match (case-insensitive)	Hello -like H*
-notlike	Reversed wildcard match (case-insensitive)	Hello -notlike W*
-match	Regular expression match (case-sensitive)	123abc -match [0-9]+

Operator	Description	Example
-notmatch	Reversed regular expression match (case-sensitive)	hello -notmatch [0-9]+
-and	Logical AND	$A -gt 10 -and $B -lt 20
-or	Logical OR	$A -eq yes -or $B -eq y

Table 3.1: *Most common PowerShell comparison and logical operators*

Recipe 10: Create advanced conditional statements using comparison and logical operators

Using comparison and logical operators for creating advanced conditional statements allows you to make complex choices depending on different values which are then used to control the flow in different statements like **if/elseif/else** blocks, **switch** statements and loops, in scripts and applications:

```
function WhatAmI ([int]$Age){
    if ($Age -lt 13){
        Write-Output "You are a child"
    }
    elseif ($Age -ge 13 -and $Age -lt 20){
        Write-Output "You are a teenager"
    }
    elseif ($Age -ge 20){
        Write-Output "You are an adult"
    }
}
```

In this first example we have created a simple function with an **if/elseif** block. The function has one parameter of the integer type, called **Age**.

- The first condition in the **if/elseif** block, states that if the provided argument is less than 13, then this evaluates to **$true**, and the code inside this block is executed.

- The next statement states that if the provided argument is greater than or equals to 13 AND less than 20, this evaluates to **$true** and this code block is executed.

- The last statement states that: If the provided parameter is greater than or equals to 20, this evaluates to **$true** and this code block is executed.

Note: An if/elseif/else block is evaluated from top to bottom and only the first $true condition is evaluated and executed. The rest of the conditions and blocks are skipped. This ensures only one block of code is executed depending on the first $true condition. In a switch block, multiple conditions can be evaluated as $true and be executed.

This is a simple example, but we can control the flow of the code and make different decisions and execute different blocks of code depending on the provided arguments value, due to the conditional statements that we used in the **if/elseif block**. There is no limit to the size and complexity of conditional statements, but the greater and more complex they are, the harder they might be to create, and they are also going to be more prone to errors, ending with unexpected results. Let us explore some more complex conditions.

Let us say we have a **hero** and a **villain** with different properties like we created in *Chapter 2, Advanced PowerShell function*. If we wanted them to engage in a fight, we do not just want to compare their **strength** against the opponent's **armor** to figure out who would win. We want to have a more complex fight mechanic that would include both **strength, luck, greed** and then some sort of randomness, so it would not always be obvious who would be victorious. In a scenario where a hero attacks a villain, the mechanics that states that the hero will successfully land a hit, could be more a more complex matter.

Such a scenario could be as follows:

To incorporate randomness to calculate a victor, both the hero and the villain rolls a dice that would return an integer between 1 and 50. We will call this a HeroDiceRoll or VillainDiceRoll. The hero´s strength combined with the hero´s luck must be greater than the villain's armor. Then the hero´s greed combined with the random **HeroDiceRoll** must be less than the combination of the villain's greed and the **VillainDiceRoll**. And the hero´s luck in combination with the **HeroDiceRoll** must be greater than the villains luck combined with the VillainDiceRoll, thus incorporating the randomness factor into the calculation of the outcome.

This sounds a lot more complex, so how can this be broken down into a conditional statement?

We use the following hero and villain for this scenario:

```
Name       : Tornado Tim
Alignment : Hero
Abilities : {Pyrokinesis, Mind Control}
Strength   : 59
Armor      : 54
Luck       : 27
Greed      : 21
Level      : 1
```

```
Flying     : False
Name       : Chiss
Alignment  : Villain
Abilities  : {Telepathy, Invulnerability}
Strength   : 45
Armor      : 70
Luck       : 5
Greed      : 26
Level      : 1
Flying     : False
```

The two superheroes are created using our **NewSuperhero** class and the **Wrapper-ExportCsv** function we created in *Chapter 2, Advanced PowerShell functions*. Each superhero instance is saved into each own variable: **$Hero** and **$Villain**. The first thing we do, is to roll some dice for each superhero:

```
$Superheroes = Wrapper-CsvImport -InputPath .\HeroMap.csv
$Hero = $Superheroes."Tornado Tim"
$Villain = $Superheroes."Chiss"
$HeroDiceRoll = Get-Random -Minimum 1 -Maximum 50
$VillainDiceRoll = Get-Random -Minimum 1 -Maximum 50
```

We then create the conditional statement that accommodates for the wanted scenario:

Hero strength combined with hero luck is greater than villain armor and hero greed combined with hero random dice roll is less than villain greed combined with villain random dice roll and hero luck combined with hero random dice roll is greater than villain luck combined with villain random dice roll:

```
$Hero.Strength + $Hero.luck -gt $Villain.Armor -and $Hero.Greed +
$HeroDiceRoll -lt $Villain.Greed + $VillainDiceRoll -and $Hero.Luck +
$HeroDiceRoll -gt $Villain.Luck + $VillainDiceRoll
```

This can be quite difficult to read, so we could add parentheses between the different expressions and conditions:

```
( ($Hero.Strength + $Hero.luck) -gt $Villain.Armor ) -and ( ($Hero.Greed +
$HeroDiceRoll) -lt ($Villain.Greed + $VillainDiceRoll) ) -and ( ($Hero.Luck
+ $HeroDiceRoll) -gt ($Villain.Luck + $VillainDiceRoll) )
```

We can reduce this like a mathematical expression. Let us assume that the **$HeroDiceRoll = 17** and the **$VillainDiceRoll = 34**. To see what is happening behind the scenes when the condition is evaluated, we replace the variables with their actual values:

```
( (59 + 27) -gt 70 ) -and ( (21 + 17) -lt (26 + 34) ) -and ( (27 + 17) -gt (5 + 34) )
```

We then calculate all the expressions:

```
( 86 -gt 70 ) -and ( 38 -lt 60 ) -and ( 44 -gt 39 )
```

This is what our condition really looks like. We replace the conditions with the Boolean values:

```
( $true ) -and ( $true ) -and ( $true )
```

Since we are using the logical operator **-and** all conditions must be evaluated to **$true** for the overall result to be **$true** which is the case for this statement and the result is that the hero successfully hits the villain.

The method for using conditional statements is the same whether it is being used in an **if/elseif/else block**, a **switch**, a loop, or any other kind of statement. The point is to get a Boolean result that is then used to decide if code should be executed or not, or what specific code should be executed. Conditions are not only limited to integers but can also be used with strings and other data types:

```
$VillainArray = "Chiss", "Manx", "Torque"

$HeroArray = "Tornado Tim", "Destiny", "Alias X"

# Statement evaluates to $true

("Chiss" -notin $HeroArray -and "Chiss" -in $VillainArray)

# Statement evaluates to $true

($HeroArray.GetType().BaseType.Name -eq "array")
```

In the case of this complex condition the result could be used in creating a battle between a hero and a villain, and for each attack the hero encounter, the condition would then express whether the hero hits the villain or not. A successful hit **($true)** could then be used to decrease the villains' hit points.

Bonus: Since we are using this statement to figure out if a hero hits a villain or not, based on the specified conditions, we could easily create the statement inside a loop and make a simulation that calculates the probability of the hero hitting the villain. Such kind of logic could look like this:

```
# Simulate the hero attacking multiple times
$NumberOfSimulations = 0
$HeroHits = 0
while ($NumberOfSimulations -lt 10000){
    $HeroDiceRoll = Get-Random -Minimum 1 -Maximum 50
    $VillainDiceRoll = Get-Random -Minimum 1 -Maximum 50
        # Check if the Hero hits the villain based on the provided condition
    if (( ($Hero.Strength + $Hero.luck) -gt $Villain.Armor ) -and ( ($Hero.
Greed + $HeroDiceRoll) -lt ($Villain.Greed + $VillainDiceRoll) ) -and (
($Hero.Luck + $HeroDiceRoll) -gt ($Villain.Luck + $VillainDiceRoll) )) {
```

```
        $HeroHits++
    }
    $NumberOfSimulations++
}
# Calculate the chance of the hero successfully landing a hit
[int]$ChanceOfHeroHit = ($HeroHits / $NumberOfSimulations) * 100
Write-Output "The chance of the hero successfully landing a hit is: $ChanceOfHeroHit %"
```

This will iterate and evaluate the condition 10.000 times and then calculate the average chance in percentage for the hero successfully hitting the villain. With the current hero and villain properties and the 1-50 random dice, the probability here is in the favor of the villain. The hero only has a 43-44% chance of performing a successful hit.

Advanced looping techniques

Advanced looping techniques in PowerShell can be further described as nested loops, which is loops running inside other loops. This is especially important when working with complex data, like database table data split in columns and rows, or components like multidimensional arrays. Advanced looping techniques also entail the use of labelled breaks and continue statements, which are used to control the execution flow inside loops. Knowing and utilizing such methods will give you more fine-grained control over the execution of a script, since you will be able to selectively skip or entirely stop iterations inside loops whenever necessary, based on specific conditions. This can help greatly improve the performance of scripts or applications because you can skip unnecessary steps of code execution which reduces unnecessary processing and improves the overall efficiency of your code.

Nested loops

Nested loops are the concept of placing one loop inside another which allows for iterating over multiple data objects like multidimensional arrays and nested collections, being able to go through each element and perform complex operations in each layer of data. The first loop is called the outer or main loop, and this determines the number of operations that should be performed in total. The inner loop is executed once for each iteration of the outer loop, so if you have 5 objects to iterate through in the outer loop, and 5 objects in the inner loop. The inner loop will iterate five times per iteration in the outer loop, with a total of 25 operations. There is no limit to the number of nested loops you can have inside each other, but the more nested loops, the more complex the general scenario and output might be. You can nest all types of PowerShell loops inside one another and nest a combination of different types. Below is an example of a simple nested **foreach** loop. Both the outer and inner loop in this example has a range of 1 to 5, and for each iteration in the outer loop, the inner loop will iterate five times. We multiplicate the values for the outer and inner loop in each iteration and writes it to the console, basically creating a small multiplication table:

```
foreach ($Outer in 1..5){
    foreach ($Inner in 1..5){
        Write-Output "$Outer x $Inner = $($Outer * $Inner)"
    }
}
```

Figure 3.1 shows the output of running the nested loop example above:

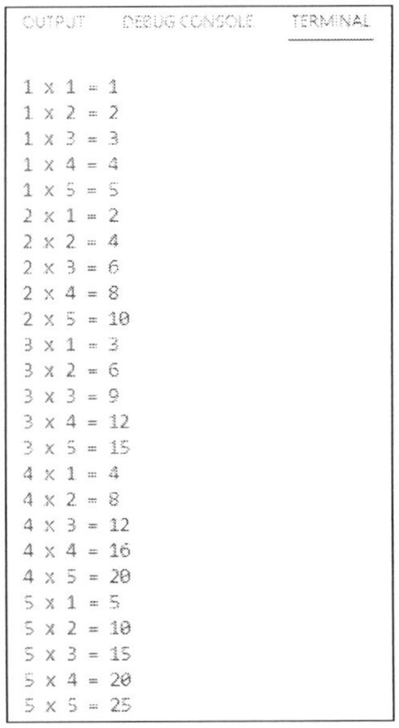

Figure 3.1: *Nested loop multiplication table output*

Below is another example of nested loops using a **while** loop as the outer and a **do-while** loop as the inner. The output results of this are the same as the previous example with the **foreach** loops. This is to show you that different types of loops can be used to create the same results:

```
$Outer = 1
while ($Outer -le 5) {
    $Inner = 1
    do {
        Write-Output "$Outer x $Inner = $($Outer * $Inner)"
        $Inner++
    } while ($Inner -le 5)
    $Outer++
}
```

Different situations might require different approaches and loops depending on the requirements and the preferred outcome. In the case with these two examples, it would not matter which approach was used, it depends on the user's preference, but for readability and simplicity reasons, the first one would be preferred. That might not have been the case with a very large dataset though, where the overall computational time might matter. In such cases, you might need to start measuring the time of your command executions and choose the one that is fastest, saving computational time and power. The shortest and less complex loop statement might not always be the fastest one.

Break and labelled break statement

A **break** is used to provide a way to exit out of loops, but it is also used in other statements like **switch** blocks and **traps** to control and stop the flow when needed, or when certain conditions are met. To use a **break**, you would simply use the **break** keyword wherever you need to exit out of the current statement. If a **break** is used inside an inner loop, it will exit the iterations of that inner loop, and the outer loop will continue with its next iteration. In the example below, we have added **break** statements to both the inner and outer loop´s inside **if** block´s. When the value in an iteration is equal to **3**, the **break** statement ensures that the loop is exited, this goes for both the inner and outer loop:

```
foreach ($Outer in 1..5){
    foreach ($Inner in 1..5){
        Write-Output "$Outer x $Inner = $($Outer * $Inner)"
        if ($Inner -eq 3){
            break
        }
    }
    if ($Outer -eq 3){
        break
    }
}
```

By adding these **break** statements, we can control the flow inside the loops, and exit them at certain points even though the provided objects still have data that could be processed. *Figure 3.2* shows the output of running the above example:

```
OUTPUT    DEBUG CONSOLE    TERMINAL

1 x 1 = 1
1 x 2 = 2
1 x 3 = 3
2 x 1 = 2
2 x 2 = 4
2 x 3 = 6
3 x 1 = 3
3 x 2 = 6
3 x 3 = 9
```

***Figure 3.2:** Output of breaking out of nested loop and its main loop at certain points*

Sometimes it can be difficult to control the flow with the **break** statement, especially inside nested loops. For managing this and making it easier we can add labels to loops and then used labelled breaks to control the flow and break out of loop´s, based on their specific label. To use a labelled break, we assign a label to each loop by using a colon : and then stating the label name, before declaring the loop. The below example shows an outer and inner labelled loop with labelled breaks:

```
:OuterLoop foreach ($Outer in 1..3) {
    Write-Host "Outer Loop: $Outer"
    :InnerLoop foreach ($Inner in 1..3) {
        Write-Host "Inner Loop: $Inner"
        if ($Outer -eq 2 -and $Inner -eq 2) {
            Write-Host "Breaking out of the inner loop..."
            break InnerLoop
        }
    }
}
```

Figure 3.3 shows the output of the example above. You can see that the labelled break in the nested loop breaks out of the iteration of the inner loop when the condition is met, and after that continues its iterations in the outer loop and the next line of iterations in the inner loop then starts over:

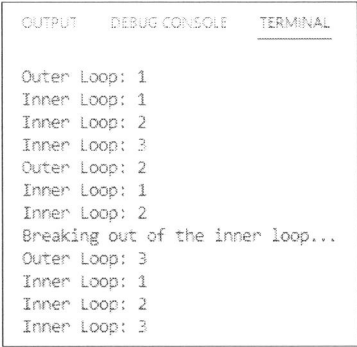

Figure 3.3: *Using labelled break to exit iteration inside the inner loop*

To further show how we can use the labels to control the flow of the statement, we can change the labelled break in the inner loop to use the outer loop´s label instead, and then exit the iterations at the outer loop, resulting in exit of this loop statement. As you can see in *Figure 3.4*, the labelled break now stopped the iterations of the outer loop instead and completely ended further executions:

```
OUTPUT      DEBUG CONSOLE      TERMINAL
Outer Loop: 1
Inner Loop: 1
Inner Loop: 2
Inner Loop: 3
Outer Loop: 2
Inner Loop: 1
Inner Loop: 2
Breaking out of the inner loop...
```

Figure 3.4: Using labelled break to exit iteration inside the inner and outer loop

With the labelled break statement, we now have better fine-grained control over how we can break out of both outer loop´s and nested loop´s. Consider a scenario where you might have four or five nested loops, then it would be much easier to break out of a specific loop by referencing its specific label, instead of having to manage it and break out, without any points of references.

Continue and labelled continue statement

Continue is another statement that is used to control the flow inside loops, and other statements like **switch** and **traps**. Whereas the **break** statement was used to break out of a loop, switch, or a trap. The **continue** statement is used to **return** the execution flow to the next iteration in line of that statement. You use the **continue** keyword to define the continue statement. And as with the **break** statement, the **continue** statement can also use labels, to control which iteration block it should continue executing from. In the example below a **continue** statement is added inside the inner loop, so if the **$Inner** iteration value equals **2**, execution of the remaining statements in that iteration is skipped and continues to the next iteration:

```
foreach ($Outer in 1..3){
    foreach ($Inner in 1..3){
        if ($Inner -eq 2){
            continue
        }
        Write-Output "$Outer x $Inner = $($Outer * $Inner)"
    }
}
```

The output of running this construct is shown in *Figure 3.5* where you can see that all output where it would have multiplied with x 2 has been skipped, due to the **continue** statement, continuing to the next iteration:

```
OUTPUT    DEBUG CONSOLE    TERMINAL
1 x 1 = 1
1 x 3 = 3
2 x 1 = 2
2 x 3 = 6
3 x 1 = 3
3 x 3 = 9
```

Figure 3.5: *Using continue statement to skip to next iteration*

As with the labelled break we can also use labelled **continue** statements. In the example below the **continue** statement is used with the **InnerLoop** label and skips to the next iteration in the inner loop, if the **$Inner** iteration value equals **2**:

```
:OuterLoop foreach ($Outer in 1..3) {
    Write-Host "Outer Loop: $Outer"
    :InnerLoop foreach ($Inner in 1..3) {
        if ($Inner -eq 2) {
            Write-Host "Continuing next iteration of the inner loop..."
            continue InnerLoop
        }
        Write-Host "Inner Loop: $Inner"
    }
}
```

The output of this construct is shown in *Figure 3.6*:

```
OUTPUT    DEBUG CONSOLE    TERMINAL

Outer Loop: 1
Inner Loop: 1
Continuing next iteration of the inner loop...
Inner Loop: 3
Outer Loop: 2
Inner Loop: 1
Continuing next iteration of the inner loop...
Inner Loop: 3
Outer Loop: 3
Inner Loop: 1
Continuing next iteration of the inner loop...
Inner Loop: 3
```

Figure 3.6: *Skipping inner loop iteration with labelled continue statement*

We can also use the **continue** statement to skip iterations to the outer loop using its label: **OuterLoop**, as shown in *Figure 3.7*:

```
OUTPUT      DEBUG CONSOLE      TERMINAL

Outer Loop: 1
Inner Loop: 1
Continuing next iteration of the inner loop...
Outer Loop: 2
Inner Loop: 1
Continuing next iteration of the inner loop...
Outer Loop: 3
Inner Loop: 1
Continuing next iteration of the inner loop...
```

Figure 3.7: *Skipping outer loop iteration from an inner loop with labelled continue statement*

Recipe 11: Use labelled breaks and continue statements

We have seen simple examples of nested loops, how to label loops, use labelled breaks and labelled continue statements. Utilizing nested loops and knowing how to break out of or skip certain iterations inside loops, and other statements like switches and traps, can be powerful tools when combined and used correctly. The examples do not provide any relevant usage and are only for showing the use of nested loops and the labelled break and continue statements, so let us create a more complex construct incorporating these, that provides usability. In the previous chapter we learned how to create superheroes, so let us create some new heroes and villains, having them battling each other on dangerous missions.

First, we need to create some new superheroes. For this we create a csv file containing heroes and villains. For now, we are not interested in neutral aligned superheroes, and we are not going to use their abilities either for these missions. What we want is to use the hero's **strength** and **luck** properties and the villains **armor** and **greed** properties.

The scenario is as follows:

Five heroes are going on different missions, always encountering the same five villains. On each mission one hero will battle one villain at a time. If a hero is defeated, the next hero in line will continue the fight, and if a villain is defeated the next villain will continue fighting. If no heroes are left after a fight, the villains win, and the mission has failed. If no villains are left, the heroes win, and the mission is successful. Since the heroes are the competitors, they use their strength to attack and the villains are the enforcers trying to protect their evil deeds from the heroes, using their armor for defense.

Since it would be easy to predict the outcome with the current strength and armor properties for the superheroes, we add a random number between 1 and 50 to the properties (we could say they use their abilities with different outcomes). This random dice roll will be added to the hero's luck points and for the villains, their greed points. Making the outcome much more unpredictable and exciting. *Figure 3.8* is the .csv file containing the superheroes we are going to create:

```
Name;Alignment;Abilities;Strength;Armor;Luck;Greed;Level
Alias X;Hero;Flying,Super Strength,Invulnerability;80;73;40;5;1
Black Commander;Hero;Telepathy,Invulnerability;45;70;23;13;1
Destiny;Hero;Necromancy,Mind Control;55;40;16;26;1
Liberator;Hero;Healing,Teleporting;63;55;30;26;1
Tornado Tim;Hero;Pyrokinesis,Mind Control;59;54;22;26;1
Atmos Fear;Villain;Flying,Super Strength,Invulnerability;80;73;10;26;1
Chiss;Villain;Telepathy,Invulnerability;45;70;10;21;1
Green Genie;Villain;Necromancy,Mind Control;55;40;10;32;1
Manx;Villain;Healing,Teleporting;63;54;10;15;1
Torque;Villain;Pyrokinesis,Mind Control;59;54;10;16;1
```

Figure 3.8: HeroMap.Csv file containing superheroes

We are going to use the **NewSuperhero** class and the **Wrapper-CsvImport** function created in *Chapter 2, Advanced PowerShell Functions* for creating a superhero object containing instances of each superhero. Following is the construct that will let our superheroes battle each other, we will walk through it in detail:

1. The superheroes are created using the wrapper function **Wrapper-CsvImport** for the **NewSuperhero** class, importing the **HeroMap.csv** file. The superheroes are saved in the **$Superheroes** variable:

   ```
   $Superheroes = Wrapper-CsvImport -InputPath .\HeroMap.csv
   ```

2. The different missions are created in an array and saved in the **$Missions** variable:

   ```
   $Missions = @("Prevent Nuclear Meltdown", "Defend the City", "Stop
   Biological Outbreak")
   ```

3. A **foreach** loop is created with the label **MissionLoop**. This is the outer loop, and it iterates over all missions in the **$Missions** array variable. The first statement in this loop is a simple **Write-Output** that writes the name of the current mission to console:

   ```
   Write-Output "`r`nMission: $Mission`r`n"
   ```

   > In PowerShell, the backtick ` is used as an escape character. When followed by certain characters, it indicates that the character should be treated literally rather than as a special character. `r represents a carriage return character and `n represents a newline character. These are often used in combination: `r`n to create a newline sequence which can be used to ensure proper formatting when dealing with strings and text output.

4. In the next statements in the **MissionLoop** we declare two new variables, **$Heroes** and **$Villains**. These variables are set as **System.Collections.Arraylist** using the **New-Object** cmdlet. The reason for using the **Arraylist** type is because it is a **.NET** class in PowerShell that creates dynamic arrays which provides more functionality compared to arrays created with the array sub-expression notation **@**

(). By using the **Arraylist** type we can modify elements in an array dynamically, such as removing specific items, which we are going to need later:

```
$Heroes = New-Object System.Collections.ArrayList
$Villains = New-Object System.Collections.ArrayList
```

> **Note: The choice between using an array sub-expression @() and the New-Object System.Collections.ArrayList depends on your specific requirements. The sub-expression is generally preferred for creating arrays due to its simplicity and readability and it is also more idiomatic and aligns with PowerShell's design principles. However, if you specifically need the features provided by an ArrayList, such as dynamic resizing, then using an ArrayList might be a suitable choice. If you are working with arrays and have no specific requirements for other collection types, using the sub-expression @() is a cleaner and more modern approach. If you have specific needs for dynamic resizing or are working with .NET methods that specifically expect an ArrayList, then an ArrayList would be the appropriate choice.**

5. We populate the variables with the names of each superhero in each alignment. For this we are going to need to be able to read the alignment property of each superhero and accordingly add the superhero name to the proper array. Since all values in the **$Superheroes** Hashtable variable is an instance of each superhero, we are going to iterate over each instance object in the values by piping them to the **Where-Object** filter cmdlet. We are then using the **alignment** property to check if it is a **hero** or a **villain**. The filtered data is then piped to the **ForEach-Object** loop where the name of the superhero is added to the array for the specific alignment. We create two statements, one for each alignment type. We could have omitted the use of the **Where-Object** filter and only have piped the values to the **Foreach-Object** loop, and inside this loop have used and **if/else** block to respectively add the heroes and villains to each respective array, this would have spared us one statement. Using the current approach will let you see the use of the **Where-Object** filter. For each iteration in the **MissionLoop** the **$Heroes** and **$Villains** variables are going to be re-declared and re-populated with the respective superheroes, starting all over again, ready for a new mission:

```
$Superheroes.values | Where-Object {$_.Alignment -eq "Hero"} |
ForEach-Object { $Heroes += $_.Name }
$Superheroes.values | Where-Object {$_.Alignment -eq "Villain"} |
ForEach-Object { $Villains += $_.Name }
```

> **Note: In PowerShell, the $_ is a special variable that is used to represent the current object in a pipeline, and it is essentially a placeholder for that object. It is also referred to as the "current object" or "pipeline" variable. The current object variable is not only limited to the pipeline but is also used in other constructs such as switch statements and more.**

6. Next is a **For** loop labelled as **HeroLoop**, this is nested inside the **MissionLoop**. We initialize the **HeroLoop** with **$i = 0** and set the condition that **$i** should be less than the number of items in the **$Heroes** array: **$i -lt $Heroes.count**. We do not specify any iteration expression in the for loop, so **$i** will always be **0**. The reason for this behavior is that we are going to need to be able to remove heroes from the **$Heroes** array whenever they lose a battle, then they would be out for the rest of that mission. If we used a **Foreach** loop instead and iterated over each hero in the **$Heroes** array, we would not be able to remove a hero from the array, since we cannot modify a collection while we are iterating over it, we would then get thrown an error. By using the **for** loop approach, we do not iterate over the array, but instead use the items count of the array as the iterator. Whenever a hero is removed, the **$Heroes.count** would have decreased by 1 for the next iteration, and when there are no heroes left in the **$Heroes** array, the loop will exit.

7. Inside the **HeroLoop** we nest another **for** loop which we label: **VillainLoop**. This has the same behavior as the **HeroLoop**, but we initialize it with **$j = 0** and use the **$Villains** array in the condition: **$j -lt $Villains.count**.

8. Inside the **VillainLoop** is where the battles take place. The first thing is to select a hero and a villain for battle. We select a random hero from the **$Heroes** array with the **Get-Random** cmdlet and assign it to the **$Hero** variable and a random villain from the **$Villains** array using the **Get-Random** cmdlet, and then assign it to the **$Villain** variable:

```
$Hero = $Heroes[(Get-Random -min 0 -max $Heroes.count)]
$Villain = $Villains[(Get-Random -min 0 -max $Villains.count)]
```

9. The next step is to calculate the battle **strength** for the hero and the battle **armor** for the villain. For the hero we get the **Strength** and **Luck** properties values from the hero's instance within the **$Superheroes** collection and add them together with a random number between 1 and 50, accumulating the total battle strength for the hero. This is assigned to the **$ChosenHeroStrength** variable. For the villain we get the **Armor** and **Greed** properties values and add them with a random number between 1 and 50, accumulating the total battle armor for the villain, assigning this to the **$ChosenVillainArmor** variable:

```
$ChosenHeroStrength = ($Superheroes.$Hero.Strength) +
    (Get-Random -Minimum 1 -Maximum 50) +
    ($Superheroes.$Hero.Luck)
$ChosenVillainArmor = ($Superheroes.$Villain.Armor) +
    (Get-Random -Minimum 1 -Maximum 50) +
    ($Superheroes.$Villain.Greed)
```

10. For the battle itself, we use an **if/else** statement. In the **if** block, If the **$ChosenHeroStrength** is greater than or equals to the **$ChosenVillainArmor**

(the hero gets the advantage if they are equal), the hero wins the battle. In this case we write the outcome to the console with the **Write-Output** statement, and then we remove the villain from the **$Villains** array using the **Remove** method on the array, the battle is over for this villain for the rest of this mission.

11. For the next part in the **if** block, we nest another **if/else** block. Whenever a hero has won a battle, we check if there are any villains left: **$Villains.count -eq 0**. If not, the heroes have successfully completed the mission. We write this to console with **Write-Output**, and then we use the labelled **continue MissionLoop** statement to skip to the **MissionLoop** labelled loop, venturing onto the next mission. If there are villains left, the mission is not yet over and we use the labelled **continue HeroLoop** statement skipping to the **HeroLoop** labelled loop and continuing the mission, fighting the next villain in the line. Notice it might not be the same hero for the next fight since we always choose an available hero (and villain for that matter) at random:

```
if ($ChosenHeroStrength -ge $ChosenVillainArmor) {
    Write-Output "Hero $Hero ($ChosenHeroStrength) defeats $Villain
($ChosenVillainArmor)"
    $Villains.Remove($Villain)
    if ($Villains.Count -eq 0) {
        Write-Output "`r`nHeroes completed the mission: $Mission"
        continue MissionLoop
    }
    else {
        continue HeroLoop
    }
}
```

12. If the hero has not won, the fight. If the **$ChosenHeroStrength** is not greater than or equals to **$ChosenVillainArmor**, the villain wins, and the statement continues to the **else** block. We write the heroes defeat to the console with **Write-Output** and then uses the **$Hero** array´s **Remove** method to remove the hero for the rest of this mission. We then nest another **if/else** block where we check if there are any heroes left: **$Heroes.count -eq 0**. If not, the mission has failed and we write this to the console, and then use the labelled **break HeroLoop** statement to **break** out of the **HeroLoop** labelled loop, moving on to the next mission, if any. If there are heroes left, we use the labelled **break VillainLoop** statement to exit the **VillainLoop** labelled loop, continuing the fight with the next random hero.

The entire construct is shown below:

```
$Superheroes = Wrapper-CsvImport -InputPath .\HeroMap.csv
$Missions = @("Prevent Nuclear Meltdown", "Defend the City", "Stop
Biological Outbreak")
```

```powershell
:MissionLoop foreach ($Mission in $Missions) {
    Write-Output "`r`nMission: $Mission`r`n"
    $Heroes = New-Object System.Collections.ArrayList
    $Superheroes.values | Where-Object {$_.Alignment -eq "Hero"} | ForEach-
Object { $Heroes += $_.Name }
    $Villains = New-Object System.Collections.ArrayList
    $Superheroes.values | Where-Object {$_.Alignment -eq "Villain"} |
ForEach-Object { $Villains += $_.Name }
    :HeroLoop for ($i = 0; $i -lt $Heroes.Count) {
        :VillainLoop for ($j = 0; $j -lt $Villains.Count) {
            # Battle
            $Hero = $Heroes[(Get-Random -min 0 -max $Heroes.Count)]
            $Villain = $Villains[(Get-Random -min 0 -max $Villains.Count)]
            $ChosenHeroStrength = ($Superheroes.$Hero.Strength) +
                (Get-Random -Minimum 1 -Maximum 50) +
                ($Superheroes.$Hero.Luck)
            $ChosenVillainArmor = ($Superheroes.$Villain.Armor) +
                (Get-Random -Minimum 1 -Maximum 50) +
                ($Superheroes.$Villain.Greed)
            # Hero Wins
            if ($ChosenHeroStrength -ge $ChosenVillainArmor) {
                Write-Output "Hero $Hero ($ChosenHeroStrength) defeats
$Villain ($ChosenVillainArmor)"
                $Villains.Remove($Villain)
                if ($Villains.Count -eq 0) {
                    Write-Output "`r`nMission Successful: $Mission"
                    continue MissionLoop
                }
                else {
                    continue HeroLoop
                }
            }
            # Villain Wins
            else {
                Write-Output "Villain $Villain ($ChosenVillainArmor)
defeats $Hero ($ChosenHeroStrength)"
                $Heroes.Remove($Hero)
                if ($Heroes.Count -eq 0) {
```

```
            Write-Output "`r`nMission Failed: $Mission"
            break HeroLoop
        }
        else {
            break VillainLoop
        }
      }
    }
  }
}
```

When we execute the code, we get an output similar to that in *Figure 3.9* depending on the outcome of the missions:

```
Mission: Prevent Nuclear Meltdown

Villain Chiss (134) defeats Liberator (126)
Hero Alias X (149) defeats Torque (83)
Hero Tornado Tim (133) defeats Green Genie (82)
Villain Manx (118) defeats Tornado Tim (117)
Villain Atmos Fear (152) defeats Black Commander (79)
Hero Destiny (125) defeats Manx (102)
Hero Alias X (149) defeats Chiss (103)
Villain Atmos Fear (110) defeats Destiny (91)
Villain Atmos Fear (138) defeats Alias X (126)

Mission Failed: Prevent Nuclear Meltdown

Mission: Defend the City

Villain Manx (114) defeats Destiny (83)
Villain Torque (114) defeats Tornado Tim (98)
Hero Liberator (139) defeats Manx (83)
Hero Liberator (106) defeats Chiss (103)
Villain Torque (104) defeats Black Commander (81)
Villain Atmos Fear (109) defeats Liberator (102)
Hero Alias X (127) defeats Atmos Fear (117)
Hero Alias X (142) defeats Green Genie (111)
Hero Alias X (148) defeats Torque (83)

Mission Successful: Defend the City

Mission: Stop Biological Outbreak

Villain Manx (121) defeats Tornado Tim (89)
Hero Liberator (99) defeats Green Genie (88)
Villain Atmos Fear (134) defeats Destiny (97)
Hero Liberator (118) defeats Manx (82)
Hero Liberator (135) defeats Atmos Fear (117)
Villain Chiss (117) defeats Black Commander (103)
Villain Torque (109) defeats Liberator (102)
Hero Alias X (167) defeats Torque (83)
Hero Alias X (129) defeats Chiss (110)

Mission Successful: Stop Biological Outbreak
```

Figure 3.9: *Output from code with nested loops, labelled breaks and continue statements, sending heroes on missions*

As we have seen we can use labelled breaks and continue statements to control the flow inside nested loops, depending on certain conditions. We can use labelled breaks to exit specific loops and nested loops, and we can use labelled continue statements to skip iterations in specific loops and nested loops. The use of labelled breaks and continue statements is not limited to loops but can also be used in other statements such as switches and traps.

Recipe 12: Usage of while and do-while loops

Previously in this chapter we saw a simple example where we could create a multiplication table using **while** and **do-while** loops. The **while** loop evaluates a condition before the loop is executed if the condition is **$false** the loop will not execute. If it is **$true**, then the loop will execute and repeat iterating as long as the condition is evaluated to **$true** on each iteration, then exit when the condition is evaluated to **$false**. A **do-while** loop is similar except that it always executes its code at least once. When the code is run once, the condition is evaluated and will continue iterating as long as the condition is evaluated to **$true** on each iteration, if it is evaluated to **$false**, the loop exits. These types of loops can be used to repeat a set of instructions until a specific condition is met, giving you more fine-grained control of the flow in scripts and other statements like functions. Let us try to make it a little more complex.

Let us have one of our superheroes engage a monster and try to defeat it, using **while** and **do-while** loops to control the flow of this encounter:

One of our hero's engages a monster and starts to attack it. A dice roll will be used in combination with the hero's strength to try and diminish the monsters hit points, whenever the hero successfully hits the monster. When the monsters hit points are below 0, the monster is defeated. Whenever the hero misses an attack, the monster retaliates and has a slim chance of defending itself and defeating the hero, by rolling the dice and diminishing the heroes hit points. This might sound like a quite complex scenario, but when we use the **while** and **do-while** loops to control the flow of the encounter, it might not be so difficult at all.

We use a hero from the **$Superheroes** collection we created from the **HeroMap.csv** file in *Figure 3.8* using the **Wrapper-CsvImport** function and our **NewSuperheroes** class. Instead of creating an entirely new class for creating monsters, we borrow the **NewSuperhero** class for this, and instantiate a monster from it.

1. A **$Monster** variable is declared, and we initialize an instance from the **NewSuperheroes** class to create a monster. Since we are going to use hit points we need to add this as a property to the monster instance. We use the **Add-Member** cmdlet to add a **NoteProperty** called **HitPoints** to the instance and then giving it a value of **1000**:

    ```
    $Superheroes = Wrapper-CsvImport -InputPath .\HeroMap.csv

    $Monster = [NewSuperhero]::new("Monster",$null,@(),52,63,0,0,25)

    $Monster | Add-Member -NotePropertyName HitPoints -NotePropertyValue 1000
    ```

2. Our hero is **Alias X**. We declare a **$Hero** variable and save the **Alias X** instance from our superhero collection into the variable. We use the **Add-Member** cmdlet to add a **HitPoints** property to our hero and sets its value to **780**:

```
$Hero = $Superheroes."Alias X"

$Hero | Add-Member -NotePropertyName HitPoints -NotePropertyValue 780
```

3. A simple function **RollDice** is created for the Dice that returns a random integer between 50 and 100 using the **Get-Random** cmdlet:

```
function RollDice {

    return Get-Random -Minimum 50 -Maximum 100

}
```

4. The next thing we do is to declare a loop control variable **$Defeated**. Moroever, then we create a **while** loop labelled **Outer**. As a condition for this loop, we use the control loop variable with the **-not** comparison operator. If the **$Defeated** variable is not equals **$true**, the while loop will execute. This loop is simply used as a placeholder of sorts for the rest of the code logic and at the end, when the monster is defeated, this is written to console, and the **$Defeated** variable is set to **$true**, breaking out of the outer loop. We can say that when this loop starts, this is where the hero encounters the monster. When the loop ends, the encounter is over, resulting in either the victory or defeat of the hero:

```
$Defeated = $false

:Outer while (-not $Defeated){

    :Center do{ ...Abbreviated Code

}

    while(...Abbreviated Code)

    Write-Output "Monster is defeated"

    $Defeated = $true

}
```

5. Inside the **Outer** labelled while loop we create a **do-while** loop labelled **Center**. The condition for this loop is: **$Monster.HitPoints -gt 0**. As long as the monsters **HitPoints** property is greater than zero, the loop will continue iterating. We can state that this loop is where the hero attacks the monster. We start this loop with the **Write-Output** statement saying that *Hero is attacking the monster*. Next, we roll the dice and declare the value in a variable called **$Roll**. This variable is the loop control variable for the next nested while loop labelled **Inner**. This variable is also used to determine whether the hero hits the monster. What happens in this loop is:

    a. The roll of the dice: **$Roll** will determine if the hero hits the monster or not. This is done using the **Inner** while loop condition. Here the **$Roll** value is compared to the value of the monsters **armor** property:

    ```
    :Inner while ($Roll -lt $Monster.Armor){}
    ```

b. If the hero's **$Roll** value is less than the monsters' **armor**, the hero miss the attack, and the monster now gets a chance to retaliate. This logic is then handled inside the inner **while** loop. This will be explained in a moment.

c. If the hero's **$Roll** value is greater than the monsters' armor, then the hero's attack successfully hit's the monster, and the inner loop is not triggered and the center loop continues its statements that are below the inner loop.

If the hero successfully hits the monster, the **Inner** while loop is not activated, and the **Center** loop carries on to its next statements. Here we declare a variable called **$Hit** where the hero's **strength** is combined with the value of the **$Roll** variable, to give the monster a massive hit. This combined value is then subtracted from the monster instance **HitPoints** property, lowering its overall remaining **HitPoints**. We write to console that the hero hit the monster, the amount of the strike and in parentheses how many **HitPoints** the monster have left. The **do-while** loop's condition then checks if the monster still have any **HitPoints** left, if it has, the attack cycle is then repeated, and the hero will keep attacking until he is either victorious or defeated:

```
:Center do{
        Write-Output "$($Hero.Name) is attacking the monster"
        $Roll = RollDice
        :Inner while ($Roll -lt $Monster.Armor){ …Abbreviated Code
}
        $Hit = ($Hero.Strength) + ($Roll)
        $Monster.HitPoints -= $Hit
            Write-Output "Hero hit monster with $hit (Left:
$($Monster.HitPoints))"
            }
        while($Monster.HitPoints -gt 0)
```

6. The **Inner while** loop is triggered if the hero misses an attack on the monster. The monster then gets the chance to retaliate. As mentioned before, the value of the dice roll **$Roll** is compared with the monster's **armor** property. The hero misses the attack on the monster if the dice roll value is less than the monster's armor. What happens further is:

a. The hero misses the attack on the monster, and this is written to console, the dice roll value is written in parentheses, and the monsters armor property value, just so we can see these values against each other. The monster then retaliates, which is written to console.

b. The monster rolls the dice, and the value of this roll is assigned to the **$MonsterRoll** variable.

c. We use an **if/else** block. The condition in the **if** block is: **$MonsterRoll -gt $Hero.Armor**. If the monsters dice roll is greater than the hero´s armor, the monster successfully hits the hero, and the **$MonsterRoll** value is subtracted from the hero´s **HitPoints** property. We write to console that the monster hit the hero with the value, and in parentheses how many HitPoints the hero have left.

d. Inside the **if** block, we nest another **if/else** block. The condition here is that **$Hero.HitPoints -le 0** checks if the hero has any HitPoints left. If not, the hero is defeated, which is then written to console, and then we use the labelled **break Outer**, to break out of the outer loop, ending the encounter, with the hero's defeat. If the hero still has **HitPoints** left, we use the labelled **continue Center** statement in the **else** block to let the hero start over with a new attack.

e. If the **$MonsterRoll** is not greater than the hero's armor, the monster misses and fails in retaliating We enter the **else** block where we write this to the console, and then use the labelled **continue Center** statement to let the hero start over with another attack:

```
:Inner while ($Roll -lt $Monster.Armor){
        Write-Output "Hero misses ($($Roll) vs. $($Monster.Armor))"
        Write-Output "Monster retaliates"
                $MonsterRoll = RollDice
        if ($MonsterRoll -gt $Hero.Armor){
            $Hero.HitPoints -= $MonsterRoll
            Write-host "Monster hits hero with $MonsterRoll
(Left: $($Hero.HitPoints))"
            if ($Hero.HitPoints -le 0){
                Write-Output "Hero is defeated"
                break Outer
            }
            else{
                continue Center
            }
        }
        else {
            Write-Output "Monster misses"
            continue Center
        }
    }
```

This might sound a bit complex but when we sum it all up, it might not be that difficult to understand. We have a hero fighting a monster. We use dice roll to bring some randomness into the equation. The hero attacks the monster and depending on the dice roll, he either hits or misses the monster upon each attack. If the hero hits the monster, the monster loses hit points. If the hero misses the monster, the monster retaliates and depending on a dice roll, the monster either hits or misses the hero. If it hits, the hero loses hit points. The process is repeated until either the hero or the monster is defeated. We could say the hero has the advantage though.

The entire construct is shown below:

```
$Superheroes = Wrapper-CsvImport -InputPath .\HeroMap.csv
$Monster = [NewSuperhero]::new("Monster",$null,@(),52,63,0,0,25)
$Monster | Add-Member -NotePropertyName HitPoints -NotePropertyValue 1000
$Hero = $Superheroes."Alias X"
$Hero | Add-Member -NotePropertyName HitPoints -NotePropertyValue 780
function RollDice {
    return Get-Random -Minimum 50 -Maximum 100
}
$Defeated = $false
:Outer while (-not $Defeated){
    :Center do{
        Write-Output "$($Hero.Name) is attacking the monster"
        $Roll = RollDice
        :Inner while ($Roll -lt $Monster.Armor){
            Write-Output "Hero misses ($($Roll) vs. $($Monster.Armor))"
            Write-Output "Monster retaliates"
            $MonsterRoll = RollDice
            if ($MonsterRoll -gt $Hero.Armor){
                $Hero.HitPoints -= $MonsterRoll
                Write-host "Monster hits hero with $MonsterRoll (Left:
$($Hero.HitPoints))"
                if ($Hero.HitPoints -le 0){
                    Write-Output "Hero is defeated"
                    break Outer
                }
                else{
                    continue Center
                }
```

```
            }
         else {
             Write-Output "Monster misses"
             continue Center
         }
      }
      $Hit = ($Hero.Strength) + ($Roll)
      $Monster.HitPoints -= $Hit
      Write-Output "Hero hit monster with $hit (Left: $($Monster.HitPoints))"
         }
   while($Monster.HitPoints -gt 0)
   Write-Output "Monster is defeated"
   $Defeated = $true
}
```

The output of running the encounter is shown in *Figure 3.10*:

```
Alias X is attacking the monster
Hero hit monster with 149 (Left: 851)
Alias X is attacking the monster
Hero misses (50 vs. 63)
Monster retaliates
Monster hits hero with 92 (Left: 688)
Alias X is attacking the monster
Hero misses (57 vs. 63)
Monster retaliates
Monster hits hero with 83 (Left: 605)
Alias X is attacking the monster
Hero hit monster with 159 (Left: 692)
Alias X is attacking the monster
Hero hit monster with 175 (Left: 517)
Alias X is attacking the monster
Hero hit monster with 171 (Left: 346)
Alias X is attacking the monster
Hero hit monster with 144 (Left: 202)
Alias X is attacking the monster
Hero hit monster with 168 (Left: 34)
Alias X is attacking the monster
Hero misses (57 vs. 63)
Monster retaliates
Monster misses
Alias X is attacking the monster
Hero hit monster with 167 (Left: -133)
Monster is defeated
```

Figure 3.10: Output of the monster encounter construct

We use the combination of labelled **while** and **do-while** loops to control the flow in the construct depending on the different outcome of the conditions. These types of loops can be used for a lot of different scenarios where you need to be able to control the flow in your scripts. This could be for validating user input like repeatedly prompting a user for input until valid data is provided, which could be a password or an email. It could be used for data or file processing, countdown timers, queue processing and a lot more. To make it even more flexible, a construct such as this could easily be created inside a function instead of directly in the global scope of the script. You could then add parameters for the hero and the monster, being able to use different heroes and monsters in such an encounter and be able to invoke the function whenever needed in your script.

Recipe 13: Use retry logic in loops

Another valuable technique when using loops to control the execution flow, is to be able to incorporate retry logic. This could be that a user enters a password which needs to be matched against a password in a database, and there are a limited number of attempts before the user gets locked out, or there might be a grace period before the user can try again after to many wrong entries. Let us look at some different examples where we use loops to incorporate retry logic:

```
$PasswordDatabase = @(
    "Passw0rd!",
    "S3cur3P@ss",
    "P@ssw0rd123",
    "MyP@ssw0rd",
    "SuperSecret!",
    "12345Password",
    "P@55word!",
    "Secret123$",
    "P@ssw0rd!",
    "P@ssword2023"
)
$Attempts = 0
$Success = $null
do{
    if ($Attempts -lt 3){
        $UserPassword = Read-Host -Prompt "Enter password"
    }
    else{
        Write-Output "To many attempts. Access denied"
```

```
        $Success = $false
        break
    }
    $Attempts ++
}while($UserPassword -notin $PasswordDatabase)
if ($Success -ne $false){
    Write-Output "Password accepted. Access granted."
}
```

In this first example we use a **do-while** loop to check if a user input password matches a password in a database. The user has 3 tries for entering the correct password or access will be denied:

1. We declare an **$Attempts** variable with the value of **0**. And a **$Success** variable with the value of **$null**. The reason for using the **$null** value and not **$true** (or any other values) is that the condition is the last thing that is checked in the **do-while** loop, and we use this condition to check if the password is a match. If the password matches, the loop exits. We then do not have other means of setting the **$Success** variable to **$true**, without incorporating another kind of logic to the structure. The easiest method here is to just use a value that is not **$false** and at the end assume that the password is accepted if **$success** is not **$false**. Any other value than **$false** could then be used as a form of acceptance value.

2. Inside the loop, we use an **if** statement to check if all number of attempts are used, with the condition: **$Attempts -lt 3**. If not, we prompt the user for entering the password and save the entered password inside the **$UserPassword** variable. The loop continues and we increment the **$Attempts** variable with **1**. The **do-while** loop condition is then checking if the **$UserPassword** value is a match to a password within the **$PasswordDatabase**.

3. If the **$Attempts** variable value is not less than **3**. All attempts are then used, and the **else** block is executed. We write to the console that too many attempts have been used and access have been denied. Setting the **$Success** variable to **$false** and then break out of the loop.

4. Outside the loop, we have a simple logic inside an **if** block that checks if the **$Success** variable is not **$false**. If it is not, then the password is assumed valid, and access is granted.

This might not be the optimal method since we are looking for a value that is anything but **$false**, but the logic is usable and shows the base mechanics of using retry logic with a **do-while** loop.

Figure 3.11 shows the output of running the construct, both when failing to provide the correct password 3 times and when successfully entering the correct password:

```
Enter password: 123456
Enter password: Abcdefg
Enter password: Qwerty
To many attempts. Access denied


Enter password: clown123
Enter password: Passw0rd!
Password accepted. Access granted.
```

Figure 3.11: *Output when entering wrong and correct*
password in do-while loop retry logic example

In the next example we use a **while** loop to create the logic, and we use the same **$PasswordDatabase** for the password database:

```
$Attempts = 0
$Success = $false
while ($Attempts -lt 3){
    $UserPassword = Read-Host -Prompt "Enter password"
    if ($UserPassword -in $PasswordDatabase){
        $Success = $true
        break
    }
    else{
        Write-Output "Wrong password. Retry."
        $Attempts ++
    }
}
if ($Success){
    Write-Output "Password accepted. Access granted."
}
else{
    Write-Output "Too many attempts. Access denied"
}
```

1. The first thing we do is to declare an **$Attempts** variable with the value of **0** and a **$Success** variable with the value **$false**.

2. Since we are using a **while** loop, the condition is checked as the first thing. We check if **$Attempts -lt 3**. If the value of the **$Attempts** variable is less than **3** the while loop is executed.

3. Inside the **while** loop, we prompt the user for entering a password and save the entered value in the **$UserPassword** variable.

4. We then use an **if/else** block for creating the inside logic. The condition in the **if** block checks if the password value in the **$UserPassword** variable is within the **$PasswordDatabase**. If it is, we set the value of the **$Success** variable to **$true** and then break out of the loop.

5. If the password entered is wrong, the **else** block is executed, and we write this to the console and then increment the **$Attempts** variable with **1**. The while loop continues its next iteration if the password is wrong, and the number of attempts is less than **3**.

6. When the loop is finished either during too many failed attempts or if the correct password is provided, an **if/else** statement is used to check the value of the **$Success** variable. If it is **$true**, the password is correct and access is granted, if not there have been to many failed attempts and access is denied.

Figure 3.12 shows the output of the example using the while loop:

```
Enter password: 123456
Wrong password. Retry.
Enter password: Abcdef
Wrong password. Retry.
Enter password: Qwerty
Wrong password. Retry.
Too many attempts. Access denied


Enter password: Passw0rd!
Password accepted. Access granted.
```

Figure 3.12: *Output when entering wrong and correct password in while loop retry logic example*

This example might be easier to understand than the first one, but the logic can be written in more ways than shown here. It depends on the specific user, requirement and preferences. It would be optimal to have logic like this inside a function and then have the function return either **$true** or **$false** depending on the outcome of the provided password. The returned value could then be used in further logic inside the script. It could be the next logic would log the user in, like: **Is the correct password provided? If $true, login the user.** This could be used to separate the logic that handles the password check, and the login function. You can see with these examples that we can use retry logic to handle temporary failures, like when we entered the wrong password, which makes the code much more resilient and a lot less error prone. Other real-world scenarios where retry logic could be used is in network and database connectivity, where we could use the retry logic to check the connection to a network or a database. If no connections are currently available, due to whatever reason, retry logic could be set to have a grace period before the next attempt at connecting to the network or database, instead of having the script entirely stop executing, because no connections are available. This makes retry logic a very powerful technique to incorporate for a lot of different reasons and scenarios.

Recipe 14: Use pipeline processing and ForEach-Object to iterate collections

Using the pipeline with the **ForEach-Object** loop allows you to iterate over collections and then perform operations on each item passed through the pipeline. Since the pipeline allows for passing an object from one cmdlet or function to another, it saves the use of storing them in variables in between the commands, which allows for an efficient and memory conserving manner of iterating through collections without the use of specific loop constructs. This makes it a very powerful way of handling large collections and processing large sets of data.

To see the real potential and memory efficiency of using the pipeline with **ForEach-Object**, we would have to work on a larger dataset. For this recipe we use a sample csv file containing 100.000 random entries.

> **Note: The used dataset is free to download and consists of random data. The dataset can be downloaded from: https://www.datablist.com/learn/csv/download-sample-csv-files. The used dataset is: organizations-100000.csv containing 100.000 randomly generated records.**

We want to compare the memory usage when working with this dataset within the pipeline and the **ForEach-Object** loop versus a **Foreach** loop that iterates over the dataset when it is stored in a variable.

The first thing we want to do is to create a function that can calculate the memory usage of commands. Since we are only interested in a **rough** estimate of the memory usage of our commands, for comparison reasons, we can create a function that returns the memory usage of the current PowerShell process where we are running our code, just before and right after the commands are executed and then subtract these numbers from each other. We can create a simple function to accommodate this. Since we are going to execute different commands, we create our commands in different script blocks assigned to variables, and then makes sure the function can execute these script blocks by adding a parameter of the **scriptblock** type:

1. We create the function called **Get-MemoryUsage** that has one parameter of the **scriptblock** type called **$Block**. To get the memory usage of our current process we use the **Get-CimInstance** with the **WIN32_PROCESS** argument. This gives us a list of all current processes on the system. The returned list has a property called **WorkingSetSize** which represents the currently allocated physical memory of the processes. Since we are only interested in the memory usage of our current PowerShell process, we pipe the **Get-CimInstance** output to **Where-Object** and filter on the property **ProcessID -eq $PID**. $PID is a PowerShell built-in variable that represents the Process ID (PID) of the current process, in this case our current PowerShell session. To get the current memory usage of the current process in bytes, we combine it to this command:

```
(Get-CimInstance WIN32_PROCESS | Where-Object {$_.ProcessID -eq
$PID}).WorkingSetSize
```

2. Inside the function we create a variable called **$BeforeMemory** where we save the memory size from the memory command, before executing the **scriptblock**. We then use the invocation operator **&** to execute the command inside the script block. After the execution we then create another variable called **$AfterMemory** where we again run and assign the output from the memory command, to get the process memory after the execution of the **scriptblock** process. We subtract the **$BeforeMemory** value from the **$AfterMemory** value and save this to the **$MemoryUsed** variable which now contains the difference in memory usage in bytes, from before and after running the **scriptblock** command. We then write the output to the console with the **$MemoryUsed** value. Note that we also divide this value with **/1MB** to get the output in **MegaBytes** (**MB**). The function looks like this:

```
function Get-MemoryUsage{
    param(
        [scriptblock]$Block
    )
    $BeforeMemory = (Get-CimInstance WIN32_PROCESS | Where-Object
{$_.ProcessID -eq $PID}).WorkingSetSize
    & $Block
    $AfterMemory = (Get-CimInstance WIN32_PROCESS | Where-Object
{$_.ProcessID -eq $PID}).WorkingSetSize
    $MemoryUsed = $AfterMemory - $BeforeMemory
    Write-Output "Memory Usage: $($MemoryUsed/1MB) MB"
}
```

3. Now we create the different script blocks that contain our commands. The first one is where we import the dataset with **Get-Content** and store it in a variable called **$Data** and then use a **Foreach** loop to iterate through the data. Just to do something with the data for demonstration purposes, we add a **$count** variable. For each iteration of the data, we add **1** to the counter variable. We assign this script block to the **$VariableBlock** variable:

```
$VariableBlock = {
    $Count = 0
    $Data = Get-Content .\organizations-100000.csv
    foreach ($Item in $Data){
        $Count++
    }
}
```

4. The next script block is the command where we use the pipeline and **ForEach-Object** to iterate over the data. We use **Get-Content** on the dataset csv file, and pipe this directly to **ForEach-Object**. Again, we simply add **1** to the **$Count** variable for each iteration. This script block is assigned to the **$PipelinedBlock** variable:

```
$PipelinedBlock = {
    $Count = 0
    Get-Content .\organizations-100000.csv | ForEach-Object
{$Count++}
}
```

5. We call the **Get-MemoryUsage** function twice, one for each script block and with the script block itself as an argument to the function **$Block** parameter:

```
Write-Output "VariableBLock:"
Get-MemoryUsage $VariableBlock
Write-Output "PipelinedBLock:"
Get-MemoryUsage $PipelinedBlock
```

It would have been a lot more complex to create a function that precisely calculated the memory usage of the processes. Since we used this simple approach to get a rough estimate of the memory usage for each process and still would like to get viable comparison values, the code needs to be executed in a new opened PowerShell shell session each time. This makes sure that the memory for this session is not already filled with the dataset and that the variables do not already exist and contain data in memory, which might pollute the end results. When the code is executed, you would get output as shown in *Figure 3.13*:

```
VariableBlock:
Memory Usage: 193.046875 MB
PipelinedBlock:
Memory Usage: 16.63671875 MB
```

Figure 3.13: Memory usage of running large dataset from variable with foreach loop and pipeline dataset to ForEach-Object

We can clearly see that using the pipeline with **ForEach-Object** use a lot less memory versus when the dataset is first stored into a variable and then used in a **Foreach** loop to iterate over each item from within the variable. This is because the pipeline allows objects to be sent directly between cmdlets and functions, without having to store the data in variables in between the commands. When we pipe the content of a dataset from a file with **Get-Content**, the pipeline processes one line at a time from within the file and passes this line to **ForEach-Object**, then each item is processed one by one as they flow through the pipeline.

Using the pipeline and **ForEach-Object** might in some cases not be faster than using another loop construct, due to the overhead of the pipeline handling. But as we can see here, it has great benefits when it comes to memory usage since we do not need to store all the data in a variable before it can be processed. For large datasets it might not be feasible at all to use the approach where data is saved in memory, unless you have a lot of memory in your system to accommodate for this. The pipeline and **ForEach-Object** approach also makes for more readable code and is easier to maintain.

Switch statements for complex scenarios

A **switch** statement is another statement that is used to control the execution flow in code. It executes different code blocks depending on the value of the provided expression. It provides a way of matching an expression against multiple possibilities, which are called **cases** and then executes the code of the matching case. Whereas an **if/elseif/else** block would only execute code for the first matching expression, a **switch** statement can match multiple cases and execute multiple code blocks depending on the provided expression. This statement is used when multiple conditions need to be checked and is an alternative instead of creating multiple **if/elseif/else** statements. We can also use both labelled and non-labelled breaks and continue statements inside nested switch blocks and switch statements can also be used inside loops. A **switch** statement is declared by using the **switch** keyword followed by an expression and then the cases that should match the expression. In *Chapter 2, Advanced PowerShell Functions* we created a simple **switch** statement in the **NewSuperhero** class:

```
switch ($this.Alignment) {
    "Hero" {
        $this.Luck += 5
        $this.Greed -= 5
    }
    "Villain" {
        $this.Luck -= 5
        $this.Greed += 5
    }
    Default {
        $this.Luck += 3
        $this.Greed += 3
    }
}
```

In this example we can see that the expression provided is the **$this.Alignment** property variable. The evaluated value of this property will be matched with the cases inside the switch block. Here we have the 3 cases: **Hero, Villain** and **Default**. If the expression evaluates to **Hero** the **Hero** block will be executed. If it evaluates to **Villain**, the **Villain** block will be executed. The **Default** is a switch built-in case, that is used if no other cases match the switch expression. If we had created the same statement as an **if/elseif/else** block it would have looked like this:

```
if ($this.Alignment -eq "Hero"){
    $this.Luck += 5
    $this.Greed -= 5
}
elseif ($this.Alignment -eq "Villain"){
    $this.Luck -= 5
    $this.Greed += 5
}
else{
    $this.Luck += 3
    $this.Greed += 3
}
```

Almost similar, and the outcome would be the same, but in the switch block the expression is only evaluated once and then matched against each case, whereas in the **if/elseif/else** block each expression would need to be evaluated until one of them is **$true**, and that code block is executed or none of them is **$true** and no code block is executed. The point is that it is evaluating all the expressions. This would also increase the performance when a **switch** statement is used instead of an **if/elseif/else** block, especially when dealing with multiple expressions or values that needs to be evaluated. Should we evaluate a single expression in a **switch** block, or multiple expressions in an **if/elseif/else**. It of course depends on the requirements and preferences.

Recipe 15: Utilize the switch statement to handle multiple conditions

Let us say that we would want to give some superheroes some benefits depending on their current levels. The higher the value of the **Level** property, the higher the chance for great improvements. It should also depend on their alignment. A hero would get more luck points, a villain would get more greed points and a superhero of neutral alignment would get both luck and greed points. We could use **switch** statements to accomplish this.

Let us define a scenario:

Each superhero will roll a dice between 1 and 3 to add some randomness as to how many luck or greed points they can obtain. The first case would be the following: If you are a superhero with a level below 10, you are a low-level superhero. For low-level superheroes the benefits would be the dice roll * 2 if you are a hero or a villain. And a dice roll * 1 for all other aligned superheroes. A level between 10 and 24 would define a mid-level superhero and the benefits would be dice roll * 3 for heroes and villains, and dice roll * 2 for other aligned superheroes. A level between 25 and 49 is defined as a high-level superhero and their benefits would be dice roll * 4 for heroes and villains, and dice roll * 3 for other aligned superheroes. If the superhero has a level of 50 or above, the superhero is already powerful enough and are not granted any benefits.

The superheroes used are defined in a csv file as shown in *Figure 3.14* and as we have done before, we are using the **NewSuperheroes** class with the **Wrapper-ImportCsv** function for importing the superheroes and save them to the **$Superheroes** variable:

```
Name;Alignment;Abilities;Strength;Armor;Luck;Greed;Level
Alias X;Hero;Flying,Super Strength,Invulnerability;80;73;40;5;5
Black Commander;Hero;Telepathy,Invulnerability;45;70;23;13;10
Destiny;Neutral;Necromancy,Mind Control;55;40;16;26;20
Liberator;Hero;Healing,Teleporting;63;55;30;26;30
Tornado Tim;Hero;Pyrokinesis,Mind Control;59;54;22;26;60
Atmos Fear;Villain;Flying,Super Strength,Invulnerability;80;73;10;26;5
Chiss;Villain;Telepathy,Invulnerability;45;70;10;21;10
Green Genie;Neutral;Necromancy,Mind Control;55;40;10;32;20
Manx;Villain;Healing,Teleporting;63;54;10;15;30
Torque;Villain;Pyrokinesis,Mind Control;59;54;10;16;50
```

Figure 3.14: Csv file HeroMap2.csv with superheroes with different levels used for switch statement recipe

1. The first thing we create in this scenario is a **Foreach** loop which we use to iterate over each value in the **$Superheroes** variable. By using the values property of the **$Superheroes** variable we get all the superhero instances and iterate over each one. We are then able to work directly on each instance in each iteration since we are creating a direct reference to each instance inside the **$Superheroes** variable. In the foreach loop, for each iteration, or superhero, we write some output telling which superhero is processed and its alignment. We then roll a dice for that superhero, resulting in a value between 1 and 3:

```
$Superheroes = Wrapper-CsvImport -InputPath .\HeroMap2.csv

foreach ($Superhero in $Superheroes.values) {

    Write-Output "`r`nProcessing $($Superhero.Name) ($($Superhero.
Alignment)):"

    $DiceRoll = Get-Random -Minimum 1 -Maximum 4

}
```

2. For each iteration, or superhero, we create a **switch** statement with the expression: **$Superhero.Level**. In this **switch** statement we create 4 conditions, or cases. The first one checks if the **$Superhero.Level** property, or **switch** statements

expressions value, is less than **10**, a low-level superhero. Notice the use of the **current object variable $_**. We can use this inside the **switch** statement as a reference to the **switch** statements expressions value. The next case checks if the value is greater than or equals to **10** and less than **25**, a mid-level superhero. The third case checks if the value is greater than or equals to **25 and** less than **50**, a high-level superhero. The last case is set as the **Default** switch case. All superheroes with a level that are equals to or above **50**, a max-levelled superhero:

```
switch ($Superhero.Level) {
    { $_ -lt 10 } {
        Write-Output "Low-level superhero"
    }
    { $_ -ge 10 -and $_ -lt 25 } {
        Write-Output "Medium-level superhero"
    }
    { $_ -ge 25 -and $_ -lt 50 } {
        Write-Output "High-level superhero"
    }
    Default {
        Write-Output "Max-level superhero"
    }
}
```

3. Inside each of these switch cases, we create a nested **switch** statement. These switch statements expressions are the **$Superhero.Alignment** property. Each of these nested **switch** statements cases are: **"Hero", "Villain"** and **Default**. The nested switch blocks is where we determine how much luck or greed each superhero should be granted, depending on the level from the main **switch** statement and the alignment due to the nested **switch** statements. We calculate the **$ExtraLuck** and **$ExtraGreed** variables depending on the superhero level, which will determine a specific multiplier that is used to multiply with the random dice roll. We also add some output statements to each block:

```
switch ($Superhero.Alignment) {
    "Hero" {
        $ExtraLuck = 3 * $DiceRoll
        Write-Output "Gains extra luck: $ExtraLuck "
        $Superhero.Luck += $ExtraLuck
    }
    "Villain" {
        $ExtraGreed = 3 * $DiceRoll
        Write-Output "Gains extra greed: $ExtraGreed"
```

```
        $Superhero.Greed += $ExtraGreed
    }
    Default {
        $ExtraLuck = 2 * $DiceRoll
        $ExtraGreed = 2 * $DiceRoll
        Write-Output "Gains extra luck: $ExtraLuck "
        Write-Output "Gains extra greed: $ExtraGreed"
        $Superhero.Luck += $ExtraLuck
        $Superhero.Greed += $ExtraGreed
    }
}
```

4. In the main switch **Default** case, we nest another **switch** statement that also used the **$Superhero.Alignment** property. Inside the nested **switch** statement, we only have the **Default** case, where we simply output that the superhero is too high powered to be granted extra benefits. You might notice that this nested **switch** statement is kind of redundant, since we only use the default case here, so all max-levelled superheroes would always result in this default block being executed. The reason for keeping this nested block is to prepare for potentially future benefits if we wanted to add some, to the max-levelled superheroes at a later time. This nested switch block could easily be omitted, and the output could be added to the main switch block´s default case directly.

5. When all superheroes are processed the **Foreach** loop is exited and here we state that all superheroes have been processed, by writing this to the console.

The entire structure would look like this:

```
$Superheroes = Wrapper-CsvImport -InputPath .\HeroMap2.csv
foreach ($Superhero in $Superheroes.values) {
    Write-Output "`r`nProcessing $($Superhero.Name) ($($Superhero.Alignment)):"
    $DiceRoll = Get-Random -Minimum 1 -Maximum 4
        switch ($Superhero.Level) {
        { $_ -lt 10 } {
            Write-Output "Low-level superhero"
                    switch ($Superhero.Alignment) {
                "Hero" {
                    $ExtraLuck = 2 * $DiceRoll
                    Write-Output "Gains extra luck: $ExtraLuck "
                    $Superhero.Luck += $ExtraLuck
                }
```

```
        "Villain" {
            $ExtraGreed = 2 * $DiceRoll
            Write-Output "Gains extra greed: $ExtraGreed"
            $Superhero.Greed += $ExtraGreed
        }
        Default {
            $ExtraLuck = 1 * $DiceRoll
            $ExtraGreed = 1 * $DiceRoll
            Write-Output "Gains extra luck: $ExtraLuck "
            Write-Output "Gains extra greed: $ExtraGreed"
            $Superhero.Luck += $ExtraLuck
            $Superhero.Greed += $ExtraGreed
        }
    }
}
{ $_ -ge 10 -and $_ -lt 25 } {
    Write-Output "Medium-level superhero"
            switch ($Superhero.Alignment) {
        "Hero" {
            $ExtraLuck = 3 * $DiceRoll
            Write-Output "Gains extra luck: $ExtraLuck "
            $Superhero.Luck += $ExtraLuck
        }
        "Villain" {
            $ExtraGreed = 3 * $DiceRoll
            Write-Output "Gains extra greed: $ExtraGreed"
            $Superhero.Greed += $ExtraGreed
        }
        Default {
            $ExtraLuck = 2 * $DiceRoll
            $ExtraGreed = 2 * $DiceRoll
            Write-Output "Gains extra luck: $ExtraLuck "
            Write-Output "Gains extra greed: $ExtraGreed"
            $Superhero.Luck += $ExtraLuck
            $Superhero.Greed += $ExtraGreed
        }
```

```
            }
        }
        { $_ -ge 25 -and $_ -lt 50 } {
            Write-Output "High-level superhero"
                    switch ($Superhero.Alignment) {
                "Hero" {
                    $ExtraLuck = 4 * $DiceRoll
                    Write-Output "Gains extra luck: $ExtraLuck "
                    $Superhero.Luck += $ExtraLuck
                }
                "Villain" {
                    $ExtraGreed = 4 * $DiceRoll
                    Write-Output "Gains extra greed: $ExtraGreed"
                    $Superhero.Greed += $ExtraGreed
                }
                Default {
                    $ExtraLuck = 3 * $DiceRoll
                    $ExtraGreed = 3 * $DiceRoll
                    Write-Output "Gains extra luck: $ExtraLuck "
                    Write-Output "Gains extra greed: $ExtraGreed"
                    $Superhero.Luck += $ExtraLuck
                    $Superhero.Greed += $ExtraGreed
                }
            }
        }
        Default {
            Write-Output "Max-level superhero"
                    switch ($Superhero.Alignment) {
                Default {
                    Write-Output "Too high powered. No new benefits."
                }
            }
        }
    }
}
Write-Output "Processed all superheroes"
```

Executing this code would result in output as shown in *Figure 3.15*:

```
Processing Green Genie (Neutral):
Medium-level superhero
Gains extra luck: 4
Gains extra greed: 4

Processing Alias X (Hero):
Low-level superhero
Gains extra luck: 6

Processing Destiny (Neutral):
Medium-level superhero
Gains extra luck: 6
Gains extra greed: 6

Processing Liberator (Hero):
High-level superhero
Gains extra luck: 4

Processing Tornado Tim (Hero):
Max-level superhero
Too high powered. No new benefits.

Processing Atmos Fear (Villain):
Low-level superhero
Gains extra greed: 6

Processing Chiss (Villain):
Medium-level superhero
Gains extra greed: 9

Processing Torque (Villain):
Max-level superhero
Too high powered. No new benefits.

Processing Black Commander (Hero):
Medium-level superhero
Gains extra luck: 3

Processing Manx (Villain):
High-level superhero
Gains extra greed: 12
Processed all superheroes
```

Figure 3.15: Output from switch statement adding benefits to superheroes

Utilizing **switch** statements in your scripts and applications can not only make the code much more readable and easier to maintain but in some cases also increase performance due to the way a switch is only evaluating a single expression and then compares the value to the cases conditions. Whereas an **if/elseif/else** block evaluates each of its conditions one by one, which sometimes leads to redundant evaluations. This of course depends on the specific use case and the size of data that needs to be processed. Choosing between the use of a switch or an **if/elseif/else** statement should be based on readability and specific requirements for that script or application.

Script blocks for dynamic and flexible flow control

Script blocks in PowerShell can be defined as a small piece of encapsulated code logic that is executed whenever it is called. It can be assigned to a variable or passed as arguments to cmdlets and functions. A script block is in some ways like functions: both are blocks of code encapsulated in curly braces **{}**. They can both accept parameters, be invoked, and return values. The differences are that functions are specifically declared using the **function** keyword, script blocks do not have a specific declaration type. A function is also named and is invoked using that specific name, whereas a script block is nameless and is usually only assigned to variables or invoked directly, depending on its usage. Another difference is that functions have their own scope containing their local variables. Script blocks do not have a personal scope but share it with the global scope whereas it can also access variables directly in the global scope. To sum up script blocks are like functions but are more lightweight and do not have their own declaration type. They are usually used for temporary or smaller pieces of code within scripts whereas functions are more suitable for reusable and larger blocks of code.

Script blocks have a variety of use cases in PowerShell such as filters for the **Where-Object cmdlet** and for the **ForEach-Object** loop, as **callbacks** in functions and **cmdlet**'s and as **event handlers** for GUI form objects and much more. In the following recipes we will learn how we can create and use script blocks for such different use cases and scenarios and how they can be utilized to dynamically modify and bring flow control to scripts.

Recipe 16: Script blocks as filters for the Where-Object cmdlet and ForEach-Object loop

A filter is a script block that allows for defining simple to complex conditions and actions based on the elements in collections and are typically used in **Where-Object** cmdlet's and **ForEach-Object** loops.

We create a filter for a **Where-Object** cmdlet that returns **$true** if the input object, in this case a superhero instance created with the **NewSuperheroes** class and **Wrapper-ImportCsv** function, is greater than or equals to **25**. We declare the variable **$HighLevelFilter** and assign a script block as the value. Within the script block we add the expression: **$_.Level -ge 25**. We use the **current object variable** directly inside the filter and derives the **Level** property from the object. If the **Level** property of the object is greater than or equals to **25**, the filter returns **$true**. We can then pipe a list of object instances to the **Where-Object** cmdlet and use the filter. All objects with a **Level** property that is greater than or equals to **25**, will be returned from the **Where-Object** cmdlet. These objects are then saved in the variable **$HighLevelSuperheroes**. With this filter we can easily create lists of superheroes with specific levels. We could create multiple filters with different conditions and depending on these conditions use a specific filter to create specific lists. Since we use the current object variable directly inside the script block, or filter, this filter can only be used in constructs that iterates over a collection and uses the current object variable where objects are being processed, typically when working with pipelines or loop constructs. To get a list with the names of the high levelled superheroes that is filtered, we would need to get all the **Name** properties of the instances in the **$HighLevelSuperheroes** variable:

```
$Superheroes = Wrapper-CsvImport -InputPath .\HeroMap2.csv

$HighLevelFilter = {

    $_.Level -ge 25

}

$HighLevelSuperheroes = $Superheroes.Values | Where-Object $HighLevelFilter

$HighLevelSuperheroes.Name
```

Next, we re-create the filter with a parameter, **$Superhero**. Inside the filter we now use an **if** block to evaluate the expression **$Superhero.Level -gt 20**. This still assumes an object with a **Level** property. If the expression is evaluated to **$true**, the filter returns the **name** property of the input object. We use the filter in a **ForEach-Object** loop, but since the filter is not using the **current object variable** directly, we need to provide this as an argument to the filter. We do this inside the script block for the **ForEach-Object** loop. We use the invocation operator **&** to explicitly call the filter script block and provides the current object variable as the argument. The names of all superheroes with a level greater than **20** is returned and saved in the **$FilteredSuperheroes** variable. This filter is not bound to constructs that uses the current object variable, and could be called anywhere, as long as an object with a **Level** and **Name** property is used as the argument. Since this filter returns the name property and not the entire superhero instances, the **$FilteredSuperheroes** variable contains a list with the names of the high levelled filtered superheroes instead of the instance objects:

```
$HighLevelFilter = {

    param($Superhero)

    if ($Superhero.Level -gt 20){

        return $Superhero.Name

    }

}

$FilteredSuperheroes = $Superheroes.values | ForEach-Object {&
$HighLevelFilter $_}

$FilteredSuperheroes
```

Both these types of filters have their pros and cons. The filter using the current object variable directly, is bound to constructs like pipelines and loops, whereas the other type of filter is not bound to such and can be called from anywhere in the code. But the filter using the parameter only returns a property and not the entire object. If you need to use a specific filter depending on, if you only need to use a list with the names or if you need the entire instance objects in a new collection. The last thing is that the filter using the current object variable, only returns a Boolean value, so it can only be used for comparison, whereas the other filter returns the specified property, in this case the **Name** property. They are similar but not the same. They are used for the same end result but in different ways.

Recipe 17: Script blocks as callback for cmdlet´s and functions

Using a script block as a callback, allows you to define custom behavior and logic that can be executed in cmdlets and functions. This allows you to dynamically change the code logic inside the cmdlet or function, without changing the structure of the cmdlet or function itself.

We create a function called **Invoke-Ability** containing one parameter of the **Scriptblock** type called **$Callback**. The function then use the invocation operator **&** to execute the callback script block that is provided as an argument for the **$Callback** parameter. The callback script block also takes an argument, in this case, a superhero instance object. In this specific function we only use the instance of the superhero **"Atmos Fear"** as an argument for the **$Callback** parameter. We then create two callback script blocks assigned to variables. The **$MyCallback** and the **$MyCallback2**. They are both similar and takes one argument, a superhero instance object. The first callback uses the first index **0** in the superhero´s ability property, which defines the first ability, and the second callback uses the second index **1** in the superhero´s ability property, which defines the second ability. Depending on which callback you invoke the function with, the superhero will use a different ability:

```
function Invoke-Ability {
    param (
        [scriptblock]$Callback
    )
    & $Callback $Superheroes."Atmos Fear"
}
$MyCallback = {
    param($Superhero)
    Write-Output "$($Superhero.Name) using ability $($Superhero.Abilities[0])"
}
$MyCallback2 = {
    param($Superhero)
    Write-Output "$($Superhero.Name) using ability $($Superhero.Abilities[1])"
}
Invoke-Ability -Callback $MyCallback
Invoke-Ability -Callback $MyCallback2
```

When we invoke the **Invoke-Ability** function with the different callback script blocks, we get the output as shown in *Figure 3.16*:

```
PS C:\Temp> Invoke-Ability -Callback $MyCallback
Atmos Fear using ability Flying
PS C:\Temp> Invoke-Ability -Callback $MyCallback2
Atmos Fear using ability Super Strength
```

Figure 3.16: Output from invoking the Invoke-Ability function with the different callback script blocks

This might seem like something that could be done by creating a parameter within the function and then provide the correct argument for this instead. But consider this: What if you create a function that has a parameter for either the entire superhero instance object or a string for a specific ability and you then later decide to change the entire structure of the superhero objects. You then might have to also change the structure of the entire function to be able to handle these changes, since the function might have a lot of other functionalities that might break other functions and statements that used this function, or even the entire script itself, depending on how and where the function is used. If you use a callback script block instead, you will only have to update or change the statements inside this callback and you can then make changes without breaking the entire function structure. You could say that we decouple the code logic from the function and then we are also making the function more dynamic and are then able to change some functionality of the function without having to change the function itself and other relevant or dependent logic inside of it.

Recipe 18: Script blocks as event handlers

An event handler is an action, in the form of specific code inside a script block, that is executed whenever an event happens. An event handler is used to create event-driven scripts and applications, making it responsive to and perform actions based on these events. An event could be a **Button click, Key press, Mouse click, Timer event, Process Start/Stop event** and much more. They are a crucial part of especially GUIs, game mechanics and any other event driven architecture.

Let us take it a step further and learn how to use script blocks as event handlers for button clicks in GUI forms:

1. In order for us to be able to create a PowerShell GUI form we need to load the **System.Windows.Forms assembly**:

   ```
   # Load the Windows Forms assembly
   Add-Type -AssemblyName System.Windows.Forms
   ```

2. We then create the main form **Windows.Forms.Form** with **New-Object** and assign this to the **$Form** variable. This is the variable reference to the form itself. We add a title and a fixed size for the form:

```
# Create the main form
$Form = New-Object Windows.Forms.Form
$Form.Text = "Superhero Abilities"
$Form.Size = New-Object Drawing.Size(400, 300)
```

3. We create a **textbox** control **Windows.Forms.Textbox** with **New-Object** for displaying output inside the form. We set some properties starting that it should be a multiline textbox, it should be read-only, have vertical scroll bars (when text goes beyond the readable area), and it should fill out the form (meaning the layout would stretch the textbox inside the form):

```
# Create a TextBox control to display output
$OutputTextBox = New-Object Windows.Forms.TextBox
$OutputTextBox.Multiline = $true
$OutputTextBox.ReadOnly = $true
$OutputTextBox.ScrollBars = "Vertical"
$OutputTextBox.Dock = "Fill"
```

4. We create a button control **Windows.Forms.Button** with **New-Object**. We set the button text and dock it at the bottom of the form:

```
# Create a Button control
$Button = New-Object Windows.Forms.Button
$Button.Text = "Click Me"
$Button.Dock = "Bottom"
```

5. Now we create the **Event Handler** script block assigned to the **$EventHandler** variable. In this event handler we use the values property of the **$Superheroes** variable and pipe this to the **Get-Random** cmdlet to select a random superhero instance object. We assign the **Name** of the selected superhero to a variable. We use **Get-Random** to select one of the superheroes abilities by random and assign this to a variable. We also assign the heroes alignment to a variable. We create a string with the information from the property values assigned to the variables (we could have spared the assignment of all the selected properties to variables and have used them directly in the string as subexpressions. The chosen method is for readability purposes). This string is then appended to the **textbox** using the **textbox** built-in method **AppendText()**:

```
# Create the event handler script block
$EventHandler = {
    # Append output to the TextBox when the button is clicked
    $Superhero = $Superheroes.Values | Get-Random
    $Name = $Superhero.Name
    $Ability = Get-Random -InputObject ($Superhero.Abilities)
```

```
$Alignment = $Superhero.Alignment
$OutputTextBox.AppendText("$Alignment $Name using $Ability`r`n")
}
```

6. Now we need to add the **event handler** to the button click event. We use the button´s built-in method **Add_Click()** for this, by using the **$EventHandler** as an argument for this method. Whenever the button is clicked (the event), the script block in the **$EventHandler** variable is executed (the event handler). In this case it appends the **string** to the **textbox**:

```
# Add a Click event handler to the button
$Button.Add_Click($EventHandler)
```

7. In order for us to be able to show the controls in the main form window, we need to add the controls to the form. This is done with the form´s control built-in method **Add()**:

```
# Add controls to the form
$Form.Controls.Add($OutputTextBox)
$Form.Controls.Add($Button)
```

8. We need to explicitly show the form, this is done with the form´s built-in method **ShowDialog()**:

```
# Show the form
$Form.ShowDialog()
```

The entire form code construct is shown below:

```
# Load the Windows Forms assembly
Add-Type -AssemblyName System.Windows.Forms
# Create the main form
$Form = New-Object Windows.Forms.Form
$Form.Text = "Superhero Abilities"
$Form.Size = New-Object Drawing.Size(400, 300)
# Create a TextBox control to display output
$OutputTextBox = New-Object Windows.Forms.TextBox
$OutputTextBox.Multiline = $true
$OutputTextBox.ReadOnly = $true
$OutputTextBox.ScrollBars = "Vertical"
$OutputTextBox.Dock = "Fill"
# Create a Button control
$Button = New-Object Windows.Forms.Button
$Button.Text = "Click Me"
```

```powershell
$Button.Dock = "Bottom"
# Create the event handler script block
$EventHandler = {
    # Append output to the TextBox when the button is clicked
    $Superhero = $Superheroes.Values | Get-Random
    $Name = $Superhero.Name
    $Ability = Get-Random -InputObject ($Superhero.Abilities)
    $Alignment = $Superhero.Alignment
    $OutputTextBox.AppendText("$Alignment $Name using $Ability`r`n")
}
# Add a Click event handler to the button
$Button.Add_Click($EventHandler)
# Add controls to the form
$Form.Controls.Add($OutputTextBox)
$Form.Controls.Add($Button)
# Show the form
$Form.ShowDialog()
```

Whenever this form is executed, it will create a GUI form window with the controls and behavior we specified. Whenever the button is clicked the **event handler** is executed and will append the **string** to the textbox control as shown in *Figure 3.17*:

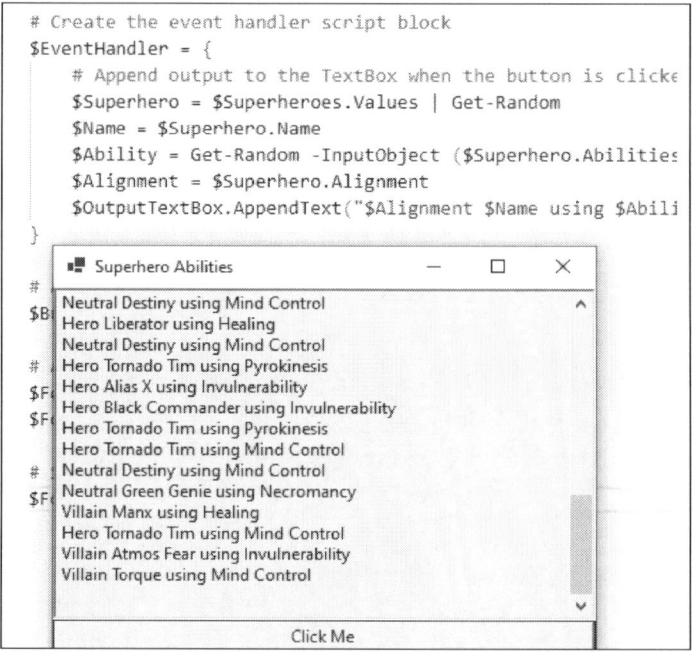

***Figure 3.17:** Using button click event handler in GUI form*

These recipes have provided an overview of script blocks and how they can be used in scripts and applications to create versatile and dynamic code constructs that can be used as filters, callbacks, and event handlers in GUI forms. These are just some of the practical use cases of script blocks in PowerShell and we have only shown a few. As you become more proficient with PowerShell you will learn how to utilize such constructs in your code to make more robust, dynamic, and sophisticated scripts and applications.

Multi-threading and parallel processing with PowerShell jobs

PowerShell does not support **real** low-level multithreading in the same way as other programming languages do. Without going into much detail about how PowerShell is built, this is due to the **Single-Threaded Apartment (STA)** mode, that the underlying components that PowerShell uses are based upon. However, PowerShell have a few methods for introducing multi-threading like capabilities. PowerShell is built upon the .NET framework which provides multithreading capabilities and PowerShell are able to utilize .NET classes like `System.Threading.Thread` and `System.Threading.Tasks.Task` from this framework to implement advanced multithreading and parallel processing support. But utilizing these classes can be complex and when working with multithreading you should always be careful of thread safety between shared resources that might end up with race conditions and concurrency issues resulting in unwanted behavior and unreliable code.

PowerShell has its own construct called `PowerShell-Jobs`. This allows for parallel processing by creating separate PowerShell processes, **jobs**, in the background of the main process. Jobs run in parallel to the main process from where you can communicate with them, and when they have finished their work, their result can be returned to the main process for further processing. PowerShell jobs are separate running processes and are not to be compared directly with multithreading, but it still allows to add the aspect of parallel processing to PowerShell mimicking multi-threading like behavior. Utilizing jobs can greatly improve the performance of scripts and applications when working with time consuming tasks such as rendering large datasets and collections or managing multiple resources simultaneously.

Recipe 19: Use PowerShell jobs and parallel processing for improving performance

When working with large datasets there can be significant performance benefits when using jobs by splitting datasets up in smaller chunks and use the jobs parallel processing capabilities to perform the operations to achieve multithreading like behavior.

First let us see how we can create and use jobs in PowerShell.

1. Start a job:

   To start a job, we use the **Start-Job** cmdlet and specify the command or script block we want to run in the background:

   ```
   Start-Job -ScriptBlock { Get-Process }
   ```

2. Receive a job:

   To retrieve the result from a job, we use the **Receive-Job** cmdlet:

   ```
   $Job = Start-Job -ScriptBlock { Get-Process }
   $Result = Receive-Job $Job
   Write-Output $Result
   ```

3. Wait for job:

   We can wait for a job to finish before continuing the execution of the script, with the **Wait-Job** cmdlet. This waits until the specified job or jobs are finished executing:

   ```
   $Job1 = Start-Job -ScriptBlock { Get-Process }
   $Job2 = Start-Job -ScriptBlock { Get-Service }
   # Wait for both jobs to complete
   Wait-Job -Job $Job1, $Job2
   ```

4. Stop and remove job:

   Jobs can be stopped and removed with the **Stop-Job** and **Remove-Job** cmdlets. **Stop-Job** stops the execution of a running job and **Remove-Job** removes a completed or stopped job. Whenever you are finished with a job you should remove it:

   ```
   $Job = Start-Job -ScriptBlock { Get-Process }
   # Stop and remove the job
   Stop-Job $Job
   Remove-Job $Job
   ```

5. Display job information:

   You can view the status and information of all jobs (that have not yet been removed) with the **Get-Job** cmdlet:

   ```
   Get-Job
   ```

These are the basic cmdlets used for handling jobs. You can create multiple jobs at a time and execute them simultaneously. You can wait for all jobs to finish their execution before continuing working on their results. When working with multiple jobs you can save the jobs within an array and do work on all jobs like wait for all the jobs with **Wait-Job $JobArray** and receive the results from all jobs with **Receive-Results $JobArray**. You can create a loop and iterate over the jobs states and perform actions like *as long as job1 state is running, perform action* with the use of **Get-Job** in combination with other code logic.

In this recipe we are going to work on data from a large dataset from a csv fil: **organizations-100000.csv** (we previously used this in an earlier recipe in this chapter). What we want is to create a function that iterates through all entries in the dataset and explicitly save all names in the **Name** column from the dataset and the store them into an array, then we return that array as the job result. This can be fairly easy achieved by importing the dataset into a variable, creating a variable declared as an empty array, iterate through the dataset in a **Foreach** loop and then extract and add the **Name** from the name column in each iteration, to the array variable. Lastly, returning the array with all the names. We can create such a function like this:

```
function Process-Csv {
    param(
        [string]$CsvPath
    )
    $CsvData = Import-Csv -Path $CsvPath
    $Results = @()
    foreach ($Row in $CsvData){
        $Results += $Row.Name
    }
    return $Results
}
```

We can then invoke the function by adding the path to the **organizations-100000.csv** as an argument, directly returning the result and showing it on the console:

```
Process-Csv -CsvPath .\organizations-100000.csv
```

Or save it to a new variable for later use:

```
$Data = Process-Csv -CsvPath .\organizations-100000.csv
```

The output of running this function would result in the list of the names from the **Name** column within the .**csv** file.

But what we are really interested in is the time it took to execute the function. Considering we need to import and save the large dataset in a variable, and we need to iterate through all entries in the dataset and extract and save the **Name** row, one by one, this might take a while and gets slower the larger the dataset is. For measuring the time, it takes to run a command, we can use the **Measure-Command** cmdlet. This runs a cmdlet, a function, or any code inside a script block, measures and returns the execution time of that command. All we need to do to measure the execution time of the **Process-Csv** function, is to add the command inside a script block and then use the **Measure-Command** cmdlet to run the script block:

```
Measure-Command {Process-Csv -CsvPath .\organizations-100000.csv}
```

Running this command gives us an output as shown in *Figure 3.18*:

```
Days              : 0
Hours             : 0
Minutes           : 5
Seconds           : 12
Milliseconds      : 784
Ticks             : 3127846796
TotalDays         : 0,00362019305092593
TotalHours        : 0,0868846332222222
TotalMinutes      : 5,21307799333333
TotalSeconds      : 312,7846796
TotalMilliseconds : 312784,6796
```

Figure 3.18: Measure-Command output of invoking the Process-Csv function with the organization-100000.csv file

As you can see, it takes a fair amount of time to process these 100.000 entries in the **organization-100000.csv** file. The results will vary depending on your systems resources and how these resources are otherwise utilized while running this command.

Let us learn how to incorporate the use of **PowerShell Jobs** to add a layer of parallel processing to speed up this process. We create a function that imports the dataset into a variable but this time we incorporate the use of multiple jobs by splitting the dataset into smaller chunks and then start a job for processing each chunk in parallel. We want to be able to adjust the number of chunks and jobs the function utilizes so we create a parameter for this. The function will wait for all jobs to finish executing and then receive the results and return them all at once. The result will be (almost) the same as the function with the foreach loop, an array containing the names from the **Name** column of the .csv file, but we add the job number to the output name string, just so we are able to see which job processed a specific row (this can of course be omitted to provide just the names to the result).

1. We create a function called **Process-CsvJob**. We add a **[String]$CsvPath** parameter that takes a path to a csv file as an argument. We create another parameter **[int]$ParallelJobs = 4**, this is used to indicate how many jobs and chunks we want to split the operation into, we set the default to 4:

```
function Process-CsvJob {
    param(
        [string]$CsvPath,
        [int]$ParallelJobs = 4
    )
```

2. Commands for a job is run in a script block. The **Start-Job** cmdlet has a **-ScriptBlock** parameter that sends the provided script block to the job so we create the process each job should execute inside a script block, inside of the

function. The script block needs two parameters, one for the specific job number and one for the data its needs to process, in this case the chunks of data we provide from the dataset. In the script block code logic, we declare a variable **$Results** as an empty array. We use a **Foreach** loop to iterate over the rows in the chunk of data provided to the job, extract the name from the **Name** column, add the result to the **$Results** array as a string where we also add the job number so we can see which job processed which data. When all rows in the chunk have been processed, we return the **$Results** array from the job back to the main process that initialized the job:

3.
```powershell
$ProcessRowScriptBlock = {
    param($JobNumber, $Chunk)
    $Results = @()
    foreach ($Row in $Chunk) {
        $Name = $Row.Name
        # Add the processed result with the job number to the results array
        $Results += "Job $jobNumber : Processed $Name"
    }
    # Return the results array
    return $Results
}
```

4. We import the dataset from the **.csv** file. It will automatically be imported as an array containing the data:
```powershell
# Import the csv file into a variable
$CsvData = Import-Csv -Path $CsvPath
```

5. We declare a variable **$Jobs** as an empty array. This is used for storing each job when they are created:
```powershell
# Create an array to store the PowerShell jobs
$Jobs = @()
```

6. We need to calculate the size of each chunk the dataset should be split into. We divide the count of the dataset with the number of parallel jobs we need to execute. To ensure that the division results in a valid and a whole number outcome, we use the **[Math]::Ceiling** .NET method of the .NET **System.Math** class. This method rounds up the division result to the nearest integer, also ensuring that each job gets at least the calculated chunk size, and any remaining data are allocated to the last job, ensuring all data elements are processed:
```powershell
# Divide the data into chunks to distribute among parallel jobs
$ChunkSize = [Math]::Ceiling($CsvData.Count / $ParallelJobs)
```

7. For the complex part, extracting the correct chunk for each job, creating, and starting the job. To ensure we get the correct number of jobs and that we can keep track of the job number, we use a **For** loop. We initialize the loop with the **$JobNumber** variable with a value of **1**. We iterate if **$JobNumber -le $ParallelJobs** and we add **1** to the **$JobNumber** variable upon each iteration. Inside this loop we do the following:

    a. We create a **$StartIndex** variable where we calculate the start index value for each chunk. The first start index value will be **0**, and the following will be **($JobNumber -1) * $ChunkSize**.

    b. We calculate the end index value for each chunk **$EndIndex**. We use the **[Math]::Min** .NET method to ensure that the last chunk might have a smaller size, if the dataset is not evenly divisible by the number of **$ParallelJobs** (even though we ensured this by using the **[Math]::Ceiling** method for calculating this earlier, we still wants to make sure we get all data processed). Since array indexing is zero based, we use **-1** for each expression, also ensuring that we do not go beyond the last index in the dataset array, which would result in an error. We end up with: **$EndIndex = [Math]::Min(($StartIndex + $ChunkSize -1), ($CsvData.Count -1))** as the end index.

    c. We use array slicing to create the relevant chunk file using the calculated start and end indexes, over the dataset array, assigning this to the **$Chunk** variable with the value of the specific chunk: **$CsvData[$StartIndex ..$EndIndex]]**.

    d. Now we create and start the job, assigning it to the **$Job** variable. We use the **Start-Job** cmdlet with the **$ProcessRowScriptBlock** as the argument for the -**ScriptBlock** parameter. We then pass the **$JobNumber** and the **$Chunk** as arguments for the script block parameters using the **Start-Job** cmdlet -**ArgumentList** parameter.

    e. Lastly, we add the **$Job** to the global **$Jobs** array, so we can keep track of all jobs:

```
# Create jobs and start parallel processing
for ($JobNumber = 1; $JobNumber -le $ParallelJobs; $JobNumber++) {
    $StartIndex = ($JobNumber - 1) * $ChunkSize
    $EndIndex = [Math]::Min(($StartIndex + $ChunkSize - 1),
($CsvData.Count - 1))
    $Chunk = $CsvData[$StartIndex..$EndIndex]
    $Job = Start-Job -ScriptBlock $ProcessRowScriptBlock
-ArgumentList $JobNumber, $Chunk
    $Jobs += $Job
}
```

8. We wait for all jobs in the **$Jobs** array to finish processing using **Wait-Job**:

    ```
    # Wait for all jobs to complete
    Wait-Job -Job $Jobs
    ```

9. When all jobs in the **$Jobs** array are finished processing, we use **Receive-Job** to receive all jobs results and combine them into the **$Results** variable:

    ```
    # Receive all job results
    $Result = Receive-Job $Jobs
    ```

10. To cleanup and make sure no finished jobs are left in the session (and memory), we use the **$Remove-Job** cmdlet to remove all jobs in the **$Jobs** array. (We could also use **Get-Job | Remove-Job** to make sure all jobs in the session are removed):

    ```
    # Remove the jobs (Cleanup)
    Remove-Job $Jobs
    ```

11. The last thing we do is to return the results from the function:

    ```
    return $Result
    ```

The entire construct will look like this:

```
function Process-CsvJob {
    param(
        [string]$CsvPath,
        [int]$ParallelJobs = 4
    )
    # Define the script block for processing each data row
    $ProcessRowScriptBlock = {
        param($JobNumber, $Chunk)
        $Results = @()
        foreach ($Row in $Chunk) {
            $Name = $Row.Name
            # Add the processed result with the job number to the results array
            $Results += "Job $jobNumber : Processed $Name"
        }
        # Return the results array
        return $Results
    }
        # Import the csv file into a variable
    $CsvData = Import-Csv -Path $CsvPath
        # Create an array to store the PowerShell jobs
    $Jobs = @()
```

```
    # Divide the data into chunks to distribute among parallel jobs
    $ChunkSize = [Math]::Ceiling($CsvData.Count / $ParallelJobs)
    # Create jobs and start parallel processing
    for ($JobNumber = 1; $JobNumber -le $ParallelJobs; $JobNumber++) {
        $StartIndex = ($JobNumber - 1) * $ChunkSize
        $EndIndex = [Math]::Min(($StartIndex + $ChunkSize - 1), ($CsvData.Count - 1))
        $Chunk = $CsvData[$StartIndex..$EndIndex]
        $Job = Start-Job -ScriptBlock $ProcessRowScriptBlock -ArgumentList
$JobNumber, $Chunk
        $Jobs += $Job
    }
    # Wait for all jobs to complete
    Wait-Job -Job $Jobs
    # Receive all job results
    $Result = Receive-Job $Jobs
    # Remove the jobs (Cleanup)
    Remove-Job $Jobs
    return $Result
}
```

We can now call our function like this:

```
Process-CsvJob -CsvPath .\organizations-100000.csv -ParallelJobs 4
```

Note that we do not need to provide the argument for the **-ParallelJobs** parameter, since we set the default for this to 4, we only add it in the command for readability purposes. Running this will return output like shown in *Figure 3.19*:

```
Job 3 : Processed Conrad, Morales and Pena
Job 3 : Processed Bonilla-Pennington
Job 3 : Processed Petty-Wu
Job 3 : Processed Hampton and Sons
Job 3 : Processed Escobar-Stone
Job 3 : Processed Cabrera, Aguirre and Martin
Job 3 : Processed Gardner, Mcmillan and Weiss
Job 3 : Processed Zavala Group
Job 3 : Processed Bond, Barajas and May
Job 4 : Processed Mcclain, Lucas and Bishop
Job 4 : Processed Benjamin-Noble
Job 4 : Processed Wright, Hoffman and Tucker
Job 4 : Processed Sheppard Ltd
Job 4 : Processed Anthony-Stephens
Job 4 : Processed Solis, Kirby and Wang
Job 4 : Processed Barron, Wiggins and Small
Job 4 : Processed Lloyd-Cervantes
```

Figure 3.19: Output when processing the dataset organization-100000.csv with multiple jobs

As you can see in this output, we have different jobs processing the data. But what about the timing of this new parallel function compared to the sequential one?

Let us use **Measure-Command** to see if we have achieved any performance improvements:

```
Measure-Command {Process-CsvJob -CsvPath .\organizations-100000.csv
-ParallelJobs 4}
```

Running this command, we get the output as shown in *Figure 3.20*:

```
Days              : 0
Hours             : 0
Minutes           : 0
Seconds           : 24
Milliseconds      : 99
Ticks             : 240996079
TotalDays         : 0,000278930646990741
TotalHours        : 0,00669433552777778
TotalMinutes      : 0,401660131666667
TotalSeconds      : 24,0996079
TotalMilliseconds : 24099,6079
```

Figure 3.20: *Measure-Command output of invoking
the Process-CsvJob function with the organization-100000.csv file*

As we can see, this is a great improvement over the previous sequential function. When measuring the execution time of the **Process-Csv** function, we got roughly 312784 MilliSeconds using the sequential function. By executing the function **Process-CsvJob** utilizing job parallelization, it only took 24099 MilliSeconds. This is an improvement by a factor of 13. Let us try another execution, this time utilizing 10 Parallel jobs instead:

```
Measure-Command {Process-CsvJob -CsvPath .\organizations-100000.csv
-ParallelJobs 10}
```

Figure 3.21 shows its output:

```
Days              : 0
Hours             : 0
Minutes           : 0
Seconds           : 12
Milliseconds      : 427
Ticks             : 124273564
TotalDays         : 0,000143835143518519
TotalHours        : 0,00345204344444444
TotalMinutes      : 0,207122606666667
TotalSeconds      : 12,4273564
TotalMilliseconds : 12427,3564
```

Figure 3.21: *Measure-Command output of invoking the Process-CsvJob function
with the organization-100000.csv file using 10 parallel jobs*

Another improvement by almost 50% against the previous execution using only 4 parallel jobs or by a total factor of 24 compared to the sequential function. This is an improvement that is worth the extra work and complexity that comes with incorporating and utilizing PowerShell jobs for parallelization.

Recipe 20: Use the ForEach-Object -Parallel parameter for non-sequential processing

PowerShell version 7.0.0 introduced a lot of new features and capabilities such as including parallel processing for the **ForEach-Object** cmdlet. This allows you to run script blocks in parallel with this cmdlet which significantly improves the performance when dealing with large datasets similar to what we have seen with the utilization of jobs.

> Note: The use of ForEach-Object with the Parallel parameter is only supported by PowerShell 7.0.0 and newer versions.

Using the **ForEach-Object** with the **-Parallel** parameter makes some operations easier than setting up jobs for processing the data. You would typically use this parameter with datasets that is stored in an array and then **ForEach-Object** will process each item in parallel across multiple processes in the background. We can then use the **ForEach-Object -ThrottleLimit** parameter to set the number of processes that should be executed in parallel. If the **ThrottleLimit** parameter is omitted, PowerShell will automatically figure out the degree of parallelism to use, depending on your systems capabilities. However, utilizing the parallel processing feature of the **ForEach-Object** might not always give the expected results in terms of performance benefits, since there is some underlying overhead when the cmdlet needs to utilize the parallelization and work with multiple processes. It depends on the type of operation and the workload, making the use of the parallel feature most optimal when working with computational heavy tasks, time consuming tasks or very large datasets. Working with relatively simple operations might even increase the time it takes to perform the operations due to this overhead when using parallelization.

Processes where parallel processing is utilized with benefits is tasks that might take some time to render or process for each operation. Consider this: we have a function that needs to access different websites. We know that accessing a single website can take from a few milliseconds to several seconds before it returns a response, and if we created a sequential loop accessing each website one by one, the combined access and response time could be quite slow. This is one place where we can utilize the benefits of parallel processing, by sending the workload to multiple processes and accessing several websites at the same time. Let us create sequential and parallel processes using **ForEach-Object** and see the difference.

Since we are only interested in the response time for websites combined and the total execution time for the process, we do not create anything fancy and create two simple functions that accepts a string array as a parameter, this array contains **URLs**. We then simply pipe this list to **ForEach-Object** where we use the **Invoke-WebRequest** cmdlet on each iterated URL. In the **ForEach-Object** loop within the first function, **Measure-ResponseTimeSequential**, we do not have any parameters other than the **$URL** parameter. In the second one, **Measure-ResponseTimeParallel**, we utilize the **-Parallel** parameter. We do not set any **ThrottleLimit** and let the system automatically utilize all its available resources.

1. We create a string array with URL´s and assign it to the **$Urls** variable. We use the same array as an argument for both functions:

```
$Urls = @(
    ”https://www.bpb.com”,
    ”https://www.example.com”,
    ”https://www.google.com”,
    ”https://www.microsoft.com”,
    ”https://www.openai.com”,
    ”https://www.github.com”,
    ”https://www.apple.com”,
    ”https://www.amazon.com”,
    ”https://www.twitter.com”,
    ”https://www.reddit.com”,
    ”https://www.yahoo.com”,
    ”https://www.wikipedia.org”,
    ”https://www.nytimes.com”,
    ”https://www.bing.com”,
    ”https://www.instagram.com”,
    ”https://www.ebay.com”,
    ”https://www.cnn.com”,
    ”https://www.espn.com”,
    ”https://www.weather.com”,
    ”https://www.twitch.tv”,
    ”https://www.youtube.com”
)
```

2. We create the first function called **Measure-ResponseTimeSequential**.

   Note that for processing each object in the pipeline we use the **current object variable $_**:

```
function Measure-ResponseTimeSequential {
    param (
```

```
        [string[]]$Urls
    )
    $Urls | ForEach-Object {
        Invoke-WebRequest $_
    }
}
```

3. We create the second function called **Measure-ResponseTimeParallel**:

```
function Measure-ResponseTimeParallel {
    param (
        [string[]]$Urls
    )
    $Urls | ForEach-Object -Parallel {
        Invoke-WebRequest $_
    }
}
```

4. We then invoke both functions using the **Measure-Command** with the **$Urls** variable as an argument for each function. We save the output from the **Measure-Command** processes in variables. We then output these variables. Notice we are only interested in **MilliSeconds**, so we only use the **TotalMilliseconds** property for the output:

```
# Measure response time - Sequential processing
$ElapsedTimeSequential = Measure-Command { Measure-
ResponseTimeSequential -Urls $Urls }
Write-Output "Results - Sequential processing:
$($ElapsedTimeSequential.TotalMilliseconds) Ms"
# Measure response time - Parallel processing
$ElapsedTimeParallel = Measure-Command { Measure-
ResponseTimeParallel -Urls $Urls }
Write-Output "Results - Parallel processing:
$($ElapsedTimeParallel.TotalMilliseconds) Ms"
```

The results of running these measurement functions are shown in *Figure 3.22*:

```
Results - Sequential processing:
10853.4445 Ms
Results - Parallel processing:
2308.7396 Ms
```

Figure 3.22: Output from running the sequential and parallel function using ForEach-Object

The result speaks for itself. The parallel process is 4-5 times faster than the sequential process, in this case. But as mentioned earlier, the performance gain can vary a lot depending on various factors like the number of CPU cores and the size and complexity of the data that is being processed. *Figure 3.23* shows a diagram of a sequential process versus a parallel process, this gives a better understanding of how these methods differ and how data are processed:

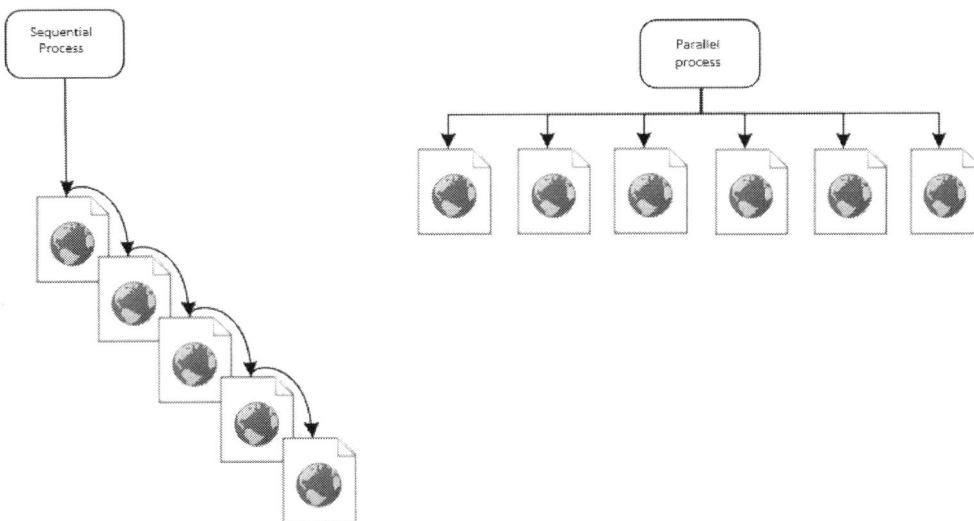

Figure 3.23: Diagram of sequential versus parallel process

We have seen that even though PowerShell does not support true multithreading, we have different options for utilizing parallel processing in the form of PowerShell jobs or using the **ForEach-Object** with its parallel parameter to add multithreading like capabilities to scripts and applications. It is essential though, to evaluate each specific use case and the kind and size of data that needs to be processes in order to determine if you should use sequential or parallel processing or if you should use PowerShell jobs for rendering and processing your data. If you have a small simple dataset that you need to process, the overhead of utilizing parallel features would make it less beneficial, but when working with larger datasets, time consuming and CPU consuming operations, there can be great performance benefits gained when utilizing parallel processing and PowerShell jobs for your tasks.

Conclusion

Being able to control the flow in your code by utilizing advanced methods and optimizing your code constructs by taking advantage of parallel processing capabilities can greatly improve the overall efficiency and effectiveness of scripts and applications. This chapter has been all about using advanced and complex methods and looping techniques to control the code flow in scripts and applications. By learning and utilizing conditions, labelled breaks and continue statements in different control structures such as loops, nested loops, `if/elseif/else` blocks, and switch statements you can make more complex decisions that are used to control and execute different processes depending on these decisions and conditions. We have also looked at script blocks and how they can be used in different constructs such as filters, callbacks for functions and cmdlets and as event handlers for GUI form code and how they can be used dynamically to execute code logic when certain events occur. It has also been about optimizing your code with implementing multithreading like capabilities in the form of parallel processing and using PowerShell built-in features such as jobs, to process data in a more effective manner and optimizing the overall performance. By using these advanced techniques and methods you should be able to write more efficient and maintainable code with a proper code flow logic and optimized performance.

The next chapter dives deep into error handling in PowerShell and introduces the reader to topics such as handling different types of errors, implementing error handling blocks in advanced scenarios and how to use the ErrorAction preference variable and the ErrorAction parameter. It also showcase how to create custom error classes for enhanced error reporting and how to handle errors in background jobs.

Join our book's Discord space

Join the book's Discord Workspace for Latest updates, Offers, Tech happenings around the world, New Release and Sessions with the Authors:

https://discord.bpbonline.com

CHAPTER 4
Error Handling

Introduction

Error handling is the process of responding to unexpected events that may occur during execution of a script or application and then managing such errors. It involves implementing mechanisms to detect, capture, and handle errors gracefully, making sure that the script or application continues execution. Errors can occur due to many different reasons, such as incorrect user input, connectivity issues, invalid operations, and a lot more. Moreover, they are usually unexpected and can be defined as both non-terminating and terminating. Without proper error handling, unexpected events can lead to script failures, data corruption and other undesirable outcomes.

Structure

The chapter covers the following topics:

- Handling different types of errors in PowerShell

    o **Recipe 21**: Techniques for handling different types of errors

- Implementing try/catch/finally blocks in advanced scenarios

    o **Recipe 22**: Use try/catch/finally blocks to handle errors, perform cleanup and ensure script liability

- Advanced error handling with the ErrorAction preference variable and the ErrorAction parameter.

  o **Recipe 23**: Use the ErrorAction preference variable and the ErrorAction parameter, to control error handling behavior and customize error actions

- Creating custom error classes for enhanced error reporting

  o **Recipe 24**: Create custom error classes to provide specific error information and enhanced error reporting capabilities

- Error handling in background jobs

  o **Recipe 25**: Use different techniques for handling errors that occur in background jobs, including capturing job specific errors and managing job states

- Debugging and logging error information

  o **Recipe 26**: Create a custom logging function for structured logging that helps with troubleshooting and debugging errors

Objectives

In this chapter you will learn how to handle and catch different types of errors in advanced scenarios. You will also learn how to implement error handling in scripts, how to handle non-terminating errors and about different error suppression techniques. you will also learn how to create your own custom error handling classes and how to debug and log error information to files. We will also cover error handling in backgroundjobs and show how to create a custom logging function that can be implemented in scripts for logging errors to files.

Handling different types of errors in PowerShell

Error handling in PowerShell is about using different techniques to capture, process and respond to different types of errors that may occur during script or application execution. PowerShell has multiple mechanisms for handling exceptions, non-terminating and terminating errors. Being able to properly handle errors is vital to the overall functionality and reliability of your scripts and applications, preventing them from crashing unexpectedly. The different types of errors can be defined as:

- **Non-terminating errors**: Are errors that do not stop the script execution. Usually when a cmdlet or function performs a command that fails, like trying to access a file that does not exists, or by dividing with zero, the command will result in a non-terminating error and the script will, in most cases, continue its execution. The behavior of cmdlets and functions that throws non-terminating errors can be controlled with the use of the **ErrorAction** parameter or by adjusting the global built-in variable **$ErrorActionPreference** and the resulting error behavior can be changed to terminating instead, which can then be caught with a **try/catch/finally** block. You might want to handle the error gracefully instead of throwing an error message. The default **$ErrorActionPreference** in PowerShell is **continue** which means that most *normal* errors result in non-terminating behavior, unless specifically specified for individual commands with the use of the **ErrorAction** parameter.

- **Terminating errors**: Are errors that will stop the script from executing any further and exits. There can be many reasons for terminating errors such as connectivity issues if your script is depending on access to external resources, or if the script consumes a lot of memory and the system then runs out of free memory and so on. Terminating errors can be caught and handled gracefully with **try/ catch/finally** blocks, resulting in non-terminating behavior. You can set the **$ErrorActionPreference** to **stop** which makes all errors behave as terminating errors, hence all errors must be caught with the use of **try/catch/finally** blocks or **traps** for the script to continue execution.

- **Exceptions**: Are specific types of errors that can occur during the execution of a script or command. They can usually be anticipated, such as dividing by zero, which results in a **RunTimeException** or when trying to access a non-existing file, which generates an **ItemNotFoundException**. These specific exceptions can be explicitly caught by their type and handled using **try/catch/finally** blocks or **traps**, allowing you to implement custom processes for the different types of exceptions when a specific error occurs.

Recipe 21: Techniques for handling different types of errors

In PowerShell, there are different kinds of techniques for handling different types of errors.

For terminating errors, you would usually use a **try/catch/finally** block to catch the exception thrown by the error, preventing it from terminating and then perform actions on the exception. This could be writing the error message to a log file or implementing some retry logic to keep trying until the process succeeds. A scenario for this could be you are trying to access a network or a website that is temporary unavailable. A **try/catch/ finally** block is created like this:

```
# Try/Catch/Finally block
try {
    <#Code logic that might throw an exception#>
}
catch {
    <#Do this if a terminating exception happens#>
```

```
}
finally {

    <#Do this after the try block regardless of whether an exception
occurred or not#>

}
```

The **try** block is where you would place your code logic that might result in an error and throw an exception. The code in the **catch** block will be executed if any potential exceptions are caught in the **try** block. The **finally** block is optional, and code placed here will be executed regardless if an error was thrown or not. You can have multiple **catch** blocks in the same statement, catching specific types of errors. In the next example, we create a **try/catch/finally** block that tries to retrieve the content of a file. If the file does not exist we catch that specific exception type, by specifying it explicitly inside the first **catch** block like this: **catch [System.Management.Automation.ItemNotFoundException]**. The next **catch** block does not specify a specific type of exception and will then catch all other types of errors that might occur. The code inside the **finally** block will be executed regardless if any errors were thrown or not and the script execution continues after the **finally** block is executed.

```
try {
    # Code that might throw an exception
    $FileContent = Get-Content -Path "NonExistentFile.txt" -ErrorAction Stop
}
catch [System.Management.Automation.ItemNotFoundException] {
    # Code to handle the specific ItemNotFoundException
    Write-Output "The file was not found $($_.Exception.Message)"
}
catch {
    # Catch-all block for handling all other exceptions
    Write-Output "An unexpected exception occurred: $_"
}
finally {
    # Optional: Code that will always execute, whether an exception occurred or not
    Write-Output "Finally block executed."
}
# Code continues executing after the try-catch-finally block
Write-Output "Script execution continues after the try-catch-finally block."
```

Notice the use of the **$_** (current object variable). In the case of error handling, we can call this the *current error variable* which refers to the current error object being processed. This object has several properties with information in regard to the current error and within the first catch block, the one with the **ItemNotFoundException**, we use it to explicitly write the message from the error object, instead of the entire error content, which is usually the default behavior.

> Note: A newer alternative to the $_ variable is the built-in $PSItem variable. This was introduced in PowerShell version 5.1. Both these variables serve the same purpose, though $PSItem is being recommended for readability and consistency. Which one you use comes down to personal preference. In this chapter we use the $_ variable.

In the **Get-Content** cmdlet inside the **try** block, we specify the **-ErrorAction** parameter for the cmdlet with the **stop** argument value. **Non-terminating** errors cannot be caught by a **try/catch/finally** block unless we make them terminating. By explicitly setting the value for this parameter to **stop**, we make this cmdlet throw a terminating error whenever it catches an exception, and we are then able to use the **try/catch/finally** block to capture exceptions that are thrown by the command. The **ErrorAction** parameter is by default built into most cmdlets and for custom advanced functions, this is one of the features that is provided by the **CmdletBinding** attribute. With this parameter we can change the error action behavior of individual cmdlets and functions. The valid values for the **ErrorAction** parameter are:

- **Stop:** This specifies that non-terminating errors should be treated as terminating errors. It stops the script execution if not captured by a statement like try/catch/finally or a trap.

- **Continue:** This is the default value. This specifies that non-terminating errors should display the error to the console and then continue with the script execution.

- **SilentlyContinue:** This will suppress all error messages for non-terminating errors and continue the execution. The script execution continues without displaying the error. Errors are still captured and processed in the background of the session.

- **Inquire:** This will display a prompt to the user when a non-terminating error occurs. The user can then decide whether to continue the execution of the script.

- **Ignore:** This completely ignores all non-terminating errors and continues execution without any error handling at all. Be cautious when using this setting as it might lead to unexpected behavior due to unnoticeable errors.

Another method for specifying the behavior of non-terminating errors, is by using the **$ErrorActionPreference** variable. This is a built-in preference variable that is usually set in the beginning of a script, and it affects the global behavior of non-terminating errors in the script, or the current session if used in a shell. This variable use the same values as the **ErrorAction** parameter, and its default value is **continue**. Setting this value to **stop** will change the error behavior of all cmdlets and commands to act as terminating errors, unless something else is specified for individual commands using the **ErrorAction** parameter:

```
# Start of script
$ErrorActionPreference = "Stop"
```

```
# All subsequential commands error behavior will
# be terminating, unless else is specified

# This will explicitly be non-terminating
# suppressing display of error, and continuing script execution
Get-Content -Path "NonExistentFile.txt" -ErrorAction SilentlyContinue

# This will result in terminating error
# and halt further script execution
Get-Content -Path "NonExistentFile.txt"
Write-Output "This will not run"
```

Another usable parameter is the **ErrorVariable** parameter, which allows you to catch error objects from non-terminating errors in cmdlets and commands, inside a variable. This variable can then be inspected and processed later in the script when needed. This is especially useful if you are interested in further analyzing potential errors and for creating custom error reports:

```
# Create an empty array to store error objects
$ErrorArray = @()
# Example code that may cause non-terminating errors
$Files = "File1.txt", "File2.txt", "File3.txt", "File4.txt"
foreach ($File in $Files) {
    Get-Content -Path $File -ErrorVariable Err -ErrorAction SilentlyContinue
    if ($Err) {
        # Add the error object to the ErrorArray
        $ErrorArray += $Err
        # Optionally, you can perform additional error handling or logging here
        Write-Output "Error occurred while processing $File : $($Err.
Exception.Message)"
    }
}
# The ErrorArray can then be inspected for all captured errors
if ($ErrorArray.Count -gt 0) {
    Write-Output "Total Errors: $($ErrorArray.Count)"
    $ErrorArray | ForEach-Object {
        Write-Output "Error Message: $($_.Exception.Message)"
    }
}
```

With the **ErrorVariable** parameter you can save errors from specific commands, but PowerShell also has a built-in **$Error** variable, that holds all errors that occurred during script execution or within a shell session. The principle usage of the **ErrorVariable** parameter and the **$Error** variable are somewhat the same, but with the **$Error** variable, you have access to the full history of errors that has occurred within the script or current session. Note that this variable is only stored in memory and is reset for each new script execution or shell session. The **$Error** variable stores the error records as objects of the type **ErrorRecord** which has different properties containing the relevant data for the error records, some of these are the error message, the error ID and the full error stacktrace. This variable is a so called **stack** which is somewhat similar to an array, but it is using the principle of **last-in, first out**. It is using indexing for access, like an array, but due to the specific stack structure, the newest item, hence the last error occurred, will always be placed at index 0.

An alternative to a **try/catch/finally** block and another method for capturing and handling terminating errors is to use a **trap**. A trap is set by using the **trap** keyword and as with a **catch** block, it can be set up to catch all terminating errors or **trap** specific exceptions like the **ItemNotFoundException**. Whenever a terminating error occurs and is trapped, the statements inside the **trap** will be executed and you are then able to suppress the error message from the failed command and continue the script execution by using the **continue** statement keyword or write the error to console and then stop further script execution by using the **break** statement inside the **trap**. Notice that when a terminating error occurs inside a statement such as a **loop** or an **if/else** block, after the statements inside the **trap** is processed, further execution will break out of and continue from outside of such a statement. You can localize **trap**s inside functions to catch specific errors relevant for that and only within that functions scope. Some of the benefits of using **trap**s is that you can define custom error handling logic for specific types of errors throughout a script. They can be used to prevent abrupt script termination and gracefully handle errors and continuing script execution. They can be used for logging purposes when errors occurs and for debugging scripts, without you having to make changes that will potentially break the current script execution flow. There are many more use cases than these that are described here, and it depends on each specific script requirement how you utilize these **trap** statements.

```
# Will trap all terminating errors and execute the statements inside the trap
trap {
    Write-Host "A terminating error occurred: $($_.Exception.Message)"
}
# Will trap only errors that throws an ItemNotFoundException
# and execute the statements inside the trap
trap [System.Management.Automation.ItemNotFoundException] {
    Write-Host "A terminating error occurred: $($_.Exception.Message)"
}
# Will trap all terminating errors and execute the statements inside the trap
```

```
# then stop further script execution
trap {
    Write-Host "A terminating error occurred: $($_.Exception.Message)"
    break
}
# Will trap all terminating errors and execute the statements inside the trap
# then will continue script execution
trap {
    Write-Host "A terminating error occurred: $($_.Exception.Message)"
    continue
}
# Will only trap terminating errors inside the function
# Then continue script execution inside the function.
function Get-Trap {
    trap {
        Write-Host "A terminating error occurred: $($_.Exception.Message)"
        continue
    }
    Get-Content -Path "NonExistentFile.txt" -ErrorAction Stop
}
# Will only trap terminating errors inside the function
# Then stop script execution inside the function.
function Get-Trap {
    trap {
        Write-Host "A terminating error occurred: $($_.Exception.Message)"
        break
    }
    Get-Content -Path "NonExistentFile.txt" -ErrorAction Stop
}
```

Another valuable statement is the **throw** statement. This can be used to manually raise an exception whenever you need to interrupt the execution flow within your code. This creates a terminating error, so **throw** statements must be caught by **try/catch/finally** blocks or **trap** statements. It takes an argument in the form of a string, for providing a custom error message:

```
$Superheroes = @("Comet", "Blue Ghost", "Evilin")
try{
    if ("Lightning Girl" -notin $Superheroes){
        throw "Lightning Girl is not yet a superhero"
```

```
    }
    Write-Output "Lightning Girl is finally a superhero"
}
catch{
    Write-Output "Error caught: $_"
}
```

In this example, if lightning girl is not in the **$superheroes** array, we **throw** an exception and the **catch** block will capture the error and execute the code within it, preventing further execution of the main statement. This can be useful if you need certain conditions to be met before continuing code execution. It can also be used to easily create custom error messages for certain conditions, breaking out of nested loops, for validating user input and so on.

Whereas the **throw** statement raises terminating errors, you can use the **Write-Error** cmdlet to create custom non-terminating errors. This cmdlet takes a string as an argument, for providing custom error messages and then writes the error to the error stream:

```
$Superheroes = @("Comet", "Blue Ghost", "Evilin")
try {
    if ("Lightning Girl" -notin $Superheroes) {
        Write-Error -Message "Lightning Girl is not yet a superhero"
    }
    else {
        Write-Output "Lightning Girl is finally a superhero"
    }
    Write-Output "Another message that will show"
}
catch {
    Write-Output "Error caught: $_"
}
```

In this example, if lightning girl is not in the **$superheroes** array, we write this to the error stream, resulting in an error output message in the console, and the execution of the main statement will continue without entering the **catch** block. The **Write-Error** cmdlet contains the **ErrorAction** parameter, so you could turn it into a terminating error by providing the **stop** argument and then the **catch** block will catch the error instead and halt further execution of the main statement.

By learning and utilizing error handling techniques, your scripts and applications will become must more reliable and robust, and you will greatly mitigate any potential errors causing your scripts and applications to fail unexpectedly and mitigate the general time you use on debugging.

Implementing try/catch/finally blocks in advanced scenarios

The **try/catch/finally** block is used to catch and gracefully handle terminating errors, making sure these errors do not stop further script execution. If these types of errors are not handled properly it will lead to potential script failure. Not only is the **try/catch/finally** block used to catch exceptions and handle errors, but it also ensures that certain code is executed regardless of the resulting state of the execution within the **try** and **catch** blocks, by always executing the code inside the **finally** block. This provides a way to perform graceful cleanup such as closing connections to databases or stopping specific processes etc. It does not matter if the statement resulted in an error or if it successfully executed its main commands without errors. By incorporating error handling using the **try/catch/finally** structure, you can significantly increase the resiliency and reliability of your scripts making sure that you gracefully handle any potential errors.

Recipe 22: Use try/catch/finally blocks to handle errors, perform cleanup and ensure script liability

In this recipe we are going to access a database and use the **try/catch/finally** block to gracefully handle potential errors that might occur when establishing a connection to the database and if queries fail on an already active database connection. Since we do not have access to a database instance and even if we did, it might not fail on cue, we are going to create our own simulation of a database instance containing databases, with the use of a PowerShell class.

```
class DatabaseInstance {
    [string] $Server
    [string] $Database
    [array] $Databases
    [bool] $Connected
        # Constructor
    DatabaseInstance([string]$Server, [string]$Database) {
        $this.Server = $Server
        $this.Database = $Database
        $this.Databases = @("Master", "TempDB", "TestDB" )
        $this.Connected = $false
    }
    # Query simulation method
    [string] Query() {
        $Rand = 1..4 | Get-Random
```

```
        if ($Rand%2 -eq 0){
            return "Simulated query result from the database."
        }
        else{
            throw "Query operation failed."
        }
    }
    # Connection simulation method
    [string] Connect() {
        if ($this.database -in $this.Databases){
            $this.Connected = $true
            return "Connected to database on server $($this.server),
database $($this.Database)."
        }
        else{
            throw "Could not connect to database $($this.Database)"
        }
    }
    # Close connection simulation method
    [string] Close() {
        return "Closed database connection to $($this.Server), $($this.Database)."
    }
}
```

This class has two parameters, **Server** and **Database** and three methods, **Query()**, **Connect()** and **Close()**. The two parameters are set as properties within the class. It also has two other properties, the array type property **$Databases** and the bool type **$Connected** property. The **$Connected** property is **$false** when no connections are made and **$true** when a connection is established. To instantiate an instance of the class we use either the **New-Object** cmdlet or the **new** static method and then provide arguments for the two parameters. To mimic a set of databases the array **$Databases** property is utilized with three databases: **@("Master", "TempDB", "TestDB")**. Using the **Connect** method will check if the provided database, saved in the **$this.Database** variable, exists in the database array. If it does exist the method will set the **$Connected** property to **$true** and then return a string, stating that you have successfully connected to the database. If it does not exist, the method will throw an error. The **Query** method mimics sending a query to the database, which results in either a successful or failed query. To mimic random query failure or success, we take a random number between 1 and 4, and use the remainder operator, also called modulo, on the random number and compares it with 0. This evaluates to **$true** if the number is even and then returning a string, mimicking a successful query. It evaluates to **$false** if the number is odd, throws an error, mimicking a failed query. The **Close** method simply returns a string stating that the database connection has been closed, mimicking close and cleanup behavior for the database. So, we can mimic connecting to a database which results in either a successful or failed connection. depending on the database existence within the instance, which in this case is the **$Databases** array. We can mimic a database query which results in randomly evaluated query success or query failure and we can also mimic the termination of the database connection with the **Close()** method.

We create a **try/catch/finally** block where we connect to a database, trying to perform some queries. We will then make sure the connection is gracefully closed when we are finished:

- In the **try** block we instantiate a connection to a database instance using the **new** static method. We set the database server as **example-server** and the database we want to connect to, as **TestDB**. This creates an instance object from the **DatabaseInstance** class assigned to the **$Connection** variable.

- We try to connect to the database using the **connect** method on the connection instance: **$Connection.Connect()**. If it fails to connect, the method will **throw** an error and the **catch** block will be executed, ending further execution within the **try** block. Upon successful connection, the **$Connected** property is set to **$true** and the statement continues and writes the **"Performing database operation"** string to the console and continues execution.

- After successful connection, we call the query method on the connection instance: **$Connection.Query()**. The result of the query, if successful, is saved into the **$Result** variable, the result is then output to the console. If the query fails, it will **throw** an error and the exception is caught by the **catch** block, ending further execution within the **try** block.

- Any exceptions caught by the **catch** block, will be written to console with the message **"An error occurred: $_"** where the current error variable **$_** contains the error message from the specific **throw** statement that raised the error.

- Within the **finally** block we ensure that a call to the **$Connection.Close()** method gracefully closes the connection if the database is connected. We check if it is connected or not using the **if/else** block. If it is not connected, it throws an error or else it successfully closes the connection. The statement in the **finally** block is executed whether or not the statements in the **try** block succeeds or fails and an error is caught by the **catch** block. One thing to note is that the call to the **close** method within the **finally** block could also fail, depending on the specifics of the **close** methods code logic. This will not be caught by the main **try** statements **catch** block, since we have passed that point, and further logic to handle the specific case of failure when trying to close the connection must be implemented explicitly. This is relevant if a connection to the database was never established, so we add a nested **try/catch** block around this statement and then handle the potential error. It will either close the connection gracefully using the **close** method, writing this to console or the **close** method will fail to close the connection, resulting in the thrown error, which is then caught by the **nested catch** block, executing the **Write-Output** statement.

This construct is shown below:

```
try {
    # Instantiate the database connection object
    $Connection = [DatabaseInstance]::new("example-server",
"NonExistingDB")
    # Connect to the database
    $Connection.Connect()
    Write-Output "Performing database operation..."
    # Creating a database query
    $Result = $Connection.Query()
    Write-Output "Query result: $Result"
}
catch {
    # Handle potential error
    Write-Output "An error occurred: $_"
}
finally {
    # Ensure the connection is closed, regardless of whether an
error occurred or not
    try{
        if ($Connection.Connected -eq $true){
            $Connection.Close()
        }
        else{
            throw "Could not close non-existing connection"
        }
    }
    catch{
        Write-Output "$_"
    }
}
```

There are a few scenarios that can happen when executing this construct. Let us have a look at each possibility. Note that we change the database we connect to, to the TestDB database. *Figure 4.1* shows the output from the first possible scenario:

```
Connected to database on server example-server, database TestDB.
Performing database operation...
Query result: Simulated query result from the database.
Closed database connection to example-server, TestDB.
```

Figure 4.1: Output from successfully connecting to a database and performing a successful query

In this scenario we have successfully establishsd a connection to the database **TestDB** and performed a query. No exceptions have been caught. All statements in the **try** block is executed and the **finally** block executes and closes the connection.

The output from the next possible scenario is shown in *Figure 4.2*:

```
Connected to database on server example-server, database TestDB.
Performing database operation...
An error occurred: Query operation failed.
Closed database connection to example-server, TestDB.
```

Figure 4.2: Output from successfully connecting to a database with a failed query

In this scenario, we still successfully connect to the database, but the query then fails, resulting in an error, which is caught by the **catch** block, ending further execution within the **try** block. The **finally** block executes and closes the connection.

In the last scenario we try to connect to another database called **NonExistingDB** (which we know does not exist), by changing the argument for the database parameter when creating the instance object from the **DatabaseInstance** class. The output from this scenario is shown in *Figure 4.3:*

```
An error occurred: Could not connect to database NonExistingDB
Could not close non-existing connection
```

Figure 4.3: Output when failing to connect to a database

As we can see here, it fails entirely to connect to the database (since it does not exist) and immediately gets caught by the **catch** block. No further execution happens in the **try** block. The **finally** block still executes. This time since we have no connection to a database, the **Close()** method is not executed and instead the **else** block is throwing an error, resulting in the **nested catch** block executing its statement.

By incorporating the **try/catch/finally** block in this scenario, where we want to connect to a database, we have ensured the reliability of the script by making sure that all potential errors are caught and handled gracefully. Errors in this scenario could be due to a variety of reasons and not just because you have tried to access a database that does not exist. It could also be due to network issues, firewall issues and so on. By making sure we handle all potential errors by utilizing the **try/catch/finally** statement we would mitigate the possibilities of a script exiting prematurely due to errors and makes sure it continues its execution. Usually, you do not want a script, application, or service for that matter, to stop executing just because of a temporary network outage. You could incorporate retry logic using loops and timers that in combination with the **try/catch/finally** statement, would keep the script execution running in a kind of paused state and then re-connect to the database when network connectivity has been re-established. Such a task could even be set to execute in parallel using a PowerShell job, whereas the script could continue other work while waiting to re-establish the connection to the database. The use of this structure also ensures that the **finally** block always executes the **close** method on the connection object whenever a connection is successfully established, making sure that we perform cleanup and making sure that on the database server side there are no remnants, in this case in the form of a stale connection to the database server, that was not properly closed by the client, waiting for timing out at the backend. We capture and handle errors gracefully, ensuring script reliability and resilience and ensure that we always perform cleanup actions by closing whatever connection we might have established.

Advanced error handling with the ErrorAction preference variable and the ErrorAction parameter

The **$ErrorActionPreference** is a PowerShell special preference variable, these kinds of preference variables are used to customize the general behavior of PowerShell and usually affects all cmdlets, functions, and other commands. The **ErrorAction** preference is used to globally set and control how the entire script or session should respond to non-terminating errors. The settings values for this variable are:

- Continue
- Stop
- SilentlyContinue
- Inquire
- Ignore

The default setting is **Continue** which displays an error message in the console and then continues script execution without interruptions when a non-terminating error occurs. More detailed information about these settings is covered in *Recipe 21: Techniques for handling different types of errors* in this chapter. The **ErrorAction** parameter is used to set the individual behavior for commands. It utilizes the same settings as the **ErrorActionPreference**, as argument values for this parameter. If the **ErrorActionPreference** is set to **Stop**, all commands would behave as terminating upon encountering errors, you can use the **ErrorAction** parameter to make a single command behave like a non-terminating error, overriding the global behavior which is set by the **ErrorActionPreference**, for that single command.

Recipe 23: Use the ErrorAction preference variable and the ErrorAction parameter, to control error handling behavior and customize error actions

If you need to change the behavior for all non-terminating errors in PowerShell, you can use the **$ErrorActionPreference** variable. It is usually set at the top of a script to change and control the general script behavior, but you can set it anywhere if you need to change the behavior back and forth at certain points. This is usually redundant since cmdlets and functions normally include the **ErrorAction** *parameter* which is used to change the error behavior for non-terminating errors for a single command. *Figure 4.4* shows the **ErrorAction** preference variable at the top of a script and its valid values:

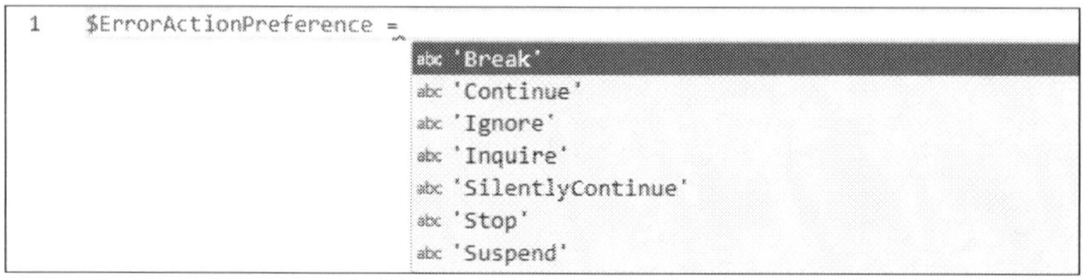

Figure 4.4: The ErrorActionVariable at the top of a script and its valid values

Note: This also shows a Break and Suspend value, these are only used for PowerShell workflow scripts and is not covered in this book.

The following figures show the usage of the **ErrorActionPreference** with the different values and the respective output:

- *Figure 4.5* shows setting **$ErrorActionPreference = "Continue"** and its output:

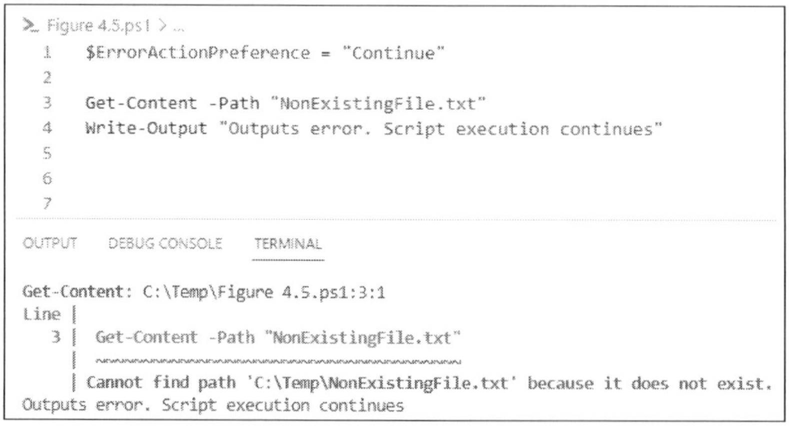

Figure 4.5: Output using the ErrorActionPreference with Continue

- *Figure 4.6* shows setting **$ErrorActionPreference = "Stop"** and its output:

```
>_ Figure 4.6.ps1 > ...
  1    $ErrorActionPreference = "Stop"
  2
  3    Get-Content -Path "NonExistingFile.txt"
  4    Write-Output "Outputs error. Script execution does not continue"
  5
  6
  7

OUTPUT    DEBUG CONSOLE    TERMINAL

Get-Content: C:\Temp\Figure 4.6.ps1:3:1
Line |
   3 |  Get-Content -Path "NonExistingFile.txt"
     |  ~~~~~~~~~~~~~~~~~~~~~~~~~~~~~~~~~~~~~~~~~
     |  Cannot find path 'C:\Temp\NonExistingFile.txt' because it does not exist.
```

Figure 4.6: *Output using the ErrorActionPreference with Stop*

- *Figure 4.7* shows setting **$ErrorActionPreference = "SilentlyContinue"** and its output:

```
>_ Figure 4.7.ps1 > ...
  1    $ErrorActionPreference = "SilentlyContinue"
  2
  3    Get-Content -Path "NonExistingFile.txt"
  4    Write-Output "No error output. Script execution continues"
  5
  6
  7

OUTPUT    DEBUG CONSOLE    TERMINAL

No error output. Script execution continues
```

Figure 4.7: *Output using the ErrorActionPreference with SilentlyContinue*

- *Figure 4.8* shows setting **$ErrorActionPreference = "Inquire"** and its output. Note that the default (**Y**) is selected in this output:

```
>_ Figure 4.8.ps1 > ...
  1    $ErrorActionPreference = "Inquire"
  2
  3    Get-Content -Path "NonExistingFile.txt"
  4    Write-Output "Prompts user for continuation.
  5    Shows error. Further execution depends on user answer"
  6
  7

OUTPUT    DEBUG CONSOLE    TERMINAL

Confirm
Cannot find path 'C:\Temp\NonExistingFile.txt' because it does not exist.
[Y] Yes  [A] Yes to All  [H] Halt Command  [S] Suspend  [?] Help (default is "Y"): []

Get-Content: C:\Temp\Figure 4.8.ps1:3:1
Line |
   3 |  Get-Content -Path "NonExistingFile.txt"
     |  ~~~~~~~~~~~~~~~~~~~~~~~~~~~~~~~~~~~~~~~~~
     |  Cannot find path 'C:\Temp\NonExistingFile.txt' because it does not exist.
Prompts user for continuation.
Shows error. Further execution depends on user answer
```

Figure 4.8: *Output using the ErrorActionPreference with Inquire*

- *Figure 4.9* shows setting **$ErrorActionPreference = "Ignore"** and its output:

```
>_ Figure 4.9.ps1 > ...
    1    $ErrorActionPreference = "Ignore"
    2
    3    Get-Content -Path "NonExistingFile.txt"
    4    Write-Output "Ignores all errors. Script execution continues"
    5
    6
    7

OUTPUT    DEBUG CONSOLE    TERMINAL

Ignores all errors. Script execution continues
```

Figure 4.9: Output using the ErrorActionPreference with Ignore

You can see that errors behave differently depending on the value of the **$ErrorActionPreference** variable. The more common choice is to use either the **Continue** or **SilentlyContinue** values, which keeps errors non-terminating.

> **Note: Other critical errors or exceptions can still occur during script execution and might result in script termination. This could be errors that the script is not directly capable of handling, such as system specific errors, memory errors and so on.**

By using either **Continue** or **SilentlyContinue**, your script will not terminate if it encounters a non-terminating error, and with the **SilentlyContinue** setting, all error console output is also suppressed. You will not be able to use a **try/catch/ finally** block to catch and handle errors for commands, unless you specifically set the **ErrorAction** parameter for specific commands to the **Stop** value, resulting in the error for these specific commands to behave as terminating. The **Ignore** setting is rarely used and should be used with caution, since you will not be informed if you encounter any errors, and your script will continue executing regardless, which might lead to undesirable behavior. **Inquire** is usually used if you need user validation for deciding whether or not to continue script execution upon encountering errors. Then there is the **Stop** value, which makes all errors behave as terminating. Using this setting can be more cumbersome to work with, since you need to account for all potential errors and try to predict and handle all possible reasons for errors, or else your script will stop executing if it encounters any unhandled errors. On the other hand, with this setting, you can be sure that your script will stop executing if it encounters an error that is not handled, which in some cases might be the behavior you want.

- *Figure 4.10* shows the **ErrorAction** parameter used to override the global **ErrorActionPreference** behavior for a single cmdlet when the **ErrorActionPreference** is set to **Stop**. Only the command where the ErrorAction parameter is set to **SilentlyContinue** will act as non-terminating, all other commands which is not specifically set to override the global behavior, acts as terminating errors and can be caught using **try/catch/finally** blocks, or **traps**:

```
>_ Figure 4.10.ps1 > ...
 1   $ErrorActionPreference = "Stop"
 2   try{
 3       Get-Content -Path "NonExistingFile.txt" -ErrorAction SilentlyContinue
 4       Write-Output "Does not get caught. Overrides global behavior"
 5
 6       Get-Content -Path "NonExistingFile.txt"
 7       Write-Output "Gets caught due to ErrorActionPreference"
 8   }
 9   catch{
10       Write-Output "Caught error. ErrorActionPreference=$ErrorActionPreference"
11   }
12

OUTPUT     DEBUG CONSOLE     TERMINAL

Does not get caught. Overrides global behavior
Caught error. ErrorActionPreference=Stop
```

Figure 4.10: *The ErrorAction parameter used to override*
the global behavior of the ErrorActionPreference for a single cmdlet

There is no incorrect way to generally set and use the **ErrorActionPreference**. It is up to the personal preference of the developer. By utilizing the **ErrorActionPreference** and the **ErrorAction** parameter, you have more control over how commands behave when encountering errors and you will be able to override this behavior for specific commands.

Creating custom error classes for enhanced error reporting

We have seen how to catch errors and exceptions and more granularly how to catch specific types of exceptions and act upon them differently, depending on specific requirements. If we loop over a set of files, we know that we might encounter a file that does not exist and an exception of the **ItemNotFoundException** type will be raised. We can catch this specific type of exception and handle this differently from any other errors that we might encounter. A typical PowerShell exception is derived from the **System.Exception** base error class. This is built in a certain way and contains specific error related properties and methods. We can create a new object from that class type and use the **Get-Member** cmdlet to see these methods and properties.

Figure 4.11 shows the methods and properties of the **System.Exception** class:

```
  1    New-Object System.Exception | Get-Member
  2

OUTPUT     DEBUG CONSOLE     TERMINAL


   TypeName: System.Exception

Name                MemberType  Definition
----                ----------  ----------
Equals              Method      bool Equals(System.Object obj)
GetBaseException    Method      System.Exception GetBaseException()
GetHashCode         Method      int GetHashCode()
GetObjectData       Method      void GetObjectData(System.Runtime.Serialization.S
GetType             Method      type GetType()
ToString            Method      string ToString()
Data                Property    System.Collections.IDictionary Data {get;}
HelpLink            Property    string HelpLink {get;set;}
HResult             Property    int HResult {get;set;}
InnerException      Property    System.Exception InnerException {get;}
Message             Property    string Message {get;}
Source              Property    string Source {get;set;}
StackTrace          Property    string StackTrace {get;}
TargetSite          Property    System.Reflection.MethodBase TargetSite {get;}
```

Figure 4.11: *Methods and properties of the System.Exception class type*

This usually provides enough information about errors that occurs, but in some cases you might need more specialized and detailed information, structured differently for making custom and enhanced error reports and messages. For this we can create and utilize custom error classes which are inherited from the base **System.Exception** class. We can include additional properties and methods that are structured for our special requirements and provides us with more capabilities for optimized error reporting and also for more effective troubleshooting.

Recipe 24: Create custom error classes to provide specific error information and enhanced error reporting capabilities

In certain circumstances or when encountering specific errors in scripts, the information provided by the default error class might not be sufficient. We might have a need for providing additional information or to be able to create custom error information in a specific format, such as json, for logging and reporting purposes.

When an error is thrown in PowerShell the default behavior is to show the string representation of the error to the console, by the **System.Exception** class **ToString()**

method. The **ToString()** method of the **System.Exception** class returns a string that includes the exception message and the errors stacktrace. This might not be the preferred output and we might need a method for creating custom error output. We also might need to be able to log errors in a specific format like Json with additional custom error information provided such as error codes, an error level, the date, and the time the error occurred and so on.

We can create a custom error class where we inherit the properties and methods from the **System.Exception** class and then add additional properties with custom information and custom methods. We can override the base class methods, such as the **ToString() method** for providing custom console output, and create additional custom methods, where we can return custom information in Json format and whatever else we might need to have customized.

The case is:

Create a custom error class that overrides the ToString method from the base class. The output from the custom ToString method should be a string containing the time and date, the specific error that occurred, the error level, the error message, and an error code. The custom error class should also contain a method that returns a JSON object containing the following information: The error message, the error code, the error level, the date and time in a combined date property, the name of the invoked script, the name of the server where the script is invoked and the stacktrace. The JSON output should be returned either as a compressed object (all data in one line) or as a JSON data object spanning multiple lines. The ToString method should be used for providing console output in a custom format, and the JSON output should be used for writing the relevant error information to a log file that is suitable for external logging monitor systems such as Datadog, DynaTrace, Seq etc.

We need to figure out the specific information we want our class to output and which properties it should contain for providing this specific information.

- **Error Message**: **[String]**. This is provided as a parameter.

- **Error Code**: **[Int]**. This is provided as a parameter.

- **Error Level**: **[String]**. This is provided as a parameter. Valid values are: **Ok**, **Debug**, **Info**, **Warning**, **Error**, **Critical**.

- **Date/Time**: **[String]**. Date and time provided as a string in the following format: (dd-mm-yyyy hh:mm:ss). This is not a parameter but handled internally within the class.

- **ScriptName**: **[String]**. The name of the invoked script. The property from the built-in **$MyInvocation** variable, **$MyInvocation.MyCommand.Name** should be used. Since **$MyInvocation** is not properly populated inside a class, the value must be provided as an argument to a parameter. In cases where **$MyInvocation** is not used, the argument should be a string containing the name, an empty string or a **$null** value.

- **Server**: **[String]**. This is only used for Json output. The value is provided from the **$Env:ComputerName** environment variable and handled inside the class.

- **Stacktrace**: **[String]**. This is handled internally inside the class. The **[System. Environment]::Stacktrace** .Net method is used to provide a string representation of the current calls stacktrace.

- **CompressJson**: **[Bool]**. This is a parameter. Set the Json string output to be either compressed (one line) or non-compressed (multi line).

Some of these properties will be provided as arguments for parameters to the class and others are handled and calculated inside the class itself. In *Chapter 2: Advanced PowerShell functions* we learned about PowerShell classes and that they can take arguments for parameters, so we need to create a class with a constructor that has parameters for the relevant arguments. We also need to figure out how the two methods we are going to use, needs to work and what they should output. The **ToString** method is an override for the base class method with the same name. This method should return a string containing the date, level, message and error code information properly formatted to our preferences. The second method will return a string object formatted as Json. This must contain the following data: message, error code, level, date, script name, server name and the stacktrace. It must also return the Json data as either a compressed or uncompressed string, depending on the value of the **CompressJson** property. To create this Json string, we start with creating a **PSCustomObject** and convert this to a Json object using the **ConvertTo-Json** cmdlet. We use an **if/else** block to return the Json data as either a compressed or uncompressed string. With this information we can begin to create the custom error class:

1. We create a class using the **class** keyword and call this **MyCustomErrorClass**. We reference the class we must inherit from, by specifying the name of that class, **System.Exception** after the name of our custom class:

    ```
    class MyCustomErrorClass : System.Exception {}
    ```

2. We specify all the class properties and their attributes. Note the use of the name **Stack** instead of **StackTrace**. Stacktrace is a PowerShell reserved keyword, so we cannot use it as a variable name. Creating the properties with a specific type, adds type validation to each property. Additional validation is added to the **Level** property in the form of a validate set with provided valid values for the **$Level** parameter:

    ```
    # Class properties
    [string]$Message
    [int]$ErrorCode
    [string]$Stack
    [string]$Date
    [string]$ScriptName
    [bool]$CompressJson
    ```

```
[ValidateSet("Ok","Debug","Info","Warning","Error","Critical")]
[string]$Level
```

3. The class constructor is created, and we add the required parameters to it. These parameters are: **Message**, **ErrorCode**, **Level**, **ScriptName** and **CompressJson**. An argument for each parameter must be provided when we use the class for throwing an error.

    The next thing we do is to pass the value of the **Message** parameter from our custom class, as an argument to the **base** class **Message** parameter. Since we are inheriting from the **System.Exception** class we also inherits its constructor, and this constructor *requires* one argument for its **Message** parameter. The Message parameter is then initialized inside the base class, and then becomes a parameter inherited into our custom class, ensuring we correctly inherit the necessary functionality from the base class. We then initialize all our properties with the values provided as arguments, within the constructor. We use the self-reference variable: **$this**, for referencing the properties within the class itself. Note that for the **$Stack** property, we use the .NET method **[System.Environment]::StackTrace** to get the value of the current calls stacktrace and assign this to the property. The **$Date** property is assigned with the current date and time values each time the constructor is initialized. We use the **Get-Date** cmdlet with the **-format** parameter to get the preferred custom date and time output as a string:

    ```
    # Constructor to initialize the properties
    MyCustomErrorClass([string]$Message, [int]$ErrorCode,
    [string]$Level, [string]$ScriptName, [bool]$CompressJson) :
        base($Message) {
        $this.Message = $Message
        $this.ErrorCode = $ErrorCode
        $this.Stack = [System.Environment]::StackTrace
        $this.Date = (Get-Date -Format "dd-MM-yyyy HH:mm:ss")
        $this.ScriptName = $ScriptName
        $this.CompressJson = $CompressJson
        $this.Level = $Level
    ```

4. We create the override **ToString** method and set the return type as **string** and then create the custom output string containing the desired properties.

    ```
    # Custom method to override the ToString() method
    [string]ToString() {
        return "Date: $($this.Date) Level: $($this.Level) Message:
    $($this.Message) (Error Code: $($this.ErrorCode))"
    }
    ```

5. For the **Json** method we create a **PSCustomObject** as value and assign it to the **$Obj** variable. We populate the **PSCustomObject** with the desired properties from the class. Note that we never initialized a **Server** property, we simply use the value from the **$Env:ComputerName** variable as the value for the **Server** property directly in the **PSCustomObject**. We then use an **if/else** block to check the value of the **CompressJson** property. If it is **$true**, we convert the **PSCustomObject** using the **ConvertTo-Json** cmdlet with the **Compression** parameter and return this. If the **CompressJson** property is **$false** we convert the **PSCustomObject** *without* using the **Compression** parameter and return it:

```
# Custom method for output custom error data in JSON
[string]Json() {
    $Obj = [PSCustomObject]@{
        Message = $this.message
        Code = $this.ErrorCode
        Level = $this.Level
        Date = $this.Date
        ScriptName = $this.ScriptName
        Server = $Env:COMPUTERNAME
        Stack = $this.Stack
    }
    if ($this.CompressJson -eq $true){
        return $Obj | ConvertTo-Json -Compress
    }
    else{
        return $Obj | ConvertTo-Json
    }
}
```

The custom error class ends up looking like this:

```
class MyCustomErrorClass : System.Exception {
    # Class properties
    [string]$Message
    [int]$ErrorCode
    [string]$Stack
    [string]$Date
    [string]$ScriptName
    [bool]$CompressJson
    [ValidateSet("Ok","Debug","Info","Warning","Error","Critical")]
    [string]$Level
```

```
    # Constructor to initialize the properties
    MyCustomErrorClass([string]$Message, [int]$ErrorCode, [string]$Level,
[string]$ScriptName, [bool]$CompressJson) :
        base($Message) {
        $this.Message = $Message
        $this.ErrorCode = $ErrorCode
        $this.Stack = [System.Environment]::StackTrace
        $this.Date = (Get-Date -Format "dd-MM-yyyy HH:mm:ss")
        $this.ScriptName = $ScriptName
        $this.CompressJson = $CompressJson
        $this.Level = $Level
    }
    # Custom method to override the ToString() method
    [string]ToString() {
        return "Date: $($this.Date) Level: $($this.Level) Message: $($this.
Message) (Error Code: $($this.ErrorCode))"
    }
    # Custom method for output custom error data in JSON
    [string]Json() {
        $Obj = [PSCustomObject]@{
            Message = $this.message
            Code = $this.ErrorCode
            Level = $this.Level
            Date = $this.Date
            ScriptName = $this.ScriptName
            Server = $Env:COMPUTERNAME
            Stack = $this.Stack
        }
        if ($this.CompressJson -eq $true){
            return $Obj | ConvertTo-Json -Compress
        }
        else{
            return $Obj | ConvertTo-Json
        }
    }
}
```

To use the custom error class, we instantiate the class with the relevant parameters, as an argument to the **throw** statement. Below, we create a **try/catch** block where we use our custom class to throw an error. In the **try** block, the first thing we do is to get the name of our script by assigning the value of **$MyInvocation.MyCommand.Name** property to a variable called **$ScriptName**. This is used as the argument for the fourth parameter in the custom error class. Then we **throw** an error and instantiate the custom error class using the **new** static method and provide the relevant arguments to it. The first argument is the error **Message**. The second is the **ErrorCode**, the third is the error **Level**, the fourth is the **ScriptName** and the last argument is for the **CompressJson** parameter. In the **catch** block, we catch the specific error, by providing the name of our custom class, **MyCustomErrorClass**. Here we have two statements. For the first one we use **Write-Output** to write a custom error message to the console using the **ToString** method. Notice that we use the current error variable followed by **Exception** and then **ToString** to call the **ToString** method. We need to refer to the **Exception** object, derived from the error class type, since we inherited from the **System.Exception** class, within the current error object. The output will be the custom string we return in the overridden **ToString** method. Within the second statement in the **catch** block, we call the **Json** method and then pipe the output from this method to **Out-File** using the path to the log file and **Append** as arguments, so we can append the output data to the file without overriding the file´s current content.

```
try {
    # Simulate an error by throwing the custom error class
    $ScriptName = $MyInvocation.MyCommand.Name
    throw [MyCustomErrorClass]::new("This is a custom error message.",
1001, "Error", $ScriptName, $false)
}
catch [MyCustomErrorClass]{
    Write-Output "Error caught: $($_.Exception.ToString())"
    $_.Exception.Json() | Out-File c:\temp\testlog.json -Append
}
```

In the example, we throw an error using the MyCustomErrorClass as an argument. We catch the MyCustomErrorClass exception in the catch block resulting in the first statement in the catch block being written to the console, as shown in *Figure 4.12*:

```
Error caught: Date: 30-07-2023 18:07:05 Level: Error Message: This is a custom error message. (Error Code: 1001)
```

Figure 4.12: Output from the Write-Output statement using the custom error class and its ToString() method

From the second statement in the catch block, where we use the **Json** method and writes its output to a file, the output within that file is shown in *Figure 4.13*:

```
   testlog.json - Notepad

 File  Edit  Format  View  Help
 {
   "Message": "This is a custom error message.",
   "Code": 1001,
   "Level": "Error",
   "Date": "30-07-2023 18:07:05",
   "ScriptName": "CustomErrorClass.ps1",
   "Server": "TestServer01",
   "Stack": "    at System.Environment.get_StackTrace()\r\n
 ingBehavior, Object dollarUnder, Object input, Object scr
 etedFrame frame)\r\n    at System.Management.Automation.In
 oolean ignoreInput, CommandParameterInternal[][] pipeElem
 eCore(CommandProcessorBase commandRequestingUpstreamComma
 s)\r\n    at System.Management.Automation.PowerShell.CoreI
 ionToken) in D:\\a\\_work\\1\\s\\src\\PowerShellEditorSer
 Host.PsesInternalHost.RunExecutionLoop(Boolean isForDebug
 rShell.EditorServices.Services.PowerShell.Host.PsesIntern
 }
```

Figure 4.13: Output from the custom error class Json() method,
saved in a file with CompressJson property set to $false

If we called the custom error class with the argument for the **CompressJson** parameter set to **$true** instead of **$false**, the output in the log file would look as shown in *Figure 4.14*, compressed to fit one line. Notice for readability purposes that the value for the **Stack** key in the **Json** output has been removed, the stacktrace would look like the one in the previous output, just spanning the one line in the file instead of multiple lines as we saw in the previous *Figure 4.13*:

```
   testlog.json - Notepad
 File  Edit  Format  View  Help
 {"Message":"This is a custom error message.","Code":1001,"Level":"Error","Date":"30-07-2023 18:11:38","ScriptName":"CustomErrorClass.ps1","Server":"TestServer01","Stack":""}
```

Figure 4.14: Output from the custom error class Json()
method, saved in a file with CompressJson property set to $true

We can also use our custom error class for handling error output from terminating errors. First we would use a **try/catch** block to catch the terminating error, as we normally would. Then we create a nested **try/catch** block, like the statement we did previously, where we **throw** our custom error class and then catch the specific **MyCustomErrorClass** exception. Instead of a custom message we would then use the error message from the first catch block as the **Message** argument for our custom class message parameter. It would look like this:

```
try{
    Get-Content -Path "NonExistingFile" -ErrorAction "Stop"
}
catch{
```

```
    try{
        $ScriptName = $MyInvocation.MyCommand.Name
        throw [MyCustomErrorClass]::new($_.Exception.Message, 1101,
"Error", $ScriptName, $false)
    }
    catch [MyCustomErrorClass]{
        Write-Output "Error caught: $($_.Exception.ToString())"
        $_.Exception.Json() | Out-File c:\temp\testlog.json -Append
    }
}
```

The console output from the **ToString** method for this would look as shown in *Figure 4.15*:

```
Error caught: Date: 30-07-2023 18:27:36 Level: Error Message: Cannot find path 'C:\Temp\NonExistingFile' because it does not exist. (Error Code: 1101)
```

Figure 4.15: *ToString console output using the custom error class with nested try/catch block to catch a terminating error*

And the **Json** output saved to a log file would look as shown in *Figure 4.16*:

```
testlog.json - Notepad
File   Edit   Format   View   Help
{
  "Message": "Cannot find path 'C:\\Temp\\NonExistingFile' because it does not exist.",
  "Code": 1101,
  "Level": "Error",
  "Date": "30-07-2023 18:27:36",
  "ScriptName": "CustomErrorClass.ps1",
  "Server": "TestServer01",
  "Stack": "    at System.Environment.get_StackTrace()\r\n    at System.Management.Automat
ingBehavior, Object dollarUnder, Object input, Object scriptThis, Pipe outputPipe, Invoc
nt.Automation.Interpreter.EnterTryCatchFinallyInstruction.Run(InterpretedFrame frame)\r\
System.Management.Automation.Internal.PipelineProcessor.SynchronousExecuteEnumerate(Obje
riptCommandProcessor.Complete()\r\n    at System.Management.Automation.CommandProcessorBa
oolean isSync)\r\n    at System.Management.Automation.PowerShell.CoreInvokeHelper[TInput,
r\n    at Microsoft.PowerShell.EditorServices.Services.PowerShell.Execution.SynchronousPo
Host\\PsesInternalHost.cs:line 990\r\n    at Microsoft.PowerShell.EditorServices.Services
, RunspaceInfo newRunspaceInfo) in D:\\a\\_work\\1\\s\\src\\PowerShellEditorServices\\Se
}
```

Figure 4.16: *Json log file output using the custom error class with nested try/catch block to catch a terminating error*

By creating custom error classes derived from the **System.Exception** class, we can customize error output that is suitable for our specific requirements, like in this case where we have created Json output for direct logging purposes and also customized the console error output. We do this by inheriting the methods and properties from the base

`System.Exception` class and then overriding and customizing these within our custom error class. This is especially useful for adding additional information in a custom format to your error messages and for incorporating custom logging and reporting capabilities into your scrips.

Error handling in background jobs

In *Chapter 3, Flow control and looping* we learned how to utilize PowerShell jobs to incorporate multithreading like behavior into scripts. For maintaining stable and reliable execution of commands running in background jobs, we need to be able to implement robust error handling for capturing job specific errors. The error handling process in background jobs is different from error handling in scripts and local sessions. In background jobs, errors are not automatically propagated to the calling script, we need to explicitly capture, and handle job errors using the jobs states or from the jobs results using the **Receive-Job** cmdlet and return information or write errors directly to log files or a logging system, from within the script block executed within a job. Jobs have different states like **Running**, **Completed**, **Stopped** and **Failed**. If an error within a **Running** job is non-terminating, the state of the job will not change, and it continues executing. When a job encounters a terminating error, it will change its state to **Failed** and stop further execution. It is essential to be able to handle both non-terminating and terminating errors within a job, to maintain the stability and reliability of your scripts and their background processes.

Recipe 25: Use different techniques for handling errors that occur in background jobs, including capturing job specific errors and managing job states

There are different techniques that can be used to capture and handle errors in background jobs. It depends on the specific type of error, is it terminating or non-terminating? Do you need your jobs to continue or halt execution upon encountering an error and how do you want to handle the error output? Do you want to log the error to a file and continue execution or do you want to stop the job and handle the error within the scope of the calling script? In this recipe, we will learn a few of the techniques for handling errors within background jobs. We will use the job state to determine if a job has failed due to a terminating error and then we handle the error in the calling script with the output returned from the job. We will use the **Receive-Job** cmdlet to catch and handle a terminating error in the calling script. And we will handle errors inside the job itself, logging the errors directly to a log file and gracefully continuing executing the job without terminating it.

When you start a job, the job is created as what is called a child job of the job object that is returned, when a job is created with the **Start-Job** cmdlet, the job object is called the parent job. The script block with the job code is the child job of the parent job object. A job is also started with a state, and this state may change during execution, like from **running** to **completed** or **failed**. This state contains information about the job and any potential error information if the job encountered an error.

The first technique will use a jobs *state* to determine if the job failed due to encountering a terminating error. The error is handled in the calling script and not within the job itself. The requirement for utilizing this technique is that the job must fail and stop further execution of its commands upon encountering an error.

> **Info: This example will use 3 files. These files must be created and exist. File1.txt, File2.txt and File3.txt. Each file has the following one-line content: Content: File X where X is the number of that specific file.**

The job will loop through an array of files, try to get the content of each file, and then write a string with the file content as the result. The result will be returned from the job. If the job fails to read the content from a file, the job will throw an error and fail. We create this job construct like this:

1. We create a script block containing the statements for the job and assign it to a variable called **$Block**. Inside the script block we create an array with the names of the files we want to get the content from. Notice that the order of the files in this example are not random. We create a **Foreach** loop that iterates over each file. Inside the **Foreach** loop we use a **try/catch** block to catch potential errors. In the **try** block, we use the **Get-Content** cmdlet to get the content of the files. We set the **ErrorAction** parameter to **Stop**, resulting in all errors from this cmdlet will behave as terminating. We can then catch errors with the **catch** block. If we successfully get the content from a file, we create a **string** stating that we successfully extracted the content. This string is not saved in a variable, it will be returned as a result from the job. If it fails to get the content from a file, the error is caught by the **catch** block. We create a **string** stating that it failed to load the content from that file and add the error message to the string using the current error variable **$_**. This is not saved in a variable either so this is returned as a result for the job. We **throw** an error, terminating the job which results in job failure:

```
$Block = {
    $Files = @("File1.txt","File2.txt","NonExistingFile.txt","File3.txt")
    foreach ($File in $Files){
        try {
            $Content = Get-Content -Path $File -ErrorAction Stop
            "Content from $($File) successfully extracted: $($Content)"
        } catch {
            "Failed to load content from $($File): $_"
            throw
        }
```

```
        }
    }
```

2. We start the job with the **Start-Job** cmdlet. Assign the job to the **$Job** variable and add the **$Block** scriptblock as an argument to the **scriptblock** parameter:

```
$Job = Start-Job -ScriptBlock $Block
```

3. We wait for the job to finish before further executing commands in the script using the **Wait-Job** cmdlet. We pipe this to **Out-Null** to suppress output from this command:

```
Wait-Job $Job | Out-Null
```

4. When the job has finished executing. We use an **if/else** block to check the state of the job. If the job state is **failed**, the job has failed, in this case because of the **throw** statement in the **catch** block. We use **Write-Error** to raise a non-terminating error for writing a custom error message to the console (and the error stream. By using **Write-Error** we also ensure that the error is saved in the scripts **$Error** variable. This is useful if we want to make a report or other kind of output with all errors that occurred within the script during its execution, at a later time). In this error message, we use the state property from the job, to write the state and then we use information from the jobs child jobs state info property. The **ChildJobs** property is an array with all child jobs within the parent job object. Since we only have one job, we use index **0** which correlates to our job, since it uses indexing for storing jobs in the job object. The **JobStateInfo** property contains information about the state of the job. The **Reason** property contains information about errors encountered if a job state is **failed**. We use the **Message** property from the **Reason** property to get the specific error message the job encountered. Within the **else** block, if the job does not fail, we write the output of the jobs **state** property, which in such case would be **completed**:

```
if ($Job.State -eq "Failed") {
    Write-Error "Job $($Job.state) $($Job.ChildJobs[0].JobStateInfo.
Reason.Message)."
} else {
    Write-Output "Job $($Job.State)."
}
```

5. The last thing we do is use **Receive-Job** to get the results from the job. We could omit this if we were just interested in the state of the job and act accordingly to this state in the **if/else** block. The **Receive-Job** cmdlet is added to this structure to show the results from the job in this specific case. Since we know that the job might result in an error, we set the **ErrorAction** parameter for the **Receive-Job** cmdlet to **SilentlyContinue**, or else this would result in a non-terminating error if the state of the job is failed:

```
Receive-Job $Job -ErrorAction SilentlyContinue
```

The construct will look like this:

```
$Block = {
    $Files = @("File1.txt","File2.txt","NonExistingFile.txt","File3.txt")
    foreach ($File in $Files) {
        try {
            $Content = Get-Content -Path $File -ErrorAction Stop
            "Content from $($File) successfully extracted: $($Content)"
        } catch {
            "Failed to load content from $($File): $_"
            throw
        }
    }
}
$Job = Start-Job -ScriptBlock $Block
Wait-Job $Job | Out-Null
if ($Job.State -eq "Failed") {
    Write-Error "Job $($Job.state) $($Job.ChildJobs[0].JobStateInfo.Reason.Message)."
} else {
    Write-Output "Job $($Job.State)."
}
Receive-Job $Job -ErrorAction SilentlyContinue
```

In this example, the job stops further execution when an error is encountered and we handle the error using the jobs state, checks if it has **failed** and accordingly manage the error. We use **Write-Error** to notify the reason *why* the job failed and use the job's state information to get the specific error message from this job. *Figure 4.17* shows the output of running this example. As you can see, we still get the job results from the successful operations from within the job, using the **Receive-Job** cmdlet that is until the error occurred. The error is also added to the job result because we created the **string** statement in the **catch** block before we threw the error:

```
Write-Error: Job Failed Cannot find path 'C:\Temp\NonExistingFile.txt' because it does not exist..
Content from File1.txt successfully extracted: Content: File 1
Content from File2.txt successfully extracted: Content: File 2
Failed to load content from NonExistingFile.txt: Cannot find path 'C:\Temp\NonExistingFile.txt' because it does not exist.
```

Figure 4.17: Output from the failed job using the jobs state for handling error

When an error is encountered in a job, the **Receive-Job** cmdlet results in a non-terminating error. We can use this with the **ErrorAction** set to **Stop** and a **try/catch** block for catching and handling this error, instead of using the approach where we checked and used the jobs state. The preferred method always depends on the specific requirements and how you want to handle the error.

For the next technique we use the **Receive-Job** with the **ErrorAction** parameter set to **stop**, within a **try/catch** block to catch and handle the error:

1. We use the same scriptblock as before:

```
$job = Start-Job -ScriptBlock {
    $Files = @("File1.txt","File2.txt","NonExistingFile.txt","File3.txt")
    foreach ($File in $Files) {
        try {
            $Content = Get-Content -Path $File -ErrorAction Stop
            "Content from $($File) successfully extracted: $($Content)"
        } catch {
            "Failed to load content from $($File): $_"
            throw

        }
    }
}
```

2. We now wait for the job to finish:

```
Wait-Job $job | Out-Null
```

3. We create a **try/catch** block. Inside the try block we call **Receive-Job** with the **ErrorAction** parameter set to **Stop**. Within the **catch** block, we catch potential errors, and we use **Write-Error** to write the error output to the console (and the error stream). We also use the current error variable **$_** to write the specific error message:

```
try {
    Receive-Job $job -ErrorAction Stop
} catch {
    Write-Error "Error occurred in the job: $_"
}
```

This construct look like this:

```
$job = Start-Job -ScriptBlock {
    $Files = @("File1.txt","File2.txt","NonExistingFile.txt","File3.txt")
    foreach ($File in $Files) {
        try {
            $Content = Get-Content -Path $File -ErrorAction Stop
            "Content from $($File) successfully extracted: $($Content)"
        } catch {
```

```
            "Failed to load content from $($File): $_"
            throw
        }
    }
}
Wait-Job $job | Out-Null
try {
    Receive-Job $job -ErrorAction Stop
} catch {
    Write-Error "Error occurred in the job: $_"
}
```

The output from running this is shown in *Figure 4.18*:

```
Content from File1.txt successfully extracted: Content: File 1
Content from File2.txt successfully extracted: Content: File 2
Failed to load content from NonExistingFile.txt: Cannot find path
'C:\Temp\NonExistingFile.txt' because it does not exist.
Write-Error: Error occurred in the job: Cannot find path 'C:\Temp\
NonExistingFile.txt' because it does not exist.
```

Figure 4.18: Output from the failed job using Receive-Job
and try/catch block for capturing and handling error

As you can see using this technique, we still get the job results using **Receive-Job** until the error occurs. The error is then raised by the job result, and we capture the error in the **catch** block, where we can handle it, in this case, using the **Write-Error** cmdlet to write the error to the console (and writing it to the error stream).

Both techniques require that the job throws a terminating error and stops further execution. This might not be what you want, you might need the job to continue execution when encountering errors, but you also still need to be informed about the errors that occurred during execution.

For the next technique we will not terminate the job when potential errors are encountered but instead handle these errors inside the job itself by logging them directly to a file, and then continue the execution of the job until it has finished processing all the files. Since we are going to log the output data to a file, we also want an output that is more readable and manageable which can be further processed, potentially by a third party logging and monitoring tool. We add a **Date**, a **Level** and a **Message** property to the output data and convert it to Json before sending it to the log file:

1. We will create a scriptblock and assign this to the **$Block** variable. Inside the scriptblock we create an array with the files we want to get the content from. We use the **Foreach** loop to iterate through each file, and for each file, we create a **PSCustomObject** which is then assigned to a **$Data** variable. Inside the **PSCustomObject** we add a **Date** property and use **Get-Date** with the **-f** format

parameter and set a proper output format for the date and time. We also add an **ErrorLevel** property and a **Message** property. Both of these are set as empty strings. These will be populated in the **try/catch** block depending on the outcome of each **Get-Content** process. In the **try** block, we use the **Get-Content** cmdlet with the **ErrorAction Stop** parameter. In both the **try** and **catch** block, we update the **$Data** object with the values for the **Message** and the **ErrorLevel** parameter, depending on the outcome. A success message and the **ErrorLevel** as *Info* for success and a failed message and the **ErrorLevel** as *Error* for a failed process. After the **try/catch** block, we take the **$Data** object, pipe this to **ConvertTo-Json** with the **compress** parameter and then further piping it to **Out-File** with the **FilePath** parameter, which is the path to the output logfile, and the **Append** parameter to make sure it appends the log line to the file and not overwrites the current content in it. The last statement within the scriptblock is that we return the **$Data** object to the job result. Note: We could also have encapsulated the output statements within another **try/catch** block and have further handled potential errors with the **ConvertTo-Json** and the **Out-File** cmdlets. For this example, we assume that the conversion can be done without errors and that the logfile exists and is writeable.

2. We will then create the job with **Start-Job** using the **$Block** scriptblock as an argument for the **ScriptBlock** parameter and then assign this to the **$Job** variable.

3. Now we wait for the job using **Wait-Job** which is piped to **Out-Null** for suppressing the output from this cmdlet, which in this case is irrelevant.

4. We can use **Receive-Job** to get the job result, assigning this to the **$JobResults** variable and then writes the output to the console.

The construct looks like this:

```
$Block = {
    $Files = @("File1.txt","File2.txt","NonExistingFile.txt","File3.txt")
    foreach ($File in $Files){
        $Data = [PSCustomObject]@{
            Date = Get-Date -f "dd-MM-yyyy HH:mm:ss"
            ErrorLevel = ""
            Message = ""
        }
        try {
            $Content = Get-Content -Path $File -ErrorAction Stop
            $Data.Message = "Content from $($File) successfully logged: $($Content)"
            $Data.ErrorLevel = "Info"
        } catch {
            $Data.Message = "Failed to load content from $($File): $_"
```

```
            $Data.ErrorLevel = "Error"
        }

                $Data | ConvertTo-Json -Compress | Out-File -FilePath "C:\
temp\ErrorLog.json" -Append
        $Data
    }
}
$Job = Start-Job -ScriptBlock $Block
Wait-Job $Job | Out-Null
$JobResults = Receive-Job $Job
$JobResults
```

Figure 4.19 shows the console output. Since we returned the **$Data PSCustomObject** from each iteration process to the job result, we get a nicely formatted output object. Note that the **RunspaceId** is automatically added specifically to the console output:

```
Date       : 01-08-2023 20:21:41
ErrorLevel : Info
Message    : Content from File1.txt successfully logged: Content: File 1
RunspaceId : 93e2b623-8f05-4b19-a0b9-3e54f230db90

Date       : 01-08-2023 20:21:41
ErrorLevel : Info
Message    : Content from File2.txt successfully logged: Content: File 2
RunspaceId : 93e2b623-8f05-4b19-a0b9-3e54f230db90

Date       : 01-08-2023 20:21:41
ErrorLevel : Error
Message    : Failed to load content from NonExistingFile.txt: Cannot find path 'C:\Temp\NonExistingFile.txt' because it does not exist.
RunspaceId : 93e2b623-8f05-4b19-a0b9-3e54f230db90

Date       : 01-08-2023 20:21:41
ErrorLevel : Info
Message    : Content from File3.txt successfully logged: Content: File 3
RunspaceId : 93e2b623-8f05-4b19-a0b9-3e54f230db90
```

Figure 4.19: *Nicely formatted console output from job that handles errors internally*

Figure 4.20 shows the output from the logfile:

```
ErrorLog.json - Notepad
File  Edit  Format  View  Help
{"Date":"04-01-2024 20:36:13","ErrorLevel":"Info","Message":"Content from File1.txt successfully logged: Content: File 1"}
{"Date":"04-01-2024 20:36:13","ErrorLevel":"Info","Message":"Content from File2.txt successfully logged: Content: File 2"}
{"Date":"04-01-2024 20:36:13","ErrorLevel":"Error","Message":"Failed to load content from NonExistingFile.txt: Cannot find
{"Date":"04-01-2024 20:36:13","ErrorLevel":"Info","Message":"Content from File3.txt successfully logged: Content: File 3"}
```

Figure 4.20: *Json formatted log output from job that handles errors internally*

Not only do we get nicely formatted output within the console but also in a log file. We also ensure that all files within the job are processed, except for the ones that raise an error of course, here we catch and handle the error accordingly and then continues the job process execution. As long as we handle all potential errors inside the job, we can continue processing all files and the job will terminate with a successful state when it has completed its work even though it encountered errors during its processing.

By gracefully handling errors in background jobs, we can mitigate potential unexpected behavior and results from running PowerShell jobs. There are cases where jobs are longer, running processes that the main script should not wait for, before execution of the main script is continued, and jobs will run in the background asynchronous with the main script. Especially in such cases, it is vital to the stability of these jobs to be able to handle any errors they encounter, log these errors, and continue the job execution. The script might be relying on the successful completion of one or more jobs, without it affecting the overall desired outcome that is needed for the script to be able to finish executing successfully.

Debugging and logging error information

To be able to properly log and debug errors is a vital part of a script development process and will help you to identify and troubleshoot any issues and capture valuable information about errors that might occur during script execution.

Logging is about capturing information about a script or applications execution of its processes and being able to save this information. Logging information is not only limited to errors but can also be about logging information from events, actions and commands that are executed within a script or application. There can be many reasons for logging specific information besides errors for troubleshooting purposes, such as for performance analysis, security monitoring, user activity tracking and auditing purposes and more. Logs should always be structured in a format such as **JSON** or **XML** which allows for additional detailed information such as timestamps, severity levels and sources to be added to logs. This not only makes it easier to read and parse with other tools but is usually also easier to send to third party logging tools or centralized logging systems. Logs can be written directly to files using cmdlets like the **Out-File** and **Add-Content**. They can be sent to the Windows event log using the **Write-EventLog** cmdlet or you can create a custom function that handles the aspects of logging to a file in a structured and custom manner. Debugging is the process of identifying and resolving errors and issues in a script or application. This also includes finding and fixing bugs, finding and solving unexpected behavior and other potential issues that you may encounter in a script or application during its execution. Proper error handling and logging makes it easier to identify and solve issues and can greatly mitigate the time you spent on debugging code. Some techniques for debugging involves stepping through your code, printing statements, inspecting variables, setting breakpoints and using specialized debugging tools. In *Chapter 1, Introduction to advanced PowerShell concepts* we briefly mentioned the use of the VS Code debugging tool which can be utilized to set breakpoints, inspect variables and help you debug other aspects of your code. You should utilize such tools wherever possible, for helping you increase debug efficiency and decrease time spent on debugging.

Recipe 26: Create a custom logging function for structured logging that helps with troubleshooting and debugging errors

It is essential to properly log not only errors but also other types of events and actions in your scripts in a structured format. By creating a custom logging function, you can provide a simple and consistent way of creating log entries for errors, events, actions, commands etc. We are going to create such a function.

The function will create Json structured logs, written directly to a log file with as little input information provided as possible:

1. We create a **function** called **Add-LogToJson** and add the **CmdletBinding** attribute. Then we create a param block with five parameters:

   a. **[String]$LogFile**: This is a mandatory parameter set at position **0**. This is the full path to the logfile.

   b. **[String]$Message**: This is a mandatory parameter set at position **1**. This is the custom log message.

   c. **[String]$Level**: This is an optional parameter with no position. This is the severity level. Valid values are **Info**, **Warning**, **Error**, **Critical**, **Debug** and **Ok**. It defaults to **Info**.

   d. **[Hashtable]$Adds**: This is an optional parameter with no position. This is for providing additional log data in the form of a **Hashtable**. **Key/value** pairs within the **Hashtable** will be converted to Json **key/values** and added to the log output data.

   e. **[Switch]$Compress**: This is a switch parameter with no position. When this is provided, the output Json will be compressed to fit one line in the file. Optimized for third party logging tools.

Each parameter has a **HelpMessage** attribute with a short explanation:

```
Function Add-LogToJson {
    [CmdletBinding()]
    Param (
        [Parameter(Position = 0, Mandatory = $true, HelpMessage =
"Path to logfile")]
        [String]$LogFile,
        [Parameter(Position = 1, Mandatory = $true, HelpMessage =
"Message String")]
        [String]$Message,
        [Parameter(HelpMessage = "Severity Level")]
```

```
        [ValidateSet("INFO", "WARNING", "ERROR", "CRITICAL", "DEBUG", "OK")]
        [String]$Level = "INFO",
        [Parameter(HelpMessage = "Add additional key/values in form
of a hashtable")]
        [hashtable]$Adds,
        [Parameter(HelpMessage = "Compress JSON output")]
        [switch]$Compress
    )
```

2. We create a **BEGIN** block. In this block we start by creating an **if** block where we use **Test-Path** to check if the log file in the **$LogFile** parameter exists. If not, we create it using the **New-Item** cmdlet with the **-Force** parameter. We add some verbose output with **Write-Verbose** if a new log file is created:

```
BEGIN {
    if (-not(Test-Path $LogFile)) {
        New-Item -Path $LogFile -ItemType File -Force | Out-Null
        Write-Verbose "Logfile created: $LogFile"
    }
}
```

3. We create a timestamp with the **Get-Date** cmdlet specifying a format with the **-f** parameter and assign this to the **$Time** variable. We create a **$LogString** variable. This is a simple string we will use later for simple verbose console output. This output string only uses the **$Time**, the **$Level** and the **$Message** variable values:

```
$Time = Get-Date -Format "dd-MM-yyyy HH:mm:ss,fff"
[String]$LogString = ”$Time - $Level : $Message”
```

4. We create a **$Body** variable as a Hashtable object. This will consist of all relevant log data and later be converted to Json. We use the Hashtables **Add** method to add the timestamp, the level and the message values from the respective variables to the Hashtable. Then we use an **if** block and check if the **$Add** variable evaluates to **$true**, if it does, meaning that a Hashtable with additional data has been provided, we then create a new **$Body** variable where the two Hashtables is combined, which overrides the first **$Body** variable, making sure we get all the added data:

```
$Body = @{ }
$Body.Add("timestamp", $Time)
$Body.Add("message", $Message)
$Body.Add("level", $Level)
        if ($Adds) {
    $Body = $Body + $Adds
}
```

5. Next is the **PROCESS** block. We create a **try/catch/finally** block. Within the **try** block we create a new object from the **System.IO.StreamWriter** .NET class. The first argument for this class parameter is the **$LogFile** variable and the second is **$true**. By setting the second parameter to **$true**, we specify we will *append* the string to the log file. If it was set to **$false** it would override the file content each time it is used. This is assigned to the **$Stream** variable. We use an **if/else** block with the **$Compress switch** as the expression. If it is set as an argument to the function **($true)** we compress the Json output to fit on one line in the log file. We create a string and within this string we pipe the **$Body** object to the **ConvertTo-Json** cmdlet with or without the **Compress** parameter depending on the **$Compress switch** value. We use the **WriteLine** method from the **$Stream** object and pass the Json string as the parameter to the **WriteLine** method. If the **$Stream** successfully writes the string to the file, we add a verbose output with **Write-Verbose**:

```
PROCESS {
    try
    {
        $Stream = [System.IO.StreamWriter]::new($LogFile, $true)
        if ($Compress){
            $Stream.WriteLine("$($Body | ConvertTo-Json -Compress)")
        }
        else{
            $Stream.WriteLine("$($Body | ConvertTo-Json)")
        }
        Write-Verbose "Successfully written log to file: $LogFile"
    }
}
```

6. In the **catch** block we simply catch any potential errors there might be raised while writing the log to the file, and use **Write-Error** to write this to the console and the error stream, making sure an error during logging is not terminating the entire script, logging can also fail:

```
catch{
    Write-Error "Could not create log entry: $_"
}
```

7. Within the **finally** block, we nest another **try/catch** block. In this **try** block we use the **Close** method from the **$Stream** object to properly unlock and save the file. We use the nested catch block here because if something should fail with the **$Stream** object, this object might never be created and then we would try to call the **Close** method on a **Null** value instead, since it then would not exist, which would result in an error. We do nothing in the **catch** block and simply ignores it if this should happen:

```
finally {
    try{
        $Stream.close()
    }
    catch{}
}
```

8. Within the **END** block we simply add a **Write-Verbose** statement that writes the **$LogString** variable value to the console if the function has been invoked with the **-Verbose** parameter:

```
END {
    Write-Verbose $LogString
}
```

The function ends up looking like this:

```
function Add-LogToJson {
    [CmdletBinding()]
    Param (
        [Parameter(Position = 0, Mandatory = $true, HelpMessage = "Path to logfile")]
        [String]$LogFile,
        [Parameter(Position = 1, Mandatory = $true, HelpMessage = "Message String")]
        [String]$Message,
        [Parameter(HelpMessage = "Severity Level")]
        [ValidateSet("INFO", "WARNING", "ERROR", "CRITICAL", "DEBUG", "OK")]
        [String]$Level = "INFO",
        [Parameter(HelpMessage = "Add additional key/values in form of a hashtable")]
        [Hashtable]$Adds,
        [Parameter(HelpMessage = "Compress JSON output")]
        [Switch]$Compress
    )
    BEGIN {
      if (-not(Test-Path $LogFile)) {
          New-Item -Path $LogFile -ItemType File -Force | Out-Null
          Write-Verbose "Logfile created: $LogFile"
      }
            $Time = Get-Date -Format "dd-MM-yyyy HH:mm:ss,fff"
      [String]$LogString = "$Time - $Level : $Message"
            $Body = @{ }
      $Body.Add("timestamp", $Time)
```

```powershell
        $Body.Add("message", $Message)
        $Body.Add("level", $Level)
            if ($Adds) {
            $Body = $Body + $Adds
        }
        }
    PROCESS {
        try
        {
            $Stream = [System.IO.StreamWriter]::new($LogFile, $true)
            if ($Compress){
                $Stream.WriteLine("$($Body | ConvertTo-Json -Compress)")
            }
            Else{
                $Stream.WriteLine("$($Body | ConvertTo-Json)")
            }
            Write-Verbose "Successfully written log to file: $LogFile"
        }
        catch{
            Write-Error "Could not create log entry: $_"
        }
        finally {
            try{
                $Stream.close()
            }
            catch{}
        }
    }
    END {
        Write-Verbose $LogString
    }
}
```

> **Info:** The reason for using the .NET System.IO.StreamWriter class instead of using the built-in Out-File or Add-Content cmdlets is that this low-level class is better at handling potential locked files. If you try to write to a file that is already opened by a file tailing tool, both the Out-File and Add-Content might result in an error due to the locked state of the file. The StreamWriter class handles locked files better and this behavior should not be an issue using this class instead of the cmdlets.

Note: For these examples we use the files: File1.txt, File2.txt and File3.txt that we created for the recipe: Use different techniques for handling errors that occur in background jobs, including capturing job specific errors and managing job states.

We can use this function for structured logging. We create a **Foreach** loop that loops over a few files, and we use **Get-Content** to try to get the content from each file. We use a **try/catch** block to catch potential errors. When the content is successfully extracted from a file, we invoke the **Add-LogToJson** function with a simple message. If we encounter an error, we create a Hashtable that contains additional information about the specific error. Besides a simple message statement, we also add the error message from the exception. We add the stacktrace and we add the filename and the file path. We then call the **Add-LogToJson** function with the additional parameters. We use *Error* as argument for the **Level** parameter and the Hashtable with additional information as an argument for the **Adds** parameter. Note that we set the **VerbosePreference** to **Continue** for always displaying all verbose output from commands. We could have set the **Verbose** parameter for each function call to **Add-LogToJson** instead. We also set the **$LogFile** variable with the path to the log file.

This construct is shown below:

```
$VerbosePreference = "Continue"
$LogFile = "CustomLog.json"
$Files = @("File1.txt","File2.txt","NonExistingFile.txt","File3.txt")
foreach ($File in $Files){
    try{
        $Content = Get-Content -Path $File -ErrorAction Stop
        $Message = "Content from $($File) successfully extracted: $($Content)"
        Add-LogToJson $LogFile $Message
    }
    catch{
        $Message = "Failed to load content from $($File)"
        $AddInfo = @{
            "errormessage" = $_.Exception.Message
            "stacktrace" = $_.Exception.StackTrace
            "file" = $File
            "filepath" = (Get-Location).Path
        }
        Add-LogToJson $LogFile $Message -Level ERROR -Adds $AddInfo
    }
}
```

When we execute this construct, we get the following verbose console output shown in *Figure 4.21*:

```
VERBOSE: Logfile created: CustomLog.json
VERBOSE: Successfully written log to file: CustomLog.json
VERBOSE: 02-08-2023 14:22:35,373 - INFO : Content from File1.txt successfully extracted: Content: File 1
VERBOSE: Successfully written log to file: CustomLog.json
VERBOSE: 02-08-2023 14:22:35,409 - INFO : Content from File2.txt successfully extracted: Content: File 2
VERBOSE: Successfully written log to file: CustomLog.json
VERBOSE: 02-08-2023 14:22:35,415 - ERROR : Failed to load content from NonExistingFile.txt
VERBOSE: Successfully written log to file: CustomLog.json
VERBOSE: 02-08-2023 14:22:35,417 - INFO : Content from File3.txt successfully extracted: Content: File 3
```

Figure 4.21: Verbose console output when using the Add-LogToJson function

And we get the following log entries in our new **CustomLog.json** log file as shown in *Figure 4.22*:

```
CustomLog.json - Notepad
File  Edit  Format  View  Help
{
  "timestamp": "02-08-2023 14:22:35,373",
  "level": "INFO",
  "message": "Content from File1.txt successfully extracted: Content: File 1"
}
{
  "timestamp": "02-08-2023 14:22:35,409",
  "level": "INFO",
  "message": "Content from File2.txt successfully extracted: Content: File 2"
}
{
  "errormessage": "Cannot find path 'C:\\Temp\\NonExistingFile.txt' because it does not exist.",
  "filepath": "C:\\Temp",
  "message": "Failed to load content from NonExistingFile.txt",
  "stacktrace": "    at System.Management.Automation.LocationGlobber.ExpandMshGlobPath("...Abbreviated Code")",
  "file": "NonExistingFile.txt",
  "level": "ERROR",
  "timestamp": "02-08-2023 14:22:35,415"
}
{
  "timestamp": "02-08-2023 14:22:35,417",
  "level": "INFO",
  "message": "Content from File3.txt successfully extracted: Content: File 3"
}
```

Figure 4.22: Log file output when using the Add-LogToJson function

As you can see with this custom logging function we can make structured logs for errors, events, actions, and other commands. We can invoke the function whenever needed and add custom information as we see fit, like with the example where we added additional information upon encountering an error. We provided simple information when a file was successfully processed. The more relevant information you add to logs, the easier it may be to debug and solve errors and issues. In this case, it is quite obvious that the error is because the file does not exist, but errors are often not that obvious and requires further debugging and a deeper insight into the script or application in order to figure out what might be the root cause for an error or other issue. Comprehensive logging aids a great deal with this and provides a structured way of debugging and solving errors and issues.

Conclusion

Being able to handle different kinds of errors is vital to the stability and reliability of scripts and applications, not only in PowerShell but in all programming languages in general. Errors can occur even though you might think you have done everything to prevent them. It is hard to predict all errors that might be raised during execution of your code, but you can do a lot to mitigate them as much as possible. In this chapter you have learned about different types of errors in PowerShell and about different statements and techniques that helps capturing and handle a lot of these errors, such as **try/catch/finally** blocks and the **ErrorAction** preference and parameter. You have explored the concepts of error handling in both the local script scope and within background jobs running in parallel, asynchronously with the calling script. You have gained an understanding of how to create custom error classes which can be utilized to provide advanced error information improving error messaging, providing user friendly error output and for logging purposes and more. You have also been introduced to debugging and logging concepts and learned how to create functions that help with logging errors in a structured and meaningful way. Leveraging these techniques will let you create more stable, user friendly and reliable scripts and applications.

The next chapter focuses on a range of different scripting techniques that are common among different programming languages but with a focus on such techniques tailored specifically for PowerShell. The chapter covers topics such as script parameters, parameter validation, string manipulation and formatting techniques and scripting for cross-platform compatibility. Additionally, it introduces the reader to PowerShell execution policies and script signing for enhancing script security. Furthermore, the chapter dives deeper into the creation of PowerShell modules and repositories which are essential for organizing and distributing PowerShell code efficiently.

Join our book's Discord space

Join the book's Discord Workspace for Latest updates, Offers, Tech happenings around the world, New Release and Sessions with the Authors:

https://discord.bpbonline.com

CHAPTER 5
Scripting Techniques

Introduction

Being able to utilize different scripting techniques is an important part of being a great developer. There are a lot of different techniques that cover all aspects of coding, and such techniques differ in each programming language. Most languages utilize script and application parameters for providing arguments upon execution. They all have methods for manipulating and formatting strings and a lot of them can be used to create platform independent scripts and applications. All of them use some form of libraries and modules and most of them have methods for signing and validating code. Even though the overall objective for each of these topics is the same across different programming languages, each language have their own specific and specialized methods. We will have a closer look into these topics within this chapter and learn how to work with those tailored specifically for PowerShell, building upon your skillset to better optimize and organize your code, streamline processes, ensure compatibility across platforms, and incorporate some security measures in the forms of execution policies and by signing scripts.

Structure

The chapter covers the following topics:

- Script parameters, parameter validation and attributes
    - **Recipe 27**: Validating script parameters using validation attributes

- Advanced string manipulation and formatting techniques

  o **Recipe 28**: Use advanced techniques for manipulating and formatting strings

- Scripting for cross-platform compatibility

  o **Recipe 29**: Techniques for writing cross platform scripts

- PowerShell execution policy and script signing

  o **Recipe 30**: Working with execution policies on Windows systems.

  o **Recipe 31**: Script signing for security purposes and signing scripts using code signing certificates.

- PowerShell modules and repositories

  o **Recipe 32**: Creating modules, module manifest files and using module within scripts

  o **Recipe 33**: Learn to package modules and work with packaged modules and repositories

Objectives

In this chapter you will learn how to create and validate script parameters using validation attributes and how to format and manipulate strings. We will glance at cross platform compatibility with PowerShell, and you will learn how to make scripts that works on multiple platforms such as Windows, Linux and MacOS. You will learn about code signing and how to sign scripts with code signing certificates and about the PowerShell execution policy. You will also be introduced to PowerShell modules and learn how to create modules for code reusability and organization, and how to package modules and create repositories for module distribution.

Script parameters, parameter validation and attributes

Parameters can be added to functions, script blocks and classes making them dynamic customizing their behavior without modifying their code. parameter input is provided in the form of arguments, as we have seen in *Chapter 2, Advanced PowerShell functions*. Argument input can be provided to parameters, both by users but also passed from other functions and commands and even through the pipeline.

We can also add parameters to scripts enabling them to accept argument input upon their execution. As with parameters within functions and other commands, we can add validation and we can specify attributes like `position`, `mandatory` and `helpmessage` and so on for the script parameters. Not only are we able to utilize parameters directly in scripts, but we can also add the **CmdletBinding** attribute and utilize the features it provides, such as adding **verbose** output and set the **ErrorAction** parameter when executing a script. You can execute a script with different input which results in different outcomes, depending on specific requirements you might have. Using parameters makes your scripts much more versatile and dynamic and you can determine what should happen depending on external circumstances or specific user input upon the invocation of a script.

Recipe 27: Validating script parameters using validation attributes.

Just as with functions and script blocks, for scripts, we initiate parameters with the use of the **param** block. This is usually placed at the start of the script and if you need to add the **CmdletBinding** attribute you would place this right above the param block. We are going to create a script called **RandomPass.ps1** it is essentially a random password generator. We are going to build upon this script as we progress through this recipe. The first thing we do is to add the **CmdletBinding** attribute and then create a param block with a few simple parameters as shown below:

```
[CmdletBinding()]
param (
    [int]$Length = 12,
    [string]$SpecialChars = "!@#$%",
    [switch]$ExcludeUpperCase,
    [switch]$ExcludeLowerCase,
    [switch]$ExcludeDigits,
    [switch]$ExcludeSpecialChars
)
```

By adding the **CmdletBinding** attribute and the param block with parameters we can see in *Figure 5.1* that we are now able to use these parameters and **CmdletBinding** features when we invoke our script:

```
PS C:\Temp> .\RandomPass.ps1 -Length 10 -SpecialChars "@#$" -ExcludeUpperCase -Verbose -ErrorAction "Stop"
```

*Figure 5.1: Script accepting parameters after adding
the CmdletBinding attribute and param block with parameters*

Currently the **Length** parameter accepts any integer and defaults to **12**, and the **SpecialChars** parameter accepts basically any string with characters and is provided with a default character set. Since we are going to create a random password generator, we should limit the **Length** parameter, so a generated password has a maximum length, we set this as **63**. We should also give it a minimum length, so it does not create vulnerable passwords, we set this as **8**. You might have noticed that these are the character limits for WIFI passwords used by the WPA2/WPA3 (Personal) security protocols that are designed for securing wireless networks. For implementing these updates, we can add validation to the parameter, by adding a validation attribute and since we are going to have a range of integers, we can use the **ValidateRange** attribute. For the **SpecialChars** parameter, we keep the current default characters, but we add a limit to the characters that are valid to a specific sub-set of characters, if we want to add a set of custom special characters instead of using the defaults. We should be able to use the following characters as valid characters for the **SpecialChars** parameter: **!@#£$€%&(){}[]**. For validating these, we could use the **ValidateSet** attribute, here we would add all characters one-by-one as strings to the validation attribute like this: **[ValidateSet("!", "@", "#", "£", "$", "€", "%", "&", "(", ")", "{", "}", "[", "]")]** but we could also use the **ValidatePattern** attribute instead and then create a RegEx (regular expression) pattern that would match all these characters. Note that creating RegEx patterns are outside of the scope of this book. There are many RegEx generators available online. What we basically need is a pattern that will match all characters in a string, in our case a string containing characters we have determined to be valid for this parameter and validate them against the specified RegEx pattern set in the **ValidatePattern** attribute. Using a random online RegEx generator **(https://regex101.com)** we have calculated this pattern **^[!@#£$€%&(){}\[\]]*$**. We add these validation attributes to the parameters:

```
[CmdletBinding()]

param (
    [ValidateRange(8, 63)]
    [int]$Length = 12,
    [ValidatePattern("^[!@#£$€%&(){}\[\]]*$")]
    [string]$SpecialChars = "!@#$%",
    [switch]$ExcludeUpperCase,
    [switch]$ExcludeLowerCase,
    [switch]$ExcludeDigits,
    [switch]$ExcludeSpecialChars
)
```

Now, invoking our script with an argument to the **Length** parameter that is out of the specified valid range, would result in an error. The same goes for a string argument to the **SpecialChars** parameter, that does not contain valid characters as specified in the pattern. *Figure 5.2* shows three attempts to invoke the script. The first attempt is with invalid special characters provided to the **SpecialChars** parameter, the second attempt is with an invalid integer provided for the **Length** parameter and the third attempt is with valid arguments for both parameters:

```
PS C:\Temp> .\RandomPass.ps1 -Length 8 -SpecialChars "ABC"
RandomPass.ps1: Cannot validate argument on parameter 'SpecialChars'. The argument "ABC"
does not match the "^[!@#£$€%&(){}\[\]]*$" pattern. Supply an argument that matches "^[!@
#£$€%&(){}\[\]]*$" and try the command again.
PS C:\Temp> .\RandomPass.ps1 -Length 6 -SpecialChars "!@#£$€%&(){}[]"
RandomPass.ps1: Cannot validate argument on parameter 'Length'. The 6 argument is less th
an the minimum allowed range of 8. Supply an argument that is greater than or equal to 8
and then try the command again.
PS C:\Temp> .\RandomPass.ps1 -Length 20 -SpecialChars "!@#£$€%&(){}[]"
v@2AXJD%iH}C€pr[o]6e
```

Figure 5.2: Running script with parameter validation attributes
where both invalid and valid arguments are provided

Using script parameters with validation ensures that a script can only be invoked and started using valid arguments. If invalid arguments are provided, the script will never run since it results in an error. Invoking a script with incorrect arguments, where the parameters have no validation, could lead to unexpected behavior upon script execution. Imagine if you have a script that must access a specific server using PowerShell remoting, let us call this server **Server001**.

The script might make changes on the server that generally would have a destructive behavior but it needs to be performed on that specific server for some (undefined) specific reason. It could be that we needed to format a disk connected as the D: drive on **Server001**. Invoking the script with a server parameter would connect to the server provided as argument and then format the drive without confirming that it is actually connected to the correct server. If the right prerequisites are present on another server, in short, if another server called **Server002** is accessible through remoting like **Server001**, and you then invoked the script with **Server002** as an argument instead of **Server001**. You would end up formatting the drive on the wrong server with severe consequences to follow. By providing validation to the parameter, we could ensure that only specific server names can be provided as valid arguments, ensuring an error will be raised and the script will never be invoked on the wrong server. This provides some context as to the benefits of using validation, not only for script parameters but in general where applicable. A good best practice would be to always analyze input that should be provided for scripts and also generally for commands and other constructs that use parameters, and approach it from a *least privileged* perspective, meaning that you should create validation rules that only accepts exactly the input that is required. In the case with the server script, it would be a **ValidationSet** attribute that would only accept certain specific server names.

Some parameter attributes can also be used as a form of parameter validation such as the **mandatory** attribute. By setting this attribute you ensure that an argument must be provided for the parameter or else the script will prompt you for providing it instead, so the script cannot be invoked before an argument is passed to that parameter. Combining validation attributes with the mandatory parameter not only ensures that an argument must be provided but also that the argument is valid accordingly to the validation attribute that is specified:

```
[CmdletBinding()]
param (
    [Parameter(Mandatory = $true, Position = 0)]
    [ValidateRange(8, 63)]
    [int]$Length,
    [Parameter(Position = 1)]
    [ValidatePattern("^[!@#£$€%&(){}\[\]]*$")]
    [string]$SpecialChars = "!@#$%",
        [switch]$ExcludeUpperCase,
    [switch]$ExcludeLowerCase,
    [switch]$ExcludeDigits,
    [switch]$ExcludeSpecialChars
)
```

As you can see above, we have added the **mandatory** attribute to the **Length** parameter. Now if we invoke the script without providing an argument for the **Length** parameter, we will be prompted to enter one before the script continues execution. *Figure 5.3* shows what happens when the script is invoked without any arguments. A prompt appears stating that you must supply a value for the **Length** parameter. As soon as a valid value is provided, the script will continue its execution, as long as it is validated by the validation attribute:

```
PS C:\Temp> .\RandomPass.ps1

cmdlet RandomPass.ps1 at command pipeline position 1
Supply values for the following parameters:
Length: 45
jk!Uqa0I8p23#loKDFOXY7trsQ9NJgyvH6TLf@mehR$ZS
```

Figure 5.3: The output of running the RandomPass.ps1 script without parameters

For optimizing the script parameters, we have also added the **position** attribute so that we can provide arguments to the parameters without stating the parameter names. This has nothing to do with parameter validation though and is purely for making it easier invoking the script. You might also have noticed that we have four **switch** parameters in the script. We do not set any parameter or validation attributes for these, since they are only used as on/off switches for certain code, in this case for excluding specific character sets when they are set upon invoking the script. The entire script is shown below:

```
[CmdletBinding()]
param (
    [Parameter(Mandatory = $true, Position = 0)]
    [ValidateRange(8, 63)]
    [int]$Length,
```

```
    [Parameter(Position = 1)]
    [ValidatePattern("^[!@#£$€%&(){}\[\]]*$")]
    [string]$SpecialChars = "!@#$%",
    [switch]$ExcludeUpperCase,
    [switch]$ExcludeLowerCase,
    [switch]$ExcludeDigits,
    [switch]$ExcludeSpecialChars
)
$CharSet = ""
if (-not $ExcludeUpperCase) { $CharSet += "ABCDEFGHIJKLMNOPQRSTUVWXYZ" }
if (-not $ExcludeLowerCase) { $CharSet += "abcdefghijklmnopqrstuvwxyz" }
if (-not $ExcludeDigits) { $CharSet += "0123456789" }
if (-not $ExcludeSpecialChars) { $CharSet += $SpecialChars }
Write-Verbose "CharSet: $CharSet"
$Password = -join (Get-Random -Count $Length -InputObject $CharSet.ToCharArray())
Write-Output $Password
```

To give a summary of this script, we start by adding the **CmdletBinding** attribute and the parameter block with the parameters. We then assign an empty string to the **$CharSet** variable. This is the placeholder for the character sets we use for creating the password. We create four **if** blocks, each for a specific character set. Upper case characters, lower case characters, digits and one for the special characters in the **$SpecialChars** variable. Each **if** block use the **-not** operator to express that it should evaluate the inverse of the provided variable value, and each variable in the **if** blocks match the **switch** parameters. So, they would state that: *if not the $ExcludeUpperCase switch is provided, add this character set to the* **$CharSet** *variable*, and so forth for each **if** block with the respective character set.

> **info: Instead of using if blocks, we could also have used a switch statement for including and excluding specific character sets.**

If none of the **switch** parameters are provided, it will add all character sets to the **$CharSet** variable. We add a verbose statement that would show the used character set if the **-Verbose** parameter is provided when the script is invoked. We create the password and assign it to the **$Password** variable. This is created in one statement, the easiest would be to walk through this backwards. Inside the parenthesis we use the **ToCharArray** method on the **$CharSet** string and return it as a **string array** which is then the **InputObject** for the **Get-Random** cmdlet. We then take **$Length** random characters from the string array and since they are returned as a new array, we use the **-join** operator to join them into a single string, this is the random password which value is assigned to the **$Password** variable. In the last statement we use **Write-Output** to write the **$Password** to the console. If we invoke the script with a length argument value of 25 and with the **verbose** parameter, we get output as shown in *Figure 5.4*:

```
PS C:\Temp> .\RandomPass.ps1 25 -Verbose
VERBOSE: CharSet: ABCDEFGHIJKLMNOPQRSTUVWXYZabcdefghijklmnopqrstuvwxyz0123456789!@#$%
dWKXpQHm6hu0CsboyAj7rMk@9
```

Figure 5.4: Output running the RandomPass.ps1 script

The **Write-Output** cmdlet not only shows the provided string object in the console, but also returns the string object, so we could use the output from the script as input for passing it through the pipeline to other cmdlets, functions, and scripts. In *Figure 5.5*, we pipe the output from our script to the **ConvertTo-SecureString** cmdlet and then save the output as a secure string, in a variable:

```
PS C:\Temp> $SecurePassword = .\RandomPass.ps1 25 | ConvertTo-SecureString -AsPlainText -Force
PS C:\Temp> $SecurePassword
System.Security.SecureString
```

*Figure 5.5: Passing output from RandomPass.ps1 script through
the pipeline to other cmdlets, functions, and scripts*

Adding parameters to scripts enables you to dynamically change the outcome depending on the provided arguments without changing the logic inside the script. However, when you enable your scripts with parameters and can provide arguments to change the outcome, it does matter what kind of arguments you provide them with. You would not want to provide the wrong kind of input since it could lead to unexpected and unwanted behavior. Let us say that you have a simple script that would add two numbers together and the resulting number should be used in another script or command for handling some important tasks. Theoretically, the resulting number might be used for setting a specific number of rotations per minute for a large industrial turbine. This turbine has a max number of rotations before it would break in a destructive manner.

What would happen if you had no validation for the size of the numbers you can provide for your addition script, and you by mistake provided the number 1000 instead of 100 as one of the integer arguments? You would then increase the turbine rotation with a greater rotation number than is actually permitted by the turbine, which would lead to a catastrophe! Setting a limit with a validation attribute for the parameters would prevent this from happening because you can account for the largest possible number that your script will output after the addition, and your script would not be invoked at all if you provided an invalid integer as one of the argument values. Keeping this scenario in mind, we can see how important it can be to add validation to parameters. There are many reasons why you would add validation to parameters in scripts, and a common best practice would be to always make sure that your script parameters have some sort of validation and only can accept the specified kind of data it needs to handle. The less validation your parameters have the more likely it as that you will encounter some sort of error or unexpected behavior at some point.

Table 5.1 shows the PowerShell validation attributes available for parameters:

Attribute	Description	Example
ValidateCount	Minimum and maximum numbers of elements in an array	ValidateCount(2,5)
ValidateDrive	Allowed drive letters in a path	ValidateDrive("C","D","Cert")
ValidateLength	Minimum and maximum length of a string	ValidateLentgh(8,63)
ValidateNotNull	Must not be $null	ValidateNotNull()
ValidateNoNull OrEmpty	Must not be $null or empty	ValidatNotNullOrEmpty()
ValidatePattern	Must match the RegEx pattern	ValidatePattern("^[!@#£$€%&(){}[\]]*$")
ValidateRange	Must be a number in the range	ValidateRange(8,63)
ValidateScript	Provided scriptblock must be evaluated to $true	ValidateScript({Test-Path $_})
ValidateSet	Must match one of the listed strings	ValidateSet("One","Two", "Three")

Table 5.1: *PowerShell validation attributes for parameters*

Advanced string manipulation and formatting techniques

Strings are one of the most common data types used in programming in general and they are the foundation for working with text-based data. Being able to manipulate and format strings is crucial for creating dynamic and adaptable code.

String manipulation is the process of modifying, extracting, and transforming strings to get specific outcome, by changing its content or structure to meet certain requirements, whereas string formatting is about controlling how data is presented in strings using placeholders and then replace these with different values from variables and other commands. You can say that we are using strings as templates and then later format them with proper data.

Examples of string manipulation: Using string concatenation for combining different strings into a new single string. Using search and replace, where you search for a specific text inside a string and replace it with another text. Using string methods for string conversions and extracting substrings from strings and using regular expressions for string pattern matching for searching, extracting, and replacing specific text patterns within strings.

Examples of string formatting: Using string interpolation to embed variables directly into strings. Using subexpressions to embed expressions directly into strings. Using escaping to escape special characters like newline and tab characters and using complex formatting with formatting operators and formatting methods.

Recipe 28: Use advanced techniques for manipulating and formatting strings

Strings can be manipulated and formatted in many ways, and it is essential for developers to know about and be able to use different techniques for manipulating and formatting strings to create strong and dynamic scripts and applications that utilizes text data. In this recipe you will learn different techniques for manipulating and formatting strings.

> **Note: For the following code examples in this recipe, we are going to add the output directly in the code block instead of adding an image figure for each example output!**

Different techniques for manipulating strings:

String concatenation

Concatenation is about combining multiple strings into a single new string. The most common method for concatenating strings in PowerShell is by using the + operator:

```
# String concatenation (+ operator)
$First = "Lightning"
$Last = "Girl"
$Name = $First + " " + $Last
PS C:\Temp> $Name
Lightning Girl
```

Here we are concatenating three strings into one. The first string is the **$First** variable value, the second is a string with a single space and the third is the **$Last** variable value.

String search and replace

Being able to search for and replace specific text or words inside strings is a quite powerful string manipulation technique. There are three ways of using search and replace in PowerShell. The string method **Replace()**, the **-replace** operator and the **-ireplace** operator. They are all used for replacing occurrences of a specific text or word within a string. The **Replace()** method is a simple case sensitive search and replacement method, whereas the **-replace** operator is a **RegEx** based operator used for pattern matching and provides more complex search and replace features. The **-ireplace** operator is basically the same as the **-replace** operator with the difference that it is case-insensitive. Below are examples using each of these methods:

```
# String search and replace (String method)
$Text = "These superheroes are Villains: Comet, Lightning Girl"
$Text = $Text.Replace("Villains", "Heroes")
PS C:\Temp> $Text
These superheroes are Heroes: Comet, Lightning Girl
# String search and replace (Operator)
$Text = "These superheroes are Villains: Comet, Lightning Girl"
$Text = $Text -replace "Villains", "Heroes"
PS C:\Temp> $Text
These superheroes are Heroes: Comet, Lightning Girl
# Above, both the Replace() method and -replace operator are used to simply
replace a word with another within the string:
# String search and replace (Operator - Case-Insensitive)
$Text = "These superheroes are Villains: Comet, Lightning Girl"
$Text = $Text -ireplace "villains", "heroes"
PS C:\Temp> $Text
These superheroes are heroes: Comet, Lightning Girl
```

In the above example, we are using the **-ireplace** method instead of the **-replace** method. They are almost the same and the only difference is that **-ireplace** is the case-insensitive equivalent to **-replace**:

```
# String search and replace (Operator - RegEx Pattern)
$Text = "Comet has 47 HitPoints, Lightning Girl has 25 HitPoints"
$Text = $Text -replace "\d+", "50"
PS C:\Temp> $Text
Comet has 50 HitPoints, Lightning Girl has 50 HitPoints
```

In the above example, we are using a simple **RegEx** pattern for replacing all grouped digits with **50**. This is only possible with the **-replace** operator due to its pattern matching abilities, this is not possible with the string **Replace()** method.

Substring extraction

Extracting a specific portion of a string can be useful if you need to parse or extract specific data from a text. The string **SubString()** method is used for this. The method takes one or two arguments. The first being the start position index within the text, or string, where the extraction should begin from. The second argument is the number of characters to extract. The **Length**. If the second argument is omitted, the substring will extend to the end of the original string. Below are different examples using this method:

```
# Substring extraction (String method, two arguments)
```

```
$Text = "Lightning Girl meets Comet"
$Substring = $Text.Substring(10,4)
PS C:\Temp> $Substring
Girl
# Substring extraction (String method, one argument)
$Text = "Lightning Girl meets Comet"
$Substring = $Text.Substring(10)
PS C:\Temp> $Substring
Girl meets Comet
```

Regular expressions

Using regular expressions for string pattern matching is a powerful way for searching strings for complex types of text data such as email addresses, IP addresses and MAC addresses especially from larger text strings or from text in files. There are a few methods for searching a string with regular expression patterns such as the **Select-String** cmdlet. This is mostly used for searching for patterns within files but, can also be used for searching for patterns inside strings which is also referred to as in-memory search. Another method is to use the static **Matches** method of the **System.Text.RegularExpression.Regex** .NET class. Using this method returns a collection of **Match** objects, with the matches found with the **RegEx** pattern, from a string. Each **Match** object has a value property containing the found text. We can use this method to search for specific patterns and then iterate through the returned object and extract all found matches which can then be saved into an array or used for values in other strings etc. The **Matches** method takes two arguments, the first one is the string to search within, and the second is the regex pattern to use for searching the string.

> **Note: For the regular expression examples, each specific regular expression has been found via google searches and are commonly available on several sites. The calculation of specific complex regular expressions is out of the scope of this book.**

```
$Text = "My personal email is email@home.com and my work email is email@
work.com"
$Emails = [regex]::Matches($Text, "[a-zA-Z0-9._%+-]+@[a-zA-Z0-9.-]+\.
[a-zA-Z]{2,}") | ForEach-Object { $_.Value }
PS C:\Temp> $Emails
email@home.com
email@work.com
```

In the above code, we searched for all email addresses in the **$Text** string using the regular expression. We collect all found matches values and store them into an array assigned to the **$Emails** variable by piping the result from the **Matches** method to **Foreach-Object** and extract the value property from all found matches:

```
$Text = "Server 1: 192.168.1.100, Server 2: 10.0.0.2, Gateway: 172.16.0.1"
```

```
$IPAddresses = [regex]::Matches($Text, "\b(?:\d{1,3}\.){3}\d{1,3}\b") |
ForEach-Object { $_.Value }
```

```
PS C:\Temp> $IPAddresses
```

```
192.168.1.100
```

```
10.0.0.2
```

```
172.16.0.1
```

```
$Text = "Device 1: AA:BB:CC:DD:EE:FF, Device 2: 11:22:33:44:55:66, Device
3: 00:11:22:33:44:55"
```

```
$MACAddresses = [regex]::Matches($Text, "([0-9A-Fa-f]{2}[:-]){5}
([0-9A-Fa-f]{2})") | ForEach-Object { $_.Value }
```

```
PS C:\Temp> $MACAddresses
```

```
AA:BB:CC:DD:EE:FF
```

```
11:22:33:44:55:66
```

```
00:11:22:33:44:55
```

The principle in the other examples is the same as the first one, though instead of searching for email addresses, we have updated the regular expressions with patterns to search for IP addresses, and in the last example, for MAC addresses. As you can see using regular expressions, searching strings for complex text patterns such as emails, IP addresses and MAC addresses is a quite powerful technique. In some scenarios it can be complicated though, due to the complexity of the regular expressions you might need, it is about finding a balance between spending time on calculating or finding a complex regular expression that will match the pattern requirements for your specific strings, and the importance of the specific text you need to extract from the string. Sometimes, it might not be worthwhile spending the time calculating or finding the correct regular expression that will be a viable pattern for your use case, it might be easier to use other methods for finding a specific string rather than finding a complex "regular expression, it comes down to weighing the cost versus the benefits. When you come accross new regular expressions, you should save them in a document for later use, they might come in handy at a later time.

Splitting strings

You might need to split a string into an array of substrings. You can use either the **Split()** string method or the **-split** operator. The **Split()** method takes a single argument in the form of a delimiter character and splits a string into substrings at the delimiter and returns an array of the substrings. The **-split** operator only takes a single argument as the delimiter but for the operator the delimiter can be a more complex regular expression pattern which provides more flexibility when splitting strings. If you need multiple delimiter characters or more complex patterns that involve spacing and other characters, then you should use the **-split** operator. This also returns an array with substrings.

If you only need to split a string with a simple single delimiter the **Split()** method is preferred, and if you need more complex split delimiter patterns, you should use the **-split** operator instead:

```
# Splitting string using Split() method
$Text = "Comet;Lightning Girl;Blue Ghost;Evilin"
$Array = $Text.Split(";")
PS C:\Temp> $Array
Comet
Lightning Girl
Blue Ghost
Evilin
# Splitting string using -split operator
$Text = "Comet;Lightning Girl;Blue Ghost;Evilin"
$Array = $Text -split ";"
PS C:\Temp> $Array
Comet
Lightning Girl
Blue Ghost
Evilin
# Splitting string using -split operator and regex delimiter pattern
$Text = "Comet;Lightning Girl,Blue Ghost#Evilin"
$Array = $Text -split "[;,#]"
PS C:\Temp> $Array
Comet
Lightning Girl
Blue Ghost
Evilin
```

Joining strings

An array of strings can be joined together to form a single string with a delimiter using the **-join** operator. This is another method for concatenating multiple strings into one single string. The **-join** operator takes a single argument in the form of a delimiter character. The delimiter can also be an empty string for combining the substrings to a single string without any space between the substrings:

```
# Joining string array with -join operator and ; as delimiter
$Array = @(
    "Comet",
```

```
    "Lightning Girl",
    "Blue Ghost",
    "Evilin"
    )
$Text = $Array -join ";"
PS C:\Temp> $Text
Comet;Lightning Girl;Blue Ghost;Evilin
# Joining string array with -join operator and empty string as delimiter
$Array = @(
    "Comet",
    "Lightning Girl",
    "Blue Ghost",
    "Evilin"
    )
$Text = $Array -join ""
PS C:\Temp> $Text
CometLightning GirlBlue GhostEvilin
```

Other string manipulation methods

There are several other string methods that can be used for manipulating strings. We are going to look at a few examples.

The string **Trim()** method can be used to remove unwanted whitespace or other specific characters at the start and the end of a string. Trimming without any arguments defaults to only removing whitespace, but you can add a specific character as an argument and trim that specific character. You can also use a regex pattern as an argument to trim multiple characters:

```
# Using string Trim() method to remove only whitespace
$Text = "    Villains vs. Heroes        "
$Text = $Text.Trim()
PS C:\Temp> $Text
Villains vs. Heroes
# Using string Trim() method to remove only *
$Text = "***    Villains vs. Heroes        ***"
$Text = $Text.Trim("*")
PS C:\Temp> $Text
```

```
    Villains vs. Heroes
# Using string Trim() method with pattern to remove whitespace and *
$Text = "***     Villains vs. Heroes        ***"
$Text = $Text.Trim("[* ]")
PS C:\Temp> $Text
Villains vs. Heroes
```

There is also a **TrimEnd()** method that only removes all trailing whitespace characters from a string and a **TrimStart()** method that only removes all leading whitespace characters from a string.

The **ToUpper()** and **ToLower()** string methods can be used to convert strings to either uppercase or lowercase characters:

```
# String conversion to UPPERCASE
$Text = "Comet is a Hero"
$Text = $Text.ToUpper()
PS C:\Temp> $Text
COMET IS A HERO
# String conversion to lowercase
$Text = "COMET is a Hero"
$Text = $Text.ToLower()
PS C:\Temp> $Text
comet is a hero
```

You can align a string within a specified width and add characters as padding for alignment, using the **PadLeft()** and **PadRight()** string methods:

```
# Left aligned padding with PadLeft() method
$Text = "Lightning Girl"
$Text = $Text.PadLeft(20)
PS C:\Temp> """$Text"""
"      Lightning Girl"
# Right aligned padding with PadRight() method
$Text = "Lightning Girl"
$Text = $Text.PadRight(20)
PS C:\Temp> """$Text"""
"Lightning Girl      "
# Using * as padding character
$Text = "Lightning Girl"
```

```
$Text = $Text.PadRight(20, "*")
PS C:\Temp> """$Text"""
"Lightning Girl******"
# Add equally left and right aligned padding with * as padding character
$Text = "Lightning Girl"
$Padding = 20
$Text = $Text.PadLeft($Padding,"*").PadRight($Padding+($Padding-$Text.
Length),"*")
PS C:\Temp> """$Text"""
"*****Lightning Girl*****"
```

Note: The use of the triple double quotes used for escaping the double quote characters is so they can be written to console output as a part of the string. This makes the output string more more readable in the examples.

Different techniques for formatting strings: String interpolation

String interpolation is about embedding variables directly into strings. When you have a double quoted string, you can directly embed variables into it. The variable will then be replaced by its value upon evaluation. String interpolation does not work on single quoted strings as they preserve the literal characters within the string and do not expand variables or interpret escape characters. Using string interpolation eliminates the need for complex concatenation and makes the code more readable:

```
# String interpolation with string variables
$Hero = "Comet"
$Villain = "Evilin"
$Text = "The hero is: $Hero and the villain is: $Villain"
PS C:\Temp> $Text
The hero is: Comet and the villain is: Evilin
# String interpolation with different datatype variables
$String = "Superhero"
$Integer = 25
$Bool = $true
$Text = "This is a string: $String This is an integer: $Integer and this is
a bool: $Bool"
PS C:\Temp> $Text
This is a string: Superhero This is an integer: 25 and this is a bool: True
```

Complex string formatting using the -f operator

The **-f** operator allows you to format strings by using placeholders that are replaced by variables. The placeholders are represented inside a string by index numbers in curly braces, like: **{0}, {1}** and so on. Each number would correspond to the index number in the **-f** operators argument list. It takes as many arguments as there are placeholders. A feature that makes the **-f** operator extra powerful is the use of format specifiers, which are patterns that can be provided to the placeholders, so you can control how values are represented when a string is evaluated. Format specifiers are most used for formatting numbers with specific decimal places, displaying dates and times in different formats and for padding strings or numbers with spaces or zeros. You provide the format specifier in the placeholder after the index divided with a colon like this: **{0:N}**. You can use the **-f** operator with both single and double quoted strings to replace the placeholders:

```
# String formatting with the -f operator
$Hero = "Comet"
$Villain = "Evilin"
$Text = "The hero is: {0} and the villain is: {1}" -f $Hero, $Villain
PS C:\Temp> $Text
The hero is: Comet and the villain is: Evilin
# String formatting with the -f operator and the Number (N) format specifier
[double]$Float = 3.16543
$Text = "The villain has {0:N2}% chance of beating this hero" -f $Float
PS C:\Temp> $Text
The villain has 3,17% chance of beating this hero
# String formatting with the -f operator and a Custom  format specifier
$Date = Get-Date
$Text = "A new superhero is born the {0:dd-MM-yyyy} at {1:HH:mm:ss}" -f $Date, $Date
PS C:\Temp> $Text
A new superhero is born the 08-08-2023 at 14:47:06
```

More information about the available format specifiers can be found in the original .NET documentation:

- Standard numeric format strings:

  https://learn.microsoft.com/en-us/dotnet/standard/base-types/standard-numeric-format-strings

- Custom date and time format strings:

  https://learn.microsoft.com/en-us/dotnet/standard/base-types/custom-date-and-time-format-strings

Subexpression operator

The subexpression operator: **$()** allows for almost any valid PowerShell code to be embedded, expressed, and evaluated within strings. The results of the evaluated expressions are then substituted into the string. This is useful for incorporating dynamic values or for performing calculations inside strings:

```
# Using subexpression operator to evaluate expression
$Hero = [PSCustomObject]@{
    Strength = 55
    Level = 7
}
$Text = "The hero´s total power is: $($Hero.Strength * $Hero.Level)"
PS C:\Temp> $Text
The hero´s total power is: 385
# Using subexpression operator to evaluate command
function New-Date{
    return Get-Date -f "dd-MM-yyyy HH:mm:ss"
}
$Text = "A new hero is born: $(New-Date)"
PS C:\Temp> $Text
A new hero is born: 09-08-2023 09:25:30
# Using subexpression operator to evaluate command
$Text = "StatusCode: $( (Invoke-WebRequest google.com).StatusCode )"
PS C:\Temp> $Text
StatusCode: 200
```

String escaping and special characters

Special characters need to be escaped when used inside strings using the backtick (`` ` ``) character. You can use special escape sequences like the newline (`` `n ``) and the tab (`` `t ``) sequences:

```
$Text = "Backtics can be used to escape `"quotes`" inside strings"
PS C:\Temp> $Text
Backtics can be used to escape "quotes" inside strings
$Text = "`"And in escape sequences like newlines`nand tabs`twhich is cool`""
PS C:\Temp> $Text
"And in escape sequences like newlines
and tabs   which is cool"
```

Check the official documentation for more special characters and escape sequences:

https://learn.microsoft.com/en-us/powershell/module/microsoft.powershell.core/ about/about_special_characters

Here-strings and multiline formatting

A here string is a multi-lined string. What makes this type of string special is that you can span code across multiple lines without the need for escaping special characters and line breaks. A double quoted here-string works like a double quoted string and will evaluate interpolated variables and subexpressions. A single quoted here-string preserves the literal characters and do not evaluate variables or subexpressions. You can still use the format operator in both single and double quoted Here-Strings.

> **Note: Here-strings preserves all whitespace including tabs and spaces within them, so it will adhere to the left side of the script. If you indent the text within, the indentation will carry to the output string.**

Below are different examples of using here-strings:

```
$Hero = "Comet"
$Text = @"
Double quoted Here-strings are perfect for creating multiline strings.
You can interpolate variables: $Hero
use subexpressions: $(Get-Date)
and even use the format {0}.
"@ -f "operator"
PS C:\Temp> $Text
Here strings are perfect for creating multiline strings.
You can interpolate variables: Comet
use subexpressions: 08/09/2023 10:02:39
and even use the format operator
inside a here-string.
$Hero = "Comet"
$Text = @'
Single quoted Here-strings are perfect for creating multiline strings.
But you cannot interpolate variables: $Hero
or use subexpressions: $(Get-Date)
But you can still use the format {0}.
'@ -f "operator"
PS C:\Temp> $Text
Single quoted Here-strings are perfect for creating multiline strings.
```

```
But you cannot interpolate variables: $Hero
or use subexpressions: $(Get-Date)
But you can still use the format operator.
```

Strings are a fundamental part of scripting and by being able to utilize string manipulation and formatting techniques, you can work effectively with textual data and create dynamic, robust and user-friendly scripts and applications. This also allows you to provide conditions for optimal data presentation for users of your scripts and applications.

Scripting for cross-platform compatibility

PowerShell core, currently known as PowerShell 7, introduced cross-platform scripting, enabling the creation of scripts that can be executed on multiple operating systems such as Windows, MacOS and Linux. PowerShell is primarily built for Windows so, there are a few things to be aware of and some best practices to follow, when it comes to creating scripts cross-platform compatible. In the next recipe, we will go through some of the best practices and dive into what it takes to make cross platform scripts.

Recipe 29: Techniques for writing cross platform scripts

Writing cross platform PowerShell scripts requires some extra care and attention to detail but by following some techniques and best practices you will be able to create scripts that can be executed on multiple platforms. In this recipe we look at such techniques and best practices and learn how to utilize and incorporate these to create cross-platform scripts.

> **Note: In this recipe we use Windows 10 and Linux Ubuntu 22.04 as platforms, but all examples should also be applicable to MacOS where non-Windows platform specific cmdlets are used.**

Use PowerShell 7

PowerShell 7 is the version that makes cross platform compatibility possible, and it supports Windows, MacOS and Linux. Make sure to use PowerShell 7.x.x and preferably the newest version. Official versions and installation guides for the different platforms can be found here:

For Windows:

https://learn.microsoft.com/en-us/powershell/scripting/install/installing-powershell-on-windows

For Linux (Ubuntu):

https://learn.microsoft.com/en-us/powershell/scripting/install/install-ubuntu

For MacOS:

https://learn.microsoft.com/en-us/powershell/scripting/install/installing-powershell-on-macos

Avoid using platform specific cmdlets and commands

PowerShell has several cmdlets that are Windows Specific such as cmdlets for handling Active Directory and HyperV, these will not work on other platforms and should be avoided when scripting for cross platform compatibility. You can use the **Get-Command** cmdlet to see the available cmdlets and functions on a specific platform. Also, note that not all **PSDrives** are available across different platforms. Windows specific drives such as the **Cert: WSMan:** and **Registry:** drives are not available on other platforms than Windows. Avoid using any platform specific cmdlets and commands in general when scripting for cross platform compatibility, including the use of **WMI** and **CIM** which are also not available on non-Windows platforms. As you can see in the next figures, using the **Get-WinEvent** cmdlet, which retrieves logs from the Windows Event viewer, only works on Windows as shown in *Figure 5.6*:

```
PS C:\Temp> Get-Winevent -LogName System | Select-Object -First 1

    ProviderName: Microsoft-Windows-Kernel-General

TimeCreated                  Id LevelDisplayName Message
-----------                  -- ---------------- -------
09-08-2023 20:48:19          16 Information      The access history in hive \??\C:\F
```

Figure 5.6: Using Get-WinEvent cmdlet on Windows platform

As you can see in *Figure 5.7* the **Get-WinEvent** cmdlet does not work in Linux, and other platforms for that matter:

```
PS /home> Get-Winevent -LogName System | Select-Object -First 1
Get-Winevent: The term 'Get-Winevent' is not recognized as a nam
e of a cmdlet, function, script file, or executable program.
Check the spelling of the name, or if a path was included, verif
y that the path is correct and try again.
```

Figure 5.7: Using Get-WinEvent cmdlet on Linux platform

Moreover, not all **PSDrives** are available on Linux as we can see in *Figure 5.8*:

```
PS /home> Get-PSDrive

Name           Used (GB)      Free (GB) Provider
----           ---------      --------- --------
/                 337.56         139.16 FileSystem
Alias                                   Alias
Env                                     Environment
Function                                Function
Temp              337.56         139.16 FileSystem
Variable                                Variable
```

Figure 5.8: Available PSDrives on Linux

In Windows, more **PSDrives** are available, shown in *Figure 5.9*:

```
PS C:\Temp> Get-PSDrive

Name            Used (GB)     Free (GB) Provider
----            ---------     --------- --------
Alias                                   Alias
C                  337,56        139,16 FileSystem
Cert                                    Certificate
Env                                     Environment
Function                                Function
HKCU                                    Registry
HKLM                                    Registry
Temp               337,56        139,16 FileSystem
Variable                                Variable
WSMan                                   WSMan
```

Figure 5.9: Available PSDrives on Windows

Here, we can clearly see the differences with cmdlets and PSDrives between the shown platforms.

Working correctly with paths

Different platforms use different separators for paths. Windows uses back slashes **C:\Temp\File.txt** and Linux and MacOS uses forward slashes **/Home/File.txt**. Use the **Join-Path** command when working with paths in cross platform scripts. This ensures that the correct separator is used independent of the chosen platform.

```
# On Windows
$Path = Join-Path "C:" "Temp" "File.txt"
PS C:\Temp> $Path
C:\Temp\File.txt
# On Linux
$Path = Join-Path "/" "home" "File.txt"
PS /home> $Path
/home/File.txt
```

Use environment variables

Some environment variables are consistent across different platforms such as the **$HOME** (Users home directory) and the **$PWD** (Current working directory) variables. Use such variables when working with system related paths or resources:

```
# On Windows
$Path = ($PWD).Path
PS C:\Temp> $Path
C:\Temp
```

```
# On Linux
$Path = ($PWD).Path
PS /home> $Path
/home
```

We can also use the **Env:** drive to check for and create our own environment variables that can be used across different platforms.

Use OS Type built-in variables

The built-in variables **$IsWindows**, **$IsLinux** and **$IsMacOS** can be used to check for and determine the current type of platform. By utilizing these built-in variables, you can ensure that specific code statements are only executed on the designated platform.

```
switch ($true) {
    { $IsWindows } {
        # Code specific to Windows
        Write-Output "This platform is Windows"
    }
    { $IsLinux } {
        # Code specific to Linux
        Write-Output "This platform is Linux"
    }
    { $IsMacOS } {
        # Code specific to MacOS
        Write-Output "This platform is MacOS"
    }
    default {
        Write-Output "This platform is Unsupported"
    }
}
```

Avoid aliases where possible

Avoid the use of command and parameter aliases where possible. Not all aliases are the same or supported across all platforms. You can access and compare current aliases on different platforms by using the **Alias:** PSDrive.

Ensure correct encoding and line endings

Inconsistent character encoding and line endings can result in issues when scripts are transferred between platforms. It is important to ensure that your cross-platform scripts have the proper character encoding and choosing a universal format is preferred. UTF-8 is widely supported and works on both Windows and Unix (Linux and MacOS) systems. It is also important to use consistent line endings such as CRLF style for Windows and LF style for Unix systems. You can choose to use a text editor that supports both UTF-8 characters and allows you to specify the line endings. A lot of IDE´s support this including VS Code.

Use a shebang line

A shebang line allows you to run a script directly without specifying the PowerShell interpreter each time you want to execute it. It is important when creating cross platform scripts to ensure the use of the correct interpreter regardless of the platform it runs on. For PowerShell scripts on Linux and MacOS the shebang line is used to specify the path to the PowerShell interpreter, and it must always be included on the first line within the script and usually looks like this: `#!/usr/bin/env pwsh` specifying the path too and the name of the interpreter. When the script is executed on Windows, the shebang line is ignored.

Be aware of case sensitivity

PowerShell is case-insensitive when it comes to naming of variables and commands just like Windows in general. But in contrast to Windows, Unix systems such as MacOS and Linux are case-sensitive so you must be aware of the differences in file and directory names etc., between the different platforms. You should avoid relying on case-insensitive behavior in general when creating cross platform scripts and be consistent in your use of case-sensitivity.

Use cross platform modules

You should use modules that are designed to work on multiple platforms. As an example, the **PowerShellGet** and the **PackageManagement** modules work on both Windows and Linux platforms for package management. In the official **PsGallery** module repository you can filter modules for specific platforms and find spublicly available cross-platform modules. Also note when you create your own modules try to make them cross platform compatible whenever possible.

Extensive testing

Testing is always a crucial part of development. It is important to test your cross-platform scripts on all platforms where they need to be executed. It is recommended that you use virtual machines or container environments to simulate different operating systems and use these for testing purposes. Extensive testing includes:

- **Functional testing**: Execute the script on all platforms to ensure it performs the intended tasks.

- **Script dependencies**: Test any modules, libraries and dependencies that are used by the script on all platforms. Avoid the use of single platform specific dependencies.

- **Automated testing**: Consider setting up automated tests of scripts across the different platforms. This can greatly mitigate the time spent on testing every time you have changed or updated a script.

- **Test input and output**: Verify operations such as reading and writing to and from files, and verify that user input and console output works as intended across all platforms.

- **Error handling and logging**: Always implement error handling and logging in your scripts. Make sure that error messages and logs are consistent across all platforms, and that they work independent of the type of platform.

- **General testing and checks**: Generally, check all aspects of the script that are relevant for cross platform compatibility, like how paths are constructed and handled including the use of environment variables. Also check how permissions are handled on each platform and ensure external tools are compatible and behaving correctly across the different platforms.

Cross platform script

The following is a simple script that is created for cross-platform compatibility between Windows, MacOS and the Linux platform. What the script does is it creates a file with some simple platform specific information and then writes this information to a file. We use a parameter for setting the path (and name) of the output file. The information also contains the aliases for the **Get-ChildItem** cmdlet. This is to showcase the differences in this specific alias across the platforms.

We start the script by creating a shebang line and then add the **CmdletBinding** attribute and a single mandatory parameter called **$FileName** which takes a file name in the form of a string as an argument. We use a **switch** block to differentiate between the different platforms using the **Is<Platform>** built-in variables. We use these to provide platform specific code, and in this case, we write the OS type to console and then use **Join-Path** to set the specific platform dependent path to a Temp directory. The output file will be created within this directory. After the switch block, we use **Join-Path** to join the **Temp** path with the file name to provide the correct path to this file, depending on the specific platform. We create a **PSCustomObject** with information we derive from the **$PSVersionTable** built-in variable which contains some PowerShell version and platform information. We also use the **Get-Alias** to get all platform specific aliases for the **Get-ChildItem** cmdlet and add this information. The **PSCustomObject** with information is piped to **ConvertTo-Json** and then piped to **Out-File** to create the output file with all the specified information.

The script ends up looking like this:

```
#!/usr/bin/env pwsh

[CmdletBinding()]

param (
```

```
    [Parameter(Mandatory = $true)]
    [String]$FileName
)
switch ($true) {
    { $IsWindows } {
        # Code specific to Windows
        Write-Output "This platform is Windows"
        $TempPath = Join-Path "C:" "Temp"
    }
    { $IsLinux } {
        # Code specific to Linux
        Write-Output "This platform is Linux"
        $TempPath = Join-Path "/" "home" "Temp"
    }
    { $IsMacOS } {
        # Code specific to MacOS
        Write-Output "This platform is MacOS"
        $TempPath = Join-Path "/" "home" "Temp"
    }
    default {
        exit "This platform is Unsupported"
    }
}
$InfoFile = Join-Path $TempPath $FileName
$Info = [PSCustomObject]@{
    OS                  = ($PSVersionTable).OS
    Platform            = ($PSVersionTable).Platform
    PSVersion           = (($PSVersionTable).PSVersion).ToString()
    "Get-ChildItem-Alias" = (Get-Alias -Definition Get-ChildItem).DisplayName
}
$Info | ConvertTo-Json | Out-File $InfoFile -Force
```

Running the script in Linux gives us the console and file output as shown in *Figure 5.10*.

Note that we use the **cat** command to output the content of the file directly in the Linux shell console:

```
PS /home> sudo ./CrossPlatformScript.ps1 -FileName TestFile.json
This platform is Linux
PS /home> cat /home/Temp/TestFile.json
{
  "OS": "Linux 4.4.0-19041-Microsoft #2311-Microsoft Tue Nov 08 17:09:00 PST 2022",
  "Platform": "Unix",
  "PSVersion": "7.3.6",
  "Get-ChildItem-Alias": [
    "dir -> Get-ChildItem",
    "gci -> Get-ChildItem"
  ]
}
```

Figure 5.10: *Console and file output after running the CrossPlatformScript.ps1 in Linux*

Also note that the aliases for the **Get-ChildItem** cmdlet on the Linux platform. Running the script in Windows gives us the console and file output as shown in *Figure 5.11*:

```
PS C:\Temp> .\CrossPlatformScript.ps1 -FileName TestFile.json
This platform is Windows
PS C:\Temp> Get-Content .\TestFile.json
{
  "OS": "Microsoft Windows 10.0.19045",
  "Platform": "Win32NT",
  "PSVersion": "7.3.6",
  "Get-ChildItem-Alias": [
    "dir -> Get-ChildItem",
    "gci -> Get-ChildItem",
    "ls -> Get-ChildItem"
  ]
}
```

Figure 5.11: *Console and file output after running the CrossPlatformScript.ps1 in Windows*

As you can see the script works on both of these platforms (and are also compatible with MacOS). Note the difference in the aliases for the **Get-ChildItem** cmdlet. This is just a very simple example script, and the more advanced the script, the more you need to be aware of the details pertaining to cross platform scripting and use the techniques and best practices for creating such scripts.

Creating cross platform scripts is easier than you might think if you adhere to the best practices and use the techniques described in this recipe. Not all scripts are suited to be made cross platform compatible, it depends on the requirements of each specific script. Whenever possible you should take different platforms into account, who knows if a script you created for one platform suddenly might be usable on another, if you have created it with cross platform in mind from the begining you should have a script that is directly portable without making any or only a few changes to it.

PowerShell execution policy and script signing

Signing your PowerShell script ensures its authenticity and integrity by allowing you to verify the identity of a scripts author and make sure that scripts originate from valid trusted sources. This help prevent any illegitimate or potentially malicious code from being executed on your systems. Some scripts also require more security in the terms of accessibility and systems running scripts should be set up with execution policies allowing them to only run trusted and validated scripts. In this topic you will learn about the PowerShell execution policy, and we will cover how to create and use code signing certificates to sign scripts. Knowing how to secure your scripts is vital to the overall security not only for the scripts themselves but also for the systems they generally are executed on.

Recipe 30: Working with execution policies on Windows systems

PowerShell's execution policy is a security feature that controls the circumstances and defines which scripts can be executed on Windows platforms. It is not a security feature that restricts users' actions since they can be bypassed, but they help administrators to define levels of trust and set rules for running scripts on different systems which prevents them from violating these rules and settings, thus reducing the risk of running malicious scripts unintentionally. Execution policies are especially important on systems and environments where users may run scripts directly and they provide a way to control script execution behavior.

> **Note: Execution policy is only available on Windows platforms. For non-Windows platforms the default execution policy is set to unrestricted and cannot be modified!**

On a windows system the execution policy can be set in different scopes. These scopes are divided into: **LocalMachine**, **CurrentUser** and **Process**, The first ones are quite self-explanatory and the process defines the current PowerShell session process. There are also two other scopes which is set using Group Policies, the **MachinePolicy** which defines all users of a computer, and the **UserPolicy** which defines the current user of a computer. Using Group Policies to set the execution policy would be a preferred method in environments where scripts are run on multiple servers and computers by different users. The list below shows the precedence order of the execution policy scopes. The policy that takes precedence will always be in effect even if a more restrictive policy is set at a lower precedence level:

- MachinePolicy
- UserPolicy
- Process

- CurrentUser

- LocalMachine

When you set the execution policy for the local computer or the current user, the settings are saved into the registry, so you don't need to use your PowerShell profile to configure these policies. For sessions, the execution policy settings are stored in-memory and is lost when the session is closed.

The different execution policies determine the behavior of PowerShell scripts, these policies are defined as follows:

- **Restricted**: This is the most restrictive policy, and no scripts are allowed to run, but individual commands in the shell are permitted. This policy is typically used in high-security environments where scripts are (almost) never going to be executed. This is the default execution policy for windows client computers.

- **AllSigned**: Requires that <u>all</u> scripts are signed by a trusted publisher, including scripts that are written on the local computer. You will be prompted before running scripts from publishers that are yet to be classified as trusted or untrusted. This policy is useful for environments where scripts need to be verified before execution.

- **RemoteSigned**: Scripts that are locally written are allowed to run without being signed, but scripts downloaded from external locations, such as the internet, must be signed by a trusted publisher, unless they are unblocked using the **Unblock-File** cmdlet. This is the default execution policy for Windows servers.

- **Unrestricted**: All scripts can run regardless of their signature, but users will be warned before running scripts that are not from the local intranet zone. This policy poses the highest security risk and should be used with caution. It is not recommended to use this policy on any production servers or computers. This is the default execution policy for non-Windows systems and cannot be changed on such platforms.

- **Bypass**: All scripts can run without any restrictions since no execution policy is enforced. You will not be prompted with any warnings. This policy poses a security risk and should be used with caution. It is not recommended to use this policy in any production environments.

PowerShell has two execution policy specific built-in cmdlets. The **Get-ExecutionPolicy** and the **Set-ExecutionPolicy**. Usage and short explanations with examples are shown below:

Note: You must be running your shell or script as an administrator in order to be able to set and change the execution policy!

```
# Get the current effective execution policy

Get-ExecutionPolicy
```

```
# Get a list of execution policies for all scopes
Get-ExecutionPolicy -List
# Get execution policy for a specific scope
# Get-ExecutionPolicy -Scope <Scope>
Get-ExecutionPolicy -Scope Process
# Set the current effective execution policy
# Set-ExecutionPolicy -ExecutionPolicy <Policy>
Set-ExecutionPolicy -ExecutionPolicy AllSigned
# Set the execution policy for a specific scope
# Set-ExecutionPolicy -ExecutionPolicy <Policy> -Scope <Scope>
Set-ExecutionPolicy -ExecutionPolicy AllSigned -Scope Process
# Remove the current effective execution policy (Set as undefined)
Set-ExecutionPolicy -ExecutionPolicy Undefined
# Remove the execution policy for a specific scope (Set as undefined)
Set-ExecutionPolicy -ExecutionPolicy Undefined -Scope CurrentUser
```

Note: If you set all execution policy scopes on a Windows client computer to undefined, the current effective policy will be set as Restricted which is the default. On Windows servers this behavior will default the execution policy to RemoteSigned.

Best practices for the execution policies entirely depends on the security requirements of your infrastructure and environment and the level of trust you have in your scripts in general. The choice of execution policy should align with your organizations general security policies. Remember that security must always be prioritized!

Some environments like production might have a low level of trust and requires a high level of security and the execution policy might be set to Restricted and a high level of trust such as a test environment, might require a low level of security and the policy could be set as either **RemoteSigned** or **AllSigned**.

Here are some usage tips and best practices in general for using execution policies:

- The execution policy must be set at the appropriate scope based on your requirements.

- Use Group policy to enforce execution policies across multiple systems especially in large enterprise environments.

- Combine execution policies with other security measures relevant for your organization and your scripting policies.

- Regularly review and update execution policies based on changes in your environment and changes to your organization security policies.

- Educate users on the risks for running scripts, especially in less restrictive environments. Introduce them to general best scripting security practices.

- Always review scripts for security before running them, regardless of the execution policy. Newer blindly trust a script and its content.

Recipe 31: Script signing for security purposes and signing scripts using code signing certificates

Why sign scripts? First and foremost is provides authenticity to your scripts by allowing you to identify and verify the scripts author ensuring that it originates from a trusted source. It also adds integrity by ensuring that a script has not been tampered with since it was signed. If a script is modified after it is signed, the signature becomes invalid. When a script is signed with a valid signature it can be executed even when strict execution policies are in place which further enforces security policies and adds a trust model inside organizations. Such a model can be used to trust only scripts that are signed by a trusted publisher or by a specific set of trusted certificates from your organization.

PowerShell scripts are signed with code signing certificates that are issued from a trusted source. This source can either be a public trusted source or you can create your own self-signed trusted source that you allow to be trusted on specific systems. The source depends on if you are going to use your scripts solely in your own infrastructure and depends on the environments they are going to be executed within. Self-signed certificates should primarily be used for test environments. For production environments and if you need to distribute scripts to external users such as other companies and other third parties you should use a public trusted authority for issuing your code signing certificates.

By issuing a code signing certificate from a trusted public source such as DigiCert or Globalsign, you would have to go through a process where the issuer identifies and validates your organization and issues a certificate upon validation success. Such a certificate will generally be trusted on systems where the issuing authority is in the trust store like on Windows where DigiCert and Globalsign are a general part of the Trusted root certificate authorities.

 A self-signed certificate is only trusted on systems that you specifically specify by adding the public key of the certificate or the self-signed **Certificate Authority (CA)** that signed the certificate, to the trusted root certificate authority on each system. For testing purposes, self-signed certificates are sufficient but for production and high-security environments it is encouraged to always use a code signing certificate from a public trusted source.

For signing scripts, you are going to need a code signing certificate. You can either purchase one or create a self-signed certificate.

In the following examples we are going to use a self-signed code signing certificate which we create using the **New-SelfSignedCertificate** cmdlet. Note that the command to create certificates must be run as an administrator:

```
# Create a self-signed code signing certificate
$Dns = "CodeSigning"
$Certificate = New-SelfSignedCertificate -KeyUsage DigitalSignature
-KeySpec Signature -KeyAlgorithm RSA -KeyLength 4096 -CertStoreLocation
Cert:\CurrentUser\My -Type CodeSigningCert -Subject $Dns -DNSName $Dns
-FriendlyName $Dns
```

Once created (or bought) and installed, you can view your current installed code signing certificates using the **Get-ChildItem** cmdlet as shown below:

```
# View currently installed code signing certificates (CurrentUser)
Get-ChildItem Cert:\CurrentUser\My -CodeSigningCert
# View currently installed code signing certificates (LocalMachine)
Get-ChildItem Cert:\LocalMachine\My -CodeSigningCert
```

The output of running these commands will look as shown in *Figure 5.12*:

```
PS C:\Temp> Get-ChildItem Cert:\CurrentUser\My -CodeSigningCert

    PSParentPath: Microsoft.PowerShell.Security\Certificate::CurrentUser\My

Thumbprint                                Subject              EnhancedKeyUsageList
-----------                               -------              --------------------
DE8CBF4EF84E25A3708937E4D7D96CFD8D7973BC  CN=CodeSigning       Code Signing
3CD30A86F9624F80A2A5AE2B1959BD4872742F19  CN=CodeSigning-C     Code Signing
2A55AD0862391DCDC0C89D58BD4C506BDC2A6580  CN=CodeSigning-B     Code Signing
```

Figure 5.12: Code signing certificates in CurrentUser certificate store.

For signing a script, we need to select the specific code signing certificate we want to use and reference it in a variable. When we have multiple certificates, we can distinguish between them using indexing.

```
# For multiple certificates, select a specific certificate
$CodeSign = (Get-ChildItem Cert:\CurrentUser\My -CodeSigningCert)[0]
```

Figure 5.13 shows that the **$CodeSign** variable now contains the reference to the specific selected code signing certificate:

```
PS C:\Temp> $CodeSign

    PSParentPath: Microsoft.PowerShell.Security\Certificate::CurrentUser\My

Thumbprint                                Subject              EnhancedKeyUsageList
-----------                               -------              --------------------
DE8CBF4EF84E25A3708937E4D7D96CFD8D7973BC  CN=CodeSigning       Code Signing
```

Figure 5.13: Specifically selected code signing certificate assigned to $CodeSign variable

Before we can use the certificate to sign scripts, we need to locally trust it by exporting the public key from the certificate and then import the public key into the trusted root certificate authority store. You can do this by piping the certificate to the **Export-Certificate** cmdlet and then further pipe it to **Import-Certificate**. Note that for the **Export-Certificate** command you need to provide an argument to the **-FilePath** parameter though we directly pipe the exported certificate to the Import-Certificate cmdlet. The public key certificate file will be placed and available for further use within that path. For the **Import-Certificate** cmdlet we need to specify an argument to the **-CertStoreLocation** parameter, this is the specific store the public key will be imported into. This must be either **Cert:\CurrentUser\Root** or **Cert:\LocalMachine\Root** depending on if you need the certificate to only be accessible for the current user, or for the entire local machine. Here we export and save the public certificate file to **C:\Temp\CodeSignPub.crt** and use the **Cert:\CurrentUser\Root** trusted root certificate authority store:

```
# Export public key and import it to trusted root certificate authority
(Get-Childitem Cert:\CurrentUser\my -CodeSigningCert)[0] | Export-
Certificate -FilePath C:\Temp\CodeSignPub.crt | Import-Certificate
-CertStoreLocation Cert:\CurrentUser\Root
```

You will be prompted to accept importing the public certificate into the trusted root certificate authority store. Accept this and your certificate will be trusted on this specific machine for this current user only. By viewing the certificate within the user certificate console, you can see that the certificate is trusted and is issued by itself. Shown in *Figure 5.14*:

Figure 5.14: *Self-Signed code signing certificate trusted with its own public certificate added to the trusted root certificate authority store*

Since this is a self-signed certificate for test purposes it is okay to use it for trust. We could have also created a self-signed Certificate Authority and used this CA to sign the code signing certificate, then we would need the public certificate of that CA certificate to import to the trusted root certificate authority store instead, ensuring the trust of the self-signed certificate signed by the self-signed CA.

The public certificate must be installed to the trusted root certificate authority store on all the systems where scripts signed by the code signing certificate must be executed, to validate and trust the signature of these scripts.

Now that we have created a code signing certificate, trusted it and selected it by referencing it in the **$CodeSign** variable, can sign scripts with this certificate, using the **Set-AuthentiCodeSignature** cmdlet. We create a simple script containing a simple **Write-Output** command as shown in *Figure 5.15*:

```
>_ ScriptToSign.ps1
   1    # I need to sign this script!
   2
   3    Write-Output "I need to sign this script!"
   4
   5    |
```

Figure 5.15: *Script before signing*

We sign the script using **Set-AuthentiCodeSignature** specifying the filepath to the script and the code signing certificate referenced in the **$CodeSign** variable. Note that some IDE´s include a feature that automatically sign your scripts each time they are saved. It is recommended to use such a feature where applicable:

```
# Sign Script
Set-AuthenticodeSignature -FilePath .\ScriptToSign.ps1 -Certificate $CodeSign
```

This results in output as shown in *Figure 5.16*:

```
PS C:\Temp> Set-AuthenticodeSignature -FilePath .\ScriptToSign.ps1 -Certificate $CodeSign

    Directory: C:\Temp

SignerCertificate                         Status      StatusMessage         Path
-----------------                         ------      -------------         ----
DE8CBF4EF84E25A3708937E4D7D96CFD8D7973BC  Valid       Signature verified.   ScriptToSign.ps1
```

Figure 5.16: *Output when successfully signing script*
using Set-AuthentiCodeSignature and code signing certificate

Whenever you sign a script with a code signing certificate, the script will only be valid until the expiration time of the certificate used to sign the script. To accommodate for this, we can add a timestamp to the script signature. When a script that includes a timestamp is signed, the script does not expire upon certificate expiration. However, this only works for certificates that are not self-signed and usually requires that the timestamp is from the same provider as the signing certificate. If your code signing certificate is from DigiCert, you would use their timestamp which can be found at: **http://timestamp.digicert.com**. You would add a timestamp by providing the URL for the timestamp server as an argument to the **-Timestamp** parameter in the **Set-AuthentiCodeSignature** cmdlet.

If we open the script file, we can now see that a signature block has been added, shown in *Figure 5.17*. Note that the signature block is abbreviated in this figure:

```
>_ ScriptToSign.ps1
 1    # I need to sign this script!
 2
 3    Write-Output "I need to sign this script!"
 4
 5
 6    # SIG # Begin signature block
 7    # MIIIogYJKoZIhvcNAQcCoIIIkzCCCI8CAQExDzANBglghkgBZQMEAgEFADB5Bgor
 8    # BgEEAYI3AgEEoGswaTA0BgorBgEEAYI3AgEeMCYCAwEAAAQQH8w7YFlLCE63JNLG
 9    # KX7zUQIBAAIBAAIBAAIBAAIBADAxMA0GCWCGSAFlAwQCAQUABCDIM/rFiHIaeAdn
10    # i4JDnDENV8wlGC0aXcVz/58PU0WsaqCCBRwwggUYMIIDAKADAgECAhBLMRl+OcGh
11    # nEKqERDE/gpDMA0GCSqGSIb3DQEBBQUAMBYxFDASBgNVBAMMC0NvZGVzaWduaW5n
12    # MB4XDTIzMDgxMzEyNTAxMVoXDTI0MDgxMzEzMTAxMVowFjEUMBIGA1UEAwwLQ29k
13    # ZXNpZ25pbmcwggIiMA0GCSqGSIb3DQEBAQUAA4ICDwAwggIKAoICAQCosSmXr7hH
14    # l1HEUcdDvhk9uCzgItn61j/QQHtThAUMoghwDEq4g4Paai4JzkO4kkeFrK++Ofzl
15    # yZ7GIJJ4NEA9hMKqOr2RVA+WOiUMo78qLf+mgbmI3udhqMIyzwCmq3VoWfrHhb1i
```

Figure 5.17: Script after signing with code signing certificate using Set-AuthentiCodeSignature cmdlet

To test the signature of the script let us first see what happens if we try to execute the script unsigned. We make sure the execution policy is set to **AllSigned** which requires that all scripts are indeed signed, even those created locally. This would be one of the recommendations for some production environments. *Figure 5.18* shows the output of running the unsigned script with the **AllSigned** execution policy:

```
>_ ScriptToSign.ps1
 1    # I need to sign this script!
 2
 3    Write-Output "I need to sign this script!"
 4
 5


OUTPUT    DEBUG CONSOLE    TERMINAL    AZURE

● PS C:\Temp> Get-ExecutionPolicy
  AllSigned
● PS C:\Temp> .\ScriptToSign.ps1
  .\ScriptToSign.ps1: File C:\Temp\ScriptToSign.ps1 cannot be loaded. The file C:\Temp\ScriptToSign.ps1
  is not digitally signed. You cannot run this script on the current system. For more information about
  running scripts and setting execution policy, see about_Execution_Policies at https://go.microsoft.com
  /fwlink/?LinkID=135170.
```

Figure 5.18: Running an unsigned script with the AllSigned execution policy

We then execute script after it is signed with the code signing certificate. The output is shown in *Figure 5.19*. Even though the script is now signed we get prompted to trust the publisher of the script due to the **AllSigned** execution policy, since this is the first time, we have executed a script from this specific publisher on that system. We can choose to always trust this publisher or only trust it once for this single script execution or we can choose to never trust and execute scripts from this publisher. Since this publisher is our own code signing certificate, we choose **[A] Always run**, we are going to trust this in the future on this computer and we will not be prompted for this again when executing scripts signed by our own self-signed code signing certificate, we trust our self as a valid publisher.

The script is executed as shown in *Figure 5.19*:

```
>_ ScriptToSign.ps1
 1    # I need to sign this script!
 2
 3    Write-Output "I need to sign this script!"
 4
 5
 6    # SIG # Begin signature block
 7    # MIIIogYJKoZIhvcNAQcCoIIIkzCCCI8CAQExDzANBglghkgBZQMEAgEFADB5Bgor
 8    # BgEEAYI3AgEEoGswaTA0BgorBgEEAYI3AgEeMCYCAwEAAAQQH8w7YFlLCE63JNLG
 9    # KX7zUQIBAAIBAAIBAAIBAAIBADAxMA0GCWCGSAFlAwQCAQUABCDIM/rFiHIaeAdn
10    # i4JDnDENV8wlGC0aXcVz/58PU0WsaqCCBRwwggUYMIIDAKADAgECAhBLMRl+OcGh
11    # nEKqERDE/gpDMA0GCSqGSIb3DQEBBQUAMBYxFDASBgNVBAMMC0NvZGVzaWduaW5n
12    # MB4XDTIzMDgxMzEyNTAxMVoXDTI0MDgxMzEzMTAxMVowFjEUMBIGA1UEAwwLQ29k
```

```
OUTPUT    DEBUG CONSOLE    TERMINAL    AZURE

● PS C:\Temp> Get-ExecutionPolicy
  AllSigned
● PS C:\Temp> .\ScriptToSign.ps1

  Do you want to run software from this untrusted publisher?
  File C:\Temp\ScriptToSign.ps1 is published by CN=Codesigning and is not trusted on your system. Only
  run scripts from trusted publishers.
  [V] Never run  [D] Do not run  [R] Run once  [A] Always run  [?] Help (default is "D"): A
  I need to sign this script!
```

Figure 5.19: Running a signed script with the AllSigned execution policy

Whenever you make any changes to a signed script, being it only a single space character, you will have to re-sign it with the code signing certificate. The script signature is invalidated and it cant be trusted until it is re-signed. It could as well have been changed by an unauthorized user or process. When trying to execute a tampered script you will get an error as shown in *Figure 5.20*:

```
≥_ ScriptToSign.ps1
   1    # I need to sign this script!
   2
   3    Write-Output "I need to sign this script!"
   4    # Invalid
   5
   6    # SIG # Begin signature block
   7    # MIIIogYJKoZIhvcNAQcCoIIIkzCCCI8CAQExDzANBglghkgBZQMEAgEFADB5Bgor
   8    # BgEEAYI3AgEEoGswaTA0BgorBgEEAYI3AgEeMCYCAwEAAAQQH8w7YFlLCE63JNLG
   9    # KX7zUQIBAAIBAAIBAAIBAAIBADAxMA0GCWCGSAFlAwQCAQUABCDIM/rFiHIaeAdn
  10    # i4JDnDENV8wlGC0aXcVz/58PU0WsaqCCBRwwggUYMIIDAKADAgECAhBLMRl+OcGh
  11    # nEKqERDE/gpDMA0GCSqGSIb3DQEBBQUAMBYxFDASBgNVBAMMC0NvZGVzaWduaW5n
  12    # MB4XDTIzMDgxMzEyNTAxMVoXDTI0MDgxMzEzMTAxMVowFjEUMBIGA1UEAwwLQ29k
```

| OUTPUT | DEBUG CONSOLE | TERMINAL | AZURE |

```
PS C:\Temp>
PS C:\Temp> . 'C:\Temp\ScriptToSign.ps1'
.: File C:\Temp\ScriptToSign.ps1 cannot be loaded. The contents of file C:\Temp\ScriptToSign.ps1 might
have been changed by an unauthorized user or process, because the hash of the file does not match the
hash stored in the digital signature. The script cannot run on the specified system. For more informa
tion, run Get-Help about_Signing..
```

Figure 5.20: Script with an invalid signature due to unsigned changes

By incorporating execution policies and procedures for signing scripts with valid and trusted code signing certificates you can add layers of trust to your PowerShell environments. This enhanced trust ensures that only authorized and verified scripts are executed on your systems. It also provides a layer of integrity to scripts and ensures that scripts can be trusted and have not been altered since they were signed by the original publisher. This helps strengthen the security and reliability of your PowerShell environments and scripts in general and by implementing these measures you reduce the risk of unwanted and malicious code being executed.

PowerShell modules and repositories

A fundamental practice in software development in general is to modularize and reuse code which can greatly mitigate time spent on creating scripts, reduce code duplication within scripts and promote code organization and reusability. It is relevant to mitigate repetition of creating and using the same code instead it should be modularized. Repeatable code should then be created either in separate scripts, functions or cmdlets, and these should then be embedded within modules for reusability. Modules offers methods for organizing, packaging, and distributing your reusable code, not only internally but also externally by distributing your packaged code through public repositories. You might have to import the same function on different servers for providing consistent usability and functionality within different scripts or you might need to distribute your code to a third party outside your own organization without having to de-duplicate your code. By embedding your code within a module and packaging this module, you can easily distribute it to both internal and external repositories and then easily install the module on other systems where needed. We can define a PowerShell module as a collection of scripts, functions, cmdlets, and other resources that are packaged to provide a single reusable functional unit of code and resources.

Here are some of the key features of PowerShell modules:

- **Code organization and standardization**: Modules provides a structured and standardized way of organizing code which promotes consistency and script manageability.

- **Code encapsulation:** In modules you can separate specific functions and cmdlets and only expose those you want a user to interact with. Some functions and cmdlets might rely on other functions to work, such functions might not be relevant for the end user and can be encapsulated and hidden.

- **Code reusability**: By using modules you only have to write your code once, and then it can be used multiple times across multiple systems and environments, reducing code duplication.

- **Versioning**: Modules support versioning which is important when you make updates or changes to code. Specific module versions can be chosen upon installation and when these are imported into scripts, it ensures consistency and predictability especially for old and legacy code.

- **Documentation and metadata**: Modules use module manifest files which include metadata about the specific module such as the author, version, description, dependencies and more. You can also add comment-based help to individual functions and cmdlets. This is useful for explaining the purposes of and how to use the module and the functions and cmdlets it contains.

- **Packaging and distribution**: PowerShell modules can be packaged for sharing and distribution purposes to both private and public repositories and other third parties. The official public PowerShell repository is the PSGallery: **https://www. powershellgallery.com/**

- **Shared development and collaboration**: PowerShell modules enable collaboration among developers. Multiple developers can work on different modules, and these modules can be combined to create more complex solutions. You can also create a new version with updated functionality from a module that comes from another developer.

Recipe 32: Creating modules, module manifest files and using modules within scripts

Whenever you have created a reusable function, you should add it to a module. You should preferably also organize your modules into different categories like having tools like specific functions and cmdlets used for managing Active Directory should be placed in one module and server specific tools in another and so on. For this recipe we use the **Add-LogToJson** function we created in the *Recipe 26: Create a custom logging function for structured logging that helps with troubleshooting and debugging errors* from *Chapter 4, Error Handling* and add this function to a new module we call *Logging*.

We need to create a folder for our new module, this folder is the base of the module and will contain all relevant module files. The module base folder must be named the same as the module, so in this case we create a new folder and call it *Logging*.

A PowerShell module file has the file type of **.psm1**. We create a new file and call it **Logging.psm1** and save this file within the *Logging* module base folder. Within this file we paste a copy of the **Add-LogToJson** function.

This is essentially all we need to create a PowerShell module, but it is always recommended to create a module manifest for modules. The module manifest is a file of the type **.psd1** and it contains all the metadata for the module within a hashtable. PowerShell has made it easy for us to create module manifest files using the **New-ModuleManifest** cmdlet. This cmdlet has parameters for all settings available within the manifest, but you do not need to fill them all as they can always be filled in later. We create a new manifest using the cmdlet by providing arguments to a few of the most essential parameters, as shown in *Figure 5.21*:

```
PS C:\Temp\Modules\Logging> New-ModuleManifest -Path Logging.psd1 `
>> -Author "Morten E. Hansen" `
>> -RootModule Logging.psm1 `
>> -ModuleVersion 1.0.0 `
>> -FunctionsToExport "Add-LogToJson" `
>> -Description "Contains misc. Logging functions"
```

Figure 5.21: Use New-ModuleManifest to create a module manifest file with essential settings

The module manifest file must also have the same name as the module, in this case **Logging.psd1** and must also be placed within the base module folder. We have added arguments to the following parameters:

- **Path**: This is the path for the module manifest file. This must be placed in the base module folder and must be named the same as the module.

- **Author**: Name of the author of the module.

- **RootModule**: This is a reference to the base module file.

- **`ModuleVersion`**: This is the version of the module. SemVer versioning is used for specifying module versions.
- **`FunctionsToExport`**: This is a string array containing all the functions within the module that the module should export into the process, when the module is imported. Functions that are not exported are not available to the user directly when a module is imported into a session, script etc.
- **`Description`**: This contains a description of the module.

After the command is executed, we now have a folder called logging, and two files, the module file **`Logging.psm1`** and the module manifest file **`Logging.psd1`**. *Figure 5.22* shows the folder structure and the content of the two files:

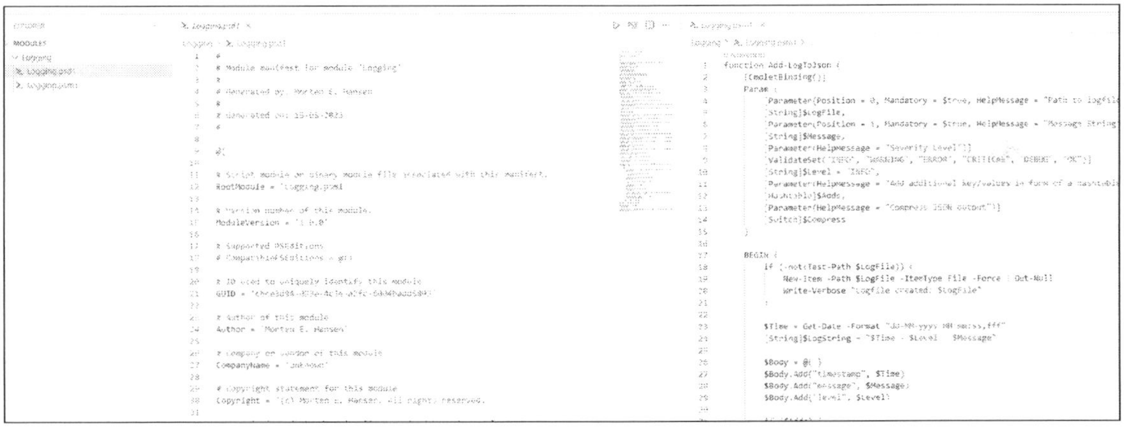

Figure 5.22: *Module folder structure and module file and module manifest file content*

This is generally all that is needed to create a module and we are now able to import the module into a PowerShell session using the **`Import-Module`** cmdlet referencing our module base folder as an argument **`.\Logging`**. After the import we can use the **`Get-Module`** cmdlet to see information about our newly imported module, as shown in *Figure 5.23*:

```
PS C:\Temp\Modules> Import-Module .\Logging
PS C:\Temp\Modules> Get-Module

ModuleType Version    PreRelease Name                                ExportedCommands
---------- -------    ---------- ----                                ----------------
Script     1.0.0                 Logging                             Add-LogToJson
Manifest   7.0.0.0               Microsoft.PowerShell.Management     {Add-Content, Clear-Content, Clear-Item, Clear-ItemProperty…}
Manifest   7.0.0.0               Microsoft.PowerShell.Security       {ConvertFrom-SecureString, ConvertTo-SecureString, Get-Acl, Get
Manifest   7.0.0.0               Microsoft.PowerShell.Utility        {Add-Member, Add-Type, Clear-Variable, Compare-Object…}
Script     0.2.0                 PowerShellEditorServices.Commands   {Clear-Host, ConvertFrom-ScriptExtent, ConvertTo-ScriptExtent,
Binary     0.2.0                 PowerShellEditorServices.VSCode     {Close-VSCodeHtmlContentView, New-VSCodeHtmlContentView, Set-VS
Script     2.2.6                 PSReadLine                          {Get-PSReadLineKeyHandler, Get-PSReadLineOption, Remove-PSReadL
```

Figure 5.23: *Import Logging module and show imported modules*

We can now invoke the function from the module within the session as shown in *Figure 5.24*:

```
PS C:\Temp\Modules> Add-LogToJson -LogFile C:\Temp\Testlog.json -Message "This is a test" -Level INFO -Compress -Verbose
VERBOSE: Successfully written log to file: C:\Temp\Testlog.json
VERBOSE: 16-08-2023 10:57:29,399 - INFO : This is a test
```

Figure 5.24: invoking the Add-LogToJson function from the Logging module

We have a fully functional module, and we can add functions as we expand our code repertoire. The module manifest can be updated whenever it is required with further information and functions that needs to be exported can be added and so on. Within the manifest file there is a short explanation for each setting, most of them are quite self-explanatory.

This is the simplest form of a module and module structure. As our module grows and as we add more functions and other resources to it, it might become harder to track all the functions the module contains, and it can end up being somewhat unorganized. Since a module is basically a PowerShell script we can import and use modules within the module itself. With this in mind we can easily set up a more organized way to handle functions. We can create every function within its own file and then import these files into the module file. By doing this we separate each function from each other, and we can easily work on one function at a time within its own file. We should also separate public and private functions within subfolders. The public folder will contain the functions that are directly imported into a session when you import the module and are available to the end user. The private folder will contain the helper functions that are used internally by the public functions, these will not be available to the end user. We create the new folder structure as shown below:

```
Modules/
├─ Logging/
│  ├─ Public/
│  │  ├─ Add-LogToJson.ps1
│  │  ├─ New-PublicFuncOne.ps1
│  ├─ Private/
│  │  ├─ New-HelperFunction.ps1
│  ├─ Logging.psm1
│  ├─ Logging.psd1
│  ├─ README.md
```

Within the public folder we create a new file called **Add-LogToJson.ps1**. As you might have guessed, within this file we paste the **Add-LogToJson** function. We also create another file in the public folder, called **New-PublicFuncOne.ps1** within this file we create a simple function that outputs a string to the console:

```
function New-PublicFuncOne {
```

```
    Write-Output "I $(New-HelperFunction)"
}
```

You can see that within the **Write-Output** statement we use the subexpression operator to call a function and replace it with the output from that function. Within the Private folder we create a new file called **New-HelperFunction.ps1** and we create the **New-HelperFunction** within this file, this function returns a string:

```
function New-HelperFunction {
    return "Helped"
}
```

The **New-PublicFuncOne** will be available to the end users and whenever this function is invoked, it will call the private function, **New-HelperFunction**. The **New-HelperFunction** is a private function that is only available to the public functions in the public folder and not to the end users.

In order for the module to work and for it to properly import the files containing the functions we create in the Public and Private folders; we need to make some changes to the **Logging.psm1** module file. Now that the **Add-LogToJson** function has its own file, we remove this from the module. We need to add some code that imports all the functions from the **.ps1** files within the Public and Private folders into the root module, whenever the Logging module is imported:

```
# Make sure to get the path where the module is placed

$ScriptRoot = Split-Path $Script:MyInvocation.MyCommand.Path

# Pull in Private files

Get-ChildItem "$ScriptRoot\Private" *.ps1 | ForEach-Object { Import-Module $_.FullName}

# Pull in Public files

Get-ChildItem "$ScriptRoot\Public" *.ps1 | ForEach-Object { Import-Module $_.FullName}
```

We use the **Split-Path $Script:MyInvocation.MyCommand.Path** to extract the directory path from the full path of the currently executing script, in this case the module. Then for each of the Public and Private folders, we use **Get-ChildItem** to get all *.ps1* files and with the **Foreach-Object** cmdlet we import each file into the root module with the **Import-Module** cmdlet. This is the only thing that is needed within the root module file. Each time we create a new file containing a new function within one of the Public or Private folders, these functions will be imported into the module if they are of the type .ps1.

The last thing we need to do is to update the module manifest file, more specifically we need to add the new public function, **New-PublicFuncOne** to the **FunctionsToExport** key in the manifest, making it available to the end users when the module is imported into a script or session. *Figure 5.25* shows the updated **FunctionsToExport** key in the module manifest, along with the new module directory structure. We also update the version key within the manifest to 1.0.1:

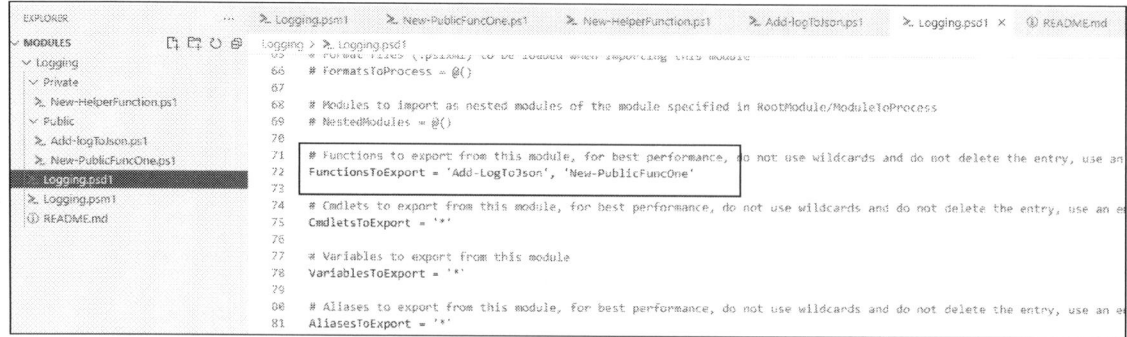

Figure 5.25: *Updated module directory structure and the updated FunctionsToExport manifest key*

We have also added a **README.md** file. This file is not mandatory and can be omitted, but it is always a good practice to document your code as much as possible.

Figure 5.26 shows the output of running the **Get-Module** command after we have imported the new module version:

```
PS C:\Temp\Modules> Import-Module .\Logging
PS C:\Temp\Modules> Get-Module

ModuleType Version   PreRelease Name                            ExportedCommands
---------- -------   ---------- ----                            ----------------
Script     1.0.1                Logging                         {Add-LogToJson, New-PublicFuncOne}
Manifest   7.0.0.0              Microsoft.PowerShell.Management  {Add-Content, Clear-Content, Clear-Item, Clear-ItemPrope
Manifest   7.0.0.0              Microsoft.PowerShell.Security    {ConvertFrom-SecureString, ConvertTo-SecureString, Get-A
Manifest   7.0.0.0              Microsoft.PowerShell.Utility     {Add-Member, Add-Type, Clear-Variable, Compare-Object…}
Manifest   7.0.0.0              Microsoft.WSMan.Management        {Connect-WSMan, Disable-WSManCredSSP, Disconnect-WSMan,
Script     0.2.0                PowerShellEditorServices.Commands {Clear-Host, ConvertFrom-ScriptExtent, ConvertTo-ScriptE
Binary     0.2.0                PowerShellEditorServices.VSCode  {Close-VSCodeHtmlContentView, New-VSCodeHtmlContentView,
Script     2.2.6                PSReadLine                       {Get-PSReadLineKeyHandler, Get-PSReadLineOption, Remove-
```

Figure 5.26: *Output of the Get-Module command after*
we have updated the module structure and imported the new version

The version of the Logging module is now 1.0.1 and the **New-PublicFuncOne** function is added to **ExportedCommands** and is now available for use. If a module contains a lot of functions, we can get a more detailed view of the module content with the **Get-Command** cmdlet using the -**Module** parameter with the module name as an argument, shown in *Figure 5.27*:

```
PS C:\Temp\Modules> Get-Command -Module Logging

CommandType     Name                Version    Source
-----------     ----                -------    ------
Function        Add-LogToJson       1.0.1      Logging
Function        New-PublicFuncOne   1.0.1      Logging
```

Figure 5.27: *Modules function overview using the Get-Command cmdlet*

The **New-PublicFuncOne** can now be invoked as it was another function or cmdlet. We get the output shown in *Figure 5.28*:

```
PS C:\Temp\Modules> New-PublicFuncOne
I Helped
```

Figure 5.28: *Invoking the New-PublicFuncOne from the Logging module*

Invoking the **New-PublicFuncOne** function we see that we get the expected output. The *Helped* string is returned from the private **New-HelperFunction** function as expected which is only available within the module for the public functions and not available to the end user.

If you have a single or a few functions only for a specific module it is not a requirement to create the advanced folder structure with the Private and Public subfolders, and it is enough to just create the base folder containing the module file (**.psm1**) and the module manifest file (**.psd1**). However, if you expect your module to grow with multiple functions and cmdlets it is recommended to keep each function and cmdlet within its own file. This provides a unified structure and a way to neatly organize your module content. It is also recommended that you keep versioning your modules as you add content to them, both for historic and legacy compatibility purposes. You might have created a version that works on an older system, that needs to undergo major updates so it can work on another newer system, by having a version of your module for each system can help make it compatible for both systems without having to create an entirely new module. Now we just need to learn to package and distribute our modules, so they can be reused across multiple systems, added to repositories and also potentially shared with third parties.

Recipe 33: Packaging modules and working with packaged modules and repositories

Before we start packaging our modules, we need a place where we can store them and easily distribute them to other systems and third parties etc. A repository is a location where you can store your PowerShell modules, it can be either private, preferably on a network share where they can be shared and accessed internally within an organization, between your systems or it can be public, like the PsGallery (**https://www.powershellgallery.com**) where you can store and share your modules with the online PowerShell community.

1. First, we need to import the **PowerShellGet** module, this module contains all functions needed for working with modules and repositories and it comes built-in with PowerShell from version 5.0. Use the **Get-Module** to see if the module is already imported into your session or import it with **Import-Module PowerShellGet**. You can view all its functions with **Get-Command -Module PowerShellGet** as shown in *Figure 5.29*:

```
PS C:\Temp\Modules> Import-Module PowerShellGet
PS C:\Temp\Modules> Get-Command -Module PowerShellGet

CommandType     Name                              Version     Source
-----------     ----                              -------     ------
Function        Find-Command                      2.2.5       PowerShellGet
Function        Find-DscResource                  2.2.5       PowerShellGet
Function        Find-Module                       2.2.5       PowerShellGet
Function        Find-RoleCapability               2.2.5       PowerShellGet
Function        Find-Script                       2.2.5       PowerShellGet
Function        Get-CredsFromCredentialProvider   2.2.5       PowerShellGet
Function        Get-InstalledModule               2.2.5       PowerShellGet
Function        Get-InstalledScript               2.2.5       PowerShellGet
Function        Get-PSRepository                  2.2.5       PowerShellGet
Function        Install-Module                    2.2.5       PowerShellGet
Function        Install-Script                    2.2.5       PowerShellGet
Function        New-ScriptFileInfo                2.2.5       PowerShellGet
Function        Publish-Module                    2.2.5       PowerShellGet
Function        Publish-Script                    2.2.5       PowerShellGet
Function        Register-PSRepository             2.2.5       PowerShellGet
Function        Save-Module                       2.2.5       PowerShellGet
Function        Save-Script                       2.2.5       PowerShellGet
Function        Set-PSRepository                  2.2.5       PowerShellGet
Function        Test-ScriptFileInfo               2.2.5       PowerShellGet
Function        Uninstall-Module                  2.2.5       PowerShellGet
Function        Uninstall-Script                  2.2.5       PowerShellGet
Function        Unregister-PSRepository           2.2.5       PowerShellGet
Function        Update-Module                     2.2.5       PowerShellGet
Function        Update-ModuleManifest             2.2.5       PowerShellGet
Function        Update-Script                     2.2.5       PowerShellGet
Function        Update-ScriptFileInfo             2.2.5       PowerShellGet
```

Figure 5.29: Functions withing the PowerShellGet module

The first thing we are interested in is to create and register a private repository on a network share. You can either use the **Universal Naming Convention (UNC)** path to the network share or map the network share to a drive letter and use the mapped path. The preferred method for compatibility is to use the UNC path.

> **Note: You might need a package management provider such as NuGet. PowerShell will poll for valid package managers. If your system is missing a valid package management provider, you will get an error and must install this manually. You can install NuGet package provider using Install-PackageProvider -Name Nuget -Force or search the web for PowerShell package manager. Further installation of a package manager is out of the scope of this book.**

Below we use the **Register-PSRepository** from the **PowerShellGet** module to register a new repository:

```
$Share = "\\Homeserver2\PsRepo"

$Repo = @{
    Name = "PsRepo"
```

```
    SourceLocation = $Share

    PublishLocation = $Share

    InstallationPolicy = "Trusted"

}

Register-PSRepository @Repo
```

The **$Share** path must be a valid network share. The **SourceLocation** parameter specifies the URI for discovering and installing modules from this repository. The **PublishLocation** parameter specifies the URI of the publish location for modules. In this case these values are the same, the **$Share** path. The **InstallationPolicy** parameter specifies PowerShell´s behavior when installing modules from this repository. If it is set to untrusted, the user will be prompted for confirmation. In this case we trust our own repository. You can create external repositories such as NuGet repositories in Azure DevOps which would require credentials. You can provide a credential argument (**Get-Credential**) to the **-Credentials** parameter for the **Register-PSRepository** for accessing such a repository.

When you execute the command you should get confirmation that the *Package source with name: PsRepo was added successfully*. If you get an error you are either missing a valid package manager or you might not have access or permissions to the network share. You should check up on these settings and try again once these prerequisites are fulfilled. When the repository is successfully registered you can list and view all your registered repositories using the **Get-PSRepository** cmdlet, as shown in *Figure 5.30*:

```
Package source with Name: PsRepo added successfully.
PS C:\Temp> Get-PSRepository


Name                        InstallationPolicy  SourceLocation
----                        ------------------  --------------
PSGallery                   Untrusted           https://www.powershellgallery.com/api/v2
PsRepo                      Trusted             \\Homeserver2\PsRepo
PowershellAzureDevopsSer... Trusted             https://pkgs.dev.azure.com/              /_packaging/PsRepo/nuget/v2
```

Figure 5.30: All *registered* PSRepositories

Note: You will have to register the repository specifically on all computers and systems that must have access to the repository, using the Register-PSRepository cmdlet. Also note that access, permissions, and firewalls might prevent you from accessing the network share used for the repository on different systems.

The repository is now registered, trusted and ready for publishing modules. We can publish a module to the repository with the **Publish-Module** command. We provide the full path to our modules base folder as an argument for the **-Path** parameter and the name of our new repository for the **-Repository** parameter:

```
Publish-Module -Path C:\Temp\Modules\Logging -Repository PsRepo
```

Within the network share a **NuGet (.nupkg)** package file is created containing the module with the version that is specified in the modules manifest file. Shown in *Figure 5.31*:

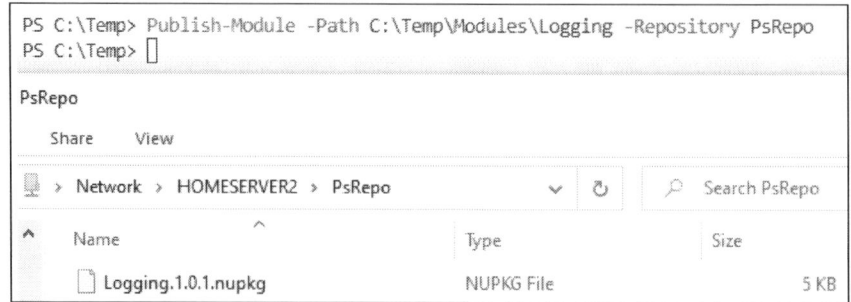

Figure 5.31: *Module published and packaged*
within the PSRepository using the Publish-Module cmdlet

Whenever you make changes to your modules, remember to update the version within the manifest file. If you try to publish a module with the same name and version as an already existing one, you will get prompted that it already exists. You can overwrite an already existing version by using the **-Force** parameter with the **Publish-Module** cmdlet. When you publish a newer version of a module the new version will be packed and published to the repository. *Figure 5.32* shows multiple packed and published versions of the Logging module:

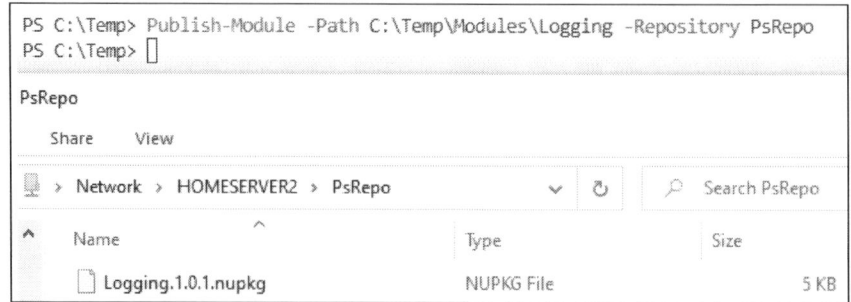

Figure 5.32: *Multiple packed and published versions of*
the Logging module in the PsRepo repository

> **Info: PowerShell modules are typically installed in specific locations on your computer. The location depends on whether you are installing modules for the current user or for all users of the system. To see the module paths configured on your system, you can use the following command: $Env:PSModulePath -split ';'. This command will display a list of directories where PowerShell looks for modules when using the Import-Module cmdlet.**

To install a module from the repository we use the **Install-Module** cmdlet. We provide the name for the module we want to install, in this case the Logging module, and use the **-Repository** parameter to specify the **PsRepo** repository. As default, when installing a module, the module will get installed in the current users' context within the directory: **C:\Users\<USERNAME>\Documents\PowerShell\Modules**. And will only be available to the current user. You can install the module for all users by providing the **AllUsers** argument to the **-Scope** parameter. This will install the module within the directory: **C:\ Program Files\WindowsPowerShell\Modules**. This requires administrator privileges so the session must be run as an administrator to install the module into this scope:

```
# Install module into current users context
Install-Module Logging -Repository PsRepo
# Install module for all users (Requires administrator privileges)
Install-Module Logging -Repository PsRepo -Scope AllUsers
```

Before we install the module, we check that it is not already installed using the **Get-Module -ListAvailable** cmdlet. The **ListAvailable** parameter lists all installed modules, not the modules that are imported into the current session. We pipe this command to **Where- Object** and specifically filter on the name *Logging*. *Figure 5.33* shows the output from the Get-Module cmdlet before and after installation of the Logging module:

```
PS C:\Temp> Get-Module -ListAvailable | Where {$_.Name -eq "Logging"}
PS C:\Temp> Install-Module Logging -Repository PsRepo
PS C:\Temp> Get-Module -ListAvailable | Where {$_.Name -eq "Logging"}

    Directory: C:\Users\███ ███     ███ ███ ███\Documents\PowerShell\Modules

ModuleType Version    PreRelease Name                         PSEdition ExportedCommands
---------- -------    ---------- ----                         --------- ----------------
Script     2.0.0                 Logging                      Desk      {Add-LogToJson, New-PublicFuncOne}
```

Figure 5.33: Get-Module cmdlet filtering on the name Logging,
before and after installation of the Logging module

Whenever you install a module from the repository, if a particular version is not specified, the newest version will be installed by default, you can also specify a specific version for installation using the **-RequiredVersion** parameter with the desired version number as an argument:

```
# Install specific module version
Install-Module Logging -Repository PsRepo -RequiredVersion 1.0.1
```

You can update an already installed module to a newer version, without having to uninstall and re-install it by using the **Update-Module** cmdlet. You can update to the newest version or to a specific version:

```
# Update to newest version
Update-Module Logging -Repository PsRepo
# Update to specific newer version
Update-Module Logging -Repository PsRepo -RequiredVersion 2.0.1
```

> **Note: You cannot downgrade to an earlier version, in this case you need to uninstall the current version of the module and specifically install an older version. Also note that in some cases you might need to restart your shell in order to be able to import a newly updated version of a module into a session.**

Usually, PowerShell modules are <u>not</u> imported automatically into a PowerShell session, with the exception being, if it is installed into the AllUsers **PsModulePath: C:\Program Files\WindowsPowerShell\Modules**. This directory is part of the system-wide module path and modules placed here are automatically loaded when a new PowerShell session is started. In all other circumstances, you will have to import the module manually using the **Import-Module** cmdlet. This imports an already installed, but not loaded, module into the current session. As with the other commands, you can also import a specific version using the **-RequiredVersion** parameter if you have multiple versions of a module installed:

```
# Import module into the current session

Import-Module Logging

# Import a specific module version into the current session

Import-Module Logging -RequiredVersion 1.0.2
```

Once a module is imported, you can use all its available functions within your current session. We import the *Logging* module, use the **Get-Module** command, which shows all imported modules within the current session, and then we invoke the **New-PublicFuncOne** from the imported module. This is shown in *Figure 5.34*:

```
PS C:\Temp> Import-Module Logging
PS C:\Temp> Get-Module

ModuleType Version   PreRelease Name                             ExportedCommands
---------- -------   ---------- ----                             ----------------
Script     2.0.0                Logging                          {Add-LogToJson, New-PublicFuncOne}
Manifest   7.0.0.0              Microsoft.PowerShell.Management   {Add-Content, Clear-Content, Clear-I
Manifest   7.0.0.0              Microsoft.PowerShell.Security     {ConvertFrom-SecureString, ConvertTo
Manifest   7.0.0.0              Microsoft.PowerShell.Utility      {Add-Member, Add-Type, Clear-Variabl
Script     1.4.8.1              PackageManagement                 {Find-Package, Find-PackageProvider,
Script     0.2.0                PowerShellEditorServices.Commands {Clear-Host, ConvertFrom-ScriptExten
Binary     0.2.0                PowerShellEditorServices.VSCode   {Close-VSCodeHtmlContentView, New-VS
Script     2.2.5                PowerShellGet                     {Find-Command, Find-DscResource, Fin
Script     2.2.6                PSReadLine                        {Get-PSReadLineKeyHandler, Get-PSRea

PS C:\Temp> New-PublicFuncOne
I Helped
```

Figure 5.34: The imported Logging module and the invoking of
the New-PublicFuncOne function from the module

When a specific module or version of a module is not required anymore, we can uninstall it entirely from the system using the **Uninstall-Module** cmdlet. We can also uninstall a specific version using the **-RequiredVersion** parameter. Once a module is removed from the sysytem you will have to re-install it again using the **Install-Module** cmdlet before it can be imported, and its functions becomes available again:

```
# Uninstall module

Uninstall-Module Logging

# Uninstall specific module version

Uninstall-Module Logging -RequiredVersion 2.0.0
```

Note: Functions from an already imported module that is then uninstalled from the current session, might still be cached within that session until the session is closed.

If you have a lot of modules and want to search for a specific module within a repository, you can use the **Find-Module** cmdlet to search within all available repositories or within a specific repository:

```
# Search for a module in a specific repository
Find-Module Logging -Repository PsRepo
# Search for a module within all available repositories
Find-Module Logging
```

Figure 5.35 shows the output of searching for the Logging module using both these methods:

```
PS C:\Temp> Find-Module Logging -Repository PsRepo

Version          Name                        Repository          Description
-------          ----                        ----------          -----------
2.0.0            Logging                     PsRepo              Contains misc. Logging functions

PS C:\Temp> Find-Module Logging

Version          Name                        Repository          Description
-------          ----                        ----------          -----------
2.0.0            Logging                     PsRepo              Contains misc. Logging functions
4.8.5            Logging                     PSGallery           Powershell Logging Module
```

***Figure 5.35:** Searching for Logging modules in PsRepo repository and all available repositories*

We can see that the Public PSGallery repository also contain a module named Logging, which brings us to naming conventions for modules and for modules functions and cmdlet´s. You can create a naming convention for your modules like: **<OrganizationName>.<ModuleName>** this minimizes the risk of having duplicates and shared names with other modules in other available repositories, or you can make sure that you only have specific repositories available where you know that modules are uniquely named. If we tried to install a duplicate named module, we would get a warning before installation as shown in *Figure 5.36*, so you will not be able to install a wrong module by accident. However, if we look at function names within modules, if you create a function with a name of an already existing built-in function, by installing and importing your module with the same function name, you will override the current function and you might end up with unwanted behavior when using other commands that might depend on the original function functionality. There is always a risk of de-duplicates, so be wary in your function and module naming conventions:

```
PS C:\Temp> install-Module Logging
WARNING: 'Logging' matched module 'Logging/2.0.0' from provider: 'PowerShellGet', repository 'PsRepo'.
WARNING: 'Logging' matched module 'Logging/4.8.5' from provider: 'PowerShellGet', repository 'PSGallery'.
Install-Package: Unable to install, multiple modules matched 'Logging'. Please specify a single -Repository.
```

***Figure 5.36:** Trying to install a module with a name that resides in multiple repositories*

Packaging modules into repositories not only allows you to organize and versioning your modules but it also provides a module distribution channel. You can register a repository on each system that need access to your modules, as long as the access and permissions prerequisites are fulfilled. You will then be able to install modules from one centralized location. By having scripts running on multiple systems that are using the same modules from the same repository, you ensure that you only need to update and manage your modules in one place and you can distribute any changes and updates to the scripts and applications on all the systems from that single centralized location. This ensures consistency and reliability in your code throughout multiple systems.

Conclusion

The ability to harness a great deal of scripting techniques can be what defines the difference between being a good developer and being a great developer. Each programming language has its own set of tools and techniques for accomplishing different tasks and even though most of them have the same end goals, they can differ a lot between the different languages and requires different techniques to accomplish. In this chapter we have learned to add parameters to scripts, enabling dynamic execution depending on external input and parameter validation to ensure input reliability. We have covered several techniques that enables you to manipulate and format textual data in PowerShell. We have also covered best practices and learned how to create scripts and applications that can be used on different platforms, mitigating limitations to only executing PowerShell scripts on Windows systems. Besides that, we have dived into PowerShells execution policy and learned how to sign scripts using code signing certificates, adding levels of trust and setting rules for running scripts on different systems. Furthermore, we have learned to organize, package and distribute code not only between local systems, but to external third parties, using modules and repositories. These are all techniques that enables you to write more reliable, secure and powerful scripts and applications. It also enables you to be more proficient, setting the foundation for organizing your code base and mitigating the use of repetitive code.

The next chapter guides you through setting up, configuring, and securely managing remote PowerShell sessions using PowerShell remoting and Windows remote management. It explains how to use session configurations to restrict and grant privileges and permissions for specific users and groups on remote hosts. The chapter also provides a more in-depth insight into securing and authenticating remote sessions using credentials, encrypted XML files, the Windows credential manager and also how to configure secure and encrypted certificate-based authentication.

CHAPTER 6

Remote Script Execution: PowerShell Remote Management

Introduction

Windows Remote Management (WinRM) and PowerShell remoting allows you to establish connections and enter session on remote computers and systems, enabling you to execute PowerShell scripts and run commands on these remote hosts. This is useful for managing and administering multiple remote systems from a centralized location. Being able to remotely manage computers and systems can save time as you no longer need to physically and manually access each system to perform tasks, execute commands and invoke scripts. It is important to always use caution when utilizing remote management features, and security measures must be implemented to ensure that only authorized users can access and control remote systems. You must set up appropriate authentication mechanisms and use encrypted communication as security measures to prevent unauthorized access to your remote systems and follow security best practices including the use of least privilege permissions to minimize security risks. Being able to remotely manage and administrate computers and systems is an invaluable tool for administrators which greatly allows for optimization and streamlining of systems management across multiple systems.

Structure

The chapter covers the following topics:

- WinRM and PowerShell remoting security, remote commands, and script execution

    o **Recipe 34**: Configuring WinRM for PowerShell remoting.

- Managing remote sessions and session configurations

    o **Recipe 35**: Create and manage remote sessions in PowerShell, including customizing and using session configurations.

- Secure Remote Session credentials and authentication

    o **Recipe 36**: Use secure strings for securely passing credentials to remote sessions.

    o **Recipe 37**: Use encrypted XML files to securely store credentials and secrets.

    o **Recipe 38**: Use the Windows Credential Manager to store credentials and secrets.

    o **Recipe 39**: Configure certificate-based authentication to establish secure and encrypted remote sessions

Objectives

In this chapter, you will be introduced to Windows Remote Management and PowerShell remoting and learn how to set up clients and hosts to allow access using PowerShell remoting for executing scripts and commands on remote computers and systems. You will learn about remote sessions and how to create, manage, use and enter remote sessions on remote hosts. We will look at security perspectives for remote sessions such as certificate-based authentication, secure credentials and credentials storage and encryption and show how to set up and use such measures for secure communication between clients and remote hosts and for securely passing credentials to scripts and sessions.

WinRM and PowerShell remoting security, remote commands, and script execution

WinRM, also known as Windows Remote Management, is a technology from Microsoft that allows you to remotely manage and administer windows systems securely over a network. It provides standardized methods for remotely running commands, executing scripts, and managing configurations on remote windows computers and servers. WinRM is built on the WS-Management protocol, also called WSMan, which is a web service-based protocol for managing hardware and software components. WinRM is used for secure remote communication and is used by various Microsoft management tools and frameworks such as PowerShell desired state configuration, which we will cover in more detail in *Chapter 13, desired state configuration*. It is also used in Windows admin center and for PowerShell remoting. By utilizing WinRM and PowerShell remoting, we can set up our systems to be able to execute commands and scripts on remote hosts from our local machine or from a centralized management server. Before setting up PowerShell remoting there are a few key aspects in terms of security to take into consideration. It is crucial to address security concerns to ensure the safety of your systems and their data, especially if you manage a lot of different systems from one or more centralized locations.

- **Secure communication and encryption**: By default, PowerShell remoting use HTTP for communication, which does not provide encryption. The default port for HTTP communication is port 5985. To secure communication between clients and hosts WinRM should be configured to use HTTPS which uses a TLS certificate for encryption. The port used for HTTPS communication is port 5986.

- **Authentication mechanisms**: PowerShell remoting supports different authentication mechanisms.

  o **Basic authentication**: The standard protocol used for HTTP access. This is insecure since it sends the username and password encoded in base64 from the client to the remote host. Do not use this authentication method unless you have to. This authentication mechanism can also be used with the HTTPS protocol which is more secure since the traffic is encrypted and protects the credentials when communicating between the client and the remote hosts.

  o **Kerberos authentication**: This requires that both the client and the remote hosts are part of the same Active Directory domain. This is a strong secure authentication mechanism that supports mutual authentication and encrypted communication. Kerberos is considered as one of the most secure authentication mechanisms and should be used whenever it is applicable.

  o **NTML authentication:** This is an older protocol that is less secure than other mechanisms and should be avoided in favor of other more secure mechanisms such as Kerberos or certificate-based authentication. This mechanism is typically used where Kerberos is not available such as when the client and remote hosts are not part of an Active Directory domain, or when you are crossing domain boundaries.

  o **CredSSP**: This authentication mechanism allows the client to send its credentials to the remote server and the remote server can then use these credentials to authenticate to other resources such as other computers and servers. This is considered less secure than other mechanisms but can be used in scenarios where so-called double-hop* authentication is required.

CredSSP is not recommended for other than trusted and closed environments and should still be used with caution in such environments.

- o **Certificate based authentication**: Uses x.509 certificates to authenticate the clients and remote hosts and provides mutual authentication capabilities and encrypted communication. Both the client and the remote hosts must have valid and trusted certificates for successful authentication. This is a secure method and is preferred when clients and hosts are not within an Active Directory domain or for workgroup scenarios.

- **Firewall configuration**: PowerShell remoting uses pre-defined ports for communication. Port 5985 is used for HTTP and port 5986 is used for HTTPS. WinRM can be configured to use custom ports instead, making it less obvious for potential intruders to guess the communication port used for PowerShell remoting. Make sure that the firewall or network security groups between the clients and remote hosts allow traffic on these or the custom ports.

- **Trusted host configuration**: You can configure a trusted host list on the local client machine. This list specifies the remote computers and systems that are allowed to establish connections. This adds an extra security layer between clients and remote hosts, but it is important to continuously keep this list updated.

- **Protect credentials**: You must never expose and hardcode sensitive information such as passwords and access tokens within scripts or within configuration files for scripts. When entering credentials for remote sessions either use the `Get-Credentials` cmdlet, create a temporary credentials object using secure strings or consider using the Windows credential manager or Azure key vault or AWS Secrets manager for secure credential storage.

- **Group policies and Access Control Lists (ACL)**: Using Group Policies and Access Control Lists can help you control who has permission to use PowerShell remoting and which actions are allowed. This allows you to restrict access to only authorized users and groups. Some organizations prevent the use of WinRM and PowerShell remoting entirely for some hosts by setting up restrictive Group policies.

- **Access management**: A best practice is to use a locked down server as a centralized client for accessing remote hosts, especially in larger company networks where client computers and systems are segmented into different virtual networks, or similar network setups. This server should only be accessible from a few select source computers and/or networks and access should be restricted as much as possible to only a select few administrators and developers if needed. Computers on client networks should generally never be able to access servers and systems on more secure networks such as application server networks and database server networks etc. unless they absolutely must and even then, the general aspect of least privileged access must be retained and only the specific relevant sources must be opened to the specific relevant destinations on the specific relevant ports in firewalls.

Note: Double-hop authentication, also known as the double hop problem, is when you authenticate to a computer or system that is used as in intermediate to connect to other systems. This is due to the security implications that arises when you try to delegate credentials across multiple systems which is not possible with most authentication mechanisms such as basic, NTLM and certificate based authentication mechanism. To address such an issue, you must use Kerberos authentication which can be configured to delegate credentials or use a mechanism such as CredSSP which delegate its credentials to the remote host, where these credentials can be used to authenticate to other resources.

By addressing these security aspects, PowerShell remoting can be used in a more secure and effectively manner while minimizing the risk of unauthorized access and security incidents. You should always follow security best practices and your company security policies.

Recipe 34: Configuring WinRM for PowerShell remoting

This recipe will help you execute commands and PowerShell scripts on remote hosts. Being able to access remote hosts from a client and execute scripts and run commands, the first thing needed is to set up and configure both the client and the remote host with WinRM for PowerShell remoting. Going forward we will refer to PowerShell Remoting as PSRemoting. The following settings and remote commands are set up for clients and remote hosts that are not domain joined, but only available on a local workgroup network and for now we are also only using basic authentication.

Note: When installing PowerShell 7 with the official Windows MSI installer, you can enable PSRemoting from within the installer wizard. Also note that you need to run PowerShell with administrative privileges to be able to properly configure PSRemoting on clients and hosts.

Setting up remote host for PSRemoting

The easiest method for setting up and enabling PSRemoting on a remote host, is to use the **Enable-PSRemoting** cmdlet. This cmdlet will configure everything that is required to setup and enable PSRemoting on the host, such as enabling the WinRM service, create a HTTP listener on the default port 5985 and enable the local firewall rules used for PSRemoting. *Figure 6.1* shows the output of running the **Enable-PSRemoting** cmdlet:

```
PS C:\Temp> enable-PSRemoting
WARNING: PowerShell remoting has been enabled only for PowerShell 6+ configurations and does n
ot affect Windows PowerShell remoting configurations. Run this cmdlet in Windows PowerShell to
 affect all PowerShell remoting configurations.
WinRM has been updated to receive requests.
WinRM service started.

WinRM has been updated for remote management.
Created a WinRM listener on HTTP://* to accept WS-Man requests to any IP on this machine.
WinRM firewall exception enabled.

PS C:\Temp> whoami
ps-host01\administrator
```

Figure 6.1: Running the Enable-PSRemoting cmdlet on a remote host for setting up PSRemoting

First, it warns us that it has only enabled PSRemoting for PowerShell 6+, in our case, we use PowerShell 7. If you are using a lower version of PowerShell, you must run the **Enable-PSRemoting** command within an administrative shell running Windows PowerShell. Since we are only using PowerShell 7 on both clients and hosts, we should not encounter any issues. As you can see it has Updated WinRM and started the WinRM service for remote management, it has created a HTTP WinRM listener and it has created the relevant local Windows firewall rules. The **whoami** command tells us that the host name is **ps-host01** and that the logged in user is **administrator**.

The remote host is now set up to receive remote commands using PSRemoting from a client if all other pre-requisites are fulfilled. It could be that the client and remote host are on different networks and a hardware firewall is set up in between these networks, then the port 5985 must be allowed between the client and the remote host, allowing the traffic between the servers within these networks. Since we are only using basic authentication, we also require a user account on the remote host to be able to authenticate from the client when running commands on the remote host. In this case we use the remote hosts administrator account. In production environments, basic authentication is not recommended, but if you for some reason need a less secure production setup that uses PSRemoting and basic authentication, you should at least be sure to create and use a non-administrator account on the remote host that only has the required permissions following the least privilege best practices.

You would have to follow the same procedure for each remote host that needs to be accessible to PSRemoting.

Setting up client for PSRemoting

The client that needs to access the remote host does not need to have WinRM and PSRemoting enabled, this is only necessary for the host that needs to receive connections. In order to access a remote host with PSRemoting enabled you have to use the **Invoke-Command** cmdlet for sending single commands to the remote host or use the **New-PSSession** and the **Enter-PSSession** cmdlets in order to create and connect to a session directly on the remote host. Let us see what happens if we from our client tries to invoke a single command on the remote host using the **Invoke-Command** cmdlet shown in Figure 6.2:

```
PS C:\Temp> Invoke-Command -ComputerName PS-Host01 -ScriptBlock {ipconfig} -Credential (Get-Credential}


PowerShell credential request
Enter your credentials.
User: Administrator
Password for user Administrator: ********

OpenError: [PS-Host01] Connecting to remote server PS-Host01 failed with the following error message :
The WinRM client cannot process the request. If the authentication scheme is different from Kerberos, o
r if the client computer is not joined to a domain, then HTTPS transport must be used or the destinatio
n machine must be added to the TrustedHosts configuration setting. Use winrm.cmd to configure TrustedHo
sts. Note that computers in the TrustedHosts list might not be authenticated. You can get more informat
ion about that by running the following command: winrm help config. For more information, see the about
_Remote_Troubleshooting Help topic.
```

Figure 6.2: Trying to connect to a remote host from a client that is not properly set up

In *Figure 6.2* we use the **Invoke-Command** cmdlet to try to send the **IpConfig** command within the **-ScriptBlock** parameter to the remote host called **PS-Host01** set as an argument for the **-ComputerName** parameter. The argument we use for the **-Credential** parameter is the **Get-Credential** cmdlet, which will prompt us to enter the username and password for the remote host. We need to add the credentials using this **-Credential** parameter, since we are using basic authentication. As you can see in *Figure 6.2*, we get an error, so what is missing?

The error message states that, **If we are not using Kerberos and the client computer is not joined to a domain, then we should either use HTTPS or add the destination machine to the TrustedHosts list**. We know that we are not using Kerberos, since we are using basic authentication and the client is not joined to a domain since we are only using workgroup servers, and we know that when we enabled PSRemoting on the remote host, it only created a HTTP listener. So, what is left is the **TrustedHosts** list. This list is a part of the WinRM configuration and determines which remote systems that the client is allowed to establish remote connections to. We would have to add the remote host to this list on the client. The TrustedHosts list can contain one of the following values:

- **No value**: If the setting is not configured (is empty), only remote hosts in the same domain or workgroup as the client is trusted. This is the most restrictive setting, and in some scenarios, depending on different system settings, security policies and the OS version, even systems within the same domain or in the same workgroup are still prohibited for establishing connections. (Which is the case in *Figure 6.2*).

- **List of specific host names and IP addresses**: Remote systems that should be allowed can be specified individually in a list by either their hostnames or IP addresses, for example: **$TrustedHosts = "PS-Host01, PS-Host02, 172.26.125.4, 172.26.125.5"** in this case, only remote hosts with these specific hostnames and IP addresses are allowed to establish a connection from the client.

- **Asterisk ("*")**: Using a wildcard indicates that all systems are allowed to establish a connection. This is the least restrictive setting and should be used with caution especially in production environments.

Below you can see how to view and add computers to the TrustedHosts list:

```
# View the list of TrustedHosts
Get-Item WSMan:\localhost\client\TrustedHosts
# Add all computers to the list of TrustedHosts
Set-Item WSMan:\localhost\client\TrustedHosts -Value *
# Add the Hostnames and IP addresses of specific computers to the list of TrustedHosts
$TrustedHosts = "PS-Host01, PS-Host02, 172.26.125.4, 172.26.125.5"
Set-Item WSMan:\localhost\client\TrustedHosts -Value $TrustedHosts
# Add a computer to an existing list of TrustedHosts
$CurrentValue = (Get-Item WSMan:\localhost\client\TrustedHosts).value
Set-Item WSMan:\localhost\Client\TrustedHosts -value "$CurrentValue, Ps-Host03"
```

Knowing this we can add the hostname of our remote host to the clients TrustedHosts list as shown in *Figure 6.3*. Before making any changes to the list, we get a confirmation prompt, and after we have accepted this by selecting yes, the remote host is added to the clients TrustedHosts list:

```
PS C:\Temp> Set-Item WSMan:\localhost\Client\TrustedHosts -Value "PS-Host01"

WinRM Security Configuration.
This command modifies the TrustedHosts list for the WinRM client. The computers in the TrustedHosts lis
t might not be
authenticated. The client might send credential information to these computers. Are you sure that you w
ant to modify
this list?
[Y] Yes  [N] No  [S] Suspend  [?] Help (default is "Y"): y
```

Figure 6.3: Adding remote host to client TrustedHosts list

Running commands and invoke scripts on remote host

After PSRemoting is enabled on the remote host and the remote host is added to the TrustedHosts list on the client, we try to run the **Invoke-Command** cmdlet again. We can now see that we have successfully established a connection and the **IpConfig** command is successfully executed on the remote host, returning the output from the command to the client, as shown in *Figure 6.4*:

```
PS C:\Temp> Invoke-Command -ComputerName PS-Host01 -ScriptBlock {ipconfig} -Credential (Get-Credential)


PowerShell credential request
Enter your credentials.
User: Administrator
Password for user Administrator: ********


Windows IP Configuration


Ethernet adapter Ethernet:

    Connection-specific DNS Suffix  . : mshome.net
    Link-local IPv6 Address . . . . . : fe80::10f3:11b0:113e:ae65%3
    IPv4 Address. . . . . . . . . . . : 172.26.125.4
    Subnet Mask . . . . . . . . . . . : 255.255.240.0
    Default Gateway . . . . . . . . . : 172.26.112.1
```

Figure 6.4: *Successfully executing a single command on remote host using Invoke-Command cmdlet*

Not only can we invoke a single command on the remote host using the **Invoke-Command** cmdlet, but we can also use this cmdlet to run a local script on the remote host by using the **-FilePath** parameter and we can also add arguments to the script using the **-ArgumentList** parameter. On the client we create a simple script in **C:\Temp** and call it **GetComputerName.ps1**.

We add the following code to the script:

```
[CmdletBinding()]
param (
    [String]$ClientHostName
)
Write-Output "This script is run on $($Env:COMPUTERNAME) from $ClientHostName"
```

The script takes a single argument for the **$ClientHostName** parameter, this argument is provided from the client. The script then use the **Write-Output** cmdlet to write the string to the console. The string writes the computer name from the computer it is invoked on, using the environment variable **$Env:COMPUTERNAME** and the value from the **$ClientHostName** parameter. The **$ClientHostName** is as mentioned provided from the client side and the **$Env:COMPUTERNAME** is the environment variable from the host the script is invoked on.

To run the script on the remote host we use the **Invoke-Command** with the **-FilePath** and **-ArgumentList** parameters instead of using the **-ScriptBlock** parameter, as shown below:

```
Invoke-Command -ComputerName PS-Host01 `
-FilePath C:\Temp\GetComputerName.ps1 `
-ArgumentList "$($Env:COMPUTERNAME)" `
-Credential (Get-Credential)
```

> **Note: We use the backtick ` to write the command over multiple lines for visibility purposes. This method will be used throughout this book!**

The **-FilePath** argument value is the path to the local script on the client and for the **-ArgumentList** we use the value from the local **$Env:COMPUTERNAME** environment variable as an argument for the scripts **$LocalHostName** parameter. When we run the command and provide credentials to the remote host, we get the output from the script running on the remote host as shown in *Figure 6.5*:

```
PS C:\Temp> Invoke-Command -ComputerName PS-Host01 `
>> -FilePath C:\Temp\GetComputerName.ps1 `
>> -ArgumentList "$($Env:COMPUTERNAME)" `
>> -Credential (Get-Credential)

PowerShell credential request
Enter your credentials.
User: Administrator
Password for user Administrator: ********

This script is run on PS-HOST01 from PS-CLIENT01
```

Figure 6.5: Running script with parameter from client on remote host

The script is successfully invoked on the remote host from the client and returns the string written to the console as expected. We can see that it was invoked on **PS-HOST01** and invoked from the **PS-CLIENT01**. Note that when using the **-ArgumentList** parameter for providing arguments to the script, the arguments must be positioned and added to the **-ArgumentList** parameter in that positioned order, since it does not provide a method for adding arguments to named parameters.

We have successfully enabled PSRemoting on the remote host and established a connection from the client, by adding the remote host to the clients TrustedHosts list and we are able to execute commands and invoke local scripts on the remote host.

Managing remote sessions and session configurations

A remote session refers to having a persistent connection or interactive session connection to a remote computer or system using PSRemoting. It allows you to interact with a remote computer or system from a local client, as if you were physically directly connected to the remote system and it enables you to execute commands, manage, configure and administrate all aspects on that system or computer remotely, from your local machine. A session configuration is a set of settings and parameters that defines how a remote session is configured and controlled when you establish a connection to a remote computer or system. Using session configurations you can customize such aspects as environments, security and general session behavior of your remote PowerShell sessions. More specifically, you can define such things as running a startup script, set environment variables, set aliases and select modules that are available on the remote system, and you can even specify specific authentication mechanisms and set the execution policy and so on.

Instead of running single commands on a remote host without establishing a direct persistent connection, as we can do with the **Invoke-Command** cmdlet, we can establish sessions that enables us to connect to a remote host as if we were logged directly into that host, and then execute multiple commands and scripts and manage and administer that host. As an administrator for remote hosts, we can also create and apply specific session configurations to remote hosts that lets us granularly specify settings for specific users and groups in order to control the level of access and which capabilities non-administrator users must have on remote hosts. Both being able to connect to and manage and administrate remote hosts and also being able to limit access and capabilities on remote hosts using session configurations are important aspects of remote administration and security. In this recipe we will first learn to create a session to a remote host that enables us to manage and administrate the remote host, as though we were directly logged into it. Then we will look at session configurations and how they can be used to not only provide but also limit certain capabilities for non-administrative users on remote hosts.

Recipe 35: Create and manage remote sessions in PowerShell, including customizing and using session configurations

As we saw in the previous recipe: we can use the **Invoke-Command** with the **-Computer Name** parameter to execute single commands and entire scripts on a remote host. Whenever we use this method we would have to re-authenticate to the remote host every time, since we are not establishing a persistent session connection to that remote host. This method is fine as long as we only need to execute one single command or invoke a single script. But, what if we needed to execute numerous commands, invoke multiple scripts or directly connect to and administrate a remote host? This is where remote sessions becomes highly relevant. By creating a remote session to a host, we only need to authenticate and establish the connection one time, and then, as long as the session is connected and persistent, we can use this session, not only to invoke commands without having to re-establish the connection and re-authenticate to the remote host each time, but we can also enter that session and manage and administer the remote host directly as if we were physically logged on to it. In order to create a session, we use the **New-PSSession** cmdlet. We specify the target remote host using the **-ComputerName** parameter and we specify the credentials to the remote host using the **-Credential** parameter with the **Get-Credential** cmdlet as an argument, prompting us for the username and password for the remote host, and we can also provide a specific name for the session using the **-Name** parameter, in case we have multiple sessions to different hosts, and we need a method for quickly identifying and selecting specific sessions. We assign the session to a variable called **$Session**. Whenever we need to execute a command or invoke a script on the remote host, we simply need to reference the **$Session** variable.

```
# Create a session to a remote host
$Session = New-PSSession -ComputerName "PS-Host01" -Credential (Get-
Credential) -Name "Host01"
```

Since we are assigning our new session to a variable we do not get any output on a successful created session, we would get error output if we encountered an error though! We can use the **Get-PSSession** cmdlet to view all current sessions. *Figure 6.6* shows the **New-PSSession** cmdlet used to create a session to the **PS-HOST01** remote host and the use of **Get-PSSession** to view all the sessions on the client. In this case we only have the one session to the **PS-HOST01** remote host with the session name **Host01**. We also get more information about the session such as the **Transport** protocol used, in this case **WSMan**, the **ComputerType** which is **RemoteMachine**, the **state** of the session, which is **opened**, and the **session configuration** that is used for this particular session, in this case **Microsoft.PowerShell** which is a default configuration that is used when no specific session configuration is applied to a session:

```
PS C:\Temp> $Session = New-PSSession -ComputerName "PS-HOST01" `
>> -Credential (Get-Credential) `
>> -Name "Host01"

PowerShell credential request
Enter your credentials.
User: Administrator
Password for user Administrator: ********

PS C:\Temp> Get-PSSession

 Id Name           Transport ComputerName   ComputerType   State    ConfigurationName    Avail
                                                                                          abili
                                                                                            ty
 -- ----           --------- ------------   ------------   -----    -----------------    -----
 29 Host01         WSMan     PS-HOST01      RemoteMachine  Opened   Microsoft.PowerShell …able
```

Figure 6.6: Creating a session with New-PSSession to a remote host and using Get-PSSession cmdlet to view all current sessions

Now that we have established a connection and created a session to the remote host, we can use the **Invoke-Command** with the **-Session** parameter whenever we need to execute a command or invoke a script on the remote host. The remote session will persist until the current shell session is closed or the remote session is explicitly removed using the **Remove-PSSession** cmdlet. The use of sessions is not limited only to the PowerShell shell, but you can also create sessions within your scripts and then use these sessions throughout your script invocation to execute multiple commands on remote hosts from within scripts without re-establishing connection and re-authenticating each time a command must be executed. Below we use the **Invoke-Command** cmdlet with the **-Session** parameter and the **$Session** variable as argument to execute multiple commands and invoke a script on the remote host using the remote session:

```
# Use session to invoke command on remote host.
Invoke-Command -Session $Session -ScriptBlock {$Env:COMPUTERNAME}
# Use session to invoke another command on remote host.
Invoke-Command -Session $Session -ScriptBlock {(Get-ComputerInfo).OsName}
# Use session to invoke script on remote host
Invoke-Command -Session $Session `
-FilePath C:\Temp\GetComputerName.ps1 `
-ArgumentList "$($Env:COMPUTERNAME)"
```

As you can see in the output from running the different commands in *Figure 6.7*, we use the session to execute the commands and invoke the script on the remote host. We do not re-establish a connection or re-authenticate each time, since the session keeps the connection and authentication established for us:

```
PS C:\Temp> whoami
ps-client01\administrator
PS C:\Temp> Invoke-Command -Session $Session -ScriptBlock {$Env:COMPUTERNAME}
PS-HOST01
PS C:\Temp>
PS C:\Temp> Invoke-Command -Session $Session -ScriptBlock {(Get-ComputerInfo).OsName}
Microsoft Windows Server 2016 Standard
PS C:\Temp>
PS C:\Temp> Invoke-Command -Session $Session `
>> -FilePath C:\Temp\GetComputerName.ps1 `
>> -ArgumentList "$($Env:COMPUTERNAME)"
This script is run on PS-HOST01 from PS-CLIENT01
```

Figure 6.7: Using remote session to invoke commands and run a script on a remote host

Instead of using the **Invoke-Command** cmdlet to invoke single commands using the **-Session** parameter, if we need to run multiple commands we can use the **Enter-PSSession** with the **$Session** variable as the first parameter, to enter the session directly and execute commands as if we were physically connected to the remote host. *Figure 6.8* shows how we enter the session directly on the remote host using **Enter-PSSession**. As you can see the command prompt changes and states the name of the entered remote host. Now whenever we execute commands they are executed directly on that host as if we were physically connected to it. To leave the remote host session and return to the client, we use the **Exit-PSSession** cmdlet within the command prompt of the entered remote host:

```
PS C:\Temp> Enter-PSSession $Session
[PS-HOST01]: PS C:\Users\Administrator\Documents> whoami
ps-host01\administrator
[PS-HOST01]: PS C:\Users\Administrator\Documents> $env:COMPUTERNAME
PS-HOST01
[PS-HOST01]: PS C:\Users\Administrator\Documents> Exit-PSSession
PS C:\Temp>
```

Figure 6.8: Enter the session directly on the remote host using Enter-PSSession
and exit the session and return to the client using Exit-PSSession

Whenever you are finished with a session it must be gracefully closed using the **Remove-PSSession** cmdlet, especially when using sessions within scripts, this ensures that there are no remnants and potential opened connections left to a remote host on the client. *Figure 6.9* shows how we first use **Get-PSSession** to check if our session is opened, then we remove the session with **Remove-PSSession**, now when we re-check with **Get-PSSession,** we can see that the session is removed, and if we try to invoke another command using that session, we get an error:

```
PS C:\Temp> Get-PSSession

 Id Name            Transport ComputerName   ComputerType    State     ConfigurationName     Avail
                                                                                             abili
                                                                                                ty

 -- ----            --------- ------------   -------------   -----     -----------------     -----
 29 Host01          WSMan     PS-HOST01      RemoteMachine   Opened    Microsoft.PowerShell  …able
PS C:\Temp> Remove-PSSession $Session
PS C:\Temp> Get-PSSession
PS C:\Temp> Invoke-Command -Session $Session -ScriptBlock {$Env:COMPUTERNAME}
Invoke-Command: Because the session state for session Host01, 146c71cb-3814-414f-bdc6-f6c9e822a384, PS-
HOST01 is not equal to Open, you cannot run a command in the session.  The session state is Closed.
Invoke-Command: No valid sessions were specified.  Ensure you provide valid sessions that are in the Op
ened state and are available to run commands.
```

Figure 6.9: *Remove session using Remove-PSSession and check that the session is successfully removed with Get-PSSession and trying to invoke a command with the removed session results in an error*

To ensure that sessions are always removed within scripts, best practices would be to either encase the entire script in a **try/catch/finally** block, where you within the **finally** block always make sure to remove all sessions. You could use the below method to ensure that you remove all sessions:

```
Get-PSSession | Remove-PSSession
```

> **Note that this would remove all sessions, not only the ones created within the script, but all opened sessions on the client computer created in the current user context, so this method should be used with caution.**

Or you should use the best practice that states to use a **Main** function within your scripts. Within the **Main** function you would create the session within the **Begin** block, execute your code, call your other functions, execute commands on remote hosts and so on, within the **Process** block and then in the **End** block you would gracefully close all your sessions. You must of course make sure you have the proper code logic and error handling in place within your **Main** function and throughout your scripts, to ensure that whatever scenario accommodates for the **End** block is always being executed or else it would defeat the purpose. A script with a **Main** function could look as shown below:

```
[CmdletBinding()]
param (
    [String]$ComputerName
)
```

```
function Main {
    [CmdletBinding()]
    param (
    )
```

This should be on line with the following command:

```
        begin {
        $Session = New-PSSession -ComputerName $ComputerName `
        -Credential (Get-Credential)
    }

        process {
        Invoke-Command -Session $Session -ScriptBlock {
            $Env:COMPUTERNAME
        }
    }

        end {
        Remove-PSSession $Session
    }
}
Main
```

Configure and use session configurations

Session configurations are primarily used by administrators to specify the settings that is available to a user or a group of users, when connecting to a remote computer or system. As an administrator you can create a session configuration file locally, and then register that session configuration using the configuration file, on a remote host or a set of remote hosts. Users with permissions to that configuration on the remote host can then use this when connecting to the host and then the remote session would adhere to these specific configured settings. These configurations can be tailored to restrict or grant specific privileges to users when they establish a remote session. It can be that some users might only have permission to connect to sessions with strong authentication mechanisms such as using a certificate and will get denied if they try to use basic authentication, it can also be that specific users might need specific environment variables available on the remote system when establishing a connection. All remote sessions that are established use a session configuration, even if you do not explicitly specify it when creating a session. A default session configuration called **Microsoft.Powershell** is used when no other session configurations are provided. When creating a new session configuration there are different session types that defines the characteristics and behavior of a remote session configuration. These session types provides varying levels of access and functionality to users that connects to remote computers and systems. The most common of these session types are:

- **Default session**: This session type provides a full set of PowerShell cmdlets and features to the user connecting remotely. It offers extensive access to the remote system, similar to what you have in a local PowerShell session.

- **Restricted Remote Server**: This session type is more restricted and is designed for secure remote administration. It limits access to a subset of cmdlets and operations, providing enhanced security by reducing the attack surface. It's suitable for environments where security is a top priority.

- **Empty**: An empty session type provides an empty environment with no predefined settings. It's a blank slate for customizing session configurations according to your specific requirements. You can use this session configuration type as a starting point to build a custom configuration from scratch.

By creating different session configurations on remote hosts, we can limit the behavior for certain users or make sure that modules and scripts are available or make sure that specific environment variables and aliases are available when a session is established to a remote host. There is a lot of settings and behavior that these session configurations can be used for, and it will be too great of a topic to cover all aspects of session configurations within this chapter. We are only going to show a simple example of creating a session configuration file that adds specific environment variables to sessions using this particular session configuration. Then we are going to show how to copy the session configuration to and register the session configuration on the remote host where it should be applied. Whenever a user creates a remote session using this specific session configuration these environment variables will be available on the remote host when the session is established.

Note that for this example, we are going to create a session configuration file on the local client, we then establish a session with the default session configuration using an administrator account, and we then use this session to copy the local session configuration file onto the remote host and use the session to register the session configuration file. For more advanced session configurations or if you need to register the same session configuration on multiple servers or systems it can be beneficial to login directly to these servers and systems and register the session configurations. By registering session configurations locally on the relevant servers and systems you can use the **Register-PSSessionConfiguration** with the **-ShowSecurityDescriptorUI** parameter, in order to granulate the permissions for the session configuration when you register your session configurations.

We want to make sure the following three environment variables are available to all users who establish a remote session with our specific session configuration:

```
"CUSTOM_DB_CONNECTION_STRING"="Server=sql.example.
com;Database=mydb;User=sqluser;Password=secretpassword"

"CUSTOM_API_KEY"="your-api-key"

"CUSTOM_CONFIG_FILE"="C:\Path\To\Your\ConfigFile.conf"
```

1. The first thing we need to do is to create a session configuration file. We do this using the **New-SessionConfigurationFile** cmdlet. We need to specify a session type for the **-SessionType** parameter, in this case we use the default. We do not want to add any restrictions to the users who use this session configuration, we are only interested in providing the environment variables. We need to save the file as a **.pssc** file type, we specify this file as an argument to the **-Path** parameter:

```
# Locally create a new session configuration file

$ConfigFile = C:\Temp\SessionConfigs\MyEnvConfig.pssc

New-PSSessionConfigurationFile -SessionType Default -Path $ConfigFile
```

2. This creates a local **.pssc** file with some initial content, like schema version, author, and description, etc. Within this file we add our environment variables as shown in *Figure 6.10*:

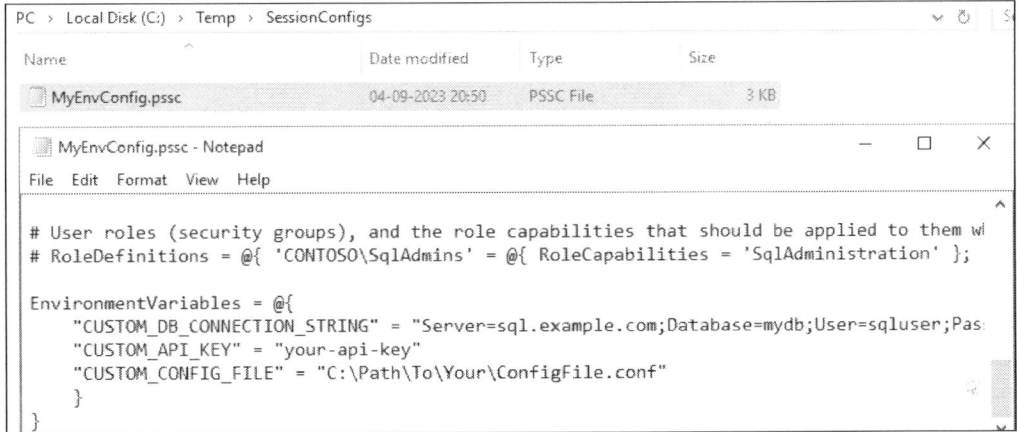

Figure 6.10: *Session configuration file created with the New-PSSessionConfigurationFile cmdlet, containing the new environment variables*

3. We create a session to the remote host using the default session configuration, meaning we do not provide any arguments and creates a session as we did in a previous example:

```
# As an Administrator, create a new session to the remote host
$Session = New-PSSession -ComputerName "PS-HOST01" `
-Credential (Get-Credential) `
-Name "Host01"
PowerShell credential request
Enter your credentials.
User: Administrator
Password for user Administrator: ********
```

4. We use the **Copy-Item** cmdlet with the **-ToSession** parameter to copy the local session configuration file to the remote host:

```
# Copy the configuration file from the local client to the remote host
# Note: Make sure the folder exists on the remote host
Copy-Item C:\Temp\SessionConfigs\MyEnvConfig.pssc `
-Destination C:\Temp\SessionConfigs\MyEnvConfig.pssc `
-ToSession $Session `
-Force
```

5. Now we enter the session so we can register the session configuration directly on the remote host:

```
# Enter the session and connect directly to the remote host.
Enter-PSSession $Session
```

6. Within the entered session of the remote host, we use the **Register-PSSessionConfiguration** cmdlet to register the session configuration. We use the **-Name** parameter to give the session configuration a specific name, in this case **MyEnvConfig** and then the **-Path** parameter specifying the path to the session configuration file as an argument:

```
# Directly logged into the remote host, register the configuration
Register-PSSessionConfiguration -Name MyEnvConfig `
-Path C:\Temp\SessionConfigs\MyEnvConfig.pssc
```

7. Once the session configuration is registered on the remote host, you will get output as shown in *Figure 6.11*:

```
[PS-HOST01]: PS C:\Users\Administrator\Documents> Register-PSSessionConfiguration -Name MyEnvConfig `
>> -Path C:\Temp\SessionConfigs\MyEnvConfig.pssc
WARNING: Register-PSSessionConfiguration may need to restart the WinRM service if a configuration using
 this name has recently been unregistered, certain system data structures may still be cached. In that
case, a restart of WinRM may be required.
All WinRM sessions connected to Windows PowerShell session configurations, such as Microsoft.PowerShell
 and session configurations that are created with the Register-PSSessionConfiguration cmdlet, are disco
nnected.


   WSManConfig: Microsoft.WSMan.Management\WSMan::localhost\Plugin

Type            Keys                             Name
----            ----                             ----
Container       {Name=MyEnvConfig}               MyEnvConfig
WARNING: Register-PSSessionConfiguration may need to restart the WinRM service if a configuration using
 this name has recently been unregistered, certain system data structures may still be cached. In that
case, a restart of WinRM may be required.
All WinRM sessions connected to Windows PowerShell session configurations, such as Microsoft.PowerShell
 and session configurations that are created with the Register-PSSessionConfiguration cmdlet, are disco
nnected.
```

Figure 6.11: Successfully registered session configuration on remote host

8. Return to the local client using the **Exit-PSSession** cmdlet:

```
# Exit entered session on remote host
Exit-PSSession
```

9. On the local client, remove the current session, using the **Remove-PSSession** cmdlet:

```
# Remove the current session
Remove-PSSession $Session
```

We have now successfully created and registered a session configuration file on the remote host, and we are now able to create a new session specifying this session configuration and we should get the settings and behavior applied to this session that is defined within the session configuration. In this case it would be the added environment variables. We use the **New-Session** cmdlet to create a new session to the remote host. This time we use the **-ConfigurationName** parameter to specify the name of the session configuration we want to use, in this case the **MyEnvConfig**:

```
# Create a new session using the MyEnvConfig session configuration
$Session = New-PSSession -ComputerName "PS-HOST01" `
-Credential (Get-Credential) `
-Name "Host01-Env" `
-ConfigurationName MyEnvConfig
```

10. Once we have established the session with the **MyEnvConfig** session configuration, we can check that the environment variables are available as expected. We use the **Invoke-Command** with the **-Session** parameter and the session variable as an argument. Within the **-ScriptBlock** parameter we call **dir env:** to list all environment variables within the **env: PSDrive** on the remote host. *Figure 6.12* shows the creation of the session using the **MyEnvConfig** session configuration and the output of the **Invoke-Command** running the **dir env:** command on the remote host. As you can see in the output the three new environment variables are created and available as expected:

```
PS C:\Temp> whoami
ps-client01\administrator
PS C:\Temp> $Session = New-PSSession -ComputerName "PS-HOST01" `
>> -Credential (Get-Credential) `
>> -Name "Host01-Env" `
>> -ConfigurationName MyEnvConfig

PowerShell credential request
Enter your credentials.
User: Administrator
Password for user Administrator: ********

PS C:\Temp> Invoke-Command -Session $Session -ScriptBlock {dir env:}

Name                       Value                                PSComputerName
----                       -----                                --------------
ALLUSERSPROFILE            C:\ProgramData                       PS-HOST01
APPDATA                    C:\Users\Administrator\AppData\Roa… PS-HOST01
CommonProgramFiles         C:\Program Files\Common Files        PS-HOST01
CommonProgramFiles(x86)    C:\Program Files (x86)\Common Files PS-HOST01
CommonProgramW6432         C:\Program Files\Common Files        PS-HOST01
COMPUTERNAME               PS-HOST01                            PS-HOST01
ComSpec                    C:\Windows\system32\cmd.exe          PS-HOST01
CUSTOM_API_KEY             your-api-key                         PS-HOST01
CUSTOM_CONFIG_FILE         C:\Path\To\Your\ConfigFile.conf      PS-HOST01
CUSTOM_DB_CONNECTION_STRING Server=sql.example.com;Database=my… PS-HOST01
HOMEDRIVE                  C:                                   PS-HOST01
HOMEPATH                   \Users\Administrator                 PS-HOST01
LOCALAPPDATA               C:\Users\Administrator\AppData\Loc… PS-HOST01
LOGONSERVER                \\PS-HOST01                          PS-HOST01
```

Figure 6.12: Environment variables on remote host when establishing
a session using the MyEnvConfig session configuration

Session configurations can be used for so much more than is shown in this example. The example in this recipe is primarily to show you how to create a session configuration file, register it on the remote host and how to create and establish a session with that specific session configuration. If you need to create more advanced session configurations, it is then encouraged to look up and become more familiar with more advanced settings of and use cases for session configurations.

Secure Remote Session credentials and authentication

So far, we have only used basic authentication and credentials with password and username for a local account on a remote host, to access that remote host using PSRemoting. Using basic authentication is considered to be insecure in most scenarios due to several limitations and vulnerabilities and should only be used between hosts in test environments or highly secure networks where other factors might limit the use of stronger authentication mechanisms. Some of the vulnerabilities and limitations using basic authentication are:

- **Unencrypted credential exposure:** Basic authentication does not encrypt credentials and the username and password are sent over the network between the hosts in plain text. This makes it vulnerable to attacks such as packet sniffing, and an attacker can easily be able to intercept and capture the credentials in transit to obtain the login information.

- **Bruce force attacks and lack of account lockout mechanisms**: Basic authentication provides no protection against brute force attacks and does not implement any account lockout mechanisms that prevents multiple failed login attempts. An attacker can repeatedly try to guess passwords using brute force mechanisms until the correct password is found, especially if weak or short passwords are used.

- **Password reuse**: Users tend to use the same password on multiple hosts and systems. If one host is compromised the chances are that the compromised credentials can be used to access other systems are high and an attacker could use this to gain access to multiple systems.

- **Password management**: It can be challenging to manage passwords securely and passwords to other systems are often stored in plain text within configuration and settings files. If an attacker gains access to one system, he might be able to gain access to other more secure systems such as database servers and other higher level accounts if the compromised system contains configuration and settings files containing credentials and other secrets to such systems and accounts.

- **Password policies:** It can be challenging to implement mechanisms to uphold passwords policies that ensures password rotations and strong password complexities for basic authentication methods. Making passwords more prone to be weak and long lived.

- **Authentication factors**: Basic authentication typically relies on a single factor, usually a password, and lacks the security that is provided by using two-factor authentication.

Due to these security vulnerabilities and limitations, it is generally recommended to use more secure authentication mechanisms such as certificate-based authentication or in domain environments using Kerberos, but it is not always possible to use these types of more secure authentication mechanisms and the only option might be to use basic authentication. When we use basic authentication, we can manually pass the credentials for remote sessions using the `Get-Credential` cmdlet. This is sufficient if we need to create a remote session manually, but what if we need to automatically invoke scripts that use remote sessions? Then we would need methods for passing the credentials securely to these scripts. Often, passwords are stored in plain text in configuration files for programs, but they can also be stored in encrypted files, in the Windows credential manager or even within cloud vaults such as Azure key vault and AWS Secrets manager.

When using basic authentication or other mechanisms that require the use of credentials for creating and authenticating remote sessions, we need methods for both storing the credentials and also for passing these credentials securely to the remote sessions or to scripts that needs to use remote sessions. We also need more secure authentication methods for environments where the use of basic authentication is too insecure or not applicable.

In the next recipes we will look at some of the methods that can be used for storing and passing credentials more securely to remote sessions and how to set up and use certificate-based authentication to provide a more secure method for authenticating remote sessions.

Recipe 36: Use secure strings for securely passing credentials to remote sessions

A SecureString is a datatype in PowerShell that is used for storing sensitive information such as passwords, connection strings and tokens. A secure string is encrypted with the machines specific **Data Protection API (DPAPI)** which is a Windows feature that provides encryption services, and it employs strong encryption algorithms such **as Advanced Encryption Standard (AES)**. Not only is DPAPI used to encrypt a SecureString, but it also use the users credentials and a machine specific key for the machine it is created on, to encrypt the SecureString. This offers strong protection, since a SecureString can only be used on a specific machine by the user who created it. This also make SecureString´s to be used primarily for in-memory protection of credential data within the context of a single user session on a specific machine, since it is not portable to other users and machines. It would not be optimal to store SecureStrings within files, since the SecureStrings with these files would then only be usable by the user who created it, on the machine it was created on.

To create a SecureString we use the **ConvertTo-SecureString** cmdlet with the **-AsPlainText** and **-Force** parameters. This cmdlet by default, expects a SecureString, so we use the **-AsPlainText** parameter to explicitly indicate that the input string must be a plain text string. We use the **-Force** parameter to suppress any potential confirmation prompts, this ensures that we can use the command within scripts without any user intervention:

```
$SecurePassword = ConvertTo-SecureString "MyPassword" -AsPlainText -Force
```

When we try to output the content of the **$SecurePassword** variable that contains the SecureString, we only get the type name of the variable returned, as shown in *Figure 6.13*:

```
● PS C:\Temp> $SecurePassword
  System.Security.SecureString
```

Figure 6.13: Type name when trying to output a variable with a SecureString

This is intended since SecureString´s are designed to keep sensitive data secure, exposing its content would defeat its purpose. Now that we have the password stored as a SecureString, we can use that SecureString to create a credential object containing both username and password (as a SecureString). Such a credential object can be used by any cmdlet that have a **-Credential** parameter, such as the **New-PSSession** cmdlet. To create a credential object, we create a new object of the **System.Management.Automation.PSCredential** type and provide a username and the variable with our SecureString as arguments:

```
$Credential = New-Object System.Management.Automation.
PSCredential("Username", $SecurePassword)
```

Now we can pass this credential object to any cmdlet that have a **-Credential** parameter, such as the **New-PSSession** cmdlet:

```
New-PSSession -ComputerName "PS-HOST01" -Credential $Credential
```

This is equivalent to the **Get-Credential** cmdlet, without the need for user intervention, so this is the method that should be used for creating credential objects within scripts that needs to be invoked automatically.

As you can see when we use the **ConvertTo-SecureString** cmdlet, we need to provide the password in plain text, so at some point the plain text password needs to be kept somewhere, if it is to be used within automation scripts that does not require any user intervention, like within configuration files. By keeping plain text passwords, or connection strings and tokens for that matter, within files, exposes the sensitive data to all users who have access to the system the data is stored in. At least you should never hardcode sensitive data directly within your scripts, and at least use a configuration file instead for such data for scripts and then import the data from the configuration file. A configuration file can be placed together with the script, and whenever the script needs to be copied to another system or used elsewhere, an empty configuration file can be provided, and then sensitive data can be provided to the new configuration file on that system. This is still not a secure method for storing passwords on systems, but at least they are only available to the users of that system, and they are not hardcoded within scripts and applications that might reside in public places or repositories. You could also obfuscate data placed within configuration files by encoding them as base64, so they are not directly human readable, and then have a base64 decode function within your scripts. This only provides a false sense of security though, since the data could easily be decoded, but at least it is not directly readable. If you need users to manually input passwords for some of your scripts, you can use the **Read-Host** cmdlet with the**: AsSecureString** parameter, this returns a SecureString and masks the input when typing in the string.:

```
$SecurePassword = Read-Host -Prompt "Enter password" -AsSecureString
```

```
$Credential = New-Object System.Management.Automation.
PSCredential("Username", $SecurePassword)
```

```
New-PSSession -ComputerName "PS-HOST01" -Credential $Credential
```

Being it manual or automatic, you should always use SecureString´s for sensitive data within scripts and sessions and use them to make credential objects that should be passed to cmdlets.

In case you need to decrypt the SecureString back to a plain text password, you can use the **System.Net.NetworkCredential** .Net method. This is only possible within the same user context and on the machine the SecureString was created:

```
$PlainTextPassword = [System.Net.NetworkCredential]::new("",
$SecurePassword).Password
```

Recipe 37: Use encrypted XML files to securely store credentials and secrets

We can create SecureString´s from plain text strings containing sensitive data such as passwords, connection strings and tokens, but we still need methods for locally storing the sensitive data, or any user who have access to the system can easily view the sensitive data, if it is saved within config files etc. By using encrypted xml files, we can store credential data and other types of secrets, within files as credential objects. Such a file will then contain the credential object encrypted in that user context and for the machine it is created on, similar to SecureString´s.

You should manually create an encrypted XML file in the user context and on the machine the credential object should be used. Once created, only that specific user on that specific machine can import the credential from that XML file and use it within scripts and sessions:

```
$Credential = Get-Credential
```

```
$Credential | Export-Clixml -Path C:\Temp\Encrypted.xml
```

This will create an XML file containing the username and the encrypted password as shown in *Figure 6.14*:

```
※ PS C:\Temp> $Credential = Get-Credential
  >> $Credential | Export-Clixml -Path C:\Temp\Encrypted.xml

   PowerShell credential request
   Enter your credentials.
   User: Test
   Password for user Test: ********

※ PS C:\Temp> Get-Content C:\Temp\Encrypted.xml
  <Objs Version="1.1.0.1" xmlns="http://schemas.microsoft.com/powershell/2004/04">
    <Obj RefId="0">
      <TN RefId="0">
        <T>System.Management.Automation.PSCredential</T>
        <T>System.Object</T>
      </TN>
      <ToString>System.Management.Automation.PSCredential</ToString>
      <Props>
        <S N="UserName">Test</S>
        <SS N="Password">01000000d08c9ddf0115d1118c7a00c04fc297eb01000000a4e3a25fd8873848be43fa40e2ed783000000000002000000000003660000c0000000100000000f2b7
f379a81e6d93a5e0b1247f0de9df000000000048000000a0000000100000005ea2b5e3d484cae9a7cf6b6210b1687d180000003728f29b30c117572c6bb76eae33ee3d3171914669477114140
00000e4eb539d1aff3b8762e0344f54fd8a9e7f799938</SS>
      </Props>
    </Obj>
  </Objs>
```

Figure 6.14: Content of encrypted XML file containing credential object

> **Note: The password could be any string, such as a database connection string, an API key or a token. Any string that must be stored securely. The username <u>must</u> be provided, but is in some cases it is not needed, so it could be any string, as long as it is provided to the Get-Credential cmdlet.**

When you need to use the credential, you have to import the content from the file, and you can than use the credential object in any cmdlet that has a **-Credential** parameter:

```
$Credential = Import-CliXml -Path C:\Temp\Encrypted.xml
New-PSSession -ComputerName "PS-HOST01" -Credential $Credential
```

If the imported credential object does not contain a credential with username and password, but another sensitive datatype such as a connection string, you can use the **System.Net. NetworkCredential** method to decrypt and store it in a variable:

```
$ConnString = [System.Net.NetworkCredential]::new("", $Credential.
Password).Password
```

In *Figure 6.15* we can see the connection string that was securely stored within the password property of the **$ConnString** credential object:

```
PS C:\Temp> $Credential = Import-CliXml -Path C:\Temp\Encrypted.xml
PS C:\Temp> $Credential


  UserName                     Password
  --------                     --------
  Test       System.Security.SecureString

PS C:\Temp> $ConnString = [System.Net.NetworkCredential]::new("", $Credential.Password).Password
PS C:\Temp> $ConnString
  "Server=ServerName;Database=DatabaseName;Integrated Security=True;"
```

Figure 6.15: Connection string imported from an encrypted xml file and decrypted and saved in a variable

Note: The credential object stored within the $Credential variable and the connection string within the $ConnString variable are stored in memory and will be available throughout the session or script where they are imported and assigned as long as the script or session is running. If you want to remove the objects from memory as soon as they are used, you can use the Remove-Variable cmdlet to remove them. This is beneficial for long running scripts and sessions to ensure no secrets are stored within memory longer than it is required.

Remember that encrypted XML files can only be used within the user context and on the machine where they are created, so they are not portable to other users, computers and systems. If you need to run the same script that imports credentials or other secrets from encrypted XML files on multiple computers or systems, you have to create a new encrypted XML file on each computer and system and for each user. If you have a lot of scripts on multiple systems that needs credentials or secrets this might not be the most beneficial method for storing credentials and secrets and you should consider using a more centralized secrets storage, such as HashiCorp Vault, Azure Key Vault or AWS Secrets Manager.

Recipe 38: Use the Windows Credential Manager to store credentials and secrets

On Windows computers and servers, you can use the Windows Credential Manager to securely store credentials and other secrets. This is a windows feature that provides secure and encrypted storage. This is generally used for storing credentials used for network resources, file shares and remote desktop connections but it is also used to store web credentials and certificate-based credentials. Many Windows applications and browsers can directly access the stored credentials within the credential manager which makes it easy to authenticate with various services and resources. You can manually add generic credentials to the credential manager and use these credentials to store not only credentials but also other types of secrets such as connections strings, tokens and API keys and use these within PowerShell. You can find and open Windows Credential Manager by clicking on the Windows start button and type **credential manager**. Within credential manager you have a **Web Credentials** and a **Windows Credentials** section. Within the **Windows Credentials** section there are different sub-sections such as **Windows Credentials**, where remote desktop and file share credentials are stored, there is a **Certificate-Based Credentials** section, where certificate-based credentials are stored and then there is the **Generic Credentials** and **Other Items** sections. *Figure 6.16* shows the Windows Credential Manager with the Windows Credentials section:

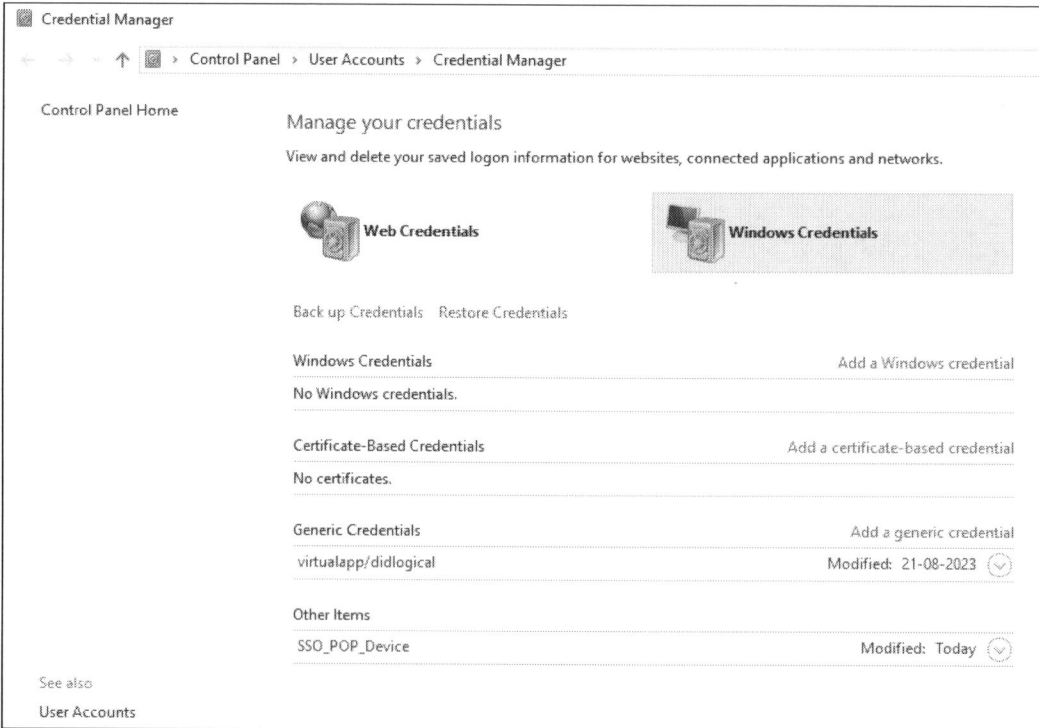

Figure 6.16: Windows Credential Manager

If we want to create credentials and other secrets we can use within PowerShell scripts and sessions, we can manually add them to the **Generic Credentials** section by clicking on the **Add a generic credential**. For this example, we create two new generic credentials:

The first credential is for the administrator account on the PS-HOST01 remote server:

CredentialName: PS-HOST01

Username: User

Password: Abcd1234

And for the second credential, we use this to store a fictive API key. In this case, the username is irrelevant, but must still be provided:

CredentialName: ApiKey

Username: ApiKey

Password: Sdfhjkpsg1234sdfgjksdpf

PowerShell does not have a built-in method for directly connecting to and using credentials stored within the credential manager, but within the PSGallery public PowerShell repository, there is a module that provides access to credentials within the Windows Credential Manager, this module is called **CredentialManager**. We install this module and import it into our current session:

```
# Install CredentialManager
Install-Module CredentialManager -Scope AllUsers
# Import CredentialManager into current session/Script
Import-Module CredentialManager
```

CredentialManager offers four cmdlets:

- **Get-StoredCredential**: This is used to retrieve credential objects from the Windows Credential Manager.

- **New-StoredCredential**: This is used to generate new credential objects within the Windows Credential Manager.

- **Remove-StoredCredential**: This is used to remove credential objects from the Windows Credential Manager.

- **Get-StrongPassword**: This is used to generate strong random passwords.

We can use the **Get-StoredCredential** cmdlet to retrieve all credential objects from credential manager:

```
# Retrieve all credential objects
Get-StoredCredential
```

Figure 6.17 shows the output of running the cmdlet:

```
PS C:\Temp> Get-StoredCredential
WARNING: Unable to convert Credential object without username or password to PSCredential object
WARNING: Unable to convert Credential object without username or password to PSCredential object

UserName                      Password
--------                      --------
User     System.Security.SecureString
ApiKey   System.Security.SecureString
```

Figure 6.17: *Credentials in Windows Credential Manager*
retrieved with Get-StoredCredential cmdlet

We can see the **User** and the **ApiKey** credential objects are found in the credential manager. Notice that there are a few warnings. These are irrelevant in our case and indicate that some credential objects placed in the credential manager, are not convertible due to a missing username or password. We can use the **Get-StoredCredential** cmdlet with the **-Target** parameter and the name of the specific credential object as an argument to retrieve a specific credential object which can then be assigned to a variable. You might have noticed that the **Get-StoredCredential** cmdlet only returns the **Username** and **Password** property of the credential object and not the object name, so we need to use the Windows Credential Manager GUI to view the object name. The object we are currently interested in is the credential object named **PS-HOST01**:

```
# Retrieve a specific credential object

$Credential = Get-StoredCredential -Target PS-HOST01
```

Once we have retrieved the correct credential object, we can use it as any other credential, in this case we use this specific credential to connect to and invoke a command on the **PS-HOST01** remote host using the **Invoke-Command** cmdlet as shown in *Figure 6.18*:

```
PS C:\Temp> $Credential = get-StoredCredential -Target PS-HOST01
PS C:\Temp> $Credential

UserName                      Password
--------                      --------
User     System.Security.SecureString

PS C:\Temp> Invoke-Command -ComputerName PS-HOST01 `
>> -ScriptBlock {$Env:COMPUTERNAME} `
>> -Credential $Credential
PS-HOST01
```

Figure 6.18: *Using credential object from Windows Credential*
Manager to invoke command on remote host

If we want to retrieve the **ApiKey** credential, we use the **Get-StoredCredential** cmdlet to retrieve the credential object and the **NetworkCredential** .Net method to retrieve the password property from the credential object which stores the **ApiKey**:

```
# Retrieve a credential object and assign the password property to a
variable

$Credential = Get-StoredCredential -Target ApiKey

$ApiKey = [System.Net.NetworkCredential]::new("", $Credential.Password).Password
```

In *Figure 6.19* we can see the **ApiKey** from the credential object is assigned to the **$ApiKey** variable:

```
PS C:\Temp> $Credential = Get-StoredCredential -Target ApiKey
PS C:\Temp> $ApiKey = [System.net.networkCredential]::new("", $Credential.password).password
PS C:\Temp> $ApiKey
Sdfhjkpsg1234sdfgjksdpf
```

Figure 6.19: *Api Key retrieved from Windows Credential Manager credential object and assigned to a variable*

As with SecureString´s and encrypted XML files, the Windows Credential Manager is isolated to the specific users context, so credential objects created by one user is only available to and can only be decrypted by that specific user and only on that specific machine. When using encrypted XML files and credential objects stored within Windows Credential Manager, you have secure methods for storing credentials and secrets. Whereas an XML file is a physical file saved in a directory which is easy to copy and distribute, credentials within the Windows Credential Manager are stored within the encrypted storage for the credential manager and are not directly distributable. Credential objects within the credential manager can be backed up to a file, using the built-in backup feature, and this backup file can then be distributed, but due to the way both types of storage are encrypted with, and bound to, both the user context and the specific machine they are created on, makes them impossible to use and decrypt when distributed to other systems and for other users.

So far and throughout the chapter, we have used Administrator and user accounts to connect to remote hosts and for running scripts, creating SecureString´s, creating encrypted XML files and working with Windows Credential Manager within the user context. It is never recommended to use such accounts for accessing systems remotely or running scripts automatically either by using schedulers or running them as services. A strong recommendation and a fundamental security best practice is to always use service accounts with least privileges for such tasks. By using service accounts instead of user and administrator accounts and limiting the privileges and permissions for such service accounts, you can greatly reduce the attack surface and limit the potential impact of security breaches and the damage it may cause. You should create service accounts and limit the permissions and levels of access as much as possible and for remote sessions to remote hosts, you should also use session configurations to limit cmdlets and other settings. For scripts that should execute automatically within a scheduler or a service, it is recommended that you create encrypted XML files or store credentials and secrets in Windows Credential Manager in the context of the particular service accounts, or use vaults such as HashiCorp Vault, Azure Key Vault or AWS Secrets Manager.

Recipe 39: Configure certificate-based authentication to establish secure and encrypted remote sessions

Certificate-based authentication for PowerShell remote sessions is a secure method for establishing trust between the local client and remote host when using PSRemoting. It relies on certificates to authenticate the client to the remote host instead of usernames and passwords. It uses HTTPS for establishing a secure connection and ensures that all communication between the client and the host is encrypted. This method enhances security especially in environments where basic authentication is not nearly secure enough such as production and less secure environments. The process for using certificate-based authentication is as follows:

1. **Certificate enrollment/issuance**: Both the client and the remote host needs a server certificate to establish trust. This is used to prove the identity between the remote host and the client.

2. **Remote host setup**: The remote host needs to allow certificate-based authentication and it needs a HTTPS listener for Windows remote management and a firewall rule allowing inbound traffic on port 5986 for WinRM HTTPS.

3. **Authentication**: When a PSRemoting session is initiated from the client to the remote host, the client certificate is presented for proving its identity to the remote host during the handshake process.

4. **Server verification**: The remote host verifies the client's certificate to ensure it trusts the certificate issuer. If the verification is successful, the connection is established.

5. **Secure communication**: Once the trust and connection is established, all communication between the remote host and the client is encrypted.

6. **Mutual authentication**: In some cases, certificate-based authentication can provide mutual authentication, meaning that both the client and server prove their identities to each other using certificates. This adds an extra layer of security.

> **Note: Certificate-based authentication is a complex topic, and this guide provides a simplified example using self-signed certificates for learning and testing purposes. In a production environment, you would typically use certificates issued by a trusted Certificate Authority (CA) and set up mutual authentication for enhanced security.**

The following steps explain how to configure and use certificate-based authentication for establishing secure and encrypted remote sessions. First, we need to set up the remote host for certificate-based authentication and create a certificate. The following steps are performed on the remote host.

1. We are going to issue a self-signed certificate. The important thing here is that the DNS name of the certificate must match the name of the remote host. The certificate is placed in the personal **LocalMachine** certificate store and assigned to the **$Cert** variable:

```
$Dns = "ps-host01"

$Cert = New-SelfSignedCertificate -DnsName $Dns `

-CertStoreLocation Cert:\LocalMachine\My
```

2. The public key of the certificate needs to be exported. This is used for the client to ensure that it trusts the certificate issuer:

```
$Cert | Export-Certificate -FilePath C:\Temp\ps-host01.cer
```

3. You should also export the certificate with the private key. Save the certificate securely for future references:

```
$Cert | Export-PfxCertificate -FilePath C:\Temp\ps-host01.pfx `

-Password (ConvertTo-SecureString "CertPass" -AsPlainText -Force)
```

4. We need to make sure that certificate-based authentication is enabled for PSRemoting on the remote host. You can use this command to check the configuration of Windows Remote Management on the remote host:

```
winrm get winrm/config
```

5. Within the configuration output, there is an **Auth** section where it should state if certificate-based authentication is enabled or not, as shown in *Figure 6.20*:

```
Auth
    Basic = true
    Digest = true
    Kerberos = true
    Negotiate = true
    Certificate = true
    CredSSP = false
DefaultPorts
    HTTP = 5985
    HTTPS = 5986
```

Figure 6.20: Certificate-based authentication is enabled

6. If it is not yet enabled, it must be enabled:

```
Set-Item WSMan:\localhost\Service\Auth\Certificate -Value $true
```

7. The next step is to create a new HTTPS WinRM listener. This enables the WinRM to listen for connections on HTTPS and port 5986. For now, we have only used an HTTP listener for basic authentication. We use the **New-Item** cmdlet and set the **-Path** parameter to the **WSMan PSDrive** path for listeners. The argument for the **-Transport** parameter is set to **HTTPS**. We need to specify which clients are allowed to access this listener on the remote host by using the **-Address** parameter. For this example, we use the wildcard ***** which allows all clients. In

secure environments, you should only allow specific clients by specifying their IP addresses or hostnames as argument for this parameter. We need to provide the thumbprint of the certificate that this listener should use, in this case the thumbprint for the self-signed certificate we created. This is set as an argument for the **-CertificateThumbprint** parameter. We also need to provide the hostname for our remote host as an argument to the **-HostName** parameter. We use the **-Force** parameter to suppress any potential prompts:

```
New-Item -Path WSMan:\localhost\listener -Transport HTTPS `
-Address * `
-CertificateThumbPrint $Cert.Thumbprint `
-HostName ps-host01 `
-Force
```

8. We can use the **Get-ChildItem** to view all current listeners as shown in *Figure 6.21*:

Get-ChildItem WSMan:\localhost\Listener

```
PS C:\Temp> Get-ChildItem WSMan:\localhost\Listener\

    WSManConfig: Microsoft.WSMan.Management\WSMan::localhost\Listener

Type             Keys                              Name
----             ----                              ----
Container        {Address=*, Transport=HTTPS}      Listener_1362561727
Container        {Address=*, Transport=HTTP}       Listener_902018458
```

Figure 6.21: Use Get-ChildItem to view all listeners

9. Once we have created the new HTTPS listener we can delete the HTTP listener to prevent the use of less secure authentication mechanisms such as basic authentication. If you still want to be able to authenticate using basic authentication and other less secure mechanisms you can keep the HTTP listener, it is strongly recommended to delete this and use stronger authentication mechanisms. We remove the HTTP listener:

```
winrm delete winrm/config/listener?Address=*+Transport=HTTP
```

Now when we list all listeners again, we are left with the HTTPS listener, as shown in *Figure 6.22*:

```
PS C:\Temp> Get-ChildItem WSMan:\localhost\Listener\

    WSManConfig: Microsoft.WSMan.Management\WSMan::localhost\Listener

Type             Keys                              Name
----             ----                              ----
Container        {Address=*, Transport=HTTPS}      Listener_1362561727
```

Figure 6.22: View of listeners after removing the HTTP listener.

10. If we try to connect to the remote host from the client after the HTTP listener is removed using basic authentication, we get an error as shown in *Figure 6.23* which confirms that the removal of the HTTP worked as intended and limited the use of less secure mechanisms:

```
PS C:\Temp> $Session = New-PSSession -ComputerName "PS-HOST01" -Credential (Get-Credential)

PowerShell credential request
Enter your credentials.
User: Administrator
Password for user Administrator: ********

New-PSSession: [PS-HOST01] Connecting to remote server PS-HOST01 failed with the following error messag
e : WinRM cannot complete the operation. Verify that the specified computer name is valid, that the com
puter is accessible over the network, and that a firewall exception for the WinRM service is enabled an
d allows access from this computer. By default, the WinRM firewall exception for public profiles limits
 access to remote computers within the same local subnet. For more information, see the about_Remote_Tr
oubleshooting Help topic.
```

Figure 6.23: Denied access using basic authentication after removal of HTTP listener on remote host

11. The HTTPS listener use port 5986 by default. This port needs to be open for inbound connections within the local firewall on the remote host. You can create a new firewall rule allowing inbound traffic on this port:

```
$Rule = "Windows Remote Management (HTTPS-In)"

New-NetFirewallRule -DisplayName $Rule `

-Name $Rule `

-Group $Rule `

-Profile Any `

-LocalPort 5986 `

-Protocol TCP
```

12. Once the set-up is complete, we can now go to the client and try to access the remote host by creating a new session with the **New-PSSession** cmdlet. Instead of using the **-Credential** parameter we need to specify the **-UseSSL** parameter. This parameter indicates that we want to establish an HTTPS connection instead of using the default HTTP connection:

```
$Session = New-PSSession -ComputerName PS-HOST01 -UseSSL
```

13. *Figure 6.24* shows the first attempt to create a session to the remote host:

```
PS C:\Temp> whoami
ps-client01\administrator
PS C:\Temp> $Session = New-PSSession -ComputerName "PS-HOST01" -UseSSL
New-PSSession: [PS-HOST01] Connecting to remote server PS-HOST01 failed with the following error messag
e : The server certificate on the destination computer (PS-HOST01:5986) has the following errors:
The SSL certificate is signed by an unknown certificate authority. For more information, see the about_
Remote_Troubleshooting Help topic.
```

Figure 6.24: Using certificate-based authentication to establish
a session to a remote host with untrusted certificate

14. As you can see we get an error that states that **The SSL certificate is signed by an unknown certificate authority**. This is because we do not yet trust the remote host certificate on the client. We need to add the certificate to the trusted root certificate authority on the client. Copy the certificate's public key file we exported in the previous step 2. To the client and then import this certificate into the trusted root certificate authority:

```
Import-Certificate -FilePath C:\Temp\ps-host01.cer `
-CertStoreLocation Cert:\LocalMachine\Root
```

15. Once the certificate is imported, we are now able to successfully establish a secure and encrypted session to the remote host using certificate-based authentication, as shown in *Figure 6.25*:

```
PS C:\Temp> Import-Certificate -FilePath C:\Temp\ps-host01.cer `
>> -CertStoreLocation Cert:\LocalMachine\Root

   PSParentPath: Microsoft.PowerShell.Security\Certificate::LocalMachine\Root

Thumbprint                                Subject             EnhancedKeyUsageList
----------                                -------             -------------------
041FFE584173BBBB894B0ABF46327E6217D08A59  CN=PS-HOST01        {Client Authentication, Server Authent…

PS C:\Temp> $Session = New-PSSession -ComputerName "PS-HOST01" -UseSSL
PS C:\Temp> Enter-PSSession $Session
[PS-HOST01]: PS C:\Users\Administrator\Documents> whoami
ps-host01\administrator
```

Figure 6.25: Successfully established remote session to remote host using certificate-based authentication

16. We are now able to use the certificate-based authentication and the trust it provides from that client to that remote host, both within PowerShell sessions but also within scripts that are invoked on the client that needs to establish sessions to the remote host, without having to store any credentials in files or in the Windows Credential Manager etc. *Figure 6.26* shows a simple script that establishes a remote session using the trust the certificate-based authentication provides between the client and the remote host:

```
PS C:\Temp> whoami
ps-client01\administrator
PS C:\Temp> Get-Content .\RemoteScript.ps1
$Session = New-PSSession -ComputerName "PS-HOST01" -UseSSL

Invoke-Command -Session $Session -ScriptBlock {"I am $($Env:COMPUTERNAME)"}

Remove-PSSession $Session
PS C:\Temp> .\RemoteScript.ps1
I am PS-HOST01
```

Figure 6.26: Script invoked from client that establishes a remote session to the remote host using the trust provided by the certificate-based authentication

17. As mentioned earlier, this is a simple example of using certificate-based authentication using a self-signed certificate. For production and other critical environments, it is strongly recommended to use certificates issued by trusted certificate authorities. Furthermore, when creating the HTTPS listener and the firewall rule on the remote hosts, in such low-trust environments, these must be limited to only allowing connections from the specific clients that must be allowed to access the remote host.

18. There are several authentication mechanisms that can be used for remote sessions, and it is recommended that you always implement the most secure mechanism available for your environments. In active directory domains the Kerberos authentication mechanism is recommended since it provides secure and encrypted communication between clients and hosts, and they need to be a member of the domain before they can even be allowed to create remote sessions. For local network and workgroup computers and systems, certificate-based authentication is always preferred over mechanisms such as basic authentication and CredSSP, even though it is more complex to set up and configure. You must never compromise your security due to complex and time-consuming configurations. Always follow security best practices and chose the most secure methods available for your environments.

Conclusion

Windows Remote Management and PowerShell remoting are valuable tools for administrators, enabling efficient and centralized management of remote computers and systems. This chapter has introduced WinRM and PowerShell remoting, covering the setup of clients and remote hosts for secure access with certificate-based authentication, the creation and management of remote sessions, remote command and script execution and methods for securing remote sessions and how to securely store and use credentials and secrets. By being able to utilize remote management between multiple remote hosts and systems you can greatly optimize time consuming tasks, execute commands, invoke and distribute scripts, and manage all aspects of these systems and remote hosts from a few clients or from one centralized secure location.

The next chapter introduces you to the Pester PowerShell testing framework. The chapter will guide you through setting up the Pester framework and it dives into Pesters structure and components. The chapter covers how to create unit tests for PowerShell functions, how to group and organize tests and how to mock dependencies. Furthermore, the chapter will provide strategies for testing infrastructure components and also how to implement code coverage analysis in tests.

Join our book's Discord space

Join the book's Discord Workspace for Latest updates, Offers, Tech happenings around the world, New Release and Sessions with the Authors:

https://discord.bpbonline.com

## CHAPTER 7

Testing with Pester

Introduction

Ensuring the reliability and functionality of your code is an essential part of writing powerful and well-functioning code. It is not enough to just write code and expect it to work as intended without encountering any issues. Testing helps you identify and fix bugs, errors and issues in your scripts and ensures that your scripts work as intended and that they are reliable under various conditions and scenarios. Testing is also used to verify that your codes functionality aligns with the requirements and specifications that is set for your scripts and applications. As changes or updates are made to your code over time, testing can help you catch unintended issues that might break existing functionality and in the long run by implementing tests and cohere to testing best practices encourages you to write cleaner and more maintainable code. Tests can serve as a form of documentation for your code and provide examples of how your code should function and be used. While it can take some time to write tests for your code, in the end it can help you save time and resources by reducing the need for manual testing and troubleshooting and in some organizations both compliance and security regulations might even require extensive testing of code before being deployed to critical production environments in order to prevent vulnerabilities and other compliance issues being introduced.

Structure

The chapter covers the following topics:

- Introduction to Pester PowerShell Testing Framework

    o **Recipe 40**: Learning how to set up Pester and about its structure and components

    o **Recipe 41**: Use Pester to set up test files, and write unit tests for functions and execute test cases

- Test organization and grouping

    o **Recipe 42**: Learn to organize tests into logical groupings

- Mocking dependencies in tests

    o **Recipe 43**: Use mocking in tests to isolate functions and simulate dependencies

- Testing infrastructure components with Pester

    o **Recipe 44**: Strategies for testing infrastructure components

- Implementing code coverage analysis in tests

    o **Recipe 45**: Learn how to measure code coverage

Objectives

In this chapter we will make an introduction to the Pester testing framework and show how to set up Pester and learn about its structure and components and we will also dive moreinto organizing and grouping tests. We will show how to set up test files and learn how to write unit tests for PowerShell functions and how to use Pester and Pester configurations to configure and execute tests. On a more advanced approach we will learn how to mock functions and cmdlets to isolate external dependencies and overwrite behavior so testcases can be created and executed without interfering with or making changes to external systems. We will also look at strategies for creating test cases for infrastructure components that can help you ensure your systems are working as intended and behave as expected.You will be briefly introduced to code coverage and learn how this can be used to ensure you have tests that cover all aspects of your code base and its commands and functions.

Introduction to Pester PowerShell Testing Framework

Pester is a powerful and versatile testing framework for PowerShell that allows you to write and execute tests for your modules, scripts and functions but pester is not limited to that and can also be used as a base tool for testing infrastructure components such as active directory, database configurations, computer deployments, cloud resources and much more. Pester can also be used for code coverage which gives an indication as to how much of your code is covered by tests and how many functions and commands might still need to have tests implemented.

So why do we need to write tests and test our code? We can look at tests as the process of evaluating and validating a script or applications code to ensure the reliability and functionality according to its intended purpose and required specifications. Testing code helps to prevent issues by catching bugs and errors within your code so that these can be fixed before they can make an impact and before scripts or applications are deployed to production and other critical environments. Testing can be divided into different types of tests, like unit tests where you test individual units of code such as functions and cmdlets. Integration tests which are used for testing interactions between different components such as multiple functions, cmdlets and between modules. Regression tests to ensure that changes to code have not introduced new bugs, errors, or other issues. This is usually accomplished by running a group of previously passed tests, whenever changes are made to the code. Smoke tests, which are quick and simple tests and checks to verify the basic functionality of scripts, modules, and applications. Functional testing is used to test the general functionality of the code from a user perspective and if the code lives up to its specifications and requirements.

Recipe 40: Learn how to set up Pester and about Pesters structure and components

Before being able to use Pester for testing, it is vital that you have installed the correct Pester version for your version of PowerShell. Pester comes pre-installed with Windows PowerShell but it might be outdated and missing some features and components. Pester is not included with PowerShell and should be installed separately. For both Windows PowerShell and PowerShell, you should download and install the newest version from the PSGallery. Furthermore, it is essential to know the general structure and the different components that make Pester, which we will go through in this recipe.

> **Info: Windows PowerShell is a reference to PowerShell version 5.x (and earlier versions). PowerShell is a reference to PowerShell versions 7.x.**

1. The first thing you need to do is to make sure that Pester is installed and available. It might be that you already have an older version of Pester installed on your

system, but you should update to or install the newest version from the PSGallery to get the newest functionality and features that Pester provides.

We can use the **Get-Module** command with the **-ListAvailable** parameter to list current versions of Pester:

```
Get-Module -ListAvailable | Where-Object {$_.Name -eq Pester"}
```

2. The output in *Figure 7.1* shows that an older version of Pester is already installed. This is installed in the context of Windows PowerShell (PowerShell 5.x) as we can see by its directory path: **C:\Program Files\WindowsPowerShell\Modules**:

```
PS C:\Temp> Get-Module -ListAvailable | Where-Object {$_.Name -eq "Pester"}

    Directory: C:\Program Files\WindowsPowerShell\Modules

ModuleType Version    PreRelease Name                     PSEdition ExportedCommands
---------- -------    ---------- ----                     --------- ----------------
Script     3.4.0                 Pester                   Desk      {Describe, Context, It, Should...}
```

Figure 7.1: Pester version 3.4.0 installed in the context of Windows PowerShell for all users

Note: It is important to distinguish between PowerShell (Pwsh - Version 7) and Windows PowerShell (PowerShell - Version 5.x) Pester might come pre-installed as a module with some versions of PowerShell. In this case we can see that version 3.4.0 is already installed on the system. This version can still be used with PowerShell 7, but its functionality might not work as expected. For PowerShell 7 we are going to install the newest version from the PSGallery repository and have both Pester module versions available on the system.

3. Use the **Install-Module** command to install the newest version of Pester from the PSGallery repository. The **-Force** parameter is used to suppress a prompt stating that there already is a version of Pester installed. The newer version will be installed without removing the older version (this is still used in the context of Windows PowerShell). Upon installation we also get a warning stating that the older version will be superseded by the newer version:

```
Install-Module Pester -Force
```

4. Once installed we can import the Pester module into the current session:

```
Import-Module Pester
```

5. We can use the **Get-Module** command to check that the correct version of Pester has been imported. Unless anything else is specified, it is always the newest version that gets imported into a session:

```
Get-Module Peste
```

6. With **Get-Module** we can see that version 5.5.0 is imported into the current session and if we use the **Get-Module** with the **-ListAvailable** parameter again, we can see that both versions are now installed and are available for import into sessions and scripts.

Note that for this chapter we use the current latest version of Pester: Version 5.5.0.

The output of the above commands that are used to install and check the Pester module can be viewed in *Figure 7.2*:

```
PS C:\Temp> Install-Module Pester -Force
WARNING: Module 'Pester' version '3.4.0' published by 'CN=Microsoft Windows, O=Microsoft Corporation, L=Redmond, S=W
ashington, C=US' will be superceded by version '5.5.0' published by 'CN=Jakub Jareš, O=Jakub Jareš, L=Praha, C=CZ'.
If you do not trust the new publisher, uninstall the module.
PS C:\Temp>
PS C:\Temp> Import-Module Pester
PS C:\Temp>
PS C:\Temp> Get-Module Pester

ModuleType Version     PreRelease Name                                ExportedCommands
---------- -------     ---------- ----                                ----------------
Script     5.5.0                  Pester                              {Add-ShouldOperator, AfterAll, AfterEach, Ass…

PS C:\Temp>
PS C:\Temp> Get-Module -ListAvailable | Where-Object {$_.Name -eq "Pester"}

    Directory: C:\Users\                        \Documents\PowerShell\Modules

ModuleType Version     PreRelease Name                                PSEdition ExportedCommands
---------- -------     ---------- ----                                --------- ----------------
Script     5.5.0                  Pester                              Desk      {Invoke-Pester, Describe, Context, …

    Directory: C:\Program Files\WindowsPowerShell\Modules

ModuleType Version     PreRelease Name                                PSEdition ExportedCommands
---------- -------     ---------- ----                                --------- ----------------
Script     3.4.0                  Pester                              Desk      {Describe, Context, It, Should…}
```

Figure 7.2: Installation and import of Pester version 5.5.0 and list of all installed Pester versions

Describe, Context and It blocks

Before we start writing tests we need to know the structure and components that makes Pester. Pester use different types of scriptblock components to segment code and each type resides in different levels within each other. During this chapter we will refer to these scriptblock components as blocks!

Each block within Pester has its own distinct function, and together they are used to create, organize, and structure tests. The primary block types include:

- **Describe**: This is the most fundamental block, and it is used to group and organize related test cases. It serves as a container within which you can define, and structure tests and its primary purpose is to provide a logical hierarchy for tests and groups of tests.

- **Context**: This is an optional block that resides inside the Describe block and it is used to provide a more logical grouping of multiple It blocks. It is also used for defining test scopes.

- **It**: These blocks can reside either within a Describe block or a Context block. This is the block where the actual tests are created and where assertions for the test cases are made.

The general structure of a **Describe** block with both a **Context** and **It** block is shown here:

```
# Pester Blocks
Describe "Password-Generator" {
    # Describe code here
    Context "Test password output" {
        # Context code here
        It "Returns a password of length 10 characters" {
            # It code here
        }
    }
}
```

Below, you can see how the different blocks are used to organize and structure different types of tests for two functions:

```
Describe "Function-One" {
    Context "INPUT tests for Function-One" {
        It "Function-One INPUT is a valid String" {
            # It code here
        }
        It "Function-One INPUT is a valid Integer" {
            # It code here
        }
    }
    Context "OUTPUT tests for Function-One" {
        It "Function-One OUTPUT is a valid String" {
            # It code here
        }
        It "Function-One OUTPUT is a valid Integer" {
            # It code here
        }
    }
}
Describe "Function-Two" {
    Context "INPUT tests for Function-Two" {
        It "Function-Two INPUT is a valid String" {
            # It code here
```

```
        }
        It "Function-Two INPUT is a valid Integer" {
            # It code here
        }
    }
    Context "OUTPUT tests for Function-Two" {
        It "Function-Two OUTPUT is a valid String" {
            # It code here
        }
        It "Function-Two OUTPUT is a valid Integer" {
            # It code here
        }
    }
}
```

Note that the **Context** block is optional and is not specifically needed. **It** blocks can be placed directly within **Describe** blocks and not just within **Context** blocks, but it is always a good practice to organize tests into smaller groups and segments for readability purposes, but if you only have one or a few similar tests, this might be overkill and you can simply create the **It** blocks with the tests directly inside a **Describe** block. Another valuable feature is that, **Describe** blocks can be tagged using the **-Tag** parameter when defined:

```
Describe -Tag "One" "Function-One" {}
```

Tags are used to invoke specific sets of tests with a specific tag when Pester is executed. Imagine you have a cross-platform script and test cases for Linux and Windows parts of the code, you can then tag the **Describe** blocks with **"Linux"** or **"Windows"**. You can use the **Filter.Tag** property within a Pester configuration or the legacy **-TagFilter** parameter (which is deprecated) to only invoke the particular groups of tests relevant to the tagged platform when you execute Pester.

Before and After blocks

Besides these primary block types there are also additional blocks for running arbitrary code before or after **It** blocks are executed. These additional block types are:

- **BeforeAll**: Is used to run arbitrary code *before any* **It** block is executed.

- **AfterAll**: Is used to run arbitrary code *after all* **It** blocks have been executed.

- **BeforeEach**: Is used to run arbitrary code *before each* **It** block is executed.

- **AfterEach**: Is used to run arbitrary code *after each* **It** block is executed.

You might need to open and close database connections, or you might need to get some return value from a function and assign it to a variable that should be used for tests within **It** blocks. This is where these **Before** and **After** types of blocks come in handy. They can be used both within **Describe** and **Context** blocks. **Before** blocks are placed before the first **It** block and **After** blocks are placed after the last **It** block within either **Describe** or **Context** blocks. Variables in **Before** and **After** blocks that reside within **Describe** blocks are available to **It** blocks in the scope of both **Describe** and **Context** blocks, and **Before** and **After** blocks inside **Context** blocks are available to **It** blocks within that **Context** blocks scope. Variables in **Before** and **After** blocks can only be used within the scope of the **Describe** block where they reside, and not within other **Describe** blocks scope. You can also create **Before** and **After** blocks outside of the scope of **Describe** and **Context** blocks to make variables and other resources available to all of these blocks scopes.

Below is a simulated example of how the test structure using **Before** and **After** blocks in a **Describe** block and the **Context** block within it, might be defined:

```
Describe -Tag "Database" "Database-Connection" {
    BeforeAll{
        $Connection = Open-DatabaseConnection
    }
    It "Connection Established"{z
        $Connection | Should -Not -BeNullOrEmpty
    }
    Context "Test connection data" {
        BeforeEach{
            $StringData = $Connection.GetRandomStringData()
        }
        It "Should be a String" {
            $StringData.GetType().Name | Should -Be "String"
        }
        It "Should not be Integer" {
            $StringData.GetType().Name | Should -Not -Be "Int32"
        }
        AfterEach{
            New-LogToFile $StringData
        }
    }
    AfterAll{
        $Connection.Close()
    }
}
```

The test structure can become quite complex if it contains a lot of tests, so it is always recommended to organize your test cases within the **Describe** and **Context** blocks for readability and organizational purposes.

Assertions

An assertion is a statement or expression in test cases used within **It** blocks to verify whether a specific condition or expectation is met, within a piece of code. Examples of assertions include:

- Asserting that: **"String" | Should -Contain "S" #Pass**

- Asserting that: **"String".length | Should -Be 6 #Pass**

- Asserting that: **"String".GetType().Name | Should -Be "Int32" #Fail**

When assertions evaluate to true, the test is considered successful and when they evaluate to false the test is considered as failed. The most common method for asserting a test case is by using the **Should** keyword. In the examples above, we assert that *an object* **Should** match *an expression*. We basically use this keyword to compare an object against an expected object by piping that object to the **Should** assertion. We use an operator, such as **-Contain** or **-Be** to create an expression. The object is then compared against the **Should** assertion expression. This can be compared to using and **if/else** statement where the expression is evaluated to **$true** (**if**), the assertion is correct and the test succeeds and if the expression evaluates to **$false** (**else**), the assertion is incorrect, and the test fails.

Assertion operators

As mentioned before you use operators to create assertion expressions. There are many different operators, and they should cover most test cases but if you have a particular case where an operator does not fulfill your requirements you can create your own custom assertion operator using the **Add-AssertionOperator** cmdlet that comes with Pester. Creating custom assertion operators is out of the scope of this chapter, but as you learn to create more advanced tests and test cases it is recommended that you look into this topic. The most common assertion operators are listed below with a short description:

```
# -Be - Checks Equality. Case Insensitive
"STRING" | Should -Be "String" #Pass
# -BeExactly - Checks Equality. Case Sensitive
"STRING" | Should -BeExactly "String" #Fail
"STRING" | Should -BeExactly "STRING" #Pass
# -Exist - Checks if file/directory exists
"C:\Temp\TestFile.txt" | Should -Exist
# Fails if file/direcotry does not exist
# Pass if file/direcotry exists
# -Contain - Check if collection, file or string contains a specific value
```

```
# Case Insensitive
"String" | Should -Contain "s" #Pass
"String" | Should -Contain "M" #Fail
"Blue", "Green", "Red" | Should -Contain "blue" #Pass
"Blue", "Green", "Red" | Should -Contain "Yellow" #Fail
"C:\Temp\TestFile.txt" | Should -Contain "Word"
# Fails if file content does not contain "Word"
# Pass if file content contains "Word"
# -ContainExactly - Check if collection, file or string contains a specific
value
# Case Sensitive
"String" | Should -ContainExactly "s" #Fail
"String" | Should -ContainExactly "S" #Pass
"Blue", "Green", "Red" | Should ContainExactly "blue" #Fail
"Blue", "Green", "Red" | Should ContainExactly "Red" #Pass
"C:\Temp\TestFile.txt" | Should ContainExactly "Word"
# Fails if file content does not contain "Word"
# Fails if file content contains "word"
# Pass if file content contains "Word"
# -Match - Uses a RegEx for comparison. Case Insensitive
"This is True" | Should -Match "This is" #Pass
"This is True" | Should -Match "This is not true" #Fail
# -MatchExactly - Uses a RegEx for comparison. Case Sensitive
"This is True" | Should MatchExactly "This is" #Pass
"This is True" | Should MatchExactly "This Is" #Fail
# -Throw - Checks if expression is thrown.
# Note: Input object must be within a scriptblock or else
# it is processed outside of the assertion!
{ String } | Should -Throw #Pass
{ String } | Should -Not -Throw #Fail
{ $Var = "String" } | Should -Throw #Fail
{ $Var = "String" } | Should -Not -Throw #Pass
{ throw "Error" } | Should -Throw "Error" #Pass
{ throw "Error" } | Should -Not -Throw "Error" #Fail
# -BeNullOrEmpty - Checks values for null or empty
```

```
$null | Should -BeNullOrEmpty #Pass
$null | Should -Not -BeNullOrEmpty #Fail
"" | Should -BeNullOrEmpty #Pass
"String" | Should -BeNullOrEmpty #Fail
```

More operators exist than the ones listed here, such as **-BeGreaterThan**, **-BeLessThan**, **-BeOfType** and more. They are more or less quite self-explanatory and once you start to create an assertion, any good PowerShell IDE, such as VS Code using a Pester extension, should be able to list all available operators for the Pester version you are using.

Now that we have learned about Pesters structure and some of its main components, we are ready to write some tests.

Writing unit tests for functions

Unit tests are usually written before or during a code development process, and they are used to ensure that each unit of code behaves as expected and produces the expected output when given specific input or some other conditions are met, and they help to catch bugs and issues early in that process. A unit of code can be a function, a cmdlet, a class method or even a class, that is tested individually and in isolation from the rest of the code. Several test cases can be created for each unit for testing different aspects of the behavior and output and whenever you make changes to a unit you re-run the tests to check that the changes have not broken the functionality of that unit. Since units can be dependent on external factors or other dependencies it can be difficult to write test cases that are isolated from such external dependencies and factors. Imagine a function that upon execution and given the correct input, creates a user in Active Directory, you certainly do not want to create a new user every time you run your unit tests. For such scenarios we use so-called **mocks** to create new behavior for existing commands for the test cases or in rarer circumstances, stubs to create empty placeholders for commands that are not available or can't be mocked. We will cover mocks in more detail later in this chapter.

Recipe 41: Use Pester to set up test files, write unit tests for functions and execute test cases

All test cases are placed within a test file that must end with **.Tests.ps1**. If your script is called **MyScript.ps1** the file containing the tests for the functions within the script must be called **MyScript.Tests.ps1** and both files must be placed within the same directory. Pester introduces a cmdlet called **New-Fixture** that creates both a main script and a test script respectively containing the functions and the tests. When you use the **New-Fixture** cmdlet to create these script files, an example function is created within the main script and an example test case is created within the test script. *Figure 7.2* shows the creation of the main and test scripts using the **New-Fixture** cmdlet and the respective example content of each file:

```
PS C:\Temp\Tests> New-Fixture -Name MyScript

    Directory: C:\Temp\Tests

Mode                 LastWriteTime         Length Name
----                 -------------         ------ ----
-a---          15-09-2023     10:27             91 MyScript.ps1
-a---          15-09-2023     10:27            192 MyScript.Tests.ps1

PS C:\Temp\Tests> Get-Content .\MyScript.ps1
function MyScript {
    throw [NotImplementedException]'MyScript is not implemented.'
}
PS C:\Temp\Tests> Get-Content .\MyScript.Tests.ps1
BeforeAll {
    . $PSCommandPath.Replace('.Tests.ps1', '.ps1')
}

Describe "MyScript" {
    It "Returns expected output" {
        MyScript | Should -Be "YOUR_EXPECTED_VALUE"
    }
}
```

***Figure** 7.3: Creating script and tests file using New-Fixture*
and the example content within these files

The command inside the **BeforeAll** block within the main script is used to effectively load and execute the corresponding main (**.ps1**) script associated with the test script. It does this by modifying the script's file extension from **.Tests.ps1** to **.ps1** and then dot sourcing it into the test script. This can be useful if you have shared code between your test script and the main script, and you want to ensure that the shared code is executed within the context of your test script. It loads all functions and variables etc. from the main script into the test script. Note the sentence *"Executed within the context of your test script"*. If your script is executing code that is not placed inside functions, this code will be executed when running the tests. This might not be the behavior you want or expect, and you should modify the code inside this **BeforeAll** block accordingly to your specific requirements. If your script primarily consists of functions, these functions will be imported into the test script and test can be executed for these functions without further modification of the imported code. It is recommended to always write tests for your code, and it is a good practice to use the **New-Fixture** cmdlet to create the initial script and test files for your projects whenever you create scripts that should include tests. For some development processes, test cases are written before code is even developed, like in test-driven development processes, but for this chapter we start by creating the functions and then afterwards, the test cases.

For the next examples we will create a simple function called **Blend-Colors** inside the main script file. It takes two arguments in the form of strings of colors. These two inputs are added to an array and then we use a **switch** with the **-RegEx** parameter. In the expression for the **switch**, we use the **-join** operator to combine the two color strings from the array, into a single string delimited by a space. Since we are using the **-RegEx** parameter we can test that each expression is either **"$Color1 $Color2"** or **"$Color2 $Color1"** within a single result by using the | (Pipe) operator, which in regex is equivalent to an **OR** operator. We can then settle for using one result for each color combination instead of two. For each color combination, we return the color they would be blended into, as a string. As the default result for the switch statement, we return a string stating that the color combination is unsupported, if arguments with unsupported colors are provided to the functions parameters. The function ends up looking like this:

```
function Blend-Colors {
    param (
        [String]$Color1,
        [String]$Color2
    )
    $ColorCombination = @("$Color1", "$Color2")
    switch -Regex ($ColorCombination -join " ") {
        "Red Blue|Blue Red" { return "Purple" }
        "Red Green|Green Red" { return "Brown" }
        "Blue Green|Green Blue" { return "Teal" }
        default { return "Unsupported Color Combination" }
    }
}
```

We need to create tests that are going to check that the behavior of the functions output will be as expected when provided with different input colors. The first set of tests will be checking if the output is correct when valid colors are provided as input arguments. We need to test if red and blue returns purple, if red and green returns brown and if blue and green returns teal. The next set of tests will be used to check if the default string is returned if any unsupported colors are provided as either one of the arguments to the function.

We start by creating a **Describe** block within the test script (you can delete the example **Describe** block created by the **New-Fixture** cmdlet) and tag this with **-Tag**, **"Colors"** and we name it the same as the function: **Blend-Colors**. Since we already know that we are going to create multiple sets of tests we use **Context** blocks to organize these sets into different sections. The first **Context** block will contain tests for valid color combinations and the second **Context** block will be for unsupported color combinations. We have three possible valid color combination outputs, so we know that we need to create at least three test cases in this section. For the unsupported color combinations tests we have several possibilities, and we could create a test for each possible invalid combination that exists, this might be overkill, so we start by only creating a few tests within this section. For the actual test cases we use **It** blocks. What we need to do is, that within each **It** block, we call the **Blend-Colors** function with different color arguments and assign the output to a variable **$Color**. We then make the assertion that makes the test cases: *We assert that $Color should be equal to the expected output color.* The expected output is either: *Purple, Brown, Teal,* or *Unsupported Color Combination.* We create the three test cases for the valid combinations and only a few test cases for the unsupported combinations.

```
Describe -Tag "Colors" "Blend-Colors" {
    Context "Test Valid color combinations" {
      It "Blue and Red should be Purple" {
          $Color = Blend-Colors "Blue" "Red"
          $Color | Should -Be "Purple"
      }
      It "Red and Green should be Brown" {
          $Color = Blend-Colors "Red" "Green"
          $Color | Should -Be "Brown"
      }
      It "Blue and Green should be Teal" {
          $Color = Blend-Colors "Blue" "Green"
          $Color | Should -Be "Teal"
      }
    }
    Context "Test unsupported color Combinations" {
      It "Black and White should be Unsupported" {
          $Color = Blend-Colors "Black" "White"
          $Color | Should -Be "Unsupported Color Combination"
      }
      It "Green and Yellow should be Unsupported" {
          $Color = Blend-Colors "Green" "Yellow"
          $Color | Should -Be "Unsupported Color Combination"
      }
    }
}
```

Now that we have these five test cases, let us invoke Pester and execute the tests. You can invoke Pester in a few ways. You can simply run the test script within your IDE (usually by pressing the F5 button) or by dot sourcing it or you can use the **Invoke-Pester** cmdlet which is usually the preferred method. If you run **Invoke-Pester** without any arguments, it will look for all **.Tests.ps1** files within the current folder and its subfolders and run all tests within all found test files and then list the test results in a combined test summary result. You can also specify a specific test file to run, using the **Invoke-Pester** cmdlet with the **-Path** parameter. *Figure 7.4* shows the test summary result of invoking Pester specifically for the **MyScript.Tests.ps1** file using the **-Path** parameter. Note the verbosity level is by default set to **Normal** which does not show the individual test cases in the summary result:

```
● PS C:\Temp\Tests> Invoke-Pester -Path MyScript.Tests.ps1

  Starting discovery in 1 files.
  Discovery found 5 tests in 8ms.
  Running tests.
  [+] C:\Temp\Tests\MyScript.Tests.ps1 91ms (18ms|65ms)
  Tests completed in 93ms
  Tests Passed: 5, Failed: 0, Skipped: 0 NotRun: 0
```

Figure 7.4: Test results for invoking Pester for the MyScript.Tests.ps1 test file

As you can see it returns information about how many test files it has discovered containing test cases. Since we specified a specific test file, it only discovers this one particular file. It also shows how many test cases (It blocks) it has found within this file, and then it runs all the discovered test cases. You can see that these five test cases completed in 93 milliseconds and that all five tests have passed. In the summary result, we not only have **Passed** and **Failed** tests, but it also includes output results for **Skipped** and **NotRun**. *Passed* indicates how many of the defined test cases were executed successfully. **Failed** indicates how many of the defined test cases failed to meet the expected outcome. Sometimes you might want to skip certain tests temporarily or it might be that they are not relevant in the current context or the functions they test might be undergoing maintenance. **Skipped** indicates all the test cases that you have specifically chosen to skip. There might be an issue with the test setup or execution, such as a problem with the test script and some tests might not execute, or you might simply have chosen to exclude specific test cases. **NotRun** indicates how many test cases that are defined but are not executed.

The test summary result shown above is the default output when invoking Pester with no additional configuration settings or parameters. We might be interested in a more detailed output that shows the specific test cases that were executed.

Pester has a different syntax for specifying properties, such as the output verbosity level, depending on the Pester version. Generally, the use of parameters and arguments are deprecated after Pester version 4 in favor of using Pester configurations to specify settings instead, besides using the **-Configuration** parameter for specifying the configuration. You could use a parameter for specifying the required output verbosity like: **Invoke-Pester -Output Detailed** but since this is a deprecated parameter, we are solely going to use Pester configurations in this chapter instead of using deprecated and legacy parameters. You should look up Pester documentation for current and updated Pester configuration settings and properties available. The reason for using configurations to set properties instead of using parameters are for flexibility and consistency purposes and it allows you to define settings that are applied consistently across multiple test scripts, ensuring the same settings are used for multiple tests without the need for specifying the same parameters in each test script or upon the invocation of Pester. Specifying settings such as output verbosity at the configuration level ensures that all tests can adhere to the same standard, in this case it would be the output verbosity level.

We can directly define Pester configurations within the current session we are working in using the **New-PesterConfiguration** cmdlet that comes with Pester, and then this configuration will be available as long as the current session is active. But we can also save the configuration within a script, dot source this configuration script, and use this configuration in different contexts, scripts, and sessions whenever we need it.

Our current main script with our **Blend-Colors** function and its test script is placed in **C:\Temp\Tests**. We create a new folder and a new script for the configuration in **C:\Temp\PesterConfigs\PesterConfig-Detailed.ps1**. We create a simple Pester configuration that sets the verbosity level to a more detailed output and add this configuration code to the configuration script.

```
$PesterConfig = New-PesterConfiguration
$PesterConfig.Output.Verbosity = "Detailed"
```

To provide an overview, this gives us the file structure shown in *Figure 7.5*:

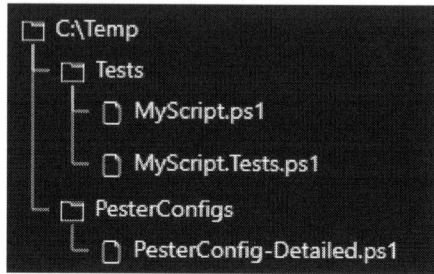

Figure 7.5: *Structure with main script, test script and Pester configuration script*

Now that we have the Pester configuration defined within the configuration file, we can dot source the configuration file into our current session and the configuration is then available within the **$PesterConfig** variable. In *Figure 7.6* we can see that the **$PesterConfig** variable is of the **PesterConfiguration** type, and we can see that the variable contains different Pester configuration properties:

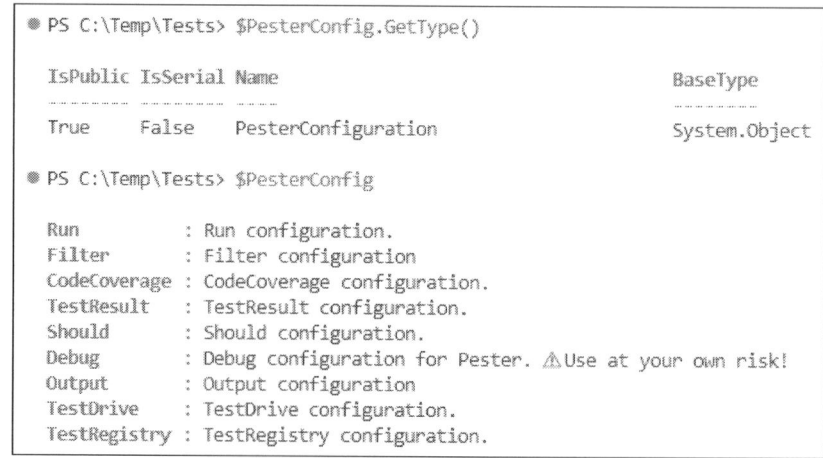

Figure 7.6: *$PesterConfig variable dot sourced into session and containing Pester Configuration settings*

We can invoke Pester with the **-Configuration** parameter and the **$PesterConfig** as argument. *Figure 7.7* shows the new detailed summary result of invoking Pester with the specified Pester configuration:

```
PS C:\Temp\Tests> . ..\PesterConfigs\PesterConfig-Detailed.ps1
PS C:\Temp\Tests> Invoke-Pester -Configuration $PesterConfig
Pester v5.5.0

Starting discovery in 1 files.
Discovery found 5 tests in 6ms.
Running tests.

Running tests from 'C:\Temp\Tests\MyScript.Tests.ps1'
Describing Blend-Colors
 Context Test Valid color combinations
    [+] Blue and Red should be Purple 3ms (1ms|2ms)
    [+] Red and Green should be Brown 6ms (6ms|0ms)
    [+] Blue and Green should be Teal 2ms (1ms|1ms)
 Context Test unsupported color Combinations
    [+] Black and White should be Unsupported 2ms (1ms|1ms)
    [+] Green and Yellow should be Unsupported 1ms (1ms|0ms)
Tests completed in 65ms
Tests Passed: 5, Failed: 0, Skipped: 0 NotRun: 0
```

Figure 7.7: Invoking Pester using Pester configuration with output verbosity set to Detailed

The test summary result is now more detailed, and we can see the specific test cases that was executed and the grouped structure.

> **Note: Using Invoke-Pester with the -Configuration parameter and the -Path parameter at the same time is not supported since they are part of different parameter sets. When using Pester configurations, you should invoke Pester from within the root directory of your tests.**

Now that we have a function, **Blend-Colors**, and test cases for this function, we can be sure that whenever we execute the test cases and if all tests pass successfully, that our function will work properly, behave as expected and return the expected output. Whenever we make changes to the function, we can re-execute the tests and make sure that the changes have not broken the function behavior and that it still returns the expected output. Let us try to update the function by adding the **CmdletBinding** attribute and add some verbose output. We will also remove the **$ColorCombination** variable and change the **switch** expression so it now looks like this:

```
function Blend-Colors {
    [CmdletBinding()]
    param (
        [String]$Color1,
        [String]$Color2
    )
```

```
Write-Verbose "Input colors: $Color1 and $Color2"
switch -Regex ("$Color1 $Color2") {
    "Red Blue|Blue Red" {
        Write-Verbose "Output color: Purple"
        return "Purple" }
    "Red Green|Green Red" {
        Write-Verbose "Output color: Brown"
        return "Brown" }
    "Blue Green|Green Blue" {
        Write-Verbose "Output color: Teal"
        return "Teal" }
    default { return "Unsupported Color Combination" }
    }
}
```

We invoke Pester again and execute the test cases. As you can see in *Figure 7.8* all tests still pass, so even though we have made changes to the functions structure, the behavior and return output is the same, as was expected in this case.

```
● PS C:\Temp\Tests> Invoke-Pester -Configuration $PesterConfig
  Pester v5.5.0

  Starting discovery in 1 files.
  Discovery found 5 tests in 8ms.
  Running tests.

  Running tests from 'C:\Temp\Tests\MyScript.Tests.ps1'
  Describing Blend-Colors
   Context Test Valid color combinations
     [+] Blue and Red should be Purple 3ms (1ms|2ms)
     [+] Red and Green should be Brown 1ms (1ms|0ms)
     [+] Blue and Green should be Teal 2ms (1ms|1ms)
   Context Test unsupported color Combinations
     [+] Black and White should be Unsupported 2ms (1ms|1ms)
     [+] Green and Yellow should be Unsupported 5ms (4ms|0ms)
  Tests completed in 64ms
  Tests Passed: 5, Failed: 0, Skipped: 0 NotRun: 0
```

Figure 7.8: Executing tests after the Blend-Colors function has been updated

The changes did not affect the overall functionality of the function but let us try to see what happens if we made some damaging changes. While working on the function we somehow managed to delete the **e** in the **"Purple"** return output by mistake, so it now looks like this: **return "Purpl"**. We did not perceive this mistake so we just assume the function work, but we execute our tests, as we should each time, we make any changes.

Figure 7.9 shows the new test summary result:

```
● PS C:\Temp\Tests> Invoke-Pester -Configuration $PesterConfig
  Pester v5.5.0

  Starting discovery in 1 files.
  Discovery found 5 tests in 6ms.
  Running tests.

  Running tests from 'C:\Temp\Tests\MyScript.Tests.ps1'
  Describing Blend-Colors
   Context Test Valid color combinations
     [-] Blue and Red should be Purple 5ms (3ms|2ms)
       Expected strings to be the same, but they were different.
       Expected length: 6
       Actual length:   5
       Strings differ at index 5.
       Expected: 'Purple'
       But was:  'Purpl'
                 -----^
       at $Color | Should -Be "Purple", C:\Temp\Tests\MyScript.Tests.ps1:11
       at <ScriptBlock>, C:\Temp\Tests\MyScript.Tests.ps1:11
     [+] Red and Green should be Brown 2ms (1ms|1ms)
     [+] Blue and Green should be Teal 1ms (1ms|0ms)
   Context Test unsupported color Combinations
     [+] Black and White should be Unsupported 3ms (1ms|1ms)
     [+] Green and Yellow should be Unsupported 2ms (1ms|1ms)
  Tests completed in 72ms
  Tests Passed: 4, Failed: 1, Skipped: 0 NotRun: 0
```

Figure 7.9: *Test summary result after introducing breaking behavior to the Blend-Colors function*

Four tests passed and one failed! The failed test is highlighted, and we get detailed information which helps us to easily locate the error. It tells us what it expected, in this case that the strings should be the same. It tells us the expected length of the string and even at what index within the string it differs. It also tells us exactly what string it expected and what string it got instead. This is a quick fix and after adding the missing **e** again and re-executing the tests, they will all pass, and the functions behavior and output will be as expected.

The more advanced the function is, the more test cases you might have to write to cover all aspects of the expected behavior, but it is not always easy to predict all potential issues and outcomes and you might have to write new or update current test cases as you are evolving your functions. With the **Blend-Color** function we could end up with hundreds of test cases if were to add more valid color combinations and also if we wanted to cover all the unsupported color combinations that exists, depending on what color schemes we might chose that the function should cover.

Knowing how to write and implement unit tests for our functions is a powerful tool to have in our toolbox. It helps us validate the expected behavior and return output for our functions without having to manually invoking and testing them whenever we have made any changes. It makes our code much more reliable, and we can be sure that our functions work as expected when we implement them into larger scripts and applications or update scripts and applications that are already running in critical environments.

Test organization and grouping

The larger your codebase grows and the more tests you write, the more important it becomes to organize and group your test cases, as it contributes to more effective and efficient testing practices. Grouping tests using **Describe** and **Context** blocks provides a clear and readable structured layout that makes it easier to understand the specific purpose and context of each test. Organizing tests allows for a logical grouping of related test cases and then selective tests can be executed for a set of specific groups. This is especially useful in very large codebases where running all test cases each time might be quite time consuming.

Recipe 42: Learn to organize tests into logical groupings

Not only is it beneficial for readability purposes that you organize and group your tests. But by implementing a grouped structure and by tagging your groups, you can selectively execute specific test cases and exclude others that might not be relevant under specific circumstances. Let us imagine that you are writing a cross-platform script that works on both Linux, MacOS and Windows and that your script functions are platform specific. You would of course, write unit test cases for all (or most of) the functions, and the functions for specific platforms will in most cases not work on a different platform than the one it was designed for, hence the test cases for these functions would also result in errors or unexpected behavior when we invoke the Pester tests. We can accommodate for this by using mocked functions, but we will get back to this later in this chapter. Another method to accommodate for this, is to selectively execute specific test cases that are designed for the platform we invoke the tests on. This is, of course not the only reason for grouping and executing selective sets of tests. As we also mentioned earlier, your codebase can have become quite extensive and running all tests might be very time-consuming. If you have only made smaller adjustments or changes to a small part of the code that will not affect most of the other functions behavior, and if you have organized, grouped, and tagged your test cases in an effectively manner, you might only need to execute a small portion of the relevant test cases. Below we have made example functions for different platforms. Some of the functions will work on all platforms, since they only return a string, but the functions named **-Other** are platform dependent and will only work on the platform it is intended for. The goal here is to show how unit tests for such functions can be grouped and selectively executed.

```
function Linux-String {
    return "I am a Linux String"
}
function Windows-String {
    return "I am a Windows String"
```

```
}
function MacOS-String {
    return "I am a MacOS String"
}
function Linux-RootPath {
    return "/"
}
function Windows-RootPath {
    return "c:\"
}
function MacOS-RootPath {
    return "/"
}
function Linux-Other {
    sudo apt-get update && sudo apt-get upgrade
}
function Windows-Other {
    Get-PSDrive WSMan
}
function MacOS-Other {
    sw_vers -productVersion
}
```

Now that we have created the functions, we need to write and group the relevant test cases. These could be written and grouped like this:

```
Describe -Tag "Linux" "Linux Tests - Platform independent" {
    Context "Strings" {
        It "Must be a Linux String" {
            $String = Linux-String
            $String | Should -Be "I am a Linux String"
        }
    }
    Context "Paths" {
        It "Must be the Root Path" {
            $Path = Linux-RootPath
            $Path | Should -Be "/"
        }
```

```
    }
}
Describe -Tag "Linux" "Linux Tests - Platform dependent" {
    It "Must not throw an error" {
        $Other = Linux-Other
        {$Other} | Should -Not -Throw
    }
}
Describe -Tag "Windows" "Windows Tests - Platform independent" {
    Context "Strings" {
        It "Must be a Windows String" {
            $String = Windows-String
            $String | Should -Be "I am a Windows String"
        }
    }
    Context "Paths" {
        It "Must be the Root Path" {
            $Path = Windows-RootPath
            $Path | Should -Be "C:\"
        }
    }
}
Describe -Tag "Windows" "Windows Tests - Platform dependent" {
    It "Must not throw an error" {
        $Other = Windows-Other
        {$Other} | Should -Not -Throw
    }
}
Describe -Tag "MacOS" "MacOS Tests - Platform independent" {
    Context "Strings" {
        It "Must be a MacOS String" {
            $String = MacOS-String
            $String | Should -Be "I am a MacOS String"
        }
    }
    Context "Paths" {
```

```
        It "Must be the Root Path" {
            $Path = MacOS-RootPath
            $Path | Should -Be "/"
        }
    }
}
Describe -Tag "MacOS" "MacOS Tests - Platform dependent" {
    It "Must not throw an error" {
        $Other = MacOS-Other
        {$Other} | Should -Not -Throw
    }
}
```

For each platform we have two **Describe** blocks, or groups. One for platform independent test cases and one for platform dependent test cases. One of the important things here is the **-Tag** for each **Describe** block or group. As you can see the groups for each platform are tagged with the specific platform name. In case you have not yet noticed, the platform independent test cases are asserting that the functions output is a string and should be equal to the assertion expression. The platform dependent test cases assert that the function it tests does not result in a thrown error! If we invoke all the test cases on a Windows platform, we get the summary result as shown in *Figure 7.10*:

> **Note: In the next examples we are not using a script for the Pester configuration, but we are using and adapting the Pester configuration directly within the current session for readability purposes. Also note that the new main script and test file are called: Organization.ps1 and Organization.Tests.ps1 and is placed in the C:\Temp\Tests-Organization directory. We will also refer to Describe blocks as groups.**

```
● PS C:\Temp\Tests-Organization> $PesterConfig = New-PesterConfiguration
● PS C:\Temp\Tests-Organization> $PesterConfig.Output.Verbosity = "Detailed"
● PS C:\Temp\Tests-Organization> Invoke-Pester -Configuration $PesterConfig
  Pester v5.5.0

  Starting discovery in 1 files.
  Discovery found 9 tests in 8ms.
  Running tests.

  Running tests from 'C:\Temp\Tests-Organization\Organization.Tests.ps1'
  Describing Linux Tests - Platform independent
   Context Strings
     [+] Must be a Linux String 3ms (1ms|2ms)
   Context Paths
     [+] Must be the Root Path 2ms (1ms|1ms)

  Describing Linux Tests - Platform dependent
    [-] Must not throw an error 64ms (62ms|2ms)
     CommandNotFoundException: The term 'sudo' is not recognized as a name of a cmdlet, function, script file,
  or executable program.
     Check the spelling of the name, or if a path was included, verify that the path is correct and try again.
     at Linux-Other, C:\Temp\Tests-Organization\Organization.ps1:21
     at <ScriptBlock>, C:\Temp\Tests-Organization\Organization.Tests.ps1:22

  Describing Windows Tests - Platform independent
   Context Strings
     [+] Must be a Windows String 4ms (1ms|3ms)
   Context Paths
     [+] Must be the Root Path 2ms (1ms|1ms)

  Describing Windows Tests - Platform dependent
    [+] Must not throw an error 8ms (6ms|2ms)

  Describing MacOS Tests - Platform independent
   Context Strings
     [+] Must be a MacOS String 6ms (4ms|2ms)
   Context Paths
     [+] Must be the Root Path 2ms (1ms|1ms)

  Describing MacOS Tests - Platform dependent
    [-] Must not throw an error 58ms (57ms|1ms)
     CommandNotFoundException: The term 'sw_vers' is not recognized as a name of a cmdlet, function, script fil
  e, or executable program.
     Check the spelling of the name, or if a path was included, verify that the path is correct and try again.
     at MacOS-Other, C:\Temp\Tests-Organization\Organization.ps1:27
     at <ScriptBlock>, C:\Temp\Tests-Organization\Organization.Tests.ps1:66
  Tests completed in 237ms
  Tests Passed: 7, Failed: 2, Skipped: 0 NotRun: 0
```

Figure 7.10: Test result summary of executing the test cases for the cross-platform functions

You can see the that two platform dependent test cases for Linux and MacOS failed. This was to be expected as they depend on their specific platform. The **sudo** command only works on Linux and the **sw_vers** command only works on MacOS. Since we are invoking the tests on a Windows machine, and we can only rely on the Windows specific tests to pass with certainty, we need some way to only execute these specific tests. This is where the tags become valuable, and we can use the Pester configuration to filter on the specific tags:

```
# Use the Filter option to filter specific tags
$PesterConfig = New-PesterConfiguration
$PesterConfig.Output.Verbosity = "Detailed"
```

```
$PesterConfig.Filter.Tag = "Windows"
```

Now if we filter on the specific tag: *"Windows"* we should only get the groups with this tag executed. *Figure 7.11* shows the test summary result when we use the tag filter option and **"Windows"** as the value for this property:

```
PS C:\Temp\Tests-Organization> $PesterConfig = New-PesterConfiguration
PS C:\Temp\Tests-Organization> $PesterConfig.Output.Verbosity = "Detailed"
PS C:\Temp\Tests-Organization> $PesterConfig.Filter.Tag = "Windows"
PS C:\Temp\Tests-Organization> Invoke-Pester -Configuration $PesterConfig
Pester v5.5.0

Starting discovery in 1 files.
Discovery found 9 tests in 10ms.
Filter 'Tag' set to ('Windows').
Filters selected 3 tests to run.
Running tests.

Running tests from 'C:\Temp\Tests-Organization\Organization.Tests.ps1'
Describing Windows Tests - Platform independent
 Context Strings
   [+] Must be a Windows String 3ms (1ms|2ms)
 Context Paths
   [+] Must be the Root Path 2ms (1ms|1ms)

Describing Windows Tests - Platform dependent
  [+] Must not throw an error 7ms (5ms|2ms)
Tests completed in 71ms
Tests Passed: 3, Failed: 0, Skipped: 0 NotRun: 6
```

Figure 7.11: Output summary result of invoking Pester with a tag filter for only including "Windows" tagged test cases

We can see that all nine tests were discovered within the test script, but only three where selected and executed due to the specified tag and all three passed successfully. The *NotRun* result indicates the six tests that were not executed, the ones with a different tag than the one specified. Everything is as expected and only the Windows specific test cases were executed. Just to note, it is also possible to select multiple tags at the same time. Let us say that you needed to filter on all tests that were tagged with both Linux and MacOS, you could do that by specifying a string array with the tags you want to include.

```
# Multiple tags are a valid option
$PesterConfig.Filter.Tag = "Linux", "MacOS"
```

And we can exclude a specific tag using the **ExcludeTag** property:

```
# Specific tags can be excluded
$PesterConfig.Filter.ExcludeTag = "Windows"
```

However, what if we wanted to only include the platform independent test cases from within all the groups and exclude the platform dependent ones? Both groups are tagged with the same specific platform, so how would we accommodate for that scenario? We can select specific groups by their name, so we could create a string array with the names of the specific groups we want to execute:

```
# Filter by group (Describe block) name
$Groups = @(
    "Linux Tests - Platform independent"
    "Windows Tests - Platform independent"
    "MacOS Tests - Platform independent"
)
$PesterConfig.Filter.FullName = $Groups
```

Moreover, to make it even more reduced and readable, we can even use a wildcard (*) to filter the group names:

```
# Use wildcard for filtering group (Describe block) names
$PesterConfig.Filter.FullName = "* independent"
```

Figure 7.12 shows the test summary result of invoking groups of tests filtered by their group names using a wildcard:

```
⊛ PS C:\Temp\Tests-Organization> $PesterConfig = New-PesterConfiguration
⊛ PS C:\Temp\Tests-Organization> $PesterConfig.Output.Verbosity = "Detailed"
⊛ PS C:\Temp\Tests-Organization> $PesterConfig.Filter.FullName = "* independent"
⊛ PS C:\Temp\Tests-Organization> Invoke-Pester -Configuration $PesterConfig
  Pester v5.5.0

  Starting discovery in 1 files.
  Discovery found 9 tests in 15ms.
  Filter 'FullName' set to ('* independent').
  Filters selected 6 tests to run.
  Running tests.

  Running tests from 'C:\Temp\Tests-Organization\Organization.Tests.ps1'
  Describing Linux Tests - Platform independent
   Context Strings
     [+] Must be a Linux String 3ms (1ms|2ms)
   Context Paths
     [+] Must be the Root Path 2ms (1ms|1ms)

  Describing Windows Tests - Platform independent
   Context Strings
     [+] Must be a Windows String 3ms (1ms|2ms)
   Context Paths
     [+] Must be the Root Path 2ms (1ms|1ms)

  Describing MacOS Tests - Platform independent
   Context Strings
     [+] Must be a MacOS String 3ms (1ms|2ms)
   Context Paths
     [+] Must be the Root Path 2ms (1ms|1ms)
  Tests completed in 110ms
  Tests Passed: 6, Failed: 0, Skipped: 0 NotRun: 3
```

Figure 7.12: *Test summary result of invoking tests filtered by group names using wildcard*

Only the test cases in groups that include *independent* in their names are being executed. Six tests are passed successfully and three are not executed at all, excluded by the filter.

By organizing and grouping test cases and by using tags or group names you can select specific test cases that should be executed. You can include or exclude groups by their tags or by their names and even use a wildcard to filter the group names. Being able to properly organize and structure your tests is a valuable skill that not only save you time executing tests, especially for large codebases, but also makes it a lot easier to get an overview of your test cases and as a bonus, it also serves as a form of documentation for your code as it helps not only yourself but also others to understand how your code should be used and what functionality is expected of it.

Mocking dependencies in tests

Mocking in Pester allows you to isolate the code you're testing from external dependencies, making it easier to focus on testing specific functionality in isolation. This is crucial for unit testing, as it ensures that the test focuses solely on the behavior of the code being tested and not on the behavior of external systems or components. Mocks are used to replace real commands or functions with custom behavior during the execution of your tests. This is especially useful when testing code that interacts with external systems, databases, web services, or other components that you want to control or simulate for testing purposes. With mocks, you have full control over the behavior of the command you're mocking. You can make it return specific values, throw exceptions, log data, or any other custom behavior that helps you test your code effectively.

Recipe 43: Use mocking in tests to isolate functions and simulate dependencies

In Pester, you use the **Mock** cmdlet to create mocks. The **Mock** command contains two parameters, the name of the function or cmdlet you want to mock and a scriptblock that defines the behavior of the mocked functionality:

```
Mock <function/cmdlet> {<Mocked functionality>}
```

1. Let us assume that we have a function that makes a request to a website and then checks the status code, we call this: **Get-WebData**. If the status code is 200 the website is running as expected and the function returns a string stating this. If the website for some reason is not running and the returned status code is not 200, another function is then triggered. This function is called: **Restart-WebServer**. This function uses the **Stop-Service** and **Start-Service** cmdlets to restart the **Internet Information Services (IIS)** service, which can be considered as an external dependency. The **Restart-WebServer** function use a **try/catch** block and returns a string stating that the webserver was restarted upon a successful restart of the webserver and if it fails to restart the webserver it returns a string stating this instead.

2. This return status is used within the **Get-WebData** function! We want to write test cases for the result of the **Get-WebData** function whether the website is running or not. However, what we do not want is that the test case triggers the **Restart-**

WebServer function and restarts the webserver, whenever we execute the tests. We need to **Mock** the behavior of the **Restart-WebService** function and overwrite its functionality, so we can use the mocked behavior in our tests, ensuring that the webserver is not actually restarted when we execute the tests. Another thing is, that we cannot guarantee that the **Invoke-WebRequest** cmdlet always will return the status code 200 whenever we execute our tests.

3. The requested site might be unavailable and return an unexpected status code at the moment where the tests are executed. We need to **Mock** the **Invoke-WebRequest** cmdlet, to make sure that it returns the expected status code (200) for **Get-WebData** tests where we check if the website is running. We also need to **Mock** the behavior when status codes other than 200 are returned. This will be an indication that the website is unavailable (or has other issues) and is the scenario where the **Restart-WebServer** function would be triggered. Sounds a bit complicated! Let us try to visualize it.

```
function Get-WebData {
    $Response = Invoke-WebRequest -Uri "Bio-Rent.dk"
        if ($Response.StatusCode -eq 200){
          return "Website is running"
    }
    else{
        $Status = Restart-WebServer
        return $Status
    }
}
function Restart-WebServer {
    try {
        Stop-Service -Name "W3SVC" -Force
        Start-Sleep -Seconds 30
        Start-Service -Name "W3SVC"
        return "Webserver Restarted"
    }
    catch {
        return "Could not restart webserver"
    }
}
```

Info: W3SVC is the service name for the IIS webserver publishing Windows service. The service display name for this service is: World Wide Web Publishing Service.

We use the **New-Fixture** cmdlet to create a new set of test scripts: **Mock.ps1** and **Mock. Tests.ps1** in the **C:\Temp\Test-Mock** directory. We write the following test cases within the test script:

```
BeforeAll {
    . $PSCommandPath.Replace('.Tests.ps1', '.ps1')
}
Describe "Get-WebData Function" {
    BeforeAll {
        Mock Restart-WebServer {return "Webserver Restarted"}
    }
    Context "Tests: Website is running" {
        BeforeAll {
            Mock Invoke-WebRequest {
                [PSCustomObject]@{
                    StatusCode = 200
                }
            }
        }
        It "Website should be Running" {
            $WebData = Get-WebData
            $WebData | Should -Be "Website is running"
        }
    }
    Context "Tests: Website is down" {
        BeforeAll {
            Mock Invoke-WebRequest {
                [PSCustomObject]@{
                    StatusCode = 503
                }
            }
        }
        It "Webserver should have been restarted" {
            $WebData = Get-WebData
            $WebData | Should -be "Webserver Restarted"
        }
    }
}
```

4. Within the **Describe** block (group), we create a **BeforeAll** block. Code within this block is executed before any other tests in the group and is available to the entire set of groups, including all the **Context** blocks. Within this **BeforeAll** block we **Mock** the **Restart-WebServer** function thus making it available to all the scopes in the group:

```
Mock Restart-WebServer {return "Webserver Restarted"}
```

5. All test cases (in this group) that tests a function containing the **Restart-WebServer** function, is now using the **Mocked** version. As you can see we overwrite the normal behavior by returning the string *"Webserver Restarted"* and no original functionality within the **Restart-WebServer** function is executed ensuring that it will never trigger the **Stop/Start-Service** cmdlets. Since we are going to **Mock** the **Invoke-WebRequest** cmdlet twice, one where the status code returned is 200 (website is available) and one for all other status codes (triggering the **Restart-WebServer** function), we create two **Context** blocks.

6. Each **Context** block has its own scope, so we can create a **BeforeAll** block in each **Context**. The code within one **BeforeAll** block in one **Context** block, is not available to the other, hence we can isolate different scenarios using these **Context** blocks. In the first **Context** blocks **BeforeAll**, we **Mock Invoke-WebRequest** to return the Status code 200 and within the other **Contexts BeforeAll** we **Mock Invoke-WebRequest** to return the status code 503 (which usually means *service unavailable*).

7. In each **Context** block, we create **It** blocks containing the tests. The **It** block in the first **Context** block, tests the behavior and than return output if the website is running (status code 200), and the **It** block in the second **Context** block tests the behavior and return result if the website is down (status code 503), the scenario where the webserver would be restarted if it was not mocked! Since we are mocking the behavior of the **Invoke-WebRequest** cmdlet and the **Restart-WebServer** function, we ensure that when the tests are executed, no actual call to the website is made using the **Invoke-WebRequest** cmdlet and also that the webserver is not actually restarted by the **Restart-WebServer** function. If we created both of these tests without mocking the cmdlet and function, not only would we make real requests to the website and actually restart the webserver each time we executed the tests, but we would also have one of the tests resulting as failed, since the **Get-WebData** function only returns one of the states, either *"Website is running"* or *"Webserver Restarted"* (it could also return *"Could not restart webserver"* if for some reason the **Restart-WebServer** function failed to restart the webserver, since we have not created any tests for this particular state. So, we could potentially end up with both tests as failed if this was the case. But since we are mocking the function we control the behavior and output).

8. Still confused? Let us summarize: We **Mock** the **Restart-WebServer** function to always return *"Webserver Restarted"*. For the first test case, we **Mock Invoke-WebRequest** to return the status code 200. This results in the *"Website is running"* return output from the **Get-WebData** function and we assert that this should be the result for this test case. In the second test case, we **Mock Invoke-WebRequest** to return the status code 503, which we know would result in the invoking of the **Restart-WebServer** function. In this case, the **Restart-WebServer** function is mocked and *"Webserver Restarted"* is then returned as the result output for the **Get-WebData** function. We assert that this should be the result of this test case. Upon execution, both tests should pass as shown in *Figure 7.13*:

```
⬤ PS C:\Temp\Test-Mock> $PesterConfig = New-PesterConfiguration
⬤ PS C:\Temp\Test-Mock> $PesterConfig.Output.Verbosity = "Detailed"
⬤ PS C:\Temp\Test-Mock> Invoke-Pester -Configuration $PesterConfig
  Pester v5.5.0

  Starting discovery in 1 files.
  Discovery found 2 tests in 8ms.
  Running tests.

  Running tests from 'C:\Temp\Test-Mock\Mock.Tests.ps1'
  Describing Get-WebData Function
   Context Tests: Website is running
     [+] Website should be Running 4ms (3ms|2ms)
   Context Tests: Website is down
     [+] Webserver should have been restarted 10ms (9ms|1ms)
  Tests completed in 107ms
  Tests Passed: 2, Failed: 0, Skipped: 0 NotRun: 0
```

Figure 7.13: Test Summary result for Get-WebData function using mocked Invoke-WebRequest cmdlet and Restart-WebServer function

9. Both tests pass as expected and we have ensured that the **Restart-WebServer** function never actually restarts the webserver due to the mock. We also control the behavior of the **Invoke-WebRequest** cmdlet by mocking its different return values depending on the status code. We can still test the functionality of the **Get-WebData** function and any changes to its current behavior would most likely result in failed tests, thus validating that these test cases work as intended. To show this, we introduce and simulate a small unintended change to the functions functionality by changing the return output. When we execute the tests again, we can see that the first test now fails and that the simulated changes broke the general expected functionality of the **Get-WebData** function. We must either accommodate for this change by fixing our mistake within the function or by updating our test case to reflect the new behavior, if this actually was the intended purpose. *Figure 7.14* shows the test summary result with the broken functionality. We changed *Website is running* to *Website is Up*:

```
● PS C:\Temp\Test-Mock> $PesterConfig = New-PesterConfiguration
● PS C:\Temp\Test-Mock> $PesterConfig.Output.Verbosity = "Detailed"
● PS C:\Temp\Test-Mock> Invoke-Pester -Configuration $PesterConfig
  Pester v5.5.0

  Starting discovery in 1 files.
  Discovery found 2 tests in 8ms.
  Running tests.

  Running tests from 'C:\Temp\Test-Mock\Mock.Tests.ps1'
  Describing Get-WebData Function
   Context Tests: Website is running
     [-] Website should be Running 11ms (9ms|2ms)
       Expected strings to be the same, but they were different.
       Expected length: 18
       Actual length:   13
       Strings differ at index 11.
       Expected: 'Website is running'
       But was:  'Website is Up'
       -----------^
       at $WebData | Should -Be "Website is running", C:\Temp\Test-Mock\Mock.Tests.ps1:35
       at <ScriptBlock>, C:\Temp\Test-Mock\Mock.Tests.ps1:35
   Context Tests: Website is down
     [+] Webserver should have been restarted 5ms (4ms|1ms)
  Tests completed in 110ms
  Tests Passed: 1, Failed: 1, Skipped: 0 NotRun: 0
```

Figure 7.14: Test summary result after the expected behavior of the Get-WebData function was changed

Mocking is a valuable technique that ensures that your tests are verifying your code without causing unintended changes to external systems. It eliminates the need to perform time-consuming or potentially destructive actions during testing, such as creating users, modifying databases, or restarting services. We would not want to create a new Active Directory user each time we tested a function that uses the **New-ADUser** cmdlet, updated a database table each time we tested a function that would add data to a database or restarted a webserver each time we tested a function that would restart a webserver. Also, if tests fail while using mock, you can be almost sure that the issue lies within your code that is being tested and not within the external dependencies.

Testing infrastructure components with Pester

Pester is not only limited to writing unit tests for functions and cmdlets but can also be used to create tests for infrastructure components such as testing network connectivity to a remote computer, testing network port availability, testing database connectivity, test the availability of cloud resources and much more. Whatever you can write code for with PowerShell, you can almost definitely be sure that there is a way to write tests for it.

Recipe 44: Strategies for testing infrastructure components

This section will discuss the strategies for testing infrastructure components such as network, database, and cloud resources. Infrastructure serves as the foundation for your IT environment and ensuring that your infrastructure components are reliable and running as expected is crucial to prevent downtime and loss of functionality in critical systems. In the long run, it can potentially save your organization money by making sure that everything runs as expected. Even the smallest issue with a single component can end up having a high impact for your entire environment, so why not find issues and fix them before your users or supervisor becomes aware that there even was an issue in the first place? By writing and implementing tests for your infrastructure, you can quickly and easily get an overview of the overall status of your systems and of external dependencies such as websites, API connections and even cloud components, that your critical systems might be dependent on.

We are not going to go into detail about the following tests within this recipe, instead we are simply going to show how some smaller infrastructure tests could be written and show the outcome of executing such tests. They can serve as a foundation for creating much more advanced and complicated infrastructure test cases.

You might need to test website connections, server connections, database connections or test if cloud resources exist or are running as expected. As an example, we have written and organized the following groups of tests:

> **Note: You are not bound by having both a main script and a test script, it is enough to have a stand-alone test script and to write infrastructure tests within this test script directly. Within this recipe we use a single test script called Infrastructure.Tests.ps1 that contains all the following infrastructure test cases.**

```
Describe -Tag "Network" "Website connections" {
    Context "Google site Tests" {
        It "Test Google network connectivity" {
            $Result = Test-NetConnection "www.google.com"
            $Result.PingSucceeded | Should -Be $true
        }
        It "Test google port 443 availability" {
            $Result = Test-NetConnection "www.google.dk" -Port 443
            $Result.TcpTestSucceeded | Should -Not -Be $false
        }
    }
    Context "Bio-Rent site Tests" {
```

```
        It "Test Bio-Rent network connectivity" {
            $Result = Test-NetConnection "Bio-Rent.dk"
            $Result.PingSucceeded | Should -Be $true
        }
        It "Test Bio-Rent port 443 availability" {
            $Result = Test-NetConnection "Bio-Rent.dk" -Port 443
            $Result.TcpTestSucceeded | Should -Not -Be $false
        }
    }
}
# Servers must exist!
Describe -Tag "Network" "Server connections" {
    Context "Webservers" {
        It "Should be able to ping PS-HOST01" {
            $Result = Test-Connection -ComputerName "PS-HOST01" -Count 1
            $Result.Status | Should -Be "Success"
        }
        It "Should be able to ping PS-CLIENT01" {
            $Result = Test-Connection -ComputerName "PS-CLIENT01" -Count 1
            $Result.Status | Should -Be "Success"
        }
    }
    Context "Domain Controllers" {
        It "Should be able to ping DC01.Moppleit.dk" {
            $Result = Test-Connection -ComputerName "DC01" -Count 1
            $Result.Status | Should -Be "Success"
        }
    }
}
# Requires sqlserver module (Install-Module sqlserver)!
Describe -Tag "Database" "Database tests" {
    Context "Database tests: MyDatabase" {
        It "Should connect to the database and retreive data" {
            $databaseServer = "DBServer"
```

```
                $databaseName = "MyDatabase"
                $query = "SELECT COUNT(*) FROM MyTable"
                $result = Invoke-Sqlcmd -ServerInstance $databaseServer
-Database $databaseName -Query $query
                $result[0].Column1 | Should -BeGreaterThan 0
            }
        }
    }
}
# An Azure subscription is required!
Describe -Tag "Azure" "Cloud Tests" {
    BeforeAll {
        # Requires AzureCLI
        if (-not ((az account list --query "[].id" --output tsv) -contains
"<AZURE SUBSCRIPTION ID>") ){
            az login
        }
    }
    Context "Test Resource Groups" {
        It "Resource group: RG-Test should exist" {
            $Result = Az group exists --name "RG-Test"
            $Result | Should -Match true
        }
    }
    Context "Other Azure tests" {
        It "App Registration should exist" {
            $Result = az ad app list --display-name "TestApp" --query "[0].
appId" --output tsv
            $Result | Should -Not -BeNullOrEmpty
        }
    }
    AfterAll {
        Az logout
    }
}
```

Looking through these tests, we can see that we have four groups (Describe blocks), covering three themes: Network, database and Azure. The first network group is used to test website connections that primarily use the **Test-NetConnection** cmdlet. The second group is used for testing connections to servers using the **Test-Connection** cmdlet. The third group is used for database tests and the fourth group is for Azure cloud tests. The cloud tests are a bit more advanced than the other tests and require a smaller explanation. First, you need an Azure subscription and the AzureCLI installed. This is covered in more detail in Chapter 10, Managing Azure with PowerShell.I

t uses a **BeforeAll** block and within that block is an **if** block. The **if** block uses the AzureCLI query command: **az account list** to return all current Azure subscriptions that are available to your user. If the returned list does not contain your Azure subscription ID (insert your own Azure subscription ID within the test case) it runs the **az login** command which will prompt you to login to your Azure subscription (this requires human intervention each time the tests are executed, but this can be automated!). The first Azure test case checks if a specific Azure resource group exists and the second test checks if a specific Azure application registration exists. After the last Azure test is executed, we use the **AfterAll** block to ensure that the **az logout** command is executed, making sure we do not leave an open session to the Azure subscription.

Let us see what happens when we invoke the tests with Pester as shown in *Figure 7.15*:

```
PS C:\Temp\Test-Infra> $PesterConfig = New-PesterConfiguration
PS C:\Temp\Test-Infra> $PesterConfig.Output.Verbosity = "Detailed"
PS C:\Temp\Test-Infra> Invoke-Pester -Configuration $PesterConfig
Discovery found 10 tests in 194ms.
Running tests.

Running tests from 'C:\Temp\Test-Infra\Infrastructure.Tests.ps1'
Describing Website connections
 Context Google site Tests
   [+] Test Google network connectivity 1.34s (1.31s|30ms)
   [+] Test google port 443 availability 130ms (129ms|1ms)
 Context Bio-Rent site Tests
WARNING: Ping to 5.186.57.95 failed with status: TimedOut
   [-] Test Bio-Rent network connectivity 4.62s (4.62s|2ms)
     Expected $true, but got $false.
     at $Result.PingSucceeded | Should -Be $true, C:\Temp\Test-Infra\Infrastructure.Tests.ps1:
15
     at <ScriptBlock>, C:\Temp\Test-Infra\Infrastructure.Tests.ps1:15
   [+] Test Bio-Rent port 443 availability 103ms (103ms|0ms)

Describing Server connections
 Context Webservers
Test-Connection: C:\Temp\Test-Infra\Infrastructure.Tests.ps1:28:23
Line |
  28 |     ...         $Result = Test-Connection -ComputerName "PS-HOST01" -Count 1
     |                           ~~~~~~~~~~~~~~~~~~~~~~~~~~~~~~~~~~~~~~~~~~~~~~~~~~~~
     | Testing connection to computer 'PS-HOST01' failed: Cannot resolve the
     | target name.
   [-] Should be able to ping PS-HOST01 2.79s (2.79s|3ms)
     Expected 'Success', but got $null.
     at $Result.Status | Should -Be "Success", C:\Temp\Test-Infra\Infrastructure.Tests.ps1:29
     at <ScriptBlock>, C:\Temp\Test-Infra\Infrastructure.Tests.ps1:29
Test-Connection: C:\Temp\Test-Infra\Infrastructure.Tests.ps1:32:23
Line |
  32 |     ...         $Result = Test-Connection -ComputerName "PS-CLIENT01" -Count 1
     |                           ~~~~~~~~~~~~~~~~~~~~~~~~~~~~~~~~~~~~~~~~~~~~~~~~~~~~~~
     | Testing connection to computer 'PS-CLIENT01' failed: Cannot resolve the
     | target name.
   [-] Should be able to ping PS-CLIENT01 2.71s (2.71s|0ms)
     Expected 'Success', but got $null.
     at $Result.Status | Should -Be "Success", C:\Temp\Test-Infra\Infrastructure.Tests.ps1:33
     at <ScriptBlock>, C:\Temp\Test-Infra\Infrastructure.Tests.ps1:33
 Context Domain Controllers
Test-Connection: C:\Temp\Test-Infra\Infrastructure.Tests.ps1:38:23
Line |
  38 |                 $Result = Test-Connection -ComputerName "DC01" -Count 1
     |                           ~~~~~~~~~~~~~~~~~~~~~~~~~~~~~~~~~~~~~~~~~~~~~~~
     | Testing connection to computer 'DC01' failed: Cannot resolve the target
     | name.
   [-] Should be able to ping DC01.Moppleit.dk 2.73s (2.72s|11ms)
     Expected 'Success', but got $null.
     at $Result.Status | Should -Be "Success", C:\Temp\Test-Infra\Infrastructure.Tests.ps1:39
     at <ScriptBlock>, C:\Temp\Test-Infra\Infrastructure.Tests.ps1:39
Describing Database tests
 Context Database tests: MyDatabase
Invoke-Sqlcmd: C:\Temp\Test-Infra\Infrastructure.Tests.ps1:52:23
Line |
  52 |     ...   $result = Invoke-Sqlcmd -ServerInstance $databaseServer -Database $ ...
     |                     ~~~~~~~~~~~~~~~~~~~~~~~~~~~~~~~~~~~~~~~~~~~~~~~~~~~~~~~~~~~~~
     | A network-related or instance-specific error occurred while establishing a connection
     | to SQL Server. The server was not found or was not accessible. Verify that the
     | instance name is correct and that SQL Server is configured to allow remote
     | connections. (provider: Named Pipes Provider, error: 40 - Could not open a connection
     | to SQL Server)
   [-] Should connect to the database and retreive data 14.71s (14.71s|4ms)
     BatchParserException: Incorrect syntax was encountered while parsing ''.
     at <ScriptBlock>, C:\Temp\Test-Infra\Infrastructure.Tests.ps1:52

WARNING: A web browser has been opened at https://login.microsoftonline.com/organizations/oau
th2/v2.0/authorize. Please continue the login in the web browser. If no web browser is availa
ble or if the web browser fails to open, use device code flow with `az login --use-device-cod
e`.
Describing Cloud Tests
 Context Test Resource Groups
   [-] Resource group: RG-Test should exist 556ms (543ms|13ms)
     Expected regular expression 'true' to match $null, but it did not match.
     at $Result | Should -Match true, C:\Temp\Test-Infra\Infrastructure.Tests.ps1:69
     at <ScriptBlock>, C:\Temp\Test-Infra\Infrastructure.Tests.ps1:69
 Context Other Azure tests
   [-] App Registration should exist 434ms (433ms|1ms)
     Expected a value, but got $null or empty.
     at $Result | Should -Not -BeNullOrEmpty, C:\Temp\Test-Infra\Infrastructure.Tests.ps1:74
     at <ScriptBlock>, C:\Temp\Test-Infra\Infrastructure.Tests.ps1:74
Tests completed in 37.03s
Tests Passed: 3, Failed: 7, Skipped: 0 NotRun: 0
```

Figure 7.15: *Test summary result of invoking infrastructure tests cases*

Our infrastructure is not very healthy! Only 3 out of 10 tests passed. One website is not pingable, no servers are available, the database has a network related or instance-specific issue (which indicates the it is not accessible on the network, usually due to missing firewall rules, or that the database instance is not running) and none of the Azure cloud resources exists. Notice the warning before the Cloud Tests are executed. It opens a web browser and prompts you to login to your Azure subscription. Let us fix all these issues and make the infrastructure healthy again. *Figure 7.16* shows the test summary result after all issues have been addressed and fixed:

```
● PS C:\Temp\Test-Infra> $PesterConfig = New-PesterConfiguration
● PS C:\Temp\Test-Infra> $PesterConfig.Output.Verbosity = "Detailed"
● PS C:\Temp\Test-Infra> Invoke-Pester -configuration $PesterConfig
  Pester v5.5.0

  Starting discovery in 1 files.
  Discovery found 10 tests in 14ms.
  Running tests.

  Running tests from 'C:\Temp\Test-Infra\Infrastructure.Tests.ps1'
  Describing Website connections
   Context Google site Tests
      [+] Test Google network connectivity 96ms (94ms|2ms)
      [+] Test google port 443 availability 95ms (95ms|0ms)
   Context Bio-Rent site Tests
      [+] Test Bio-Rent network connectivity 94ms (93ms|2ms)
      [+] Test Bio-Rent port 443 availability 87ms (87ms|0ms)

  Describing Server connections
   Context Webservers
      [+] Should be able to ping PS-HOST01 1.02s (1.02s|3ms)
      [+] Should be able to ping PS-CLIENT01 1.02s (1.01s|0ms)
   Context Domain Controllers
      [+] Should be able to ping DC01.Moppleit.dk 1.03s (1.03s|1ms)

  Describing Database tests
   Context Database tests: MyDatabase
      [+] Should connect to the database and retreive data 1.27s (1.27s|3ms)

  Describing Cloud Tests
   Context Test Resource Groups
      [+] Resource group: RG-Test should exist 1.09s (1.08s|3ms)
    Context Other Azure tests
      [+] App Registration should exist 1.21s (1.21s|1ms)
  Tests completed in 91.51s
  Tests Passed: 10, Failed: 0, Skipped: 0 NotRun: 0
```

Figure 7.16: Test summary result after all infrastructure issues is addressed and fixed

We have made sure that all websites are pingable. We have restarted all servers. We have created a firewall rule so that we can access our database server instance and we have created the missing Azure resources. All test cases now pass successfully. Our infrastructure is healthy again.

Sometimes you might have found that some smaller systems or particular servers have been down for hours or even days without no one noticing and some data might not have been updated properly for a while. Even the smallest deviation in data can be catastrophic in the long run and you might end up with incorrect or even invalid data that is a part of a much larger and critical system. Imagine if this data was for some part of your budget or for invoices being shipped to customers, it might end up being a very expensive affair. By writing and implementing tests for your infrastructure components, you can test almost all infrastructure aspects and make sure that every component behaves and runs as expected. If you have a very large infrastructure it might be beneficial to run daily tests or even schedule automatic hourly tests that provides you with reports if something is not as it should be, you will be able to find and fix such issues, before the consequences might become too severe.

Implementing code coverage analysis in tests

Code coverage analysis helps you identify which parts of your code have been executed during testing and which portions may have been overlooked. In very large code bases it is not always easy to get a total overview of your code and you might end up missing writing test cases for some smaller functions or commands that would actually be quite beneficial having test cases for. Even the tiniest flaw in the smallest code snippet has the potential to affect the entire code base and break a script or an applications functionality entirely. Keep in mind that you can almost never have too many test cases and the broader your test coverage is, the more reliable your code becomes and the less likely it would be that you end up breaking the general functionality when making any changes.

Recipe 45: Learn how to measure code coverage

In this recipe you will learn how to measure code coverage in scripts and identify code that is not covered by tests. Code coverage is used to measure the extent to which your code is covered by a set of tests, and it gives an indication of how thoroughly code is being tested. It is not enough to just say: *"I have 10 functions and I have tests for 5 of them, so my code coverage is 50%"*. Each command within functions in your code is a potential for testing, so we could make test cases that targets these individual commands to ensure that each of them is covered by tests. Such commands encompass various elements like: **If** statements, **throw** statements, assigned variables, **return** statements and so on.

Pester has a code coverage feature to analyse and generate code coverage metrics and even reports, when tests are being invoked.

We enable code coverage by setting the **CodeCoverage.Enabled** property to **$true** in the Pester configuration we want to use when invoking our tests. We can also set a code coverage percent target value, which we can use to indicate the minimum code coverage percentage that we accept. If the code coverage is below this target value the test summary result will indicate this with a red color, and if it is above the accepted value, the result indicates this with a green color. The default value in Pester is 75%. We are a bit stricter in our coverage, so we set this to 85%:

```
$PesterConfig = New-PesterConfiguration
$PesterConfig.Output.Verbosity = "Detailed"
$PesterConfig.CodeCoverage.Enabled = $true
$PesterConfig.CodeCoverage.CoveragePercentTarget = 85
```

We need some functions with commands to test and for analysing code coverage. The following functions are very simple and is purely for giving an insight as to how code coverage works. These functions are created within a script called **CodeCoverage.ps1**:

```
function One {
    param (
        [Bool]$Parameter
    )
    if ($Parameter){
        return "Parameter is true"
    }
    else{
        return "Parameter is false"
    }
}
function Two {
    param (
        [Bool]$Parameter = $false
    )
    try{
        if ($Parameter){
            throw "Failed"
        }
        $Output = "Success"
    }
    catch{
        $Output = "$_"
    }
    return $Output
}
```

Function **One** takes a **bool** as an argument and executes either the **if** or **else** block dependent on the **bool** value specified. Function **Two** takes a **bool** as an argument and use a **try/catch** block. In this case the **$Parameter** is used to **throw** an error within the **if** block. If the **bool** value is **$true**, the **catch** block "catches" the error and assign the "Failed" throw error message to the **$Output** variable. If the **bool** value is **$false**, the **$Output** variable is assigned the string value: "Success". The function returns the **$Output** string variable.

It might not be obvious at first how many commands are a potential for tests so let us write some test cases and see if we can get a high code coverage. We create the tests within a test script called **CodeCoverage.Tests.ps1**:

```
Describe "CodeCoverage" {
    Context "It tests function One" {
        It "Should return Parameter is true" {
            One $true | Should -Be "Parameter is true"
        }
    }
    Context "It tests function Two" {
        It "Should return Failed" {
            Two $true | Should -Be "Failed"
        }
    }
}
```

We create a group for the tests and a context for each functions test cases. The first case tests the return value of the **One** function if it is invoked with **$true** as an argument for the parameter. The second case tests the return value of the **Two** function if it is invoked with **$true** as an argument for the parameter.

Figure 7.17 shows the test summary result including the code coverage analysis of the commands within the functions in the **CodeCoverage.ps1** script:

```
⊕ PS C:\Temp\CodeCoverage> $PesterConfig = New-PesterConfiguration
⊕ PS C:\Temp\CodeCoverage> $PesterConfig.output.Verbosity = "Detailed"
⊕ PS C:\Temp\CodeCoverage> $PesterConfig.CodeCoverage.Enabled = $true
⊕ PS C:\Temp\CodeCoverage> $PesterConfig.CodeCoverage.CoveragePercentTarget = 85
⊕ PS C:\Temp\CodeCoverage> Invoke-Pester -configuration $PesterConfig
  Pester v5.5.0

  Starting discovery in 1 files.
  Discovery found 2 tests in 13ms.
  Starting code coverage.
  Code Coverage preparation finished after 7 ms.
  Running tests.

  Running tests from 'C:\Temp\CodeCoverage\CodeCoverage.Tests.ps1'
  Describing CodeCoverage
   Context It tests function One
     [+] Should return: Parameter is true 5ms (3ms|3ms)
   Context It tests function Two
     [+] Should return Failed 4ms (2ms|2ms)
  Tests completed in 78ms
  Tests Passed: 2, Failed: 0, Skipped: 0 NotRun: 0
  Processing code coverage result.
  Code Coverage result processed in 6 ms.
  Covered 75% / 85%. 8 analyzed Commands in 1 File.
  Missed commands:

  File              Class Function Line Command
  ----              ----- -------- ---- -------
  CodeCoverage.ps1        One        9 return "Parameter is false"
  CodeCoverage.ps1        Two       20 $Output = "Success"
```

Figure 7.17: Test summary result including code coverage of commands within the CodeCoverage.ps1 script

Besides the usual test results, we also get information about the code coverage within the script. Eight commands in one file have been analysed with a code coverage of 75%, meaning that we have six commands covered by tests and two that are not. The 85% value is the indication of the target percentage coverage that we specified within the Pester configuration. We are not quite there yet, so let us see if we can write some more tests to cover all aspects of the code. Lucky for us, Pester gives us an overview of missing commands that are not yet covered by tests, which makes it quite easy for us to find and write tests that covers these commands:

```
Describe "CodeCoverage" {
    Context "It tests function One" {
        It "Should return: Parameter is true" {
            One $true | Should -Be "Parameter is true"
        }
        It "Should return: Parameter is false" {
            One $false | Should -Be "Parameter is false"
        }
    }
```

```
Context "It tests function Two" {

    It "Should return Failed" {

        Two $true | Should -Be "Failed"

    }

    It "Should return Success" {

        Two $false | Should -Be "Success"

    }

}

}
```

We create two more test cases, so our test script contains the test as shown above. *Figure 7.18* shows the test summary result of invoking Pester after we have updated our test cases with tests that covers the missing commands:

```
● PS C:\Temp\CodeCoverage> $PesterConfig = New-PesterConfiguration
● PS C:\Temp\CodeCoverage> $PesterConfig.output.Verbosity = "Detailed"
● PS C:\Temp\CodeCoverage> $PesterConfig.CodeCoverage.Enabled = $true
● PS C:\Temp\CodeCoverage> $PesterConfig.CodeCoverage.CoveragePercentTarget = 85
● PS C:\Temp\CodeCoverage> Invoke-Pester -configuration $PesterConfig
  Pester v5.5.0

  Starting discovery in 1 files.
  Discovery found 4 tests in 12ms.
  Starting code coverage.
  Code Coverage preparation finished after 6 ms.
  Running tests.

  Running tests from 'C:\Temp\CodeCoverage\CodeCoverage.Tests.ps1'
  Describing CodeCoverage
   Context It tests function One
     [+] Should return: Parameter is true 16ms (13ms|3ms)
     [+] Should return: Parameter is false 15ms (14ms|1ms)
   Context It tests function Two
     [+] Should return Failed 12ms (3ms|9ms)
     [+] Should return Success 12ms (11ms|1ms)
  Tests completed in 123ms
  Tests Passed: 4, Failed: 0, Skipped: 0 NotRun: 0
  Processing code coverage result.
  Code Coverage result processed in 52 ms.
  Covered 100% / 85%. 8 analyzed Commands in 1 File.
```

Figure 7.18: *Test summary result after writing tests for the missing commands in the CodeCoverage.ps1 script*

Our code is now covered 100% and all tests have passed. We can be confident that we have tests that covers our entire code base in our script. Of course, as we write and add more code to our script, the coverage will change accordingly and we have to make sure that we write tests to cover the new code and commands, or as a minimum at least write tests that cover commands to reach our acceptable coverage percentage target. Keep in mind that in some cases it might not be possible to cover all code 100%. It depends on how advanced and complicated the code, the functions, and the commands you write might be and how it all works together.

One last thing to note is that you can create code coverage reports with Pester. If you have followed this recipe, you might have noticed that by enabling code coverage, a coverage.xml file might have been created within the test script path. We will not go into any more detail covering these report files, other than mention that such a report (in default JaCoCo format) can be used to publish code covering metrics within an Azure DevOps pipeline. For more information about this we refer to the official Pester online documentation which can be found here: **https://pester.dev/docs/quick-start**

Conclusion

Every developer should know how to write test cases and implement testing as an integral part of their coding workflow to ensure their code is reliable and its functionality is as expected. But testing is not only limited to developers, as we have seen within this chapter, IT administrators and IT Technicians can greatly benefit from implementing tests for their organizations IT infrastructure. For PowerShell developers and administrators, Pester is the framework that is used to not only create unit and infrastructure tests for PowerShell but also to organize tests and analyze and report code coverage for your code base.

The next chapter presents a detailed introduction to XML and JSON that are used for representing and structuring data in formats that are both human readable and easy for scripts and applications to interpret. While the main focus is targeted at XML, you will learn how to read and write XML files using cmdlets, the XML accelerator and by using .NET classes. You will also learn how to read and write JSON files and how to convert between JSON and PowerShell objects. It also dives into querying and extracting data from XML files using XPath expressions and how to serialize and deserialize PowerShell objects using CliXml.

Join our book's Discord space

Join the book's Discord Workspace for Latest updates, Offers, Tech happenings around the world, New Release and Sessions with the Authors:

https://discord.bpbonline.com

CHAPTER 8
Working with XML and JSON

Introduction

Scripts and applications are often dependent on data from external sources or need to load settings from configuration files or write logs to files. Such data comes in a variety of different formats, and the choice of format depends on the specific requirements of your scripts and applications and personal preferences. Two commonly used data formats in PowerShell for external data, configuration files and for logs, amongst others, are XML and JSON. **XML** stands for **eXtensible Markup Language** which is a hierarchical structured data format and **JSON** stands for **JavaScript Object Notation**, which is a lightweight key-value pair structured data format. Being able to properly navigate, parse, write, read, and convert data in these formats with PowerShell are essential skills needed for creating powerful scripts and applications that relies on data from external sources, uses configuration files and for writing logs to files.

Structure

The chapter covers the following topics:

- Introduction to XML
- Introduction to JSON
- Reading and writing XML files using PowerShell

- o **Recipe 46**: Write XML files using the Out-File and Set-Content cmdlets.

- o **Recipe 47**: Write XML files using the XML accelerator

- o **Recipe 48**: Write XML files using the System.Xml.XmlDocument .NET class

- o **Recipe 49**: Read XML files using the XML accelerator and extract and manipulate XML data

- Querying and extracting XML document data using XPath expressions

  - o **Recipe 50**: Use XPath expressions to query and extract XML document data

- Serializing and deserializing PowerShell objects with CliXml

  - o **Recipe 51**: How to serialize and deserialize PowerShell objects using CliXml

- Reading and writing JSON files using PowerShell

  - o **Recipe 52**: Write JSON files using the ConvertTo-Json cmdlet

  - o **Recipe 53**: Read JSON files using the ConvertFrom-Json cmdlet

Objectives

In this chapter you will be introduced to XML and JSON, their structure, and components and how these formats can be used in PowerShell for configuration files, log files and for storing data. You will learn about and how to create XML data documents using different methods and how to read and write XML data documents to and from files. You will also learn how to query and filter XML data documents using XPath expressions and how to serialize and deserialize PowerShell objects using PowerShell´s own CliXml format, for saving and restoring the states of such objects to and from XML files. You will learn how to read and extract data from JSON files and how to convert JSON data into PowerShell objects, how to convert PowerShell objects into JSON data and how to write JSON data to files.

Introduction to XML

eXtensible Markup Language or **XML** for short, is a data format that is used for structuring and representing data in a hierarchical manner. It is made to be both human readable and machine readable which makes it a good choice for data exchange between different systems, for configuration files, for webservices and for structured data storage. It is a self-descriptive format which means that data is described using descriptive tags and it allows you to define your own tags and build a structure that is based on your specific preferences and requirements. It includes elements that can contain multiple sub-elements, attributes, content, and additional information. The tree-like structure within an XML file is usually referred to as the XML *document* and each part of the document is divided into so called nodes. A node is any component such as elements, attributes, and text content within the

XML document. XML parsers are usually used to read and process XML to extract the data within documents while also for checking the syntax and rules of documents. It is also used to validate the rules and syntax against so called XML schemas. An XML schema is used to describe specific rules and limits to the structure of a particular set of XML documents. If there are syntax or any other validation errors as described within a schema, the XML parser will not process the XML document. This could be because of a missing end tag or that a schema condition has not been met. This makes XML a strict markup language. It is also important to note that XML is case-sensitive.

The general structure of an XML document consists of the following components:

- **XML Declaration**: An XML document typically begins with the XML declaration. This is used to define that this is an XML formatted document. It also specifies the XML version being used and the character encoding.

```
<?xml version="1.0" encoding="UTF-8"?>
```

Root element: This is the top-level element of an XML document and all other elements in the XML document go inside this root element. We can say that this is a representation of the XML document.

```
<publisher>
    <!-- Elements within the root element -->
</publisher>
```

- **Elements**: Are what is used to build the structure of the XML document. It is defined by an opening tag followed by the elements content and is then closed using a closing tag. The content within a tag can be text or other elements such as arrays.

```
<publisher>
  <book>
    <title>Python for Developers</title>
  </book>
  <book>
    <title>PowerShell Advanced Cookbook</title>
  </book>
</publisher>
```

- **Attributes**: Elements can have attributes in the form of name-value pairs. These attributes provide additional information about the element.

```
<publisher>
  <book id="1">
    <title lang="en">Python for Developers</title>
  </book>
```

```
  <book id="2">
    <title lang="en">PowerShell Advanced Cookbook</title>
  </book>
</publisher>
```

Id is an attribute of the book element and *Lang* is an attribute of the title element!

- **Comment**: Are used for documenting the XML structure and for providing additional information that is relevant for the XML document but are not a part of the documents structure. Comments are not processed by XML parsers. Below is an XML comment example.

  ```
  <!-- This is a comment -->
  ```

- **Whitespace**: Whitespace within XML documents are usually ignored by XML parsers, but leading and trailing whitespace characters within element content are preserved. Whitespace elements are spaces, tabs, and line breaks etc.

- **Node**: A node represents the individual parts of an XML documents data, such as the root element, elements, and attributes. Nodes are used to navigate the XML document structure. The node types within an XML document depend on the documents structure and content.

An XML document can be structured as shown below:

```
<?xml version="1.0" encoding="UTF-8"?>
<publisher>
  <book id="1">
    <title lang="en">Python for Developers</title>
    <author>Mohit Raj</author>
    <technology>Python</technology>
    <year>2019</year>
    <isbn format="paperback">978-8194401872</isbn>
  </book>
  <book id="2">
    <title lang="en">PowerShell Advanced Cookbook</title>
    <author>Morten E. Hansen</author>
    <technology>PowerShell</technology>
    <year>2023</year>
    <isbn format="paperback">978-XXXXXXXXX</isbn>
  </book>
</publisher>
```

This is a general example of how an XML document could be structured. This consists of the declaration, a root element (publisher) with two (parent) elements (book), and each of these elements have their own sub or nested (child) elements (title, author, technology, year and isbn). You can also see that some of the elements have attributes like **<book id="1">**, **<title lang="en">** and **<isbn format="paperback">**.

Introduction to JSON

JSON is a short for **JavaScript Object Notation** and it is a lightweight data format that is used for structuring and representing data in a collection of key-value pairs. Each key is represented as a string and each value can be a string, number, array, object, boolean, null or another JSON object. This data format is easy for both humans and machines to read and write and is a widely used format for data exchange between servers and web applications such as API´s. It is also used for configuration files, for structured data storage and for logging script and application logs to files. Though JSON was created specific for Javascript, it is a language independent format, and it is supported by many programming languages. It is flexible and allows you to define custom structures to meet specific requirements. The structure of JSON is simpler than that of XML making it usable for many scenarios where you might want a simpler structure that might be easier to read and parse.

The general structure of a JSON file consists of the following elements:

- **Top-level object**: The top-level structure of a JSON file is an object that is enclosed in curly braces **{ }**. Within this object all the elements are placed.

```
{
# JSON elements are placed inside the JSON object
}
```

- **Key-value pairs**: Data is organized in key-value pairs within a JSON object. The keys are strings in double quotes: **"key"**, followed by a colon **:** and values can be elements of the different data types.

```
{
  "publisher": "book"
}
```

- **Arrays**: Are ordered lists of values enclosed in square brackets **[ ]**. Arrays can contain values of the different data types such as other arrays, booleans and objects.

```
{
  "publisher": {
    "book": ["book1", "book2"]
  }
}
```

- **Strings, numbers and boolean values**: Strings in JSON are enclosed within double quotes and can contain any valid Unicode character. Numbers can be integers or floating-point numbers. JSON also supports the boolean values **true** and **false**.

```
{
  "publisher": {
    "book": [{
      "id": 1,
      "title": "Python for Developers",
      "author": "Mohit Raj",
      "year": 2019,
      "released": true
    }]
  }
}
```

- **Null value**: If a value is missing or undefined, JSON allows the use of the null value as an empty placeholder.

```
{
  "publisher": null
}
```

The below example shows the general structure and the usage of JSON elements, except for the null value element:

```
{
  "publisher": {
    "book": [
      {
        "id": 1,
        "title": {
          "lang": "en",
          "content": "Python for Developers"
        },
        "author": "Mohit Raj",
        "technology": "Python",
        "year": 2019,
        "isbn": {
          "format": "paperback",
```

```
            "content": "978-8194401872"
        }
    },
    {

        "id": 2,
        "title": {
            "lang": "en",
            "content": "PowerShell Advanced Cookbook"
        },
        "author": "Morten E. Hansen",
        "technology": "PowerShell",
        "year": 2023,
        "isbn": {
            "format": "paperback",
            "content": "978-XXXXXXXXXX"
        }
    }
    ]
  }
}
```

This example JSON structure is equivalent to the previous XML document example. Within the top-level object, we create a **publisher** key that contains another object with a key called **book**. The value of **book** is an array that contains different book objects and their specific data. These book objects each contain the same elements that describe the different books contained within the JSON object, such as id, title, author and so on.

With these XML and JSON examples, we can imagine that these could be the result of a query made to a database containing these books and their information data, and these examples are the return data from such a query either as XML or JSON format. Return data for such a query could be structured as shown in these examples. When such return data is parsed, as either XML or JSON it is easy to search for and derive information for a specific book or book information, within the returned data structure.

Reading and writing XML files using PowerShell

It is common to be able to read and write data in XML format in PowerShell especially when dealing with configuration files, data that should be interchanged with other systems or for storing data as XML formatted documents. PowerShell provides different methods and built-in cmdlets for such operations.

For reading XML files we can use the **[XML]** type accelerator with the **Get-Content** cmdlet to import and store XML data within a PowerShell object, or we can use the **Select-Xml** cmdlet to read, query and extract specific data from XML document files using XPath expressions. We will cover the **Select-Xml** cmdlet and XPath expressions in more detail later in this chapter.

The **[XML]** type accelerator can also be used to manipulate and write XML data in PowerShell by creating an **[XML]** object, set the required properties and then save it to an XML file using the **save()** method. The **New-Object** cmdlet can be used with the **System.Xml.XmlDocument** .NET class to create XML documents. Different elements can be created and manipulated using the objects methods such as the **CreateXmlDeclaration()**, **CreateElement()** and **CreateAttribute()** methods. Once the object and all elements are created, it can be saved to a file using the **save()** method. Besides the **System.Xml.XmlDocument** class there are other .NET classes that can be used for writing XML data such as the **System.Xml.XmlTextWriter** class. As a more low-level approach you can also use the **Out-File** and **Set-Content** cmdlets to write XML text data directly to files. But you need to ensure that the XML content is properly formatted as text before writing it to a file using these cmdlets, making this more prone to errors in syntax and the XML document structure.

In the next recipes we will look at these methods and cmdlets that is used for parsing, reading, and writing XML document data using PowerShell.

Recipe 46: Write XML files using the Out-File and Set-Content cmdlets

We can create an XML document structure directly within a **Here-String** assigned to a variable and then we can pipe this variable to the **Out-File** or **Set-Content** cmdlets to create an XML configuration file. This is one of the most readable and straight forward methods for creating an XML file with PowerShell programmatically, but it is more prone to errors in the syntax and structure because the XML data is simply a string that is not in any way parsed by any XML classes or accelerators which also means that no validation is made before saving the document structure to a file. The example below shows how this structure is created, assigned to a variable, and then piped to both the **Out-File** and **Set-Content** cmdlets:

```
$XmlText = @"
<?xml version="1.0" encoding="UTF-8"?>
<Config>
    <Database id="database">
        <Instance>DBServer</Instance>
```

```
        <Port>1433</Port>
        <Database>TestDB</Database>
    </Database>
    <Azure id="azure">
        <SubscriptionID>9c4b3e8a-2d1f-6a7b-5e9c-8d3a6f1c4b9e</
SubscriptionID>
        <TenantID>1e9d4a5f-9b2a-6e7b-3a7d-2c4d60b7ca7</TenantID>
        <ClientID>a8d2c4b6-1f7e-4e6a-b2d9-8c3a9d5e1f4c</ClientID>
        <ClientSecret>5e2d4b3a-7c8d-9b2a-6e4f-7a1f6c3b2d8a</ClientSecret>
    </Azure>
    <ServiceAccount id="serviceaccount">
        <UserName>Service.DBUser</UserName>
        <Password>ThisIsARandomPwd</Password>
    </ServiceAccount>
</Config>
"@
$XmlText | Out-File C:\Temp\Config1.xml
$XmlText | Set-Content C:\Temp\Config2.xml
```

If we pipe the **$XmlText** variable to **Get-Member** we can see that this variable is of the string type. Shown in *Figure 8.1*:

```
● PS C:\Temp> $XmlText | Get-Member

    TypeName: System.String

Name            MemberType          Definition
----            ----------          ----------
Clone           Method              System.Object Clone()
CompareTo       Method              int CompareTo(System.(
Contains        Method              bool Contains(string \
```

Figure 8.1: *Get-Member showing the data type of the $XmlText variable*

Both the **Out-File** and the **Set-Content** output results in the same structured XML document within each output file. So why not just create the document directly in a file? Because we might need to create multiple files for different applications with the same XML structure but with different content values. Instead of creating each XML file separately, we could have a file, such as a .csv file, containing multiple content values, and then build several XML configuration files from that data. It also serves as a template for future configuration files that should have the same document structure. It would be very easy to create a function with a parameter for each content value, and for the name of the output file, and then create configuration files with this document structure when needed, but of course if the structure becomes very large, you would need a function with a lot of parameters for each content value, and a better approach might be to create a parameter that takes and object such as a Hashtable or **PSCustomObject** as an argument containing the data instead.

Recipe 47: Write XML files using the XML accelerator

This method looks almost similar to the previous method, but there are some major differences. We create the XML document within a **Here-String**, but instead of directly assigning it to the variable, we assign it to the variable using the **[XML]** accelerator. The accelerator automatically converts the string content into an XML document of the System. Xml.XmlDocument type, and furthermore, it adds validation so if the syntax or structure in the string is not properly formatted as XML, the accelerator will throw an error:

```
[xml]$XmlObject = @"
<?xml version="1.0" encoding="UTF-8"?>
<Config>
    <Database id="database">
        <Instance>DBServer</Instance>
        <Port>1433</Port>
        <Database>TestDB</Database>
    </Database>
    <Azure id="azure">
        <SubscriptionID>9c4b3e8a-2d1f-6a7b-5e9c-8d3a6f1c4b9e</SubscriptionID>
        <TenantID>1e9d4a5f-9b2a-6e7b-3a7d-2c4d60b7ca7</TenantID>
        <ClientID>a8d2c4b6-1f7e-4e6a-b2d9-8c3a9d5e1f4c</ClientID>
        <ClientSecret>5e2d4b3a-7c8d-9b2a-6e4f-7a1f6c3b2d8a</ClientSecret>
    </Azure>
    <ServiceAccount id="serviceaccount">
        <UserName>Service.DBUser</UserName>
        <Password>ThisIsARandomPwd</Password>
    </ServiceAccount>
</Config>
"@
```

If we pipe the **$XmlObject** variable to **Get-Member** we can see that this is an object of the **System.Xml.XmlDocument** type, shown in *Figure 8.2*:

```
● PS C:\Temp> $XmlObject | Get-Member

    TypeName: System.Xml.XmlDocument

Name                    MemberType        Definition
----                    ----------        ----------
ToString                CodeMethod        static string XmlNode(psobject
AppendChild             Method            System.Xml.XmlNode AppendChild
Clone                   Method            System.Xml.XmlNode Clone(), Sy
CloneNode               Method            System.Xml.XmlNode CloneNode(b
CreateAttribute         Method            System.Xml.XmlAttribute Create
CreateCDataSection      Method            System.Xml.XmlCDataSection Cre
CreateComment           Method            System.Xml.XmlComment CreateCo
.........
RemoveAll               Method            void RemoveAll()
RemoveChild             Method            System.Xml.XmlNode RemoveChild
ReplaceChild            Method            System.Xml.XmlNode ReplaceChil
Save                    Method            void Save(string filename), vo
SelectNodes             Method            System.Xml.XmlNodeList SelectN
SelectSingleNode        Method            System.Xml.XmlNode SelectSingl
```

Figure 8.2: Showing methods of the $XmlObject variable using Get-Member (Methods abbreviated)

We get a whole new set of methods we can use to work with and manipulate the XML object, such as the **save()** method which can be used to directly save the XML document to a file:

```
$XmlObject.Save("C:\Temp\Config3.xml")
```

The **[XML]** accelerator actively converts the XML text inside the **Here-String** into a valid XML document of the **XmlDocument** type and validates the structure and syntax within the **Here-String**. Whereas the first method that writes the XML structure using the **Out-File** or **Set-Content** cmdlets are basically just writing a string to a file and provides no validation for the syntax and structure. In this case, it is up to the developer to make sure that the structure and syntax in the **Here-String** is formatted as proper and valid XML.

Recipe 48: Write XML files using the System.Xml.XmlDocument .NET class

The next method for writing XML files with PowerShell is also the most difficult one. We create a new object using the **System.Xml.XmlDocument** **.NET** class and then use the methods this class provides for building the XML document structure, and for adding each element within the document and the content within each element.

1. First, we create the XML document using the **New-Object** cmdlet and the **System.**

Xml.XmlDocument class. This is assigned to the **$XmlDocument** variable which is the base for our XML document:

```
# Create an XML document

$XmlDocument = New-Object System.Xml.XmlDocument
```

2. Next, we need to create the XML declaration. Since **$XmlDocument** is the base, we use the methods within the base to create all components such as the declaration, elements, and attributes. A component is assigned to its own variable and this component can then be appended to another component. In this case with the declaration, we append it to the **$XmlDocument** using its **AppendChild()** method. It is worth noticing that all components have an **AppendChild()** method which is used to append other components to it. This is the method we use for building the structure of the XML document one element and component at a time, as you will see in the next steps:

```
# Create the XML declaration

$XmlDeclaration = $XmlDocument.CreateXmlDeclaration("1.0", "UTF-8", $null)

$XmlDocument.AppendChild($XmlDeclaration)
```

3. The root element is created using the **CreateElement()** method, which is also used to create all the XML elements within the document structure. The root element is assigned to the **$Config** variable, which is used for reference when we need to add components to this element. This is also appended to the base document just like we did with the declaration element:

```
# Create the root element

$Config = $XmlDocument.CreateElement("Config")

$XmlDocument.AppendChild($Config)
```

4. We create the database section. First we create a database element using the **CreateElement()** method and assign this to the **$Database** variable which is the reference for this sections element. Since the database element has an attribute, we add this using the **SetAttribute()** method for the **$Database** element. We need to append the database section to the root element, so we use the **AppendChild()** method for the **$Config** element variable (which is the root element reference). Now we need to add all the remaining elements for the database section, such as the instance, port and database name elements, these are also referred to as child elements of the database element. We use the base´s **CreateElement()** method to create the elements and assign them to respective variables. Each of these elements are the ones that hold the data thus the element content. Within each element, this is referred to as the *InnerText*, and each element has an **InnerText** property. We set this property with the content accordingly. Each element is then appended to the database element using the database elements **AppendChild()** method:

```
# Create Database element with Id attribute
$Database = $XmlDocument.CreateElement("Database")
$Database.SetAttribute("Id", "database")
$Config.AppendChild($Database)
# Add child elements to the Database element
$Instance = $XmlDocument.CreateElement("Instance")
$Instance.InnerText = "DBServer"
$Database.AppendChild($Instance)
$Port = $XmlDocument.CreateElement("Port")
$Port.InnerText = "1433"
$Database.AppendChild($Port)
$DatabaseName = $XmlDocument.CreateElement("Database")
$DatabaseName.InnerText = "TestDB"
$Database.AppendChild($DatabaseName)
```

5. The next step is to create the Azure and the ServiceAccount sections and add their components accordingly. This is basically the same approach as we previously used in step 4. We add the elements for both of these sections:

```
# Create Azure element with Id attribute
$Azure = $XmlDocument.CreateElement("Azure")
$Azure.SetAttribute("Id", "azure")
$Config.AppendChild($Azure)
# Add child elements to the Azure element
$SubscriptionId = $XmlDocument.CreateElement("SubscriptionId")
$SubscriptionId.InnerText = "9c4b3e8a-2d1f-6a7b-5e9c-8d3a6f1c4b9e"
$Azure.AppendChild($SubscriptionId)
$TenantId = $XmlDocument.CreateElement("TenantId")
$TenantId.InnerText = "1e9d4a5f-9b2a-6e7b-3a7d-2c4d60b7ca7"
$Azure.AppendChild($TenantId)
$ClientId = $XmlDocument.CreateElement("ClientId")
$ClientId.InnerText = "a8d2c4b6-1f7e-4e6a-b2d9-8c3a9d5e1f4c"
$Azure.AppendChild($ClientId)
$ClientSecret = $XmlDocument.CreateElement("ClientSecret")
$ClientSecret.InnerText = "5e2d4b3a-7c8d-9b2a-6e4f-7a1f6c3b2d8a"
$Azure.AppendChild($ClientSecret)
# Create ServiceAccount element with Id attribute
```

```
$ServiceAccount = $XmlDocument.CreateElement("ServiceAccount")

$ServiceAccount.SetAttribute("Id", "serviceaccount")

$Config.AppendChild($ServiceAccount)

# Add child elements to the ServiceAccount element

$UserName = $XmlDocument.CreateElement("UserName")

$UserName.InnerText = "Service.DBUser"

$ServiceAccount.AppendChild($UserName)

$Password = $XmlDocument.CreateElement("Password")

$Password.InnerText = "ThisIsARandomPwd"

$ServiceAccount.AppendChild($Password)
```

6. When these steps are put together, we have the building blocks for creating the entire structure and components that makes the XML document, using the **XmlDocument** class. The last thing to do is to use the base's **save()** method to save the XML document to a file:

```
# Save the XML document to a file
$XmlDocument.Save("C:\Temp\Config4.xml")
```

As you can see, using this method is a much more advanced and complex approach than that of the previous methods where we have the XML document structure built within a **Here-String**. It can be quite cumbersome to create very large XML documents using this method, but it has its advantages. One of the advantages is that it ensures that the structure and syntax is always created the same way, and that it is valid. Another advantage is that we can use loops to create XML documents that contain a lot of similar sections that contain the same types of elements. It could be that we need to create a document containing book information for a lot of books, like the example that was used in the XML introduction topic in this chapter. In this example it could be an advantage to loop through a set of data, such as a .csv file that contains the book information, and then create each book element using a loop, as shown in the example below:

```
# Sample book data
$BooksData = @(
    @{ Title = "Book 1"; Author = "Author 1" },
    @{ Title = "Book 2"; Author = "Author 2" },
    @{ Title = "Book 3"; Author = "Author 3" }
)
# Create book elements using a loop
foreach ($BookInfo in $BooksData) {
    $Book = $XmlDocument.CreateElement("Book")
    $Books.AppendChild($Book)
```

```
$Title = $XmlDocument.CreateElement("Title")
$Title.InnerText = $BookInfo.Title
$Book.AppendChild($Title)
$Author = $XmlDocument.CreateElement("Author")
$Author.InnerText = $BookInfo.Author
$Book.AppendChild($Author)
}
```

7. The method you use is up to your preferences and specific requirements. In some scenarios it might be enough to create a simple XML document structure within a **Here-String** and save it to a file, but for other more complex scenarios, the use of the **System.Xml.XmlDocument** .NET class might be the preferred method to ensure consistency and validity.

    All methods in the previous recipes create XML configuration files with the same XML document content. One single thing to note though, is that the document created with the **System.Xml.XmlDocument** .NET class might set another tab indentation that you use as default. *Figure 8.3* shows the content of one of these XML configurations files.

```
۞ PS C:\Temp> Get-Content .\Config3.xml
  <?xml version="1.0" encoding="UTF-8"?>
  <Config>
    <Database Id="database">
      <Instance>DBServer</Instance>
      <Port>1433</Port>
      <Database>TestDB</Database>
    </Database>
    <Azure Id="azure">
      <SubscriptionId>9c4b3e8a-2d1f-6a7b-5e9c-8d3a6f1c4b9e</SubscriptionId>
      <TenantId>1e9d4a5f-9b2a-6e7b-3a7d-2c4d60b7ca7</TenantId>
      <ClientId>a8d2c4b6-1f7e-4e6a-b2d9-8c3a9d5e1f4c</ClientId>
      <ClientSecret>5e2d4b3a-7c8d-9b2a-6e4f-7a1f6c3b2d8a</ClientSecret>
    </Azure>
    <ServiceAccount Id="serviceaccount">
      <UserName>Service.DBUser</UserName>
      <Password>ThisIsARandomPwd</Password>
    </ServiceAccount>
  </Config>
```

Figure 8.3: *Content of XML configuration files created with the three methods for writing an XML file*

Recipe 49: Read XML files using the XML accelerator and extract and manipulate XML data

1. The simplest method for reading XML files is to use the **[XML]** accelerator and the **Get-Content** cmdlet:

```
# Read XML file using accelerator
[xml]$Config = Get-Content C:\Temp\Config3.xml
```

2. If we tried to read an XML file with an invalid structure or syntax, we would get an error as shown in *Figure 8.4*:

```
PS C:\Temp> [xml]$Config = Get-Content C:\Temp\Config3.xml
MetadataError: Cannot convert value "System.Object[]" to type "System.Xml.XmlDocument". Error:
  "Unexpected end of file has occurred. The following elements are not closed: Config. Line 18,
  position 9."
```

Figure 8.4: Error when trying to read an invalid XML file using the XML accelerator

3. Using the accelerator to read XML document files ensures that the XML document data is properly structured, and that the syntax is valid.

    Since we have a simple structure in our XML document data, we can use dot notation to access the nested elements within the XML document.

Note: XML elements might not always be accessible using dot notation. It depends on the complexity of the structure in your XML documents.

We can view the parent elements and child elements including their content for each section:

View Section (Database)

$Config.Config.Database

View Section (Azure)

$Config.Config.Azure

View Section (ServiceAccount)

$Config.Config.ServiceAccount

Shown in *Figure 8.5*:

```
PS C:\Temp> $Config.Config.Database

Id       Instance Port Database
--       -------- ---- --------
database DBServer 1433 TestDB
```

```
PS C:\Temp> $Config.Config.Azure

Id             : azure
SubscriptionId : 9c4b3e8a-2d1f-6a7b-5e9c-8d3a6f1c4b9e
TenantId       : 1e9d4a5f-9b2a-6e7b-3a7d-2c4d60b7ca7
ClientId       : a8d2c4b6-1f7e-4e6a-b2d9-8c3a9d5e1f4c
ClientSecret   : 5e2d4b3a-7c8d-9b2a-6e4f-7a1f6c3b2d8a
```

```
PS C:\Temp> $Config.Config.ServiceAccount

Id             UserName        Password
--             --------        --------
serviceaccount Service.DBUser  ThisIsARandomPwd
```

Figure 8.5: View of each XML document sections elements and their content

We can extract the data from the XML document and use the element content when needed within scripts and applications. We can assign all content values to variables at the beginning of our script or application or we can extract the values directly from the **$Config** variable whenever we need it. We can consider the **$Config** variable as our loaded configuration file, which is available to us as long as the script or application is running or until we specifically delete it (remove it from memory using the **Remove-Variable** cmdlet etc.):

```
# Example of using extracted XML data
$AzureSub = $Config.Config.Azure.SubscriptionId
$AzureTen = $Config.Config.Azure.TenantId
$SaName = $Config.Config.ServiceAccount.UserName
Write-Output "Azure information:

    Subscription: $AzureSub

    Tenant: $AzureTen
"

Write-Output "Database information:

    Instance: $($Config.Config.Database.Instance)

    Port: $($Config.Config.Database.Port)

    Database: $($Config.Config.Database.Database)
"

Write-Output "ServiceAccount:

    UserName: $SaName

    Password: $($Config.Config.ServiceAccount.Password)
"
```

Figure 8.6 shows the output of running the above example of extracting and using the XML data:

```
● Azure information:
      Subscription: 9c4b3e8a-2d1f-6a7b-5e9c-8d3a6f1c4b9e
      Tenant: 1e9d4a5f-9b2a-6e7b-3a7d-2c4d60b7ca7

   Database information:
      Instance: DBServer
      Port: 1433
      Database: TestDB

   ServiceAccount:
      UserName: Service.DBUser
      Password: ThisIsARandomPwd
```

Figure 8.6: *Example output of extracting and using XML data*
loaded into script or application from and XML file

Not only can we use the data from our loaded XML configuration file within our scripts and applications, but we can also change and manipulate the data if needed and update and save the changes to the XML configuration file accordingly. Let us imagine that the password for the service account that our application use to connect to the database has to be changed occasionally, but our application is system critical and cannot just be shut down for updating a password. We could have a function that receives the new password accordingly (this could be from a webservice or an API etc.), and then updates the loaded configuration with the new password. Then another function that connects to the database using the service account, just has to re-establish a new connection using the new credentials. Then we update and save the new password to our configuration file from within the application, so we do not have to do this manually. The password will be updated and ready the next time the application has to be restarted, or we could even create logic that could handle this without ever having to restart the application. All this without ever having to schedule a maintenance window and having the application restarted unintentionally. We will not go into any details on how to create such a setup, but we show how to update the loaded configuration with a new password and save the changes to the XML file. It is quite simple. We just assign a new value to the specific XML element content and then use the **$Config** variable objects **save()** method to update and save the new password within the XML configuration file:

```
# View the Old password
Write-Output "Old Password: $($Config.Config.ServiceAccount.Password)"
# Update/Change the password for the SA in memory
$Config.Config.ServiceAccount.Password = "ThisIsANewPassword"
# View the new Password
Write-Output "New Password: $($Config.Config.ServiceAccount.Password)"
# Save the changes to and update the XMl file
$Config.Save("C:\Temp\Config3.xml")
# View the new saved content of the XML file
Get-Content "C:\Temp\Config3.xml"
```

As you can see in *Figure 8.7* not only have, we changed the password within our loaded XML configuration document, but also updated the configuration file to reflect the changes with the new password. Next time the application has to be restarted, we have ensured that the password is updated, without having to manually update the configuration file and without having to schedule a maintenance window for a restart of the application in order to load the new password. The password is updated on the fly, both within the application but also within the configuration file.

```
● PS C:\Temp> Write-Output "Old Password: $($Config.Config.ServiceAccount.Password)"
  Old Password: ThisIsARandomPwd
● PS C:\Temp> $Config.Config.ServiceAccount.Password = "ThisIsANewPassword"
● PS C:\Temp> Write-Output "New Password: $($Config.Config.ServiceAccount.Password)"
  New Password: ThisIsANewPassword
● PS C:\Temp> $Config.Save("C:\Temp\Config3.xml")
● PS C:\Temp> Get-Content "C:\Temp\Config3.xml"
  <?xml version="1.0" encoding="UTF-8"?>
  <Config>
    <Database Id="database">
      <Instance>DBServer</Instance>
      <Port>1433</Port>
      <Database>TestDB</Database>
    </Database>
    <Azure Id="azure">
      <SubscriptionId>9c4b3e8a-2d1f-6a7b-5e9c-8d3a6f1c4b9e</SubscriptionId>
      <TenantId>1e9d4a5f-9b2a-6e7b-3a7d-2c4d60b7ca7</TenantId>
      <ClientId>a8d2c4b6-1f7e-4e6a-b2d9-8c3a9d5e1f4c</ClientId>
      <ClientSecret>5e2d4b3a-7c8d-9b2a-6e4f-7a1f6c3b2d8a</ClientSecret>
    </Azure>
    <ServiceAccount Id="serviceaccount">
      <UserName>Service.DBUser</UserName>
      <Password>ThisIsANewPassword</Password>
    </ServiceAccount>
  </Config>
```

Figure 8.7: Content of XML configuration file after update of the service account password

We have several methods for writing XML documents and for saving these as files. We can read XML document files and extract the data to use within our scripts and applications and we can make changes and update XML document files from within scripts and applications. We have only seen simpler examples of how to read and write such configuration files and use configuration data but the methods in this recipe can be used for different types of XML document files and scenarios and are not only limited to configuration files usage.

Querying and extracting XML document data using XPath expressions

XPath, which stands for XML Path Language, is a query language that is used for navigating XML documents using so called XPath expressions. With XPath you can filter and extract data from XML documents using a path-like structure by creating expressions that resembles paths through the structure of an XML document which enables you to access specific elements, attributes and values based on their location within the XML document. The **Select-Xml** cmdlet in PowerShell is used for querying XML documents using XPath expressions. You might notice that some XPath expressions use a single forward slash **/** and others are using a double forward slash **//**. The differences between these are significant and will affect the scope of the query selection. A single forward slash is used to specify an absolute path within the XML document. You should use this when you want to specify an exact path and work with nodes within that path. A double forward slash is used for relative paths and will search for nodes throughout the entire XML document regardless of their location and selects all nodes that match the specified XPath expression criteria. This is useful when you want to find nodes that can appear in different levels within the XML document. Below are a few examples of XPath expressions:

```
# XPath expressions
# List all nodes in the XML document
"//node()"
# List all node in the XML document
# Excluding whitespace nodes (spaces, tabs, and line breaks)
"//node()[normalize-space()]"
# Select the Root node in the XML document
"/*"
# Select all elements with a specific name
# regardles of their location in the XML document:
"//ElementName"
# Select Parent element and its child elements
"/ParentElement/ChildElement"
# Select all elements in a specific path
"//RootElement/Element1/Element2"
# Select elements with a specific attribute
# regardless of its value. (Check presence of an attribute)
"//Element[@AttributeName]"
# Select elements with a specific attribute name and value
# Find elements with attributes such as "Id=database"
"//Element[@AttributeName='Value']"
```

These are just a few simpler examples of XPath expressions and more complex expressions can be made to match your specific requirements. You can create expressions that use indexing to find and select a specific occurrence of an element. You can create expressions with multiple conditions using logical operators such as **AND** and **OR** and you can select elements based on their positions and so on.

The **Select-Xml** cmdlet is used with the **-Path** parameter specifying the path to the XML document file and the **-Xpath** parameter specifying the XPath expression. The output of the **Select-Xml** cmdlet is an object containing the specific data filtered with the Xpath expression query:

```
# Select-Xml using XPath expression
Select-Xml -Path <PathToXMLDocument> -XPath <XPathExpression>
```

Recipe 50: Use Xpath expressions to query and extract XML document data

We use the **Select-Xml** with Xpath expressions to query, extract and manipulate the data within an XML document file.

> **Note: For the next examples we use one of the XML configuration files we created earlier (they all contain the same XML document content).**

1. First, we use **Select-Xml** to list and view all the nodes within the XML document configuration file. Since we are not interested in whitespace nodes we use the special **node()** XPath method with the **normalize-space()** method: **"//node() [normalize-space()]"**. The square brackets are used to specify a condition that the **node()** method must meet, in this case we use the **normalize-space()** method to filter out nodes that contain whitespace, tabs and line breaks:

    ```
    Select-Xml -Path C:\Temp\Config3.xml -XPath "//node()[normalize-
    space()]"
    ```

2. This results in the output as shown in *Figure 8.8*:

```
● PS C:\Temp> Select-Xml -Path C:\Temp\Config3.xml -XPath "//node()[normalize-space()]"

Node            Path                    Pattern
----            ----                    -------
Config          C:\Temp\Config3.xml     //node()[normalize-space()]
Database        C:\Temp\Config3.xml     //node()[normalize-space()]
Instance        C:\Temp\Config3.xml     //node()[normalize-space()]
#text           C:\Temp\Config3.xml     //node()[normalize-space()]
Port            C:\Temp\Config3.xml     //node()[normalize-space()]
#text           C:\Temp\Config3.xml     //node()[normalize-space()]
Database        C:\Temp\Config3.xml     //node()[normalize-space()]
#text           C:\Temp\Config3.xml     //node()[normalize-space()]
Azure           C:\Temp\Config3.xml     //node()[normalize-space()]
SubscriptionID  C:\Temp\Config3.xml     //node()[normalize-space()]
#text           C:\Temp\Config3.xml     //node()[normalize-space()]
TenantID        C:\Temp\Config3.xml     //node()[normalize-space()]
#text           C:\Temp\Config3.xml     //node()[normalize-space()]
ClientID        C:\Temp\Config3.xml     //node()[normalize-space()]
#text           C:\Temp\Config3.xml     //node()[normalize-space()]
ClientSecret    C:\Temp\Config3.xml     //node()[normalize-space()]
#text           C:\Temp\Config3.xml     //node()[normalize-space()]
ServiceAccount  C:\Temp\Config3.xml     //node()[normalize-space()]
UserName        C:\Temp\Config3.xml     //node()[normalize-space()]
#text           C:\Temp\Config3.xml     //node()[normalize-space()]
Password        C:\Temp\Config3.xml     //node()[normalize-space()]
#text           C:\Temp\Config3.xml     //node()[normalize-space()]
```

Figure 8.8: Output from Select-Xml with Xpath expression listing nodes within XML document (without whitespace elements)

3. We do not get the tree structure of the XML document, but we get a list of all the nodes (elements) within the XML document. We know that the root node in our configuration file is the "**Config**" node, which is also the first one in the list, but it is not always necessarily guaranteed that the first item listed is the **root** node. We can use the XPath expression: **"/*"** to specifically select the **root** node within our XML document. We assign the result to a variable:

```
$Root = Select-Xml -Path C:\Temp\Config3.xml -XPath "/*"
```

4. We can then use the node property of the result variable to list all parent nodes found within the **root** node, as shown in *Figure 8.9*:

```
 PS C:\Temp> $Root = Select-Xml -Path C:\Temp\Config3.xml -XPath "/*"
● PS C:\Temp> $Root.Node

 Database Azure ServiceAccount
 -------- ----- --------------
 Database Azure ServiceAccount
```

Figure 8.9: Selecting the root node and list all parent nodes in the root node

5. Using dot sourcing we can further access the child nodes of the parent nodes and eventually their elements content data, as shown in *Figure 8.10*:

```
● PS C:\Temp> $Root.Node.Azure

 id            : azure
 SubscriptionID : 9c4b3e8a-2d1f-6a7b-5e9c-8d3a6f1c4b9e
 TenantID      : 1e9d4a5f-9b2a-6e7b-3a7d-2c4d60b7ca7
 ClientID      : a8d2c4b6-1f7e-4e6a-b2d9-8c3a9d5e1f4c
 ClientSecret  : 5e2d4b3a-7c8d-9b2a-6e4f-7a1f6c3b2d8a


● PS C:\Temp> $Root.Node.Azure.TenantID
 1e9d4a5f-9b2a-6e7b-3a7d-2c4d60b7ca7
```

Figure 8.10: Dot sourcing nodes to get the content of elements

6. Using this method, where we start at the **root** node and dot source the way through the structure can be useful if you do not know the exact structure of the XML document you are working with in advance. If we knew the structure, we could be more specific with our XPath queries and we could use expressions such as the one below, to directly filter the elements of a specific node:

```
$AzureNode = Select-Xml -Path C:\Temp\Config3.xml -XPath "/Config/
Azure"
```

```
$AzureNode.Node
```

7. We can select the specific elements content shown in *Figure 8.11*:

```
● PS C:\Temp> $AzureNode = Select-Xml -Path C:\Temp\Config3.xml -XPath "/Config/Azure"
● PS C:\Temp> $AzureNode.Node


  id           : azure
  SubscriptionID : 9c4b3e8a-2d1f-6a7b-5e9c-8d3a6f1c4b9e
  TenantID       : 1e9d4a5f-9b2a-6e7b-3a7d-2c4d60b7ca7
  ClientID       : a8d2c4b6-1f7e-4e6a-b2d9-8c3a9d5e1f4c
  ClientSecret   : 5e2d4b3a-7c8d-9b2a-6e4f-7a1f6c3b2d8a

●
  PS C:\Temp> $AzureNode.Node.ClientID
● a8d2c4b6-1f7e-4e6a-b2d9-8c3a9d5e1f4c
  PS C:\Temp> $AzureNode.Node.ClientSecret
○ 5e2d4b3a-7c8d-9b2a-6e4f-7a1f6c3b2d8a
```

Figure 8.11: Using XPath expressions to select specific nodes and the element content

8. Another valuable expression is to search for the presence of specific element attributes. In the example below, we search the entire document structure for elements containing the **"id"** attribute:

```
Select-Xml -Path C:\Temp\Config3.xml -XPath "//*[@id]"
```

> **Note: Remember that XML is case-sensitive. "Id" is not the same as "id".**

9. The output in *Figure 8.12* shows the nodes (elements) that contain an *id* attribute:

```
● PS C:\Temp> Select-Xml -Path C:\Temp\Config3.xml -XPath "//*[@id]"

Node           Path                    Pattern
----           ----                    -------
Database       C:\Temp\Config3.xml //*[@id]
Azure          C:\Temp\Config3.xml //*[@id]
ServiceAccount C:\Temp\Config3.xml //*[@id]
```

Figure 8.12: Nodes that contain the "id" attribute

10. This only provides us with the nodes that have an *id* attribute but not the specific attribute values. We can pipe the output to a **Foreach-Object** loop and iterate over each result to get the node **name** and the **id** attribute value for each node:

```
$SearchAttributePresence = Select-Xml -Path C:\Temp\Config3.xml
-XPath "//*[@id]"

$SearchAttributePresence | ForEach-Object {
    "$($_.Node.Name) : $($_.Node.id)"
}
```

11. We can see in *Figure 8.13* that each node has an id attribute value corresponding to its node name:

```
● PS C:\Temp> $SearchAttributePresence = Select-Xml -Path C:\Temp\Config3.xml -XPath "//*[@id]"
>> $SearchAttributePresence | ForEach-Object {
>>      "$($_.Node.Name) : $($_.Node.id)"
>> }
Database : database
Azure : azure
ServiceAccount : serviceaccount
```

Figure 8.13: Using Foreach-Object to loop through XPath result to
get node names and corresponding id attribute values

12. Now that we know the specific id attribute values, we can use the below expression
to search for specific elements with specific attributes, such as **id=serviceaccount**
and get a filtered result containing these particular nodes:

$Att = Select-Xml -Path C:\Temp\Config3.xml -XPath "//*[@
id='serviceaccount']"

13. *Figure 8.14* shows the result when selecting elements with the **id=serviceaccount**
attribute value. In this case we only have a single element, but there could be
several elements with the same attribute and value, it depends on the specific
structure of the XML document. Attributes can be used as a unique identifier
such as: **id=1**, **id=2** etc. or as an identifier for groups or sets of elements like
genre=horror, **genre=crime** and so on to identify and filter specific content
within XML documents:

```
 PS C:\Temp> $Att = Select-Xml -Path C:\Temp\Config3.xml -XPath "//*[@id='serviceaccount']"
● $Att.Node

 id              UserName       Password
 --              --------       --------
 serviceaccount Service.DBUser ThisIsARandomPwd

● PS C:\Temp> $Att.Node.UserName
 Service.DBUser
● PS C:\Temp> $Att.Node.Password
○ ThisIsARandomPwd
```

Figure 8.14: Searching for and filtering nodes with specific attributes

We have filtered and selected the **ServiceAccount** node with the **id=serviceaccount**
attribute value, and we now have direct access to the content within the different elements
within that node. Using XPath expressions with the **Select-Xml** cmdlet is quite a powerful
method for reading, querying, and extracting data from XML document files. Hence, what
are the differences between using **the [XML]** accelerator and the **Select-Xml** cmdlet with
Xpath expressions? Both approaches have their own advantages, so the choice depends on
the specific use case and scenario along with personal preferences. The advantages of using
the [XML] accelerator are that it provides an object-oriented approach for working with
the XML document. The document is loaded as an object into PowerShell which makes it

easier to navigate. Furthermore, the accelerator allows you to make changes to the XML document data, by adding, modifying and deleting different elements and attributes.

The accelerator also loads the entire XML document into memory which can have several advantages when working with both small and large documents, performance wise and by using the memory as a cache, making it more beneficial to perform multiple operations on the same document, instead of accessing and reading from the same file multiple times. The `Select-Xml` with XPath method is ideal when you need to query and extract more specific data from within an XML document file and when you want to perform simpler searches and filter the XML document data and for smaller tasks that does not require you to modify the XML document. Another benefit is that using this method does not load the entire document into memory, but instead only extracts the queried data directly from within the XML document file. This is especially beneficial when working with large XML document files where you need to extract specific data, since you do not need to load the entire file into memory. To sum up, the accelerator is used when you need to manipulate and make changes to the XML document data and structure and the `Select-Xml` cmdlet using XPath expressions approach, is a read-only more efficient way of querying, extracting, and filtering XML document data. Again, the choice depends on the specific task, requirements, and preferences.

Serializing and deserializing PowerShell objects with CliXml

PowerShell introduces an XML variant format, called CliXml. This format is specifically designed for and is unique to PowerShell. It is used for serializing and deserializing PowerShell objects and the purpose of CliXml is to save and restore the state of PowerShell objects such as Hashtables, PSCustomObject's and variables while preserving their structure and their properties. This allows you to save such objects to files and re-load them into other PowerShell sessions. In the next recipe we will show you how to save Hashtables, PSCustomObject's and variables in files and how to re-load these objects into other sessions.

Recipe 51: How to serialize and deserialize PowerShell objects using CliXml

Serialization is the process of converting an object such as a Hashtable or PSCustomObject into a format that can be saved to a file. Deserialization is the reverse process where a serialized, stored object is re-loaded from a file and converted back into an object. In PowerShell we use the `Export-CliXml` cmdlet to serialize and save an object into a file, and the `Import-CliXml` cmdlet to load and deserialize an object that is saved within a file back into a script or session.

We use the following Hashtable as the object we want to serialize and save to a file:

```
$BooksTable = @{
    Publisher = @{
        Books = @(
            @{
                Id = 1
                Title = "Python for Developers"
                Author = "Mohit Raj"
                Technology = "Python"
                Year = 2019
                Isbn = "978-8194401872"
            }
            @{
                Id = 2
                Title = "PowerShell Advanced Cookbook"
                Author = "Morten E. Hansen"
                Technology = "PowerShell"
                Year = 2023
                Isbn = "978-XXXXXXXXXX"
            }
        )
    }
}
```

It could as easily have been a **PSCustomObject**:

```
$BooksObject = [PSCustomObject]@{
    Publisher = @{
        Books = @(
            @{
                Id = 1
                … # Abbreviated data
            }
            @{
                … # Abbreviated data
            }
        )
    }
}
```

To serialize and save the object to a file we pipe the object to the **Export-CliXml** cmdlet:

```
$BooksTable | Export-Clixml C:\Temp\Books.xml
```

If we look at the Books.xml file, we can see that the XML structure within this file is different than that of a typical XML document. This is the structure that **CliXml** use to keep track of the type, structure, and content of the serialized object. *Figure 8.15* shows an abbreviated view of the Books.xml file and the CliXml structure used to store the hashtable:

```
Books.xml - Notepad
File  Edit  Format  View  Help
<Objs Version="1.1.0.1" xmlns="http://schemas.microsoft.com/powershell/2004/04">
  <Obj RefId="0">
    <TN RefId="0">
      <T>System.Collections.Hashtable</T>
      <T>System.Object</T>
    </TN>
    <DCT>
      <En>
        <S N="Key">Publisher</S>
        <Obj N="Value" RefId="1">
          <TNRef RefId="0" />
          <DCT>
            <En>
              <S N="Key">Books</S>
              <Obj N="Value" RefId="2">
                <TN RefId="1">
                  <T>System.Object[]</T>
                  <T>System.Array</T>
                  <T>System.Object</T>
                </TN>
                <LST>
                  <Obj RefId="3">
                    <TNRef RefId="0" />
                    <DCT>
                      <En>
                        <S N="Key">Author</S>
                        <S N="Value">Mohit Raj</S>
                      </En>
                          # Abbreviated data
```

Figure 8.15: *Abbreviated view of the Books.xml file and the CliXml structure used to save the object*

We can now use the **Import-CliXml** cmdlet to load and deserialize the saved object within the Books.xml file into a new PowerShell session:

```
# In a new PowerShell session

$NewBooksTable = Import-Clixml C:\Temp\Books.xml
```

Figure 8.16 shows a new PowerShell session that does not contain any **$BooksTable** or **$NewBooksTable** variables. We load the object from the Books.xml file and assign it to the **$NewBooksTable** variable. We can see that the structure and data from the original **$BooksTable** Hashtable object, that we serialized and saved into the Books.xml file, is restored and loaded into the **$NewBooksTable** variable in the new PowerShell session:

```
# PS C:\Temp> $BooksTable
# PS C:\Temp> $NewBooksTable
  PS C:\Temp>
# PS C:\Temp> $NewBooksTable = Import-Clixml C:\Temp\Books.xml
# PS C:\Temp> $NewBooksTable

  Name                        Value
  ----                        -----
  Publisher                   {[Books, System.Collections.Hashtable System.Collections.Hashtable]}

# PS C:\Temp> $NewBooksTable.Publisher.Books | Where-Object {$_.Id -eq 1}

  Name                        Value
  ----                        -----
  Technology                  Python
  Author                      Mohit Raj
  Year                        2019
  Title                       Python for Developers
  Id                          1
  Isbn                        978-8194401872

  PS C:\Temp>
# PS C:\Temp> $NewBooksTable.Publisher.Books | Where-Object {$_.Author -eq "Morten E. Hansen"}

  Name                        Value
  ----                        -----
  Technology                  PowerShell
  Author                      Morten E. Hansen
  Year                        2023
  Title              []       PowerShell Advanced Cookbook
  Id                          2
  Isbn                        978-XXXXXXXXXX
```

Figure 8.16: Loading a saved Hashtable data structure from a
CliXml formatted file into a new PowerShell session

Not only can we save objects such as Hashtables and PSCustomObject´s but we can also use CliXml to save states from one session and load it into other sessions. It could be that we wanted to save all variables from one session and load them into another session. We could do this by serializing and saving the output from the **Get-Variable** cmdlet into a file, and then load and deserialize the session variables in another session:

```
# Save the Variable session state to a file
Get-Variable | Export-Clixml C:\Temp\Variables.xml
# Restore the session state from the file
Import-Clixml C:\Temp\Variables.xml | ForEach-Object {
    Set-Variable -Name $_.name -Value $_.value -ErrorAction
SilentlyContinue
}
```

Note that some variables are constants and read-only such as the **$PSVersionTable**, **$PSStyle**, **$PSHOME** and other built-in variables. Such variables cannot be replaced, so in the case where you would want to load variables into other sessions, you should create some proper logic to only load variables that are relevant and not built-in variables or at least be aware that this might result in multiple non-terminating errors, when trying to overwrite such variables.

Using PowerShell's CliXml format for storing object data structures can be useful in certain situations such as state persistence where you want to store variables and other data objects for later use. It can simplify storage of more complex objects and larger data structures, and it can even be used for caching purposes, to help reduce loads on external resources such as API responses or database query results. Even though it might not always be beneficial, you can also use the CliXml format for your configuration files and logs instead of using the standard XML format as we did in the previous recipes. The usage of the different XML formats depends on each individual scenario, requirements, and also personal preferences. As we have seen, for storing complex data objects such as Hashtables and PSCustomObject's or for storing specific session states, CliXml is the recommended choice, but for simpler structures such as configuration files, the standard XML format might be preferred.

Reading and writing JSON files using PowerShell

JSON is commonly used in PowerShell for configuration files, when working with interchangeable data between systems, for storing data in a format that is both easy for humans and machines to read and interpret and for logging purposes for scripts and applications.

PowerShell has a simpler approach to handling JSON compared to XML. In PowerShell we use the **ConvertTo-JSON** and **ConvertFrom-JSON** type conversion cmdlets to convert JSON data to and from PowerShell objects and with the use of read and write cmdlets such as **Get-Content** and **Out-File**, to read and write JSON data from and to files.

In the next recipes we will use the **ConvertTo-Json** and **ConvertFrom-Json** cmdlets with the **Get-Content** and **Out-File** cmdlets to read, convert and write JSON data to and from files, and learn how to use this data for creating configuration files

Recipe 52: Write JSON files using the ConvertTo-Json cmdlet

The **ConvertTo-Json** cmdlet converts a PowerShell object to JSON formatted data. The Object can be a PSCustomObject or hashtable. The PowerShell object keys are converted to the JSON keys or field names and the object values are converted to the JSON property values.

1. We want to create a configuration file in JSON format from a PowerShell hashtable object. We structure the different levels, or *depts* as Hashtables within Hashtables. The level, or depth, can be seen as the number of nested elements within each other within the JSON structure. As JSON can easily handle arrays of data, we

have added an array containing service accounts within the **ServiceAccount** section. This configuration file has almost the same structure in JSON format, in comparison with the one we created in the previous recipe in XML format. The only difference here is the added service account array. The Hashtable configuration structure is assigned to the **$Config** variable:

```
$Config = @{
    Config = @{
        Database = @{
            Instance = "DBServer"
            Port     = 1433
            Database = "TestDB"
        }
        Azure = @{
            SubscriptionID = "9c4b3e8a-2d1f-6a7b-5e9c-8d3a6f1c4b9e"
            TenantID       = "1e9d4a5f-9b2a-6e7b-3a7d-2c4d60b7ca7"
            ClientID       = "a8d2c4b6-1f7e-4e6a-b2d9-8c3a9d5e1f4c"
            ClientSecret   = "5e2d4b3a-7c8d-9b2a-6e4f-7a1f6c3b2d8a"
        }
        ServiceAccount = @(
            @{
                Id = 1
                UserName = "Service.DBUser"
                Password = "ThisIsARandomPwd"
            }
            @{
                Id = 2
                UserName = "Service.AzureUser"
                Password = "VerySecretPwd"
            }
        )
    }
}
```

2. If we output the **$Config** variable as it is, we can see the PowerShell object structure containing the Hashtables and arrays that makes the configuration data object, shown in *Figure 8.17*:

```
PS C:\Temp> $Config

Name                          Value
----                          -----
Config                        {[ServiceAccount, System.Object[]], [Database, System.Collections.Hashtable], [Azure, System.Collections.Hashtable]}
```

Figure 8.17: PowerShell object structure containing the configuration data as Hashtables and arrays

3. Now we can use the **ConvertTo-Json** cmdlet to convert this configuration structure to JSON and then use **Out-File** to write the converted data to a file:

   `$Config | ConvertTo-Json | Out-File C:\Temp\Config1.json`

4. When we execute the command, you might notice the warning shown in *Figure 8.18*:

```
PS C:\Temp> $Config | ConvertTo-Json | Out-File C:\Temp\Config1.json
WARNING: Resulting JSON is truncated as serialization has exceeded the set depth of 2.
```

Figure 8.18: Warning shown when converting PowerShell Object to JSON

This warning specifies that the resulting JSON output has been truncated since its *depth* has exceeded the default set depth of 2, which means that our structure has more than two levels of nested components. If we do not accommodate for this, the resulting JSON serialization of the output will truncate the data as shown in *Figure 8.19*:

```
PS C:\Temp> $Config | ConvertTo-Json | Out-File C:\Temp\Config1.json
WARNING: Resulting JSON is truncated as serialization has exceeded the set depth of 2.
PS C:\Temp>
PS C:\Temp> Get-Content C:\Temp\Config1.json
{
  "Config": {
    "Database": {
      "Instance": "DBServer",
      "Port": 1433,
      "Database": "TestDB"
    },
    "ServiceAccount": [
      "System.Collections.Hashtable",
      "System.Collections.Hashtable"
    ],
    "Azure": {
      "TenantID": "1e9d4a5f-9b2a-6e7b-3a7d-2c4d60b7ca7",
      "ClientID": "a8d2c4b6-1f7e-4e6a-b2d9-8c3a9d5e1f4c",
      "SubscriptionID": "9c4b3e8a-2d1f-6a7b-5e9c-8d3a6f1c4b9e",
      "ClientSecret": "5e2d4b3a-7c8d-9b2a-6e4f-7a1f6c3b2d8a"
    }
  }
}
```

Figure 8.19: JSON output with truncated data due to serialization exceeding the default depth of 2

5. This is of course not what we wanted since the truncated data now only represents string values containing the text: **"System.Collections.Hashtable"**. This will

not be converted back to the original content if we reverse the operation. The **ConvertTo-Json** cmdlet has a parameter called **-Depth** which by default is set to 2. This can be set to values between 0 and 100 and is used to specify at which depth the cmdlet should serialize the data when converting it. We set the **-Depth** parameter to 3, to accommodate for our structures levels of depth:

```
$Config | ConvertTo-Json -Depth 3 | Out-File C:\Temp\Config1.json
```

Figure 8.20 shows the JSON file output with the depth parameter set to 3:

```
PS C:\Temp> $Config | ConvertTo-Json -Depth 3 | Out-File C:\Temp\Config1.json
PS C:\Temp> Get-Content C:\Temp\Config1.json
{
  "Config": {
    "Database": {
      "Instance": "DBServer",
      "Port": 1433,
      "Database": "TestDB"
    },
    "ServiceAccount": [
      {
        "Id": 1,
        "UserName": "Service.DBUser",
        "Password": "ThisIsARandomPwd"
      },
      {
        "Id": 2,
        "UserName": "Service.AzureUser",
        "Password": "VerySecretPwd"
      }
    ],
    "Azure": {
      "TenantID": "1e9d4a5f-9b2a-6e7b-3a7d-2c4d60b7ca7",
      "ClientID": "a8d2c4b6-1f7e-4e6a-b2d9-8c3a9d5e1f4c",
      "SubscriptionID": "9c4b3e8a-2d1f-6a7b-5e9c-8d3a6f1c4b9e",
      "ClientSecret": "5e2d4b3a-7c8d-9b2a-6e4f-7a1f6c3b2d8a"
    }
  }
}
```

Figure 8.20: JSON output with the depth parameter set to
accommodate for the configuration objects nested objects

We now get the PowerShell configuration object converted as properly JSON formatted content within the configuration file.

JSON formatted data is often used for scripts and application logs to store log data in a human readable format. One of the optimal methods for storing log data in files is by storing the data as one line per log, instead of having it span multiple lines. This is also optimal if you need to use third-party log monitoring tools, such as Datadog and Dynatrace which monitors and reads logs from files, one line at a time. **ConvertTo-Json** has a switch parameter, **-Compress** which omits whitespace characters, such as spaces, tabs, and line breaks (except within content values) when converting an object to JSON. This helps us make sure that the JSON output is created as a one-line JSON object within the output file:

```
$Log=@{
    Timestamp="01-01-2023 10:00:00"
    Level="INFO"
    Message="This is a log message"
}
$Log | ConvertTo-Json -Compress | Out-File C:\Temp\JsonLog.json
```

Figure 8.21 shows the JSON file output when using **ConvertTo-Json** with the **-compress** parameter:

```
● PS C:\Temp> Get-Content C:\Temp\JsonLog.json
○ {"Timestamp":"01-01-2023 10:00:00","Message":"This is a log message","Level":"INFO"}
```

Figure 8.21: *JSON file output compressed to omit whitespace*
characters and to fit on one line in the file

It is fairly easy to convert objects to JSON format and write the JSON content data to a file. Remember to be aware of the depth of your data structure before converting it or else data might be truncated, resulting in an unexpected structure and content values. If you need to store multiple JSON data entries within the same file, such as logs, it is recommended to compress the data to fit into one line. For configuration files and for storing other kind of data in JSON format, it might be more readable and optimal to store the data without compression.

Recipe 53: Read JSON files using the ConvertFrom-Json cmdlet

The **ConvertFrom-Json** cmdlet is used to convert JSON formatted data to a PowerShell object. It does not matter if the JSON data is compressed or not within the file, the input result will be the same. We use the configuration file, **Config1.json** we created earlier (see *figure 8.19*) as the JSON configuration file we want to read.

To read the JSON configuration file data and convert it to a PowerShell object is as simple as using **Get-Content** and pipe this to the **ConvertFrom-Json** cmdlet. We assign the input to the **$Config** variable:

```
$Config = Get-Content C:\Temp\Config1.json | ConvertFrom-Json
```

If we look at the content of the **$Config** variable we can see that it contains our data and using the **GetType()** method we can see that it is converted into a **PSCustomObject** object as shown in Figure 8.22. We might actually have expected it to be loaded as a Hashtable, which we previously used as the object we stored into a file using the ConvertTo-Json cmdlet. This is the default behavior for the ConvertFrom-Json cmdlet. If we want to load the object as a hashtable instead, we can use the cmdlets -AsHashTable switch parameter:

```
⊕ PS C:\Temp> $Config

  Config
  ------
  @{Database=; ServiceAccount=System.Object[]; Azure=}

⊕ PS C:\Temp> $Config.GetType()

  IsPublic IsSerial Name                                    BaseType
  -------- -------- ----                                    --------
  True     False    PSCustomObject                          System.Object
```

Figure 8.22: *Content and type of the $Config variable reading JSON data from a file using Get-Content and converting it from JSON with the ConvertFrom-Json cmdlet*

Now we can use dot notation to traverse the **$Config** variable and get the specific configuration data property values from the **$Config** object, as you can see in *Figure 8.23*:

```
⊕ PS C:\Temp> $Config.Config.Azure.TenantID
  1e9d4a5f-9b2a-6e7b-3a7d-2c4d60b7ca7
⊕ PS C:\Temp> $Config.Config.Azure.ClientID
  a8d2c4b6-1f7e-4e6a-b2d9-8c3a9d5e1f4c
⊕ PS C:\Temp> $Config.Config.Database.Instance
  DBServer
```

Figure 8.23: *Using dot notation to get specific configuration data properties from the $Config variable*

However, what about the **ServiceAccount** section? This was specified as an array within the JSON configuration file! If we try to use dot notation, we will get all the content in that array, as shown in *Figure 8.24*:

```
⊕ PS C:\Temp> $Config.Config.ServiceAccount

  UserName          Password          Id
  --------          --------          --
  Service.DBUser    ThisIsARandomPwd  1
  Service.AzureUser VerySecretPwd     2

⊕ PS C:\Temp> $Config.Config.ServiceAccount.UserName
  Service.DBUser
  Service.AzureUser
⊕ PS C:\Temp> $Config.Config.ServiceAccount.Password
  ThisIsARandomPwd
  VerySecretPwd
```

Figure 8.24: *Using dot notation to return the data from the ServiceAccount array within the configuration data*

We could of course create a new variable containing this data and extract our property values from this variable, but since this is an array, we can use indexing to get the specific data we need, shown in *Figure 8.25*:

```
● PS C:\Temp> $Config.Config.ServiceAccount[0].UserName
  Service.DBUser
● PS C:\Temp> $Config.Config.ServiceAccount[0].Password
  ThisIsARandomPwd
● PS C:\Temp> $Config.Config.ServiceAccount[1].UserName
  Service.AzureUser
● PS C:\Temp> $Config.Config.ServiceAccount[1].Password
  VerySecretPwd
```

Figure 8.25: Using indexing to get specific data from the ServiceAccount array within the configuration data

This might suffice if we only have a small array like the one in this configuration file, and if we know the specific data and its index. But, what if it was a very large array, or an array that might have been dynamically updated with several service accounts? How would we go about finding the data for a specific account? For this we can use the **Where-Object** filter to search for specific property values within the keys of the **ServiceAccount** array, such as **Id=2** or **UserName=Service.DBUser** and so on. We assign the output to a variable, and that variable will contain the object with the specific data we wanted to extract from the array, as shown in *Figure 8.26*:

```
● PS C:\Temp> $AzureUser = $Config.Config.ServiceAccount | Where-Object {$_.Id -eq 2}
● PS C:\Temp> $AzureUser

  UserName            Password         Id
  --------            --------         --
  Service.AzureUser VerySecretPwd    2

● PS C:\Temp> $AzureUser.Password
  VerySecretPwd
● PS C:\Temp> $DBUser = $Config.Config.ServiceAccount | Where-Object {$_.UserName -eq "Service.DBUser"}
● PS C:\Temp> $DBUser

  UserName            Password         Id
  --------            --------         --
  Service.DBUser ThisIsARandomPwd   1

● PS C:\Temp> $DBUser.Password
  ThisIsARandomPwd
```

Figure 8.26: Using Where-Object to filter array content within the configuration data

With the lightweight structure of JSON, it is easy to convert data between PowerShell objects and JSON, parse JSON data and read and write JSON data from and too files, while compared to using the XML format. The **ConvertTo-Json**, **ConvertFrom-Json**, **Get-Content** and **Out-File** cmdlets are essentially all that is needed to work with JSON formatted data in PowerShell.

Conclusion

Both XML and JSON have their advantages and disadvantages and the choice for selecting a specific format to use for scripts and applications strongly depends on the specific requirements and use case, but also the personal preferences of the developer or administrator. For logging purposes, it could be recommended to use the JSON format with compression for writing logs to files, this is not only easy to read and parse, but it is also a format that is used by many external monitoring systems and will be applicable to such systems without further conversion or parsing. For configuration files it might be a better choice to use XML structured document files and for larger and more complex objects or if you want to store session states for later use, CliXml might be the better choice. Again, it depends on each individual use case and preferences, but it might also depend on other systems and services that your scripts and applications might be dependent on and communicating with. If a specific system that your scripts or applications rely on or interchange data with, is built upon one format, it is of course obvious to choose the same format instead of having to convert between them. you should choose the format wisely.

The next chapter delves into the essentials of managing and automating Active Directory tasks using PowerShell. This chapter introduces the ActiveDirectory module which is an essential tool in PowerShell for interacting with AD environments. You will learn how to manage AD users and groups efficiently. The chapter also introduces techniques for performing bulk operations, which are crucial in larger organizations where managing numerous accounts manually is impractical. Furthermore, it explores how to query and filter AD objects effectively, using PowerShell's filtering capabilities to streamline administrative Active Directory tasks.

Join our book's Discord space

Join the book's Discord Workspace for Latest updates, Offers, Tech happenings around the world, New Release and Sessions with the Authors:

https://discord.bpbonline.com

## CHAPTER 9

Active Directory Management

Introduction

Active Directory or AD for short, is a directory service and identity management system developed by Microsoft. It is used to manage and organize resources such as users, computers, groups, and other types of resources within a Windows based network environment. **Active Directory (AD)** is organized in a hierarchical structure where the top-level is called a forest. A forest can contain multiple domains where each domain serves as an individual segment that contains its own set of objects, permissions, and policies. Within a domain you can organize and segregate objects into **Organizational Units (OUs).** One of the primary use cases of Active Directory is for authenticating and authorizing users and computers within a domain network. It enables users to log in to their computers and access other network resources such as mailboxes, servers, database instances and file shares based on their permissions and AD group memberships. Active Directory provides security features such as **Role-Based Access Control (RBAC)** for managing permissions and access rights which allows administrators to grant or deny access to resources based on user and group memberships. It also supports single sign in so that users can log on to their computers and access their resources without having to login to multiple applications and resources. Another feature is Group Policies that allow administrators to define and enforce configuration settings and security policies for users and computers within the domain network ensuring a consistent and secure environment.

Active Directory is a fundamental part of Windows networks within both small and larger organizations for managing and securing resources and as an identity and user access management solution.

Being able to optimize and automate Active Directory tasks and processes can be quite beneficial, efficient and time saving for administrators, especially when working in larger organizations where there are many users, computers, and resources to manage. PowerShell provides a set of cmdlets that makes it easy to create scripts and applications for optimizing, automating, and managing Active Directory tasks and processes.

Structure

The chapter covers the following topics:

- Pre-requisites and the ActiveDirectory module
- Managing AD users and groups with PowerShell
    - **Recipe 54**: Creating, modifying, and deleting AD users and AD groups
    - **Recipe 55**: Use filters to query AD users and AD groups information
- Performing Bulk operations on AD objects
    - **Recipe 56**: How to perform bulk operations on AD users and AD groups
- Automating AD account provisioning
    - **Recipe 57**: Developing automation scripts for creating AD users and AD users in bulk

Objectives

In this chapter, we will explore Active Directory Management using PowerShell and the **ActiveDirectory** module. The primary focus in this chapter will be AD users and AD groups which are some of the most important aspects when it comes to Active Directory management. You will learn how to use the **ActiveDirectory** module and its cmdlets to create, modify and delete AD users and AD groups. You will learn to use filters to query specific AD user and AD group information and we will delve into the differences between the **ActiveDirectory** cmdlets filter parameter and the Where-Object filter cmdlet. We will also look at using distinguished names as search bases for optimizing search queries when querying AD object information. You will learn how to perform bulk operations on AD users and AD groups, by querying specific AD objects and then modifying multiple users at once and how to add multiple users to specific AD groups depending on specific filter and search queries. Furthermore, we will show how to automate AD account provisioning and learn how to create scripts that can be used to automatically provisioning users and for provisioning multiple users in bulk.

Pre-requisites and the ActiveDirectory module

Before you can work with Active Directory and to fully benefit from the recipes and examples in this chapter, you need to have access to a domain with *Domain Admin* privileges, or at least have permissions to work with and edit domain resources. If you work in a small or larger organization you might already be a member of and have access to your work domain as an administrator, preferably a test domain. If not, you can install Windows Server 2016 or newer, on a stand-alone virtual machine and then install the Active Directory Domain Services role and then use this virtual server as your test domain controller for working with and managing AD domain resources using PowerShell.

The **ActiveDirectory** module in PowerShell is a collection of cmdlets that allow administrators to manage and interact with Active Directory domain resources and objects. On Windows Server operating systems, the **ActiveDirectory** module is typically available when the Active Directory Domain Service role is installed and on client systems such as Windows 10 and Windows 11, you can install the **Remote Server Administration Tools (RSAT)** to gain access to the module and its cmdlets. Note that in an AD environment, clients and domain controllers should be able to communicate on specific network ports in order to access the AD-related services. It is essential that firewall and network configurations are set up properly to ensure that communication between the different client and server resources within the AD infrastructure functions correctly.

Once you have access to a domain as an administrator, you can use the ActiveDirectory module cmdlets to manage almost all aspects of the domain resources such as creating, modifying, deleting, querying, and searching for AD objects like users, groups, and organizational units. It also includes cmdlets for password and group policy management and cmdlets for access control management and for reporting and logging purposes. The ActiveDirectory module can also be used for remote management, making it possible to manage Active Directory on other domain controllers. Many cmdlets in the module support this using the **-Server** parameter, which enables you target specific domain controllers in your network.

Note: The ActiveDirectory module is only compatible with PowerShell 7 on Windows Server build 1809+. For Windows Server 2016 and earlier versions of Windows Server, you need to use PowerShell 5.1 or else the ActiveDirectory module will be loaded in Windows PowerShell as an WinPSCompatSession remoting session. This will result in deserialization of all input and output objects which might further result in unexpected input and output behavior. It is strongly recommended to use the ActiveDirectory module with a compatible version of PowerShell.

Figure 9.1 shows the **WinPSCompatSession** remote session warning when importing the ActiveDirectory module in PowerShell 7 on a Windows Server version below build 1809, in this case, Windows Server 2016:

```
PS C:\Users\Administrator> (Get-CimInstance -ClassName Win32_OperatingSystem).Caption
Microsoft Windows Server 2016 Standard
PS C:\Users\Administrator>
PS C:\Users\Administrator> Import-Module ActiveDirectory
WARNING: Module ActiveDirectory is loaded in Windows PowerShell using WinPSCompatSession remoting
 session; please note that all input and output of commands from this module will be deserialized
 objects. If you want to load this module into PowerShell please use 'Import-Module -SkipEditionC
heck' syntax.
```

Figure 9.1: Importing the ActiveDirectory module in PowerShell 7 on a Windows Server 2016

A newer Windows Server version, such as Windows Server 2022 do not have the same compatibility issue with PowerShell 7 and the ActiveDirectory module, as shown in *Figure 9.2*.

```
PS C:\Users\Administrator> (Get-CimInstance -ClassName Win32_OperatingSystem).Caption
Microsoft Windows Server 2022 Standard
PS C:\Users\Administrator>
PS C:\Users\Administrator> Import-Module ActiveDirectory
PS C:\Users\Administrator>
PS C:\Users\Administrator> _
```

Figure 9.2: Importing the ActiveDirectory module in PowerShell 7 on a Windows Server 2022

> **All recipes and examples in this chapter are created and executed in PowerShell 7 on a Domain Controller running Windows Server 2022 Standard! You can use the Get-CimInstance cmdlet with the Win32_OperatingSystem class name to get your current operating system as shown in the figures. For more detailed information about your version and operating system product name, you can use the Get-ComputerInfo cmdlet: Get-ComputerInfo | Select-Object WindowsProductName, WindowsVersion.**

You should import the ActiveDirectory module into your current session or script using **Import-Module** to use the cmdlets it provides, though the module will automatically be imported once you use one of its cmdlets, but there is some overhead loading the module, so it is recommended to import the module before running any ActiveDirectory commands, especially when used in scripts. It is generally recommended to always load modules that are used in scripts before running any commands. Once the module is imported, we can check that it is loaded using the **Get-Module** cmdlet and we can use the **Get-Command** with the **-Module** parameter to view all the cmdlets the module provides:

```
# Import the ActiveDirectory module
Import-Module ActiveDirectory
# Check that module is imported
Get-Module ActiveDirectory
# Get all ActiveDirectory module commands
Get-Command -Module ActiveDirectory
```

You will get a list of all the cmdlets provided by the **ActiveDirectory** module as shown in *Figure 9.3*:

```
PS C:\Users\Administrator> Import-Module ActiveDirectory
PS C:\Users\Administrator>
PS C:\Users\Administrator> Get-Module ActiveDirectory

ModuleType Version    PreRelease Name                          ExportedCommands
---------- -------    ---------- ----                          ----------------
Manifest   1.0.1.0               activedirectory               {Add-ADCentralAccessPolicyMember


PS C:\Users\Administrator> Get-Command -Module ActiveDirectory

CommandType     Name                                              Version   Source
-----------     ----                                              -------   ------
Cmdlet          Add-ADCentralAccessPolicyMember                   1.0.1.0   activedirectory
Cmdlet          Add-ADComputerServiceAccount                      1.0.1.0   activedirectory
Cmdlet          Add-ADDomainControllerPasswordReplicationPolicy   1.0.1.0   activedirectory
Cmdlet          Add-ADFineGrainedPasswordPolicySubject            1.0.1.0   activedirectory
Cmdlet          Add-ADGroupMember                                 1.0.1.0   activedirectory
Cmdlet          Add-ADPrincipalGroupMembership                    1.0.1.0   activedirectory
Cmdlet          Add-ADResourcePropertyListMember                  1.0.1.0   activedirectory
Cmdlet          Clear-ADAccountExpiration                         1.0.1.0   activedirectory
Cmdlet          Clear-ADClaimTransformLink                        1.0.1.0   activedirectory
Cmdlet          Disable-ADAccount                                 1.0.1.0   activedirectory
Cmdlet          Disable-ADOptionalFeature                         1.0.1.0   activedirectory
Cmdlet          Enable-ADAccount                                  1.0.1.0   activedirectory
Cmdlet          Enable-ADOptionalFeature                          1.0.1.0   activedirectory
Cmdlet          Get-ADAccountAuthorizationGroup                   1.0.1.0   activedirectory
Cmdlet          Get-ADAccountResultantPasswordReplicationPolicy   1.0.1.0   activedirectory
Cmdlet          Get-ADAuthenticationPolicy                        1.0.1.0   activedirectory
Cmdlet          Get-ADAuthenticationPolicySilo                    1.0.1.0   activedirectory
Cmdlet          Get-ADCentralAccessPolicy                         1.0.1.0   activedirectory
Cmdlet          Get-ADCentralAccessRule                           1.0.1.0   activedirectory
Cmdlet          Get-ADClaimTransformPolicy                        1.0.1.0   activedirectory
```

Figure 9.3: List of cmdlets in the ActiveDirectory module

Notice that the *Noun* in the *Verb-Noun* naming convention for all the cmdlet names starts with the characters *AD*. This makes it easier to distinguish cmdlets that are provided by the ActiveDirectory module, and that it is directly linked to Active Directory management.

Managing AD users and groups with PowerShell

It is essential for administrators that works with Windows environments and Active Directory domains to know how to utilize available tools such as the ActiveDirectory module with PowerShell to be able to optimize and automate tasks like creating, modifying, and deleting or disabling users and groups and how to query and filter specific user and group information. PowerShell and the ActiveDirectory module provide several cmdlets for Active Directory domain management. Some of the most common tasks when working with Active Directory are the management of AD users and AD groups.

An AD user account is an object that represents a person or individual within a domain and it consists of different characteristics and attributes such as identity information that could be the *UserPrincipalName* and *SamAccountName* which are unique identifiers. It also consists of profile information such as a specified home directory, a profile path and credentials which covers a user's password and account status, is the account enabled or disabled. each object also has a unique security identifier or SID.

These are just some of the key characteristics and attributes that an AD User consists of, and further attributes such as phone numbers, email addresses, addresses and job title etc. can be added to the AD User object. AD Users can be members of security groups (AD groups) that are used to grant access to specific resources such as file shares, servers, computers, databases and so on. Users can also be assigned different roles that grant different levels of access and permissions within a domain, such as the *Domain Users* and *Domain Admins* roles. A newly created user is by default a member of the Domain Users role. This role is amongst others used for granting *user* permissions by default, to servers and computers that are joined to the domain and allows a user to login to all such resources with user privileges. The Domain Admins role will grant *administrator* permissions to all domain joined servers and computers and allows for managing and modifying AD Objects within the Active Directory itself.

An AD group is a *collection* of AD objects such as user accounts, computer accounts (server and computer objects) and other AD groups within a domain and they are used for organizing access control, permissions, and resource assignments for such objects. Members of an AD group share the same set of permissions that the group grants to different resources and you can nest AD groups within each other to create a hierarchical delegation of permissions. There are different kinds of AD groups and scopes such as security groups and distribution groups. A security group is used for managing access control and permissions and a distribution group is primarily used for sending emails to a group of recipients simultaneously and are not meant for access control and permissions. The different group scopes are:

- **Domain Local Groups:** Used to assign permissions within a single domain. Members can be from the same domain or trusted domains.

- **Global Groups:** Used to group users from the same domain. These groups can be added to domain local groups in the same domain.

- **Universal Groups:** Used to group users from different domains within a forest and are typically used in multi-domain environments.

All AD Objects are placed within Organizational Units (OUs) which is a type of container that is used to organize and structure AD objects in a hierarchical manner within a domain or a domain forest. It allows for access control and permission delegation to all objects within specific OUs for a more granular control over the resources within a domain.

Recipe 54: Creating, modifying, and deleting AD users and AD groups

In this recipe you are going to learn how to use the ActiveDirectory module to create, modify and delete AD users and AD groups. The ActiveDirectory module provides specific cmdlets for these tasks, such as the **New-ADUser** and **New-ADGroup** cmdlets for creating users and groups, **Set-ADUser** and **Set-ADGroup** for modifying existing users and groups and **Remove-ADUser** and **Remove-ADGroup** for deleting users and groups. We can use the **Get-Command** cmdlet to view all the specific user and group management cmdlets that the module provides:

```
# List all AD User management cmdlets

Get-Command -Module ActiveDirectory -Noun "*User*"

# List all AD Group management cmdlets

Get-Command -Module ActiveDirectory -Noun "*Group*"
```

The output of these commands are shown in *Figure 9.4*:

```
PS C:\Users\Administrator> Get-Command -Module ActiveDirectory -Noun "*User*"

CommandType     Name                              Version     Source
-----------     ----                              -------     ------
Cmdlet          Get-ADUser                        1.0.1.0     activedirectory
Cmdlet          Get-ADUserResultantPasswordPolicy 1.0.1.0     activedirectory
Cmdlet          New-ADUser                        1.0.1.0     activedirectory
Cmdlet          Remove-ADUser                     1.0.1.0     activedirectory
Cmdlet          Set-ADUser                        1.0.1.0     activedirectory


PS C:\Users\Administrator> Get-Command -Module ActiveDirectory -Noun "*Group*"

CommandType     Name                              Version     Source
-----------     ----                              -------     ------
Cmdlet          Add-ADGroupMember                 1.0.1.0     activedirectory
Cmdlet          Add-ADPrincipalGroupMembership    1.0.1.0     activedirectory
Cmdlet          Get-ADAccountAuthorizationGroup   1.0.1.0     activedirectory
Cmdlet          Get-ADGroup                       1.0.1.0     activedirectory
Cmdlet          Get-ADGroupMember                 1.0.1.0     activedirectory
Cmdlet          Get-ADPrincipalGroupMembership    1.0.1.0     activedirectory
Cmdlet          New-ADGroup                       1.0.1.0     activedirectory
Cmdlet          Remove-ADGroup                    1.0.1.0     activedirectory
Cmdlet          Remove-ADGroupMember              1.0.1.0     activedirectory
Cmdlet          Remove-ADPrincipalGroupMembership 1.0.1.0     activedirectory
Cmdlet          Set-ADGroup                       1.0.1.0     activedirectory
```

*Figure 9.4: Cmdlets provided by the ActiveDirectory module
for AD user and AD group management*

To get more detailed information about specific cmdlets in general, you can use the **Get-Help** cmdlet. This will include parameter explanations and usage examples. Use the **-Detailed** or the **-Full** parameters to retrieve additional information. Use the **Update-Help** cmdlet to update and fetch the newest help files to your computer. Below are some simple examples using the **Get-Help** cmdlet to retrieve cmdlet information:

```
# Use Get-Help to view detailed cmdlet info and usage examples

Get-Help New-ADUSer -Detailed

Get-Help New-ADGroup -Full
```

Create AD Users

To create a new AD User within a domain, we use the **New-ADUser** cmdlet. It has a lot of parameters for setting the user account attribute properties but not all of them are mandatory and you can add additional properties later by modifying the AD User object after it is created if needed. Notice that all new users are by default a member of the *Domain Users* AD group.

We can create a new AD User using parameters and set the arguments for the parameters as shown below:

```
# Create a new AD user using parameter arguments
New-ADUser -Name "Morten E. Hansen" `
-GivenName "Morten" `
-SurName "E. Hansen" `
-SamAccountName "meh" `
-UserPrincipalName "meh@moppleit.dk" `
-Path "OU=DK,OU=ADUsers,DC=moppleit,DC=dk" `
-AccountPassword (ConvertTo-SecureString "Pa$$w0rd" -AsPlainText -Force) `
-Enabled $true
```

In this case, the **-Path** and the **-Enabled** parameters are optional. If the **-Path** parameter is not specified, the user will automatically be created within the *Users* container in the domain hierarchy. This container is not a typical Organizational Unit, but a default container created by Active Directory that holds user accounts. Unlike OUs, it does not support the same level of administrative control, organizational features and sub-containers and OUs cannot be created within this container. This is also why you would typically create a custom OU for your users to provide a more organized and manageable structure of your domain hierarchy. Using a custom user OU also allow you to create nested OUs within the custom user OU to divide users into sub segments such as country divisions and departments etc. For the hierarchy structure of the domain used for this chapter, we have created a specific user OU called **ADUsers** containing sub-OUs for country segregation, as shown in *Figure 9.5*:

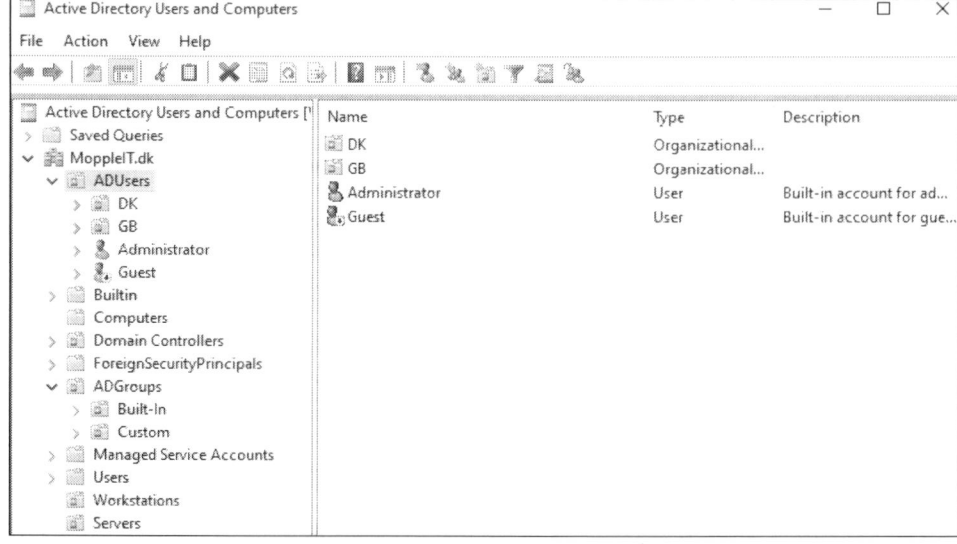

Figure 9.5: *Domain tree structure with custom OUs for users and groups*

The path argument is provided as an LDAP formatted `Distinguished Name: OU=DK,OU=ADUsers,DC=moppleit,DC=dk`. This format is used by Active Directory to uniquely identify objects within a directory hierarchy. All objects in Active Directory have a distinguished name in this format, identifying its location within the hierarchy. If the `-Enabled` parameter is not specified, the user will be created as a **Disabled** account by default, and it needs to be enabled manually. Also note that for the `-AccountPassword` parameter we convert the password to a secure string, which is the required type for this parameter. Some parameters might not be defined within the cmdlet for specific attributes such as *Info* and *TelephoneNumber* etc. The **New-ADUser** cmdlet has a parameter called `-OtherAttributes` that is used for adding such attributes to the user object. This parameter takes a Hashtable as an argument and additional attributes can be specified using this Hashtable.

Another method for specifying arguments to cmdlets that has a lot of parameters is by using splatting. Splatting allows you to pass a Hashtable containing parameter names and their corresponding values to a cmdlet or a function as arguments:

```
# Create a new AD user using splatting
$Params = @{
    Name = "Morten E. Hansen"
    GivenName = "Morten"
    SurName = "E. Hansen"
    DisplayName = "Morten E. Hansen"
    SamAccountName = "meh" # Max 20 characters
    UserPrincipalName = "meh@moppleit.dk"
    Path = "OU=DK,OU=ADUsers,DC=moppleit,DC=dk"
    AccountPassword = (ConvertTo-SecureString "Pa$$w0rd" -AsPlainText
-Force)
    Enabled = $true
    OtherAttributes = @{
        Info = "Administrator, Developer and DevOps"
        TelephoneNumber = "+4512345678"
    }
}
New-ADUser @Params
```

We have changed the command for creating our AD user to use this *splatting* method, and also added additional attributes using the **OtherAttributes** parameter within a nested Hashtable. Once we execute the command, a new AD user with the provided property values is created. The **New-ADUser** cmdlet do not return any output when a user is successfully created, so if no errors are returned, the user should be successfully created in Active Directory. We can use the **Get-ADUser** cmdlet with the **SamAccountName** as an argument (for the 0 positioned **-Identity** parameter), to double check that the user is actually created and exists. Also note that we use the **-Properties** parameter for specifying additional attributes the cmdlet must return. By default, the cmdlet returns a minimum number of properties for the user account. The new user is created and viewed as shown in *Figure 9.6*:

```
PS C:\Users\Administrator> $Params = @{
>>      Name = "Morten E. Hansen"
>>      GivenName = "Morten"
>>      SurName = "E. Hansen"
>>      DisplayName = "Morten E. Hansen"
>>      SamAccountName = "meh" # Max 20 characters
>>      UserPrincipalName = "meh@moppleit.dk"
>>      Path = "OU=DK,OU=ADUsers,DC=moppleit,DC=dk"
>>      AccountPassword = (ConvertTo-SecureString "Pa$$w0rd" -AsPlainText -Force)
>>      Enabled = $true
>>      OtherAttributes = @{
>>          Info = "Administrator, Developer and DevOps"
>>          TelephoneNumber = "+4512345678"
>>      }
>> }
PS C:\Users\Administrator> New-ADUser @Params
PS C:\Users\Administrator> Get-ADUser meh -Properties Info,TelephoneNumber,DisplayName

DisplayName       : Morten E. Hansen
DistinguishedName : CN=Morten E. Hansen,OU=DK,OU=ADUsers,DC=MoppleIT,DC=dk
Enabled           : True
GivenName         : Morten
Info              : Administrator, Developer and DevOps
Name              : Morten E. Hansen
ObjectClass       : user
ObjectGUID        : 2f91806a-0e9e-4844-8cb0-1b0133fb9d6e
SamAccountName    : meh
SID               : S-1-5-21-1225418253-179372207-2133877867-1108
Surname           : E. Hansen
TelephoneNumber   : +4512345678
UserPrincipalName : meh@moppleit.dk
```

Figure 9.6: Successful creation of a new AD User account

Note: AD Objects can contain a lot of properties which is why the returned properties are limited when using Get-AD... cmdlets. You can use the -Properties parameter to return and view specific properties that are not returned by the default view. To return and view all properties for an AD object you can use the -Properties parameter with a wildcard: Get-ADUser -Properties *.

Modify AD Users

Sometimes you might need to modify an existing AD user by updating current attribute properties or by adding properties to attributes that have no values specified. For this we use the **Set-ADUser** cmdlet. This cmdlet almost contains the same parameters as the **New-ADUser** cmdlet, except parameters for attributes that are not changeable such as **UserPrincipalName**, **ObjectGUID** and **SID** since such attributes are unique identifiers for the specific user account object. Let us add some additional and change some current attribute properties using the **Set-ADUser** cmdlet:

```
# Update current and add missing attributes
$Params = @{
    EmailAddress = "Moppleit@hotmail.com"
    Description = "
    IT SystemAdministrator and DevOps at Energi Danmark A/S.
    Owner of Bio-Rent.dk
    Author"
    City = "Ryomgaard"
    Country = "DK"
    MobilePhone = "+4512345678"
    SurName = "Hansen"
    DisplayName = "Morten Hansen"
}
Set-ADUSer -Identity "meh"  @Params
```

We need to use the **-Identity** parameter to specify the AD user account we want to modify or use the **Get-ADUser** cmdlet to retrieve the AD user object, and then pipe this to the **Set-ADUser** cmdlet. This method can also be used to retrieve and modify multiple AD User objects in bulk, which will be covered in more detail, later within this chapter:

```
Get-ADUser -Identity "meh" | Set-ADUser @Params
```

Once we have modified our AD user, we can use the **Get-ADUser** cmdlet to check and view that the changes have been applied, as shown in *Figure 9.7*:

```
PS C:\Users\Administrator> $Params = @{
>>      EmailAddress = "Moppleit@hotmail.com"
>>      Description = "
>>      IT SystemAdministrator and DevOps at Energi Danmark A/S.
>>      Owner of Bio-Rent.dk
>>      Author"
>>      City = "Ryomgaard"
>>      Country = "DK"
>>      MobilePhone = "+4512345678"
>>      SurName = "Hansen"
>>      DisplayName = "Morten Hansen"
>> }
PS C:\Users\Administrator> Set-ADUser -Identity "meh"  @Params
PS C:\Users\Administrator> Get-ADUser meh -Properties DisplayName,EmailAddress,Description,City

City              : Ryomgaard
Description       :
                        IT SystemAdministrator and DevOps at Energi Danmark A/S.
                        Owner of Bio-Rent.dk
                        Author
DisplayName       : Morten Hansen
DistinguishedName : CN=Morten E. Hansen,OU=DK,OU=ADUsers,DC=MoppleIT,DC=dk
EmailAddress      : Moppleit@hotmail.com
Enabled           : True
GivenName         : Morten
Name              : Morten E. Hansen
ObjectClass       : user
ObjectGUID        : 2f91806a-0e9e-4844-8cb0-1b0133fb9d6e
SamAccountName    : meh
SID               : S-1-5-21-1225418253-179372207-2133877867-1108
Surname           : Hansen
UserPrincipalName : meh@moppleit.dk
```

Figure 9.7: *Successful modification of existing AD User account*

The splatting method works well for adding and modifying parameterized attributes, but what if we needed to update or add values to attributes that the **Set-ADUser** cmdlet does not provide a specific parameter for, such as the **Info** and **TelephoneNumber** attributes? The **Set-ADUser** cmdlet provides parameters such as **-Remove**, **-Add**, **-Replace** and **-Clear**. These parameters are used for adding, modifying, and removing values of an attribute property that cannot be modified using a cmdlet parameter. These parameters can be used together, and the operations are performed in the order as they are listed above:

```
# Add a non-parameterized attribute property value

$Add = @{EmployeeType="Manager"}

Set-ADUser -Identity "meh" -Add $Add

# Replace a non-parameterized attribute property value

$Replace = @{Info="Administrator, Developer, DevOps and author"}

Set-ADUser -Identity "meh" -Replace $Replace

# Remove a non-parameterized attribute property value

$Remove = @{TelephoneNumber="+4512345678"}

Set-ADUser -Identity "meh" -Remove $Remove

# Clear a non-parameterized attribute property value
```

```
$Clear = "EmployeeType"
Set-ADUser -Identity "meh" -Clear $Clear
```

Figure 9.8 shows the execution of these commands and the modifications they make to the AD user object:

```
PS C:\Users\Administrator> $Add = @{EmployeeType="Manager"}
PS C:\Users\Administrator> Set-ADUser -Identity "meh" -Add $Add
PS C:\Users\Administrator> $Replace = @{Info="Administrator, Developer, DevOps and author"}
PS C:\Users\Administrator> Set-ADUser -Identity "meh" -Replace $Replace
PS C:\Users\Administrator>
PS C:\Users\Administrator> Get-ADUser meh -Properties EmployeeType,Info,TelephoneNumber

DistinguishedName : CN=Morten E. Hansen,OU=DK,OU=ADUsers,DC=MoppleIT,DC=dk
EmployeeType      : Manager
Enabled           : True
GivenName         : Morten
Info              : Administrator, Developer, DevOps and author
Name              : Morten E. Hansen
ObjectClass       : user
ObjectGUID        : 2f91806a-0e9e-4844-8cb0-1b0133fb9d6e
SamAccountName    : meh
SID               : S-1-5-21-1225418253-179372207-2133877867-1108
Surname           : Hansen
TelephoneNumber   : +4512345678
UserPrincipalName : meh@moppleit.dk


PS C:\Users\Administrator> $Remove = @{TelephoneNumber="+4512345678"}
PS C:\Users\Administrator> Set-ADUser -Identity "meh" -Remove $Remove
PS C:\Users\Administrator> $Clear = "EmployeeType"
PS C:\Users\Administrator> Set-ADUser -Identity "meh" -Clear $Clear
PS C:\Users\Administrator>
PS C:\Users\Administrator> Get-ADUser meh -Properties EmployeeType,Info,TelephoneNumber

DistinguishedName : CN=Morten E. Hansen,OU=DK,OU=ADUsers,DC=MoppleIT,DC=dk
Enabled           : True
GivenName         : Morten
Info              : Administrator, Developer, DevOps and author
Name              : Morten E. Hansen
ObjectClass       : user
ObjectGUID        : 2f91806a-0e9e-4844-8cb0-1b0133fb9d6e
SamAccountName    : meh
SID               : S-1-5-21-1225418253-179372207-2133877867-1108
Surname           : Hansen
UserPrincipalName : meh@moppleit.dk
```

Figure 9.8: *Modification of an AD user object using the Set-ADUser cmdlet with the -Remove, -Add, -Replace and -Clear parameters*

We can use the **Set-ADUser** and its parameters to add, modify and delete common attribute properties. For additional attributes that are not specified as a parameter for the cmdlet, we have to use the **-Remove, -Add, -Replace** and **-Clear** parameters. Remember that some attribute property values cannot be modified or removed such as the **UserPrincipalName**, **ObjectGUID** and **SID** attributes.

Delete and disable AD Users

Usually when an employee leaves a company or for some other reason should be denied access to a domain, you can either disable or delete the user's account. By disabling a user, the AD user object and all its settings and properties are still available in Active Directory, but the user will not be able to login to and access any resources. A disabled user account can be re-enabled if needed and all the permissions and access re-apply for that user. You can use the **Disable-ADAccount** cmdlet to disable a user either by specifying the user account identity or the distinguished name as an argument to the **-Identity** parameter or by using **Get-ADUser** and pipe the result to the **Disable-ADAccount** cmdlet. You can also use the **Set-ADUser** cmdlet and set the **-Enabled** parameter to **$false**:

```
# Disable AD user using -Identity parameter

Disable-ADAccount -Identity "meh"

# Disable AD user using Get-ADuser and Pipe

Get-ADUser "meh" | Disable-ADAccount

# Disable AD user using Set-ADUser and the -Enabled parameter

Set-ADUser -Identity "meh" -Enabled $false
```

You can check if a user is enabled or disabled by checking the value of the **Enabled** attribute property. In *Figure 9.9* we can see that the specific account is disabled:

```
PS C:\Users\Administrator> Get-ADUser meh

DistinguishedName : CN=Morten E. Hansen,OU=DK,OU=ADUsers,DC=MoppleIT,DC=dk
Enabled           : False
GivenName         : Morten
Name              : Morten E. Hansen
ObjectClass       : user
ObjectGUID        : 2f91806a-0e9e-4844-8cb0-1b0133fb9d6e
SamAccountName    : meh
SID               : S-1-5-21-1225418253-179372207-2133877867-1108
Surname           : Hansen
UserPrincipalName : meh@moppleit.dk
```

Figure 9.9: Using the Get-ADUser cmdlet to check the Enabled state for a user account

If you know that a user should never be used again or for some other reason should be deleted entirely from Active Directory, you can delete a user account object with the **Remove-ADUser** cmdlet either by specifying the **-Identity** parameter or by piping the output from the **Get-ADUser** cmdlet to **Remove-ADUser**:

```
# Delete AD User using -Identity parameter

Remove-ADUser -Identity "meh"

# Delete AD user using Get-ADuser and Pipe

Get-ADUser "meh" | Remove-ADUser
```

Since this is a destructive command, you will be prompted for confirmation before deletion of the account. If you are sure about the command you are executing, you can use the **,Confirm:$false** parameter switch to override the confirmation prompt:

```
# Delete AD User without confirmation prompt
Remove-ADUser -Identity "meh" -Confirm:$false
```

Figure 9.10 shows the confirmation prompts when running the two commands described above and the deletion of a user account using the **-Confirm:$false** switch parameter:

```
PS C:\Users\Administrator> Remove-ADUser -Identity "meh"

Confirm
Are you sure you want to perform this action?
Performing the operation "Remove" on target "CN=Morten E. Hansen,OU=DK,OU=ADUsers,DC=MoppleIT,DC=dk".
[Y] Yes  [A] Yes to All  [N] No  [L] No to All  [S] Suspend  [?] Help (default is "Y"): n
PS C:\Users\Administrator> Get-ADUser "meh" | Remove-ADUser

Confirm
Are you sure you want to perform this action?
Performing the operation "Remove" on target "CN=Morten E. Hansen,OU=DK,OU=ADUsers,DC=MoppleIT,DC=dk".
[Y] Yes  [A] Yes to All  [N] No  [L] No to All  [S] Suspend  [?] Help (default is "Y"): n
PS C:\Users\Administrator> Remove-ADUser -Identity "meh" -Confirm:$false
PS C:\Users\Administrator> Get-ADUser meh
Get-ADUser: Cannot find an object with identity: 'meh' under: 'DC=MoppleIT,DC=dk'.
```

Figure 9.10: *Deletion of an AD user account object*

Once the user account is deleted the user is not entirely removed from Active Directory, yet. What typically happens is the following:

1. The user account is deactivated and is no longer accessible. The user will not be able to login and the account is marked as *disabled*.

2. By default, a deleted user object is moved to the *Deleted Items* container. This is a temporary storage space for deleted objects.

   a. A recycle bin can be enabled for Active Directory, which allows for easier recovery of deleted objects. If this is enabled, deleted objects are placed in the recycle bin.

3. Deleted objects may be retained within the deleted items container or the recycle bin for a retention period. This depends on the AD settings and policies.

4. After the retention period expires the object is permanently removed from AD and cannot be recovered.

With the correct AD settings and policies, a deleted object might be recoverable for a shorter period of time, after that, objects are permanently deleted from the AD and would have to be re-created from scratch if similar objects should ever be required.

Create AD groups

To create AD groups within a domain we use the **New-ADGroup** cmdlet. If we do not explicitly specify a *path* when creating groups, they will by default be placed within the built-in *users* container in the domain forest. The -**Name** and the -**GroupScope** parameters are mandatory, whereas the group scope can be either **DomainLocal**, **Global** or **Universal**. The -**GroupCategory** parameter is used to specify if it should be a **Security** or **Distribution** group. This parameter is optional and if not specified, it will by default be created as a security group. The **New-ADGroup** cmdlet also have a few other optional parameters like -**DisplayName**, -**Description** and -**SamAccountName**. If the **SamAccountName** is not specified upon creation, it will automatically be added as a derivative of the group name.

```
# Create a new AD Group
$Params = @{
    Name = "TestServerAccess"
    DisplayName = "TestServerAccess"
    GroupScope = "Global"
    Path = "OU=Custom,OU=ADGroups,DC=moppleit,DC=dk"
    Description = "Grants access to all test servers"
}

New-ADGroup @Params
```

We can use the **Get-ADGroup** cmdlet to check and view the new group. We specify the -**Properties** parameter with additional properties we want to have returned as an argument. Just like the **Get-ADUser** cmdlet, only a limited set of the most general properties are returned from this cmdlet by default. *Figure 9.11* shows the newly created group:

```
PS C:\Users\Administrator> $Params = @{
>>      Name = "TestServerAccess"
>>      DisplayName = "TestServerAccess"
>>      GroupScope = "Global"
>>      Path = "OU=Custom,OU=ADGroups,DC=moppleit,DC=dk"
>>      Description = "Grants access to all test servers"
>> }
PS C:\Users\Administrator> New-ADGroup @Params
PS C:\Users\Administrator>
PS C:\Users\Administrator> Get-ADGroup -Identity TestServerAccess -Properties Description,DisplayName

Description       : Grants access to all test servers
DisplayName       : TestServerAccess
DistinguishedName : CN=TestServerAccess,OU=Custom,OU=ADGroups,DC=MoppleIT,DC=dk
GroupCategory     : Security
GroupScope        : Global
Name              : TestServerAccess
ObjectClass       : group
ObjectGUID        : 3e7b47a4-13e1-444d-bad6-9cb23f8fc088
SamAccountName    : TestServerAccess
SID               : S-1-5-21-1225418253-179372207-2133877867-1113
```

Figure 9.11: *Creation of the TestServerAccess AD group using the New-ADGroup cmdlet*

Modifying AD groups and adding and listing group members

The **Set-ADGroup** cmdlet is used to modify the properties of groups. It provides a set of parameters for modifying common properties and like the **Set-ADUser** cmdlet, the **Set-ADGroup** cmdlet also contains the **-Remove**, **-Add**, **-Replace** and **-Clear** parameters used for modifying properties that cannot be modified using a parameter. You can use the **Set-ADGroup** cmdlet with the **-Identity** parameter to modify a specific group, or you can use the **Get-ADGroup** cmdlet and pipe the output to the **Set-ADGroup** cmdlet. This approach can be used to modify multiple groups in bulk, which will be covered later in this chapter:

```
# Modify AD Group
$Params = @{
    Description = "Test server access group"
    DisplayName = "Test Server Access"
}
Set-ADGroup -Identity TestServerAccess @Params
# Modify AD Group using Get-ADGroup
Get-ADGroup -Identity TestServerAccess | Set-ADGroup @Params
```

Figure 9.12 shows the group after modification:

```
PS C:\Users\Administrator> $Params = @{
>>      Description = "Test server access group"
>>      DisplayName = "Test Server Access"
>> }
PS C:\Users\Administrator> Set-ADGroup -Identity TestServerAccess @Params
PS C:\Users\Administrator>
PS C:\Users\Administrator> Get-ADGroup -Identity TestServerAccess -Properties Description,DisplayName

Description       : Test server access group
DisplayName       : Test Server Access
DistinguishedName : CN=TestServerAccess,OU=Custom,OU=ADGroups,DC=MoppleIT,DC=dk
GroupCategory     : Security
GroupScope        : Global
Name              : TestServerAccess
ObjectClass       : group
ObjectGUID        : 3e7b47a4-13e1-444d-bad6-9cb23f8fc088
SamAccountName    : TestServerAccess
SID               : S-1-5-21-1225418253-179372207-2133877867-1113
```

Figure 9.12: Modification of the TestServerAccess AD Group using the Set-ADGroup cmdlet

Some of an AD group´s purpose is to provide access control and resource permissions to its members. A member is not only limited to user objects but can also be another AD group. We can add members to a group using the **Add-ADGroupMember** cmdlet. The **-Identity** parameter is used to specify the group that members should be added too and the **-Members** parameter is used to specify the *users* that should be added to the group:

```
# Add members to an AD Group
```

```
Add-ADGroupMembers -Identity TestServerAccess -Members meh
```

You can use the **Get-ADGroupMember** cmdlet to list all members of an AD group:

```
# Get members of an AD Group
Get-ADGroupMember -Identity TestServerAccess
```

In *Figure 9.13* we add the **meh** user to the **TestServerAccess** group and then list all members of that group:

```
PS C:\Users\Administrator> Add-ADGroupMember -Identity TestServerAccess -Members meh
PS C:\Users\Administrator>
PS C:\Users\Administrator> Get-ADGroupMember -Identity TestServerAccess

distinguishedName : CN=Morten E. Hansen,OU=DK,OU=ADUsers,DC=MoppleIT,DC=dk
name              : Morten E. Hansen
objectClass       : user
objectGUID        : 9694d6c1-34a9-4beb-b021-a4601021fe7c
SamAccountName    : meh
SID               : S-1-5-21-1225418253-179372207-2133877867-1114
```

Figure 9.13: *Adding members too and listing members of an AD group*

As stated before, members of an AD group are not only limited to AD user objects. We can also add and nest other groups as group members:

```
# Add AD Group to an AD Group
Add-ADGroupMember -Identity TestServerAccess -Members "Domain users"
```

This is shown in *Figure 9.14*:

```
PS C:\Users\Administrator> Add-ADGroupMember -Identity TestServerAccess -Members "Domain users"
PS C:\Users\Administrator>
PS C:\Users\Administrator> Get-ADGroupMember -Identity TestServerAccess

distinguishedName : CN=Domain Users,OU=Built-In,OU=ADGroups,DC=MoppleIT,DC=dk
name              : Domain Users
objectClass       : group
objectGUID        : a3f34be9-dcbf-45da-ae42-bf13e2b3e9c3
SamAccountName    : Domain Users
SID               : S-1-5-21-1225418253-179372207-2133877867-513

distinguishedName : CN=Morten E. Hansen,OU=DK,OU=ADUsers,DC=MoppleIT,DC=dk
name              : Morten E. Hansen
objectClass       : user
objectGUID        : 9694d6c1-34a9-4beb-b021-a4601021fe7c
SamAccountName    : meh
SID               : S-1-5-21-1225418253-179372207-2133877867-1114
```

Figure 9.14: *Nest another AD group as a member of a group*

All AD users that are direct members of a group and all users within nested groups that are members of that group, will inherit the access controls and permissions that are defined for the group and will be able to access all the resources the group grants permissions to.

You can list all the groups that an AD user or AD group is a member *of*, using the **Get-ADPrincipalGroupMembership** cmdlet:

```
# View MemberOf groups for a User or Group
Get-ADPrincipalGroupMembership -Identity meh | Select-Object Name
```

To limit the output view, we are only interested in the **names** of the groups that the user with the username **meh** is a member of, so we pipe the command to **Select-Object** for filtering the group names, which gives us the output shown in *Figure 9.15*:

```
PS C:\Users\Administrator> Get-ADPrincipalGroupMembership -Identity meh | Select-Object Name

Name
----
Domain Users
TestServerAccess
```

Figure 9.15: Listing all the AD groups that a user (or group) is a member of

Remove members from and delete AD groups

You can use the **Remove-ADGroupMember** cmdlet to remove specific users or groups that are members of an AD group. This is a destructive action so you will be prompted for confirmation, or you can set the **-Confirm** switch parameter to **$false** for overriding the confirmation prompt:

```
# Remove user and group from AD Group
Remove-ADGroupMember -Identity TestServerAccess -Members meh -Confirm:$false
```

Shown in *Figure 9.16*:

```
PS C:\Users\Administrator> Remove-ADGroupMember -Identity TestServerAccess -Members meh

Confirm
Are you sure you want to perform this action?
Performing the operation "Set" on target "CN=TestServerAccess,OU=Custom,OU=ADGroups,DC=MoppleIT,DC=dk".
[Y] Yes  [A] Yes to All  [N] No  [L] No to All  [S] Suspend  [?] Help (default is "Y"): n
PS C:\Users\Administrator>
PS C:\Users\Administrator> Remove-ADGroupMember -Identity TestServerAccess -Members meh -Confirm:$false
PS C:\Users\Administrator> Get-ADGroupMember -Identity TestServerAccess

distinguishedName : CN=Domain Users,OU=Built-In,OU=ADGroups,DC=MoppleIT,DC=dk
name              : Domain Users
objectClass       : group
objectGUID        : a3f34be9-dcbf-45da-ae42-bf13e2b3e9c3
SamAccountName    : Domain Users
SID               : S-1-5-21-1225418253-179372207-2133877867-513
```

Figure 9.16: Remove members from AD groups

You can delete an AD group entirely using the **Remove-ADGroup** cmdlet. This is also a destructive action and requires confirmation or confirmation override, using the **-Confirm** switch. Members of a group will not be deleted from the AD, but all references to that group are removed from the members objects:

```
# Delete AD Group
```

```
Remove-ADGroup -Identity TestServerAccess -Confirm:$false
```

Figure 9.17 shows the deletion of the **TestServerAccess** group. We use the **Get-ADGroup** to confirm that the group does not exist in the AD after deletion:

```
PS C:\Users\Administrator> Remove-ADGroup -Identity TestServerAccess

Confirm
Are you sure you want to perform this action?
Performing the operation "Remove" on target "CN=TestServerAccess,OU=Custom,OU=ADGroups,DC=MoppleIT,DC=dk".
[Y] Yes  [A] Yes to All  [N] No  [L] No to All  [S] Suspend  [?] Help (default is "Y"): n
PS C:\Users\Administrator>
PS C:\Users\Administrator> Remove-ADGroup -Identity TestServerAccess -Confirm:$false
PS C:\Users\Administrator>
PS C:\Users\Administrator> Get-ADGroup -Identity TestServerAccess
Get-ADGroup: Cannot find an object with identity: 'TestServerAccess' under: 'DC=MoppleIT,DC=dk'.
```

Figure 9.17: *Deletion of the TestServerAccess AD group*

The cmdlets and techniques shown in this recipe are the essentials for working with and managing AD users and AD groups with PowerShell.

In the next recipe you will learn how to use the **Filter** parameter for the **Get-ADUser** and **Get-ADGroup** cmdlets for more fine-grained object querying and also how this filter option differentiates from the **Where-Object** filter cmdlet. You will also learn how to use search bases to search and query within specific object paths.

Recipe 55: Use filters to query AD users and AD groups information

The **Get-ADUser** and **Get-ADGroup** cmdlets has a mandatory **-Filter** parameter. This parameter specifies a query string that is used to retrieve specific AD objects and the syntax used for the filter is in a specific *PowerShell expression language*. You can get more information about the filter parameter with the **Get-Help about_ActiveDirectory_Filter** command.

> **Note: The -Filter parameter is mandatory when using the Get-ADUser and Get-ADGroup cmdlets if you do not specifically use the -Identity parameter to query for a specific user or group. If you want to query and search for all objects of a given type, you can use a wildcard as an argument for the filter: Get-ADUser -Filter *. Notice when using the filter with a wildcard in domains that contain a lot of AD objects, the query might take some time to retrieve and return all objects.**

This filter can be used to query AD users and AD groups containing specific property values. You might want to make a query that filters all users or groups within your domain that is employed in a specific country, or you might want to query and filter users that have a specific job title and so on:

```
# Filter examples using string
Get-ADUser -Filter "Title -eq 'Manager'"
$Country = "DK"
Get-ADUser -Filter "Country -eq '$Country'"
# Filter examples using script block
Get-ADuser -Filter {Title -eq "Manager"}
$Country = "GB"
Get-ADuser -Filter {Country -like $Country}
```

For the examples in this recipe, we have a domain with a select few users and groups that are divided into departments residing in two different countries. An overview of these users and groups are shown in *Figure 9.18*:

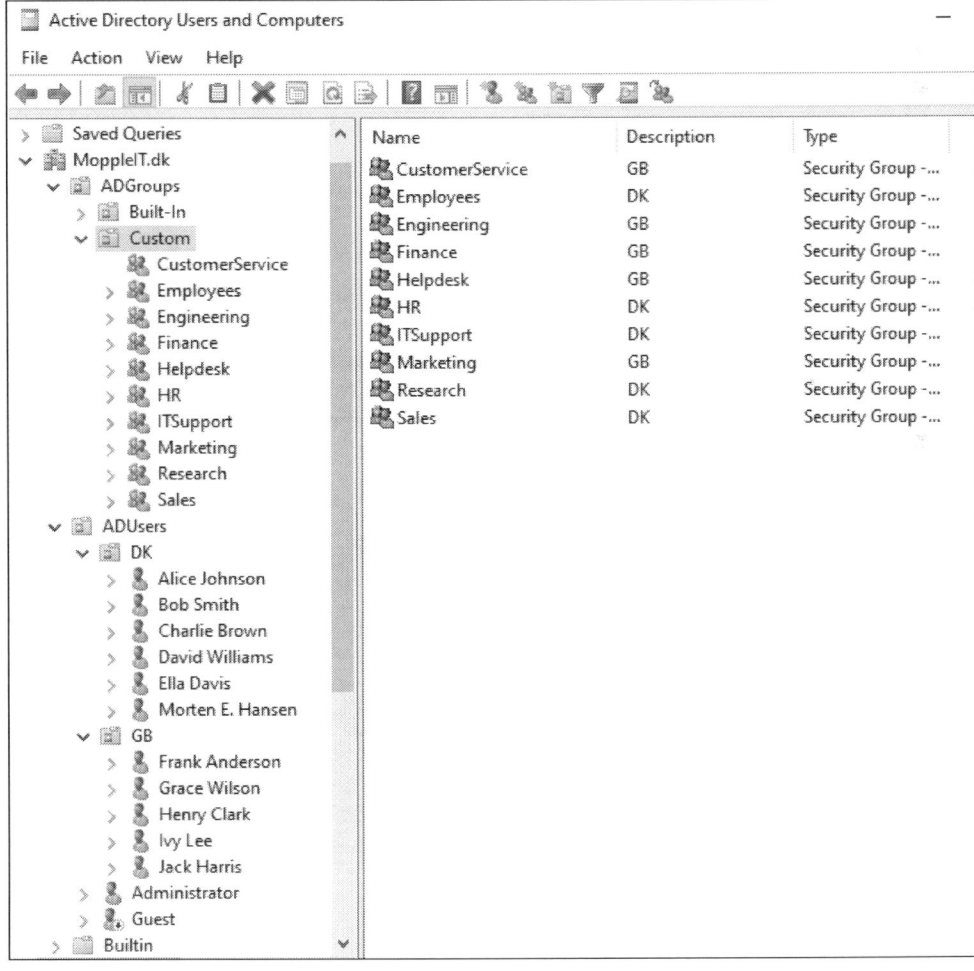

Figure 9.18: Domain users and groups used for examples.

To get an overview of *all* users within the domain and a select few of their properties, we can use the **Get-ADUser** with the **-Filter** parameter and a wildcard (*) as an argument. To select the specific relevant properties from the object, we pipe the command to the **Select-Object** cmdlet:

```
# Query all AD users. Selecting specific properties
Get-ADUser -Filter * `
-Properties Country,Title | `
Select-Object Name,SamAccountName,Country,Title
```

The output of this command is shown in *Figure 9.19*:

```
PS C:\Users\Administrator> Get-ADUser -Filter * `
>> -Properties Country,Title | `
>> Select-Object Name,SamAccountName,Country,Title

Name              SamAccountName Country Title
----              -------------- ------- -----
Administrator     Administrator
Guest             Guest
krbtgt            krbtgt
Alice Johnson     AlJo           DK      Employee
Bob Smith         BoSm           DK      Employee
Charlie Brown     ChBr           DK      Helpdesk
David Williams    DaWi           DK      Helpdesk
Ella Davis        ElDa           DK      Manager
Frank Anderson    FrAn           GB      Helpdesk
Grace Wilson      GrWi           GB      Helpdesk
Henry Clark       HeCl           GB      Employee
Ivy Lee           IvLe           GB      Employee
Jack Harris       JaHa           GB      Manager
Morten E. Hansen  meh            DK      Owner
```

Figure 9.19: *Listing all AD users and a selection of their properties*

As you can see, we need to use the **-Properties** parameter to specify that we want the command to also return the **Country** and **Title** property, since these are not returned by default from the cmdlet. By default, the cmdlet only returns a sub-set of properties for the AD user, so we need to specify additional properties besides the defaults, that we want to have returned.

Note: When you enclose a filter in double quotes, comparison values and variables must be enclosed within single quotes like: "Title -eq 'Employee'" and "Title -eq '$Employee'". When you enclose a filter using curly braces, values are enclosed within double quotes, but variables should not be quoted at all: {Title -eq "Employee"} and {Title -eq $Employee}.

We can use the filter to query **all** users in a specific **country**:

```
# Query AD users in a specific country
Get-ADuser -Filter "Country -eq 'DK'" `
```

```
-Properties Country,Title | `
Select-Object Name,SamAccountName,Country,Title
```

The output of this command is shown in *Figure 9.20*:

```
PS C:\Users\Administrator> Get-ADuser -Filter "Country -eq 'DK'"
>> -Properties Country,Title | `
>> Select-Object Name,SamAccountName,Country,Title

Name              SamAccountName Country Title
----              -------------- ------- -----
Alice Johnson     AlJo           DK      Employee
Bob Smith         BoSm           DK      Employee
Charlie Brown     ChBr           DK      Helpdesk
David Williams    DaWi           DK      Helpdesk
Ella Davis        ElDa           DK      Manager
Morten E. Hansen  meh            DK      Owner
```

Figure 9.20: *Querying and filtering users in a specific country*

Furthermore, we can use the filter to query users in a specific *country* and with a specific *job title*:

```
# Query AD users in a specific country with a specific job title
Get-ADuser -Filter "Country -eq 'DK' -and Title -eq 'Employee'" `
-Properties Country,Title | `
Select-Object Name,SamAccountName,Country,Title
```

The output of this command is shown in *Figure 9.21*:

```
PS C:\Users\Administrator> Get-ADuser -Filter "Country -eq 'DK' -and Title -eq 'Employee'"
>> -Properties Country,Title | `
>> Select-Object Name,SamAccountName,Country,Title

Name           SamAccountName Country Title
----           -------------- ------- -----
Alice Johnson  AlJo           DK      Employee
Bob Smith      BoSm           DK      Employee
```

Figure 9.21: *Querying and filtering users in a specific country and with a specific job title*

The principal for querying and filtering specific AD groups are the same as when querying and filtering AD users, instead we use the **Get-ADGroup** with the **-Filter** parameter. Below, we query for AD groups that have a *Description* property value that equals *"GB"*:

```
# Query AD Groups with a specific Description property
Get-ADGroup -Filter "Description -eq 'GB'" `
-Properties Description | `
Select-Object Name,Description
```

The output of this command is shown in *Figure 9.22*:

```
PS C:\Users\Administrator> Get-ADGroup -Filter "Description -eq 'GB'" `
>> -Properties Description | `
>> Select-Object Name,Description

Name            Description
----            -----------
Helpdesk        GB
Finance         GB
Marketing       GB
Engineering     GB
CustomerService GB
```

Figure 9.22: Querying and filtering groups with a specific Description property value

By using filtering, we can return a specific selection of AD objects based on the filter query. This selection can then be used to perform bulk operations on those specific objects such as adding multiple users from one country to a specific AD group or changing the job title for specific employees and so on. In the previous examples we used the **Select-Object** cmdlet to select and return specific properties from the users and groups. The caveat of using the **Select-Object** cmdlet is that the objects base type gets converted into a *PSCustomObject* which is returned instead of the **ADAccount** type returned by the **Get-ADUser** cmdlet and the **ADPrincipal** type returned by the **Get-ADGroup** cmdlet. The **PSCustomObject** object returned by **Select-Object** cannot be used for performing bulk and other operations by piping this to other AD cmdlets. We simply use **Select-Object** in these examples, to return lists that only contains a few select properties that we are interested in, making it easier to get an overview of the properties for specific objects and making it easier to read the objects and their properties in the console. You can also use this method to create specific lists and save these as files or use them for reports. But when you need to perform operations such as bulk or making changes etc. on the filtered objects, you will have to omit piping the commands to Select-Object.

Filter parameter vs. Where-Object

You might be wondering, why not just use the **Where-Object** cmdlet to filter the results instead of using the AD cmdlets with the **-Filter** parameter? The AD cmdlets with the **-Filter** parameter performs its filtering on the *server-side*, meaning that the filtering is done at the Active Directory server, and only the matching results are returned to the PowerShell session, whereas the **Where-Object** filter cmdlet performs *client-side* filtering, meaning that it retrieves all object results from the Active Directory server to the AD cmdlet first and then filters all the returned objects within the PowerShell session. The **-Filter** parameter is more efficient especially when working with large amounts of AD objects. Imagine if you have a few thousand user objects in your domain and whenever you make a query, the **Get-ADUser** cmdlet would retrieve them all and return them to the session, then you could use **Where-Object** to filter all the returned users to find a select few. The **-Filter** parameter would instead send the query to the AD server and then only the specific filtered selection objects would be returned to the session.

To show the difference we can make two simple **Get-ADUser** queries. One using the filter parameter and one using **Where-Object**. To mimic a domain with a lot of users while also preventing false positives that might occur if each command was only executed once, we can use a loop to execute each command multiple times. The **Measure-Command** can be used to time each command. *Figure 9.23* shows the execution of these commands:

```
PS C:\Users\Administrator> (Measure-Command {
>>     foreach ($i in 0..10000){
>>         Get-ADUser -Filter "Country -eq 'DK'"
>>     }
>> }).TotalMilliseconds
17988,0186
PS C:\Users\Administrator> (Measure-Command {
>>     foreach ($i in 0..10000){
>>         Get-ADUser -Filter * | Where-Object {$_.Country -eq "DK"}
>>     }
>> }).TotalMilliseconds
28676,2551
```

Figure 9.23: Execution of timed commands using the Filter parameter and the Where-Object filter cmdlet.

You can see that the execution of the timed command using the **-Filter** parameter is about 10 seconds faster than using the **Where-Object** filter cmdlet in this case. The performance gain relies on the number of AD objects the command has to process. For small domains with a few users and groups, the gain would be minimal, but in large domains with a lot of users and groups, you can save a significant amount of time by using the **-Filter** parameter instead of the **Where-Object** filter cmdlet, especially if you have to execute several commands and query the AD multiple times:

Use the SearchBase parameter to query and search for AD objects in specific paths

Another valuable parameter when using the **Get-ADUser** and **Get-ADGroup** cmdlets are the **-SearchBase** parameter. This parameter enables you to specify an Active Directory path to search in. If not specified, the AD cmdlets generally search within the entire domain. By specifying a search base, which can be a container or an Organizational Unit, the query will only search within that particular object path. This is especially useful when searching within domains that contain a lot of organizational units and containers as long as the AD objects are properly organized and structured within these organizational units and containers. Specifying the search base when making AD queries makes these queries more efficient since it do not need to crawl through all containers and OUs within the domain searching for specific AD objects. Note that it will also search in all nested containers and OUs within the specified path.

The **-SearchBase** parameter use the Distinguished Name (DN) of the container or the OU where you want to start the search:

```
# Search within the default Users container
Get-ADUser -Filter * -SearchBase "CN=Users,DC=moppleit,DC=dk" | `
Select-Object Name,SamAccountName,DistinguishedName
# Search within the DK OU.
Get-ADUser -Filter * -SearchBase "OU=DK,OU=ADUsers,DC=moppleit,DC=dk" | `
Select-Object Name,SamAccountName,DistinguishedName
```

Running these commands will return the output shown in *Figure 9.24*:

```
PS C:\Users\Administrator> Get-ADUser -Filter * -SearchBase "CN=Users,DC=moppleit,DC=dk" | `
>> Select-Object Name,SamAccountName,DistinguishedName

Name    SamAccountName DistinguishedName
----    -------------- -----------------
krbtgt  krbtgt         CN=krbtgt,CN=Users,DC=MoppleIT,DC=dk

PS C:\Users\Administrator> Get-ADUser -Filter * -SearchBase "OU=DK,OU=ADUsers,DC=moppleit,DC=dk" |
>> Select-Object Name,SamAccountName,DistinguishedName

Name            SamAccountName DistinguishedName
----            -------------- -----------------
Alice Johnson   AlJo           CN=Alice Johnson,OU=DK,OU=ADUsers,DC=MoppleIT,DC=dk
Bob Smith       BoSm           CN=Bob Smith,OU=DK,OU=ADUsers,DC=MoppleIT,DC=dk
Charlie Brown   ChBr           CN=Charlie Brown,OU=DK,OU=ADUsers,DC=MoppleIT,DC=dk
David Williams  DaWi           CN=David Williams,OU=DK,OU=ADUsers,DC=MoppleIT,DC=dk
Ella Davis      ElDa           CN=Ella Davis,OU=DK,OU=ADUsers,DC=MoppleIT,DC=dk
```

Figure 9.24: *Using the SearchBase parameter to search for AD objects within specific containers and OUs*

Using the **-SearchBase** parameter in combination with the **-Filter** parameter, not only enables us to make specific targeted searches, but also optimizes the efficiency of the search query by not having to crawl through all objects within the domain to find the queried AD objects. *Figure 9.25* shows a query using both the **-Filter** parameter and the **-SearchBase** parameter to find users with a specific *job title* within a specific *OU*:

```
PS C:\Users\Administrator> Get-ADUser -Filter "Title -eq 'Helpdesk'" `
>> -SearchBase "OU=DK,OU=ADUsers,DC=moppleit,DC=dk" `
>> -Properties Title | `
>> Select-Object Name,SamAccountName,Title,DistinguishedName

Name            SamAccountName Title    DistinguishedName
----            -------------- -----    -----------------
Charlie Brown   ChBr           Helpdesk CN=Charlie Brown,OU=DK,OU=ADUsers,DC=MoppleIT,DC=dk
David Williams  DaWi           Helpdesk CN=David Williams,OU=DK,OU=ADUsers,DC=MoppleIT,DC=dk
```

Figure 9.25: *Search query using both Filter and SearchBase parameters*

Making filtered queries is an efficient way to search for AD objects within a domain, especially in combination with the SearchBase parameter, which narrows the search parameters to specific paths. The results of such search queries can be used to perform bulk operations on the specific sets of AD objects that are returned by the query. It could be that you need to update all users with the *Helpdesk* job title to *supporters* or you might need to *move* users within a specific OU into another OU and so on.

Performing bulk operations on AD objects

A real efficient and optimal way of working with Active Directory in PowerShell is the ability to perform bulk operations such as creating multiple users and groups, modifying properties on multiple objects, or moving multiple objects between Organizational Units and so on. In combination with filtered queries, this allows for performing operations on specific sets of multiple AD objects with specific properties as single operations.

Recipe 56: How to perform bulk operations on AD users and AD groups

Targeting all AD objects of a type such as users or groups or by using search queries to find specific AD objects like users or groups with specific properties or objects residing within specific paths, by using the **Get-AD** cmdlets, we can pipe the results to other AD cmdlets or to the **Foreach-Object** loop, to perform bulk operations on multiple objects as single operations.

Update property for all users

Users within our domain have their *company* property set to either *DK*, *GB* or it is not set at all. We want to update all users *company* property to match that of our company name. We can use the **Get-ADUser** cmdlet with a wildcard filter to return all users within our domain. To get an overview of all the current users in our domain and their current company property values, we use the **Get-ADUser** and **Select-Object** cmdlets. *Figure 9.26* shows all the current users in our domain and their company property:

```
PS C:\Users\Administrator> Get-ADUser -Filter * `
>> -Properties Company | `
>> Select-Object Name,Company

Name              Company
----              -------
Administrator
Guest
krbtgt
Alice Johnson     DK
Bob Smith         DK
Charlie Brown     DK
David Williams    DK
Ella Davis        DK
Frank Anderson    GB
Grace Wilson      GB
Henry Clark       GB
Ivy Lee           GB
Jack Harris       GB
Morten E. Hansen
```

Figure 9.26: All AD users in our domain and their company property

We use the **-Properties** parameter to specifically select the **Company** property and then we use the **Select-Object** cmdlet to return a minimized view with the properties we are interested in. We use this to verify that the users the query return, only contain the users that we want to modify.

> **Note: It is always a good idea to verify the output result of a query before making any changes, or you might end up modifying objects that were not intended to be modified. In worst case, this might lead to unexpected destructive behavior. This is of course not easy when executing such commands within automation scripts but be sure that commands in such scripts are extensively tested before being deployed to production environments. It could have serious consequences in your production Active Directory domain if commands are executed using wrong queries!**

Now that we have verified that the command returns all the expected users, we can update the command by removing **Select-Object** and then pipe the command to the **Set-ADUser** cmdlet to update the Company property for all the users in bulk:

```
# Update the Company property for all users
Get-ADUser -Filter * `
-Properties Company | `
Set-ADUser -Company "MoppleIT"
```

Once we execute this command, all users *Company* property should be updated. *Figure 9.27* shows the execution of the command. We verify the outcome using the **Get-ADUser** cmdlet with **Select-Object**:

```
PS C:\Users\Administrator> Get-ADUser -Filter * `
>> -Properties Company | `
>> Set-ADUser -Company "MoppleIT"
PS C:\Users\Administrator>
PS C:\Users\Administrator> Get-ADUser -Filter * `
>> -Properties Company | `
>> Select-Object Name,Company

Name              Company
----              -------
Administrator     MoppleIT
Guest             MoppleIT
krbtgt            MoppleIT
Alice Johnson     MoppleIT
Bob Smith         MoppleIT
Charlie Brown     MoppleIT
David Williams    MoppleIT
Ella Davis        MoppleIT
Frank Anderson    MoppleIT
Grace Wilson      MoppleIT
Henry Clark       MoppleIT
Ivy Lee           MoppleIT
Jack Harris       MoppleIT
Morten E. Hansen  MoppleIT
```

Figure 9.27: Modifying the company property for all AD users in bulk

Add specific users to a specific group

Within our domain we have an AD group called *Employees* with a description stating that this group is for employees within *DK*. We also know that we have some users in the *DK* OU with the job title *Employee*. We want to add these specific users to that specific AD group.

The first thing we do is to verify that our queries return the expected users and group:

```
# Query the specific group:
Get-ADGroup `
-Filter "Name -eq 'Employees' -and Description -eq 'DK'" `
-Properties Members
# Query the specific users
Get-ADUser `
-Filter "Country -eq 'DK' -and Title -eq 'Employee'" `
-Properties Country,Title | `
Select-Object Name,Country,Title
```

Figure 9.28 shows the output of these commands. We can verify that the returned group and the returned users are the ones we expect. Note that the group currently has no members:

```
PS C:\Users\Administrator> Get-ADGroup `
>> -Filter "Name -eq 'Employees' -and Description -eq 'DK'" `
>> -Properties Members

DistinguishedName : CN=Employees,OU=Custom,OU=ADGroups,DC=MoppleIT,DC=dk
GroupCategory     : Security
GroupScope        : Global
Members           : {}
Name              : Employees
ObjectClass       : group
ObjectGUID        : d23577ee-41de-4354-bbe8-5aaf5004f325
SamAccountName    : Employees
SID               : S-1-5-21-1225418253-179372207-2133877867-1156


PS C:\Users\Administrator> Get-ADUser `
>> -Filter "Country -eq 'DK' -and Title -eq 'Employee'" `
>> -Properties Country,Title | `
>> Select-Object Name,Country,Title

Name          Country Title
----          ------- -----
Alice Johnson DK      Employee
Bob Smith     DK      Employee
```

***Figure 9.28:** Verification of the commands for finding specific users and group*

The eagle-eyed reader might have noticed that it might be redundant to use the **Get-ADGroup** command with the filter, since we only have one group called *Employees*. All AD groups **Name** property is unique within the domain, so we could as easily have just executed **Get-ADGroup -Identity Employees**, but we might not have known that this was the specific group with the description matching *DK*. The group´s description might have been changed at some point. If we do not use the filter, we might end up adding users to the wrong group. We use the filter to verify that the group is the correct one.

Now that the commands are verified, we can bulk add the users as members to the group by updating the commands to make changes:

```
# Bulk add users to group
$Group = Get-ADGroup `
-Filter "Name -eq 'Employees' -and Description -eq 'DK'"
Get-ADUser `
-Filter "Country -eq 'DK' -and Title -eq 'Employee'" | `
ForEach-Object {
    Add-ADGroupMember -Identity $Group -Members $_
}
```

We assign the output from **Get-ADGroup** to the **$Group** variable, to ensure that we have a reference for the group object. The **Get-ADUser** command is piped to **Foreach-Object**. We need to use the **Add-ADGroupMember** to add the users to the group. This cmdlet´s **-Members** parameter does not accept pipeline input directly, which is why the **Foreach-Object** loop is used in this example. The **-Members** parameter do accept a list of **ADUser** objects, so instead of using the **Foreach-Object** loop approach, we could also have assigned the **Get-ADUser** output to a variable, and then use this variable as an argument for the **-Members** parameter, as shown below:

```
$Group = Get-ADGroup `
-Filter "Name -eq 'Employees' -and Description -eq 'DK'"
$Users = Get-ADUser `
-Filter "Country -eq 'DK' -and Title -eq 'Employee'"
Add-ADGroupMember -Identity $Group -Members $Users
```

The first approach using the **Foreach-Object** loop, adds some overhead that might influence the performance negatively if there are a lot of users since this approach executes the **Add-ADGroupMember** command once for each user. The second approach only executes the **Add-ADGroupMember** command once and then the cmdlet itself handles the addition of each user to the group. The general principal is that we can filter a specific set of users by their properties and then add them in bulk to the group.

Figure 9.29 shows that the expected users have been added as members to the group:

```
PS C:\Users\Administrator> Get-ADGroup `
>> -Filter "Name -eq 'Employees' -and Description -eq 'DK'" `
>> -Properties Members

DistinguishedName : CN=Employees,OU=Custom,OU=ADGroups,DC=MoppleIT,DC=dk
GroupCategory     : Security
GroupScope        : Global
Members           : {CN=Bob Smith,OU=DK,OU=ADUsers,DC=MoppleIT,DC=dk, CN=Alice Johnson,OU=DK,OU=ADUsers,DC=MoppleIT,DC=dk}
Name              : Employees
ObjectClass       : group
ObjectGUID        : d23577ee-41de-4354-bbe8-5aaf5004f325
SamAccountName    : Employees
SID               : S-1-5-21-1225418253-179372207-2133877867-1156
```

Figure 9.29: Confirmation that users have been added as members of the group

Being able to perform bulk operations using PowerShell is an efficient and time saving way to work with Active Directory objects. Even though we have only shown a few examples in this recipe, the general principal is the same. It is about using filter functions to retrieve objects you want to perform operations on, such as modifying properties on multiple or a set of specific AD users or adding specific users to a specific group, and then perform these operations on multiple objects at once. Imagine if you had to use the Active Directory users and computers GUI, to add tens, hundreds, or thousands of users manually to a group! This would be quite a cumbersome task, that can be done in mere seconds using PowerShell and the ActiveDirectory module, to perform bulk operations.

Automating AD account provisioning

Whenever an employee starts within a company a new account needs to be created and several other aspects might have to be configured, such as creating accounts and access for other systems that are not covered by Active Directory accounts and have mailboxes set up on the exchange server and so on. We refer to this as provisioning. When an employee stops, the account needs to be disabled or entirely removed and some other tasks and configurations might need to be performed, such as closing accounts and removing permissions for other systems, and exchange mailboxes needs to be disabled etc. This is referred to as deprovisioning. If you only have a few employees that start or stops at your company occasionally, it might suffice to perform these tasks manually. However, what if you work at a large company where multiple employees start and stops all the time? Then it can be quite time consuming to perform such tasks manually and it is then strongly recommended to optimize and automate such tasks. By automating the provisioning and deprovisioning of users, you not only save a lot of time, but you also ensure that all tasks are always performed consistent and all aspects of the provisioning and deprovisioning always follow the exact same procedures. PowerShell can be used to create, disable, and remove AD accounts in bulk, but can also be used for tasks such as creating accounts and logins for other systems depending on the methods that are used to access such systems.

Creating an AD user is usually not only the process of just creating the AD user account, but it is also about making sure that a similar user with the same name does not already exist in the system and figuring out the username for the new user, and check that a similar user does not already exist in your Active Directory. Each new user should also be given a unique one-time password, instead of using the same password for all new accounts. You would not want a disgruntled employee to know the default password and be able to login to new user accounts. There is always a security aspect when working with passwords, even if it is a temporary password for a new account, and even if this is going to be changed soon. The new user might already have access and permissions to secure and secret systems that other users should not be able to access. Another important aspect for a user account is a mailbox. A new user typically needs a mailbox created and associated with their account, this is a task for your on-prem exchange server, online exchange server or other mail server your company use. A mailbox usually can only be set-up for and associated with a user after the initial AD account is created. These are just some of the tasks needed whenever you have to create a new user and depending on your companies' requirements for accounts and system access, you might have a lot of other tasks that must be provisioned for a new user. When an employee stops, all these tasks might have to be done in reverse to deprovision all the access, permissions and accounts that have been associated with that user. Provision or deprovision users manually for each employee that starts and stops in your company can end up being quite time consuming and are also more prone to errors. What if you forget to disable an account for an employee that has just been terminated on bad terms? Then such an account quickly ends up being a security incident waiting to happen! By automating such tasks, you ensure that all aspects of the provisioning and deprovisioning of users will follow the same steps and procedures.

Recipe 57: Developing automation scripts for creating AD users and AD users in bulk

In this recipe we create two scripts that can be used as templates for automating and optimizing the process of creating AD users and for performing provisioning tasks and for creating and provisioning multiple users in bulk.

We want to create a script that can be used to automate the creation of AD users within our Active Directory. This script will be an essential part of a larger task for provisioning a user. Creating the user account within Active Directory is the first important step in the larger provisioning process. The task of automating the creation of an AD user consists of a subset of smaller tasks.

- Create a 4-character username (**SamAccountName**) that is derived from the users first and last names. Check and make sure that the username does not already exist in AD. If it already exists, re-create the username until an unused unique username if found.

- Create a unique one-time password with 10 characters. This could be sent directly to the new employees' manager, or placed within that specific managers private file share etc. In this script though, we write it to a file that could later be handed over to the respective manager.

- Create the user in the correct AD user's country OU, depending on the country provided for the user.

- Set the relevant attribute property values for the user.

- Make sure that the account is set as Enabled and that the user is required to change password at first login.

- Create the user in AD with the required settings and properties.

- Add the user to an AD group depending on the country. If the user is from DK add the user to the AD group *EmployeesDK* and if the user is from GB add the user to the AD group *EmployeesGB*.

Creating users requires at least some input information such as the users first and last names. We want to rely on minimal input to create these users. Besides the names, we would require their job title, the country they are going to work in, the department they are going to work in and their mobile phone number, which could be used for 2 factor authentication etc. With this type of information, we can create a script to accommodate all the requirements mentioned above.

The first thing is to add the **CmdletBinding** attribute and a **param** block, so the script will be able to handle the required input arguments. After the **param** block we set the **$ErrorActionPreference** variable to **stop**, so that we are able to catch and handle errors using **try/catch** blocks within the script:

```
[CmdletBinding()]

param (
    [Parameter(Mandatory = $true, Position = 0)]
    [String]$GivenName,
    [Parameter(Mandatory = $true, Position = 1)]
    [String]$SurName,
    [Parameter(Mandatory = $true, Position = 2)]
    [String]$JobTitle,
    [Parameter(Mandatory = $true, Position = 3)]
    [String]$Department,
    [Parameter(Mandatory = $true, Position = 4)]
    [ValidateSet("DK", "GB")]
    [String]$Country,
    [Parameter(Mandatory = $true, Position = 5)]
    [String]$MobilePhone
)

$ErrorActionPreference = "Stop"
```

Next, we create a function called **New-UserName**. This function takes one argument, which is the full name of the user, more precise a combination of the users **GivenName** and **SurName**. This function is used to calculate the four charactered username that will be used as the users **SamAccountName**. Some users might only have one name like *cher* or *prince*, but most users have at least one, two or three last names. We want to create a username that is derived from these names. The naming convention will be as follows:

- One name like **Morten**: Would take the first four characters for the username: **Mort**.

- Two names like **Morten Hansen**: Would take the first two characters in each name for the username:

  Moha.

- Three names like **Morten Elmstrøm Hansen**: Would take the first two characters in the first name and the first character from each of the last names for the username:

  Moeh.

- Four names like: **Morten Elmstrøm Larsen Hansen**: Would take the first character in each name for the username:

  Molh.

- Five + names: If a user has five or more names, only the first four will be used to calculate the username. The switch block can have more expressions added to accommodate for this in a different way if explicitly required.

It does this by splitting the full name using the space character (" ") as a delimiter, into an array and then save this array into the **$SplitName** variable. We ensure that only the first four names are selected, so the resulting **$SplitName** variable always only contains the first four names if a user should have more than four names.

Now we introduce a **do-while** loop and within this loop a **switch** block. This **switch** block takes the numbers of items in the **$SplitName** array as an expression. If the matching result equals 1, meaning that the user only has one name, the action is to **join** the first four characters in that name into the *username*.

The username is then assigned to the **$Init** variable. If the matching result equals 2, meaning that the user has two names, the action is to take the first two characters from each name and **join** them into the *username*, and so forth for matching results equals to 3 and 4. According to the naming convention described earlier.

Once the username is calculated from the naming convention, using the **switch** block, we use a **try/catch** block to check if the username already exists in Active Directory. If it already exists, the **$Exists** variable is assigned the **$true** value.

To re-create a new username, we remove the first character from the last name within the

$SplitName array. If the name is: **Morten Hansen**, which would result in the username **Moha**, and this username already exists in AD, the step will remove the *H* in *Hansen* and calculate a new username from the name: *Morten Ansen*, resulting in the username *Moan*. This process will continue until a username that does not exist in AD is found.

When the call to **Get-ADUser** in the **try** block results in a username that does not exist, it will throw an error, and the catch block will set the **$Exists** variable to **$false**, exiting the **do-while** loop.

The function calculates a username from the users names that does not already exist in AD and it is returned as lowercase characters. This might be a lot to take in, for one "simple" function, but by doing this we ensure that we can automate the process of calculating a unique username for new users without the command resulting in an error because a username already exists in AD. One thing this function do not accommodate for though, is the result of 4 charactered foul or swear words, such as *pigs* and *ugly* and so on. You do not want a user to be given such a username. You should incorporate a blacklist containing such words, and then make the proper code logic within this function, that would result in a re-calculation of the username if it resulted in any words within such a blacklist, until a proper valid username is calculated.

```
function New-UserName {
    [CmdletBinding()]
    param (
        [String]$FullName
    )
        $SplitName = ($FullName -split " ") | Select-Object -First 4
    do {
        switch ($SplitName.Length) {
            1 { $Init = -Join $SplitName[0][0..3] }
            2 { $Init = -Join ($SplitName[0][0..1] `
                + $SplitName[1][0..1]) }
            3 { $Init = -Join ($SplitName[0][0..1] `
                + $SplitName[1][0..0]) `
                + $SplitName[2][0..0] }
            4 { $Init = -Join ($SplitName[0][0..0] `
                + $SplitName[1][0..0]) `
                + $SplitName[2][0..0] `
                + $SplitName[3][0..0] }
        }
```

```
        try {
            Get-ADUser $Init | Out-Null
            $Exists = $true
            $SplitName[-1] = $SplitName[-1].Substring(1)
        }
        catch {
            $Exists = $false
        }
    } while ($Exists)
    return $Init.ToLower()
}
```

Next, we create a function for generating a random password. For this function we use the password generator we created in *Chapter 5, Scripting Techniques* in *recipe 27: Validating script parameters using validation attributes*. We make some few adjustments to the code and use it to create a function called **Random-Pwd** that that return a random password instead of just writing it to the console:

```
function Random-Pwd {
    [CmdletBinding()]
    param (
        [Parameter(Mandatory = $true, Position = 0)]
        [ValidateRange(8, 63)]
        [int]$Length,
        [Parameter(Position = 1)]
        [ValidatePattern("^[!@#£$€%&(){}\[\]]*$")]
        [string]$SpecialChars = "!@#$%",
        [switch]$ExcludeUpperCase,
        [switch]$ExcludeLowerCase,
        [switch]$ExcludeDigits,
        [switch]$ExcludeSpecialChars
    )
    $CharSet = ""
    if (-not $ExcludeUpperCase) { $CharSet += "ABCDEFGHIJKLMNOPQRSTUVWXYZ"
}
    if (-not $ExcludeLowerCase) { $CharSet += "abcdefghijklmnopqrstuvwxyz"
}
```

```
    if (-not $ExcludeDigits) { $CharSet += "0123456789" }
    if (-not $ExcludeSpecialChars) { $CharSet += $SpecialChars }


    Write-Verbose "CharSet: $CharSet"
    $Password = -join (Get-Random -Count $Length -InputObject $CharSet.
ToCharArray())
    Return $Password
  }
```

The next function is a smaller function that is used to select the correct **OU** path for the user, depending on the specified country. If a user works in **DK**, the path the user will be created in is the **DK OU** under the ADUser **OU**. For **GB** it would be the **GB OU** under the ADUser **OU**. If other countries are provided, the user will be placed within the ADUser **OU** by default. The function will return the correct paths *Distinguished Name*, which is then used to place the user in the correct country user **OU** upon creation:

```
function Select-CountryPath {
    param (
        [String]$Country
    )
    switch ($Country) {
        "DK" { return "OU=DK,OU=ADUsers,DC=moppleit,DC=dk" }
        "GB" { return "OU=GB,OU=ADUsers,DC=moppleit,DC=dk" }
        default { return "OU=ADUsers,DC=moppleit,DC=dk" }
    }
}
```

The next function is somewhat similar, but instead of returning an **OU** path, it uses the **Add-ADGroupMember** cmdlet to place a user within a specific employee AD group, depending on the specified country. Users in **DK** will be placed within the **EmployeesDK** group, and users in **GB** will be placed within the **EmployeesGB** group. If a user is created with another country property than **DK** or **GB**, the user will <u>not</u> be placed in any additional employees' group. In this function we have added some **verbose** output and placed the code logic within a **try/catch** block, resulting in an error if for some reason it should fail to place the user within a group, while also ensuring that it would not result in a terminating error, we use **Write-OutPut** to write a simple statement. This function is used after the user is created within the AD, since it of course requires the user exists, before the user can be placed in a group:

```
function Add-UserToCountryGroup {
    param (
```

```
        [String]$UserName,
        [ValidateSet("DK","GB")]
        [String]$Country
    )
    try {
        switch ($Country) {
            "DK" { Add-ADGroupMember -Identity EmployeesDK -Members $UserName;
            Write-Verbose "User $UserName added to AD group: EmployeesDK" }
            "GB" { Add-ADGroupMember -Identity EmployeesGB -Members $UserName;
            Write-Verbose "User $UserName added to AD group: EmployeesGB" }
        }
    }
    catch {
        Write-OutPut "Could not add user $UserName to country specific AD Group"
    }
}
```

We only want the temporary password to be written to a file and placed in the same location as the script. The optimal would be that it was either placed in a private share directory where only the user's manager have access or it can be sent directly to the manager by email or sms or something similar. But for now, we are satisfied with the file approach.

We create a simple function called **New-PwdDoc** that takes two parameters, **$UserName** and **$Password**. This function writes the password to a file called **$UserName.txt** using the **New-Item** cmdlet and assign this to the **$File** variable. This ensures that we get the full name of the file it creates returned, which is then used to write some verbose output:

```
function New-PwdDoc {
    param (
        [String]$UserName,
        [String]$Password
    )
    $File = New-Item -ItemType file -Path ".\$UserName.txt" -Value
"$($Password)"
    Write-Verbose "Created password document: $($File.FullName)"
}
```

The last function we create is a **Main** function. This is used to combine and handle all the code logic, and this is where we call all the other functions and gather the functions output that is used to create the AD user.

1. First, we create a variable, **$FullName** which is simply a string combination of the first and last names. We invoke the **New-UserName** function and assign the output to the **$UserName** variable. We invoke the **Random-Pwd** function and assign the output to the **$Password** variable and we invoke the **Select-CountryPath** function, assigning the output to the **$CountryOU** variable.

2. Next, we create a **$Params** hashtable containing all the settings for our new user. We use the **$UserName** variable value for both the **SamAccountName**, the **UserPrincipalName** and **EmailAddress** properties. The **$Password** is converted to a **secure-string** and we ensure that the user is created as *Enabled* and that we set the *password must be changed at first logon* setting.

3. Next, we invoke the **New-ADUser** cmdlet and create the AD user. This is invoked in a **try/catch** block, and we use *splatting* to provide all the parameters within the **$Params** hashtable variable. If the user is successfully created, we provide some verbose output, and the **Main** function continues executing the additional code, which could be further provisioning tasks. If for some reason the command fails to create the AD user, we write an error stating this with the error message, and make sure that our script exits before any other commands are executed.

4. When the user is successfully created, the function can be used to perform other provisioning tasks such as creating and associating a user mailbox to the user, creating logins for other systems and other requirements for the provisioning of the user. In this function, we only have two provisioning tasks besides the actual AD user creation. The one that adds the user to the country relevant AD group by invoking the **Add-UserToCountryGroup** function and the other that writes the users password to a file using the **New-PwdDoc** function. The last step in our script, is to invoke the **Main** function, making sure the entire process is started:

```
function Main {
```

Align this with the following commands:

```
$FullName = "$($GivenName) $($SurName)"
$UserName = New-UserName $FullName
Write-Verbose "Calculated initials: $UserName"
$Password = Random-Pwd -Length 10
Write-Verbose "Created Random Password: XXXXXXXXXX"
$CountryOU = Select-CountryPath $Country
Write-Verbose "Selected Country OU: $CountryOU"
$Params = @{
    Name              = $FullName
    DisplayName       = $FullName
    GivenName         = $GivenName
    SurName           = $SurName
```

```
        SamAccountName        = $UserName

        UserPrincipalName     = "$($Username)@moppleit.dk"

        EmailAddress          = "$($Username)@moppleit.dk"

        Path                  = $CountryOU

        AccountPassword       = (ConvertTo-SecureString
"$($Password)" -AsPlainText -Force)

        Enabled               = $true

        MobilePhone           = $MobilePhone

        Title                 = $JobTitle

        Department            = $Department

        Country               = $Country

        Company               = "MoppleIT"

        ChangePasswordAtLogon = $true

    }

    try {

        New-ADUser @Params

        Write-Verbose "New AD User created: $UserName"

    }

    catch {

        Write-Error "Could not create new AD user: $UserName`r`n$($_)"

        Exit 1

    }

    # Perform other provisioning tasks!

    # Add DK employees to the EmployeesDK AD group and

    # GB employees to the EmployeesGB AD group.

    Add-UserToCountryGroup -UserName $UserName -Country $Country

    # Create password file

    New-PwdDoc -UserName $UserName -Password $Password

    # Create and associate mailbox with user.

    # Use API to create login to System XX.

    # etc...

}

Main
```

5. These functions and processes combined makes the script that can be used for creating AD users by providing minimal input, it is not quite automated yet

though, but the process of creating AD users have been optimized and some of the sub-processes have been fully automated such as the calculation of the username from the users full name and the creation of a random password that is written to a file after the user is created. We save the script as **CreateADUser.ps1**. Before we continue, let us first check that the script works as intended, by creating a test user. *Figure 9.30* shows the creation of an AD user using the **CreateADUser.ps1** script:

```
PS C:\Temp> .\CreateADUser.ps1 `
>> -GivenName "john" `
>> -SurName "Wilkins" `
>> -JobTitle "Senior Developer" `
>> -Department "Development" `
>> -Country "DK" `
>> -MobilePhone "+4532165487" `
>> -Verbose
VERBOSE: Calculated initials: jowi
VERBOSE: CharSet: ABCDEFGHIJKLMNOPQRSTUVWXYZabcdefghijklmnopqrstuvwxyz0123456789!@#$%
VERBOSE: Created Random Password: XXXXXXXXXX
VERBOSE: Selected Country OU: OU=DK,OU=ADUsers,DC=moppleit,DC=dk
VERBOSE: New AD User created: jowi
VERBOSE: User jowi added to AD group: EmployeesDK
VERBOSE: Created password document: C:\Temp\jowi.txt
PS C:\Temp>
PS C:\Temp> Get-Content .\jowi.txt
ZB4QcmUJHs
PS C:\Temp>
PS C:\Temp> Get-ADUser jowi `
>> -Properties EmailAddress,Title,Department,Country,Company,MemberOf,PasswordExpired

Company           : MoppleIT
Country           : DK
Department        : Development
DistinguishedName : CN=john Wilkins,OU=DK,OU=ADUsers,DC=MoppleIT,DC=dk
EmailAddress      : jowi@moppleit.dk
Enabled           : True
GivenName         : john
MemberOf          : {CN=EmployeesDK,OU=Custom,OU=ADGroups,DC=MoppleIT,DC=dk}
Name              : john Wilkins
ObjectClass       : user
ObjectGUID        : 049188ff-ad8f-4d23-92fa-738982a39a30
PasswordExpired   : True
SamAccountName    : jowi
SID               : S-1-5-21-1225418253-179372207-2133877867-1222
Surname           : Wilkins
Title             : Senior Developer
UserPrincipalName : jowi@moppleit.dk
```

Figure 9.30: *Creation of AD user using automation script*

6. In the figure you can see the content of the password document and we use **Get-ADUser** to check that the user is created with the expected attribute property values. It is created within the correct **OU** path. It is added as a member of the **EmployeesDK** AD group, and the password is set as expired, which is an indication that the password is set to be changed at next logon. All in all, the script works as intended and all properties are set. The user is successfully created and provisioned as expected.

7. Now to the next step, using the script to create users in **bulk**. This could be done using various methods, but for simplicity we have decided to use a **.csv** file. The csv file will contain the required information needed to create users and each entry

will create a new user from that specific information. *Figure 9.31* shows a **csv** file containing **ten** new users that should be created:

```
BulkUsers.csv - Notepad

File  Edit  Format  View  Help
GivenName;SurName;JobTitle;Department;Country;MobilePhone
Olivia;Smith;Employee;HR;GB;+4477665544
William;Brown;Manager;Finance;DK;+4588991100
James;Wilson;Developer;Development;DK;+4599118877
Benjamin;Harris;Manager;Finance;GB;+4477663344
Lucas;Johnson;Developer;Development;GB;+4489887766
Emma;Lee;Helpdesk;IT;GB;+4477112233
Sophia;Anderson;Helpdesk;IT;DK;+4555447799
Liam;Clark;Employee;HR;DK;+4533221100
Mia;Davis;Manager;Finance;DK;+4577889900
Ava;Williams;Employee;HR;GB;+4433554477
```

Figure 9.31: Csv file containing users that should be created in bulk

8. We are going to create another simpler script for handling the bulk creation of the users from the csv file. This script takes one argument, the path to a csv file. We create a **Main** function, as best practice dictates, and within this function we simply: Import the csv file content. Use a **Foreach** loop to loop through all entries from the csv file, and then use the properties from each entry as arguments for the **CreateADUser.ps1** script and invoke this script for creating each user. We encase the code in a **try/catch** block, so it does not terminate if the creation of a single or a few users might fail for some reason. Finally, we call the **Main** function. The script is saved as **CreateBulkADUsers.ps1**.

```
[CmdletBinding()]
param (
    [Parameter(Mandatory=$true,Position=0)]
    [String]$CsvFilePath
)
$ErrorActionPreference = "Stop"
function Main {
    $CsvContent = Import-Csv $CsvFilePath -Delimiter ";"
    foreach ($User in $CsvContent){
        $Params = @{
            GivenName = $User.GivenName
            SurName = $User.SurName
            JobTitle = $User.JobTitle
            Department = $User.Department
            Country = $User.Country
            MobilePhone = $User.MobilePhone
```

```
        }
        try{
            .\CreateADUser.ps1 @Params
            Write-Verbose "Created user for: $($User.GivenName)
$($User.SurName)"
        }
        catch{
            Write-Output "Could not create user: $($User.GivenName)
$($User.SurName)"
                $_
        }
    }
}
Main
```

9. We execute the script with the path to our csv file containing the new users as an argument for the **-CsvFilePath** parameter, all the users are created in bulk. *Figure 9.32* shows the execution of the **CreateBulkADUsers.ps1** script and confirms that it creates multiple users in bulk as expected:

```
PS C:\Temp> .\CreateBulkADUsers.ps1 -CsvFilePath .\BulkUsers.csv -Verbose
VERBOSE: Calculated initials: olsm
VERBOSE: CharSet: ABCDEFGHIJKLMNOPQRSTUVWXYZabcdefghijklmnopqrstuvwxyz0123456789!@#$%
VERBOSE: Created Random Password: XXXXXXXXXX
VERBOSE: Selected Country OU: OU=GB,OU=ADUsers,DC=moppleit,DC=dk
VERBOSE: New AD User created: olsm
VERBOSE: User olsm added to AD group: EmployeesGB
VERBOSE: Created password document: C:\Temp\olsm.txt
VERBOSE: Created user for: Olivia Smith
VERBOSE: Calculated initials: wibr
VERBOSE: CharSet: ABCDEFGHIJKLMNOPQRSTUVWXYZabcdefghijklmnopqrstuvwxyz0123456789!@#$%
VERBOSE: Created Random Password: XXXXXXXXXX
VERBOSE: Selected Country OU: OU=DK,OU=ADUsers,DC=moppleit,DC=dk
VERBOSE: New AD User created: wibr
VERBOSE: User wibr added to AD group: EmployeesDK
VERBOSE: Created password document: C:\Temp\wibr.txt
VERBOSE: Created user for: William Brown
VERBOSE: Calculated initials: jawi
VERBOSE: CharSet: ABCDEFGHIJKLMNOPQRSTUVWXYZabcdefghijklmnopqrstuvwxyz0123456789!@#$%
VERBOSE: Created Random Password: XXXXXXXXXX
VERBOSE: Selected Country OU: OU=DK,OU=ADUsers,DC=moppleit,DC=dk
VERBOSE: New AD User created: jawi
VERBOSE: User jawi added to AD group: EmployeesDK
VERBOSE: Created password document: C:\Temp\jawi.txt
VERBOSE: Created user for: James Wilson
VERBOSE: Calculated initials: beha
VERBOSE: CharSet: ABCDEFGHIJKLMNOPQRSTUVWXYZabcdefghijklmnopqrstuvwxyz0123456789!@#$%
VERBOSE: Created Random Password: XXXXXXXXXX
VERBOSE: Selected Country OU: OU=GB,OU=ADUsers,DC=moppleit,DC=dk
VERBOSE: New AD User created: beha
VERBOSE: User beha added to AD group: EmployeesGB
VERBOSE: Created password document: C:\Temp\beha.txt
VERBOSE: Created user for: Benjamin Harris
```

Figure 9.32: *Creation of new AD users in bulk*

We have two scripts that significantly optimize the AD user creation and provisioning process. One script that takes the minimum required input in order to provision a user and that automates some of the sub-processes required for creating an AD user account such as calculating a unique username derived from the users first and last names and creating a random password for the user. It then creates the user account in Active Directory. The purpose of the script is to not only create and AD user, but it is a user account provisioning script that should be used to create most of the aspects that is required when a new employee starts in a company such as creating and associating a mailbox with the created AD user, add the created user to specific access granting AD groups, automatically send the users password to a specific manager and create access and login to other required third party systems using API´s and so on. In this template script we simply created a few simple provisioning tasks that is executed after the user account is created such as adding the user account to a country specific AD group and saving the users temporary password within a file. But the possibilities for adding additional provisioning tasks are almost endless and once you start adding additional tasks and optimize the script, you will find that the entire user provisioning task becomes more efficient.

The second script is used to execute the provisioning script and for creating and provisioning users in bulk. It reads a simple csv file where minimal required information is added and it use this information as the parameter arguments for the provisioning script. In combination, these scripts can be built upon to become quite powerful and time efficient. You can add numerous other tasks depending on your specific requirements and use these scripts as a building block or template to create scripts that handles all kinds of processes and tasks that is required when a new employee starts at your company, almost fully automatically, the only thing required is a file containing simple information about each new user. The next step for further optimizing the provisioning tasks with scripts such as these might be to create code logic that not only reads a csv file and starts the provisioning task when executed, but that can automate this by creating it as a scheduled task or even as a service script, so that it automatically reads when there is a new csv file with new information available, provisioning the users accordingly and then remove the file once it is finished, being ready for the next file to provision. You would only have to feed it new files with new employee information whenever you want to provision new users, the rest of the provisioning is then handled automatically by the script.

When an employee stops at your company, the user must be deprovisioned and all accounts must be either disabled or deleted and access must be revoked etc. The same principals for the provisioning and bulk scripts can be used for deprovisioning. Instead of creating accounts and granting access and permissions, you would have to create scripts that does the opposite. These tasks can easily be scripted and automated like the provisioning scripts, and you would not even have to provide more information than the *username* of the user accounts you want to deprovision. You could simply provide a list containing the usernames to a deprovisioning script and then it would disable or delete the AD user, remove, or disable the associated mailbox and perform all other necessary tasks that is required when an employee stops, and when users have to be deprovisioned.

One last thing to note: You should of course implement proper error handling to accommodate for potential errors and handle such accordingly within your scripts in general. We could have easily incorporated much more error handling within the provisioning and bulk scripts.

Conclusion

When working in a Windows environment managed by Active Directory it is essential for administrators to be able to control and manage all aspects of Active Directory such as AD users, AD groups and other AD Objects like Organizational Units. The ActiveDirectory module enables you to manage all aspects of Active Directory using PowerShell which has great advantages over the GUI tools provided by Windows. By using PowerShell, you can optimize and automate almost all Active Directory tasks such as creating, modifying, and removing AD objects by creating scripts that can be used to manage such tasks not only automatically but also in bulk. This is not only timesaving but also help you streamline your Active Directory tasks and processes, enhances your overall productivity, and allows you to focus on other prioritized tasks instead of using a lot of time managing your Active Directory manually.

The next chapter examens Azure cloud services management using the Azure command line interface (AzureCLI) and PowerShell. This chapter covers working with and managing Azure virtual machines, storage accounts, blobs, and file shares. It also dives deeper into Azure EntraID and focuses on the creation and management of users, groups, and resource access permissions. Additionally, it provides insight into automating resource provisioning and management focusing on creating service principals that are used for programmatically connecting to Azure using scripts and also how to create scripts that are used for configuration and automatic provisioning of Azure resources.

Join our book's Discord space

Join the book's Discord Workspace for Latest updates, Offers, Tech happenings around the world, New Release and Sessions with the Authors:

https://discord.bpbonline.com

CHAPTER 10

Managing Azure with PowerShell

Introduction

In this modern world, it becomes more common to implement cloud computing, services, and features into corporate infrastructures. Some companies operate in hybrid environments relying on some systems being on-premises and some in the cloud. Other companies have made full transitions to the cloud and swear solely to this approach. One of the more generally known cloud providers is Microsoft Azure. Azure is a versatile and powerful platform that offers a great variety of cloud services and features such as: Virtual machines, databases, storage, Active Directory, Kubernetes and much more. It is easy to scale resources, it offers high levels of reliability, it provides security measures and can also be cost effective, reducing the upfront investments in hardware and infrastructure. However, harnessing the full potential of Azure while ensuring resource optimization for cost-efficiency, performance, and security often requires programmatic optimization and automation. That is where PowerShell comes into the picture. PowerShell together with Azure´s command line interface, the Azure CLI enable you to manage almost all aspects of Azures services and features programmatically and allows you to create scripts and applications for automating and optimizing processes. Azure CLI and PowerShell are valuable tools for developers, system administrators and DevOps managers who want to be able to utilize and manage the Azure Cloud programmatically.

Structure

The chapter covers the following topics:

- Introduction to the Azure command line interface
  - **Recipe 58**: Installation and general usage of the Azure CLI
- Working with Azure Virtual Machines
  - **Recipe 59**: Create, configure, and manage VMs and VM network resources
- Managing Azure storage accounts, blob containers, blobs and file shares
  - **Recipe 60**: Create and manage storage accounts
  - **Recipe 61**: Create and manage blob containers and blobs
  - **Recipe 62**: Create and manage file shares
- Azure EntraID: Users, groups and permissions
  - **Recipe 63**: Managing users, groups, and resource access permissions
- Automating Azure resource provisioning and management
  - **Recipe 64**: Create a Service principal to automatically connect to Azure using scripts
  - **Recipe 65**: Create scripts for automatically provision and configure Azure resources

Objectives

In this chapter we will look into Azure services and resources and learn how to use PowerShell in combination with the Azure Command Line Interface, the Azure CLI, to create, configure and manage Azure resources. We will cover how to set up Azure CLI and how to login to your Azure subscriptions. You will learn how to create a Virtual Machine and how to configure Windows Remote access to a Virtual Machine by creating and configuring network security group rules and by executing scripts on a Virtual Machine using Azure CLI commands to configure and create local firewall rules. You will learn how to create, manage, and delete storage accounts and storage resources such as blob containers, blobs and file shares. We will also go through Azure EntraID previously known as Azure Active Directory used for managing users, groups and permissions in Azure and learn how to manage these using Azure CLI. We will look into automating Azure resource provisioning and learn how to set up service principals that can be used to access Azure programmatically and you will learn how to create scripts for automatically provisioning Azure resources.

Introduction to the Azure command line interface

The Azure Command-Line Interface, or Azure CLI, is a cross-platform command-line tool that is used to connect to Azure and execute commands on Azure resources. In Windows, it allows for execution of commands through PowerShell using interactive command-line prompts or scripts. It is designed to help developers, system administrators and DevOps managers to manage their Azure resources, automate tasks and integrate Azure management tasks into scripts. Azure CLI is an essential component for Azure administrators who want to manage Azure cloud infrastructure and automate routine tasks.

Recipe 58: Installation and general usage of the Azure CLI

In Windows, you can install Azure CLI directly using PowerShell. Start PowerShell as an administrator and run the following command:

```
$ProgressPreference = 'SilentlyContinue'; `

Invoke-WebRequest -Uri https://aka.ms/installazurecliwindowsx64 `

-OutFile .\AzureCLI.msi; `

Start-Process msiexec.exe -Wait `

-ArgumentList '/I AzureCLI.msi /quiet'; `

Remove-Item .\AzureCLI.msi
```

This will download and install the latest 64-bit version of Azure CLI for Windows:

> **Note: If you prefer a 32-bit version of Azure CLI instead of the 64-bit version, change the URL to: https://aka.ms/installazurecliwindows. If Azure CLI is already installed on the system, the installer will overwrite the existing version. Also note that you might need to restart PowerShell after installation before you can use Azure CLI commands.**

Once installed, you can check that Azure CLI has successfully been installed by executing the **az version** command, as shown in *Figure 10.1*:

```
PS C:\Temp> az version
{
  "azure-cli": "2.53.0",
  "azure-cli-core": "2.53.0",
  "azure-cli-telemetry": "1.1.0",
  "extensions": {}
}
```

Figure 10.1: *Check installation and version of Azure CLI*

All Azure CLI commands start with the **az** statement followed by a command, such as **az account, az aks, az storage, az vm** and so on. Some of these commands contain a sub-set of other commands like **az account list, az account show, az aks create, az storage account, az vm delete** and so on, and these can also contain further sub-commands. Some commands are quite self-explanatory such as the **az vm delete**, that are used to delete virtual machines and **az aks create** which creates a new **Azure Kubernetes Service (AKS)** cluster.

You can view the reference list containing all the **az** commands at the official documentation page: **https://learn.microsoft.com/en-us/cli/azure/reference-index?view=azure-cli-latest**.

Login to Azure

The first thing you need in order to be able to use the Azure CLI commands is to use the **az login** command to login to your azure account, or else you will be met with a short error statement specifying that you need to login to use the **az** commands, as shown in *Figure 10.2*:

```
PS C:\Temp> az account show
Please run 'az login' to setup account.
```

Figure 10.2: *Error statement when running az commands before being logged in*

When you execute the **az login** command, it will open a web browser window where you should continue the login process. Once you have successfully logged in, the command will return a list of the available subscriptions for your account. *Figure 10.3* shows a successful login and the available subscriptions:

```
PS C:\Temp> az login
WARNING: A web browser has been opened at https://login.microsoftonline.com/organizations/oauth2/v2.0/authorize. Please
continue the login in the web browser. If no web browser is available or if the web browser fails to open, use device co
de flow with `az login --use-device-code`.
[
  {
    "cloudName": "AzureCloud",
    "homeTenantId": "57f387c6-3587-4ae7-a156-c9c7d10d7df6",
    "id": "50c527e4-b726-4c71-b507-de6cfa9aefa4",
    "isDefault": true,
    "managedByTenants": [],
    "name": "MainSubscription",
    "state": "Enabled",
    "tenantId": "57f387c6-3587-4ae7-a156-c9c7d10d7df6",
    "user": {
      "name": "Morten@█████ █████.dk",
      "type": "user"
    }
  }
]
```

Figure 10.3: *Successful login to Azure account using the az login command*

In this case there is only one subscription available for the account, so this is selected by default. If you have multiple subscriptions, you would use the **az account set** command with the **--subscription** parameter to select and set the specific subscription you want to work in.

```
az account set --subscription <Subscription ID>
```

You can always switch between your different subscriptions using this command. To view a list of your available subscriptions, use the `az account list` command.

After you are logged in and have selected the subscription you want to work with, you can use Azure CLI to manage your Azure cloud by creating, modifying, and deleting resources such as resource groups, key vaults, virtual machines, Kubernetes clusters (AKS), SQL instances, databases and so on.

The az find command

You can always refer to the official documentation and the command reference list for more information about and how to use the different Azure CLI commands, but Azure CLI has a built-in **az find** command which is a *robot* that is built upon AI technology. The **az find** command is not only based on the Azure documentation but also upon the usage patterns of Azure users. The *robot* will provide usage examples for the most possible and logical CLI command that matches your search term. You use the **az find** command by specifying a string with a search term **([CLI_TERM])** as a parameter to the command. You can specify a sentence such as: **az find "How to create a resource group"** or if you know the specific command and want to find examples you can specify the command directly like: **az find "az group create"**. *Figure 10.4* shows the output from the **az find** command using such search terms:

```
PS C:\Temp> az find "how to create a resource group"
Finding examples...

Here are the most common ways to use [how to create a resource group]:

Create a new resource group in the West US region. (autogenerated)
az group create --location westeurope --resource-group ASEv3ResourceGroup

create a resource. (autogenerated)
az resource create --location westus2 --name "{sitename+slot}/siteextensions/Contrast.NetCore.Azure.SiteExtension" --pro
perties "{ \"id\": \"Contrast.NetCore.Azure.SiteExtension\", \
                \"location\": \"West US\", \"version\": \"1.9.0\" }" --resource-group myRG --resource-type Microsoft.Web
/sites/siteextensions

Create a read-only resource group level lock. (autogenerated)
az group lock create --lock-type CanNotDelete --name lockName --resource-group MyResourceGroup

PS C:\Temp> az find "az group create"
Finding examples...

Here are the most common ways to use [az group create]:

Create a new resource group in the West US region. (autogenerated)
az group create --location westeurope --resource-group ASEv3ResourceGroup

Create Resource Group, vNet and app service environment v2 with default values.
az group create --resource-group MyResourceGroup --location westeurope

az network vnet create --resource-group MyResourceGroup --resource-group MyVirtualNetwork \
   --address-prefixes 10.0.0.0/16 --subnet-name MyAseSubnet --subnet-prefixes 10.0.0.0/24

az appservice ase create --resource-group MyAseName --resource-group MyResourceGroup --vnet-name MyVirtualNetwork \
   --subnet MyAseSubnet
```

Figure 10.4: *Using the az find AI robot command to find examples for creating resource groups using different search terms*

As you can see, it provides us with a general example of how to create a new resource group. It does not provide details about the command's parameters, but the examples are usually shown with the mandatory parameters that is at least required for a command. If you want to view additional available parameters for commands, you should use the command reference list and official documentation, but the **az find** command does provide some useful cases.

Resource groups

Azure uses resource groups to provide a structured approach to resource organization and uses such resource groups to create logical groupings and manage relatable resources. They provide a way to streamline resource management, simplify access control, and organize resources based on specific projects, environments, or applications by using tagging. You can create a new resource group using the **az group create** command. A resource group requires a **name** and a **location**:

```
$GroupName = "TestVM"

$Location = "westeurope"

az group create --name $GroupName --location $Location
```

Figure 10.5 shows the execution of the **az group create** command and the output provided when a resource group is successfully created:

```
PS C:\Temp> $GroupName = "TestVM"
PS C:\Temp> $Location = "westeurope"
PS C:\Temp> az group create --name $GroupName --location $Location
{
  "id": "/subscriptions/50c527e4-b726-4c71-b507-de6cfa9aefa4/resourceGroups/TestVM",
  "location": "westeurope",
  "managedBy": null,
  "name": "TestVM",
  "properties": {
    "provisioningState": "Succeeded"
  },
  "tags": null,
  "type": "Microsoft.Resources/resourceGroups"
}
```

Figure 10.5: *Successfully creation of a resource group using the az group create command*

To list all resource groups within the selected subscription, and to also verify that the new resource group exists within that subscription, you can use the **az group list** command:

```
az group list | ConvertFrom-Json | Select-Object Name,Location,Properties
```

Note: Azure CLI commands in general, return their output in JSON format. To convert the commands output to PowerShell objects you can pipe the commands to the ConvertFrom-Json cmdlet. You can then further pipe the command to Select-Object to filter and list specific attribute property values from the commands return output. Note that some output might contain keys with different casing, in such case you might need to use the ConvertFrom-Json with the -AsHashtable parameter. You can also use the –output table parameter at the end of az commands to list the output in a readable table format without converting it to a PowerShell object.

Figure 10.6 shows the converted and filtered output from the **az group list** command. Note that we have added the Properties attribute property values to the output, to show how this nested property is added within a Hashtable as the value to the properties key in the PowerShell object after it is converted from the JSON output data format.

```
PS C:\Temp> az group list | ConvertFrom-Json | Select-Object Name,Location,Properties

name       location     properties
----       --------     ----------
TestVM     westeurope   @{provisioningState=Succeeded}
RG-Test01  westeurope   @{provisioningState=Succeeded}
RG-Test02  westeurope   @{provisioningState=Succeeded}
RG-Test03  northeurope  @{provisioningState=Succeeded}
RG-Test04  eastus       @{provisioningState=Succeeded}
```

Figure 10.6: *Converted and filtered output from the az group list command*

We get a list of all the resource groups within the subscription, their locations, and additional properties.

You should divide and place your resources into resource groups based on a logical grouping. Resources within the same group should be closely related and serve a common purpose. It could be that you have a resource group for each application and for different environments for that application, such as development, testing and production.

> **Note: Whenever you delete a resource group, all resources within that group is also deleted. Be careful when you delete a resource group and be sure that you intend to delete all resources within that group.**

Regions and availability zones

All Azure resources must reside within a region. An Azure region is a set of regional datacenters that are connected through a dedicated low-latency network. You can choose to deploy your resources within datacenters in specific regions close to you, or some of your resources might require to be located within specific countries, you can then deploy resources in regions that meet such requirements. As you can see in the previous figures, regions in Azure resources are usually referred to as *location´s*. There can be a slight variation in cost prices for resources depending on their region, and by placing resources within regions far away from your physical location, might introduce more latency when accessing such resources. You can get a list of available and supported regions for your current selected subscription, using the **az account list-locations** command:

```
# List all locations Converted to and filtered as a PowerShell object.
az account list-locations | `
ConvertFrom-Json | `
Select-Object Name,DisplayName | `
Sort-Object Name
```

Some resources also provide the possibility of zone redundant services which is used to specify specific zones to place resources in. These are referred to as **Availability Zones**. An Azure availability zone is a physical location within an Azure region that protects applications and data from datacenter failures. Each zone is made up of one or more datacenters that are equipped with their own independent power supply, cooling, and network. A zone redundant service replicates the applications and data across Azure availability zones and protects from single points of failure and from datacenter facility-level issues. As an example, you can create a Virtual Machine (VM) as zone redundant by specifying multiple zones to place the resource in upon creation:

```
# Example for creating VM as zone redundant

az vm create `

--resource-group <resource-group-name> `

--name <vm-name> `

--image <vm-image-sku> `

--size <vm-size> `

--admin-username <admin-username> `

--admin-password <admin-password> `

--location <region-name> `

--zone 1 2 3
```

By distributing the VM across different availability zones you increase its availability and mitigate the probability of failures. If a failure occurs in one zone, the VM continues running in one of the other availability zones. This provides high availability and a level of fault tolerance for your resources.

> **Once you are finished working with the Azure CLI you should log out of your account to remove the access to the Azure subscription within the current shell session, using the az logout command.**

Working with Azure virtual machines

Azure **virtual machines** (**VM**) are a fundamental compute resource in Azure and a core component of Azure's **Infrastructure as a Service (IaaS)** offerings. It provides the ability to run virtualized Windows and Linux servers and clients in the cloud for a wide range of purposes such as webservers, databases and custom applications and it offers a wide variety of pre-configured VM images, or you can provide your own custom image. Some of the key advantages by using virtual machines in the cloud is the ability to scale to accommodate for changing workloads and also the offering of high availability and fault tolerance when deployed in availability sets or in different availability zones. Azure offers various VM types for different kinds of workloads such as general purpose VMs, compute, memory, and storage optimized VMs. These types of VMs vary in the terms of

CPU, memory, and storage. You should create VMs that are optimized for your specific purpose. Note that you can always up-scale a VMs resources.

Recipe 59: Create, configure, and manage VMs and VM network resources

When you want to create a VM there are few things to keep in mind like what image do you want for your VM and what size you want for your VM in terms of processing power, memory, and storage capacity. Azure offers a wide variety of images and sizes to support any types of use cases.

> **Note: Azure charges an hourly prize based on the VM´s size and operating system type.**

Azure also offers VM pre-defined configurations referred to as SKU´s which represents a combination of VM size and an operating system image. A SKU defines the precise characteristics of a VM, including the hardware configuration (VM size) and the base OS image. For example, a SKU might represent a *Windows Server 2022* VM with a *Standard_D2s_v3* VM size.

You can choose to use a SKU, or you can specify an image and a size for creating your VM. The following commands are used to list available VM OS images, VM sizes and SKU´s:

```
# List VM OS Images
az vm image list --location westeurope --output table
# List VM sizes
az vm list-sizes --location westeurope --output table
# List SKU´s
az vm list-skus --location westeurope --output table
```

These lists might contain a lot of JSON data that can be difficult to parse, so we use the **--output table** parameter for the **az** command, to provide readable lists in the console. We also provide it with the location parameter to only list the resources available in the region we want to create our VM´s in. Once we have found the correct SKU or image and size, we can continue to create a VM.

Create a Virtual Machine

For our VM we have chosen to specify the image and the size we want to use instead of using a SKU. We are going to use *Windows Server 2022 Datacenter* as the Operating System. In the OS images list, we can find the correct image and use the *UrnAlias* of the image for our commands **--image** parameter. The next is to find a size for the VM. In the size list we find a smaller size with 2 vCPU´s (Virtual CPU´s) and 4GB of memory. It also has an OS disk size of 1TB. This fits the size of a **Standard_B2s**, which is the name to use for the **--size** parameter. Note that there are a lot of different sizes in all price ranges from a few dollars to hundreds of dollars per month for a VM, so choose carefully, especially for testing purposes, so you do not end up with large unintended bills. We use the **az vm create** command to create a new VM. It has a few mandatory parameters such as the **--resource-group**, the **--name** and the **--location** parameters. Besides these and the **--image** and **--size** parameters, you must also provide parameters for an administrator username and password. The minimum required parameters for the command (when using **--image** and **--size** parameters) are shown here:

```
# Create a Virtual machine
az vm create `
--resource-group "TestVM" `
--name "TestVM" `
--image "Win2022Datacenter" `
--size "Standard_B2s" `
--admin-username "TestUser" `
--admin-password "@Test123456789" `
--location "westeurope"
```

Creating Azure resources might take some time to complete. If the creation of a resource is in progress, Azure CLI will notify this by the *Running* statement as shown in *Figure 10.7*. Note that commands might show different warnings and recommendations. If you have provided wrong arguments or for some other reason the progress fails, it will result in an error output statement that provides more information about that specific error:

```
PS C:\Temp> az vm create `
>> --resource-group "TestVM" `
>> --name "TestVM" `
>> --image "Win2022Datacenter" `
>> --size "Standard_B2s" `
>> --admin-username "TestUser" `
>> --admin-password "@Test123456789" `
>> --location "westeurope"
WARNING: Selecting "uksouth" may reduce your costs. The region you've selected may cost more for the same services. You can disable this m
essage in the future with the command "az config set core.display_region_identified=false". Learn more at https://go.microsoft.com/fwlink/
?linkid=222571
WARNING: Ignite (November) 2023 onwards "az vm/vmss create" command will deploy Gen2-Trusted Launch VM by default. To know more about the
default change and Trusted Launch, please visit https://aka.ms/TLaD
WARNING: It's recommended to create with `--public-ip-sku Standard`. Please be aware that the default Public IP will be changed from Basic
 to Standard in the next release. Also note that Basic option will be removed in the future.
[K - Running ...
```

Figure 10.7: Creation of a VM using image and size and the output while the creation is in progress

Once the progress has completed and the Azure resource, in this case the VM, is created the statement changes to *Finished* and some output relevant for the created resource such as the *public IP address* and its *power state*, is returned as shown in *Figure 10.8*:

```
[K[| Finished ..
  "fqdns": "",
  "id": "/subscriptions/50c527e4-b726-4c71-b507-de6cfa9aefa4/resourceGroups/TestVM/providers/Microsoft.Compute/virtualMachines/TestVM",
  "location": "westeurope",
  "macAddress": "60-45-BD-94-5C-97",
  "powerState": "VM running",
  "privateIpAddress": "10.0.0.4",
  "publicIpAddress": "20.224.74.16",
  "resourceGroup": "TestVM",
  "zones": ""
}
```

Figure 10.8: Completed creation of a VM and the returned output from the successful az command

You can assign a command to a variable like: **$NewVM = `az vm create`** and the JSON formatted output from the command will be stored within the variable for further usage, such as converting it into a PowerShell object. If you assign a command to a variable, no further output like the **warning** or the **Running** and **Finished** statements will be shown. The shell will be in a busy state until the command completes its progress.

By default, a VM with a Windows OS is created with a network security group rule that opens port 3389 (**RDP – Remote Desktop Protocol**) and for a Linux OS it is created with a network security group rule that opens port 22 (SSH - Secure Shell). These network security group rules are created with a wildcard (*) allowing *any* source to access the VM on these ports from the public internet. Since we have created a VM with a Windows OS, we should be able to access it directly using RDP from a client, by the VM´s public IP address. We can also test that the RDP port is open from our location using telnet or the PowerShell **Test-NetConnection** cmdlet: **Test-NetConnection 20.224.74.16 -Port 3389.** You could also use other port scanning tools to test the port availability.

When a VM is created in a resource group it creates additional resources that is required for the VM such as a *disk*, a *network interface*, a *virtual network*, a *public IP address* and a *network security group*. You can use the **`az resource list`** command to list all resources in a specific resource group:

```
# List resources in a specific resource group
# Using Azure CLI table output
az resource list --resource-group "TestVM" --output table
# Using converted and filtered output
az resource list --resource-group "TestVM" | `
ConvertFrom-Json | `
Select-Object Name,Type
```

Figure 10.9 shows the output of running both of these commands:

```
PS C:\Temp> az resource list --resource-group "TestVM" --output table
Name                                                ResourceGroup   Location    Type                                         Status
--------------------------------------------------  --------------- ----------  -------------------------------------------  --------
TestVM_OsDisk_1_d4110a26c79b45de873a3143055e56db    TestVM          westeurope  Microsoft.Compute/disks
TestVM                                              TestVM          westeurope  Microsoft.Compute/virtualMachines
TestVMVMNic                                         TestVM          westeurope  Microsoft.Network/networkInterfaces
TestVMNSG                                           TestVM          westeurope  Microsoft.Network/networkSecurityGroups
TestVMPublicIP                                      TestVM          westeurope  Microsoft.Network/publicIPAddresses
TestVMVNET                                          TestVM          westeurope  Microsoft.Network/virtualNetworks
PS C:\Temp>
PS C:\Temp> az resource list --resource-group "TestVM" | ConvertFrom-Json | Select-Object Name,Type

name                                                type
----                                                ----
TestVM_OsDisk_1_d4110a26c79b45de873a3143055e56db    Microsoft.Compute/disks
TestVM                                              Microsoft.Compute/virtualMachines
TestVMVMNic                                         Microsoft.Network/networkInterfaces
TestVMNSG                                           Microsoft.Network/networkSecurityGroups
TestVMPublicIP                                      Microsoft.Network/publicIPAddresses
TestVMVNET                                          Microsoft.Network/virtualNetworks
```

Figure 10.9: *Listing resources in a specific resource group using both the Azure CLI table output and the converted and filtered output as a PowerShell object*

The different additional resources for the VM are listed. We are particularly interested in the **network security group** (**NSG**) resource.

Updating network security group rule and limit public access to VM

As we mentioned earlier in this recipe, the network security group is created with a rule allowing *any* source to access our VM on port 3389 using RDP. This introduces a security risk and opens the VM up for potential attacks on this port. A hacker could try to brute-force the username and password or try to use other vulnerabilities to try to access the VM. We want to update the network security group rule to limit the access to this port by only allowing our own public IP address as a valid source.

First, we use the `az network nsg rule list` command which allows us to list and view the current NSG rules:

```
az network nsg rule list --nsg-name "TestVMNSG" --resource-group "TestVM"
```

Figure 10.10 shows the list of the current NSG rules:

```
PS C:\Temp> az network nsg rule list --nsg-name "TestVMNSG" --resource-group "TestVM"
[
  {
    "access": "Allow",
    "destinationAddressPrefix": "*",
    "destinationAddressPrefixes": [],
    "destinationPortRange": "3389",
    "destinationPortRanges": [],
    "direction": "Inbound",
    "etag": "W/\"0af8563f-900e-4475-88a0-62602afd3ca9\"",
    "id": "/subscriptions/50c527e4-b726-4c71-b507-de6cfa9aefa4/resourceGroups/TestVM/providers/Microsoft.Network/networkSecurityGroups/TestVMNSG/securityRules/rdp",
    "name": "rdp",
    "priority": 1000,
    "protocol": "TCP",
    "provisioningState": "Succeeded",
    "resourceGroup": "TestVM",
    "sourceAddressPrefix": "*",
    "sourceAddressPrefixes": [],
    "sourcePortRange": "*",
    "sourcePortRanges": [],
    "type": "Microsoft.Network/networkSecurityGroups/securityRules"
  }
]
```

Figure 10.10: List of all current network security group rules for the VM

There is currently only one rule. We can see that it is named **rdp** and *allows inbound* traffic on port **3389** from **any** (*) source. What we are interested in here, is to update the **sourceAddressPrefix** attribute value from a wildcard to only contain our own public IP address instead.

For retrieving our own public IP address, we can use any service on the internet that provides us with our own public IP, such as **httpbin.org** or we can use either PowerShell's **Invoke-RestMethod** cmdlet or Azure CLI's **az rest** command to retrieve the public IP from such a source:

```
# Retrieve Public IP address from httpbin.org

# Using PowerShell's Invoke-RestMethod

$MyIp1 = (Invoke-RestMethod "http://httpbin.org/ip").origin
```

```
$MyIp1
# Using Azure CLI´s az rest command
$MyIp2 = az rest --method get --uri "http://httpbin.org/ip" --query
"origin" --output tsv
$MyIp2
```

As you can see in *Figure 10.11*, both methods returns the public IP address. By assigning the IP address to a variable, we can use the variable in the next commands:

```
PS C:\Temp> $MyIp1 = (Invoke-RestMethod "http://httpbin.org/ip").origin
PS C:\Temp> $MyIp1
5.186.57.95
PS C:\Temp> $MyIp2 = az rest --method get --uri "http://httpbin.org/ip" --query "origin" --output tsv
PS C:\Temp> $MyIp2
5.186.57.95
```

Figure 10.11: *Fetching public IP address using both*
PowerShell Invoke-RestMethod cmdlet and Azure CLI´s az rest command

To update the NSG rule we use the **az network nsg rule update** command:

```
# Update NSG Rule
az network nsg rule update `
--resource-group "TestVM" `
--nsg-name "TestVMNSG" `
--name "rdp" `
--source-address-prefix $MyIp1
```

We need to provide the resource group, the name of the NSG, the name of the NSG rule and then we use the **--source-address-prefix** parameter to specify our Public IP address. When the command is successfully executed, it outputs the updated NSG rule with the new attribute values, as shown in *Figure 10.12*:

```
PS C:\Temp> az network nsg rule update `
>> --resource-group "TestVM" `
>> --nsg-name "TestVMNSG" `
>> --name "rdp" `
>> --source-address-prefix $MyIp1
{
  "access": "Allow",
  "destinationAddressPrefix": "*",
  "destinationAddressPrefixes": [],
  "destinationPortRange": "3389",
  "destinationPortRanges": [],
  "direction": "Inbound",
  "etag": "W/\"faf48355-7eaa-46c0-b441-e5d8f39e681a\"",
  "id": "/subscriptions/50c527e4-b726-4c71-b507-de6cfa9aefa4/resourceGroups/TestVM/providers/Microsoft.Network/networkSecurityGroups/TestV
MNSG/securityRules/rdp",
  "name": "rdp",
  "priority": 1000,
  "protocol": "TCP",
  "provisioningState": "Succeeded",
  "resourceGroup": "TestVM",
  "sourceAddressPrefix": "5.186.57.95",
  "sourceAddressPrefixes": [],
  "sourcePortRange": "*",
  "sourcePortRanges": [],
  "type": "Microsoft.Network/networkSecurityGroups/securityRules"
}
```

Figure 10.12: *Output from the successful update of the NSG rule to*
only allow a specific IP address to access VM with RDP

We can see that the rule now only allows our own public IP address to access the VM using RDP. You can test that you can still access the VM with RDP, by using telnet or with the **Test-NetConnection** cmdlet from your location. If possible, you could also try to access it from another location, to verify that access is only allowed from your own public IP address.

Set up Windows Remote Management access to VM with NSG and local firewall rules

We can also configure our VM to be accessed using *Windows Remote Management*, in this recipe we set it up to use *basic authentication*. Since WinRM use port 5985 for HTTP access and basic authentication, we need to create a new *inbound NSG rule* that allows us to access that port on the VM. To create a new NSG rule we use the **az network nsg rule create** command:

```
# Create NSG rule to allow WinRM
az network nsg rule create `
--resource-group "TestVM" `
--nsg-name "TestVMNSG" `
--name "WinRM" `
--source-address-prefix $MyIp1 `
--destination-port-range 5985 `
--priority 1001 `
--protocol "TCP"
```

We specify the resource group where the NSG is located. The name of the NSG where we want to create the new rule. We use the **--name** parameter to specify a new name for the rule and we use the **--source-address-prefix** to only allow our public IP address as a source. The **--destination-port-range** is used to specify the destination port that should be allowed. The **--priority** parameter is a mandatory parameter that must be unique for each rule collection (inbound or outbound rule collection) in the NSG. The lower the priority number, the higher the priority. In *Figure 10.12* you can see that the *rdp* rule have a priority of 1000, so we just specify the next priority number in line for this parameter. We explicitly set the **--protocol** parameter as TCP, since the default value for this parameter is a wildcard, applying all available protocols (Ah, Esp, Icmp, Tcp and Udp). We only need the TCP protocol allowed. We could also specify the **--allow** parameter and the **--direction** parameter, but they default to *allow* and *inbound*, which are the values we are going to need anyways. Once the command is successfully executed, the new NSG rule is created, and the command outputs the new rule as shown in *Figure 10.13*:

```
PS C:\Temp> az network nsg rule create `
>> --resource-group "TestVM" `
>> --nsg-name "TestVMNSG" `
>> --name "WinRM" `
>> --source-address-prefix $MyIp1 `
>> --destination-port-range 5985 `
>> --priority 1001 `
>> --protocol "TCP"
{
  "access": "Allow",
  "destinationAddressPrefix": "*",
  "destinationAddressPrefixes": [],
  "destinationPortRange": "5985",
  "destinationPortRanges": [],
  "direction": "Inbound",
  "etag": "W/\"202b84ba-c79e-4afc-98b5-d33cb6733352\"",
  "id": "/subscriptions/50c527e4-b726-4c71-b507-de6cfa9aefa4/resourceGroups/TestVM/providers/Microsoft.Network/networkSecurityGroups/TestV
MNSG/securityRules/WinRM",
  "name": "WinRM",
  "priority": 1001,
  "protocol": "Tcp",
  "provisioningState": "Succeeded",
  "resourceGroup": "TestVM",
  "sourceAddressPrefix": "5.186.57.95",
  "sourceAddressPrefixes": [],
  "sourcePortRange": "*",
  "sourcePortRanges": [],
  "type": "Microsoft.Network/networkSecurityGroups/securityRules"
}
```

Figure 10.13: *Successfully creation of a new NSG rule using
the az network nsg rule create command*

We are not done yet. Since Windows own local firewall typically comes with a firewall rule that denies access to Windows Remote Management from public locations and only allows public access to *local subnet* remote addresses, we are still not able to access port 5985 even though the NSG rule is created. The NSG is not to be mistaken with Windows local firewall. *Figure 10.14* shows the current firewall rules for Windows Remote Management within the VM:

Inbound Rules							
Name	Group	Profile	Enabled	Remote Address	Local Address	Local Port	Action
Windows Remote Management (HTTP-In)	Windows Remote Manage...	Domain, Private	Yes	Any	Any	5985	Allow
Windows Remote Management (HTTP-In)	Windows Remote Manage...	Public	Yes	Local subnet	Any	5985	Allow

Figure 10.14: *Current Windows Remote Management firewall rules on the VM*

We need to create a firewall rule in the local firewall allowing our public IP address access to the port 5985.

The **az vm run-command invoke** allows us to execute a script on the VM. We can use this command to execute the **New-NetFirewallRule** cmdlet on the VM, creating a new firewall rule that allows our IP address to access the port 5985:

```
az vm run-command invoke `

--command-id RunPowerShellScript `

--name "TestVM" `

--resource-group "TestVM" `

--scripts 'New-NetFirewallRule -Name Allow_WinRM_from_MyIP -DisplayName
Allow_WinRM_from_MyIP -Direction Inbound -Action Allow -Protocol TCP
-LocalPort 5985 -RemoteAddress 5.186.57.95'
```

The `--name` and `--resource-group` parameters are the name of the VM and the resource group the VM resides in. The `--command-id` parameter is an Azure command id that can be found using the `az vm run-command list` command that list available command id´s that can be used for this command. Since we are going to run a cmdlet we use the `RunPowerShellScript` command id. It is used to run scripts, but in this case we can compare a cmdlet to a simple script. In the `--scripts` parameter we specify the script, or in this case the `New-NetFirewallRule` cmdlet we want to execute. Note that the cmdlet and its parameters are enclosed within single quotes. For the parameters for the `New-NetFirewallRule` cmdlet, we specify that we want to `allow inbound` traffic on *TCP* port *5985* from the specified IP address *5.186.57.95*. *Figure 10.15* shows the successful execution of the command:

```
PS C:\Temp> az vm run-command invoke `
>> --command-id RunPowerShellScript `
>> --name "TestVM" `
>> --resource-group "TestVM" `
>> --scripts 'New-NetFirewallRule -Name Allow_WinRM_from_MyIP -DisplayName Allow_WinRM_from_MyIP -Direction Inbound -Action Allow -Protoco
l TCP -LocalPort 5985 -RemoteAddress 5.186.57.95'
{
  "value": [
    {
      "code": "ComponentStatus/StdOut/succeeded",
      "displayStatus": "Provisioning succeeded",
      "level": "Info",
      "message": "Name                        : Allow_WinRM_from_MyIP\nDisplayName                : Allow_WinRM_from_MyIP\nDescriptio
n                        : \nDisplayGroup                : \nGroup                : \nEnabled                : True\nProfile                :
                : Any\nPlatform                : {}\nDirection                : Inbound\nAction                : 
Allow\nEdgeTraversalPolicy        : Block\nLooseSourceMapping        : False\nLocalOnlyMapping        : False\nOwner
                : \nPrimaryStatus                : OK\nStatus                : The rule was parsed successfully from the store. (
65536)\nEnforcementStatus                : NotApplicable\nPolicyStoreSource        : PersistentStore\nPolicyStoreSourceType        : Lo
cal\nRemoteDynamicKeywordAddresses : {}\nPolicyAppId                : \n\n\n",
      "time": null
    },
    {
      "code": "ComponentStatus/StdErr/succeeded",
      "displayStatus": "Provisioning succeeded",
      "level": "Info",
      "message": "",
      "time": null
    }
  ]
}
```

Figure 10.15: Successful execution of the az vm run-command invoke command

The command outputs the messages from either *StdOut* (standard out stream) or *StdErr* (standard error stream) from the cmdlet executed on the VM. If the message is returned in the StdOut stream, the cmdlet has been successfully executed on the VM. In case of any errors running the cmdlet on the VM, it would return a message in the StdErr stream output. In this case the cmdlet was successfully executed on the VM. *Figure 10.16* shows that the new firewall rule is added to the local firewall on the VM:

Inbound Rules

Name	Group	Profile	Enabled	Remote Address	Local Address	Local Port	Action
Allow_WinRM_from_MyIP		All	Yes	5.186.57.95	Any	5985	Allow
Windows Remote Management (HTTP-In)	Windows Remote Management	Public	Yes	Local subnet	Any	5985	Allow
Windows Remote Management (HTTP-In)	Windows Remote Management	Domain, Private	Yes	Any	Any	5985	Allow

Figure 10.16: Firewall rule successfully created on the VM using
the az vm run-command invoke command

We should now be able to access the VM on port 5985 from clients using our public IP address. To verify this, we use the `Test-NetConnection` cmdlet: `Test-NetConnection`

5.186.57.95 -Port 5985. Again, we could also use telnet or any other port scanning tool.

Since we are going to use basic authentication with Windows Remote Management to the VM, we need to add the VM IP address to the clients **TrustedHosts** list:

```
set-item wsman:\localhost\Client\TrustedHosts -value 20.224.74.16
```

Once the IP is added to the **TrustedHosts** list, all pre-requisites for accessing the VM using Windows Remote Management should be in place, and we should be able to create a session too and access the VM using Windows Remote Management:

```
# Create a new WinRM remote session to the VM

$Session = New-PSSession -ComputerName 20.224.74.16 -Credential (Get-Credential)
```

Figure 10.17 shows the successful creation of a session to the VM and how we can use that session to access and enter the VM directly using Windows Remote management:

```
PS C:\Temp> set-item wsman:\localhost\Client\TrustedHosts -value 20.224.74.16

WinRM Security Configuration.
This command modifies the TrustedHosts list for the WinRM client. The computers in the TrustedHosts list might not be authenticated. The
client might send credential information to these computers. Are you sure that you want to modify this list?
[Y] Yes  [N] No  [S] Suspend  [?] Help (default is "Y"): y
PS C:\Temp>
PS C:\Temp> $Session = New-PSSession -ComputerName 20.224.74.16 -Credential (Get-Credential)

PowerShell credential request
Enter your credentials.
User: TestUser
Password for user TestUser: **************

PS C:\Temp> $Session

 Id Name          Transport ComputerName    ComputerType    State   ConfigurationName       Availability
 -- ----          --------- ------------    ------------    -----   -----------------       ------------
  2 Runspace2     WSMan     20.224.74.16    RemoteMachine   Opened  Microsoft.PowerShell      Available

PS C:\Temp> Enter-PSSession -Session $Session
[20.224.74.16]: PS C:\Users\TestUser\Documents> $Env:COMPUTERNAME
TestVM
```

Figure 10.17: Creating and entering a session to
the VM after all pre-requisites for WinRM is set up

Delete virtual machine and resource group

Once we are done working with a VM we can delete it using the **az vm delete** command:

```
# Delete a vm

az vm delete `

--resource-group "TestVM" `

--name "TestVM" `

--yes
```

We only need to provide the name of the resource group and the name of the specific VM to delete it. The **--yes** switch parameter allows for deletion without being prompted for confirmation. This command does not return any output upon successful deletion, and it only deletes the VM and not its associated resources. *Figure 10.18* shows the content of the resource group after the VM have been successfully deleted:

```
PS C:\Temp> az vm delete `
>> --resource-group "TestVM" `
>> --name "TestVM" `
>> --yes
PS C:\Temp> az resource list --resource-group "TestVM" --output table
Name                                          ResourceGroup   Location     Type                                          Status
--------------------------------------------  --------------  -----------  --------------------------------------------  --------
TestVM_OsDisk_1_d4110a26c79b45de873a3143055e56db  TESTVM          westeurope   Microsoft.Compute/disks
TestVMVMNic                                   TestVM          westeurope   Microsoft.Network/networkInterfaces
TestVMNSG                                     TestVM          westeurope   Microsoft.Network/networkSecurityGroups
TestVMPublicIP                               TestVM          westeurope   Microsoft.Network/publicIPAddresses
TestVMVNET                                    TestVM          westeurope   Microsoft.Network/virtualNetworks
```

Figure 10.18: Content of the resource group after deletion of the VM

The VM is gone but the other VM resources are still available in the resource group. Resources such as the disk and the public IP are billable resources so you should remove these resources unless you might still need them for other reasons. You can remove each resource individually using the specific **az delete** command for that type of resource:

```
# Delete disk

az disk delete `

--resource-group "TestVM" `

--name "TestVM_OsDisk_1_d4110a26c79b45de873a3143055e56db"

# Delete network interface (NIC)

az network nic delete `

--resource-group "TestVM" `

--name "TestVMVMNic"

# Delete NSG

az network nsg delete `

--resource-group "TestVM" `

--name "TestVMNSG"

# Delete Public IP address

az network public-ip delete `

--resource-group "TestVM" `

--name "TestVMPublicIP"

# Delete virtual network (VNET)

az network vnet delete `

--resource-group "testVM" `

--name "TestVMVNET"
```

Or you can delete the entire resource group which will not only delete the group itself but also all resources within it:

```
az group delete `
--name "TestVM"
```

It could take a while deleting a resource group, depending on the number and types of resources it contains. Once it is deleted all the resources within and the reference to that resource is completely removed from your subscription, as shown in *Figure 10.19*:

```
PS C:\Temp> az group delete `
>> --name "TestVM"
Are you sure you want to perform this operation? (y/n): y
PS C:\Temp> az resource list --resource-group "TestVM" --output table
(ResourceGroupNotFound) Resource group 'TestVM' could not be found.
Code: ResourceGroupNotFound
Message: Resource group 'TestVM' could not be found.
```

Figure 10.19: Successful deletion of a resource group and all of its resources

We have created a new VM. Updated the NSG rule for port 3389 (RDP) to only allow a specific public IP address as a source for accessing the VM. We have created a new NSG rule allowing a specific public IP address to access port 5985 (WinRM) for Windows Remote Management and we have created a firewall rule allowing a specific public IP address to access port 5985 (WinRM) in the local firewall of the VM. The VM´s public IP address is added to the **TrustedHosts** list on the client that needs to access the VM. This client is now able to access the VM using Windows Remote Management where we can manage all aspects of the VM using PowerShell. Finally, we have deleted the VM and after that, deleted the resource group and all the remaining associated resources.

Managing Azure storage accounts, blob containers, blobs and file shares

When working with Azure resources such as virtual machines, databases, Kubernetes clusters etc. The data for such resources needs to be placed somewhere. Disks for virtual machines and databases can be placed in storage accounts, you can create file shares to store your log files from Kubernetes and you can use blob containers to store **Virtual Machine Disks (VHDs)** or as backup containers for files and so on.

Azure Storage accounts, blob containers and file shares are key components of Microsoft Azure's cloud storage services, offering scalable, durable, and highly available data storage for various use cases. Managing Azure storage accounts, blob containers, blobs and file shares are common tasks when working with Azure resources.

An Azure Storage Account is a logical container that holds all your Azure Storage data objects, including blob containers and blobs, files, queues, tables, and disks. Each storage account is associated with a specific region and is defined by a unique name within the Azure namespace.

Azure Blob Containers are specific storage entities within an Azure Storage Account that are used to organize and manage blobs. Blobs are unstructured data objects, and blob containers provide a way to group related blobs together.

Azure File shares also called Azure file Storage provides fully managed, scalable file shares in the cloud that can be mounted as network drives by cloud or on-premises machines. It offers a way to share files and data across multiple machines and applications.

Recipe 60: Create and manage storage accounts

In this recipe we will look at some of the basic operations for creating and managing Azure Storage Accounts using Azure CLI and PowerShell. Azure Storage Accounts offer various features and settings that can be configured for creating, accessing and managing storage accounts. Be sure to check the official Azure documentation for more advanced updated configurations and options.

Create a storage account

We start by creating a new resource group for the storage account. Then, we can create a new storage account using the **az storage account create** command. We specify a name for the storage account. The name must be unique across Azure. We specify the resource group and the region to place the storage account in. Furthermore, we specify the **--sku** parameter which is used to choose the desired replication type. In this case, we specify the **Standard_LRS** type, which is *locally redundant storage*. The different available sku types can be found here: **https://learn.microsoft.com/en-us/rest/api/storagerp/srp_sku_types**. We also specify the **--access-tier** parameter with the **Hot** value. The access tier specifies how frequently we might want to access, and use data and how to manage the cost. Cool and archive tiers are used for data that are infrequently accessed such as archived and backup data, and hot and premium tiers for data that are frequently accessed. There are a lot of other optional parameters for this command. Refer to the official Azure documentation for more details:

```
# Create a new resource group
$Group = az group create `
--name "RG-Storage" `
--location westeurope
# Assign the group name from the return data to the $GroupName variable
$GroupName = $Group | ConvertFrom-Json | Select-Object -ExpandProperty Name
# Create a storage account
az storage account create `
--name "moppleitstorage" `
--resource-group $GroupName `
```

```
--location "westeurope" `
--sku "Standard_LRS" `
--access-tier "Hot"
```

List storage accounts

You can list all your Azure storage accounts in a specific resource group or across all your Azure subscriptions using the **az storage account list** command. A storage account contains a lot of attributes that will be listed by the return output. You can convert and filter the command to list specific attributes:

```
# List All storage accounts
az storage account list
# List storage accounts in specific resource group
az storage account list `
--resource-group $GroupName
# List storage account as table output
az storage account list `
--resource-group $GroupName `
--output table
# List storage account and specific properties
az storage account list `
--resource-group $GroupName | `
ConvertFrom-Json | `
Select-Object Name,Location,Sku,Kind,AccessTier
```

Update storage account settings

You can update the settings of an existing storage account such as changing the access tier or changing the minimum TLS version to be permitted on requests to storage and so on. We use the **az storage account update** command:

```
# Update an existing storage accounts settings
az storage account update `
--name "moppleitstorage" `
--resource-group $GroupName `
--access-tier "Cool" `
--min-tls-version "TLS1_2"
```

Retrieve storage account connection string

For applications to be able to access storage accounts, it often requires the connection string for the storage account. This connection string can be retrieved using the **az storage account show-connection-string** command:

```
az storage account show-connection-string `
--name "moppleitstorage" `
--resource-group $GroupName
```

Retrieve storage account keys

You can retrieve and list the access keys for a storage account using the **az storage account keys list** command. These keys are used to authenticate and authorize access to the storage account:

```
# Retrieve storage account keys
az storage account keys list `
--account-name "moppleitstorage" `
--resource-group $GroupName
```

Delete a storage account

You can delete a storage account and all its data using the **az storage account delete** command:

```
# Delete a storage account
az storage account delete `
--name "moppleitstorage" `
--resource-group $GroupName `
--yes
```

Recipe 61: Create and manage blob containers and blobs

In this recipe we will look at some of the basic operations for creating and managing Azure blob containers and blobs using Azure CLI and PowerShell. Blob containers are a component inside storage accounts and blobs are data objects inside blob containers. A *blob* in the context of blob containers typically refers to a type of data that is used for storing large amounts of unstructured data, such as text or binary data. *Blob* simply stands for: *Binary Large Object*. For the following examples we create a new resource group and storage account. We also need to use a storage account key as credentials for the blob commands. This key is retrieved from the storage account and assigned to a variable.

We also assign the names of the group and storage account to variables which are used throughout this recipe:

```
# Create a resource group for blobs
$GroupName = az group create `
--name "RG-Blobs" `
--location westeurope | `
ConvertFrom-Json | `
Select-Object -ExpandProperty Name
# Create a storage account for blobs
$StorageName = az storage account create `
--name "moppleitblobs" `
--resource-group $GroupName `
--location "westeurope" `
--sku "Standard_LRS" `
--access-tier "Hot" | `
ConvertFrom-Json | `
Select-Object -ExpandProperty Name
# Retrieve storage account key
$StorageKey = az storage account keys list `
--account-name $StorageName `
--resource-group $GroupName | `
ConvertFrom-Json | `
Select-Object -ExpandProperty value -First 1
```

Create a blob container

To create a blob container within a storage account we use the **az storage container create** command. We specify the name of the new blob container using the **--name** parameter. The --**account-name** parameter is the storage accounts name and the **--account-key** parameter is the storage accounts access key:

```
# Create a blob container
az storage container create `
--name "blobcontainer" `
--account-name $StorageName `
--account-key $StorageKey
```

Note: We need to specify the storage account name and the storage account key, using the --account-name and --account-key parameters for almost all of the blob and container commands. You could omit the --account-key parameter, but you will get a warning when you execute the commands stating that there are no credentials provided in your command and environment, you will then be prompted for the account key for your storage account. It is recommended to provide --connection-string, --account-key or --sas-token in your command as credentials.

List blob containers

We can list all blob containers within a storage account using the **az storage container list** command:

```
# List blob containers
az storage container list `
--account-name $StorageName `
--account-key $StorageKey
```

Upload local file to blob container

We can upload local files to a blob container using the **az storage blob upload** command. The **--container-name** parameter is used to specify the name of the specific bloc container and the **--file** parameter is used to specify the path to a local file. The **--type** parameter is used to indicate that this is a *block* type blob. If we were to upload a .vhd file, the type would default to *page* instead:

```
# Upload a file to a blob container
az storage blob upload `
--account-name $StorageName `
--account-key $StorageKey `
--type block `
--file C:\Temp\test.txt `
--container-name "blobcontainer"
```

List blobs in a blob container

To list all blob files within a blob container we use the **az storage blob list** command:

```
# List all blobs in a blob container
az storage blob list `
--account-name $StorageName `
--account-key $StorageKey `
```

```
--container-name "blobcontainer"
```

Download blobs from blob container

You can download a file from a blob container using the **az storage blob download** command. The **--name** parameter is used to specify the file within the blob container that we want to download, and the **--file** parameter is used to specify a local path to save the file too. You can also use this parameter to rename the file if needed:

```
# Download a file from a blob container
az storage blob download `
--account-name $StorageName `
--account-key $StorageKey `
--container-name "blobcontainer" `
--name "test.txt" `
--file C:\Temp\NewTest.txt
```

Delete blobs from blob container

To delete blobs from a blob container we use the **az storage blob delete** command. The **--name** parameter is used to specify the file in the blob container that we want to delete:

```
# Delete a blob (file) in a blob container
az storage blob delete `
--account-name $StorageName `
--account-key $StorageKey `
--container-name "blobcontainer" `
--name "test.txt"
```

Delete a blob container

You can delete a blob container and all the containing blobs using the **az storage container delete** command:

```
# Delete a blob container
az storage container delete `
--account-name $StorageName `
--account-key $StorageKey `
--name "blobcontainer"
```

Recipe 62: Create and manage file shares

In this recipe we will look at some of the basic operations for creating and managing Azure file shares using Azure CLI and PowerShell. We will use the same storage account that we created in the previous recipe. The name of the storage account is assigned to the **$StorageName** variable and the access key for the storage account is assigned to the **$StorageKey** variable. You can also create a new storage account if needed, then re-assign the new storage account name and key to these variables.

Create a file share

You can create a file share using the **az storage share create** command. You must provide a name for the share using the **--name** parameter and you must also add a quota, which specifies the maximum size of the share in Gigabytes, using the **--quota** parameter. The quota must be greater than 0 and no more than 5 Terabytes (5120GB):

```
# Create a file share
az storage share create `
--account-name $StorageName `
--account-key $StorageKey `
--name "myshare" `
--quota 5
```

List file shares

You can list all file shares within a storage account using the **az storage share list** command:

```
# List file shares
az storage share list `
--account-name $StorageName `
--account-key $StorageKey
```

Generate a Shared Access Signature (SAS) for a file share

A shared access signature or SAS token can be used to grant temporary access to a file share without sharing the storage account key. You can generate a SAS token using the **az storage share generate-sas** command. We need to specify a set of permissions using the **--permissions** parameter. Valid values are: *(c)reate (d)elete (l)ist (r)ead (w)rite* and they can be used in combination. We also need to specify an expiry date for the token using the **--expiry** parameter in *UTC datetime (Y-m-d'T'H:M'Z')* format. Note that the command will return the token as an output. Copy and save the token or assign it to a variable for later use within the same session:

```
# Generate SAS token for file share
az storage share generate-sas `
--account-name $StorageName `
--account-key $StorageKey `
--name "myshare" `
--permissions "lrw" `
--expiry "2023-12-31T23:59:59Z"
```

Map a file share to a local network drive

A file share can be mapped locally as a network drive.

1. Create a credential object using the storage account key (**$StorageKey**) as the password and the storage account name as the username (**$StorageName**):

   ```
   # 1: Create a Credential Object
   $Pwd = $StorageKey | Convertto-SecureString -AsPlainText -force
   $Username = $StorageName
   $Creds = New-Object PSCredential -ArgumentList $Username, $Pwd
   ```

   You can also store the credentials in credential manager to ensure that the drive will be persistent on server/client reboot. We can use the **cmd** command **cmdkey** for this task:

   ```
   # 1.1: Save the password so the drive will persist on reboot
   cmd.exe /C "cmdkey /add:`"$StorageName.file.core.windows.net`" /
   user:`"localhost\$StorageName`" /pass:`"$StorageKey`""
   ```

2. Map the drive locally using the **New-PSDrive** cmdlet:

   ```
   # 2: Map the drive locally
   New-PSDrive -Name "Z" `
   -PSProvider FileSystem `
   -Root "\\$StorageName.file.core.windows.net\myshare" `
   -Credential $Creds `
   -Persist
   ```

Note: If you store the credentials in credential manager, you should omit the -credential parameter. Also change the drive name/letter if needed. The drive should now be mapped locally as a network drive with the specified drive letter.

3. When you are finished working with the drive, you can remove it:

```
# 3. Remove PS drive
Remove-PSDrive -Name "Z"
```

Delete a file share

You can delete a file share using the **az storage share delete** command. This will delete all files and directories within the file share. If *soft-delete* is enabled for the file share, you are able to undelete it within a retention period:

```
# Delete a file share
az storage share delete `
--account-name $StorageName `
--account-key $StorageKey `
--name "myshare"
```

There are many ways to work with data and files in Azure. This recipe provides the most common commands used for working with and managing storage accounts, blob containers, blob data and file shares in Azure. A lot of the commands used for storage management are quite similar such as **az storage container create, az storage share create**, **az storage container delete**, **az storage blob delete**, **az storage share delete** and so on. A lot of the commands also provides additional parameters. You can refer to the official updated Azure documentation when working with Azure CLI commands in general or use the **az find** robot command for examples of command usage.

Azure EntraID: Users, groups and permissions

Azure provides a vast amount of services and features such as Azure EntraID (previously called Azure Active Directory), AKS (Azure Kubernetes Service), SQL Databases and Data warehouses, Servicebus (message queues), backups, virtual machines (VMs) and many more. All of these services and features can be managed using PowerShell and Azure CLI. It is all about finding the right commands for specific services and the right sub commands for performing particular tasks and creating and managing specific resources.

However, Azure is not only about creating and managing specific resources it is also about managing and controlling the access *too* and permissions *for* these resources. Not all users in your company should have access to all resources and you should always work on the principal of *least privileged* access. Which means that users should only have access to the specific resources they need and nothing more.

Azure provides an Active Directory service called EntraID which uses some of the same principals as on-premise Active Directory Domain Service for managing users, groups and access control and permissions to resources.

Recipe 63: Managing users, groups, and resource access permissions

Working with users in Azure is much like working with users in Active Directory. You create, manage, and delete users. Users can be members of groups and users and groups can be granted access permissions to different resources using Azure **Role-Based-Access-Control (RBAC).** In Azure you can grant permissions for all resources from the subscription level down to a single specific resource. Usually, administrators might be global admins and have access to manage all resources within a subscription, but employees and users should be granted access and permissions to only the specific resources they should be able to work with. Azure use inheritance meaning that whenever you grant a user or group permission to a resource, the permissions will be inherited for all resources within or under that resource. If a user or group is granted permissions to a *subscription* all resources under that subscription such as resource groups and the specific resources within these resource groups will inherit these permissions. If a user or group is granted permissions to a specific resource group all resources within that resource group will inherit these permissions for the user and group. You can set permissions on all kinds of resources within Azure and grant users and groups direct permission to only specific resources. Each type of resource can have different and specific roles for that kind of resource, which can be assigned to users and groups. But all resources have three common general permission roles:

- **Owner**: Grants full access to manage all resources including the assignment of roles.

- **Contributor**: Grants full access to manage all resources but does not allow role assignment.

- **Reader**: View all resources but does not allow to make any changes.

It is also possible to create custom roles that grants custom access to resources. To grant access to resources you assign a role to a user or a group.

The case in this recipe is: We need to create a new set of resources within a new resource group. Three new users' needs access as *contributors* to this resource group and all the resources that will be created within it. These users must not have access to any other resources within Azure besides those in this specific resource group.

1. We create the resource group using the **az group create** command. We convert the output from JSON and assign the output to the **$RG** variable:

```
# Create resource group
$RG = az group create `
--name "RG-App01" `
--location "westeurope" | `
ConvertFrom-Json
```

2. We create the EntraID group using the **az ad group create** command. Converting the output and assigning it to the **$ADGroup** variable:

```
# Create EntraID group
$AdGroup = az ad group create `
--display-name "AccessTo-RG-App01" `
--mail-nickname "AccessTo-RG-App01" | `
ConvertFrom-Json
```

3. To create new EntraID users we need a few required parameters: **--display-name**, **--user-principal-name** and **--password**. We create an array and assign it to the **$Users** variable. Within the array we create a Hashtable for each user with properties for each of the required parameters:

```
# Create 3 new EntraID users
$Users = @(
    @{
        name = "Liam Anderson"
        upn = "Lian@bio-rent.dk"
        password = "@Test123456789"
    }
    @{
        name = "Mia Garcia"
        upn = "Miga@bio-rent.dk"
        password = "@Test123456789"
    }
    @{
        name = "Oliver Patel"
        upn = "Olpa@bio-rent.dk"
        password = "@Test123456789"
    }
)
```

4. We use a **foreach** loop to loop through the **$Users** array and we create each EntraID user using the **az ad user create** command and apply the parameters from the users properties in the Hashtable. We convert the command output from JSON and assign it to the **$ADUser** variable. For each EntraID user that is created we add that user as a member of the EntraID group **$ADGroup** using the **az ad group member add** command. As you can see we use the **$ADGroup.id** property to specify the specific EntraID group and the specific **$User.id** property to specify the user to add to the group:

```
foreach ($User in $Users){
    # Create EntraID user
    $ADUser = az ad user create `
    --display-name "$($User.name)" `
    --user-principal-name "$($User.upn)" `
    --password "$($User.password)" | `
    ConvertFrom-Json
    # Add user to EntraID group
    az ad group member add `
    --group "$($AdGroup.id)" `
    --member-id "$($ADUser.id)"
}
```

5. We use the **az role assignment create** command to assign the **contributor** role for the resource group **$RG** to the **EntraID** group **$ADGroup**. We use the **$ADGroup.id** property for the **--assignee** parameter and the **$RG.id** property for the **--scope** parameter:

```
# Assign contributor role for resource group to EntraID Group
az role assignment create `
--assignee "$($AdGroup.id)" `
--role "Contributor" `
--scope "$($RG.id)"
```

To summarize, we create a new resource group called **RG-App01** and an EntraID group called **AccessTo-RG-App01**. We then create three new EntraID users by looping through an array containing the minimum required properties for each user within a Hashtable in the array. After each user is created, we add the user as a member of the **AccessTo-RG-App01** EntraID group. Finally, we assign the **contributor** role to the **AccessTo-RG-App01** EntraID group for the **RG-App01** resource group. All resources that are created within the **RG-App01** resource group will inherit the specified role permissions and all users within the **AccessTo-RG-App01** EntraID group will be granted access to these resources due to the inheritance.

6. We can verify the role assignment to the resource group has been granted to the EntraID group using the **az role assignment list** command using the scope id for the resource group, as shown in *Figure 10.20*:

```
PS C:\Temp> az role assignment list --scope "$($RG.id)"
[
  {
    "condition": null,
    "conditionVersion": null,
    "createdBy": "df582b3d-ea77-4ccf-a743-2d021f9e4f96",
    "createdOn": "2023-10-18T07:51:44.178517+00:00",
    "delegatedManagedIdentityResourceId": null,
    "description": null,
    "id": "/subscriptions/50c527e4-b726-4c71-b507-de6cfa9aefa4/resourceGroups/RG-App01/providers/Microsoft.Authorization/roleAssignments/8
ef41cc0-fbaa-4881-92e5-2ba71b843340",
    "name": "8ef41cc0-fbaa-4881-92e5-2ba71b843340",
    "principalId": "3809c23f-45dd-46ff-8459-206696c21730",
    "principalName": "AccessTo-RG-App01",
    "principalType": "Group",
    "resourceGroup": "RG-App01",
    "roleDefinitionId": "/subscriptions/50c527e4-b726-4c71-b507-de6cfa9aefa4/providers/Microsoft.Authorization/roleDefinitions/b24988ac-61
80-42a0-ab88-20f7382dd24c",
    "roleDefinitionName": "Contributor",
    "scope": "/subscriptions/50c527e4-b726-4c71-b507-de6cfa9aefa4/resourceGroups/RG-App01",
    "type": "Microsoft.Authorization/roleAssignments",
    "updatedBy": "df582b3d-ea77-4ccf-a743-2d021f9e4f96",
    "updatedOn": "2023-10-18T07:51:44.178517+00:00"
  }
]
```

Figure 10.20: Listing role assignments for a specific resource
group using the resource groups scope id

7. We can see that the **contributor** role has been assigned to the **AccessTo-RG-App01** EntraID group for the **RG-App01** resource group scope. We can then check the members of the **AccessTo-RG-App01** EntraID group using the **az ad group member list** command to verify that the expected users not only are actually created as EntraID users but also that they are members of the EntraID group as expected. This is shown in *Figure 10.21*:

```
PS C:\Temp> az ad group member list --group "$($AdGroup.displayname)" | `
>> ConvertFrom-Json | `
>> Select-Object DisplayName,UserPrincipalName

displayName     userPrincipalName
-----------     -----------------
Liam Anderson   Lian@bio-rent.dk
Mia Garcia      Miga@bio-rent.dk
Oliver Patel    Olpa@bio-rent.dk
```

Figure 10.21: Listing members of the EntraID group,
verifying the correct members but also that the users exist in EntraID

These relatively few commands give a clear insight into creating and managing EntraID users and groups and how to assign permissions using role-based-access-control to Azure resources. You use the **az ad** and its sub-commands such as **az ad user** and **az ad group** to manage EntraID users and groups and the **az role** and its sub-commands to manage role-based-access-control and resource permissions.

These commands can be combined into and executed as a single script. The principals from the *Recipe 57: Developing automation scripts for creating AD users and AD users in bulk in Chapter 9, Active Directory management* can be applied to the creation of users, groups and role assignments in Azure for automating the processes of creating and managing users, groups and permissions and for performing such operations in bulk.

Automating Azure resource provisioning and management

By automating the provisioning and management of Azure resources you can not only create and manage EntraID users, groups, and permissions but you can also create entire Azure infrastructures in a matter of minutes and then tear them down just as easily when they have fulfilled their purpose. For automating the provisioning of Azure resources, we can create PowerShell scripts that utilizes the Azure CLI commands, from the previous recipes and examples and combine these commands into powerful scripts for automation and bulk processing purposes.

Azure also introduces the use of **Azure Resource Manager Templates (ARM templates)** for implementing infrastructure as code. ARM templates are JSON files that defines the infrastructure and configurations for the required deployments. In the template you specify the resources to deploy and the properties for those resources. The use of ARM templates are outside of the scope of this book. If you want to learn more about ARM templates refer to the official ARM template documentation: **https://learn.microsoft.com/ en-us/azure/azure-resource-manager/templates/**.

Before we can begin to automatically deploy resources in Azure whether it being by utilizing the Azure CLI commands in scripts and applications or by using ARM templates, we need a method that does not require us to manually logging in to Azure.

Recipe 64: Create a Service principal to automatically connect to Azure using scripts

Instead of having to sign in manually and for having applications to sign in as a fully privileged user, Azure offers service principals. An Azure service principal is an identity created for use with scripts and applications but is also used for hosted services and other automation tools. Scripts, applications and other automation tools should have restricted permissions to ensure that access to Azure resources is secure and should always adhere to the principal of *least privileges*. A service principal identity is used to access Azure resources.

For this recipe we create a new resource group called **RG-Infrastructure** and then we create a service principal called **SP-RG-Infrastructure** with **Contributor** permissions to that resource group using the **az ad sp create-for-rbac** command. We assign the output from this command to the **$SP** variable:

```
# Create resource group
$RG = az group create `
--name "RG-Infrastructure" `
--location "westeurope" | `
ConvertFrom-Json
```

```
# Create a service principal with contributor permissions
# to a resource group
$SP = az ad sp create-for-rbac `
--name "SP-RG-Infrastructure" `
--role "Contributor" `
--scopes "$($RG.id)" | `
ConvertFrom-Json
```

When you create a service principal the output includes credentials for that service principal identity such as the **app id** and **password**. The service principal creation output is shown in *Figure 10.22*:

```
PS C:\Temp> $RG = az group create `
>> --name "RG-Infrastructure" `
>> --location "westeurope" | `
>> ConvertFrom-Json
PS C:\Temp> $SP = az ad sp create-for-rbac `
>> --name "SP-RG-Infrastructure" `
>> --role "Contributor" `
>> --scopes "$($RG.id)" | `
>> ConvertFrom-Json
WARNING: Creating 'Contributor' role assignment under scope '/subscriptions/50c527e4-b726-4c71-b507-de6cfa9aefa4/resourceGroups/RG-Infrast
ructure'
WARNING: The output includes credentials that you must protect. Be sure that you do not include these credentials in your code or check th
e credentials into your source control. For more information, see https://aka.ms/azadsp-cli
PS C:\Temp> $SP

appId                                displayName        password                                       tenant
-----                                -----------        --------                                       ------
7e78e975-3d6e-45ca-8d9a-4614087ae284 SP-RG-Infrastructure -aT8Q~pe6f9Jz_q3V-wK7uVWV.eVISIh5aVJFcjL 57f387c6-3587-4ae7-a156-c9c7d10d7df6
```

Figure 10.22: Creation of a service principal identity and using the az ad sp create-for-rbac command and its output

Note: Always store credentials for service principals that should be used in scripts and applications in a secure fashion, or at least provide them in configuration files. Never hardcode credentials and other kinds of secrets directly into scripts and applications.

To use the service principal to login to Azure in a script or application, use the **az login** command with the **--service-principal** switch parameter and then provide the **--username**, **--password** and **--tenant** parameters for that service principal:

```
# Login to Azure using service principal
az login --service-principal `
--username <APP_ID> `
--password <CLIENT_SECRET/SP_PASSWORD> `
--tenant <TENANT_ID>
```

Note that when the first character of a password is **"-"** (dash/minus sign) you must specify the password parameter like this: **--password=<SP_PASSWORD>**. This will also be stated in an error message if it is applied incorrectly:

```
# Login to Azure using service principal (Special)
az login --service-principal `
```

```
--username <APP_ID> `
--password=<CLIENT_SECRET/SP_PASSWORD> `
--tenant <TENANT_ID>
```

To test the service principal, we can create a simple script that use the service principal to login and then create a resource within the **RG-Infrastructure** resource group. Below we login using the service principal and create a storage account in the resource group. We save this as a script called **CreateSAScript.ps1**:

```
# Login to Azure using Service Principal
az login --service-principal `
--username "7e78e975-3d6e-45ca-8d9a-4614087ae284" `
--password="-aT8Q~pe6f9Jz_q3V-wK7uVWV.eVISIh5aVJFcjL" `
--tenant "57f387c6-3587-4ae7-a156-c9c7d10d7df6"
# Create resource in RG-Infrastructure
az storage account create `
--name "strginfrastructure" `
--resource-group "RG-Infrastructure" `
--location "westeurope" `
--sku "Standard_LRS" `
--access-tier "Cool"
# Logout of Azure
az logout
```

Once we execute the **CreateSAScript.ps1** script, it creates the expected resource using the service principal. We can verify that the storage account is created as expected using the **az storage account list** command as shown in *Figure 10.23*:

```
PS C:\Temp> az storage account list `
>> --resource-group "RG-Infrastructure" | `
>> ConvertFrom-Json | `
>> Select-Object Name,ResourceGRoup

name                resourceGroup
----                -------------
strginfrastructure RG-Infrastructure
```

Figure 10.23: *Verification that the Storage Account is successfully created as expected using the service principal login*

If we were to try to use the service principal to create resources in other resource groups or try to create other resource groups, it would result in an authentication error since this service principal is created with permissions solely for the *RG-Infrastructure* resource group.

Recipe 65: Create scripts for automatically provision and configure Azure resources

As we saw in the previous *Recipe 64: Create a Service principal to automatically connect to Azure using scripts.* We basically created a script for automatically provisioning the storage account using the service principal to login and authenticate to Azure. We can apply the same principals from this and the other recipes within this chapter, to create scripts for automatically provisioning and configuring any Azure resources and combine this knowledge with knowledge from previous chapters to create scripts that builds larger infrastructures or whatever resource combinations required. As an example, we can make a script that creates several virtual machines from a string array of VM names and make it more versatile by specifying such an array as a parameter to the script. For more versatility we also provide parameters for the resource group, the region and for the configuration file. The service principal credentials is provided from an XML configuration file. By doing so we can easily specify another resource group and another configuration file that contains another service principal with permissions for another resource group, to create virtual machines in other specified resource groups, and also change the region if needed.

The XML configuration file (**Infrastructure.config**) content looks like this:

```xml
<?xml version="1.0" encoding="UTF-8"?>
<Azure>
  <UserName>7e78e975-3d6e-45ca-8d9a-4614087ae284</UserName>999999
  <Password>-aT8Q~pe6f9Jz_q3V-wK7uVWV.eVISIh5aVJFcjL</Password>
  <TenantID>57f387c6-3587-4ae7-a156-c9c7d10d7df6</TenantID>
</Azure>
```

And the general script (**Infrastructure.ps1**) looks like this:

```powershell
[CmdletBinding()]
param (
    [Parameter(Position=0)]
    [String]$ResourceGroup = "RG-Infrastructure",
    [Parameter(Position=1)]
    [String]$Location = "westeurope",
    [Parameter(Position=2)]
    [String[]]$VMs = @("VmOne", "VmTwo", "VmThree"),
    [Parameter(Position=3)]
    [String]$ConfigPath = ".\Infrastructure.config"
)
[xml]$Config = Get-Content $ConfigPath
```

```
# Login to Azure using Service Principal
az login --service-principal `
--username "$($Config.Azure.UserName)" `
--password="$($Config.Azure.Password)" `
--tenant "$($Config.Azure.TenantID)"
foreach ($Vm in $VMs){
    az vm create `
    --resource-group $ResourceGroup `
    --name $Vm `
    --image "Win2022Datacenter" `
    --size "Standard_B2s" `
    --admin-username "TestUser" `
    --admin-password "@Test123456789" `
    --location $Location
}
# Logut
az logout
```

When executed without arguments it will create the three default VMs specified in the **$VMs** variable within the *RG-Infrastructure* resource group in the **westeurope** region and the service principal credentials are fetched from the **Infrastructure.config** file. You could specify any number of VMs to create, in a specific region in a specific resource group. Note that you need to create a configuration file that contains service principal credentials for a service principal identity with permissions to the specified resource group. Below is shown an example execution using a different resource group, location, new VM names and another configuration file that would contain a service principal with permissions for that resource group:

```
.\Infrastructure.ps1 -ResourceGroup "RG-New" `
-Location "East Us" `
-VMs "TestVm", "DevVM", "StagingVM", "PocVM", "ProdVM" `
-ConfigPath "C:\Configs\RG-New.config"
```

You should of course implement the proper error handling and general script logic in order to accommodate for any errors or issues. Some resources might fail where other resources are dependent on such, you should then implement the proper retry logic or other logic that might skip specific resources or entirely removes current created resources if dependent resources cannot be created as expected and so on. It might take some trial and error. In such a script you can then add any resource besides the VMs to accommodate your needs for infrastructure resource requirements.

Please keep in mind that you might have limits to the number of compute resources you can create in your current account subscription, or you might have other limits due to billing issues. In such cases, you should check your general account and make sure you have the proper subscription and/or billing methods set for your Azure account.

Conclusion

When working with Azure cloud and Azure resources it is essential to have the right tools and know how to utilize such tools to be able to manage all aspects of Azure and its resources programmatically, without relying on the Azure portal and other GUIs. By using PowerShell in combination with Azures Command Line Interface, the Azure CLI, you can perform any task and create and manage any resource within Azure using PowerShell. This not only allows you to create resources such as Virtual Machines and storage accounts but also enable you to manage users, groups and permissions. In this chapter we have walked through different aspects of creating and managing different types of resources in Azure and used EntraID for managing users, groups and permissions. The topics in this chapter provides a general idea how to manage Azure, its resources and the usage of the Azure CLI and its commands. You can utilize this knowledge to start working with more advanced resources such as creating AKS clusters, database instances and so on. Moreover, by adhering to the concepts in this chapter, you should be able to both optimize and automate a lot of Azure tasks and be able to create scripts for not only automating provision of resources and performing bulk operations, but also for creating entire infrastructures in Azure.

The next chapter walks through AWS cloud services management and introduces the AWS tools for PowerShell. It describes how to install and configure these tools and also how to configure credentials for accessing AWS programmatically. The chapter dives deeper into AWS identity and access management (IAM) showcasing how to manage IAM users and groups and how to create and manage access keys, permissions, and policies. Furthermore, the chapter not only describes how to create and manage EC2 instances, key pairs and security groups but also how to manage S3 buckets and how to upload and download objects to such buckets.

Join our book's Discord space

Join the book's Discord Workspace for Latest updates, Offers, Tech happenings around the world, New Release and Sessions with the Authors:

https://discord.bpbonline.com

CHAPTER 11
Managing AWS with PowerShell

Introduction

Amazon Web Services or AWS is a cloud computing platform provided by Amazon. It offers cloud resources, services and features that enable you to build, deploy and manage applications and entire infrastructures in the cloud with ease. AWS is a popular choice for a cloud provider, and it is known for its scalability and reliability. Whether you are a sole developer or an administrator for a large organization, AWS provides a wide range of services and resources and provides tools for your toolbox that enables you to manage, optimize, and automate such services and resources with PowerShell. You can create virtual machine instances for hosting your websites or for larger computational requirements. You can build storage buckets for a multitude of data storage purposes. You can create different kinds of databases. You can start, run, and scale Kubernetes services, build blockchains and dive deep into machine learning resources. These are just some of the resources, services and features AWS provides. AWS provides datacenters on a global scale distributed across multiple geographic locations that ensures low-latency and high redundancy with minimal to no downtime. AWS is also dedicated to security and data protection providing reliable trust that ensures your resources and data are safe. As a developer or and administrator you will greatly benefit from learning how to utilize tools for managing AWS using PowerShell and by being able to programmatically create, manage, scale and automate AWS cloud resources and services with PowerShell, you can greatly minimize your time spent on creating and managing resources for your infrastructure from a small to a large scale and in general lower your costs for your infrastructure resources. When working with AWS cloud services and resources, the AWS Tools for PowerShell is an invaluable tool for managing AWS with PowerShell.

Structure

The chapter covers the following topics:

- Introduction to AWS Tools for PowerShell and credentials configuration
    - o **Recipe 66**: Installation of AWS tools for PowerShell
    - o **Recipe 67**: Configuring credentials for accessing AWS programmatically
- AWS Identity and Access Management
    - o **Recipe 68**: Managing IAM users and groups
    - o **Recipe 69**: Managing IAM access keys, permissions and policies
- Managing AWS EC2 instances
    - o **Recipe 70**: Create and manage EC2 instances, key pairs and security groups
- Managing AWS S3 buckets
    - o **Recipe 71**: Create and manage S3 buckets including uploading and downloading objects
    - o **Recipe 72**: Create policies allowing only IAM users in specific IAM groups to access S3 buckets

Objectives

AWS is one of the most used cloud services today. Learning about and being able to manage different aspects of AWS are essential skills to have in an administrator or developer's toolkit. In this chapter we will cover how to install and configure AWS Tools for PowerShell that are used for managing AWS with PowerShell and how to configure and manage credentials for accessing AWS programmatically. You will also learn how to use the tools for AWS Identity and Management that allows you to create and manage users and groups and manage their access and permissions for AWS services and resources. You will learn how to create and manage policies that enables you to limit permissions and access to resources and services. We will also dive into EC2 computational instances and S3 storage buckets and learn how to manage such resources using PowerShell.

Note: Using AWS requires an active account. When you create an account, you will initially be granted a root user that is the account owner with unlimited access. It is highly recommended that you create an IAM user with least privileged permissions for accessing AWS services and resources programmatically. You can get a free AWS account and select from different tiers that grants access to more than 100 available products.

Introduction to AWS tools for PowerShell and credentials configuration

AWS introduces packaged modules for managing and working with AWS services and resources using PowerShell, referred to as *AWS Tools for PowerShell*. There are currently three package types of this tool that depends on the release and edition of Windows and the version of PowerShell:

- **AWSPowerShell**: Single, large-module version and legacy module used for Windows PowerShell and are compatible with Windows PowerShell version 2 – 5.1. All AWS services are supported by this module.

- **AWSPowerShell**.**NetCore**: Single, large-module version compatible with Windows PowerShell 3+ versions and PowerShell Core 6+ (PowerShell 7). Provides support for all AWS services in a single module.

- **AWS.Tools**: Modularized version of the AWS tools for PowerShell. Each AWS service is supported by its own individual, small module, with shared support modules **AWS.Tools.Common** and **AWS.Tools.Installer**. Compatible with Windows PowerShell 3+ versions and PowerShell Core 6+ (PowerShell 7).

You can use the **AWSPowerShell.NetCore** package that provides all cmdlets in one module. Notice that it contains a lot of cmdlets and provides some overhead when importing this large module into a PowerShell session. The **AWS.Tools** modularized package only installs an **installer** module and then you will have to install single service modules when you need cmdlets and tools for specific kinds of services and resources. This provides less overhead and only installs the specific tools needed for the services and resources you are working with. If you are using Windows PowerShell, you should use the legacy **AWSPowerShell** package module.

The AWS tools for PowerShell is an essential component in the toolkit for AWS administrators and developers who want to manage, optimize and automate their AWS cloud infrastructure.

Recipe 66: Installation of AWS tools for PowerShell

All AWS Tools for PowerShell packages are installed using the **Install-Module** cmdlet.

> **Note: For this chapter we use the modularized AWS.Tools package with PowerShell 7 on a Windows 10 client. Required service modules will be installed when needed. Due to potential security risks, Amazon recommends not to install AWS modules with elevated privileges unless you need these privileges for your tasks at hand. Also note that it is only recommended to have one variant of the AWS Tools for PowerShell installed, to avoid potential cmdlet auto-import issues.**

1. We will install the **AWS.Tools.Installer** module:

   ```
   # Install AWS.Tools installer module (Modularized package)
   Install-Module AWS.Tools.Installer
   ```

2. After installation of the **AWS.Tools.Installer** module we can use the **Install-AWSToolsModule** cmdlet to install specific service modules. When using this cmdlet, it also installs any dependency modules that are required for specific modules to work. Once you install the first service module, the installer also installs the **AWS.Tools.Common** module which is a shared module that is required by all AWS service modules. The cmdlet also removes older module versions and updates current installed modules to their newest versions. As an example, you would have to install the **AWS.Tools.S3** module for working with the AWS **Simple Storage Service (S3)** or install the **AWS.Tools.EC2** module for working with the Elastic **Compute Cloud service (EC2)**:

   ```
   # Install module for Simple Storage Service (S3)
   Install-AWSToolsModule AWS.Tools.S3
   # Install module for Elastic Compute Cloud service (EC2)
   Install-AWSToolsModule AWS.Tools.EC2
   ```

3. Once installed you can import the modules into your current session. *Figure 11.1* shows the output from the **Get-Module** cmdlet after these modules are imported into a session:

```
PS C:\Temp> Import-Module AWS.Tools.S3
PS C:\Temp> Import-Module AWS.Tools.EC2
PS C:\Temp> Get-Module

ModuleType Version   PreRelease Name                             ExportedCommands
---------- -------   ---------- ----                             ----------------
Binary     4.1.434              AWS.Tools.Common                 {Add-AWSLoggingListener, Clear-AWSCredential, Cle…
Binary     4.1.434              AWS.Tools.EC2                    {Add-EC2CapacityReservation, Add-EC2ClassicLinkVp…
Script     1.0.2.4              AWS.Tools.Installer              {Install-AWSToolsModule, Uninstall-AWSToolsModule…
Binary     4.1.434              AWS.Tools.S3                     {Add-S3PublicAccessBlock, Copy-S3Object, Get-S3AC…
Script     0.0                  ImportGuard
Manifest   7.0.0.0              Microsoft.PowerShell.Management  {Add-Content, Clear-Content, Clear-Item, Clear-It…
Manifest   7.0.0.0              Microsoft.PowerShell.Security    {ConvertFrom-SecureString, ConvertTo-SecureString…
Manifest   7.0.0.0              Microsoft.PowerShell.Utility     {Add-Member, Add-Type, Clear-Variable, Compare-Ob…
Script     1.4.8.1              PackageManagement                {Find-Package, Find-PackageProvider, Get-Package,…
Script     2.2.5                PowerShellGet                    {Find-Command, Find-DscResource, Find-Module, Fin…
Script     2.2.6                PSReadLine                       {Get-PSReadLineKeyHandler, Get-PSReadLineOption, …
```

Figure 11.1: *Output from the Get-Module cmdlet after importing AWS modules into a session*

Note: If modules are not explicitly imported into a session, in general a module will be auto imported when you invoke a cmdlet from such a module.

4. You can list all cmdlets in a specific module using the **Get-Command** cmdlet specifying the name of the module as an argument for the **-Module** parameter as shown in *Figure 11.2*:

```
PS C:\Temp> Get-Command -Module AWS.Tools.S3

CommandType     Name                                            Version    Source
-----------     ----                                            -------    ------
Alias           Remove-S3MultipartUploads                       4.1.434    AWS.Tools.S3
Cmdlet          Add-S3PublicAccessBlock                         4.1.434    AWS.Tools.S3
Cmdlet          Copy-S3Object                                   4.1.434    AWS.Tools.S3
Cmdlet          Get-S3ACL                                       4.1.434    AWS.Tools.S3
Cmdlet          Get-S3Bucket                                    4.1.434    AWS.Tools.S3
Cmdlet          Get-S3BucketAccelerateConfiguration             4.1.434    AWS.Tools.S3
Cmdlet          Get-S3BucketAnalyticsConfiguration              4.1.434    AWS.Tools.S3
Cmdlet          Get-S3BucketAnalyticsConfigurationList          4.1.434    AWS.Tools.S3
Cmdlet          Get-S3BucketEncryption                          4.1.434    AWS.Tools.S3
Cmdlet          Get-S3BucketIntelligentTieringConfiguration     4.1.434    AWS.Tools.S3
Cmdlet          Get-S3BucketIntelligentTieringConfigurationList 4.1.434    AWS.Tools.S3
Cmdlet          Get-S3BucketInventoryConfiguration              4.1.434    AWS.Tools.S3
Cmdlet          Get-S3BucketInventoryConfigurationList          4.1.434    AWS.Tools.S3
Cmdlet          Get-S3BucketLocation                            4.1.434    AWS.Tools.S3
Cmdlet          Get-S3BucketLogging                             4.1.434    AWS.Tools.S3
```

Figure 11.2: *Listing all cmdlets in a module using the Get-Command cmdlet with the -Module parameter*

You can always install and import additional AWS modules when needed.

Recipe 67: Configuring credentials for accessing AWS programmatically

Before you can start using AWS Tools cmdlets, you need to configure credentials for your AWS account for programmatic access. If you have not configured credentials for your account, you will get an error when trying to execute AWS Tools cmdlets as shown in *Figure 11.3*:

```
PS C:\Temp> Get-S3Bucket
Get-S3Bucket: No credentials specified or obtained from persisted/shell defaults.
```

Figure 11.3: Error when trying to execute AWS Tool cmdlets without being authorized and authenticated

AWS offers different methods for configuring credentials for your account for programmatic access.

- **IAM Identity Center authentication**: AWS IAM Identity Center is the recommended method for providing AWS credentials when developing on a non-AWS compute service.

- **IAM roles anywhere**: You can use IAM Roles Anywhere to get temporary security credentials in IAM for workloads such as servers, containers, and applications that run outside of AWS. To use IAM Roles Anywhere, your workloads must use X.509 certificates.

- **Short term credentials**: You can copy and use temporary credentials that are available in the AWS access portal. New credentials will need to be copied when these expire. You can use the temporary credentials in a profile or use them as values for system properties and environment variables.

- **Long term credentials**: You can copy and use credentials that are available in the AWS access portal for long term programmatic access. This type of credential does not expire.

IAM stands for Identity and Access Management which is a service provided by AWS. It is a fundamental component that allows managing and controlling access to AWS resources and services.

Besides these methods, AWS offers authentication options for code running within an AWS environment such as *IAM roles for EC2 instances*, *AWS CloudShell* and *AWS Cloud9*. These are not covered by this chapter, but are worth looking into if needed.

Within this chapter we will focus on using long term credentials in the form of access keys for IAM users. Using long termed credentials is not the preferred method for authenticating and accessing AWS and should only be used for development and testing purposes. For production environments you should use the *AWS IAM Identity Center* for authentication and programmatic access to AWS. Configuration and usage of the IAM Identity Center can be quite comprehensive and is therefore outside of the scope of this book. The AWS documentation provides detailed information on how to configure and use the different authentication methods: **https://docs.aws.amazon.com/sdkref/latest/guide/access.html**. You should refer to this documentation for other authentication methods that are not used in this chapter.

Access keys are made up of an access key pair which is the combination of an *access key id* and a *secret access key*. Both are required for authenticating to AWS programmatically. To create your first access key pair, you must first create a non-root IAM user from within the console and create an access key for that user. It is not recommended to use the *root* user for programmatic access. Each IAM user can have two access keys which can be either active or inactive which allows for the keys to be rotated. Rotating keys is a crucial and recommended security practice where new keys are generated and old ones are deactivated periodically. When creating access keys, it is also crucial to account for the permissions that are associated with the IAM user which determines the scope of access level that the key provides. Be sure to always follow security best practices by storing your keys safely, rotate keys regularly and never embed keys directly in code.

Within the console, you can create access keys using the *Create access key* feature. To create your first IAM user and access key for that user, follow these steps:

1. Once logged into the AWS console, click on your **account name** in the **top right corner**.

2. Select **Security Credentials**. You will then be switched to your **IAM (Identity and Access Management)** console.

3. In the left side menu, select **Users**.

4. Click on the **Create user** button. Follow the steps to create a user. Only give it **least privileged** permissions needed for your tasks. For the user in this chapter, we add the **AdministratorAccess** policy.

    a. You can create a **group** to manage user permissions and add the user to that group. Then attach policies and permissions to the group.

    b. You can attach a user directly to a **policy** or create a **new custom policy** with custom permissions and attach the user to this policy.

    c. You can **copy** permissions from an existing user.

5. Once the user is **created**, you can select the user in the users overview list. This will lead to the specific users overview page where you can create access keys using the **Create access key** link in the summary pane.

Note: An IAM user can only have two access keys at a time. Also note that these steps for creating an IAM user and access key might change over time as AWS makes updates to its console content and design.

Figure 11.4 shows the successful creation of an access key pair for the *IAM Test* user created within the AWS portal:

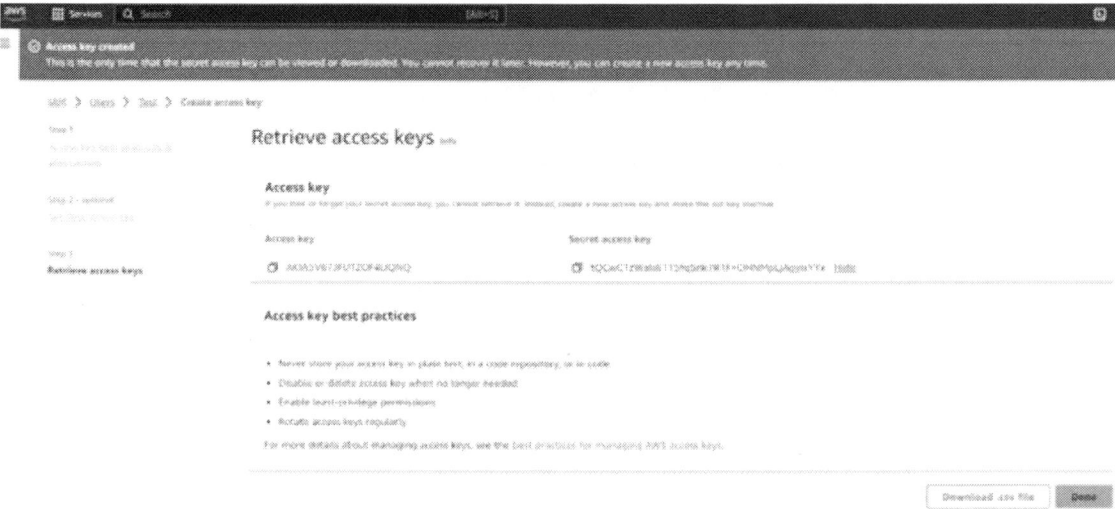

Figure 11.4: *Successful creation of an access key pair for the IAM Test user within the AWS portal*

Note that the secret access key is only shown once and cannot be recovered later. You should store or download the access key. If you lose the access key you can create a new one at any time though. Also notice the access keys best practices mentioned:

- Never store your access key in plain text, in a code repository, or in code.

- Disable or delete access key when no longer needed.

- Enable least-privilege permissions.

- Rotate access keys regularly.

For more details about managing your access keys securely, see the AWS access keys best practices documentation: **https://docs.aws.amazon.com/console/general/access-keys-best-practices**.

To generally help securing your AWS resources, you can refer to the general security best practices for IAM here: **https://docs.aws.amazon.com/IAM/latest/UserGuide/best-practices.html**.

Once we have created a user and an access key, there are a few methods for using the access key for authenticating programmatically to AWS. The following list is in preceding order, from highest to lowest:

1. Explicitly set credentials in code using specific AWS cmdlets **-AccessKey** and **-SecretKey** parameters. Not all AWS cmdlets contain these parameters, and they should be considered as legacy/deprecated. They can be quite useful though for testing single commands. The access key will only be available for this single cmdlet execution:

```
# Specify credentials for a single cmdlet
Get-S3Bucket `
-AccessKey "AKIA5V67JFUTZOF4UQNQ" `
-SecretKey "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"
```

2. Explicitly set credentials in a session using the **Set-AWSCredentials** cmdlet. By setting the credentials using this cmdlet they will only be available for the duration of this session:

```
# Configure credentials using the Set-AWSCredentials cmdlet
Set-AWSCredentials `
-AccessKey "AKIA5V67JFUTZOF4UQNQ" `
-SecretKey "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"
```

3. Set credentials using environment variables. You can configure and define the access key pair as environment variables. Credentials defined as environment variables in a session, will only be available for the duration of that session. For persisting the credentials, you should add them as system or user environment variables. Also note that AWS offers additional environment variables for configuring other settings such as region etc.:

```
# Configure credentials using Environment variables
$Env:AWS_ACCESS_KEY_ID="AKIA5V67JFUTZOF4UQNQ"
$Env:AWS_SECRET_ACCESS_KEY="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"
$Env:AWS_DEFAULT_REGION="eu-north-1"
```

4. Set credentials using an AWS shared credentials file. This file is a plaintext file that resides in the **%USERPROFILE%\.aws** directory. If the directory and/or file does not exist, you can create it:

```
New-Item -Path "$($env:USERPROFILE)\.aws\credentials" -ItemType file
-Force
```

Add the following content to the file:

```
# Specify credentials using credentials file
[default]
aws_access_key_id = AKIA5V67JFUTZOF4UQNQ
aws_secret_access_key = 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
```

AWS cmdlets will look for this file and use the credentials within this file if no other preceding credential methods are specified. You can use the following environment variable to change the location or the name of the credentials file. This can also be persistent by setting this as a system or user environment variable:

```
$ENV:AWS_SHARED_CREDENTIALS_FILE="C:\New\Path\To\credentials"
```

Note: For the recipes and examples within this chapter we use a credentials file for authentication unless something else is specified. The user is an AWS account administrator with permissions to perform the required tasks for the recipes and examples. You should in general never use IAM users with administrator permission for programmatic access. Always adhere to the principal of least privilege and create a user with the least required permissions for your specific requirements.

As mentioned earlier in this recipe there are several ways for authenticating and accessing AWS and going through all of them could fit into a whole chapter. The methods used in this chapter is not the recommended solution but are chosen due to its simplicity. Once you get more accustomed to AWS and IAM you should transition to using the IAM Identity Center or other temporary methods for authenticating as soon as possible to avoid unnecessary security risks. You should in general follow the AWS best practices and guides from the AWS official documentation.

AWS Identity and Access Management

AWS **Identity and Access Management (IAM)** is a fundamental web service component that allows you to control and manage access to your AWS resources in a secure manner. IAM enables you to create and manage users, groups, roles, and set permissions to ensure that the right people or services have the right level of access to your AWS services, resources, and environment.

IAM allows you to create individual users in your AWS account and each user can have unique permissions and security credentials enabling you to give specific employees or applications access to specific resources and services. By following the principle of least privilege, you can grant individual users and applications the minimum access that is required for your AWS resources.

IAM users can be organized into groups for managing permissions collectively instead of assigning permissions to each individual user. They simplify user management and permissions management and are particularly useful when managing access to teams or roles that require more consistent access to resources. You can also apply specific password policies to groups for enforcing password complexity and password rotation policies for users in specific groups.

Roles defines what actions and permissions are allowed for specific AWS resources and are a way to grant temporary or short-termed permissions to access AWS resources without the need for long-term credentials like access and secret keys. Services, such as an EC2 instance, assume roles during their execution. These roles define what the service can do and which AWS resources it can access. For example, an EC2 instance can assume an IAM role to access an S3 bucket or a database and so on. They are also used for granting temporary permissions to other AWS accounts for cross account access and for federated identity management where external providers such as SAML and OpenID connect can authenticate users and provide temporary security credentials for accessing AWS accounts resources.

Policies are used to define sets of permissions that can be attached to users, groups, roles and other AWS resources, to specify which actions they can perform on which resources. AWS provides a set of managed policies that are created and maintained by AWS. These are designed to cover common use cases such as AdministratorAccess, Billing and AWSSupportAccess etc. You can also create custom policies to define specific access requirements for your specific requirements.

Users, groups, roles, and policies are essential components of AWS and are critical for ensuring the security of your AWS environment.

Working with Identity and Access management using PowerShell requires the AWS **IdentityManagement** module for the **AWS.Tools** modularized version. If you are using the **AWSPowerShell.NetCore** or **AWSPowerShell** legacy module, the **IdentityMangement** cmdlets should already be available:

```
# Install the IAM Identity management module for the modularized AWS tools
module

Install-AWSToolsModule AWS.Tools.IdentityManagement
```

Recipe 68: Managing IAM users and groups

AWS Tools for PowerShell consist of a large set of cmdlets for managing AWS resources. It is a bit more manageable to get an overview of the cmdlets that are relevant for specific purposes and for managing specific resource types when using the modularized version. When working with users you would need cmdlets that are used to manage users and so on for groups, policies, EC2 instances, S3 buckets and for all other kinds of AWS resources. AWS gives their cmdlets resource relevant names, meaning that cmdlets for managing IAM resources are named by starting the verb with IAM and then the name of a particular resource type. Resources for managing users are named in conventions like **Get-IAMUser**, **New-IAMUser** and **Update-IAMUser**. Cmdlets for managing groups are named **Get-IAMGroup**, **New-IAMGroup** and **Update-IAMGroup**. Likewise, cmdlets for managing EC2 instances and S3 buckets are named in the same way as **New-EC2Instance**, **Start-EC2Instance**, **New-S3Bucket**, **Remove-S3Bucket** and so on. This makes it quite easy to search for, filter and list cmdlets that are relevant for specific resources. You can use these conventions in combination with the **Get-Command** cmdlet and the **Where-Object** filter cmdlet to list resource specific cmdlets:

```
# List and view AWS User cmdlets

Get-Command | Where-Object {$_.Noun -like "IAMuser"}

# List and view AWS Group cmdlets

Get-Command | Where-Object {$_.Noun -like "IAMGroup"}

# List and view AWS Policy cmdlets

Get-Command | Where-Object {$_.Noun -like "IAMPolicy"}

# List and view AWS EC2 Instance cmdlets
```

```
Get-Command | Where-Object {$_.Noun -like "EC2Instance"}
# List and view AWS S3 Bucket cmdlets
Get-Command | Where-Object {$_.Noun -like "S3Bucket"}
```

Figure 11.5 shows the output when using the **Get-Command** and the **Where-Object** filter cmdlet to filter and list all cmdlets that contain *IAMUser* in the Noun part of the name. These are cmdlets that are relevant for working with IAM users:

CommandType	Name	Version	Source
Alias	Get-IAMUserPolicies	4.1.438	AWS.Tools.IdentityManagement
Alias	Get-IAMUserPolicies	4.1.436	AWS.Tools.IdentityManagement
Alias	Get-IAMUsers	4.1.438	AWS.Tools.IdentityManagement
Alias	Get-IAMUsers	4.1.436	AWS.Tools.IdentityManagement
Cmdlet	Add-IAMUserTag	4.1.438	AWS.Tools.IdentityManagement
Cmdlet	Add-IAMUserToGroup	4.1.438	AWS.Tools.IdentityManagement
Cmdlet	Get-IAMUser	4.1.438	AWS.Tools.IdentityManagement
Cmdlet	Get-IAMUserList	4.1.438	AWS.Tools.IdentityManagement
Cmdlet	Get-IAMUserPolicy	4.1.438	AWS.Tools.IdentityManagement
Cmdlet	Get-IAMUserPolicyList	4.1.438	AWS.Tools.IdentityManagement
Cmdlet	Get-IAMUserTagList	4.1.438	AWS.Tools.IdentityManagement
Cmdlet	New-IAMUser	4.1.438	AWS.Tools.IdentityManagement
Cmdlet	Register-IAMUserPolicy	4.1.438	AWS.Tools.IdentityManagement
Cmdlet	Remove-IAMUser	4.1.438	AWS.Tools.IdentityManagement
Cmdlet	Remove-IAMUserFromGroup	4.1.438	AWS.Tools.IdentityManagement
Cmdlet	Remove-IAMUserPermissionsBoundary	4.1.438	AWS.Tools.IdentityManagement
Cmdlet	Remove-IAMUserPolicy	4.1.438	AWS.Tools.IdentityManagement
Cmdlet	Remove-IAMUserTag	4.1.438	AWS.Tools.IdentityManagement
Cmdlet	Set-IAMUserPermissionsBoundary	4.1.438	AWS.Tools.IdentityManagement
Cmdlet	Unregister-IAMUserPolicy	4.1.438	AWS.Tools.IdentityManagement
Cmdlet	Update-IAMUser	4.1.438	AWS.Tools.IdentityManagement
Cmdlet	Write-IAMUserPolicy	4.1.438	AWS.Tools.IdentityManagement

Figure 11.5: *Listing AWS cmdlets relevant for working with and managing IAM users*

> **Tip: Remember you can always use the Get-Help cmdlet and provide the name of a specific cmdlet as an argument for displaying that cmdlets help file. This provides you with more information about the cmdlet, its usage syntax, usage examples and parameter explanations etc. Get-Help New-IAMUser -Full. You can update the module help files using the Update-Help cmdlet to the newest versions. Note that some modules do not support updatable help. In such case you can view the online help for a modules cmdlets, if it is available, using the -Online parameter: Get-Help New-IAMUser -Online. This will open the updated help site for that cmdlet in a browser.**

- To list all IAM users in an account, you would use the **Get-IAMUsers** cmdlet. *Figure 11.6* shows the output of running this cmdlet:

```
● PS C:\Temp> Get-IAMUsers

   Arn                  : arn:aws:iam::940529233191:user/NoConsoleAccess
   CreateDate           : 26-10-2023 20:18:22
   PasswordLastUsed     : 01-01-0001 00:00:00
   Path                 : /
   PermissionsBoundary  :
   Tags                 : {}
   UserId               : AIDA5V67JFUT3VQCUTUDS
   UserName             : NoConsoleAccess

   Arn                  : arn:aws:iam::940529233191:user/Test
   CreateDate           : 24-10-2023 13:40:16
   PasswordLastUsed     : 01-01-0001 00:00:00
   Path                 : /
   PermissionsBoundary  :
   Tags                 : {}
   UserId               : AIDA5V67JFUTX3AOLVSDR
   UserName             : Test
```

Figure 11.6: Listing all AWS users in an account using the Get-IAMUsers cmdlet

The objects returned by the AWS Tools for PowerShell cmdlets are .NET objects and not the JSON text objects that would typically be returned from such API´s. As an example, the **Get-IAMUser** cmdlet returns a **user** collection (**Amazon.IdentityManagement.Model.User**). Such a collection object can be placed in the PowerShell pipeline and managed as any other PowerShell object. As you can see in *Figure 11.7* we can pipe the command output to a cmdlet like **Select-Object** and select specific properties without any additional conversion:

```
● PS C:\Temp> Get-IAMUsers | Select-Object UserName,UserId

   UserName          UserId
   --------          ------
   NoConsoleAccess   AIDA5V67JFUT3VQCUTUDS
   Test              AIDA5V67JFUTX3AOLVSDR
```

Figure 11.7: Managing and piping AWS cmdlet output as a .NET PowerShell native like object

- You can use the **Get-IAMUser** (no trailing *s*) cmdlet to list the user used by the current context (dependent on the access key used) or you can provide it with the

-UserName parameter and provide a specific username to list that specific user if it is known to you and if it exists, as shown in *Figure 11.8*:

```
⦿ PS C:\Temp> Get-IAMUser

  Arn                  : arn:aws:iam::940529233191:user/Test
  CreateDate           : 24-10-2023 13:40:16
  PasswordLastUsed     : 01-01-0001 00:00:00
  Path                 : /
  PermissionsBoundary  :
  Tags                 : {AKIA5V67JFUT4URIYD5S}
  UserId               : AIDA5V67JFUTX3AOLVSDR
  UserName             : Test


⦿ PS C:\Temp> Get-IAMUser -UserName NoConsoleAccess

  Arn                  : arn:aws:iam::940529233191:user/NoConsoleAccess
  CreateDate           : 26-10-2023 20:18:22
  PasswordLastUsed     : 01-01-0001 00:00:00
  Path                 : /
  PermissionsBoundary  :
  Tags                 : {}
  UserId               : AIDA5V67JFUT3VQCUTUDS
  UserName             : NoConsoleAccess
```

Figure 11.8: Listing current user and specific user using the Get-IAMUser cmdlet

- You can create a new IAM user using the **New-IAMUser** cmdlet. The only required parameter is **-UserName**. The username must be unique within the account and is not distinguished by lower- and upper-case characters. *Figure 11.9* shows what happens when you try to create a user with a username that already exists in the account and the creation of a new user that does not already exist:

```
⦿ PS C:\Temp> New-IAMUser -UserName Test
  New-IAMUser: User with name Test already exists.
○ PS C:\Temp>
⦿ PS C:\Temp> New-IAMUser -UserName ApiAccess

  Arn                  : arn:aws:iam::940529233191:user/ApiAccess
  CreateDate           : 27-10-2023 20:47:15
  PasswordLastUsed     : 01-01-0001 00:00:00
  Path                 : /
  PermissionsBoundary  :
  Tags                 : {}
  UserId               : AIDA5V67JFUTVMYUOI6PN
  UserName             : ApiAccess
```

Figure 11.9: Output when trying to create a user with an already existing username and the creation of a unique new user

- You can update the information for a user such as changing the username using the **Update-IAMUser** cmdlet:

```
# Update an IAM user (Change username)
```

```
Update-IAMUser -UserName ApiAccess -NewUserName AppAccess
```

- To delete a user, you would use the **Remove-IAMUser** cmdlet. You will be prompted for confirmation, or you can override the confirmation prompt using the **-Confirm:$false** switch parameter or the **-Force** parameter:

```
# Delete an IAM user

Remove-IAMUser -UserName AppAccess

# Do not prompt for confirmation

Remove-IAMUser -UserName AppAccess -Confirm:$false
```

IAM groups allows you to group users together and instead of attaching policies directly to individual users, policies can be attached to groups, granting permissions to multiple users with similar roles or responsibilities at once. When you update a policy that is attached to a group, the changes automatically apply to all the group members. Using groups and attaching policies simplifies policy management. Groups are usually used to delegate responsibilities and isolate resource permissions. For example, you might create an Administrator group that provides full access to resources and users added to this group are granted these privileges. Or you can use groups to segregate user permissions based on different projects, departments or roles within organizations and so on.

- To list all current groups in an AWS account, use the **Get-IAMGroups** cmdlet:

```
# List all AWS account groups

Get-IAMGroups
```

- To get information about a specific group, use the **Get-IAMGroup** cmdlet. The below command will list the group named **AdminUsers**:

```
# Get specific IAM Group

Get-IAMGroup -GroupName AdminUsers
```

It is also worth noticing that the returned object from the **Get-IAMGroup** cmdlet, gives information about its group members within the **Users** property of that object. You can use this property to get the full list of a group's members.

- To create a new group, use the **New-IAMGroup** cmdlet and specify a name for the group using the **-GroupName** parameter. The below command will create a new group called **ApiUsers**:

```
# Create new IAM group

New-IAMGroup -GroupName ApiUsers
```

- You can add IAM users to IAM groups using the **Add-IAMUserToGroup** cmdlet. Use the **-UserName** parameter to specify the user and the **-GroupName** parameter to specify the group. The below command will add the user **ApiAccess** to the **ApiUsers** group:

```
# Add IAM user to IAM Group

Add-IAMUserToGroup -UserName ApiAccess -GroupName ApiUsers
```

- Likewise, you can remove a user from a group using the **Remove-IAMUserFromGroup** cmdlet. The below command removes the **ApiAccess** user from the **ApiUsers** group. Since this is a destructive behavior, you will be prompted for confirmation. Use the **-Confirm:$false** switch or the **-Force** parameter to override the confirmation prompt:

```
# Remove IAM user from IAM Group

Remove-IAMUserFromGroup -UserName ApiAccess -GroupName ApiUsers

# Override confirmation prompt

Remove-IAMUserFromGroup -UserName ApiAccess -GroupName ApiUsers
-Confirm:$false
```

- To delete a group from the AWS account, use the **Remove-IAMGroup** cmdlet. Specify the group name using the **-GroupName** parameter and override the confirmation prompt using the **-Confirm:$false** switch or the **-Force** parameter. The below command will delete the **ApiUsers** group from the account. Note that you cannot delete a group containing users. You must first remove all users from the group:

-
```
# Delete an IAM Group

Remove-IAMGroup -GroupName ApiUsers

# Override confirmation prompt

Remove-IAMGroup -GroupName ApiUsers -Confirm:$false
```

- You can list all groups that a user is a member of using the **Get-IAMGroupForUser**. The below command will list all groups that the **ApiAccess** user is a member of:

```
# List an IAM user group memberships

Get-IAMGroupForUser -UserName ApiAccess
```

IAM users and IAM groups are not worth much without permissions. In the next recipe you will learn how to manage permissions using policies and how to enable portal access for users and how to create access keys.

Recipe 69: Managing IAM access keys, permissions, and policies

When you create a new IAM user using the **New-IAMUser** cmdlet, the user is created with no groups, no permissions, no access keys and with no password and console access. If an IAM user should only be used programmatically you would not enable console access or set a password for the user, but if you are programmatically creating users that should be able to access and login to the AWS portal, you should enable console access and create a password.

1. For enabling console access and creating a password we can use the **New-IAMLoginProfile** cmdlet. In *Figure 11.10* we create a new user called **ConsoleAccess** and enables console access and set the password for the user. We also specify that the user should change the password at first login. Note that the password is provided as plaintext and not as a secure string for this cmdlet:

```
◉ PS C:\Temp> New-IAMUser -UserName ConsoleAccess

 Arn                    : arn:aws:iam::940529233191:user/ConsoleAccess
 CreateDate             : 29-10-2023 19:25:03
 PasswordLastUsed       : 01-01-0001 00:00:00
 Path                   : /
 PermissionsBoundary    :
 Tags                   : {}
 UserId                 : AIDA5V67JFUT7OPSRPA53
 UserName               : ConsoleAccess


◉ PS C:\Temp> New-IAMLoginProfile -UserName ConsoleAccess `
>> -PasswordResetRequired $true `
>> -Password "New@Password"


 CreateDate            PasswordResetRequired UserName
 ----------            --------------------- --------
 29-10-2023 19:26:05 True                    ConsoleAccess
```

Figure 11.10: Creating a new IAM user, enabling console access and set a new password for that user

2. If an IAM user only needs programmatic access, we can enable and create a new access key for that user using the **New-IAMAccessKey** cmdlet. In *Figure 11.11* we create a new user called **NoConsoleAccess** and create a new access key for that user:

```
◉ PS C:\Temp> New-IAMUser -UserName NoConsoleAccess

 Arn                    : arn:aws:iam::940529233191:user/NoConsoleAccess
 CreateDate             : 29-10-2023 19:35:03
 PasswordLastUsed       : 01-01-0001 00:00:00
 Path                   : /
 PermissionsBoundary    :
 Tags                   : {}
 UserId                 : AIDA5V67JFUT7Z6YN2A2C
 UserName               : NoConsoleAccess


◉ PS C:\Temp> New-IAMAccessKey -UserName NoConsoleAccess

 AccessKeyId     : AKIA5V67JFUT27ZTTORG
 CreateDate      : 29-10-2023 19:35:23
 SecretAccessKey : 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
 Status          : Active
 UserName        : NoConsoleAccess
```

Figure 11.11: Creating a new user and enable programmatic/
Api access by creating an access key for that user

Note: When creating a new access key, the SecretAccessKey will only be available and shown once. You should store this key in a safe location. You can also redirect the command output to a file, this might be useful when creating multiple users and you need to provide them with the access key, you can then securely send the file to the user, at a later time.

An IAM user can both be enabled for console and Programmatic access at the same time. This might be applicable for testing purposes, but users that are used for programmatic access rarely has the need for being able to access and login to the console.

3. Once a new user is created it still requires permissions for relevant resources and services before it is useful. As an example, we can use the new **NoConsoleAccess** user to try to list all IAM users within the account. To override the current user context that are set in the AWS credentials file, we use the **-AccessKey** and **-SecretKey** parameters specifically in the cmdlet and provide the access key property values for the **NoConsoleAccess** user as arguments. Then this specific cmdlet will be executed in that specific user´s context, overriding the credentials file. In *Figure 11.12* you can see what happens if we try to list all IAM users with the context of the **NoConsoleAccess** user:

```
PS C:\Temp> Get-IAMUsers -AccessKey AKIA5V67JFUT27ZTTORG `
>> -SecretKey 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
Get-IAMUserList: User: arn:aws:iam::940529233191:user/NoConsoleAccess is not authorized to perform: iam:ListUsers on
resource: arn:aws:iam::940529233191:user/ because no identity-based policy allows the iam:ListUsers action
```

Figure 11.12: Trying to list all IAM users in the context of the NoConsoleAccess user without permissions

This user does not have the permissions required for listing IAM users in the account and contains no other permissions for that matter. No policy allows this action. We have not added any policies or permissions to this user yet.

4. There are different types of policies in AWS such as **Resource-Based** policies which are policies that you attach to resources such as S3 Buckets and EC2 instances and **Identity-Based** policies which are policies you apply to identities such as users and groups. AWS provides a large set of pre-defined identity-based policies called **AWS managed policies**. A policy that you define and create is called a **customer managed policy**. These allow you to create more fine-grained policies than provided by AWS managed policies. You can also create so-called Inline policies which are directly attached to single identities and are only available for that identity. When you delete the identity, you also delete the inline policy attached to it. Besides these, AWS have a few other policy types such as permissions boundaries, organizations service control policy, access control lists and *session policies*. In this recipe we focus on the Identity-Based policy types for users and groups.

Policies are JSON structured documents that look more or less like the simple policy definition in the example below. For further information about the policy structure and elements, refer to the AWS policy elements page here: **https://docs. aws.amazon.com/IAM/latest/UserGuide/reference_policies_elements.html**:

```
{
    "Version": "2012-10-17",
    "Statement": [
        {
            "Effect": "Allow",
            "Action": "iam:ListUsers",
            "Resource": "*"
        }
    ]
}
```

A policy consists of a version and an array with one or more statements. A statement states which *effect* an *action* has on a *resource*. This specific policy allows the IAM **ListUsers** action on all resources. To create a policy, we use the **New-IAMPolicy** cmdlet. The policy must be named using the **-PolicyName** parameter and then you specify the defined JSON document policy using the **-PolicyDocument** parameter. You can define the policy document within a JSON file and then use the **Get-Content** cmdlet to import the policy definition from that file, as an argument for the **-PolicyDocument** parameter:

```
# Create a new policy using a policy document defined in a JSON file
New-IAMPolicy -PolicyName "ListUsers" `
-PolicyDocument (Get-Content -Raw ListUserPolicy.json) `
-Description "This grants ListUsers permissions for all resources"
```

Or you can specify the policy document within a **Here-String** and assign it to a variable, then use the variable as an argument for the **-PolicyDocument** parameter:

```
# Create a new Policy defining the policy document in a Here-String
$ListUsersPolicy = @"
{
    "Version": "2012-10-17",
    "Statement": [
        {
            "Effect": "Allow",
            "Action": "iam:ListUsers",
```

```
            "Resource": "*"
        }
    ]
}
"@
New-IAMPolicy -PolicyName "ListUsers" `
-PolicyDocument $ListUsersPolicy `
-Description "This grants ListUsers permissions for all resources"
```

Note: The version value is not a free text date, we must specify this specific date and use this as the version.

Now it is worth mentioning that instead of using **Here-Strings** for creating policies as JSON we can put together the policy in the form of a hashtable and pass that through the `ConvertTo-Json` cmdlet. This is more PowerShell conventional and will also be easier to read and edit. First create the policy in a hashtable and store that in a variable:

```
# Create a new Policy defining the policy document in a Hashtable
$PolicyHash = @{
    Version = "2012-10-17"
    Statement = @(
        @{
        Effect = "Allow"
        Action = "iam:ListUsers"
        Resource = "*"
        }
    )
}
```

Then we convert this hashtable to JSON and use it as the argument for the **-PolicyDocument** parameter:

```
New-IAMPolicy -PolicyName "ListUsers" `
-PolicyDocument (ConvertTo-Json -InputObject $PolicyHash) `
-Description "This grants List Users permissions for all resources"
```

Figure 11.13 shows the successful creation of the **ListUsers** custom managed identity policy:

```
New-IAMPolicy -PolicyName "ListUsers" `
-PolicyDocument $ListUsersPolicy `
-Description "This grants ListUsers permissions for all resources"

Arn                            : arn:aws:iam::940529233191:policy/ListUsers
AttachmentCount                : 0
CreateDate                     : 30-10-2023 20:06:20
DefaultVersionId               : v1
Description                    :
IsAttachable                   : True
Path                           : /
PermissionsBoundaryUsageCount  : 0
PolicyId                       : ANPA5V67JFUTSUAV3CXFB
PolicyName                     : ListUsers
Tags                           : {}
UpdateDate                     : 30-10-2023 20:06:20
```

Figure 11.13: Successful creation of the ListUsers custom managed identity policy

To view a specific policy, we use the **Get-IAMPolicy** cmdlet with the **-PolicyArn** parameter:

```
# View a specific policy

Get-IAMPolicy -PolicyArn "arn:aws:iam::940529233191:policy/
ListUsers"
```

The resulting object from this cmdlet does not contain the policy document itself but only information about the policy such as the creation date, policy id, policy name etc. To access and view the policy document from a policy, we can use the **Get-IAMPolicyVersion** cmdlet:

```
$PolicyDoc = Get-IAMPolicyVersion -PolicyArn
"arn:aws:iam::940529233191:policy/ListUsers" -VersionId v1
```

Unfortunately, the returned document is in an encoded format under the **Document** property. We can use the **WebUtility** .NET class to decode this:

```
[System.Net.WebUtility]::UrlDecode($PolicyDoc.Document)
```

It will then output the policy document in a readable format.

5. **ARN** is short for **Amazon Resource Name** which is used to uniquely identify AWS resources. ARN´s are usually required when you need to specify a resource across all of AWS, such as a policy. The specific ARN format depends on the resource, but these are the general formats:

```
arn:partition:service:region:account-id:resource-id
arn:partition:service:region:account-id:resource-type/resource-id
arn:partition:service:region:account-id:resource-type:resource-id
```

Note: Some resources can omit the account ID, the region, or both.

In order to better understand the specific content of an ARN we can create a function that extends an AWS object with ARN properties. We do this by splitting up the ARN and then adding each "section" of the ARN as individual properties. This also allows for more precise filtering and sorting of AWS objects:

```powershell
function Resolve-ARN {

    param(

        [Parameter(ValueFromPipeline = $true)]

        [PSObject]

        $AwsObject

    )

    process{

        if(!($AwsObject.arn)){

            return $AwsObject

        }

        else{

            $null, $Partition, $Service, $Region, $AccountID,
$ResourceType, $ResourceID = $AwsObject.arn -split "[:/]"

            if(!($ResourceID)){

                $ResourceID = $ResourceType

                $ResourceType = $null

            }

            foreach($Prop in 'partition', 'service', 'region',
'accountid', 'resourcetype', 'resourceid'){

                Add-Member -InputObject $AwsObject -MemberType NoteProperty
-Name "_$Prop" -Value (Get-Variable -Name $Prop -ValueOnly) -Force

            }

            $AwsObject

        }

    }

}
```

We can then pipe an AWS Object that contains an ARN property to this function and then pipe that to **Format-List** ***** to view the extended properties of the AWS object, as shown below:

```powershell
$Policy = Get-IAMPolicy -PolicyArn "arn:aws:iam::940529233191:policy/
ListUsers"

$Policy | Resolve-ARN | fl *
```

The output will contain the new and extended properties for the AWS object as shown here:

```
_partition                     : aws
_service                       : iam
_region                        :
_accountid                     : 940529233191
_resourcetype                  : policy
_resourceid                    : ListUsers
Arn                            : arn:aws:iam::940529233191:policy/ListUsers
AttachmentCount                : 0
CreateDate                     : 30-10-2023 20:26:29
DefaultVersionId               : v1
Description                    :
IsAttachable                   : True
Path                           : /
PermissionsBoundaryUsageCount  : 0
PolicyId                       : ANPA5V67JFUTSUAV3CXFB
PolicyName                     : ListUsers
Tags                           : {}
UpdateDate                     : 30-10-2023 20:26:29
```

With this extension, we are now able to distinguish the **partition**, **service**, **region** (if any), **account id** (if any), **resource type** and the **resource id** from the AWS object, by extending its properties with the properties derived from the AWS objects ARN.

6. To list all policies that are available, use the **Get-IAMPolicies** cmdlet. This returns a list with both AWS and custom managed policies. You can pipe the **Get-IAMPolicies** cmdlet to the **Where-Object** filter cmdlet and **Select-Object** cmdlet to search for available policies by name. You can search for all policies that contain a word like *EC2*, *Account* or *List* in its name to narrow down possible usable policies for your specific use cases. In *Figure 11.14* we search through all policies containing *List*. For more specific information about each individual policy, you should refer to the official AWS documentation:

```
PS C:\Temp> Get-IAMPolicies | Where-Object {$_.PolicyName -match "List"} | Select-Object PolicyName,Arn

PolicyName                        Arn
----------                        ---
ListUsers                         arn:aws:iam::940529233191:policy/ListUsers
AWSQuickSightListIAM              arn:aws:iam::aws:policy/service-role/AWSQuickSightListIAM
AWSPriceListServiceFullAccess     arn:aws:iam::aws:policy/AWSPriceListServiceFullAccess
```

Figure 11.14: *Using Where-Object and Select-Object to search for possible relevant available policies*

7. Now that we have created a policy that grants `iam:ListUser` permissions, we can create a new group, attach the policy to that group and add the relevant users as members to the group. All members within that group will inherit the permissions to *List* all IAM users in the AWS account. In this case we add the **NoConsoleAccess** user that was previously not allowed to list all IAM users to the group, granting it the permissions:

```
# Create ListUsers Group

New-IAMGroup -GroupName ListUsers

# Attach ListUsers policy to ListUsers group

Register-IAMGroupPolicy -GroupName ListUsers `
-PolicyArn "arn:aws:iam::940529233191:policy/ListUsers"

# Add NoConsoleAccess user to ListUsers group

Add-IAMUserToGroup -UserName NoConsoleAccess -GroupName ListUsers
```

We can list all the policies registered to a group using the **Get-IAMAttachedGroupPolicies** cmdlet:

```
# Get groups registered policies

Get-IAMAttachedGroupPolicies -GroupName ListUsers
```

8. The **NoConsoleAccess** user now has permission to list all IAM users in the AWS account. We re-execute the same command as we did in *Figure 11.12* using the **Get-IAMUsers** cmdlet with the access key for the **NoConsoleAccess** user, to make sure the cmdlet is executed in the context of that specific user. We pipe the command to **Select-Object** to filter the names and ARN´s to get a more readable output list. *Figure 11.15* shows the output of running this command:

```
● PS C:\Temp> Get-IAMUsers -AccessKey AKIA5V67JFUT27ZTTORG `
  >> -SecretKey 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 | `
  >> Select-Object UserName,Arn

  UserName         Arn
  --------         ---
  ApiAccess        arn:aws:iam::940529233191:user/ApiAccess
  ConsoleAccess    arn:aws:iam::940529233191:user/ConsoleAccess
  NoConsoleAccess  arn:aws:iam::940529233191:user/NoConsoleAccess
  Test             arn:aws:iam::940529233191:user/Test
  Test1            arn:aws:iam::940529233191:user/Test1
  Test2            arn:aws:iam::940529233191:user/Test2
```

Figure 11.15: Listing all IAM users in the context of the NoConsoleAccess user

9. The permissions work as expected and the **NoConsoleAccess** user now have the permissions to list all IAM users in the AWS account. This is the only permission this user currently has due to the limited permissions attached to the policy.

You should create custom policies with only the required permissions whenever it is applicable, instead of using the AWS managed policies if there are no managed policies that are strict enough depending on your permission requirements. Be aware that some permissions might be dependent on other permissions. You will not be able to use the **GetSecretValue** permission on a secret manager and get a specific secret, without being able to list the secrets with the **ListSecrets** permission etc. The **GetSecretValue** permission is dependent on the **ListSecrets** permission. Such a policy could look like this, where you define both permissions within the specific policy document:

```
{
  "Version": "2012-10-17",
  "Statement": [
    {
      "Effect": "Allow",
      "Action": [
        "secretsmanager:GetSecretValue",
        "secretsmanager:ListSecrets"
      ],
      "Resource": "*"
    }
  ]
}
```

> **Note: You can define multiple permissions for specific resources granting the same effect by specifying the action key as an array and adding the permissions within.**

For the rest of the recipes and examples in this chapter, we are going to need an IAM user with permissions to create, manage and delete EC2 instances and S3Buckets. We also want this user to be able to Get information about itself using the **Get-IAMUser** cmdlet and we want it to be able to also list and delete IAM users. It should also be able to read and write secrets in the AWS secrets manager. For permissions to manage EC2 instances, S3Buckets and the AWS secret manager, we use AWS managed policies. For listing and deleting users, we are going to create a custom policy with the required permissions. For deleting a user, it is not just enough to have the **iam:DeleteUser** permission. It also requires other dependent permissions for resources associated with a user, such as access keys, policies, and groups. So, the user also needs to be able to list and delete access keys, list and delete user policies and list a user's group memberships and be able to remove a user from groups. We create a custom policy with all the required permissions. The policies will be attached to a group and the user will be added as a member to this group. The user also require an access key, so it can be used programmatically. To summarize:

We create a new user that can manage different resources. We call it **RM** (short for **ResourceManager User**).

We create an access key for the user.

We create a new group called **RMGroup** (short for **ResourceManager Group**) and add the *RM* user as a member to this group.

We define the custom policy as described above in a policy document and create a new custom policy with the defined permissions called **RMPolicy** (**ResourceManager Policy**).

We create an array containing the ARN´s of all the policies we are going to apply to the **RMGroup** and then we use a loop to register each policy for the **RMGroup**.

We use the **Set-AWSCredentials** cmdlet to override the credentials file and switch the credential context to the new RM user for this shell session.

All output of the cmdlets, besides the **Register-IAMGroupPolicy** cmdlet, are assigned to variables so that those can be used as arguments for the following cmdlets parameters. The **New-IAMAccessKey** output is assigned to the **$RMUserKey** variable and the properties for the access key from this variable are later used as arguments for the **Set-AWSCredentials** cmdlets parameters and so on. This process can be created with the combination of commands shown here:

```
# Create a new user with permission for EC2,S3, Secrets manager and for
listing and deleting users
# Create the IAM user
$User = New-IAMUser -UserName RM
# Create access key for the user
$RMUserKey = New-IAMAccessKey -UserName $User.UserName
#Create the IAM group
$Group = New-IAMGroup -GroupName RMGroup
# Add the user to the group
Add-IAMUserToGroup -UserName $User.UserName `
-GroupName $Group.GroupName
# Create a policy that have permissions to delete a user
$CustomPolicy = @"
{
    "Version": "2012-10-17",
    "Statement": [
        {
            "Effect": "Allow",
```

```
            "Action": [
                "iam:GetUser",
                "iam:ListUsers",
                "iam:DeleteUser",
                "iam:ListAccessKeys",
                "iam:DeleteAccessKey",
                "iam:ListUserPolicies",
                "iam:DeleteUserPolicy",
                "iam:ListGroupsForUser",
                "iam:RemoveUserFromGroup"
            ],
            "Resource": "*"
        }
    ]
}
"@
$NewCustomPolicy = New-IAMPolicy -PolicyName "RMPolicy" `
-PolicyDocument $CustomPolicy `
-Description "This grants custom permissions"
# Define relevant policies
$Policies = @(
    "arn:aws:iam::aws:policy/AmazonEC2FullAccess"
    "arn:aws:iam::aws:policy/AmazonS3FullAccess"
    "arn:aws:iam::aws:policy/SecretsManagerReadWrite"
    "$($NewCustomPolicy.Arn)"
)
foreach ($Policy in $Policies){
    Register-IAMGroupPolicy -GroupName $Group.GroupName `
    -PolicyArn $Policy
}
Set-AWSCredentials -AccessKey $RMUserKey.AccessKeyId `
-SecretKey $RMUserKey.SecretAccessKey
```

When we execute these commands the **RM** user and the **RMGroup** is created. The group is assigned the policies with the permissions and the user is added to the group, inheriting these permissions. The context is switched to the RM user as we can see in *Figure 11.16* when listing the current user with the **Get-IAMUser** cmdlet:

```
● PS C:\Temp> Get-IAMUser

  Arn                   : arn:aws:iam::940529233191:user/RM
  CreateDate            : 02-11-2023 19:50:49
  PasswordLastUsed      : 01-01-0001 00:00:00
  Path                  : /
  PermissionsBoundary   :
  Tags                  : {}
  UserId                : AIDA5V67JFUT7EN25ZRC3
  UserName              : RM
```

Figure 11.16: Listing the context of the current user using the Get-IAMUser cmdlet, confirming that the RM user have been created and the context is set to this user

We can check if the different permissions that we have assigned to the RM user through the RMGroup membership work as expected by executing a few commands. In *Figure 11.17* we list the Test3 user, then we delete this user and try to list it again after it is deleted. Confirming that both the list users and the delete users permissions are assigned and working as expected for the RM user:

```
● PS C:\Temp> Get-IAMUser Test3 | Select-Object UserName

  UserName
  --------
  Test3

● PS C:\Temp> Remove-IAMUser Test3 -Confirm:$false
● PS C:\Temp> Get-IAMUser Test3 | Select-Object UserName
  Get-IAMUser: The user with name Test3 cannot be found.
```

Figure 11.17: Confirming that list users and delete users permissions are working as expected for the RM user by listing and deleting the Test3 user

> To work with and manage the AWS Secrets manager you must install the AWS.Tools.SecretsManager module when using the modularized version of AWS Tools for PowerShell: Install-AWSToolsModule AWS.Tools.SecretsManager. When we do an install of a sub-module and then we want to import them, we may get an error stating that assemblies are already in use. In this case we may need to restart our PowerShell session.

Furthermore, we can check if we can create a new secret in the secrets manager using the **New-SECSecret** cmdlet and that these permissions are working as expected for the RM user, as shown in *Figure 11.18*:

```
⊕ PS C:\Temp> New-SECSecret -Name "TestSecret" -SecretString "VerySecret" -Region "eu-north-1"

  ARN                                                                  Name       ReplicationStatus VersionId
  ---                                                                  ----       ----------------- ---------
  arn:aws:secretsmanager:eu-north-1:940529233191:secret:TestSecret-DMoPmD TestSecret {}                      ad619ebe-5d7f-4967-8743-2c157278bfdb
```

Figure 11.18: Creating a new secret in AWS secrets manager using the context of the RM user

We could do the same to check the permissions for EC2 and S3 by trying to create an EC2 instance and an S3 Bucket, but for now we assume that these also work as expected. The commands for creating the RM user, the RMGroup, assigning the permissions and creating the access key can easily be ported to a script that have parameters for the user and group names, the access key credentials could easily be saved to a file or a secure location by some other means. Instead of creating the specific policies with permissions inside such as script, you could pre-define sets of policies within your account that could be attached to IAM groups. With some tweaks to the code logic, you could easily create a script that can be used to create different IAM users with different group memberships with different permissions for a variety of tasks.

Managing AWS EC2 instances

Elastic Compute Cloud (EC2) is a fundamental service offered by AWS that provides scalable and resizable virtual machines known as instances. EC2 offers a wide range of instance types optimized for various use cases that differ in the terms of CPU, memory, storage, and network performance allowing for the creation of instances for almost any types of scenarios and workloads. EC2 is scalable both vertically (by resizing instances) and horizontally (by launching multiple instances) to accommodate changing workloads depending on your demands. EC2 instances supports both Windows, macOS and Linux based images with a variety of different operating systems to choose from. EC2 instances can use different kinds of storage such as **Elastic Block Store Volumes (EBS)** for block storage, **Elastic File System (EFS)** for file storage and S3 Buckets for storing, sharing, and transferring data and files between different EC2 instances. EC2 instances are typically launched from so-called **Amazon Machine Images (AMI´s)** which is an AWS maintained and pre-configured image that includes the operating system and provides all information and configurations that are required to launch an instance. Multiple instances can be launched from the same AMI ensuring consistent and concise configurations and you can also create your own custom AMI´s that include your own configurations and applications allowing you to launch instances that matches your desired setup whenever needed. EC2 is a versatile service resource that allows you to run applications, host websites, store data and handling a wide range of workloads on virtual machine instances in AWS not limited to a single type of use case.

Recipe 70: Create and manage EC2 instances, key pairs and security groups

To create an EC2 instance, you need at least an image id for an AMI. An instance type, which defines the instances resources such as CPU and memory. A security group, which will be created if no one is specified or exists. You would also need to specify the region where your instance will be hosted and furthermore you need a set of key pairs which are used to securely connect to your instance. For Windows instances, the key pair is used to decrypt the administrator password. You then use the decrypted password to connect to your instance. In this recipe we are going to go through and learn about each of these dependencies that are required to be able to create and manage an EC2 instance.

Amazon Machine Images

There are numerous **Amazon Machine Images (AMI´s)** available between AWS, the AMI marketplace and community created AMI´s. It can be a hurdle to find a specific image if you have very specific needs, but Amazon offers so-called quick start AMI´s which is a collection of the most used AMI´s for all types of operating systems and there is also public free tier eligible AMI´s available. You can use the **Get-EC2Image** cmdlet with the **-Region** parameter to list all available AMI´s. As mentioned, this is currently a big list so it could take a while. *Figure 11.19* shows the count of all available AMI´s in the **eu-north-1** region as the writing of this chapter:

```
⊛ PS C:\Temp> (Get-EC2Image -Region eu-north-1).count
  53753
```

Figure 11.19: Listing all available AMIs in the eu-north-1 region using the Get-EC2Image cmdlet

The **Get-EC2Image** cmdlet have a **-Filter** parameter that can help narrow the search for AMI´s. The filter is an array of Hashtables that are used to define the properties and the specific property values we want to filter:

```
$Filter = @{
    Name = "architecture"; Values = "x86_64"
}, @{
    Name = "description"; Values = "Amazon Linux 2 AMI*"
}, @{
    Name = "is-public"; Values = "true"
}, @{
    Name = "state"; Values = "available"
}
```

In this example we are filtering for Amazon Linux 2 AMI´s that are x86_64 (64-bit), have descriptions that match "Amazon Linux 2 AMI*", are public (free), and are in the available state. Figure 11.20 shows the count when executing the **Get-EC2Image** cmdlet with this filter applied:

```
● PS C:\Temp> (Get-EC2Image -Region eu-north-1 -Filter $Filter).count
  132
```

Figure 11.20: *Listing AMIs with a filter searching for specific architecture, description, availability, and state*

This narrows the list. You can change the values to search for images with Windows, Ubuntu and so on to look for specific images. You can of course always use the console or other means to find a specific image id that is suitable for your specific requirements. Once you have found a suitable image, you should note its id or store it in a variable in your session. It is also a good idea to make and save a list with image id´s you are going to use frequently. An image ID has a format such as this:

ami-0fe8bec493a81c7da

Instance types

An instance type is used to define instance resources such as CPU, memory, network speed and in some cases GPU. To search for instance types, you use the **Get-EC2InstanceType** cmdlet. There are over 350 instance types to choose from. This cmdlet also provides a **-Filter** parameter that works like the parameter for the **Get-EC2Image** cmdlet. You can also use the **Where-Object** filter cmdlet to search and filter for different properties like the number of CPU cores, the memory size, and the memory size for the GPU if you need this resource. Here are two examples filtering for specific instance type properties using the **Where-Object** cmdlet. Note that memory is specified in MiB:

```
Get-EC2InstanceType -Region $Region | `

Where-Object {

    $_.VCpuInfo.DefaultVCpus -eq 2 `

    -and $_.MemoryInfo.SizeInMib -eq 1024

}
```

There are only two instance types with these properties. 2 VCPUs and 1GB of memory. These are the t4g.micro and the t3.micro which are common instance types usually used for testing purposes and very small and simple workloads.

The next example searches for instances containing a GPU:

```
Get-EC2InstanceType -Region $Region | `

Where-Object {

    $_.VCpuInfo.DefaultVCpus -eq 8 `

    -and $_.MemoryInfo.SizeInMib -ge 24576 `

    -and $_.GpuInfo.TotalGpuMemoryInMiB -ge 24576

}
```

We search for an instance type with 8 VCPUs, at least 24GB of memory and with a GPU with at least 24 GB of dedicated memory. There are only one instance type matching these properties, the g5.2xlarge type. Make a note of the instance type name you want to use.

Security groups

EC2 instances are upon instantiation, by default assigned a public IP address so that the resource is accessible. Windows systems are usually accessible from port 3389 using **Remote Desktop Protocol (RDP)** and Linux systems are accessible from port 22 with **SSH**. For security reasons an instance must have a security group, which is a set of firewall rules that controls the traffic for your instance. You can create a security group with a set of your own pre-defined rules and attach this security group to an instance when it is created. You can use the same security group for multiple instances that needs the same set of rules. Or you can create a new security group specifically for a new instance, with its own set of rules.

> **Note: When you create an EC2 instance from within the console, the default is to allow access from all IP addresses. It is recommended to create security group rules to allow access from known IP addresses only. If you create an EC2 instance programmatically using the AWS Tools for PowerShell cmdlets, the default is that all IP addresses are denied. You should create a security group rule that allows at least your own IP address for allowing access to an instance.**

You should create security group rules in your security group that only allows the IP addresses that are required for accessing and managing your instance. You can also use security group rules to allow traffic between specific instances on specific ports.

Key pairs

Key pairs are a set of public and private keys that are used to authenticate and securely access your Linux instances through SSH. For Windows instances the key pair are used for decrypting the administrator password for the built-in administrator account. Once you create a key pair, the private key is private for you and must be saved and stored securely on your system or machine. The public key is stored in AWS. You can either use the same set of key pairs for all instances, or specify different key pairs for specific instances. When you log into an instance using SSH you must specify the private key that matches the public key.

> **Info: AWS never stores the private key, so if you lose it, there is no way to recover it. AWS have alternative methods for accessing instances if you have lost the private key. You should refer to the latest updated AWS documentation in such situations.**

To create a new key pair, you use the `New-EC2KeyPair` cmdlet. A key pair requires a name, a key type that can be either ed25519 or RSA. This type defines the cryptographic algorithms and the key size used for encryption, where the rsa is a longer key than the ed25519 type and provides a larger computational overhead but also a stronger encryption due to its larger size. A key pair can be in either .pem or .ppk format where pem is usually used for

OpenSSH and the ppk format is used by putty.

When you log in to a Linux instance using the key pair, you simply have to specify the path to the private key file on your system or machine. If you use SSH it could look like this:

```
# Connect to a Linux instance using SSH
ssh -i <PathToPrivateKey.pem file> ec2-user@<PublicIpForEC2Instance>
ssh -i C:\Temp\SSHKey.pem ec2-user@123.10.10.123
```

For windows you can use the **Get-EC2PasswordData** cmdlet, the instance id of your instance and the key pair to decrypt the Administrator password like this:

```
# Decrypt Windows administrator password using key pair
$InstanceId = "YourInstanceId"
$PasswordData = Get-EC2PasswordData -InstanceId $InstanceId -KeyPair
"YourKeyPairName"
$DecryptedPassword = [System.Text.Encoding]::UTF8.GetString([System.
Convert]::FromBase64String($PasswordData.PasswordData))
Write-Output $DecryptedPassword
```

Replace **YourInstanceId** with the actual id of your EC2 instance and **YourKeyPairName** with the name of your key pair.

Create and manage EC2 instances

The minimum requirements for creating an EC2 instance is to have a key pair, an image id and the instance type. If you do not specify a security group one will be created, or it uses the default if you have previously created one.

> **Note: That you should still be in the context of the previously created RM IAM user with the permissions granted by the policies attached to the RMGroup IAM group. Or in the context of an administrator user with the required permissions to create EC2 instances.**

Most EC2 instance cmdlets requires a region to be specified. You should create all relevant and dependent resources within the same region. In this recipe we are going to create an EC2 instance using an Ubuntu AMI and we use the **eu-north-1** region which we assign to the **$Region** variable:

```
$Region = "eu-north-1"
```

1. First, we create the key pair and assign it to the **$SSHKey** variable:

   ```
   # Create a new Key Pair
   $SSHKey = New-EC2KeyPair -KeyName "SSHKey" `
   -KeyType "ED25519" `
   ```

```
-KeyFormat pem `
```

```
-Region $Region
```

> **The *-KeyType* should be either Ed25519 or Rsa which is the default. Ed25519 keys are not supported for Windows instances.**

2. The private key in the output from the command is placed in the **KeyMaterial** property in the **$SSHKey** variable. We save this key to a file for later use:

```
# Save the Private Key to a file
```

```
$SSHKey.KeyMaterial | Out-File C:\Temp\SSHKeys\SSHKey.pem
```

3. For this instance, we want to use an Ubuntu 22.04 AMI and noted the specific AMI id as: ***ami-0fe8bec493a81c7da.***

4. We are also going to use a small instance type and have selected the *t3.micro* that comes with 2VCPUs and 1GB memory.

5. Now that a region is specified, we have created a key pair and we have chosen the AMI and instance type to use, we can create a new EC2 instance using the **New-EC2Instance** cmdlet and provide the relevant arguments to the **-ImageId**, **-InstanceType**, **-KeyName** and **-Region** parameters, but before we create it, we also want to tag the instance to provide it with a name.

6. Tagging instances is a bit special in AWS. First we create a Hashtable with a key name named **Key**, where we specify that the key we want to tag is called **Name** by setting this as the value. We then add the key called **Value** and specify the value of the name we want the instance to be named. Now we have to create a new object of the **Amazon.EC2.Model.TagSpecification** type where we need to set the **ResourceType** property as "**instance**" and then use the **Tags.Add()** method to add the tag we defined in the Hashtable. We then use the **-TagSpecification** parameter of the **New-EC2Instance** cmdlet and provide the tag specification as an argument. Adding a name tag to the instance makes it easier to get an overview of your instances, especially if you are using the AWS console. We create the tag and the EC2 instance:

```
# Create an EC2 instance with a Name tag
```

```
$Tag_Name = @{Key="Name";Value="TestUbuntu"}
```

```
$TagSpec = new-object Amazon.EC2.Model.TagSpecification
```

```
$TagSpec.ResourceType = "instance"
```

```
$TagSpec.Tags.Add($Tag_Name)
```

```
$EC2 = New-EC2Instance `
```

```
-ImageId "ami-0fe8bec493a81c7da" `
```

```
-InstanceType "t3.micro" `
```

```
-KeyName $SSHKey.KeyName `
```

```
-Region $Region `
-TagSpecification $TagSpec
```

It can take a few moments before the EC2 instance is created and running.

7. The new EC2 instance is now referenced in the **$EC2** variable, but since this variable was created and assigned at the moment the command was executed, not all properties such as the instance public IP address have not yet been populated. It takes a moment for a new instance to start up and get its properties. We still have the reference to the instance in this variable, but if we want to make sure it is populated with properties after the instance is fully created, we can update the **$EC2** variable using the **Get-EC2Instance** cmdlet:

    ```
    $EC2 = ($EC2 | Get-EC2Instance -Region $Region)
    ```

8. Now we can get the public IP address for the instance, which we are going to need before we can connect to it. We can find this in the **$EC2** instance variable. But we also know that the security group by default blocks all incoming traffic, we need to create a new security group rule that allows our public IP address. For creating this rule, we need the GroupID property value from the security group attached to the instance, which we can also find in the **$EC2** instance variable. We save the public IP address for the instance in the **$PublicIP** variable and the security groups **GroupID** in the **$SECGroupID** variable. Since instances is stored in an array in the instance variable, we use indexing:

    ```
    $PublicIP = $EC2.Instances[0].PublicIPAddress
    $SECGroupID = $EC2.Instances[0].SecurityGroups.GroupID
    ```

9. To create a new security group rule we use a Hashtable to specify the properties and values like protocol, source and destination ports and the IP address or IP range we want to allow. We assign this to the **$IpPermission** variable. But first we need to get our public IP address. We use the **Invoke-RestMethod** to call the **https://httpbin.org/ip** site where we can retrieve our public IP and assign this to a variable called **$MyIP**. The source and destination ports are set to **22** for SSH and the protocol to use is **TCP**:

    ```
    $MyIP = (Invoke-RestMethod "http://httpbin.org/ip").origin
    $IpPermission = @{
        "IpProtocol" = "tcp"
        "FromPort" = 22
        "ToPort" = 22
        "IpRanges" = "$MyIP/32"
    }
    ```

10. We can now create the inbound security group rule using the **Grant-EC2SecurityGroupIngress** cmdlet. We specify the **-GroupID**, the **-IpPermission**

and the **-Region** parameters:

```
Grant-EC2SecurityGroupIngress `
-GroupId $SECGroupID `
-IpPermission $IpPermission `
-Region $Region
```

11. Now that we have created a key pair, the EC2 instance and a security group rule that allows our public IP address to access the instance, we should now be able to access the instance directly using SSH. But we need one more thing. The username for the instance default user. The default username for an EC2 instance is determined by the AMI. For Debian AMI´s the username would be admin, for Amazon Linux AMI´s it would be ec2-user and for Ubuntu it would be ubuntu. Windows AMI´s are always created with the default Administrator user.

Note: Default usernames for all AMI types can be found in AWS documentation: https://docs.aws.amazon.com/AWSEC2/latest/UserGuide/managing-users.html. You can always create more users within an instance for individual users.

12. Since we have created an EC2 instance with an Ubuntu AMI, the default username in our case is ubuntu. We can assign this to a variable. **$UserName**:

```
$UserName = "ubuntu"
```

13. Now we should be able to directly connect to the instance using SSH. We use the **-i** parameter to specify the path to the private key file and specify the username and the public IP address for the instance from their respective variables:

```
ssh -i C:\Temp\SSHKeys\SSHKey.pem $UserName@$PublicIP
```

14. *Figure 11.21* shows the successful SSH connection to the EC2 Ubuntu instance:

```
PS C:\Temp> ssh -i C:\Temp\SSHKeys\SSHKey.pem $UserName@$PublicIP
Welcome to Ubuntu 22.04.3 LTS (GNU/Linux 6.2.0-1012-aws x86_64)

  System information as of Sun Nov  5 12:00:30 UTC 2023

  System load:  0.0              Processes:               100
  Usage of /:   20.7% of 7.57GB  Users logged in:         0
  Memory usage: 21%              IPv4 address for ens5:   172.31.22.219
  Swap usage:   0%

The list of available updates is more than a week old.
To check for new updates run: sudo apt update

Last login: Sun Nov  5 11:49:22 2023 from 5.186.57.95
To run a command as administrator (user "root"), use "sudo <command>".
See "man sudo_root" for details.

ubuntu@ip-172-31-22-219:~$ whoami
ubuntu
```

Figure 11.21: *Using ssh to connect to the EC2 Ubuntu instance*

The EC2 instance is successfully created, the security group rule successfully allows our public IP address to access the instance on port 22 using SSH and the key pair allows us to authenticate to the instance as the ubuntu user.

You can list all the relevant cmdlets for working with EC2 instances using the **Get-Command** cmdlet:

```
Get-Command | Where-Object {$_.Name -match "EC2Instance"}
```

You can list all EC2 instances in your account and region:

```
# List all EC2 Instances in your account/Region
Get-EC2Instance -Region eu-north-1
# List all EC2 instances and their instance properties
(Get-EC2Instance -Region eu-north-1).Instances
```

There are commands for stopping, starting, restarting and resetting instances:

```
# Get instance iD for specific instance (referenced in a variable)
$InstanceID = $EC2.Instances.InstanceId
# Stop EC2 Instance
Stop-EC2Instance -Region $Region -InstanceId $InstanceId
# Start EC2 Instance
Start-EC2Instance -Region $Region -InstanceId $InstanceId
# Restart EC2 Instance
Restart-EC2Instance -Region $Region -InstanceId $InstanceId
# Reset EC2 Instance
Reset-EC2Instance -Region $Region -InstanceId $InstanceId
```

You can terminate and remove instances:

```
# Terminate and remove EC2 Instance
Remove-EC2Instance -Region $Region -InstanceId $InstanceId
# Terminate and remove EC2 Instance without confirmation prompt
Remove-EC2Instance -Region $Region -InstanceId $InstanceId -Confirm:$false
```

> **Note that when you terminate and remove your instances the associated key pairs and security group are not removed. If these are not needed anymore you should remove them using the Remove-EC2KeyPair and Remove-EC2SecurityGroup cmdlets.**

The example EC2 instance in this recipe is created with the minimum required settings and configurations. When you create a new EC2 instance using the **New-EC2Instance** cmdlet there are a lot more settings that can be configured such as setting a specific network interface, specifying subnets and enabling IPV6 addresses and so on. You should refer to the official AWS documentation for the **New-EC2Instance** cmdlet for specific configurations and parameters that are available.

You can use the examples in this recipe as a template for creating scripts that can automatically create EC2 instances, create the proper security group rules and create and save the private key file at specific locations enabling you to quickly provision and de-provision EC2 instance resources when needed.

> **Note: EC2 instances are billable by-the-hour resources, and you should remove instances as soon as they are not needed, or at least stop them so they do not use computational resources. Also pay attention to the instance types and AMI´s that you are using. Large instances with GPUs can be quite expensive and some AMI´s might require additional licensing.**

Managing AWS S3 buckets

S3 stands for Simple Storage Service which is an object storage service that allows you to store and retrieve data such as files, images, and other objects. S3 is highly scalable, durable, and secure. A bucket is a container for storing data in S3. Note that buckets must have a unique name across all of AWS. Buckets are used for storing objects which is the actual data. Each object in a bucket is uniquely identified by a key which can be compared to a file and its path. Data can be replicated across multiple availability zones within a region or between regions which ensures high availability and data redundancy. It is highly scalable and can in principle store an almost unlimited amount of data. It also provides security features in the terms of encryption of data, access control and **Identity and Access Management (IAM)** for securing data. You can control who exactly can access and modify objects and buckets. You can also manage the lifecycle of buckets that includes automatic archiving of infrequently used data, automatic deletion, and versioning. S3 also offers different classes of storage each with its own configurations, costs, and access patterns. Standard storage is designed for frequently accessing data or you can choose storage classes for infrequently used data and data that should be archived. The versatility and scalability of S3 make it suitable for a wide range of use cases, from data storage and backup to content distribution and application data hosting.

Recipe 71: Create and manage S3 buckets including uploading and downloading objects

Working with S3 buckets requires the **AWS.Tools.S3** module when using the modularized version of AWS Tools for PowerShell. Install the module using the **Install-Module AWS.Tools.S3** command.

You can use the **Get-Command** cmdlet to list all relevant S3 bucket cmdlets available in the module:

```
# List all S3 Bucket cmdlets
Get-Command | Where-Object {$_.Name -match "S3"}
```

> Note: All cmdlets in this recipe that requires an argument for the -Region parameter uses the $Region variable that are set to eu-north-1. Also note that we use the RM IAM user and the permissions that is granted by policies attached to the RMGroup IAM group. We can also globally set the default region, so we don't need to specify the -Region parameter for each cmdlet: Set-DefaultAWSRegion -Region eu-north-1.

- To create a new S3 bucket, use the **New-S3Bucket** cmdlet. You need to at least provide a bucket name that must be unique across all of AWS. If you do not provide a region, it will be placed in your default region:

```
New-S3Bucket `
-BucketName "moppleit-test-bucket" `
-Region $Region
```

> Note: The bucket name scheme is quite restrictive so all characters in the bucket name must be lowercase.

- To list all of your AWS accounts S3 buckets, use the **Get-S3Bucket** cmdlet. This will list all buckets across all regions. Figure 11.22 shows a list of the current S3 buckets:

```
 PS C:\Temp> Get-S3Bucket

    CreationDate          BucketName
    ------------          ----------
    05-11-2023 16:05:39  moppleit-development-bucket
    05-11-2023 16:05:49  moppleit-production-bucket
    05-11-2023 15:42:16  moppleit-test-bucket
```

Figure 11.22: Listing all S3 buckets across all regions using the Get-S3Bucket cmdlet

AWS Tools for PowerShell contains different cmdlets that can be used to retrieve different information and properties about buckets such as attached access control lists, encryption scheme used by a bucket, a buckets region, attached policies and tags etc.:

```
# Get different information and properties of a specific bucket
# Get bucket Access Controll List (ACL)
Get-S3ACL -BucketName moppleit-test-bucket
# Get bucket encryption scheme
Get-S3BucketEncryption moppleit-test-bucket
# Get bucket location (Region)
Get-S3BucketLocation moppleit-test-bucket
```

```
# Get bucket attached policies
Get-S3BucketPolicy moppleit-test-bucket
# Get bucket tags
Get-S3BucketTagging moppleit-test-bucket
```

- For writing (uploading) data to a bucket, we use the **Write-S3Object** cmdlet. Use the **-File** parameter to specify the path to a local file that you want to upload to the bucket:

```
# Upload a file to a bucket
Write-S3Object -BucketName moppleit-test-bucket `
-File "C:\Temp\Data.zip"
```

- We can use the **-Key** parameter to specify a key in the bucket where files should be placed. This is equivalent to specifying a path:

```
# Upload a file to a bucket in specific key (path)
Write-S3Object -BucketName moppleit-test-bucket `
-File "C:\Temp\MoreData.zip" `
-Key "ZipFiles/MoreData"
# Upload a file to a bucket in specific key (path)
Write-S3Object -BucketName moppleit-test-bucket `
-File "C:\Temp\MostData.zip" `
-Key "ZipFiles/MoreData/MostData.zip"
```

- You can also write (upload) all files within a folder using the **-Folder** parameter specifying a path to a local folder as an argument. You also need to specify the **-KeyPrefix** parameter for applying a key prefix to all files in the folder if you would add it to a specific key (path) within the bucket. You also need to set the **-Recurse** switch parameter if you want to include all sub-folders and their content. If you omit this parameter, only files in the specified path will be uploaded to the bucket:

```
Write-S3Object -BucketName moppleit-test-bucket `
-Folder "C:\Temp\Files" `
-KeyPrefix "Temp/Files" `
-Recurse
```

- To list all objects in a bucket you use the **Get-S3Object** cmdlet:

```
# List all objects in an S3 bucket
Get-S3Object -BucketName moppleit-test-bucket
```

- You can list a specific object using the **-Key** parameter:

```
# List a specific object in an S3 bucket
```

```
Get-S3Object -BucketName moppleit-test-bucket `
-Key "Temp/Files/Books.xml"
```

- To list all objects in a specific key, you use the **-KeyPrefix** parameter:

```
Get-S3Object -BucketName moppleit-test-bucket `
-KeyPrefix "Temp/Files"
```

- To read (download) files from a bucket, you use the **Read-S3Object** cmdlet. The **-Key** parameter is used to specify a specific file within the bucket and the **-File** parameter is used to specify the path where the file should be saved locally. You could also use this parameter to rename the file before downloading it:

```
# Read (download) a specific file from a bucket
Read-S3Object -BucketName moppleit-test-bucket `
-Key "Temp/Files/Books.xml" `
-File "C:\Temp\Books.xml"
```

- You can also read (download) an entire folder from the bucket. Use the **-KeyPrefix** parameter to specify the key (folder) in the bucket that you want to download. Use the **-Folder** parameter to specify a local folder where the folder should be saved. If you specify a local folder that does not exist, it will be created:

```
# Read (download) all content from a keyprefix (folder) in a bucket
Read-S3Object -BucketName moppleit-test-bucket `
-KeyPrefix "Temp/Files" `
-Folder "C:\Temp\NewTemp"
```

- To delete a specific file in a bucket, you use the **Remove-S3Object** cmdlet with the **-Key** parameter specifying the file to delete:

```
# Delete a specific file in a bucket
Remove-S3Object -BucketName moppleit-test-bucket `
-Key "Temp/Files/Books.xml" `
-Confirm:$false
```

- The **Remove-S3Object** cmdlet does not have a **-KeyPrefix** parameter, so in order to delete an entire folder from the bucket, we instead use the **Get-S3Object** cmdlet with the **-KeyPrefix** parameter to retrieve all files in that specific key (folder) and then pipe the command to the **Remove-S3Bucket** cmdlet. This command will also output all deleted files:

```
# Delete a folder in a bucket
Get-S3Object -BucketName moppleit-test-bucket `
-KeyPrefix "Temp/Files" | `
```

```
Remove-S3Object `

-Force
```

To override the confirmation prompt when using the Remove-S3Object cmdlet to delete a file or a folder in a bucket, you can use either the -Confirm:$false or the -Force parameter.

- For deleting an entire S3 bucket you use the **Remove-S3Bucket** cmdlet and specify the bucket name as an argument to the **-BucketName** parameter. You cannot delete a bucket that contains files unless you specify the **-DeleteBucketContent** parameter. Use the **-Confirm:$false** or the **-Force** parameter to override the confirmation prompt:

```
# Delete an S3 bucket

Remove-S3Bucket -BucketName moppleit-test-bucket `

-DeleteBucketContent `

-Force
```

Figure 11.23 show how easy it is to create a new S3 bucket, upload a file called **Data.zip** to it, download the file back locally with a new name, **NewData.zip** and then deleting the bucket:

```
PS C:\Temp> $BucketName = "moppleit-s3"
New-S3Bucket -BucketName $BucketName -Region $Region

CreationDate        BucketName
------------        ----------
05-11-2023 18:10:02 moppleit-s3

PS C:\Temp>
PS C:\Temp> Write-S3Object -BucketName $BucketName `
-File "C:\Temp\Data.zip"
PS C:\Temp>
PS C:\Temp> Read-S3Object -BucketName $BucketName `
-Key "Data.zip" `
-File "C:\Temp\NewData.zip"

Mode                LastWriteTime         Length Name
----                -------------         ------ ----
-a---         05-11-2023     19:10           2508 NewData.zip

PS C:\Temp>
PS C:\Temp> Remove-S3Bucket -BucketName $BucketName `
-DeleteBucketContent `
-Force
PS C:\Temp> Get-S3Bucket moppleit-s3
PS C:\Temp>
```

Figure 11.23: *Creation of an S3 bucket, writing a file, reading a file and saving it with a new name and then the deletion of the bucket*

Working with S3 buckets is quite easy with the AWS tools for PowerShell. Remember that the IAM user that is used must have the proper permissions, like the *RM* IAM user that is used in this recipe. You should limit the access to specific S3 buckets to only users or groups that specifically require access using policies or else all users and groups with permissions to manage S3 buckets in general, will be able to access them.

Recipe 72: Create policies allowing only IAM users in specific IAM groups to access S3 buckets

You can limit access to specific S3 buckets using policies. It is recommended to attach a policy to specific IAM users or an IAM group, so that only users in that group are allowed to access specific buckets. In this recipe we create a new bucket and a new IAM group. Then we create a policy that only provides access to read (download) and write (upload) files to that bucket, and then attach this policy to the IAM group.

> Note: **We need to use a user with permissions to create IAM groups and policies. If you are still working in the context of the RM user that was previously set using the Set-AWSCredentials cmdlet, you should switch back to the user with full permissions that was set in the AWS credentials file. To remove the context of a user and go back to use the credentials from the AWS credentials file, you can either restart the PowerShell session or remove the current users context with the Clear-AWSCredentials cmdlet.**

1. First we create a new IAM Group called **BucketAccess**:

   ```
   # Create a new IAM Group

   New-IAMGroup -GroupName BucketAccess
   ```

2. Then we create a new S3 bucket called **moppleit-access-limit**. Access to this bucket will be limited to users in the **BucketAccess** IAM group:

   ```
   # Create a new S3 bucket

   New-S3Bucket -BucketName moppleit-access-limit `
   -Region eu-north-1
   ```

3. We need to define a policy that allows the **BucketAccess** group to **Get** and **Put** objects in the bucket, which grants access to read and write files from and to the bucket. The policy is defined in a **hashtable** and assigned to the **$AccessPolicy** variable. Note that we specify the name of the specific bucket within the **Resource** key within the policy document:

   ```
   $AccessPolicy = @{
       "Version" = "2012-10-17"
       "Statement" = @(
           @{
               "Effect" = "Allow"
   ```

```
            "Action" = @(
                "s3:GetObject",
                "s3:PutObject"
            )
            "Resource" = "arn:aws:s3:::moppleit-access-limit/*"
        }
    )
}
```

4. We use the **New-IAMPolicy** to create the policy. We assign the command to the **$GroupPolicy** variable, so that we can easily retrieve the ARN we need to use for registering the policy to the **BucketAccess** group:

```
# Create the new policy
$GroupPolicy = New-IAMPolicy -PolicyName "AccessS3-moppleit-access-
limit" `
    -PolicyDocument  (ConvertTo-Json $AccessPolicy -Depth 10) `
-Description "This grants Get/Put on S3 moppleit-access-limit"
```

5. Then we need to attach the policy to the group using the **Register-IAMGroupPolicy** cmdlet:

```
# Attach the policy to IAM the group
Register-IAMGroupPolicy -GroupName "BucketAccess" `
-PolicyArn $GroupPolicy.Arn
```

6. Now users that are member of the **BucketAccess** IAM group will be granted permissions to read (download) and write (upload) files from and too the **moppleit-access-limit** bucket. Unless they have other memberships or permissions that grants them more permission to S3 buckets in general that supersedes the permissions granted by the **BucketAccess** group. If you grant a user permissions to this specific S3 bucket by being a member of the **BucketAccess** group, thus limiting their permissions to only read and write from the bucket, make sure that they are not members of other groups or have policies attached that grants additional permissions to S3 bucket.

    Figure 11.24 shows the following scenario:

    a. Using **Get-IAMUser** to check the current user context, which is the IAM **Test2** user.

    b. Trying to write a file to the **moppleit-access-limit** bucket. This results in an Access denied error.

    c. We clear the credentials for the **Test2** user and switch the context to the **Test** user with more access (which is the credentials set in the AWS credentials file).

    d. The **Test** user adds the **Test2** user to the **BucketAccess** group.

    e. We then switch back to the context of the **Test2** user using the **Set-AWSCredentials** cmdlet, and then confirm that the context is switched back to the **Test2** user.

    f. Now we read and write files to the **moppleit-access-limit** bucket using the **Test2** users context. It has been granted these permissions from the **BucketAccess** group membership.

    g. We test further access to the bucket by trying to list all the content from the bucket using the **Get-S3Bucket** cmdlet. This is denied since the policy only allows read (Get) and write (Put) permissions to the bucket:

```
⬤ PS C:\Temp> Get-IAMUser | Select-Object -ExpandProperty Username
  Test2
⬤ PS C:\Temp> Write-S3Object -BucketName moppleit-access-limit -File C:\Temp\Books.xml
  Write-S3Object: Access Denied
⬤ PS C:\Temp> Clear-AWSCredentials
⬤ PS C:\Temp> Get-IAMUser | Select-Object -ExpandProperty Username
  Test
⬤ PS C:\Temp> Add-IAMUserToGroup -UserName Test2 -GroupName BucketAccess
⬤ PS C:\Temp> Set-AWSCredentials -SecretKey 3iI7hNRO2nlU62AseLanf/VjcRC+8WQnOVETHImo -AccessKey AKIA5V67JFUTYTPPXCT2
⬤ PS C:\Temp> Get-IAMUser | Select-Object -ExpandProperty Username
  Test2
⬤ PS C:\Temp> Write-S3Object -BucketName moppleit-access-limit -File C:\Temp\Books.xml
⬤ PS C:\Temp> read-S3Object -BucketName moppleit-access-limit -Key Data.zip -File c:\temp\Test.zip

  Mode              LastWriteTime          Length Name
  ----              -------------          ------ ----
  -a---          05-11-2023    20:49         2508 Test.zip

⬤ PS C:\Temp> Get-S3Bucket moppleit-access-limit
  Get-S3Bucket: Access Denied
```

Figure 11.24: *Confirming the permissions granted by the BucketAccess group works as intended*

7. We have confirmed that the policy attached to the **BucketAccess** IAM group <u>only</u> permits the **read** and **write** actions on the **moppleit-access-limit** S3 bucket.

8. You can fine grain permissions to specific resources and limit specific user and groups to only allow certain actions using policies. If you add the **s3:ListBucket** action you will allow users or groups to list the specific bucket resource that is specified in the policy, or you could add the **s3:GetBucketLocation** to grant permissions for listing the buckets region and so on.

You should always use the principal of least privilege when granting permissions for resources to users or groups and it is recommended to use group memberships and apply policies to groups instead of directly attaching policies to users in general. This not only makes permission management much more manageable but also makes it easier to create permission sets for specific resources and granting access to multiple users.

Conclusion

Amazon Web Services enables you to create numerous different resources for almost any task imaginable. If you need computational resources, you create an EC2 instance and if you need storage for backups or for storing other data objects in general you create an S3 bucket. In this chapter we have only scratched the surface and laid the foundation for working with AWS using PowerShell by showing you how to install the AWS Tools for PowerShell and giving you an insight into configuring and using credentials for programmatic access to AWS. We have walked through Identity and Access Management and shown how to create and manage IAM users and groups and learned how to create and manage access keys, permissions, and policies, which are essential for being able to manage and work with AWS in a secure fashion, especially when using and accessing AWS programmatically. We have worked more in-depth with EC2 computational instances and S3 storage buckets and provided you with the initial tools for working with all kinds of AWS resources and services.

While the AWS module is built to comply with the general PowerShell concepts in mind, there are still a few minor discrepancies to highlight. When working with EC2 instances you might have noticed that an instance object does not contain a region property which we might have expected. So, when we pipe this type of object to **Get-EC2Instance** we need to specify the region. We can also see that having both **Get-IAMGroup** and **Get-IAMGroups**, **Get-IAMUser** and **Get-IAMUsers** cmdlets is not common PowerShell practice. Instead, we should have a single cmdlet such as **Get-IAMGroup**, which should work by default without parameters as **Get-IAMGroups**. We could then have an **-Identity** or a **-Name** parameter to restrict the result to a specific instance. For **Get-IAMUser** we should have something like a **-Self** switch to get the context of the current AWS user. The **Update-IAMUser** cmdlet does not follow PowerShell verb usage recommendations. We should instead have a **Set-IAMUser** cmdlet in order to follow these recommendations. All these are minor observations and overall, the AWS module is a great and functional module that makes it easy and secure to work with AWS resources using PowerShell and it is a great and invaluable tool for your toolkit.

With what you have learned in this chapter you are ready to take it further and start migrating some of your infrastructure to the cloud and managing it with PowerShell. The AWS Tools for PowerShell provides modules for working with all kinds of AWS resources and services. Just remember to install the correct modules if you are using the modularized version of the tool, and within a short time you will be able to create and manage any kind of resources and service that AWS provides.

The next chapter showcases how to install and use specific application modules that focus on different aspects of Microsoft 365 applications management. The chapter covers management of SharePoint online, Exchange online and Microsoft Teams using PowerShell. Additionally, it introduces the Microsoft Graph API and the Microsoft Graph PowerShell SDK module describing installation, configuration, and authentication. Furthermore, the chapter gives an overview of how to manage Entra ID users and licenses using PowerShell and the modules.

## CHAPTER 12

Microsoft 365 Applications Management

Introduction

Microsoft is one of the leading companies in providing office tools that targets all audiences from single individuals to large organizations. They offer tools that are not only used for word processing and spreadsheet creation but also tools for online collaboration and communication between individuals and entire teams both inside and outside organizations. SharePoint online is used for storing, sharing, and managing digital information within organizations and provides services such as newsfeeds that keeps you updated on the latest news and trends within your organization and SharePoint sites offers a web-based collaborative platform that can be used for creating both personal sites for your employees and intranet sites that provide a centralized news and information hub.

It also provides a central repository for storing and managing documents making it easy for team members to access and collaborate on files. Exchange online is a cloud-based messaging solution that not only allows you to create, send, and receive emails but also offer additional features such as calendars, contacts and tasks, making it easy to communicate with anyone everywhere and also let you keep track of your meetings, schedules and tasks and allows you to manage your personal and professional contacts within a single application. Teams is a communication and collaboration platform that takes real-time communication both inside and outside organizations to a new level by providing chat, calls, and video messaging capabilities within a single platform. Not only that, but it also enables you to easily collaborate on and share files and applications such as

Planner and GitHub and adds the ability to install and set up integrations for almost any kind of applications that can be shared between your teams. You can create channels where you can post news or discuss specific topics with specific team members, and you can host meetings with up to a thousand attendees at a time. Within organizations it is essential for administrators to be able to manage such online applications in a secure, easy, and effective manner. Microsoft provides a set of modules to interact with and manage various Microsoft 365 services like SharePoint Online, Exchange Online and Microsoft Teams and by utilizing PowerShell, you can easily optimize and automate tasks for managing these applications. With the SharePoint module you can manage tasks such as creating, retrieving, and deleting SharePoint Online sites and site collections and managing site and collections permissions. With the Exchange module you can retrieve information about, create, modify and remove exchange mailboxes and distribution groups and managing permissions and mail flows. With the Teams module you can retrieve, create, modify and remove teams and teams channels. You can manage teams and channel memberships and you can manage policies and permissions. Microsoft also offers a unified API that enables you to access data and services across Microsoft 365 and Entra ID. It provides a single endpoint to interact with the various Microsoft online and cloud services, making it easier to build applications that integrate with Microsoft 365 services. This API also allows you to manage Entra ID and enables you to manage and assign licenses for users. These application modules are invaluable tools for administrators and developers who need to work with and manage Microsoft 365 applications programmatically.

Note: Microsoft 365 services such as SharePoint, Exchange and Teams requires valid licenses. You should acquire a license from you organization or as an individual, licenses can be bought from Microsoft or third-party resellers.

Structure

This chapter covers the following topics:

- Microsoft 365 application specific PowerShell modules and Microsoft Graph API

- Managing Microsoft SharePoint Online

    o **Recipe 73**: SharePoint Online management's module installation and authentication

    o **Recipe 74**: SharePoint Online management and creating sites and managing permissions

- Managing Microsoft Exchange Online

    o **Recipe 75**: Exchange Online management and module installation and authentication

    o **Recipe 76**: Exchange Online management and managing mailboxes, distribution groups and mail contacts

- Managing Microsoft Teams
    - **Recipe 77**: Teams management and module installation and authentication
    - **Recipe 78**: Teams management and managing teams, members, and channels
- Microsoft Graph API and the Microsoft Graph PowerShell SDK module
    - **Recipe 79**: Microsoft Graph's Module installation and authentication
    - **Recipe 80**: Microsoft Graph and managing users and licenses

Objectives

This chapter will dive into the different PowerShell modules used for managing Microsoft applications and you will learn how to utilize the different modules to manage different aspects of Microsoft 365 services such as creating, modifying, and deleting SharePoint sites and collections, Exchange mailboxes, distribution groups, team channels and teams, and, how to manage permissions. We will also look into the Microsoft Graph API and you will learn how to use the Microsoft Graph PowerShell SDK to manage and assign user licenses for Microsoft 365 applications.

Microsoft 365 application specific PowerShell modules and Microsoft Graph API

Microsoft Graph is a RESTful API created and provided by Microsoft that allows you to access and manage data from Microsoft 365 services and applications including SharePoint Online, Exchange Online and Teams. This API is a unified endpoint for interacting with all Microsoft 365 services, essentially making it easier to develop applications and automate administrative tasks.

While Microsoft Graph is a RESTful API it is not directly built and designed for PowerShell, but PowerShell provides a module with a rich set of cmdlets that builds upon the Microsoft Graph PowerShell SDK (software development kit). The **Microsoft.Graph** module. This enables you to interact with the Microsoft Graph API with PowerShell. This module provides a broad range of capabilities for working with and manage Microsoft 365 applications and services but there are certain specialized functionalities and advanced features that are specific for each application and service that are not supported by the Microsoft Graph PowerShell module. These applications have their own sets of application specific modules that is built upon and leverage the Microsoft Graph API. You can utilize the respective modules for SharePoint Online, Exchange Online and Teams, which provides additional cmdlets and features specific for these services when you need to leverage these specialized functionalities and advanced features.

The `Microsoft.Online.Sharepoint.PowerShell` module focuses on SharePoint Online. The `MicrosoftTeams` PowerShell module is designed specifically for managing Microsoft Teams and the `ExchangeOnlineManagement` module is designed for managing and performing administrative tasks in Exchange Online. Some of these modules utilize the Microsoft Graph API to interact with the relevant Microsoft 365 resources and simplifies the process of managing such resources and performing the application specific operations.

There is one especially important thing to notice when working with the `Microsoft.Online.Sharepoint.PowerShell` module. This module is not natively supported in PowerShell 7 and Core versions unless it is imported in Windows PowerShell compatibility mode. You should either import and utilize this module within earlier versions of PowerShell such as PowerShell 5.1 or import it into your PowerShell 7 session using the `-UseWindowsPowerShell` parameter, which imports and loads the module in Windows PowerShell using a WinPSCompatSession remoting session. This will deserialize all input and output from commands in the imported module, which might result in unwanted behavior when providing input to commands or working with output from commands. This might not necessarily affect your behavior depending on your specific use cases and requirements, but you should consider using Windows PowerShell if the behavior of using these module commands is not what you expected when executed in PowerShell 7 or Core versions.

When objects are deserialized, they are converted into a format that can be easily transmitted between different PowerShell sessions. This process can have implications for the behavior of the objects, especially when you're piping the output of such commands to other commands. Deserialized objects are represented in a simple, text-based format during transmission between sessions. When you receive these objects in your local session, they are rehydrated back into PowerShell objects. Deserialized objects may not behave exactly like normal PowerShell objects, for instance, you might not be able to access certain properties or methods directly. When you pipe the output of a command that produces deserialized objects to another command, PowerShell will attempt to rehydrate the objects before passing them to the next command in the pipeline. While most operations will work seamlessly, you may encounter scenarios where certain operations or accessing properties do not behave as expected due to the deserialization process. It is always a good idea to test and verify the behavior of your required commands when working with modules in compatibility mode.

The `Microsoft.Graph`, `ExchangeOnlineManagement` and `MicrosoftTeams` modules are supported by PowerShell 7, and you should not encounter compatibility issues when working with these modules in a PowerShell 7 session or script. Make sure to use the latest version though.

Note: Always make sure that you have the necessary administrative permissions before executing any management tasks when working with Microsoft 365 services and applications.

Managing Microsoft SharePoint Online

SharePoint Online is a collaborative cloud-based platform that allows organizations to create, manage and share digital content and information within departments, teams and across the entire organization. SharePoint Online provides a centralized location for storing and managing files and documents which makes it easy for teams and departments to collaborate on these in real-time. Organizations can create SharePoint sites for projects, teams and departments that serve as collaborative spaces where members can share information, documents, files, and updates. Sites can contain features such as newsfeeds, announcements and discussion boards that facilitate communication within teams and departments. SharePoint Online also allows organizations to build their intranet portals that provide a centralized hub for company news, announcements, and vital information. Sites and content can also be shared externally allowing partners, customers, and clients access to information relevant for externally shared projects. SharePoint Online also supports the creation of workflows by using tools such as Power Automate to automate processes like streamlining approval processes and document reviews. With the PowerShell SharePoint module **Microsoft.Online.SharePoint.PowerShell** you can manage and automate SharePoint related tasks programmatically using PowerShell such as creating, deleting and managing user and group permissions for sites and site collections and more.

Recipe 73: SharePoint Online management's module installation and authentication

In this recipe we are going to install the **Microsoft.Online.SharePoint.PowerShell** module. This module is specifically created for managing SharePoint online and it can be downloaded and installed from the **PSGallery**. We are also going to cover how to authenticate and login to the SharePoint online admin center which is required in order to be able to use the cmdlets from the module to manage SharePoint online.

1. Install the **Microsoft.Online.SharePoint.PowerShell** module from the **PSGallery** using the **Install-Module** cmdlet. Use the **-Scope** parameter to specify if it should be installed for all users or only for the current user:

   ```
   Install-Module -Name "Microsoft.Online.SharePoint.PowerShell" -Scope
   "AllUsers"
   ```

2. When installed, you can import the module into the current session. Use the **-UseWindowsPowerShell** parameter if you need to import it in Windows PowerShell compatibility mode when using PowerShell 7:

   ```
   Import-Module "Microsoft.Online.SharePoint.PowerShell"
   ```

   ```
   Import-Module "Microsoft.Online.SharePoint.PowerShell"
   -UseWindowsPowerShell
   ```

3. To login and connect to your SharePoint Online administration center you have to use the **Connect-SPOService** cmdlet. You have to be a *SharePoint Online Administrator* or *Global Administrator* to run this cmdlet. The **-Url** parameter is required, and you need to specify the URL of your *SharePoint Online Administration center site* as an argument for this parameter. A SharePoint URL would typically look like this:

```
https://<Tenant>-admin.sharepoint.com
```

In this case it would be:

```
https://biorentdk-admin.sharepoint.com
```

4. If you do not specify any other parameters, a Microsoft interactive login prompt will appear, and you can login by entering the user principal name and password for your SharePoint administrator account. This will also work if the account is set up for two factor authentication:

```
# Connect interactively
Connect-SPOService -Url "https://biorentdk-admin.sharepoint.com"
```

5. If you need to login programmatically you need to use the **-Credential** parameter and provide a credential object as an argument:

```
# Connect using credential object
$User = "SharePoint@bio-rent.dk"
$Password = "Share@Point2023_Apps123"
# Convert the client secret to a secure string
$SecurePassword = ConvertTo-SecureString -String $Password
-AsPlainText -Force
# Create the PSCredential object
$Credentials = New-Object System.Management.Automation.
PSCredential($User, $SecurePassword)
# Connect
Connect-SPOService -Url "https://biorentdk-admin.sharepoint.com"
-Credential $Credentials
```

6. It is never recommended to use a *Global Administrator* account for programmatic tasks. If you need to login and connect programmatically you should create a specific account for your specific purpose and provide only the required permissions. In this case we have created a SharePoint user with the *SharePoint Administrator role* assigned. The **Connect-SPOService** cmdlet does not support

login using Azure identities so the only available option is to use an account with the *SharePoint Administrator role* or the *Global Administrator role*.

7. Once you are logged in to your SharePoint administration center site you can start using the available cmdlets to manage SharePoint Online. Use the **Get-Command** cmdlet to list all available cmdlets and use **Get-Help** to get detailed information about cmdlet parameters and syntax:

```
# List all cmdlets in the SharePoint module

Get-Command -Module Microsoft.Online.SharePoint.PowerShell

# Use Get-Help to get detailed information about cmdlet parameters
and syntax

Get-Help Get-SPOSite -Full
```

Recipe 74: SharePoint Online management and creating sites and managing permissions

In this recipe we are going to create a new collaboration project site and learn how to manage site permissions. We are going to remove unnecessary user permissions and add specific user permissions using SharePoint site permissions groups, to limit the general access to the project site. This shows some of the fundamental usage of the SharePoint module and gives insights into managing SharePoint sites using PowerShell.

When you get access to SharePoint Online, assuming it is a part of your Microsoft 365 subscription, you will typically be provided with a default or main site collection. This is also often referred to as the root site or root site collection. The root site collection is the top-level site in your SharePoint Online environment and serves as the starting point for your organization's SharePoint sites. By default, it includes features such as document libraries, lists, and other collaboration tools. If your domain is **Bio-Rent.dk** your root site collection would be associated with the URL: **https://biorentdk.sharepoint.com**. Within a site collection you can create new sites, also called sub-sites, which are used to separate and support collaboration and information among different departments and teams within organizations. When you create a new site, its permissions will be inherited from the root site collection, and you should limit the permissions and access to sites for specific departments and teams.

Sites are built from site design templates and Microsoft offers a few templates to choose from. For a team site you would choose the team site template and for a project site you would choose the project site template and so on. You can also create custom templates by defining the structure and settings for a custom design template using a JSON file and then define actions you want to perform during site creation using other JSON files. Such a design template can then be applied to an existing site or used when creating a new site. It's important to note that SharePoint Online site designs and site scripts have limitations, and not all settings and configurations can be used in custom templates. Additionally,

Microsoft may introduce changes or enhancements to these features over time. We will not go into detail about custom site design templates and for this recipe we use the default project site template. You can list available templates using the **Get-SPOWebTemplate** cmdlet.

Note that SharePoint can use different languages for site user interfaces enabling you to create sites in different languages and different time zones. Languages are specified using the **-LocaleId** parameter and time zones are specified using the **-TimeZoneId** parameter. Your SharePoint module cmdlet output language might depend on the global language specified for your tenant and you can change the cmdlet output language by specifying the **-LocaleId** parameter. Within this chapter we use the locale id 1033 which defines English and for the time zone id we use 3 which specifies GMT+01:00. You can lookup relevant id´s by referring to documentation about the **Language.Lcid** property and the **RegionalSetting.TimeZones** property for SharePoint.

Figure 12.1 shows the available templates:

```
● PS C:\Temp> Get-SPOWebTemplate -LocaleId 1033

  Name                        Title                                    LocaleId
  ----                        -----                                    --------
  STS#3                       Team site (no Microsoft 365 group)           1033
  STS#0                       Team site (classic experience)               1033
  BDR#0                       Document Center                              1033
  DEV#0                       Developer Site                               1033
  OFFILE#1                    Records Center                               1033
  EHS#1                       Team Site - SharePoint Online configuration  1033
  SRCHCEN#0                   Enterprise Search Center                     1033
  BLANKINTERNETCONTAINER#0    Publishing Portal                            1033
  ENTERWIKI#0                 Enterprise Wiki                              1033
  PROJECTSITE#0               Project Site                                 1033
  COMMUNITY#0                 Community Site                               1033
  COMMUNITYPORTAL#0           Community Portal                            1033
  SITEPAGEPUBLISHING#0        Communication site                          1033
  SRCHCENTERLITE#0            Basic Search Center                         1033
```

Figure 12.1: *Listing available SharePoint site design templates using the Get-SPOWebTemplate cmdlet*

1. To create a new site for our project, we use the **New-SPOSite** cmdlet. We specify a title using the **-Title** parameter. We use the **-LocaleId** and **-TimeZoneId** parameters to specify the language and time zone. The **-Template** parameter is used to specify which template we are going to use, and we specify the relevant template name from the **Get-SPOWebTemplate** cmdlet as an argument. In this case the template name is: **PROJECTSITE#0**. We need to specify a URL for the new site using the **-Url** parameter. This must be a valid path within the company´s site. We also specify storage quota in megabytes using the **-StorageQuota** parameter. This must not exceed the company´s overall available quota. We specify a site owner using the **-Owner** parameter. This must be a user and not a group. We create a new project site called ProjectX:

```
New-SPOSite `
-Title "ProjectX" `
-Template "PROJECTSITE#0" `
-Url "https://biorentdk.sharepoint.com/sites/ProjectX" `
-LocaleId 1033 `
-TimeZoneId 3 `
-StorageQuota 1000 `
-Owner "SharePoint@Bio-Rent.dk"
```

2. We can list all sites using the **Get-SPOSite** cmdlet without specifying any parameters. By specifying the **-Identity** parameter and adding a specific site URL as an argument, we can list a specific site. Use **Select-Object** to select additional properties. *Figure 12.2* shows the output of the **Get-SPOSite** cmdlet listing all sites, and listing the ProjectX site using the **-Identity** parameter:

```
* PS C:\Temp> Get-SPOSite

  Url                                                      Owner  Storage Quota
  ---                                                      -----  -------------
  https://biorentdk.sharepoint.com/sites/Bio-RentShare            26214400
  https://biorentdk.sharepoint.com/sites/Bio-Rent994              26214400
  https://biorentdk.sharepoint.com/sites/ProjectX                 26214400
  https://biorentdk-my.sharepoint.com/                            26214400
  https://biorentdk.sharepoint.com/sites/Bio-Rent                 26214400
  https://biorentdk.sharepoint.com/sites/allcompany               26214400
  https://biorentdk.sharepoint.com/sites/Teams                    26214400
  https://biorentdk.sharepoint.com/                               26214400
  https://biorentdk.sharepoint.com/search                         26214400

* PS C:\Temp> Get-SPOSite `
  >> -Identity https://biorentdk.sharepoint.com/sites/ProjectX | `
  >> Select-Object Title,Url,Owner,StorageQuota,Status

  Title        : ProjectX
  Url          : https://biorentdk.sharepoint.com/sites/ProjectX
  Owner        : 9ec7856f-f9ed-4865-9367-cdbc91b33719
  StorageQuota : 26214400
  Status       : Active
```

Figure 12.2: Listing all sites and the new ProjectX site using the Get-SPOSite cmdlet

3. The new ProjectX site can be accessed in a browser by visiting the URL. *Figure 12.3* shows the new ProjectX site in a browser:

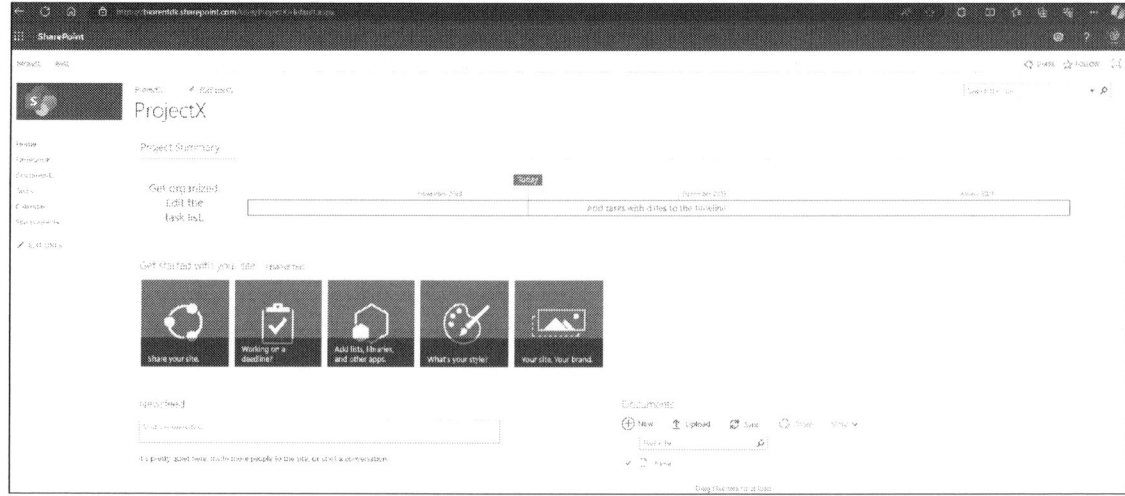

Figure 12.3: Visiting the new ProjectX site in a browser

Since we have not made any changes to the permissions for the root site collection, the special accounts: *Everyone* and *everyone except external users* by default have access to the ProjectX site due to the site inheritance. The purpose why these are added by default is to ensure that a wide range of users have some level of access to the site when it is created, without requiring explicit permission assignments. The *Everyone* account references and includes all authenticated users within the organization. The *Everyone except external users* account references and includes all authenticated users within the organization but excludes external users. It is crucial for administrators to review and adjust default permissions based on the specific security and access requirements for your organization. Granting broad access might not be suitable for all sites, especially those containing sensitive information and you should only allow the relevant department or team members access. Administrators should carefully manage permissions to adhere to security best practices in general.

4. Use the **Get-SPOUser** cmdlet with the site URL as an argument for the **-Site** parameter to list all user accounts and security groups from the site, as shown in *Figure 12.4*:

```
● PS C:\Temp> Get-SPOUser `
>> -Site https://biorentdk.sharepoint.com/sites/ProjectX

Display Name                        Login Name                                          Groups              User Type
------------                        ----------                                          ------              ---------
Everyone                            true                                                {}                  Member
Everyone except external users      spo-grid-all-users/57f387c6-3587-4ae7-a156-c9c7d10d7df6 {}               Member
Global Administrator                9ec7856f-f9ed-4865-9367-cdbc91b33719                {}                  Member
Morten Hansen                       morten@bio-rent.dk                                  {}                  Member
NT Service\spsearch                 nt service\spsearch                                 {}                  Member
SharePoint                          sharepoint@bio-rent.dk                              {}                  Member
SharePoint Administrator            963789b6-9944-45fa-9586-41f0e968679e                {}                  Member
SharePoint App                      app@sharepoint                                      {}                  Member
System Account                      SHAREPOINT\system                                   {ProjectX Owners}   Member
```

Figure 12.4: *Listing all ProjectX site members*

Note: The -Site parameter is required for most of the *SPO* cmdlets to specify the specific site, and it should be implied that this is set to the specific site URL in each command.

Note that the owner GUID returned in *Figure 12.2* from the **Get-SPOSite** cmdlet, matches that of the *Global Administrator role* as listed in *Figure 12.4* instead of the owner that was specified when the site was created, the **SharePoint@Bio-Rent. dk** user. This is default behavior in SharePoint to ensure that there is always at least one user with full control over the newly created site. If the **SharePoint@ Bio-Rent.dk** user was a Global Administrator, this would have been set as the site owner as you might have expected.

5. We will remove the *Everyone* and *Everyone except external user's* accounts from the site. The login name for the *Everyone* account is only listed as *true* in the **Get-SPOUser** output. This is not the correct name for this account, and it is not obvious how to reference this without looking it up. The same goes for the *Everyone except external users* account. The login names for these accounts are quite complex and will look something like this for *Everyone*: "**c:0(.s|true**" and something like this for *Everyone except external users*: "**c:0-.f|rolemanager|spo-grid-all-users/57f387c6-3587-4ae7-a156-c9c7d10d7df6**". The text after the last pipe in each account name is the login name as shown in the output from the **Get-SPOUser** cmdlet. Everything before the last pipe is a special reference to that special account:

c:0(.s|<LOGINNAME>
c:0-.f|rolemanager|<LOGINNAME>

The easiest alternative method for finding the exact names for such special accounts is to open the site in a browser and go to the site settings and look at the *People and Groups* section and then view the information for the special group you want, as shown in *Figure 12.5*:

Figure 12.5: Viewing the information for a special group to find the correct account name

6. We can remove site members using the **Remove-SPOUser** cmdlet. Then specify the account that should be removed using the **-LoginName** parameter:

```
# Remove "Everyone""
Remove-SPOUser `
-Site https://biorentdk.sharepoint.com/sites/ProjectX `
-LoginName "c:0(.s|true"
# Remove "Everyone except external users"
Remove-SPOUser `
-Site https://biorentdk.sharepoint.com/sites/ProjectX `
-LoginName "c:0-.f|rolemanager|spo-grid-all-users/57f387c6-3587-
4ae7-a156-c9c7d10d7df6"
```

When we execute the **Get-SPOUser** cmdlet again, we can see that these accounts are removed as expected, shown in *Figure 12.6*:

```
● PS C:\Temp> Get-SPOUser -site https://biorentdk.sharepoint.com/sites/ProjectX

Display Name              Login Name                            Groups            User Type
-----------               -----------                           ------            ---------
Global Administrator      9ec7856f-f9ed-4865-9367-cdbc91b33719  {}                Member
Morten Hansen             morten@bio-rent.dk                    {}                Member
NT Service\spsearch       nt service\spsearch                   {}                Member
SharePoint                sharepoint@bio-rent.dk                {}                Member
SharePoint Administrator  963789b6-9944-45fa-9586-41f0e968679e  {}                Member
SharePoint App            app@sharepoint                        {}                Member
System Account            SHAREPOINT\system                     {ProjectX Owners} Member
```

Figure 12.6: Listing site members after removal of accounts

When you create a site, SharePoint will also create SharePoint specific groups that can be used for easily granting permissions for that site. In this case where the site is called *ProjectX*, SharePoint will create the following site groups: *ProjectX Visitors*, which grants *read* permissions to the site. *ProjectX Members*, which grants *contribute* permissions to the site, and *ProjectX Owners* which is used to grant *full control* of the site. Members of the *Excel Services Viewers* group can view pages, list items and documents. You should use these groups to manage the permissions for the site by adding the relevant users to these groups. To list all SharePoint groups for a site, use the **Get-SPOSiteGroup** cmdlet as shown in *Figure 12.7*:

```
PS C:\Temp> Get-SPOsitegroup `
-Site https://biorentdk.sharepoint.com/sites/ProjectX | `
Select-Object Title,Users,Roles | `
Format-Table -AutoSize


Title                   Users               Roles
-----                   -----               -----
Excel Services Viewers  {}                  {View Only}
ProjectX Members        {}                  {Contribute}
ProjectX Owners         {SHAREPOINT\system} {Full Control}
ProjectX Visitors       {}                  {Read}
```

Figure 12.7: *Listing site specific SharePoint groups*

Note: The SHAREPOINT\system account, also known as the SharePoint Farm Account, that is listed in the ProjectX Owners group, is a system account used by SharePoint itself to run various service applications, timer jobs, and background processes within SharePoint. This account is a SharePoint managed account that is granted specific permissions to access SharePoint resources.

7. To add users to SharePoint groups we use the **Add-SPOUser** cmdlet and specify the users login name as an argument for the **-LoginName** parameter and the specific group name using the **-Group** parameter:

```
# Add existing 365 users to SharePoint Groups

Add-SPOUser `

-Site https://biorentdk.sharepoint.com/sites/ProjectX `

-LoginName lian@bio-rent.dk `

-Group "ProjectX Members"

Add-SPOUser `

-Site https://biorentdk.sharepoint.com/sites/ProjectX `

-LoginName morten@bio-rent.dk `

-Group "ProjectX Owners"

Add-SPOUser `

-Site https://biorentdk.sharepoint.com/sites/ProjectX `
```

```
-LoginName miga@bio-rent.dk `
-Group "ProjectX Visitors"
```

Once the users have been added to the SharePoint groups we can use the **Get-SPOSiteGroup** cmdlet to list the groups and its members, shown in *Figure 12.8*:

```
PS C:\Temp> Get-SPOsitegroup `
 -Site https://biorentdk.sharepoint.com/sites/ProjectX | `
 Select-Object Title,Users,Roles | `
 Format-Table -AutoSize

Title                   Users                                  Roles
-----                   -----                                  -----
Excel Services Viewers  {}                                     {View Only}
ProjectX Members        {lian@bio-rent.dk}                     {Contribute}
ProjectX Owners         {morten@bio-rent.dk, SHAREPOINT\system} {Full Control}
ProjectX Visitors       {miga@bio-rent.dk}                     {Read}
```

*Figure 12.8: Listing SharePoint groups and their members
after members have been added to the groups*

These users now have the assigned permissions for the site through the SharePoint group memberships.

> **Info: You can also add Microsoft 365 groups as members to the SharePoint groups. Just as with users, you must specify the Microsoft 365 group login name, which would be the email address assigned to that specific Microsoft 365 group. All members in that Microsoft 365 group will inherit the SharePoint group permissions.**

8. You can use the **Remove-SPOUser** cmdlet to remove users and Microsoft 365 groups from SharePoint groups. Specify the user or Microsoft 365 group login name as an argument for the **-LoginName** parameter and the specific SharePoint group name using the **-Group** parameter:

```
# Remove users from SharePoint groups
Remove-SPOUser `
-Site https://biorentdk.sharepoint.com/sites/ProjectX `
-LoginName miga@bio-rent.dk `
-Group "ProjectX Visitors"
```

We can use the SharePoint module to create SharePoint sites for different purposes using web templates and we can manage site permissions for users and Microsoft 365 groups. This is especially useful if you manage a lot of sites and users within your organization. This also allows you to automate tasks that create new sites for new teams or departments and manage permissions for sites using scripts.

The **Microsoft.Online.SharePoint.PowerShell** module versions might change often, and cmdlets might be deprecated in favor of **Microsoft.Graph** implementations. You should check for module updates frequently and make sure that the cmdlets for your requirements are available in newer versions of the module. Check the **PSGallery** for the newest version by using the **Find-Module** cmdlet to list the most recent module version. Use the **-AllVersions** parameter to list all available module versions from the **PSGallery**:

```
Find-Module Microsoft.Online.SharePoint.PowerShell
```

```
Find-Module Microsoft.Online.SharePoint.PowerShell -AllVersions
```

For finding specific cmdlets from the SharePoint module for your specific requirements and for more information about the individual cmdlets, you should lookup official module and cmdlet documentation.

Managing Microsoft Exchange Online

Exchange Online is a cloud-based email hosting service provided by Microsoft as a part of Microsoft 365 services. It offers email, calendar, contacts and tasks functionality and it is designed to provide a reliable and secure messaging platform for organizations. With PowerShell and the **ExchangeOnlineManagement** module you can manage important exchange online tasks such as creating new mailboxes, enabling mailboxes for existing users and perform tasks like adding and removing full access permissions, forwarding emails, and enabling auto replies. Even though the tasks you can perform with this module might seem limited it is still quite powerful when you need to manage certain aspects of your organizations Exchange Online accounts. You can also add, manage and remove external contacts enabling you to include important contacts into distribution groups and receive calendar invitations and you can create, manage and remove mail distribution groups.

The **ExchangeOnlineManagement** module is supported in PowerShell 7 with versions 2.0.4 or later.

> **Note: Version 3.0.0 and later (2022) of the ExchangeOnlineManagement module is known as the Exchange Online PowerShell V3 module (abbreviated as the EXO V3 module). Version 2.0.5 and earlier (2021) is known as the Exchange Online PowerShell V2 module (abbreviated as the EXO V2 module).**

Recipe 75: Exchange Online management and module installation and authentication

Install the **ExchangeOnlineManagement** module from the **PSGallery** using the **Install-Module** cmdlet. Use the **-Scope** parameter to specify if it should be installed for all users or only for the current user:

```
Install-Module -Name "ExchangeOnlineManagement" -Scope "AllUsers"
```

When installed, you can import the module into the current session:

```
Import-Module "ExchangeOnlineManagement"
```

Note: For readability purposes, for the rest of this chapter, the *Exchange Online Management* module will be referred to as the *Exchange* module.

To login and connect to exchange online you have to use the **Connect-ExchangeOnline** cmdlet. You have to be an *Exchange Administrator* or *Global Administrator* to manage most exchange tasks such as creating mailboxes and distribution groups and to grant full access permissions to mailboxes etc. If you execute the cmdlet without any parameters or only specify the **-UserPrincipalName** parameter, a Microsoft interactive login prompt will appear, and you can login by entering the user principal name and password for your Exchange Administrator account. This will also work if the account is set up for two factor authentication:

```
# Connect to Exchange Online interactively

Connect-ExchangeOnline

Connect-ExchangeOnline -UserPrincipalName Exchange@bio-rent.dk
```

You can also login using a credential object as an argument for the **-Credential** parameter:

```
# Connect to Exchange Online using credential object

$User = "Exchange@bio-rent.dk"

$Password = "ExcOnline@4321"

# Convert the client secret to a secure string

$SecurePassword = ConvertTo-SecureString -String $Password -AsPlainText
-Force

# Create the PSCredential object

$Credentials = New-Object System.Management.Automation.PSCredential($User,
$SecurePassword)

# Connect

Connect-ExchangeOnline -Credential $Credentials
```

This module also supports log in with an Azure user or system assigned managed identity, but this method is not supported in a PowerShell session on your local computer, instead you connect in the context of the Azure resource that's associated with the managed identity. This could be an Azure automation account or an Azure VM. To login using a managed identity use the **-ManagedIdentity** switch parameter and specify your organization using the **-Organization** parameter from the associated Azure resource:

```
# Connect to Exchange Online using Azure managed identity

Connect-ExchangeOnline -ManagedIdentity -Organization <YourDomain>.
onmicrosoft.com
```

The creation of managed identities is out of the scope of this book, and you should refer to the official *Exchange Online PowerShell: Connect using Azure managed identity* documentation which can be found here: **https://learn.microsoft.com/en-us/powershell/exchange/connect-exo-powershell-managed-identity?view=exchange-ps**.

When you connect to Exchange Online using the **Connect-ExchangeOnline** cmdlet, the cmdlet establishes a connection to the Exchange Online REST API. This connection is used for various management operations involving RESTful web services that it requires to interact with Exchange Online. The cmdlet also creates a Remote PowerShell Session (RPS) to the Exchange Online server. This session allows you to run PowerShell commands remotely on the Exchange server, enabling you to manage Exchange Online using PowerShell cmdlets locally.

The Exchange module contains a limited set of cmdlets in itself such as **Get-EXOMailbox**, **Get-EXOMailboxPermissions** and **Get-EXOMailboxStatistics**. Use the **Get-Command -Module ExchangeOnlineManagement** command to list the available cmdlets. The RPS and REST API connections enables the Exchange cmdlets that resides on the remote Exchange Online server and make these available within your logged in session. These are cmdlets that you would find in the *Exchange Management Shell* for Exchange servers, such as the **Get-Mailbox**, **Get-DistributionGroup** and **Get-Contacts** cmdlets. In *Figure 12.9* we try to use the **Get-Mailbox** and **Get-EXOMailbox** cmdlets before we are connected to Exchange Online. The **Get-Mailbox** cmdlet does not exist at all. The **Get-EXOMailbox** cmdlet do exist and is provided by the Exchange module, but it requires a connection to Exchange Online. When we are connected to Exchange Online, the **Get-Mailbox** (and other REST API and RPS backed cmdlets) becomes available and we can use these cmdlets within the session. As an example, we are now able to get the Hostmaster mailbox using the **Get-Mailbox** cmdlet. If we inspect the **Get-Mailbox** cmdlet using **Get-Command** we can see that the cmdlet is a function command from the remote source module called: **tmpEXO_beufp24s.wox**. We can inspect this remote source module using **Get-Command** and provide this module name as an argument for the **-Module** parameter and list all remote cmdlets that is now available through the remote session:

Figure 12.9: *Connecting to Exchange Online and get REST API and RPS backed cmdlets available in the current session*

We can now use the available Exchange cmdlets from both the local Exchange module and the remote module to manage Exchange Online.

Recipe 76: Exchange Online management and managing mailboxes, distribution groups and mail contacts

We are going to create a new mailbox and granting full access permissions to this mailbox for another user. We are going to forward emails sent to this mailbox, to another mailbox and we are going to create an auto reply. Then we are creating mail distribution groups and adding members to these groups, and we are going to make some external mail contacts that can be added to distribution groups. This will give an insight into the Exchange module and its capabilities and give you a general idea how to use this module to manage different aspects of Exchange Online.

Exchange Online Mailbox

When you create a new mailbox, you also create a new Entra ID user account associated with that mailbox. To create a new mailbox, use the **New-Mailbox** cmdlet provided by the remote Exchange module. The **-MicrosoftOnlineServicesID** parameter is the specific user ID for the object, this only applies to objects in Azure (not on-premises) and is used to provide the user principal name. The password argument for the **-Password** parameter must be provided as a secure string. It is recommended to set the **-ResetPasswordOnNextLogon** parameter to **$true** to ensure that the user changes the password on the first login. You should also at least specify arguments for the **-Alias**, **-Name**, **-FirstName**, **-LastName** and the **-DisplayName** parameters:

```
New-Mailbox `
-MicrosoftOnlineServicesID "John@bio-rent.dk" `
-Alias John `
-Name JohnAmbrose `
-FirstName John `
-LastName Ambrose `
-DisplayName "John Ambrose" `
-Password (ConvertTo-SecureString -String "ThisIs#VerySecret2468"
-AsPlainText -Force) `
-ResetPasswordOnNextLogon $true
```

Figure 12.10 shows the successful creation of a new mailbox, and the Entra ID user account associated with it:

```
PS C:\Temp> New-Mailbox `
-MicrosoftOnlineServicesID "John@bio-rent.dk" `
-Alias John `
-Name JohnAmbrose `
-Password (ConvertTo-SecureString -String "ThisIs#VerySecret2468" -AsPlainText -Force) `
-FirstName John `
-LastName Ambrose `
-DisplayName "John Ambrose" `
-ResetPasswordOnNextLogon $true

Name              Alias      Database           ProhibitSendQuota        ExternalDirectoryObjectId
----              -----      --------           -----------------        -------------------------
JohnAmbrose       John       EURP192DG108-db361    99 GB (106,300,440,…  212f1dfe-fb8c-488a-b1e5-7c0
6c9dab716
WARNING: After you create a new mailbox, you must go to the Office 365 Admin Center and assign the mailbox a license, or
it will be disabled after the grace period.
```

Figure 12.10: Successful creation of an Entra ID user account and the associated mailbox

> **Info:** Notice the warning stating that you must assign a license for the mailbox, or it will be disabled after a grace period. After a 30 days grace period, the mailbox data is deleted, and cannot be recovered. If you assign an exchange license to the user during the grace period, access is restored, and the mailbox will become fully active.

In Exchange Online you cannot enable a mailbox for an already existing user using the **Enable-Mailbox** cmdlet. Instead, you would have to assign an exchange license to that user to enable the mailbox associated with that account. In Exchange Online, the **Enable-Mailbox** cmdlet is used to add archive mailboxes and to enable auto-expanding archives for existing users.

To list permissions to show who have full access permission to a mailbox, use the **Get-MailboxPermissions** cmdlet. Use the **-Identity** parameter to specify the mailbox you want to view the permissions for. You can use any value that uniquely identifies the mailbox such the email address, Name, Alias, **MicrosoftOnlineServicesID** (UPN) etc. This also lists other permissions for the mailbox. Here we list the permissions for *John´s* mailbox:

```
# List full access permissions for a mailbox

Get-MailboxPermission -Identity john@bio-rent.dk
```

Figure 12.11 show the output of this command:

```
⚫ PS C:\Temp> Get-MailboxPermission -Identity john@bio-rent.dk

   Identity              User                 AccessRights
   --------              ----                 ------------
   JohnAmbrose           NT AUTHORITY\SELF    {FullAccess, ReadPermission}
```

Figure 12.11: *Listing mailbox permissions*

We can see that only John himself has *full access* and *read* permission for his mailbox.

To grant a user full access permissions to another mailbox we use the **Add-MailboxPermissions** cmdlet. The **-Identity** parameter is used to specify which user mailbox the permissions should be assigned too. The **-User** parameter is used to specify which user the permissions should be assigned to. The **-AccessRights** parameter is used to specify the type of permissions that should be granted. In this case it would be **FullAccess**. Valid values are: **ChangeOwner**, **ChangePermission**, **DeleteItem**, **ExternalAccount**, **FullAccess** and **ReadPermission**. The parameter accepts a string array with multiple permissions, so you can assign more than one type of permission. The **-InheritanceType** parameter is used to specify how permissions are inherited by folders within the mailbox. **All** is the default value. To limit inheritance, you can specify one of the other valid values: **None**, **Children**, **Descendents**, **SelfAndChildren**. For more information about values for these parameters, refer to the official cmdlet documentation.

Here we grant **Morten@bio-rent.dk** full access permissions to *John´s* mailbox:

```
# Grant full access permissions to a mailbox

Add-MailboxPermission `

-Identity "john@bio-rent.dk" `

-User "morten@bio-rent.dk" `
```

```
-AccessRights FullAccess `

-InheritanceType All
```

After the command is executed and we have granted the permissions, we can use the **Get-MailboxPermission** cmdlet to view the new permissions for *John´s* mailbox, as shown in *Figure 12.12*:

```
● PS C:\Temp> Get-MailboxPermission -Identity john@bio-rent.dk

   Identity              User                    AccessRights
   --------              ----                    ------------
   JohnAmbrose           NT AUTHORITY\SELF       {FullAccess, ReadPermission}
   JohnAmbrose           Morten@bio-rent.dk      {FullAccess}
```

***Figure 12.12:** Listing mailbox permissions after another user have been granted full access*

We can see that **Morten@bio-rent.dk** have been granted the expected permissions.

To remove permissions from a mailbox, use the **Remove-MailboxPermission** cmdlet. We must specify the **-Identity** parameter and provide the mailbox we want to remove permissions from. The **-User** parameter specifies the user that should have permissions removed and the **-AccessRights** parameter specifies the type of permissions that should be removed. If a user has been granted both **FullAccess** and **ReadPermission**, you can settle for removing either or you can remove both. The **-AccessRights** parameter accepts a string array with the permission types you want to remove. Since this is considered destructive behavior, you will be prompted for confirmation. Use the **-Confirm:$false** parameter to continue without confirmation:

```
# Remove full access permission from a mailbox

Remove-MailboxPermission `

-Identity "john@bio-rent.dk" `

-User "morten@bio-rent.dk" `

-AccessRights "FullAccess"
```

The **Set-Mailbox** cmdlet is used to modify the settings of existing mailboxes. This cmdlet can also be used to enable mail forwarding if emails need to be forwarded to another mailbox. We do this by specifying the **-ForwardingAddress** parameter and add the email address for the mailbox that we need to forward mails too, as an argument. This only applies to email addresses within your organization. The **-DeliverToMailboxAndForward** parameter is used to indicate whether the emails should be delivered to the original mailbox in addition to being forwarded. This parameter takes a boolean as an argument. If this is set to **$false**, the original mailbox will not receive a copy and the mail is only forwarded to the forwarding address. The cmdlet also has a parameter called **-ForwardingSmtpAddress**. This is typically used to specify external email addresses that aren't validated and accessible within your organization. If you specify both the **-ForwadingAddress** and the **-ForwardingSmtpAddress**, the **-ForwardingSmtpAddress** parameter is ignored. We need to use the **-Identity** parameter to specify which mailbox should be forwarded. Below we enable mail forward for *John´s* mailbox and forward emails to **Morten@bio-rent.dk** internally within the organization. The second example forward John´s emails to an external email address outside of the organization:

```
# Forward emails (to internal organization email address) and keep a copy
in the original mailbox
```

```
Set-Mailbox -Identity "john@bio-rent.dk" `
```

```
-ForwardingAddress "morten@bio-rent.dk" `
```

```
-DeliverToMailboxAndForward $true
```

```
# Forward emails (to external email address) and keep a copy in the
original mailbox
```

```
Set-Mailbox -Identity "john@bio-rent.dk" `
```

```
-ForwardingSmtpAddress "morten@hotmail.com" `
```

```
-DeliverToMailboxAndForward $true
```

Now mail will be forwarded to either the internal address: **Morten@bio-rent.dk** og to the external address: **Morten@hotmail.com** depending on which of the commands we execute,and John will keep a copy of the forwarded email in his own mailbox, since the **-DeliveToMailboxAndForward** parameter is set to **$true**. You can list the addresses a mailbox is forwarded too using the **Get-Mailbox** cmdlet and then use **Select-Object** to specify the relevant properties as shown in *Figure 12.13*:

```
PS C:\Temp> Get-Mailbox "john@bio-rent.dk" | `
● Select-Object ForwardingAddress,ForwardingSmtpAddress,DeliverToMailboxAndForward

ForwardingAddress                           ForwardingSmtpAddress DeliverToMailboxAndForward
-----------------                           --------------------- --------------------------
df582b3d-ea77-4ccf-a743-2d021f9e4f96                                                    True
```

Figure 12.13: Listing a mailbox forwarding addresses and settings

If the forwarding address is returned with the id as shown in *Figure 12.13*, you can use the **Get-Mailbox** cmdlet and select properties such as **DisplayName**, **WindowsLiveID** and **WindowsEmailAddress** to view who the account belongs to, as shown in *Figure 12.14*:

```
PS C:\Temp> Get-Mailbox df582b3d-ea77-4ccf-a743-2d021f9e4f96 | `
● Select-Object Name,DisaplyName,WindowsLiveId,WindowsEmailAddress,Id

Name                : df582b3d-ea77-4ccf-a743-2d021f9e4f96
DisaplyName         :
WindowsLiveID       : Morten@bio-rent.dk
WindowsEmailAddress : Morten@bio-rent.dk
Id                  : df582b3d-ea77-4ccf-a743-2d021f9e4f96
```

Figure 12.14: Listing a mailbox using the Id as an argument
for the identity parameter. Selecting account defining properties

The **Set-Mailbox** cmdlet is not only used for configuring and enabling mailbox forwarding, but you can use this cmdlet to configure numerous different settings for your mailbox such as quotas, hide the mailbox from the address list, setting a mail tip, reset the password and configure values for custom attributes. Refer to the official cmdlet documentation for all available parameters and configurations.

You can set an auto reply for a mailbox using the **Set-MailboxAutoReplyConfiguration** cmdlet. The **-Identity** parameter is used to specify the mailbox. Use the **-AutoReplyState** parameter to Enable or Disable auto reply for the mailbox. The mailbox will save the last auto- reply messages, so you can re-use these messages by enabling a disabled auto reply without specifying new messages. The **-ExternalMessage** parameter is used to specify auto-reply messages for people outside of your organization and the **-InternalMessage** parameter is used to specify auto reply messages for colleagues inside of your organization. Auto reply messages supports HTML so you can create more stylish auto-reply messages by creating messages using HTML. Below we enable auto reply for *John's* mailbox and set different HTML styled messages for internal and external recipients:

```
# Set an auto reply for a mailbox
$InternalMessage = @"
<h1 style="color: blue">Dear Colleagues.</h1>
<p>I am out of the office until tomorrow<br><br>
Best regard<br>
John
</p>
"@
$ExternalMessage = @"
<h1 style="color: red">Dear friend.</h1>
<p>I am out of the office until tomorrow<br><br>
Best regard<br>
John
</p>
"@
Set-MailboxAutoReplyConfiguration `
-Identity "john@bio-rent.dk" `
-AutoReplyState Enabled `
-ExternalMessage $ExternalMessage `
-InternalMessage $InternalMessage
```

Figure 12.15 shows the auto replies that are received for both an internal and external recipient:

Figure 12.15: *Auto replies sent to both an internal and external recipient*

Disable an auto reply for a mailbox by setting the **-AutoReplyState** parameter to **Disabled**:

```
# Disable an auto reply (Messages are saved)
Set-MailboxAutoReplyConfiguration `
-Identity "john@bio-rent.dk" `
-AutoReplyState Disabled
```

An auto reply can also be scheduled. Set the **-AutoReplyState** to Scheduled and use the **-StartTime** parameter to specify the time the auto reply should automatically enable and the **-EndTime** parameter for when it should automatically disable. If you do not specify any arguments for the **-InternalMessage** and **-ExternalMessage** parameters, the last used (saved) messages will be used, if any exists:

```
# Schedule an auto reply
Set-MailboxAutoReplyConfiguration `
-Identity "john@bio-rent.dk" `
-AutoReplyState Scheduled `
-StartTime "7/10/2023 08:00:00" `
-EndTime "7/15/2023 17:00:00" `
-InternalMessage $InternalMessage `
-ExternalMessage $ExternalMessage
```

You can delete a mailbox and the associated user account using the **Remove-Mailbox** cmdlet. The mailbox will be soft deleted and remain in the Exchange Online database for the retention period that is configured for that database. Specify the mailbox you want to delete using the **-Identity** parameter. This is a destructive behavior, and you will be prompted for confirmation. Suppress the confirmation prompt by specifying the

-Confirm:$false parameter:

```
# Remove a mailbox and the associated user account

Remove-Mailbox -Identity "john@bio-rent.dk" -Confirm:$false
```

Once a mailbox (and the associated user) is soft-deleted, it cannot be found and listed using the conventional **Get-Mailbox** cmdlet, unless you use the **-SoftDeletedMailbox** switch parameter. Shown in *Figure 12.16*:

```
● PS C:\Temp> Get-Mailbox "john@bio-rent.dk"
  Get-Mailbox: Ex6F9304|Microsoft.Exchange.Configuration.Tasks.ManagementObjectNotFoundException|The operation couldn't be
  performed
  because object 'john@bio-rent.dk' couldn't be found on 'DB6P192A04DC002.EURP192A004.PROD.OUTLOOK.COM'.
● PS C:\Temp> Get-Mailbox "john@bio-rent.dk" -SoftDeletedMailbox

  Name                Alias          Database           ProhibitSendQuota        ExternalDirectoryObjectId
  ----                -----          --------           ----------------         -------------------------
  JohnAmbrose         John           EURP192DG108-db361 99 GB (106,300,440,...   212f1dfe-fb8c-488a-b1e5-7...
```

Figure 12.16: Listing a soft-deleted mailbox

You can delete a soft-deleted mailbox using the **Remove-Mailbox** cmdlet with the **-PermanentlyDelete** parameter. First find the specific soft-deleted mailbox using the **Get-Mailbox** cmdlet with the **-SoftDeletedMailbox** parameter and pipe this to the **Remove-Mailbox** cmdlet. This will purge the mailbox and you will not be able to recover it. Note that you cannot permanently delete/purge a mailbox as long as the associated user account is still in its retention period (users and mailboxes are automatically permanently deleted 30 days after they are soft-deleted), if you need to permanently delete the mailbox before the retention period expires, you must first purge the soft-deleted user account:

```
# Permanently delete a soft-deleted mailbox (After the user account has
been purged)

Get-Mailbox "john@bio-rent.dk" `

-SoftDeletedMailbox | `

Remove-Mailbox -PermanentlyDelete `

-Confirm:$false
```

Instead of removing a mailbox and the associated user account, you can disable the mailbox and remove all mailbox attributes from a user while keeping the user account intact. Use the **Disable-Mailbox** cmdlet:

```
# Disable a mailbox while keeping the user account intact

Disable-Mailbox john@bio-rent.dk
```

The Exchange module contain exclusive **Get-EXO*** cmdlets. These cmdlets are optimized for speed in bulk data retrieval scenarios. Another benefit of using the **Get-EXO*** cmdlets is that their return output properties have been categorized into property sets. This means that they won't return all properties, and by default only returns the bare minimum properties specified in the *Minimum* property set. You can use the **-PropertySet** parameter for specifying one or more property sets, for the properties you want these cmdlets to return:

```
# Use Get-EXOMailbox with property sets
Get-EXOMailbox `
-Identity "morten@bio-rent.dk" `
-PropertySets Minimum,Delivery
```

You can get a list of all the available property sets for each of the EXO cmdlets in the official documentation: **https://learn.microsoft.com/en-us/powershell/exchange/cmdlet-property-sets?view=exchange-ps**. Use the EXO cmdlets instead of the ordinary similar cmdlets if you need to perform bulk operations on numerous mail objects.

Distribution groups

Distribution groups are used for sending emails to multiple recipients. It is a way to simplify the process of sending messages to a group of people rather than having to enter each recipient's email address individually. To create a new distribution group, use the **New-DistributionGroup** cmdlet. **-Name** is the only required parameter but you should at least also add a description using the **-Description** parameter. You can add members to the group using the **-Members** parameter. This takes a string array as an argument for specifying multiple users. The **-RequireSenderAuthenticationEnabled** parameter is used for allowing people outside of your organization to send mails to a group. If you need to allow external senders, the value must be set to **$false**. The **-PrimarySmtpAddress** is used for specifying the primary return email address that is used for the recipient, if not specified the primary address will be something like **<Name>@<Domain>.onmicrosoft.com**:

```
# Create a distribution group
New-DistributionGroup `
-Name "Employees" `
-Description "Mail list for all employees" `
-Members "miga@bio-rent.dk", "lian@bio-rent.dk" `
-PrimarySmtpAddress "Employees@bio-rent.dk" `
-RequireSenderAuthenticationEnabled $true
```

To list all distribution groups, use the **Get-DistributionGroup** cmdlet without specifying any parameters:

```
# List all distribution groups
Get-DistributionGroup
```

To list a specific distribution group, use the **Get-DistributionGroup** cmdlet and specify the name of the group as an argument for the **-Identity** parameter:

```
# List specific distribution group
```

```
Get-DistributionGroup -Identity "Employees"
```

List all members of a distribution group using the **Get-DistributionGroupMember** cmdlet. The default view might show the id for the members instead of their names. Use **Select-Object** to specify properties such as the **DisplayName** and **WindowsLiveID** to view the user's names and Windows Id´s etc.:

```
# List distribution group members
Get-DistributionGroupMember `
-Identity "Employees" | `
Select-Object DisplayName,WindowsLiveId
```

Figure 12.17 shows the current members of the *Employees* distribution group:

```
PS C:\Temp> Get-DistributionGroupMember `
-Identity "Employees" | `
Select-Object DisplayName,WindowsLiveId


DisplayName    WindowsLiveID
-----------    -------------
Mia Garcia     Miga@bio-rent.dk
Liam Anderson  Lian@bio-rent.dk
```

Figure 12.17: *Listing members of the Employees distribution group, selecting specific properties*

You can add members to a distribution group using the **Add-DistributionGroupMember** cmdlet. Use the **-Identity** parameter to specify the group you want to add a member to and the **-Member** parameter to specify the member to add. The **-Member** parameter does not take a string array so you can only add one member. Use a **Foreach-Object** loop to add multiple members to a group:

```
# Add members to a distribution group
$Members = "olpa@bio-rent.dk", "miriam@bio-rent.dk"
$Members | Foreach-Object {
    Add-DistributionGroupMember `
    -Identity "Employees" `
    -Member $_
}
```

Likewise, you can remove members from a group using the **Remove-DistributionGroupMember** cmdlet. This is destructive behavior, and you will be prompted for confirmation. Suppress the confirmation prompt by specifying the **-Confirm:$false** parameter:

```
# Remove members from a distribution group
```

```
$Members = "lian@bio-rent.dk", "miga@bio-rent.dk"
$Members | Foreach-Object {
    Remove-DistributionGroupMember `
    -Identity "Employees" `
    -Member $_ `
    -Confirm:$false
}
```

You can delete a distribution group using the **Remove-DistributionGroup** cmdlet. Specify the **-Identity** of the group you want to delete. Use the **-Confirm:$false** parameter to suppress the confirmation prompt:

```
# Delete a distribution group
Remove-DistributionGroup `
-Identity "Employees" `
-Confirm:$false
```

When you delete a distribution group it is permanently deleted from the account. There is no soft delete option for such groups. Users and their associated mailboxes, that are members of distribution groups will not be affected by the deletion of distribution groups, only their membership and reference to such groups will be removed.

Mail contacts

A mail contact is an object that represents a person or entity external to your Exchange organization. It contains information about an individual or entity's external email address and other details. Mail contacts are typically used when you need to send emails to external recipients and want to include them in distribution groups or allow them to receive calendar invitations. Mail contacts provide a way to include external recipients in your organization's communication and collaboration processes, making it easier to manage and streamline interactions with individuals outside your organization.

To create a new mail contact, use the **New-MailContact** cmdlet. Specify parameters such as **-DisplayName**, **-FirstName**, **-LastName**, **-Name** and **-Alias**. To specify the contacts external email address, use the **-ExternalEmailAddress** parameter:

```
# Create a new contact
New-MailContact `
-DisplayName "Mads Sommer (Private)" `
-ExternalEmailAddress "madssommer1234@gmail.com" `
-FirstName "Mads" `
-LastName "Sommer" `
-Name "Mads Sommer" `
```

```
-Alias "MadsSommer"
```

You can list all contacts using the **Get-MailContact** cmdlet. Use the **-Identity** parameter to list a specific contact. Pipe to **Select-Object** for listing specific properties in the output:

```
# List all contacts
Get-MailContact | `
Select-Object DisplayName,Name,ExternalEmailAddress
# List a specific contact
Get-MailContact `
-Identity "MadsSommer"| `
Select-Object DisplayName,Name,ExternalEmailAddress
```

The output from these commands is shown in *Figure 12.18*:

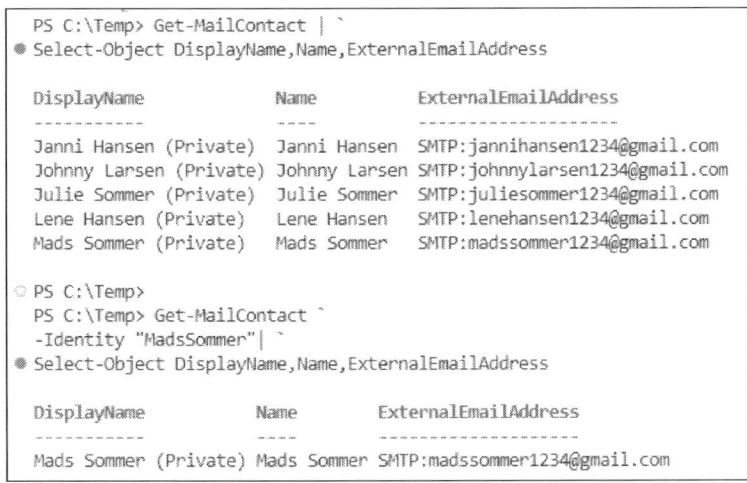

Figure 12.18: *Listing all and specific mail contacts*

Use the **Set-MailContact** cmdlet to modify the properties for a contact:

```
# Modify properties of existing contact
Set-MailContact `
-Identity "MadsSommer" `
-ExternalEmailAddress madssommer@hotmail.com
```

Mail contacts can be added to distribution groups:

```
# Add contacts to a distribution group
$Members = "MadsSommer", "JulieSommer", "JohnnyLarsen", "JanniHansen",
"LeneHansen"
$Members | Foreach-Object {
```

```
    Add-DistributionGroupMember `
    -Identity "External" `
    -Member $_
}
```

Figure 12.19 shows that the mail contacts have been added to the distribution group named *External*:

```
● PS C:\Temp> Get-DistributionGroupMember External | Select-Object DisplayName,EmailAddresses

  DisplayName            EmailAddresses
  -----------            --------------
  Mads Sommer (Private)    {SMTP:madssommer@hotmail.com}
  Julie Sommer (Private)   {SMTP:juliesommer1234@gmail.com}
  Janni Hansen (Private)   {SMTP:jannihansen1234@gmail.com}
  Lene Hansen (Private)    {SMTP:lenehansen1234@gmail.com}
  Johnny Larsen (Private)  {SMTP:johnnylarsen1234@gmail.com}
```

Figure 12.19: Mail contacts added to the External distribution group

These external contacts will now receive emails sent to the *External* distribution group.

To delete a mail contact, use the **Remove-MailContact** cmdlet. Use the **-Confirm:$false** parameter to suppress the confirmation prompt:

```
# Remove a mail contact

Remove-MailContact `

-Identity "MadsSommer" `

-Confirm:$false
```

The exchange module can be used for managing a lot of different aspects of Exchange Online. It can be used for creating and managing mailboxes and mailbox permissions and for forwarding emails to other mailboxes and for configuring mailbox auto replies. It can be used for creating and managing distribution groups and you can create and manage mail contacts so that external users to your organization can be included as members of internal distribution groups. These are just some of the more common use cases when working with Exchange and the Exchange module provides a lot more cmdlets that can be used for tasks such as getting mailbox statistics, restore soft deleted mailboxes, configuring malware filter policies and rules, configuring retention policies and much more.

For finding specific cmdlets from the exchange module for your specific requirements and for more information about the individual cmdlets, you should lookup official module and cmdlet documentation.

Managing Microsoft teams

Teams is a communication and collaboration platform provided by Microsoft as a part of Microsoft 365 services. It provides a centralized hub for teamwork and communication both inside and outside of your organization regardless of the user's physical location. It brings together chat, calls, video meetings and conferencing, file storage and application integration. The *MicrosoftTeams* PowerShell module provides cmdlets that allow administrators to manage and configure various aspects of Microsoft Teams such as team and channel management, permissions control and user configuration and policies management within Teams. You can configure messaging policies and managing notifications and alert settings. You can configure and manage integrations with third party applications and services and other Microsoft 365 services and much more.

Microsoft are constantly improving the **MicrosoftTeams** module, and you should keep up to date by referencing the *Teams PowerShell Module – Supported Versions* page: **https:// learn.microsoft.com/en-us/microsoftteams/teams-powershell-supported-versions**. And the official module release notes: **https://learn.microsoft.com/en-us/microsoftteams/ teams-powershell-release-notes**.

Recipe 77: Teams management and module installation and authentication

Install the **MicrosoftTeams** module from the **PSGallery** using the **Install-module** cmdlet. Use the **-Scope** parameter to specify if it should be installed for all users or only for the current user:

```
Install-Module -Name "MicrosoftTeams" -Scope "AllUsers"
```

When installed, you can import the module into the current session:

```
Import-Module "MicrosoftTeams"
```

> **Note: For readability for the rest of this chapter, the MicrosoftTeams module will be referred to as the Teams module.**

To login and connect to Microsoft Teams you have to use the **Connect-MicrosoftTeams** cmdlet. You have to be a *Teams Administrator* or *Global Administrator* to manage all Teams-related tasks. If you execute the command without any parameters, a Microsoft interactive prompt will appear, and you can login by entering the user principal name and password for your Teams administrator account. If the account if set up for two factor authentication you can only login and authenticate using the interactive prompt:

```
# Connect to Teams interactively

Connect-MicrosoftTeams
```

You can also login using a credential object as an argument for the **-Credential** parameter:

```
# Connect to Teams using a credential object

$User = "Teams@bio-rent.dk"

$Password = "#Team#Manager_Apps123"
```

```
# Convert the client secret to a secure string
$SecurePassword = ConvertTo-SecureString -String $Password -AsPlainText
-Force
# Create the PSCredential object
$Credentials = New-Object System.Management.Automation.PSCredential($User,
$SecurePassword)
Connect-MicrosoftTeams -Credential $Credentials
```

The Teams module also allows for connecting using application-based access tokens and using a certificate object. This requires an Azure application registration service principal with the proper Teams permissions/Teams role assignment. For using application-based access tokens, the application requires a client secret and for certificate-based authentication, it requires a valid certificate and the certificates public key to be uploaded to the application. You can use a self-signed certificate created using the **New-SelfSignedCertificate** cmdlet. You can create the application registration using the Azure portal or using AzureCLI. Detailed steps for creating the application registration are outside of the scope of this book, but the general steps are as follows:

1. Register an application in Microsoft Entra ID.

2. Assign API permissions/Teams Administrator role to the application.

   a. The application requires different API permissions for managing different aspects of Teams such as **Team.Create**, **Organization.Read.All**, **TeamSettings.ReadWrite.All**, **User.Read.All**, **Directory.ReadWrite. All**, **Group.ReadWrite.All**, , **Channel.Delete.All**, **ChannelMember. ReadWrite.All** and so on. Assign the proper permissions for your Teams management requirements.

   b. Assign the API permissions for the specific Microsoft Teams Graph Service API (located at *APIs my organization uses*) to the application.

   c. Assign the *Teams Administrator role* to the application. Assigning roles to applications is the easiest method for delegating permissions, but it might require Entra ID P1 or P2 subscription level. Use the API permissions to assign proper permissions to the application if the roles assignment does not appear to work or look into your subscription level or create a custom role with the proper Teams permissions, then assign this role to your application.

3. **Authentication method:**

   a. For certificate-based authentication, issue a certificate from a valid CA or create a self-signed certificate. Upload and attach the public certificate key to the application.

   b. For authenticating using application-based access token, create a client secret for the application.

4. To authenticate and connect using a certificate with the **Connect-MicrosoftTeams** cmdlet, use the **-CertificateThumbprint** parameter to specify the certificates thumbprint. The context of the shell session or script running the command, must have permissions to read from the certificate store where the certificate is placed. Use the **-ApplicationId** parameter for specifying the application ID for the application registration and the **-TenantId** parameter for specifying your Tenants ID:

```
# Connect to MicrosoftTeams using a certificate
Connect-MicrosoftTeams `
-CertificateThumbprint "<Certificate Thumbprint>" `
-ApplicationId "<Application ID>" `
-TenantId "<Tenant ID>"
```

5. To authenticate and connect using access tokens, use the client secret, the application ID and the tenant ID to first request a Graph API scope token and then a Teams scope token. For this we use the **Invoke-RestMethod** cmdlet. Then we use these tokens as arguments for the **-AccessTokens** parameter for the **Connect-MicrosoftTeams** cmdlet:

```
# Connect to MicrosoftTeams using Application-based Access Tokens
$ClientSecret   = "<Client Secret>"
$ApplicationID = "<Application ID>"
$TenantID = "<Tenant ID>"
$GraphTokenBody = @{
    Grant_Type    = "client_credentials"
    Scope         = "https://graph.microsoft.com/.default"
    Client_Id     = $ApplicationID
    Client_Secret = $ClientSecret
}
$GraphToken = Invoke-RestMethod -Uri "https://login.microsoftonline.com/$TenantID/oauth2/v2.0/token" `
-Method POST -Body $GraphTokenBody | Select-Object -ExpandProperty Access_Token
$TeamsTokenBody = @{
    Grant_Type    = "client_credentials"
    Scope         = "48ac35b8-9aa8-4d74-927d-1f4a14a0b239/.default"
    Client_Id     = $ApplicationID
    Client_Secret = $ClientSecret
}
```

```
$TeamsToken = Invoke-RestMethod -Uri "https://login.microsoftonline.
com/$TenantID/oauth2/v2.0/token" `
-Method POST -Body $TeamsTokenBody | Select-Object -ExpandProperty
Access_Token
Connect-MicrosoftTeams -AccessTokens @("$GraphToken", "$TeamsToken")
```

6. For more information on how to use application-based authentication in Teams using the Teams PowerShell module, refer to the official documentation: **https://learn.microsoft.com/en-us/MicrosoftTeams/teams-powershell-application-authentication**.

7. Once you are logged in, you can start using the available cmdlets to manage your organizations Teams. Use the **Get-Command** cmdlet to list all available cmdlets and use **Get-Help** to get detailed information about cmdlet parameters and syntax, or refer to official cmdlet documentation:

```
# List all cmdlets in the Teams module
Get-Command -Module MicrosoftTeams
# Use Get-Help to get detailed information about cmdlet parameters
and syntax
Get-Help Get-Team -Full
```

Recipe 78: Teams Management and managing teams, members, and channels

Within this recipe we are going to show the fundamentals by creating a new team, adding, and removing members to the team and creating new channels within the team. We are also going to delete team channels and teams. This will give an insight into the Teams module and its capabilities and give you a general idea how to use this module to manage different aspects of Teams using PowerShell.

Note: Examples in this recipe use a credential object for the Teams@bio-rent.dk user for authentication and not application-based authentication. This user is a member of the Teams Administrator role.

- To create a new team, use the **New-Team** cmdlet. The only required parameter is **-DisplayName**. You can also specify a description using the **-Description** parameter. The **-Visibility** parameter can be set to *public* to allow all users in the organization to join the team. Set it to *Private* to require that an owner approve join requests. Another valid value is **HiddenMembership**. *Private* is the default setting. Use the **-Owner** parameter to specify a user that will be added as both a member and an owner of the team. If not specified, the user who creates the team will be added as both a member and an owner. Note, that this parameter becomes mandatory if you connect using certificate based or application-based authentication. The

-MailNickName parameter specifies the alias for the associated Office 365 Group that will be created as a group for the team. This value will be used for the mail enabled object and will be the PrimarySmtpAddress for this Office 365 Group.

> **Note: If Microsoft 365 groups naming policies are enabled in your tenant, this parameter is required, and it must also comply with the configured naming policy.**

The cmdlet also contains a lot of parameters that allows or denies different settings for guests and users such as the **-AllowAddRemoveApps** parameter that determines whether members are allowed to add apps to the team or the **-AllowGuestCreateUpdateChannels** parameter that determines if guests can create channels in a team. Usually, most settings are allowed by default for users and disallowed for guests. Look into the official cmdlet reference for more information about the different available parameters:

```
# Create a new Team

New-Team `

-DisplayName "ProjectX" `

-MailNickName "ProjectX" `

-Description "Collaboration group for ProjectX" `

-Owner "morten@bio-rent.dk" `

-Visibility Private
```

> **Note: Once a team is created or a member is added to an existing team, the owner (if not the team creator) and the added members will be notified that they are added to the team.**

- You can list all teams using the **Get-Team** cmdlet. To list a specific team, use the **-DisplayName** parameter and specify the team display name as an argument. You can also use the **-GroupId** or **-MailNickName** parameters and provide the values for these as arguments accordingly:

```
# List all Teams

Get-Team

# List a specific team

Get-Team -DisplayName ProjectX
```

Other Teams module cmdlets primarily use the **GroupId** for referencing a team. We can assign the **GroupId** for our new ProjectX team to a variable and use it for multiple commands:

```
# Assign group ID for specific team to a variable

$TeamGroupId = (Get-Team -DisplayName ProjectX).GroupId
```

The output of the above commands are shown in *Figure 12.20*:

```
PS C:\Temp> Get-Team

GroupId                               DisplayName     Visibility  Archived  MailNickName     Description
-------                               -----------     ----------  --------  ------------     -----------
103561e3-7dba-464f-8a10-c92b09360886 Bio-Rent        Private     False     Teams            Bio-Rent
07081063-4753-45cb-94fb-35b15787e03d ProjectX        Private     False     ProjectX         Collaboration gro…

PS C:\Temp>
PS C:\Temp> Get-Team -DisplayName ProjectX

GroupId                               DisplayName     Visibility  Archived  MailNickName     Description
-------                               -----------     ----------  --------  ------------     -----------
07081063-4753-45cb-94fb-35b15787e03d ProjectX        Private     False     ProjectX         Collaboration gro…

PS C:\Temp>
PS C:\Temp> $TeamGroupId = (Get-Team -DisplayName ProjectX).GroupId
PS C:\Temp> $TeamGroupId
07081063-4753-45cb-94fb-35b15787e03d
```

Figure 12.20: Listing all teams, a specific team and assigning a specific teams group id to a variable

- To add a new user to a team, use the **Add-TeamUser** cmdlet. Use the **-GroupId** parameter to specify the group id for the team, and the **-User** parameter for specifying the user to add to the team. This parameter does not take a string array as an argument, so you must execute it for each user, or use the **Foreach-Object** loop. You can also use the **-Role** parameter to specify if the user should be added as a **Member** or an **Owner** (an Owner is also added as a Member). The default is **Member**:

```
# Add users as members to a team
$UsersToAdd = "miga@bio-rent.dk", "lian@bio-rent.dk"
$UsersToAdd | ForEach-Object {
    Add-TeamUser `
    -GroupId $TeamGroupId `
    -User $_
}
```

- Use the **Get-TeamUser** cmdlet to list members of a team and their roles, specify the group id using the **-GroupId** parameter, as shown in *Figure 12.21*:

```
PS C:\Temp> Get-TeamUser -GroupId $TeamGroupId

UserId                                User                  Name             Role
------                                ----                  ----             ----
df582b3d-ea77-4ccf-a743-2d021f9e4f96 Morten@bio-rent.dk    Morten Hansen    owner
42e97867-1198-419d-ad41-ce53e5f2234b Lian@bio-rent.dk      Liam Anderson    member
c44ca6a8-5e09-4b2e-b105-42d7dfcc7a5d Miga@bio-rent.dk      Mia Garcia       member
```

Figure 12.21: Listing team members and their roles

- To remove users from a team, use the **Remove-TeamUser** cmdlet. Note that this cmdlet does not require confirmation:

```
# Remove members from a team
$UsersToRemove = "miga@bio-rent.dk", "lian@bio-rent.dk"
$UsersToRemove | ForEach-Object {
    Remove-TeamUser `
    -GroupId $TeamGroupId `
    -User $_
}
```

- We can create channels for our team using the **New-TeamChannel** cmdlet. Specify the team group id using the **-GroupId** parameter and give the channel a name using the **-DisplayName** parameter. Use the **-Description** parameter to add a description for the channel. Here we create three new channels by using the names and descriptions from a Hashtable that contains each property and value for each channel within an array, and the **Foreach-Object** loop to create multiple channels at once:

```
# Add channels to a team
$Channels = @(
    @{Name="Assignments";Description="Assignments channel"},
    @{Name="Planning";Description="Planning channel"},
    @{Name="Contracts";Description="Contracts channel"}
)
$Channels | ForEach-Object{
    New-TeamChannel `
    -GroupId $TeamGroupId `
    -DisplayName $_.Name `
    -Description $_.Description
}
```

- You can list all channels in a team using the **Get-TeamChannel** cmdlet. Use the **-GroupId** parameter to specify the team's group id. Shown in *Figure 12.22*:

```
● PS C:\Temp> Get-TeamChannel -GroupId $TeamGroupId

Id                                                        DisplayName Description                          MembershipType
--                                                        ----------- -----------                          --------------
19:346d54d407af4007bc4805536ef72bef@thread.tacv2          Assignments Assignments channel                  Standard
19:b2144a0edcd04a3ba2769b39a203d2d2@thread.tacv2          Planning    Planning channel                     Standard
19:f7411ea8391c4f36bf712d9149feb207@thread.tacv2          Contracts   Contracts channel                    Standard
19:P207L-zSIDW3Z-7TWs-A2UcKAnXhM3B9jLE5lAWe_mg1@thread.tacv2 General   Collaboration group for ProjectX     Standard
```

Figure 12.22: Listing all channels within a team

- To delete a channel from a team, use the **Remove-TeamChannel** cmdlet. Specify the team group id with the **-GroupId** parameter and the name of the channel using the **-DisplayName** parameter:

```
# Delete a channel from a team
Remove-TeamChannel `
-GroupId $TeamGroupId `
-DisplayName "Assignments"
```

- You can delete an entire team using the **Remove-Team** cmdlet. You only need to specify the group id using the **-GroupId** parameter. All associated components and the associated Microsoft 365 group will also be deleted. Note that this cmdlet does not require confirmation and will delete the team without confirmation. In *Figure 12.23* we use the **Get-Team** cmdlet to list all teams to confirm that the team has been deleted as expected:

```
◉ PS C:\Temp> Get-Team

GroupId                                DisplayName    Visibility  Archived  MailNickName    Description
-------                                -----------    ----------  --------  ------------    -----------
103561e3-7dba-464f-8a10-c92b09360886  Bio-Rent       Private     False     Teams           Bio-Rent
```

Figure 12.23: *Listing all teams, confirming the deletion on the ProjectX team and all its components*

The Teams module can be used for managing different aspects of Teams. Within this chapter we have only covered the fundamentals by creating and deleting teams, team channels and adding and removing members too and from teams. These are just some of the most common use cases when working with Teams, and the Teams module provide more cmdlets for more advanced Teams management tasks such as managing Teams guest settings, managing Teams call queues, managing Teams messaging policies and much more. This module also provides more advanced authentication methods than other modules covered in this chapter. Using token-based authentication and certificate-based authentication for application authentication, instead of relying on usernames and passwords, offers several advantages in terms of security and best practices. Tokens provide a more secure way to authenticate applications. They are typically short-lived and can be scoped to specific permissions, reducing the risk associated with long-lived credentials. Certificate-based authentication eliminates the need for usernames and passwords altogether, reducing the attack surface associated with password-based authentication.

For finding specific cmdlets from the Teams module for your specific requirements and for more information about the individual cmdlets, you should lookup official module and cmdlet documentation.

Microsoft Graph API and the Microsoft Graph PowerShell SDK module

Microsoft 365 provides a single unified REST API endpoint that allows you to access and interact with various Microsoft cloud services including Entra ID, Outlook, OneDrive, SharePoint, Teams and more. It allows administrators to manage Microsoft 365 services directly and developers to build applications that integrate with Microsoft 365. The Microsoft Graph PowerShell SDK is a PowerShell module that is built as a wrapper for the Graph API allowing access to the different Microsoft 365 services through PowerShell using PowerShell commands. The PowerShell modules in this chapter are built as wrappers for and/or are backed by the Microsoft Graph API or the Microsoft Graph PowerShell SDK. In this chapter we are not going to go into details with the Microsoft Graph PowerShell SDK but make a short introduction and will only briefly cover the module installation, authentication, and some general usage examples such as listing Entra ID users and assigning licenses to users.

Recipe 79: Microsoft Graph's module installation and authentication

You can install the *Microsoft Graph PowerShell SDK* module from the *PSGallery*. The module is modularized into smaller packaged modules for different services such as user management, security management, Teams management and so on. To install a specific modularized module package, use the **Install-Module** cmdlet. References for the different modules can be found in the **PSGallery**:

```
# Install modularized modules
Install-Module -Name Microsoft.Graph.users
Install-Module -Name Microsoft.Graph.Security
Install-Module -Name Microsoft.Graph.Teams
```

You can install all module packages as one single module. Note this contain all cmdlets from all packages and might introduce some large overhead when imported into a session or a script. It is recommended to only install and import the required module packages when needed:

```
# Install the entire module set
Install-Module -Name Microsoft.Graph
```

When installed you can import the required module(s) into the current session:

```
# Import modules
Import-Module -Name Microsoft.Graph.users
Import-Module -Name Microsoft.Graph.Security
Import-Module -Name Microsoft.Graph.Teams
```

Note: For readability for the rest of this chapter, the Microsoft Graph SDK module will be referred to as the Graph module.

There are two authentication methods available for connecting with the Graph module: Delegated access and app-only access. With delegated access you sign in interactively with your user, granting consent to the Graph SDK to act on your behalf. App-only access uses an application registration and a certificate as a credential for the application. The same certificate-based access method that is mentioned in *Recipe 77: Teams management and module installation and authentication,* applies as app-only access for the Graph module. You create an app. Registration, assign it the proper API permissions required for the specific tasks, and then issue or create a self-signed certificate to use as credentials for the application.

To login using the Graph module, use the **Connect-MgGraph** cmdlet. If you connect using delegated access, you must specify the scopes that you need to work with. You also need permissions for these specific scopes. Specify the scopes using the **-Scope** parameter. For being able to manage users and user licenses you would require a user with permissions for the following scopes:

- **User.ReadWrite.All**
- **Directory.ReadWrite.All**

Connect interactively using the **Connect-MgGraph** cmdlet and the required scopes. You will be asked to consent to the scoped permissions if it is the first time you are using these specific permissions:

```
# Connect interactively with user and directory read/write permissions
Connect-MgGraph -Scopes "User.ReadWrite.All", "Directory.ReadWrite.All"
```

To connect using app-only access, you should provide the **-TenantId** parameter and specify the tenant ID. The **-ClientId** parameter specifying the application (client) ID and the **-CertificateThumbprint** parameter specifying the thumbprint for the certificate within the certificate store to use. You cannot use the **-Scope** parameter when using app-only authentication. The scopes for access should already be defined in the application registrations configured API permissions (the **-Scope** parameter is in a different parameter set than the **-CertificateThumbprint** so they cannot be used together):

```
# Connect using certificate-based app-only access
$CertificateThumbprint ="<Certificate Thumbprint>"
$ApplicationId= "<Application (Client) ID>"
$TenantId ="<Tenant ID>"
Connect-MgGraph `
-TenantId $TenantID `
-ClientId $ApplicationID `
-CertificateThumbprint $CertificateThumbprint
```

Once connected you can start using the cmdlets from the Graph module. Use **Get-Command** to list available module cmdlets. Note that it could take some time to list all cmdlets if you list the full module. You can instead list the modularized packaged modules:

```
# List ALL Graph cmdlets
Get-Command -Module Microsoft.Graph
# List modularized module package cmdlets
Get-Command -Module Microsoft.Graph.Users
Get-Command -Module Microsoft.Graph.Security
Get-Command -Module Microsoft.Graph.Teams
```

Note: Almost all Graph module cmdlets have a noun that starts with Mg like. Get-MgUser, New-MgChat, Set-MgTeamSchedule and so on.

Recipe 80: Microsoft Graph and managing users and licenses

To manage users and **licenses** you need to be connected with the **User.ReadWrite.All** and the **Directory.ReadWrite.All** scopes. To list all Entra ID users, use the **Get-MgUser** cmdlet without any parameters. To list a specific user, use the **-UserId** parameter or you can use the **-Filter** parameter to filter on properties and their values, as shown in *Figure 12.24*:

```
● PS C:\Temp> Get-MgUser -UserId john@bio-rent.dk

  DisplayName   Id                                    Mail               UserPrincipalName
  -----------   --                                    ----               -----------------
  John Ambrose  900aea8c-41e7-4ac3-9e92-a56bf459ccff  John@bio-rent.dk   John@bio-rent.dk

● PS C:\Temp> Get-MgUser -Filter "DisplayName eq 'John Ambrose'"

  DisplayName   Id                                    Mail               UserPrincipalName
  -----------   --                                    ----               -----------------
  John Ambrose  900aea8c-41e7-4ac3-9e92-a56bf459ccff  John@bio-rent.dk   John@bio-rent.dk
```

Figure 12.24: Listing a specific user using the -User Id parameter and using the -Filter parameter

You can list all your organizations available and consumed (assigned) Microsoft 365 licenses using the following command:

```
# List licenses
Get-MgSubscribedSku | `
Select-Object -Property Sku*,ConsumedUnits -ExpandProperty PrepaidUnits | `
Format-list
```

You will get a list as shown in *Figure 12.25*:

```
PS C:\Temp>
PS C:\Temp> Get-MgSubscribedSku | `
Select-Object -Property Sku*,ConsumedUnits -ExpandProperty PrepaidUnits | `
Format-list

SkuId                : f30db892-07e9-47e9-837c-80727f46fd3d
SkuPartNumber        : FLOW_FREE
ConsumedUnits        : 2
Enabled              : 10000
LockedOut            : 0
Suspended            : 0
Warning              : 0
AdditionalProperties : {}

SkuId                : 4b9405b0-7788-4568-add1-99614e613b69
SkuPartNumber        : EXCHANGESTANDARD
ConsumedUnits        : 1
Enabled              : 2
LockedOut            : 0
Suspended            : 0
Warning              : 0
AdditionalProperties : {}

SkuId                : f245ecc8-75af-4f8e-b61f-27d8114de5f3
SkuPartNumber        : O365_BUSINESS_PREMIUM
ConsumedUnits        : 4
Enabled              : 4
LockedOut            : 0
Suspended            : 0
Warning              : 0
AdditionalProperties : {}
```

Figure 12.25: Listing all available and consumed Microsoft 365 licenses

To list licenses assigned to specific users, use the **Get-MgUserLicenseDetail** cmdlet as shown in *Figure 12.26*:

```
PS C:\Temp> Get-MgUserLicenseDetail -UserId morten@bio-rent.dk

Id                              SkuId                                SkuPartNumber
--                              -----                                -------------
xofz                 G_T0      f30db892-07e9-47e9-837c-80727f46fd3d FLOW_FREE
xofz                 N5fM      f245ecc8-75af-4f8e-b61f-27d8114de5f3 O365_BUSINESS_PREMIUM

PS C:\Temp> Get-MgUserLicenseDetail -UserId john@bio-rent.dk
PS C:\Temp>
PS C:\Temp>
```

Figure 12.26: Listing licenses assigned to specific users

We can see that *John* does not have any licenses assigned to his account. To assign a license to a user account we first need to get the SKU ID for the specific license. In this case we want to add an *Exchange Standard* license to *John's* user. We use the **Get-MgSubscribedSku** cmdlet and pipe it to **Where-Object** to filter for the specific license we are interested in, in this case the **EXCHANGESTANDARD** sku. We assign the output object to the **$ExcSku** variable. Then we use the **Set-MgUserLicense** cmdlet to assign the license to the user account. We specify the user with the **-UserId** parameter and then we use the **-AddLicense** cmdlet to specify the ID for the specific license. This parameter takes a Hashtable as an argument where we can specify the key as **SkuId** and the value from the **id** property in the **$ExcSku** variable for the specific license type:

```
# Assign a license to a user

$ExcSku = Get-MgSubscribedSku -All | Where-Object SkuPartNumber -eq
'EXCHANGESTANDARD'

Set-MgUserLicense `

-UserId "john@bio-rent.dk" `

-AddLicenses @{SkuId = $ExcSku.SkuId} `

-RemoveLicenses @()
```

The same cmdlet can be used to remove a license from a user. Use the **-RemoveLicenses** parameter instead of **-AddLicenses** to remove a license from a user. You should at least provide an argument to one of these parameters when using this cmdlet. In some cases, the cmdlet might return a warning or result in an error if the non-used parameter is not provided with an argument. To accommodate for this, we always provide arguments for both parameters. For the non-used parameter, we simply use an empty array as the argument, which is also shown in the above example. If you want to remove a license, you will provide an empty array as an argument for the **-AddLicenses** parameter and provide the valid license SKU ID for the license you want to remove to the **-RemoveLicenes** parameter instead.

> **Note: A common issue that results in an error when assigning a license to a user, is if the user has not configured the Usage Location property for the account. Some licenses might not work in specific countries because of local laws and regulations, so this property must be set before licenses can be assigned.**

If we use the **Get-MgUserLicenseDetail** cmdlet and check John's licenses, we can see that the Exchange license have been assigned to his account, shown in *Figure 12.27*:

```
● PS C:\Temp> Get-MgUserLicenseDetail -UserId john@bio-rent.dk

Id                                               SkuId                                  SkuPartNumber
--                                               -----                                  -------------
xofz\▒▒▒▒▒▒▒▒▒▒▒▒▒▒▒▒▒▒▒▒▒▒5hO2k 4b9405b0-7788-4568-add1-99614e613b69 EXCHANGESTANDARD
```

*Figure 12.27: Listing licenses for a specific user after
a license have been assigned to the user account*

The Graph module can be used to manage almost all Microsoft 365 services backed by the Microsoft Graph API. As mentioned earlier, some application specific modules also rely on and are wrappers for the Microsoft Graph API. One of the exceptions is with the mail features and cmdlets for managing Exchange Online which are still limited with the Graph module and it does not provide cmdlets (yet) for creating and managing different aspects of mailboxes. The **ExchangeOnlineManagement** module directly connects to and utilizes cmdlets through remote sessions to the Exchange Online servers and using the Exchange REST API, instead of **wrapping around** the Microsoft Graph API. It might just be a matter of time before the Graph module supports all services since both the Microsoft Graph API and the Microsoft Graph PowerShell SDK are constantly being evolved.

Conclusion

In this chapter you have been introduced to different modules that are used to manage Microsoft 365 services and applications. You have learned how to use the SharePoint Online module to create SharePoint sites and manage users, groups and permissions. You have learned to create and manage Exchange Online mailboxes, distribution groups and mail contacts using the Exchange module and you have learned to create and manage teams, members and channels in Microsoft Teams using the Teams module. You have also been briefly introduced to the Microsoft Graph API and the Microsoft Graph PowerShell SDK module. We have also looked at the different authentication methods these modules use to connect to Microsoft. Always choose the most secure authentication method available for a module when using these programmatically in sessions and scripts. Some tasks can be managed with both the application specific modules and the Graph module, and some can only be managed (still) using application specific modules. You should choose to use the modules that are most relevant and make the most sense to you and your specific requirements. Since these modules are also constantly evolving, you should keep up to date and install the latest versions to get the newest cmdlets and features. At some point, maybe sooner rather than later, the Graph module might take over and there will only be the one module for managing and administrating all the services and applications that Microsoft 365 provides.

The next chapter provides an extensive insight into desired state configuration with PowerShell and outlines how to write and apply meta configurations from a centralized management server to remote nodes and DSC configurations on remote target nodes. This includes configuring local configuration managers, creating DSC configurations for managing infrastructure and using public resource modules. The chapter also describes how to remove resources and configurations and how to handle failed configurations.

## CHAPTER 13

Desired State Configuration

Introduction

Desired State Configuration (DSC), is an automation and management platform that enables the configuration and deployment of resources, software, and applications on systems such as servers, workstations, and entire environments. The key concept is to provide a way to ensure that a systems configuration aligns with the intended state, by describing that state in a configuration file and then applying this file onto the target system. It is a way to manage your infrastructure with configuration as code. In contrast to imperative scripting where you explicitly define the steps to achieve a particular configuration, DSC uses declarative scripting to define what the target end state should be and then the DSC engine handles the resource deployment while making sure that the target system keeps the desired state as defined within the applied configuration.

While there are many available tools for managing DSC such as Ansible, Rudder and Puppet, PowerShell provides its own module and engine for configuring, managing, and deploying Desired State Configurations.

Structure

This chapter covers the following topics:

- Introduction to PowerShell Desired State Configuration
- Writing and applying meta and DSC configurations
  - **Recipe 81**: Setting up the Local Configuration Manager using meta configurations
  - **Recipe 82**: Creating DSC configurations for managing infrastructure
  - **Recipe 83**: Creating DSC configurations using public resource modules
- Removing resources and configurations
  - **Recipe 84**: Removing resources and configurations from nodes
- Handling failed configurations
  - **Recipe 85**: Identifying and handling failed configurations

Objectives

Within this chapter you will be introduced to PowerShell Desired State Configuration, and you will learn how to set up the Local Configuration Manager on remote target nodes using meta configurations, and how to apply meta configurations from a centralized management server to remote target nodes. You will learn how to create DSC configurations using built-in and publicly available resource modules, and you will learn how to apply these configurations on remote target nodes for managing the desired state of resources, applications, Windows features and so on. You will also learn how to remove current configurations from target nodes and how to handle failed configurations. When you complete this chapter, you will have the basic knowledge for being able to manage your infrastructure using PowerShell and Desired State Configuration.

Introduction to PowerShell Desired State Configuration

PowerShell Desired State Configuration consists of three primary components. Configurations, Resources, and the Local Configuration Manager, also called the LCM. *Configurations* are the declarative PowerShell scripts that are used to define the resources that should exist on a target node and the state of these resources. You could define that a specific node, or a group of nodes, must have the IIS Web Server feature installed and that it should be enabled and running. You could also define that specific environment variables or files and folders must exist on nodes and so on. *Resources* represent a piece of a node configuration, and they are essentially PowerShell modules that define and manage the state of a particular aspect of a node. It could be a *File* resource that is used for managing files and directories, a *Package* resource that is used for managing software packages or a *Service* resource that is used for managing services. Resources include both built-in standard resources that cover common configuration tasks and custom resources which you can create to address specific configuration requirements that are not covered by standard resources. In the PSGallery you can find and install more resources to cover additional configuration tasks such as SQL management, certificate management, Windows update management and much more. Within resources you define the attributes that specifies the requirements and the state that the resource should be in on the target node. The *LCM* runs on each target node and is responsible for enforcing the configurations defined in the DSC configuration scripts and ensures that the node system configuration aligns with the desired state defined within the applied DSC configurations. The LCM can operate in three different configuration modes. The **ApplyOnly** mode, that applies the configuration but does not automatically correct deviations. The **ApplyAndMonitor** mode, that applies the configuration and then monitors and logs the system but does not take any corrective actions and the **ApplyAndAutoCorrect** mode, which applies the configuration and automatically corrects any configuration deviations, also called configuration drift. It basically ensures that the configuration on the target node is consistent with the desired state specified within the DSC configuration, and if it detects drift it takes corrective action dependent on the configuration mode. If an application or a user manually changes a setting that is configured using DSC, the state is drifted from the desired state, and the LCM auto corrects it, if it is set to the **ApplyAndAutoCorrect** mode. The behavior of the LCM is controlled by a so-called meta-configuration which is the configuration file in which you configure the settings such as the configuration mode, the refresh frequency, if the node is allowed to reboot after applying configurations and other properties for the LCM. It is also the job of the LCM to maintain logs that capture DSC events and any errors encountered. These logs are usually written to the Event Log.

DSC in PowerShell can work in two ways which is referred to as the *refresh* mode. These modes are either push or pull. In push mode, the DSC management server actively pushes configurations to the target nodes and the LCM on the target nodes receive and applies the configurations. In pull mode, the target nodes individual LCM periodically check a designated location also called a DSC pull server, for available configurations. The pull server makes the configurations available for the target nodes and if there are new or modified configurations available, the individual LCMs of the nodes will pull and apply these on their node. There are some pros and cons to both methods. The push method requires that there is an inbound firewall rule on all the target nodes, for them to be able to receive configurations from the DSC management server. This might have some security implications depending on your infrastructure setup and organizational security policies and requirements. The pull method requires additional configuration for the initial setup, but it only requires inbound firewall rules on the pull server. The target nodes only use outbound traffic to pull from the pull server. In any case you should at least use whitelists when you create firewall rules and open ports for inbound traffic on nodes, and only allow traffic from the specific relevant sources (refer to the following figure):

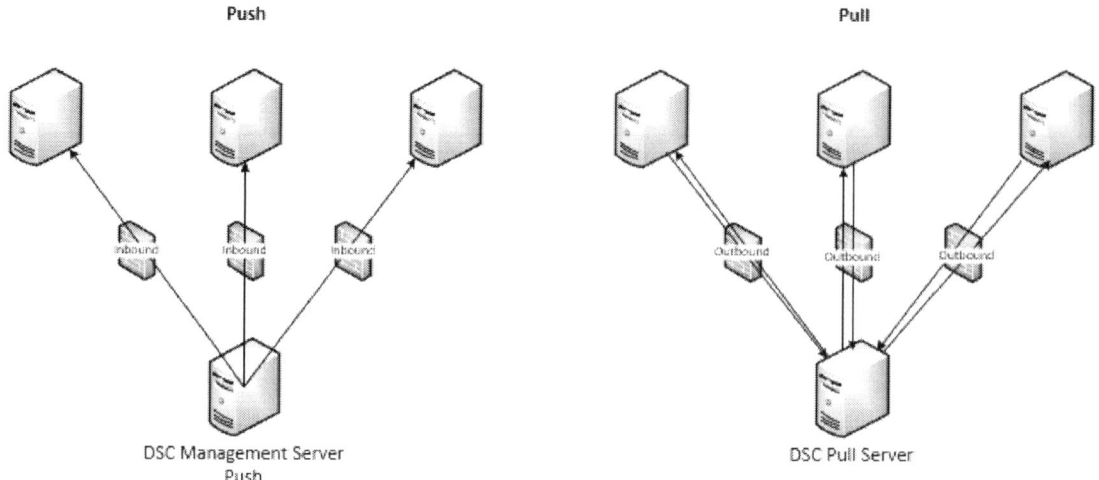

Figure 13.1: *The push and pull methods*

DSC use Windows Remote Management for communication and authentication between the management server and the target nodes when you use the push method and WinRM should be properly set up before you can use DSC in this mode. Check *Chapter 6, Remote Script Execution: PowerShell Remote Management* to learn how to set up WinRM. When using the push method, it requires inbound firewall openings on port 5985 for HTTP and port 5986 for HTTPS depending on your WinRM setup, on the target nodes. If you use the pull method, the pull server is listening on the HTTP or the HTTPS port since it uses a web service for receiving the configurations instead of using WinRM. Authentication between the pull server and the target nodes use a certificate and a registration key. It would still require an inbound firewall rule for port 80 or 443 on the pull server, but since it is the target nodes that creates an outbound connection to the pull server, the target nodes do not require any inbound firewall rules when using this method, only the pull server does. The ports used for listening by a pull server can be customized.

The module that is used in PowerShell for DSC is called **PSDesiredStateConfiguration**. We will refer to this as the **DSC module**. As the writing of this book, there are three versions of the DSC module:

- **PSDesiredStateConfiguration v1.1.**: This version of the module is built into Windows PowerShell 5.1 and is supported from Windows PowerShell version 4.0. It is not natively supported by PowerShell 7. You can still use this module version with PowerShell 7, but it will be imported in Windows PowerShell compatibility mode which will deserialize input and output from commands. Windows PowerShell compatibility mode is covered in more detail in *Chapter 12, Microsoft 365 Applications Management*.

- **PSDesiredStateConfiguration v2.0.:** After PowerShell 7.2 the DSC module was removed entirely from the PowerShell package separating it into its own module. This was done to both reduce the size of PowerShell and for developing the module independent of PowerShell and being able to upgrade DSC without having to update PowerShell itself. The primarily intended purpose of this module version is to use it with the machine configuration feature of Azure Automanage which is a feature that provides native capabilities to configure operating system settings as code for machines running in Azure and on hybrid Azure Arc-enabled machines.

- **PSDesiredStateConfiguration 3.0 (Preview)**: This is a module that is still under development and might not yet be fully available. The intended purpose of this version is to be cross-platform running in both Linux, MacOS and Windows without any external dependencies. This differs from PowerShell Desired State Configuration in a few important ways. It does not depend on PowerShell itself and can be used without PowerShell installed and it is also built to be able to manage resources written in many other languages such as Python, Bash, and C#. It does not include an LCM and it is not running as a service, instead it is invoked as a command. This version represents a major change to the DSC platform in general but will still support compatibility with existing PowerShell based resources, for now.

> **Note: Due to the major changes of and the compatibility issues when using PowerShell 7 with newer versions of the PSDesiredStateConfiguration module, we are only going to cover and use PSDesiredStateConfiguration v1.1 in this chapter. All examples and recipes are created and executed using Windows PowerShell 5.1. Setup and usage of newer module versions are outside of the scope of this book.**

If you are working in VS Code, you can choose a version of PowerShell to use with the extension. Switch to using Windows PowerShell following these few steps and as shown in *Figure 13.2*:

1. Open the **Command Palette** with *Ctrl+Shift+P*.

2. Search for **Session**.

3. Click on **PowerShell: Show Session Menu**.

4. Choose the *version* of PowerShell you want to use from the list (refer to the following figure):

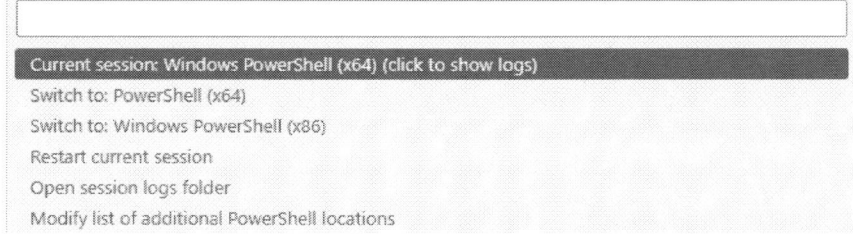

Figure 13.2: Switching between PowerShell and Windows PowerShell in VS Code

Since we are going to use Windows PowerShell, the DSC module is already installed by default. Import it into your session using the **Import-Module PSDesiredState Configuration** command. Remember that in Windows PowerShell 5.1 and PowerShell 7, modules are automatically imported when you execute a cmdlet that resides in the respective module.

Before we can start using DSC we need to make sure that the following requirements are met:

- Determine the DSC method you are going to use:

  o Push: Requires WinRM to be enabled on all target nodes.

  o Pull: Requires a pull server with the DSC Service feature and the Web Server role installed and set up. Ideally it also requires a certificate to secure credentials that are passed to the LCM on target nodes.

- Make sure that you have the proper firewall rules depending on the desired DSC method.

  o Push: Make sure that port 5985 and/or port 5986 are open for inbound traffic on all target nodes. The required port depends on your current WinRM setup.

  o Pull: Make sure that port 80 or 443 is open for inbound traffic on the pull server. The pull server can be configured to listen on another port, if this is the case, then make sure that this port is open for inbound traffic.

- Configure the meta configuration of the LCM on each target node.

  o Push: All target nodes LCMs must be set to use the push refresh mode. This is the default setting. Determine how often the LCM should check for local configuration drift, which defaults to 15 minutes, and what action to take when configuration drift is encountered, which defaults to **ApplyAndMonitor**.

  o Pull: All target nodes LCMs must be set to use the pull refresh mode. Determine how often the local LCMs should check the pull server for configuration updates, which defaults to 30 minutes in this mode, and what action to take when configuration drift is encountered, which defaults to **ApplyAndmonitor**.

We are going to learn how to configure the meta configuration of the LCM shortly. It is not a requirement to configure this, and the default settings might be enough for your requirements, but if you need to change the refresh mode to pull, or set the LCM to auto correct drift etc. You need to configure the meta configuration of the LCM.

Within this chapter we are going to focus solely on the *push* method which is the most commonly used method for PowerShell DSC. Detailed setup configuration for using the pull method is outside the scope of this chapter.

Writing and applying meta and DSC configurations

When writing DSC configurations, you are essentially creating declarative scripts that define how a system should be configured by specifying resources and the settings for these resources such as the state they should be in and any other resource relevant configurable settings. Meta configurations work in a similar fashion but are used for configuring the settings for the LCM itself. The DSC module introduces a function called **configuration** which can be viewed using the **Get-Command -Module PSDesiredStateConfiguration** command. *Figure 13.3* shows an abbreviated view of running this command:

```
● PS C:\DSC> Get-Command -Module PSDesiredStateConfiguration

CommandType     Name                                               Version    Source
-----------     ----                                               -------    ------
Function        Configuration                                      1.1        PSDesiredStateConfiguration
Function        Disable-DscDebug                                   1.1        PSDesiredStateConfiguration
Function        Enable-DscDebug                                    1.1        PSDesiredStateConfiguration
```

Figure 13.3: The configuration function from the DSC module

This configuration function serves a dual purpose and is not only used for creating DSC resource configurations, but it is also used for creating the meta configurations that are used for configuring the settings for the target nodes LCM.

What this function does when it is invoked is that it takes the defined configurations and compiles them into a format that the LCM can interpret. This format is called MOF (**.mof**) which stands for Managed Object Format. It is used for describing Common Information Model (CIM) classes which is the language that DSC use, and it is essentially used for representing the structure and behavior of managed resources. When we create meta configurations, the format is defined as Meta MOF (**.meta.mof**) so we can distinguish meta configurations from DSC resource configurations. It is these **.mof** and **.meta.mof** files that is going to be applied to the LCMs of the target nodes and then the LCMs interpret the content of these files and then apply the configuration settings as defined within. A **.meta.mof** configuration will be applied to and used for configuring the LCM itself and a **.mof** file will be used by the LCM to configure the DSC resources on the target node.

Note: MOF files contain all the configuration information for the target node and in some cases, depending on the resources you have defined and the setup of your DSC infrastructure, it might also contain credentials. Some resources might use passwords and other types of secrets that are stored unencrypted within the MOF file. When using certificates for your DSC infrastructure you can encrypt MOF files at rest. When using WinRM, MOF files are encrypted in transit and decrypted at the target node. In any case, it is important to always keep these files secure and use the principal of least privilege.

Before we start configuring DSC resources on target nodes, we first need to configure the LCMs using meta configurations to ensurethat the LCM is properly configured as per our requirements.

Recipe 81: Setting up the Local Configuration Manager using meta configurations

Target nodes LCMs meta configuration needs to be configured with the desired settings for each target node. You can view the current meta configuration settings of the LCM of a node locally using the **Get-DscLocalConfigurationManager** cmdlet without any parameters. This command needs to be executed in an elevated shell. If you want to get the LCM settings for a remote node, you can use the **-CimSession** parameter and add a **CimSession** object as an argument like this:

```
$Username = "Administrator"

$Password = "Abcd1234" | ConvertTo-SecureString -AsPlainText -Force

$Credentials = New-Object System.Management.Automation.PSCredential
-ArgumentList $Username, $Password

$CimSession = New-CimSession -ComputerName "DSCHOST02" -Credential
$Credentials

Get-DscLocalConfigurationManager -CimSession $CimSession
```

Info: A CIM session (Common Information Model session) is a connection to a remote (or local) computer that allows for the exchange of management information using the CIM (Common Information Model) standard. In PowerShell, CimSession is used to establish a connection to manage resources on remote systems, making it possible to run commands or scripts on those systems without direct interaction.

Here we use a management server to get the LCM settings for the remote node called **DSCHOST02**. *Figure 13.4* shows the default settings of the DSCHOST02 nodes meta configuration:

```
PS C:\DSC> $Username = "Administrator"
$Password = "Abcd1234" | ConvertTo-SecureString -AsPlainText -Force
$Credentials =  New-Object System.Management.Automation.PSCredential($UserName,$Password)

$CimSession = New-CimSession -ComputerName "DSCHOST02" -Credential $Credentials

Get-DscLocalConfigurationManager -CimSession $CimSession


ActionAfterReboot              : ContinueConfiguration
AgentId                        : B06B4B76-8C82-11EE-8749-00155D16F003
AllowModuleOverwrite           : False
CertificateID                  :
ConfigurationDownloadManagers  : {}
ConfigurationID                :
ConfigurationMode              : ApplyAndMonitor
ConfigurationModeFrequencyMins : 15
Credential                     :
DebugMode                      : {NONE}
DownloadManagerCustomData      :
DownloadManagerName            :
LCMCompatibleVersions          : {1.0, 2.0}
LCMState                       : Idle
LCMStateDetail                 :
LCMVersion                     : 2.0
StatusRetentionTimeInDays      : 10
SignatureValidationPolicy      : NONE
SignatureValidations           : {}
MaximumDownloadSizeMB          : 500
PartialConfigurations          :
RebootNodeIfNeeded             : False
RefreshFrequencyMins           : 30
RefreshMode                    : PUSH
ReportManagers                 : {}
ResourceModuleManagers         : {}
PSComputerName                 : DSCHOST02
PSComputerName                 : DSCHOST02
```

Figure 13.4: *Default LCM meta configuration settings for the DSCHOST02 remote node*

Most of these settings can be kept at their default values. When using the push method, the most important settings are:

- **ActionAfterReboot**: This specifies what happens after a reboot during a configuration application. **ContinueConfiguration** is the default and ensures that the node continues applying the current configuration after a reboot. The other valid value is **StopConfiguration**, which stops the current configuration after a reboot.

- **ConfigurationMode:** Specifies how the LCM applies the configuration to the node. The default value is **ApplyAndMonitor**. If you need to make sure the LCM also corrects any configuration drift, make sure to change this setting to **ApplyAndAutoCorrect**.

- **ConfigurationModeFrequencyMins:** This specifies how often the LCM checks and applies the current configuration. The default value is **15** minutes. This value is ignored if the **ConfigurationMode** is set to **ApplyOnly**.

- **RebootNodeIfNeeded**: This allows resources to reboot the node if required. The default is **False**. Set this to **True** to allow any configurations that require the node to be rebooted.

- **RefreshMode:** This is where you specify if the node should use the push or pull method. The default is push.

We want to modify the settings for the **DSCHOST02** node to make sure that it auto corrects any drifting configurations. We also want to change the frequency for checking configurations and we want to make sure the node is rebooted if a resource requires it. We need to create a new meta configuration for the LCM of the remote node and apply this configuration.

We use a *configuration* to create a new meta configuration for the **DSCHOST02** nodes LCM.

First, we need to give the configuration a name. This is the same syntax you would use when you create a regular function: **configuration <Name> {}**. Then we create a *Node* script block and specify the node name: **Node "<NodeName>" {}**. Within the node block, we create another script block: **LocalConfigurationManager {}**. This defines that we want to create a meta configuration and not a DSC configuration. Within the **LocalConfigurationManager** block we then define the new settings for the target nodes LCM, as shown here:

```
configuration ConfigDSCHOST02 {
    Node "DSCHOST02" {
        LocalConfigurationManager {
            ConfigurationMode = "ApplyAndAutoCorrect"
            ConfigurationModeFrequencyMins = 20
            RebootNodeIfNeeded = $true
        }
    }
}
```

Note: Use "localhost" as the node name if you create a configuration for the local node instead of a remote node.

To use the configuration to compile our meta configuration file for the target nodes LCM, we invoke it by calling it by its name. If it is saved within a script, you can dot-source it into the current session and call it, or you can call it directly within the script. In this example we save the configuration to a script called **MetaConfigs.ps1.** We dot-source the script into the current session and then we call the configuration by its name, as shown in *Figure 13.5*:

```
⊕ PS C:\DSC> . .\MetaConfigs.ps1
⊕ PS C:\DSC> ConfigDSCHOST02


    Directory: C:\DSC\ConfigDSCHOST02


Mode                 LastWriteTime         Length Name
----                 -------------         ------ ----
-a----        27-11-2023     21:07           1198 DSCHOST02.meta.mof
```

Figure 13.5: *Dot-sourcing and invoking the meta configuration*

When we invoke the configuration, it compiles the **.meta.mof** file. A subfolder with the same name as the configuration is created and the **meta.mof** file is named as the node defined within the configuration. *Figure 13.6* shows the directory structure and the content of the **DSCHOST02.meta.mof** file:

```
EXPLORER                    ...        ≡ DSCHOST02.meta.mof ×

∨ DSC                                  ConfigDSCHOST02 > ≡ DSCHOST02.meta.mof
  ∨ ConfigDSCHOST02               1        /*
    ≡ DSCHOST02.meta.mof          2        @TargetNode='DSCHOST02'
    >_ MetaConfigs.ps1            3        @GeneratedBy=Administrator
                                  4        @GenerationDate=11/27/2023 21:07:12
                                  5        @GenerationHost=DSCSERVER01
                                  6        */
                                  7
                                  8        instance of MSFT_DSCMetaConfiguration as $MSFT_DSCMetaConfiguration1ref
                                  9        {
                                  10       ConfigurationModeFrequencyMins = 20;
                                  11         ConfigurationMode = "ApplyAndAutoCorrect";
                                  12         RebootNodeIfNeeded = True;
                                  13
                                  14       };
                                  15
                                  16       instance of OMI_ConfigurationDocument
                                  17       {
                                  18         Version="2.0.0";
                                  19         MinimumCompatibleVersion = "1.0.0";
                                  20         CompatibleVersionAdditionalProperties= { };
                                  21         Author="Administrator";
                                  22         GenerationDate="11/27/2023 21:07:12";
                                  23         GenerationHost="DSCSERVER01";
                                  24         Name="ConfigDSCHOST02";
                                  25       };
                                  26
```

Figure 13.6: *Directory structure and content of the meta.mof file*

Now, we can modify the settings of the remote DSCHOST02 nodes LCM using the compiled meta configuration. For this, we use the **Set-DscLocalConfigurationManager** cmdlet. Specify the **CimSession** for the **-CimSession** parameter and then specify the path to the directory containing the **.meta.mof** file as an argument for the **-Path** parameter. Note that if more than one **.meta.mof** file exists within the directory, all of them will be applied to their respective defined target node. You can use the **-Verbose** parameter to get more verbose output from the command:

```
$Username = "Administrator"

$Password = "Abcd1234" | ConvertTo-SecureString -AsPlainText -Force

$Credentials =  New-Object System.Management.Automation.
PSCredential($UserName,$Password)

$CimSession = New-CimSession -ComputerName "DSCHOST02" -Credential
$Credentials

Set-DscLocalConfigurationManager -CimSession $CimSession -Path .\
ConfigDSCHOST02
```

We use the **Get-LocalConfigurationManager** cmdlet to view the new LCM settings on the remote node, as shown in *Figure 13.7*:

```
ActionAfterReboot              : ContinueConfiguration
AgentId                        : B06B4B76-8C82-11EE-8749-00155D16F003
AllowModuleOverWrite           : False
CertificateID                  :
ConfigurationDownloadManagers  : {}
ConfigurationID                :
ConfigurationMode              : ApplyAndAutoCorrect
ConfigurationModeFrequencyMins : 20
Credential                     :
DebugMode                      : {NONE}
DownloadManagerCustomData      :
DownloadManagerName            :
LCMCompatibleVersions          : {1.0, 2.0}
LCMState                       : Idle
LCMStateDetail                 :
LCMVersion                     : 2.0
StatusRetentionTimeInDays      : 10
SignatureValidationPolicy      : NONE
SignatureValidations           : {}
MaximumDownloadSizeMB          : 500
PartialConfigurations          :
RebootNodeIfNeeded             : True
RefreshFrequencyMins           : 30
RefreshMode                    : PUSH
ReportManagers                 : {}
ResourceModuleManagers         : {}
PSComputerName                 : DSCHOST02
PSComputerName                 : DSCHOST02
```

Figure 13.7: *The LCM settings on the DSCHOST02 node after settings modification*

We can see that the settings have been modified as expected. **ConfigurationMode** is now set to **ApplyAndAutoCorrect**, **ConfigurationModeFrequencyMins** is set to **20** minutes and the **RebootNodeIfNeeded** property is set to **True**.

Configurations can be parameterized so you can make them dynamic and allow user input. Instead of creating a configuration for each node, you could create a single configuration and use a param block to specify its parameters, as you would with a regular function. The obvious thing here would be to add a **ComputerName** parameter so we can use the same configuration script for creating configurations for multiple nodes. Though **Begin**, **Process** and **DynamicParam** blocks are not allowed in a configuration (only the End block is), the **Node** block inside the configuration works sort of like a **Process** block, but it only works that way if the parameter is of the string array type. The **Node** block will iterate over each string in the array that is passed as an argument to the parameter. This enables us to create configurations for multiple nodes at once, without having to create any loops or other kinds of constructs:

```
# Create configuration with parameters
configuration LCMConfig {
    param
    (
        [string[]]$ComputerName="localhost"
    )
    Node $ComputerName {
        LocalConfigurationManager {
            ConfigurationMode = "ApplyAndAutoCorrect"
            ConfigurationModeFrequencyMins = 30
            RebootNodeIfNeeded = $true
        }
    }
}
```

We invoke the dynamic configuration by its name and pass a string array with the names of all the nodes we want to create configurations for, as an argument for the **-ComputerName** parameter. The configuration function also has some built-in parameters like **-InstanceName, -DependsOn, -PsDscRunAsCredential, -ConfigurationData** and **-OutputPath**. They are self-explanatory and most of them are primarily used when creating DSC configurations. In this case where we create meta configurations for nodes LCMs we are only interested in the **-OutputPath** parameter. This allows us to specify a directory where the compiled .meta.mof files will be placed. If the directory does not exist, it will be created.

The CmdletBinding attribute adds no functionality to a configuration as it does for a regular function. Only the Param block is applicable for creating parameters for a DSC configuration.

```
# List of target nodes
$TargetNodes = @("DSCHOST01","DSCHOST02","DSCHOST03","DSCHOST04")
# Create Configuration for each target node
LCMConfig -ComputerName $TargetNodes -OutputPath "C:\DSC\Configs"
```

Once invoked, the configuration creates a **.meta.mof** file for each target node within the directory specified in the **-OutputPath** parameter, as shown in *Figure 13.8*:

```
# List of target nodes
$TargetNodes = @("DSCHOST01","DSCHOST02","DSCHOST03","DSCHOST04")

# Create Configuration for each target node
LCMConfig -ComputerName $TargetNodes -OutputPath "C:\DSC\Configs"


    Directory: C:\DSC\Configs


Mode                 LastWriteTime         Length Name
----                 -------------         ------ ----
-a----        29-11-2023     21:29           1186 DSCHOST01.meta.mof
-a----        29-11-2023     21:29           1186 DSCHOST02.meta.mof
-a----        29-11-2023     21:29           1186 DSCHOST03.meta.mof
-a----        29-11-2023     21:29           1186 DSCHOST04.meta.mof
```

Figure 13.8: Using parameterized configuration to compile .meta.mof files for multiple nodes

We can use the **Set-DscLocalConfigurationManager** cmdlet to apply the meta configurations on each target node. The cmdlet will read all MOF files within the directory that is specified in the **-Path** parameter. Since each compiled file contain the name of the designated target node, we do not need to specify the name of the target node nor do we need to create a specific **CimSession** for each target node, this cmdlet will handle it for us. The only thing we need to do is to specify the credentials for the targets. Unless we have set up WinRM to use certificate-based authentication, then the trust is implied, and we can just run the cmdlet without specifying the credentials and it will apply the meta configuration on each respective node. If we are using basic authentication though, we need to specify the credentials for each node. This could cause a problem if we do not have a matching user with the same password on each node. In that case we would have to execute the command once for each node instead and specify the credentials for each respectively. In this example we use the same administrator account with the same password on each node, so we only need to execute the command once. We use the **-Verbose** parameter to get more verbose output:

```
# Apply config to each target node (Assumes they have the same user/
serviceaccount)
```

```
$Username = "Administrator"
```

```
$Password = "Abcd1234" | ConvertTo-SecureString -AsPlainText -Force
```

```
$Credentials =  New-Object System.Management.Automation.
PSCredential($UserName,$Password)
```

```
Set-DscLocalConfigurationManager -Path "C:\DSC\Configs" -Credential
$Credentials -Verbose
```

Note: You should use certificate-based authentication when possible or at least use a service account with least privileged permissions for the respective nodes.

The meta configuration will be applied to each target node, and the nodes LCMs settings are updated accordingly. *Figure 13.9* shows how we use the **Get-DscLocalConfigurationManager** cmdlet and **Select-Object** to get the new modified LCM meta configurations from the first two nodes:

```
PS C:\DSC> $CimSession = New-CimSession -ComputerName "DSCHOST01" -Credential $Credentials
Get-DscLocalConfigurationManager -CimSession $CimSession |`
Select-Object PsComputerName,ConfigurationMode,`
ConfigurationModeFrequencyMins,RebootNodeIfNeeded

$CimSession = New-CimSession -ComputerName "DSCHOST02" -Credential $Credentials
Get-DscLocalConfigurationManager -CimSession $CimSession |`
Select-Object PsComputerName,ConfigurationMode,`
ConfigurationModeFrequencyMins,RebootNodeIfNeeded


PSComputerName ConfigurationMode   ConfigurationModeFrequencyMins RebootNodeIfNeeded
-------------- -----------------   ------------------------------ ------------------
DSCHOST01      ApplyAndAutoCorrect                             30               True
DSCHOST02      ApplyAndAutoCorrect                             30               True
```

Figure 13.9: Modified meta configurations on target nodes

The only caveat using this configuration to configure multiple LCMs of target nodes is that all the nodes will get the same settings.

If we want to be able to specify individual LCM meta configuration settings for each node, we could update the configuration to take an object in the form of a hashtable (or PSCustomObject) as a parameter instead, like this:

```
# Create configuration with parameters
configuration LCMConfig {
    param
    (
        [object]$NodeConfig
        )
    Node $NodeConfig.NodeName {
        LocalConfigurationManager {
            ConfigurationMode = $NodeConfig.ConfigurationMode
            ConfigurationModeFrequencyMins = $NodeConfig.
ConfigurationModeFrequencyMins
            RebootNodeIfNeeded = $NodeConfig.RebootNodeIfNeeded
        }
    }
}
```

We could then create an array of Hashtables with the specific settings for each individual node, like this:

```
# List of target nodes with configurations as objects
$TargetNodes = @(
    @{
        NodeName = "DSCHOST01"
        ConfigurationMode = "ApplyAndAutoCorrect"
        ConfigurationModeFrequencyMins = 15
        RebootNodeIfNeeded = $true
    },
    @{
        NodeName = "DSCHOST02"
        ConfigurationMode = "ApplyOnly"
        ConfigurationModeFrequencyMins = 60
        RebootNodeIfNeeded = $false
    }
)
```

Since a configuration only works as a process block when we use a string array parameter type, we would have to instead use a loop to create each individual **.meta.mof** file. Here we use a **foreach** loop to iterate through each Hashtable within the **$TargetNodes** array and then call the **LCMConfig** configuration in each iteration. The **-OutputPath** is the same for each configuration so the compiled files will still be created in the same directory, named after their defined node:

```
# Create Configuration for each target node
foreach ($NodeConfig in $TargetNodes) {
    LCMConfig -NodeConfig $NodeConfig -OutputPath "C:\DSC\Configs"
}
```

Figure 13.10 shows the creation of the **.meta.mof** files for the two nodes using the configuration with the object parameter:

```
# Create Configuration for each target node
foreach ($NodeConfig in $TargetNodes) {
    LCMConfig -NodeConfig $NodeConfig -OutputPath "C:\DSC\Configs"
}


    Directory: C:\DSC\Configs


Mode                 LastWriteTime         Length Name
----                 -------------         ------ ----
-a----        03-12-2023     15:56           1186 DSCHOST01.meta.mof
-a----        03-12-2023     15:56           1168 DSCHOST02.meta.mof
```

Figure 13.10: *Configuration .meta.mof files created using the configuration with the object parameter*

We can use the **Set-DscLocalConfigurationManager** cmdlet to apply all the compiled configurations within a directory, to their respective nodes LCMs:

```
# Apply config to each target node (Assumes they have the same user,
serviceaccount or WinRM is set up with certificate)

$Username = "Administrator"

$Password = "Abcd1234" | ConvertTo-SecureString -AsPlainText -Force

$Credentials =  New-Object System.Management.Automation.
PSCredential($UserName,$Password)

Set-DscLocalConfigurationManager -Path "C:\DSC\Configs" -Credential
$Credentials -Verbose
```

When we check each nodes LCM settings, we can see that they are updated accordingly to the values specified within the respective Hashtables, as shown in *Figure 13.11*:

```
PS C:\DSC>
PS C:\DSC> $CimSession = New-CimSession -ComputerName "DSCHOST01" -Credential $Credentials
Get-DscLocalConfigurationManager -CimSession $CimSession |`
Select-Object PsComputerName,ConfigurationMode,`
ConfigurationModeFrequencyMins,RebootNodeIfNeeded

$CimSession = New-CimSession -ComputerName "DSCHOST02" -Credential $Credentials
Get-DscLocalConfigurationManager -CimSession $CimSession |`
Select-Object PsComputerName,ConfigurationMode,`
ConfigurationModeFrequencyMins,RebootNodeIfNeeded

PSComputerName ConfigurationMode   ConfigurationModeFrequencyMins RebootNodeIfNeeded
-------------- -----------------   ------------------------------ ------------------
DSCHOST01      ApplyAndAutoCorrect                             15               True
DSCHOST02      ApplyOnly                                       60              False
```

Figure 13.11: Modified meta configurations on target nodes with individual settings

Now that we have configured the target nodes LCMs using meta configurations, we can begin to create and apply DSC configurations for the target nodes.

Recipe 82: Creating DSC configurations for managing infrastructure

Resource configurations are quite similar to meta configurations and are referred to as DSC configurations. These are the configurations that are used to state that the desired resources must be either present or absent on the target nodes. In other words, these are the configurations that we use to specify which resources and applications should be installed (or not) on the target nodes and their settings and desired states. Instead of creating a **LocalConfigurationManager** block we define *Resource* blocks within the configuration to specify the desired resources. Multiple resource blocks can be defined within a configuration, which also enables you to define resources that can be dependent on other resources. As an example, you can create a configuration resource that ensures that the web server (IIS) feature is installed and after that, a configuration resource that installs a web site that should run on the web server. You can then make the web site dependent on the web server (IIS) feature. The Web Server resource must run before the web site configuration since it depends on the presence of the web server feature.

DSC Resources are used to define what type of resource you want to configure. The **Environment** resource is used to manage environment variables, the **Registry** resource is used to manage the Windows Registry and the **Service** resource is used to manage Windows Services and so on. The most common resource types are listed here:

Type name	Description
File	Manages files and directories
Registry	Manages registry keys and values
Service	Manages Windows services
Package	Manages software packages
Environment	Manages environment variables
WindowsFeature	Manages Windows features
Group	Manages local groups
User	Manages local users
Script	Executes custom scripts
Archive	Manages compressed archives (.zip files)

Table 13.1: Built-in common resource types

These common resource types are built-in to the DSC module. Besides the common resource types, you can find a great amount of public resource modules in the PSGallery to use for DSC, such as the **xWebAdministration** module that are used for Web Administration, the **xWindowsUpdate** module that are used for managing and installing Windows updates, the **xDnsServer** module that are used for managing and configuring Windows Server DNS and more. You can also create your own custom resources that enables you to manage tasks that are not covered by the built-in or public resources. Each resource has a set of properties and shared common properties. The shared common properties are available in all resources:

Property	Description
DependsOn	The configuration of another resource must run before this resource is configured. This property syntax is: DependsOn = "[ResourceType]ResourceName".

Property	Description
Ensure	Set this property to Present to ensure that the configured process exist, otherwise it should be set to Absent to ensure it does not exist. Present is the default value.
PsDscRunAsCredential	Sets the credentials for another context the configured process must be run as.

Table 13.2: Common resource properties

Note: Resources that starts with an x are experimental resources and you cannot expect any supportability by using these types of resources.

Besides the common properties, each resource have a set of its own properties that are specific for that resource type, some are mandatory, and some are optional. An Environment resource contains the **Name** and **Value** properties, and a Registry resource contains the **Key**, **ValueName** and **ValueData** properties and so on. You should look up official resource documentation for more information and the available properties for each resource.

We create a simple configuration using built-in common resources, that makes sure that a specific environment variable and a specific registry key is present on the **DSCHOST01** target node:

```
# Create the configuration
Configuration SimpleDsc {
    Import-DscResource –ModuleName "PSDesiredStateConfiguration"
    Node "DSCHOST01" {
        Environment CreateEnvironmentVariable {
            Name = "DSCNODE"
            Value = "DSCHOST01"
            Ensure = "Present"
            Path = $true
        }
        Registry CreateRegistryValue {
            Key       = "HKEY_LOCAL_MACHINE\SOFTWARE\DSC"
            ValueName = "DSCNODE"
            ValueData = "DSCHOST01"
            Ensure    = "Present"
        }
    }
}
# Compile the configuration to C:\DSC\DSCConfigs directory
SimpleDsc -OutputPath "C:\DSC\DSCConfigs"
```

Note: We specifically import the module containing the resources we use in the configuration: Import-DscResource -ModuleName "PSDesiredStateConfiguration". Explicitly importing modules containing resources into configurations not only makes it clear to anyone who is reading the script that you are using resources from that specific module, but also ensures that your DSC configurations are consistent and use the standard set of DSC resources. If your DSC configuration relies on resources from additional modules that are not guaranteed to be available on the target node, you need to ensure those modules are installed on the target node before applying the DSC configuration.

As you can see, we have specified the **Environment** and the **Registry** resource and provided the required property values. For the Environment resource we specify that a variable called **DSCNODE** must be present and have the value of **DSCHOST01**. For the Registry resource, we specify that a subkey called **DSC** must exist in the **HKLM\Software** key and that a value named **DSCNODE** must exist with the value of **DSCHOST01**.

We also specify the **-OutputPath** where the configuration should be compiled to. We compile the configuration into a **.mof** file, by calling it. *Figure 13.12* shows that the configuration is compiled to a **.mof** file in the targeted output directory:

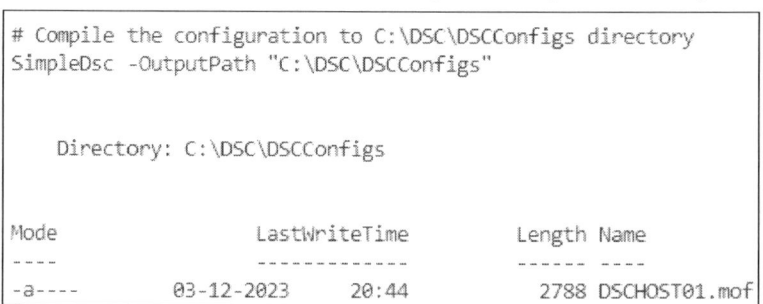

Figure 13.12: Output from compiling DSC configuration

To apply a DSC configuration to a target node (or the local node) we have to use the **Start-DscConfiguration** cmdlet. This cmdlet initiates the process of configuring the target node based on the compiled DSC configuration and then applies the settings accordingly. Use the **-Path** parameter to specify the path containing the compiled configuration **.mof** file(s). Just as with the **Set-DscLocalConfigurationManager** cmdlet, this cmdlet can also read and apply configurations to multiple nodes, depending on the hostnames defined within the .mof configuration files, but it also has the same **limitations** according to the target nodes credentials requirements. If your management server and the target nodes are set up for certificate-based authentication, it would be much simpler and secure to apply configurations to multiple target nodes. The **Start-DscConfiguration** cmdlet have a parameter for both **-Credential** and **-CimSession**, so if you are using basic authentication, you can use the parameter you prefer to specify the credentials for the target nodes. The cmdlet have a **-Wait** switch parameter, that makes the cmdlet wait until the configuration is applied, this also provides real-time feedback from the target node. You can use the **-Force** switch parameter to force the application of the configuration without prompting for confirmation. Use the **-Verbose** switch parameter for more verbose output. The workflow of the cmdlet is as follows:

1. Reads the compiled DSC configurations (**.mof** files) in the specified directory.

2. Sends the compiled DSC configurations (**.mof** files) to the LCM on the target node(s).

3. The LCM on the target node(s) processes the configuration, compares the current state with the desired state, and takes action to align the system with the desired state.

```
# Apply config to each target node (Assumes they have the same user,
serviceaccount or WinRM is set up with certificate)
$Username = "Administrator"
$Password = "Abcd1234" | ConvertTo-SecureString -AsPlainText -Force
$Credentials =  New-Object System.Management.Automation.
PSCredential($UserName,$Password)
Start-DscConfiguration -Path "C:\DSC\DSCConfigs" -Wait -Force
-Credential $Credentials -Verbose
```

Note that when you apply configurations to a target node, the new configuration generally overrides the current one.

Once the configuration is applied, we can check that the resources are created on the target node. In *Figure 13.13* we check that the expected environment variable and the Registry key exist on that target node by logging into it directly. We could use a remote session to the target node but for simplicity we just connect directly to the target node in this case, and check for the existence of the new resources:

```
PS C:\Temp> # View computer name
$Env:COMPUTERNAME
DSCHOST01
PS C:\Temp>
PS C:\Temp> # View DSCNODE environment variable
([System.Environment]::GetEnvironmentVariables([System.EnvironmentVariableTarget]::Machine)).DSCNODE

DSCHOST01
PS C:\Temp>
PS C:\Temp> # View DSCNODE Registry
Get-ItemProperty -Path "HKLM:\SOFTWARE\DSC" -Name DSCNODE

DSCNODE      : DSCHOST01
PSPath       : Microsoft.PowerShell.Core\Registry::HKEY_LOCAL_MACHINE\SOFTWARE\DSC
PSParentPath : Microsoft.PowerShell.Core\Registry::HKEY_LOCAL_MACHINE\SOFTWARE
PSChildName  : DSC
PSDrive      : HKLM
PSProvider   : Microsoft.PowerShell.Core\Registry
```

Figure 13.13: *Checking the existence of the new resources created by the DSC*

Since we have set this target node's LCM **ConfigurationMode** to **ApplyAndAutoCorrect**, the LCM should maintain the desired state for these resources. If one of these configured settings where accidentally, or for some other reason removed, the LCM would take the proper action and make sure the resource was re-created to keep the desired state as specified in the DSC configuration. *Figure 13.14* shows the manual removal of the configured Registry key and how the LCM auto corrects this by re-applying the resource:

```
PS C:\Temp> Get-ItemProperty -Path "HKLM:\SOFTWARE\DSC" -Name DSCNODE

DSCNODE       : DSCHOST01
PSPath        : Microsoft.PowerShell.Core\Registry::HKEY_LOCAL_MACHINE\SOFTWARE\DSC
PSParentPath  : Microsoft.PowerShell.Core\Registry::HKEY_LOCAL_MACHINE\SOFTWARE
PSChildName   : DSC
PSDrive       : HKLM
PSProvider    : Microsoft.PowerShell.Core\Registry

PS C:\Temp> Remove-ItemProperty -Path "HKLM:\SOFTWARE\DSC" -Name DSCNODE
PS C:\Temp> Get-ItemProperty -Path "HKLM:\SOFTWARE\DSC" -Name DSCNODE
Get-ItemProperty: Property DSCNODE does not exist at path HKEY_LOCAL_MACHINE\SOFTWARE\DSC.
PS C:\Temp> Get-ItemProperty -Path "HKLM:\SOFTWARE\DSC" -Name DSCNODE

DSCNODE       : DSCHOST01
PSPath        : Microsoft.PowerShell.Core\Registry::HKEY_LOCAL_MACHINE\SOFTWARE\DSC
PSParentPath  : Microsoft.PowerShell.Core\Registry::HKEY_LOCAL_MACHINE\SOFTWARE
PSChildName   : DSC
PSDrive       : HKLM
PSProvider    : Microsoft.PowerShell.Core\Registry
```

Figure 13.14: *The LCM re-applying the DSC configured*
Registry resource after it has been manually deleted

Note: The time it takes for the LCM to act and re-apply the resource to keep the desired state is dependent on the LCMs ConfigurationFrequencyInMins property.

To check the current DSC configurations that are present on a node, you can use the **Get-DscConfiguration** cmdlet. This cmdlet can only be used with a **CimSession**, by specifying the CimSession as an argument for the **-CimSession** parameter:

```
# Specify credentials for CimSession

$Username = "Administrator"

$Password = "Abcd1234" | ConvertTo-SecureString -AsPlainText -Force

$Credentials =  New-Object System.Management.Automation.
PSCredential($UserName,$Password)

# Create CimSession

$Session = New-CimSession -ComputerName DSCHOST01 -Credential $Credentials

# Get current DSC configuration of target node

Get-DscConfiguration -CimSession $Session
```

The cmdlet will return information about each configuration that is applied to the target node, as shown in *Figure 13.15*:

```
# Get current DSC configuration of target node
Get-DscConfiguration -CimSession $Session


ConfigurationName     : SimpleDsc
DependsOn             :
ModuleName            : PSDesiredStateConfiguration
ModuleVersion         : 1.1
PsDscRunAsCredential  :
ResourceId            : [Environment]CreateEnvironmentVariable
SourceInfo            :
Ensure                : Present
Name                  : DSCNODE
Path                  :
Value                 : DSCHOST01
PSComputerName        : DSCHOST01
CimClassName          : MSFT_EnvironmentResource

ConfigurationName     : SimpleDsc
DependsOn             :
ModuleName            : PSDesiredStateConfiguration
ModuleVersion         : 1.1
PsDscRunAsCredential  :
ResourceId            : [Registry]CreateRegistryValue
SourceInfo            :
Ensure                : Present
Force                 :
Hex                   :
key                   : HKLM:\SOFTWARE\DSC
ValueData             : {DSCHOST01}
ValueName             : DSCNODE
ValueType             : String
PSComputerName        : DSCHOST01
CimClassName          : MSFT_RegistryResource
```

Figure 13.15: *Configuration information from target node*

We can see that the two configurations specified in the **SimpleDsc** configuration is applied with the expected settings, and that these are ensured to be present on the target node.

You can create configurations for setting up your infrastructure using the different types of resources available to make sure that whatever resources, applications, files, windows features and so on is available on the target nodes and that they are kept in their desired states. For more complex scenarios you should use pre-defined public resource modules that are created for specific purposes. If no defined resource exists that covers your requirements, you can create custom resources that cover these requirements. You can also explore the *Script* resource that can be used to run Windows PowerShell script blocks on target nodes which can be used for more complex and custom scenarios, but where possible it is recommended to use pre-defined or custom created resources. Using the Script resource makes it hard to test without invoking it on a target node and there is no guarantee that it will work on any target node because it uses custom code.

Recipe 83: Creating DSC configurations using public resource modules

If no built-in resources can be used for your specific requirements, you should check the PSGallery for public available resource modules, such as the **xWebAdministration** module which is used for managing the configuration of different IIS components such as websites, application pools and virtual directories. This module is often used to create websites after you have enabled the IIS web server feature on a server. With the combination of built-in resources and the resources that the **xWebAdministration** module offers, you can not only enable the web server feature, but you can create and manage websites using DSC.

In this recipe we are going to enable the IIS web server feature on a target node and create a simple website within the same configuration using resources from the **xWebAdministration** module. The first thing you need is to make sure that the module is installed and available on both the management server and the target node, since we are going to have to import this module and use resources from it, within the configuration.

One caveat is that public DSC resource modules that you are going to use needs to be installed before you can use them in configurations. You could create an individual configuration that uses a Script resource to install the required module on the target node or create a custom resource. In some cases, it might also require that you install the **NuGet** package provider on the target node before you can install modules from the PSGallery. And it might also require that the Windows Management Instrumentation (WMI) service is restarted after the **xWebAdministration** module have been installed, in order for the LCM of the target nodes to be able to properly import the newly installed module into configurations. So, you need to accommodate for this in your Script or custom resource. For making this example easier, we use the **Invoke-Command** to install the **NuGet** package provider, the **xWebAdministration** module and for restarting the WMI service on the DSCHOST01 target node before we create and apply the new configuration.

```
# Credentials
$Username = "Administrator"
$Password = "Abcd1234" | ConvertTo-SecureString -AsPlainText -Force
$Credentials =  New-Object System.Management.Automation.
PSCredential($UserName,$Password)
# Pre-requisites for using the xWebAdministration module on target node
Invoke-Command -ComputerName "DSCHOST01" `
-Credential $Credentials `
-ScriptBlock {
    Install-PackageProvider -Name NuGet -MinimumVersion 2.8.5.201 -Force
    Install-Module xWebAdministration -Scope AllUsers -Force
```

```
    Restart-Service Winmgmt -Force
}
```

> **Note: If you need to manage a lot of nodes, it is recommended to create a custom resource or use the Script resource to make sure all pre-requisites are handled on the target nodes.**

Once the pre-requisites are taken care of, we can begin to create the configuration that enables the web server feature and creates the new website on the target node. The new web site is called **MySite** and it should contain a simple index.html file that we are also going to create using a resource within the configuration. We also need to make sure that the directory for the **MySite** website path exists on the target node, or we might get an error when applying the configuration, stating that the directory for the website does not exist. One more thing we need to do is to disable the default website that is created when the web server feature is enabled, or else we cannot bind our **MySite** website to port 80 because this will already be in use by the default website. We take care of this issue by disabling the default website since we are not going to use it anyway. Another thing you could do is to change the port for either the default or the **MySite** website to another port, such as 8080. You cannot have multiple sites bound to the same port and IP address; this combination defines a unique endpoint for network communication. Or you could use HTTPS with server name indication (SNI) which allows multiple websites to use the same IP address and port while still using distinct TLS certificates, thus this would also require a certificate for the website. We keep it simple and use HTTP for this example. The configuration would look like this:

```
Configuration WebSite {
    Import-DscResource -ModuleName "PSDesiredStateConfiguration"
    Import-DscResource -ModuleName "xWebAdministration"
    Node "DSCHOST01" {
        # Install the Web Server feature
        WindowsFeature WebServerFeature {
            Ensure = "Present"
            Name   = "Web-Server"
        }
        # Make sure the \MySite folder exists
        File MySiteFolder {
            DependsOn = "[WindowsFeature]WebServerFeature"
            Ensure          = "Present"
            Type            = "Directory"
            DestinationPath = "C:\inetpub\wwwroot\mysite"
        }
```

```
        # Create a simple index.html file in \MySite
        File NewIndexFile {
            DependsOn = "[File]MySiteFolder"
            Ensure          = "Present"
            DestinationPath = "C:\inetpub\wwwroot\mysite\index.html"
            Contents        = "<h1>This is MySite</h1>"
        }
        # Stop the default website from running (Ensures that port 80 is
not binded to this site)
        xWebsite DefaultWebsite {
            DependsOn = "[WindowsFeature]WebServerFeature"
            Ensure       = "Present"
            Name         = "Default Web Site"
            State        = "Stopped"  # Ensure the default website is stopped
            PhysicalPath = "C:\inetpub\wwwroot"
        }
        # Use the xWebAdministration resource to create a new IIS site (MySite)
        xWebsite MyWebsite {
            DependsOn = "[File]MySiteFolder"
            Ensure = "Present"
            Name = "MySite"
            State = "Started"
            PhysicalPath = "C:\inetpub\wwwroot\MySite"
            BindingInfo = @(
                MSFT_xWebBindingInformation {
                    Protocol = "HTTP"
                    Port     = 80
                    IPAddress = "*"
                }
            )
        }
    }
}
# Compile the configuration
WebSite -OutputPath "C:\DSC\WebSite"
```

We create a configuration called **WebSite** and start by importing the modules that contain the required resources, using the **Import-DscResource** cmdlet. We create the **Node** block and specify the name of the target node. Remember that we could make this more dynamic by using parameters for the node name if we wanted to. The next thing we do is to ensure that the web server feature is present, using the **WindowsFeature** resource. The **Name** parameter here indicates what specific Windows feature we want to enable, in this case it is the **web-server** (IIS) feature. When the web server feature is installed, it creates the **c:\inetpub\wwwroot** directory and place the files for the default web site within. We are going to create a sub-folder in this directory for our **MySite** website using the **File** resource called **MySiteFolder**, to ensure that this new sub-folder is present.

Since the **File** resource by default is used to define a file, we need to specify that it should create a directory instead using the **Type** parameter. The **DestinationPath** parameter is used to specify the directory we want to create. We also use the **DependsOn** parameter and specify that this resource is dependent on the presence of the **web-server** Windows feature. Usually, a website consists of multiple files and folders that combined creates the website. We could use the **File** resource to ensure that a website that exists in a file share or other directory that the target node have access to, is copied to the website root directory on the target node. In this example we are creating a simple website that only contains one file, the **index.html** file and this file only have some very simple content. We are using the **File** resource called **NewIndexFile**, to ensure the presence of the **index. html** file for the website, and we use the **Contents** parameter to set the content of this file. This resource is set to be dependent on the **MySiteFolder File** resource.

Can we create the **index.html** file, if the website directory does not exist? If you use the **File** resource to ensure the presence of a file, and if the directory that this file should reside within does not exist, the **File** resource would ensure that the directory is also created and present, so in this case, we could have omitted the **MySiteFolder File** resource, but it always a good idea to ensure the specific resources you need are present on the target node. The **WindowsFeature** and the **File** resources are both built-in resources that are a part of the DSC module. The last two resources we are creating are a part of the **xWebAdministration** module. First, we use the **xWebsite** resource, from the **xWebAdministration** module, called **DefaultWebsite** to ensure that the default website on the target node is stopped. We use the **Name** parameter to specify the name of the website to stop, in this case "Default Web Site" and the **State** parameter to specify the state of the targeted website, in this case we set the value to **Stopped**. When the default website is stopped, we can bind the new MySite website to port 80 and the IP address of the target node, making this the website that is active when accessing the node with HTTP. To ensure that our MySite website is present and correctly configured on the target node, we add another **xWebsite** resource. We specify the name of the website using the **Name** parameter, the **State** parameter to specify that it must be started and the **PhysicalPath** parameter to specify the root directory of the MySite website, in this case it is the directory we previously created with the **File MySiteFolder** resource. The **xWebsite** type of resource also have a **BindingInfo** parameter. This parameter takes an array of **MSFT_**

xWebBindingInformation objects that we use to specify the different website bindings for the website such as the protocol to use, the port and the IP address. If we were to use HTTPS and TLS we would also define the certificates thumbprint and the certificate store where the certificate that is used in the binding resides within this object. In our case, we specify that the MySite website uses the HTTP protocol, the port 80 and that the website should listen on all available IP addresses (the asterisk) on the node. Once all the resources are configured, we invoke the configuration and compile it into a **.mof** file within the **C:\ DSC\WebSite** folder.

Now we can use the **Start-DscConfiguration** cmdlet to apply the compiled configuration to the target node:

```
# Create the credentials
$Username = "Administrator"
$Password = "Abcd1234" | ConvertTo-SecureString -AsPlainText -Force
$Credentials =  New-Object System.Management.Automation.
PSCredential($UserName,$Password)
# Start the configuration
Start-DscConfiguration -Path "C:\DSC\WebSite" -Wait -Force -Credential
$Credentials
```

Figure 13.16 shows a view during the process of running the **Start-DscConfiguration** cmdlet and the view after the process has finished:

```
Start Installation...
    44% 00:00:00 44%
    [DSCHOST01] Set-TargetResource


PS C:\DSC>
PS C:\DSC> $Username = "Administrator"
$Password = "Abcd1234" | ConvertTo-SecureString -AsPlainText -Force
$Credentials =  New-Object System.Management.Automation.PSCredential($UserName,$Password)

# Start the configuration
Start-DscConfiguration -Path "C:\DSC\WebSite" -Wait -Force -Credential $Credentials


LCM
    100% 00:00:01 Applying Configuration
    [DSCHOST01] Set


PS C:\DSC>
PS C:\DSC> $Username = "Administrator"
$Password = "Abcd1234" | ConvertTo-SecureString -AsPlainText -Force
$Credentials =  New-Object System.Management.Automation.PSCredential($UserName,$Password)

# Start the configuration
Start-DscConfiguration -Path "C:\DSC\WebSite" -Wait -Force -Credential $Credentials
PS C:\DSC> █
```

*Figure 13.16: View during and after the Start-Dsc
Configuration cmdlet process has finished*

Once the configuration is successfully applied to the target node, the MySite website should be running, and we should be able to access the website on the target node, for example in a browser, as it is shown in *Figure 13.17*:

Figure 13.17: Accessing the new *website* MySite in a browser

This is a great indicator that everything is applied to the target node as expected. To double check the configuration on the target node, use the **Get-DscConfiguration** cmdlet. *Figure 13.18* shows the output of running this command on the target node. We use **Select-Object** to filter the properties we want to return in the output:

```
PS C:\DSC> # Create the credentials
$Username = "Administrator"
$Password = "Abcd1234" | ConvertTo-SecureString -AsPlainText -Force
$Credentials =  New-Object System.Management.Automation.PSCredential($UserName,$Password)

# Create a CimSession
$Session = New-CimSession -ComputerName "DSCHOST01" -Credential $Credentials

# Get the current configuration of the target node
Get-DscConfiguration -CimSession $Session | `
Select-Object ConfigurationName,ModuleName,ResourceId,Ensure

ConfigurationName ModuleName                   ResourceId                          Ensure
----------------- ----------                   ----------                          ------
WebSite           PSDesiredStateConfiguration  [WindowsFeature]WebServerFeature Present
WebSite           PSDesiredStateConfiguration  [File]MySiteFolder                  present
WebSite           PSDesiredStateConfiguration  [File]NewIndexFile                  present
WebSite           xWebAdministration           [xWebSite]DefaultWebsite            Present
WebSite           xWebAdministration           [xWebSite]MyWebsite                 Present
```

Figure 13.18: Returning the current configuration of a target node
using Get-DscConfiguration and selecting specific properties using Select-Object

We can see that all the resources in the configuration is applied as expected to the target node, we can see the resource type and name and the specific resource modules. You can also use the **Get-DscConfigurationStatus** cmdlet to get the current DSC status of a target node. It returns the information about the last configuration that was applied, and it will show the state of the configuration, the date and time it was applied, the mode that was used and the number of resources that was applied. This cmdlet use a **CimSession** to connect to the target node. *Figure 13.19* shows the output of this cmdlet connecting to the **DSCHOST01** node:

```
PS C:\DSC> # Create the credentials
$Username = "Administrator"
$Password = "Abcd1234" | ConvertTo-SecureString -AsPlainText -Force
$Credentials = New-Object System.Management.Automation.PSCredential($UserName,$Password)

# Create a CimSession
$Session = New-CimSession -ComputerName "DSCHOST01" -Credential $Credentials

# Get the DSC configuration status from the target node
Get-DscConfigurationStatus -CimSession $Session

Status     StartDate            Type         Mode  RebootRequested    NumberOfResources        PSComputerName
------     ---------            ----         ----  ---------------    -----------------        --------------
Success    10-12-2023 20:49:02  Consistency  PUSH  False              5                        DSCHOST01
```

Figure 13.19: Using the Get-DscConfigurationStatus cmdlet to get the status for the last applied configuration on a target node

As mentioned earlier, note that when you apply a new configuration to a target node, any current configurations will be overridden by the new configuration. That is the reason why we only see the new configured resources and any previous resources have been overridden by the new configuration.

In general, the built-in and the public available resource modules can be used to accomplish almost any required task, but for certain specialized scenarios these resources might not be enough, and you would have to create a custom resource. Creating custom resources is outside of the scope of this book but Microsoft have great documentation that covers how to build custom Windows PowerShell DSC resources which can be found here: **https:// learn.microsoft.com/en-us/powershell/dsc/resources/authoringresource?view=dsc-1.1**. I would recommend you first understand the documentation that covers how to write a custom DSC resource with PowerShell classes. In addition to that, you can also look into the documentation that covers the use of the Resource Designer tool.

Removing resources and configurations

In the case where you do not need the resources and the configuration on a target node anymore, you would have to remove them or else the LCM will keep the desired state on that node, depending on the LCMs meta configuration settings and the applied DSC configuration. If an LCM is set up to **ApplyAndAutoCorrect** it is not enough to just manually remove the resources from the target node, the LCM will just keep re-creating them. Depending on the resources that are configured on the target node, it might have security implications to keep resources when they are not needed. It might be that you have installed a feature, such as the web server feature that publicly exposes port 80 on the internet. Then you at some point remove the web server feature manually because you must reuse the server for other applications and you did not, at that moment, remember that the web server was installed using DSC. The new applications on the server have much stricter security procedures and must not be exposed publicly, but now you have a DSC that re-installs the web server feature and opens port 80 with the default website, exposing the server on that port onto the internet. This is not the behavior you wanted. By removing the configurations from the target node, you would ensure that no resources specified in the configuration would be re-installed or re-applied on the node. When resources are removed, the LCM should be configured to not manage the desired state anymore. You do this by removing the configurations documents that the LCM use to manage the state.

Recipe 84: Removing resources and configurations from nodes

To remove a configuration from a node we use the **Remove-DscConfigurationDocument** cmdlet. This cmdlet also does additional required cleanup on the target node, by removing some cached files used by the LCM.

Notice the word **Document** in the cmdlet. The **Document** refers to the compiled configuration files that are created on the target node based on the DSC configuration. There are three types of documents:

- **Current configuration document**: This document describes the current state of the system based on the applied DSC configuration. It represents the configuration that is currently in effect on the target node and this is the document that the LCM refers to when determining the current state of the system.

- **Pending configuration document**: This document describes the configuration that is pending application on the system. It represents a configuration that has been received by the LCM but has not yet been applied. The **pending** document is used when the LCM is waiting for the next configuration application cycle to occur.

- **Previous configuration document**: This document describes the state of the system before the most recent configuration was applied. It represents the configuration that was in effect prior to the current configuration. The **previous** document is useful for maintaining a history of configurations applied to the system.

The **Remove-DscConfigurationDocument** cmdlet allows you to selectively remove these documents based on the specified stage (current, pending, previous). This can be useful for managing the configuration history on a target node. These documents are typically stored in the **C:\Windows\System32\Configuration** directory and each document is associated with a specific configuration. The LCM references these documents to track the state of the system and to determine which configuration should be applied during the next configuration cycle. In *Figure 13.20* we can see the content of the LCMs Configuration directory and that it contains both a **Previous.mof** and a **Current.mof** document file on the target node:

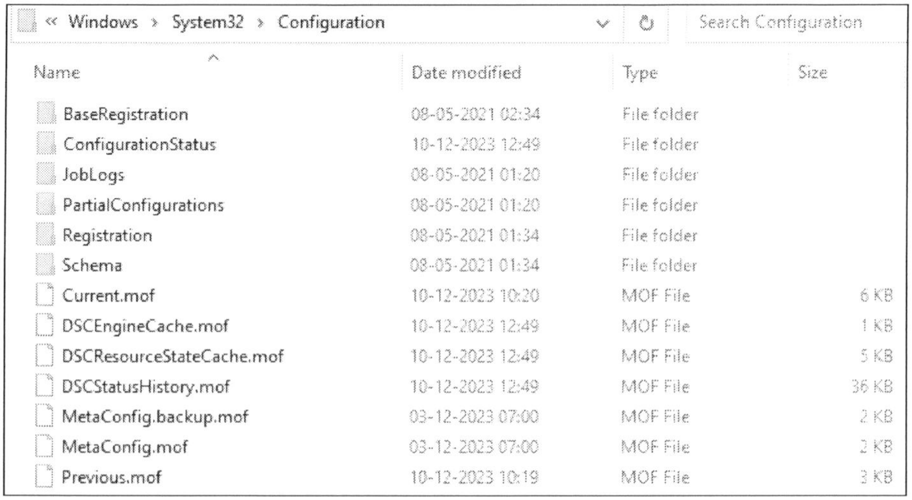

Figure 13.20: The content of the configuration directory that is used by the LCM

Keep in mind that when configuration documents are removed, the system does not automatically revert to a previous state. It mainly affects the tracking and history of configurations on the node. If you want to change the system's state, you need to apply a new configuration using **Start-DscConfiguration**. This means that if we want to ensure that all the configured resources are removed from the target node, we should first update the (or create a new) configuration where we state that all the resources should be absent instead of present, and then apply this to the target node. After the state has been updated and all the resources are removed, we can remove the documents from the target node. If we remove the configuration documents before we remove the resources, the LCM on the target node does not expect any desired state anymore, and the resources are kept as is, without being maintained by the LCM. All the resources must then be removed manually from the node.

> **Note: Remember that if you create a new configuration that states that resources should be absent, for removing the resources on a target node, and that nodes LCM is configured to RebootNodeIfNeeded, the target node might restart without any confirmation. The process will continue after reboot if there are resources remaining that still need to be configured and the ActionAfterReboot setting is set to ContinueConfiguration. You should also ensure that all resources are properly removed from the target node before you remove any configuration documents if you use a new configuration for removing resources. Some resources such as the File resource, might need to be set with the Force parameter to True in order for it being able to remove the specified files and directories.**

The updated version of a configuration that ensures that all resources are removed could look like this:

```
Configuration WebSite {
```

```
Import-DscResource -ModuleName "PSDesiredStateConfiguration"
Import-DscResource -ModuleName "xWebAdministration"
Node "DSCHOST01" {
    # Install the Web Server feature
    WindowsFeature WebServerFeature {
        Ensure = "Absent"
        Name   = "Web-Server"
    }
    # Make sure the \MySite folder exists
    File MySiteFolder {
        DependsOn = "[WindowsFeature]WebServerFeature"
        Ensure          = "Absent"
        Type            = "Directory"
        DestinationPath = "C:\inetpub\wwwroot\mysite"
        Force = $true
    }
    # Create a simple index.html file in \MySite
    File NewIndexFile {
        DependsOn = "[File]MySiteFolder"
        Ensure          = "Absent"
        DestinationPath = "C:\inetpub\wwwroot\mysite\index.html"
        Contents        = "<h1>This is MySite</h1>"
        Force = $true
    }
    # Stop the default website from running (Ensures that port 80 is
not binded to this site)
    xWebsite DefaultWebsite {
        DependsOn = "[WindowsFeature]WebServerFeature"
        Ensure       = "Absent"
        Name         = "Default Web Site"
        State        = "Stopped"  # Ensure the default website is stopped
        PhysicalPath = "C:\inetpub\wwwroot"
    }
    # Use the xWebAdministration resource to create a new IIS site (MySite)
```

```
        xWebsite MyWebsite {
            DependsOn = "[File]MySiteFolder"
            Ensure = "Absent"
            Name = "MySite"
            State = "Started"
            PhysicalPath = "C:\inetpub\wwwroot\MySite"
            BindingInfo = @(
                MSFT_xWebBindingInformation {
                    Protocol = "HTTP"
                    Port     = 80
                    IPAddress = "*"
                }
            )
        }
    }
}
```

When we use the **Remove-DscConfigurationDocument** cmdlet to remove documents, we must use the **-Stage** parameter to specify which document to remove from the target node. You can specify each document stage individually or you can specify multiple document stages. The cmdlet uses a **CimSession** for connecting to the target node:

```
# Create the credentials
$Username = "Administrator"
$Password = "Abcd1234" | ConvertTo-SecureString -AsPlainText -Force
$Credentials =  New-Object System.Management.Automation.
PSCredential($UserName,$Password)
# Create a CimSession
$Session = New-CimSession -ComputerName "DSCHOST01" -Credential
$Credentials
# Remove all documents from the target node
Remove-DscConfigurationDocument -CimSession $Session `
-Stage Current,Pending,Previous -Force
```

Once the configuration documents are removed from the target node, the LCM will not manage the desired state until a new configuration is applied. You can use the **Get-Configuration** and **Get-ConfigurationStatus** to confirm that the target node does not have any managed configurations.

Handling failed configurations

In some cases, DSC configurations might partially or fully fail to be applied on a target node. There can be several reasons for this:

- **Syntax errors in configuration**: You might have a syntax error in your configuration. Any issues with the script structure or syntax can prevent successful execution.

- **Resource availability**: Ensure that the DSC resources used in your configuration are available on the target node. If you are using custom resources, make sure they are properly registered and if you are using resources from publicly available modules from the PSGallery, make sure that the module is installed on both the management server and the target node.

- **Permissions**: Ensure that the account running the DSC configuration has the necessary permissions to make the desired changes on the target node.

- **Dependency resources**: Check for dependencies between resources in your configuration. If a resource depends on another resource, ensure that the dependent resource is configured first.

- **Pending reboot**: If a configuration requires a reboot and there is a pending reboot on the target node, it might affect the application of the configuration.

- **Configuration drift**: If the target node has configurations applied manually or through other means, it might result in configuration drift. DSC might not be able to enforce the desired state if drift is detected.

- **LCM configuration**: Check the configuration of the Local Configuration Manager on the target node. Ensure that it is set to the correct configuration mode and other properties are configured appropriately.

- **Error handling in configuration scripts**: Add proper error handling in your configuration script. This can help identify issues during execution.

- **Event viewer logs**: Review the Event Viewer on the target node for any error messages or warnings related to DSC configuration.

By investigating these aspects, you can identify and address the potential issues that might be causing the DSC configuration to fail. Besides this, you might encounter errors that are not directly linked to DSC but the system itself and you might have to thoroughly understand your network connectivity, firewall settings, disk space and system resources etc. for finding the issues.

Recipe 85: Identifying and handling failed configurations

Sometimes the application of configurations might fail and identifying and resolving issues in DSC configurations can be challenging. In order to prevent partially or fully failed configurations, the DSC module contains the **Test-DscConfiguration** cmdlet. This cmdlet checks configurations for syntax errors and test if the configuration would be applied successfully. This cmdlet is used to check the current configuration against the desired configuration without applying any changes. It also allows you to validate the configuration for correctness and identify any potential issues or errors that might occur during the application. It is always a good idea to use this cmdlet to test configurations before you apply them to target nodes, or you might end up with a failed configuration. One common issue is because of the missing resource modules on target nodes.

Consider that you have created a configuration just like the one in *Recipe 83* where we use resources from both the DSC module and the **xWebAdministration** module and the **xWebAdministration** module is not installed on the target node. If you try to apply that configuration it will result in an error. *Figure 13.21* shows the output of trying to apply the configuration when the **xWebAdministration** module is missing from the target node:

```
# Start the configuration
Start-DscConfiguration -Path "C:\DSC\WebSite" -Wait -Force -Credential $Credentials


    Directory: C:\DSC\WebSite


Mode                LastWriteTime         Length Name
----                -------------         ------ ----
-a----        12-12-2023     19:25           5656 DSCHOST02.mof
The PowerShell DSC resource MSFT_xWebSite from module <xWebAdministration,3.3.0> does not exist at the PowerShell module path n
or is it registered as a WMI DSC resource.
    + CategoryInfo          : InvalidOperation: (root/Microsoft/...gurationManager:String) [], CimException
    + FullyQualifiedErrorId : DscResourceNotFound
    + PSComputerName        : DSCHOST02
```

*Figure 13.21: Output of applying a configuration when a
resource module is missing from the target node*

The error messages states that the **xWebAdministration** module does not exist. This gives us a pretty good idea of the error.

Now if we were to use the **Get-DscConfiguration** cmdlet to get the current configuration and the **Get-DscConfigurationStatus** cmdlet to get the configuration status on the target node, we would get the output as shown in *Figure 13.22*:

```
PS C:\DSC> Get-DscConfiguration -CimSession $Session
WARNING: DSCHOST02: [DSCHOST02]:                    [] The GET operation will be carried against a pending
configuration since the latest configuration has not converged yet.
Get-DscConfiguration : The PowerShell DSC resource MSFT_xWebSite from module <xWebAdministration,3.3.0> does not exist at the P
owerShell module path nor is it registered as a WMI DSC resource.
At line:1 char:1
+ Get-DscConfiguration -CimSession $Session
+ ~~~~~~~~~~~~~~~~~~~~~~~~~~~~~~~~~~~~~~~~~~~
    + CategoryInfo          : InvalidOperation: (MSFT_DSCLocalConfigurationManager:root/Microsoft/...gurationManager) [Get-Dsc
   Configuration], CimException
    + FullyQualifiedErrorId : DscResourceNotFound,Get-DscConfiguration
    + PSComputerName        : DSCHOST02

PS C:\DSC> Get-DscConfigurationStatus -CimSession $Session

Status    StartDate              Type     Mode  RebootRequested   NumberOfResources    PSComputerName
------    ---------              ----     ----  ---------------   -----------------    --------------
Failure   12-12-2023 19:25:26    Initial  PUSH  False                                  DSCHOST02
```

Figure 13.22 Output from running the Get-DscConfiguration and
Get-DscConfigurationStatus cmdlets after a failed configuration application

We can see that the configuration is applied to the target node, but in a failed state and no resources are applied. Now we could remove the failed configuration from the target node using the **Remove-DscConfigurationDocument** cmdlet, fix the issue by installing the module on the target node and then re-apply the configuration. However, depending on the LCMs settings including the Configuration mode, and if you used the **-Force** parameter with the **Start-DscConfiguration** cmdlet, it forcefully reapplies the configuration regardless of its state, and then the LCM will automatically re-apply the configuration, after you have installed the missing module on the target node. Note that it could take the time of the **ConfigurationModeFrequencyMins** value before the configuration is automatically applied. You can see that this behavior depends on the various factors and settings of the LCM. The standard recommendation is to manually initiate the configuration after addressing the issues. This ensures a controlled and intentional application of the desired state.

Figure 13.23 shows the output of the **Get-DscConfigurationStatus** cmdlet after the missing module is installed on the target node:

```
PS C:\DSC> Get-DscConfigurationStatus -CimSession $Session

Status    StartDate              Type         Mode  RebootRequested   NumberOfResources    PSComputerName
------    ---------              ----         ----  ---------------   -----------------    --------------
Success   12-12-2023 19:45:42    Consistency  PUSH  False             5                    DSCHOST02
```

Figure 13.23: Checking the status of the configuration after the
missing module have been installed on the target node

The configuration is automatically applied after a while, and the resources are installed as initially expected.

Even though you can apply configurations and address potential issues after the fact and then wait for the LCM to re-apply the failed configuration until it succeeds, it is always recommended to use the **Test-DscConfiguration** cmdlet before you apply any configurations to make sure that it will initially succeed. A typical workflow working with DSC would be:

1. Write your DSC configuration scripts.

2. Use **Test-DscConfiguration** to test and check the configuration without making any changes to the target node.

3. Identify and address any potential issues.

4. Apply the configuration to the target node using **Start-DscConfiguration**.

There can be many reasons why configurations fail to apply. Check the error messages and go through the reasons mentioned in the start of the topic to identify and address issues. It is important to address all issues before your configurations succeed or else you might end up with failed applied configurations. In some scenarios your resources might be partially applied and some are not and your desired state will not be as you would expect.

Conclusion

Desired State Configuration can be a powerful tool, especially when managing resources and applications across numerous servers and systems, ensuring the consistent and desired state of your entire organization's infrastructure. By leveraging DSC, administrators can define and declaratively create the configuration settings for various components such as file systems, registry settings, services, applications and more. Within this chapter you have been given the foundation for configuring nodes Local Configuration Managers, creating meta configurations, creating DSC configurations, and learned how to apply such configurations to target nodes using the push method. You should be able to start managing the desired state and maintain the consistency of your organization's nodes using Windows PowerShell.

The next chapter is about using PowerShell to manage different Windows server and workstation components. The chapter covers how to create, manage, and delete windows services, how to start and manage processes, how to manage and configure network settings and how to initialize, partition and format disks. It also dives deeper into firewall rules and the Windows task scheduler.

CHAPTER 14

Managing Windows Components

Introduction

PowerShell is developed by Microsoft, and it is initially intended for administrating Windows operating systems and Windows components programmatically and was designed as a language to do so. Some will argue that PowerShell is not a programming language but simply an administrative and scripting language, but throughout this book we have seen that PowerShell is so much more. We can create advanced functions and classes. We can control the flow in scripts using loops and other types of statements such as if/else blocks and switch statements. It provides comprehensive methods and tools for handling errors and for catching and managing exceptions. It provides cross platform capabilities, incorporates modules and advanced scripting techniques. It can be used to manage servers and systems remotely using PowerShell remoting and it provides a comprehensive testing framework in Pester. It can handle advanced document types such as XML and JSON and it can be used to manage Active Directory. It also has modules that can be used to manage and administrate cloud resources, infrastructure, and Microsoft applications such as SharePoint, Teams, and Exchange. It comes with its own module and engine for providing Desired State capabilities to servers and systems. But it is so much more than that. PowerShell is a powerful language that can be used for scripting and automating numerous tasks for optimizing your daily workflow and tasks. PowerShell is positioned as a high-level programming language, but it incorporates elements of both high-level and low-level characteristics. While it is often associated with system administration, scripting, and automation, it possesses the key characteristics that define a programming language due to its scripting capabilities, structured syntax, its variables and datatypes, its flow control, its functions and modules, its object-oriented features, its integration with the .NET framework and its error handling capabilities. Developers and administrators can leverage PowerShell to create sophisticated scripts, automation solutions and even complex and advanced GUI applications and Windows services, making it a programming language in the broader sense. However, we must not forget its simpler initial purpose, administrating Windows operating systems and Windows components. In this chapter we show how to use PowerShell to manage different Windows components.

Structure

This chapter covers the following topics:

- Window services
    - **Recipe 86**: Create, manage, and delete Windows services
- Processes
    - **Recipe 87**: Start, manage, and delete Windows processes
- Network settings
    - **Recipe 88**: Manage and configure network settings for interfaces
- Disks and storage
    - **Recipe 89**: Initialize, partition and format disks
- Firewall rules
    - **Recipe 90**: Create, configure, and manage firewall rules
- The task scheduler
    - **Recipe 91**: Create and manage scheduled tasks

Objectives

Within this chapter we are going to keep PowerShell at its roots and learn how to manage different components that are built into Windows and Windows server operating systems. With a step through approach, you will learn how to manage components such as Windows services and processes. Network settings such as configuring IP addresses, DNS and default gateways for network interfaces. You will learn how to manage disks and storage. How to create and manage local firewall rules and how to create and manage scheduled tasks. These are some of the more important Windows' components and all of them can be managed using PowerShell and the built-in modules that comes with PowerShell.

Windows services

Windows services, simply referred to as services, are background processes that run independently of user interaction. They are a fundamental part of the Windows operating system and perform various tasks such as managing hardware components, running system processes, and providing essential functionalities. Unlike standard applications that require user interaction, services run in the background and can start automatically when the system boots. To interact with and manage Windows services using PowerShell, we can use cmdlets such as **Get-Service**, **Start-Service**, **Stop-Service**, **Restart-Service**. These cmdlets allow us to query information about services, start and stop services, and configure services properties. We can also create new services using the **New-Service** cmdlet, keep in mind though that this cmdlet does not create the service executable, but simply registers an executable as a Windows service. It assumes that we have an executable that is designed to be a Windows service and that contains the service code logic. Windows services are controlled by the **Service Control Manager (SCM)** which is a component of the Windows operating system. It allows the management of a systems services using the built-in GUI, the sc.exe Windows service management application and PowerShell. It is essentially this controller that the cmdlets interact with, to manage and administer services using PowerShell.

Recipe 86: Create, manage, and delete Windows services

To manage services, we use the PowerShell **service** cmdlets. These cmdlets are a part of the **Microsoft.PowerShell.Management** built-in module. Since this module contains cmdlets for a variety of tasks, to list all available service cmdlets, we can use **Get-Command**, specify the module as an argument for the **-Module** parameter and the string **service** as an argument for the **-Noun** parameter:

```
Get-Command -Module Microsoft.PowerShell.Management -Noun "service"
```

Figure 14.1 shows the output of this command and the list of specific service cmdlets:

```
PS C:\Temp> Get-Command -Module Microsoft.PowerShell.Management -Noun "service"

CommandType     Name                    Version    Source
-----------     ----                    -------    ------
Cmdlet          Get-Service             7.0.0.0    Microsoft.PowerShell.Management
Cmdlet          New-Service             7.0.0.0    Microsoft.PowerShell.Management
Cmdlet          Remove-Service          7.0.0.0    Microsoft.PowerShell.Management
Cmdlet          Restart-Service         7.0.0.0    Microsoft.PowerShell.Management
Cmdlet          Resume-Service          7.0.0.0    Microsoft.PowerShell.Management
Cmdlet          Set-Service             7.0.0.0    Microsoft.PowerShell.Management
Cmdlet          Start-Service           7.0.0.0    Microsoft.PowerShell.Management
Cmdlet          Stop-Service            7.0.0.0    Microsoft.PowerShell.Management
Cmdlet          Suspend-Service         7.0.0.0    Microsoft.PowerShell.Management
```

Figure 14.1: *Listing all service relevant cmdlets using Get-Command*

Note: The Remove-Service cmdlet only exists in newer versions of PowerShell. If you manage services using Windows PowerShell you will have to use the Windows native sc.exe to remove Windows services.

To list all services that are installed on a system, we use the **Get-Service** cmdlet without any parameters, as shown in *Figure 14.2*:

```
PS C:\Temp> Get-Service

Status     Name              DisplayName
------     ----              -----------
Stopped    AJRouter          AllJoyn Router Service
Stopped    ALG               Application Layer Gateway Service
Stopped    AppIDSvc          Application Identity
Stopped    Appinfo           Application Information
Stopped    AppMgmt           Application Management
Stopped    AppReadiness      App Readiness
Stopped    AppVClient        Microsoft App-V Client
Stopped    AppXSvc           AppX Deployment Service (AppXSVC)
Stopped    AsusUpdateCheck   AsusUpdateCheck
Stopped    AudioEndpointBu...  Windows Audio Endpoint Builder
Stopped    Audiosrv          Windows Audio
Stopped    AxInstSV          ActiveX Installer (AxInstSV)
Running    BFE               Base Filtering Engine
Stopped    BITS              Background Intelligent Transfer Ser...
Running    BrokerInfrastru...  Background Tasks Infrastructure Ser...
Stopped    bthserv           Bluetooth Support Service
Running    camsvc            Capability Access Manager Service
```

Figure 14.2: Listing all services installed on a system using the Get-Service cmdlet without parameters

As you can see, we get a default listing showing the **Status**, **Name** and **DisplayName** properties of all the services on the system. The cmdlet contains a **-Name** parameter positioned at index 0, that allows us to specify a specific service name and return that service if it exists. If not, the cmdlet returns an error, as shown in *Figure 14.3*:

```
PS C:\Temp> Get-Service -Name WSearch

Status    Name              DisplayName
------    ----              -----------
Stopped   WSearch           Windows Search


PS C:\Temp> Get-Service WSearch

Status    Name              DisplayName
------    ----              -----------
Stopped   WSearch           Windows Search


PS C:\Temp> Get-Service WSear
Get-Service : Cannot find any service with service name 'WSear'.
At line:1 char:1
+ Get-Service WSear
+ ~~~~~~~~~~~~~~~~~~
    + CategoryInfo          : ObjectNotFound: (WSear:String) [Get-Service], ServiceCommandException
    + FullyQualifiedErrorId : NoServiceFoundForGivenName,Microsoft.PowerShell.Commands.GetServiceCommand
```

Figure 14.3: Using the -Name parameter for the Get-Service cmdlet

The cmdlet also contain a **-DisplayName** parameter that allows us to return a service with a specific display name. We can use arguments with wildcards for these parameters in order to return and list multiple services that have similar names and display names, such as returning all services that have a display name that starts with *Windows*: **Get-Service -DisplayName "Windows*"** or to return all services that contain **svc** in its name: **Get-Service -Name "*svc*"**. We can further pipe such commands to **Select-Object** to select specific properties that we want to output and include relevant properties such as the **StartType** that specifies if a service should start **Automatically, Manually** or be **Disabled**. In *Figure 14.4* we output all services that starts with *Windows* in the **DisplayName** property and use **Select-Object** to list only the **Status**, **StartType** and **DisplayName** properties in the output:

```
PS C:\Temp> Get-Service -DisplayName "Windows*" | `
>> Select-Object -Property Status, StartType, DisplayName

 Status StartType DisplayName
 ------ --------- -----------
Running Automatic Windows Audio Endpoint Builder
Running Automatic Windows Audio
Running Automatic Windows Event Log
Running Automatic Windows Font Cache Service
Stopped    Manual Windows Presentation Foundation Font Cache 3.0.0.0
Stopped    Manual Windows Camera Frame Server
Stopped    Manual Windows Mobile Hotspot Service
Running    Manual Windows License Manager Service
Stopped    Manual Windows Mixed Reality OpenXR Service
Running Automatic Windows Defender Firewall
Stopped    Manual Windows Installer
```

Figure 14.4: Listing a specific set of services using Where-Object
and specific service properties using Select-Object

Once we have a list of all the services we are interested in, we can remove the pipe to **Select-Object** and save the command output into a variable containing the service objects. We remove the **Select-Object** command to make sure that the returned objects keep their initial data type since using **Select-Object** might change this. We can then pipe that variable to other service cmdlets such as the **Set-Service** for modifying the **StartType** parameter for all the selected services at once:

```
$Services = Get-Service -DisplayName "Windows*"

# Modify the StartType of all selected services

$Services | Set-Service -StartupType Automatic

# Stop all the selected services

$Services | Stop-Service

# Start all the selected services

$Services | Start-Service

# Restart all the selected services

$Services | Restart-Service
```

Note: In general, it requires elevated permissions to manage services, so make sure that PowerShell is running as an administrator. If you use scripts to manage services, make sure that the context that executes such scripts are elevated, or else you will get a permission denied error. Some services might also depend on other services, in such a case you can use the -Force parameter to make sure dependent services is also managed when working with service cmdlets.

Tip: Discovery and modification of service permissions can be done using the SC.exe (cmd) command, unfortunately this command returns permissions in SDDL syntax which is hard to translate and use directly in PowerShell. In this PowerShell blog by Rohn Edwards:

https://rohnspowershellblog.wordpress.com/2013/03/19/viewing-service-acls/ You can learn more about viewing service ACLs. The Get-ServiceACL function in this post is also a very nice example of integrating SC.exe, the Get-Service cmdlet and .NET with each other. Also note that if you want to run SC in Windows PowerShell, this is actually an alias for the Set-Content cmdlet, so you either need to start SC.exe or run Cmd /c SC in order to be able to use this command.

Each of these cmdlets are quite self-explanatory and they can be used to **Set**, **Start**, **Stop** and **Restart** individual services. We can use either the **-Name** or the **-DisplayName** parameter to specify the individual service we want to manage:

```
# Modify the StartType of an individual service
Set-Service -Name "WSearch" -StartupType Automatic
# Stop an individual service
Stop-Service -Name "WSearch"
# Start an individual service
Start-Service -DisplayName "Windows Search"
# Restart an individual service
Restart-Service -DisplayName "Windows Search"
```

If we have an executable that is designed to be a Windows service, we can use the **New-Service** cmdlet to create, or more specific, register that executable as a service. We must specify the name and display name for the service using the **-Name** and **-DisplayName** parameters. We should also specify the start type of the service using the **-StartType** parameter. We can add a description using the **-Description** parameter, and if the service depends on other services, we can use the **-DependsOn** parameter to specify the dependent services. If we want the service to run in a specific user context, we use the **-Credential** parameter to specify the credentials for that user. The most important parameter for this cmdlet though, is the **-BinaryPathName** parameter which is used for specifying the path to the executable service file:

```
# "Register" a new service from an executable
New-Service -Name "TestService" `
-DisplayName "TestService" `
-BinaryPathName C:\Temp\TestService\TestService.exe `
-Description "This is a simple test service executable" `
-StartupType Automatic
```

If the service is successfully created, it will return the status, name, and display name properties. Note that the service will start in the **Stopped** state. *Figure 14.5* shows the successful creation of a new service:

```
PS C:\Temp> # "Register" a new service from an executable
New-Service -Name "TestService" `
-DisplayName "TestService" `
-BinaryPathName C:\Temp\TestService\TestService.exe `
-Description "This is a simple test service executable" `
-StartupType Automatic


Status    Name                 DisplayName
------    ----                 -----------
Stopped   TestService          TestService
```

Figure 14.5: Successful creation of a new service using the New-Service cmdlet

In *Figure 14.6* we use **Get-Service** to get the current state of the **TestService** service and then we start and stop the service respectively, so that we can see that the service works as expected and that its state can be managed as any other Windows service using these service cmdlets:

```
PS C:\Temp> Get-Service "TestService"

Status    Name                 DisplayName
------    ----                 -----------
Stopped   TestService          TestService


PS C:\Temp>
PS C:\Temp> Get-Service "TestService" | Start-Service
PS C:\Temp>
PS C:\Temp> Get-Service "TestService"

Status    Name                 DisplayName
------    ----                 -----------
Running   TestService          TestService


PS C:\Temp>
PS C:\Temp> Get-Service "TestService" | Stop-Service
WARNING: Waiting for service 'TestService (TestService)' to stop...
WARNING: Waiting for service 'TestService (TestService)' to stop...
PS C:\Temp>
PS C:\Temp> Get-Service "TestService"

Status    Name                 DisplayName
------    ----                 -----------
Stopped   TestService          TestService
```

Figure 14.6: Getting the state before and after starting and stopping the TestService service

To remove (unregister) a service, we use the **Remove-Service** cmdlet as shown in *Figure 14.7*. The service needs to be stopped before it can be removed, or else executing the **Remove-Service** command will only mark the service for deletion and set its start type to **Disabled**, but the service will still be in its running state. As soon as the service is stopped, after it is marked for deletion, the service will then be removed by the SCM:

```
PS C:\Temp> Remove-Service "TestService"
PS C:\Temp> Get-Service "TestService"
Get-Service: Cannot find any service with service name 'TestService'.
```

Figure 14.7: *Successful removal of the Windows service*
TestService using the Remove-Service cmdlet

The executable itself will not be deleted from the system; it is only the service association (registration) for that executable that is removed by the SCM. We can easily re-create or re-register the executable again as a service, using the **New-Service** cmdlet.

These are the basic tasks that you usually encounter when working with Windows services. Utilizing PowerShell enables you to not only manage services easily but also allows you to create scripts for optimizing and automating service tasks. If for instance you have an application that consist of multiple (micro) services that needs to be stopped and started in a correct order, or if you simply want to make sure all your applications (micro) services are handled at once, you can easily create a custom application restart script for managing such tasks. Go one step further and automate such a script to execute at specific times or upon the occurrence of certain events using the Windows task scheduler.

> **Tip:** In Chapter 15, SAPIEN PowerShell Studio IDE you will learn how to create Windows Services from PowerShell scripts using the tools provided by the IDE referenced in that chapter. If you want to learn how to write Windows services in PowerShell more natively, without an IDE that creates all the underlying code for us, you should look at this article: https://learn.microsoft.com/en-us/archive/msdn-magazine/2016/may/windows-powershell-writing-windows-services-in-powershell

Processes

A process is an instance of a running program or application that has its own memory space, system resources, and execution context. Processes play a crucial role in managing the execution of programs and applications, ensuring multitasking, and provides a structured environment for running software on a Windows system. Whenever you start a program, a Windows Service or even when you create a PowerShell job, it is instantiated as a process and a unique **Process ID (PID)** and the respective required resources are allocated for that process on the system. An application can also contain multiple threads for differentiating individual internal processes and each such thread is instantiated as its own individual system process.

Recipe 87: Start, manage, and delete Windows processes

To manage processes, we use the PowerShell **Process** cmdlets. These cmdlets are a part of the **Microsoft.PowerShell.Management** built-in module. To get a list of all available process cmdlets, we can use **Get-Command**, specify the module as an argument for the **-Module** parameter and the string **process** as an argument for the **-Noun** parameter:

```
Get-Command -Module Microsoft.PowerShell.Management -Noun "process"
```

Figure 14.8 shows the output of this command and the list of specific process cmdlets:

```
PS C:\Temp> Get-Command -Module Microsoft.PowerShell.Management -Noun "process"

CommandType     Name                                               Version    Source
-----------     ----                                               -------    ------
Cmdlet          Debug-Process                                      7.0.0.0    Microsoft.PowerShell.Management
Cmdlet          Get-Process                                        7.0.0.0    Microsoft.PowerShell.Management
Cmdlet          Start-Process                                      7.0.0.0    Microsoft.PowerShell.Management
Cmdlet          Stop-Process                                       7.0.0.0    Microsoft.PowerShell.Management
Cmdlet          Wait-Process                                       7.0.0.0    Microsoft.PowerShell.Management
```

Figure 14.8: *Listing all process relevant cmdlets using Get-Command*

We can see that there are only a few cmdlets for managing processes where the most relevant are the **Get-Process**, **Start-Process** and **Stop-Process** cmdlets. The **Get-Process** cmdlet returns all running processes on a system if executed without any arguments. We can use the **-Name** parameter to specify a specific process to retrieve by its name. Note that there can be multiple processes with the same process name. When we run a PowerShell shell or script etc. it creates an individual process named **pwsh** (or **powershell** or **powershell_ise**, depending on the version and if you are running Windows PowerShell ISE) for each instance of PowerShell that are running on the system. *Figure 5.9* shows the output of using the **-Name** parameter to retrieve all **pwsh** processes. As we can see in the figure, this is equivalent to use **Where-Object** to filter the command by the **ProcessName** property. It is worth mentioning though, that using the parameters of cmdlets are always more efficient for filtering, than using **Where-Object**:

```
PS C:\Temp> Get-Process | Where-Object {$_.ProcessName -eq "pwsh"}

 NPM(K)    PM(M)    WS(M)   CPU(s)      Id  SI ProcessName
 ------    -----    -----   ------      --  -- -----------
    130    65,30   166,93     7,81    5716   2 pwsh
     74    30,47    92,97     1,08    6004   2 pwsh
     69    30,36    91,48     0,66    7692   2 pwsh

PS C:\Temp> Get-Process -Name "pwsh"

 NPM(K)    PM(M)    WS(M)   CPU(s)      Id  SI ProcessName
 ------    -----    -----   ------      --  -- -----------
    131    65,33   166,98     7,86    5716   2 pwsh
     74    30,47    92,97     1,08    6004   2 pwsh
     70    30,68    91,73     0,66    7692   2 pwsh
```

Figure 14.9: *Using the -Where-Object and the -Name parameter to list all pwsh processes running on a system*

If we want to stop all processes for a specific program such as *Notepad*, we can first retrieve all processes using the **Get-Process -Name "Notepad"** command and then pipe the command to **Stop-Process** which will then gracefully (try to) stop all the selected processes. If we use the cmdlet with the **-Force** parameter, the process will be instantly killed. Note that when running on a system with multiple users, we will have to use the **Stop-Process** cmdlet with the **-Force** parameter, in order to kill processes that are running in the context of other users. If we do not own the process, we cannot stop it unless we force it:

```
# Stop all selected processes
Get-Process -Name "Notepad" | Stop-Process
```

To target a single specific process, we should use the process id instead of the name to specify the process that we want to stop:

```
# Stop a specific process using Get-Process
Get-Process -Id 7304 | Stop-Process
# Stop a specific process using Stop-Process
Stop-Process -Id 7304
```

New processes can be started using the **Start-Process** cmdlet. To start a process, we would have to use the **-FilePath** parameter to specify the path to the specific program or application we want to start. If the program or application is specified within the PATH environment variable, it is enough to just specify the name of the program or application without specifying the entire path. *Figure 14.10* shows the usage of the **Start-Process** cmdlet to start a new *Notepad* process:

```
PS C:\Temp> Get-Process -Name "Notepad"
Get-Process: Cannot find a process with the name "Notepad". Verify the process name and call the cmdlet again.
PS C:\Temp>
PS C:\Temp> Start-Process -FilePath Notepad
PS C:\Temp>
PS C:\Temp> Get-Process -Name "Notepad"

 NPM(K)    PM(M)     WS(M)     CPU(s)      Id  SI ProcessName
 ------    -----     -----     ------      --  -- -----------
     13     2,54     17,68       0,05    7964   2 notepad
```

Figure 14.10: Using Start-Process to start a new Notepad process

Note: The Start-Process cmdlet has some limitations especially when it comes to the error and output streams. All of the output from the started process will only be displayed to the console when the process terminates, meaning it is not asynchronously displayed to the console when the process is running. If you want asynchronous output from the running process, you should look into more advanced methods that utilizes approaches such as event handlers to handle streams. One such example can be found here in the Invoke-Process.ps1 script:

https://gist.github.com/guitarrapc/dd05e671eea67059acb1.

- The **Wait-Process** cmdlet is typically used when we need to pause the execution of a script or a sequence of commands until one or more specified processes have been completed. This can be useful in certain scenarios where scripts or commands depend on the successful completion of a specific background process. It works like the **Wait-job** cmdlet we use when we wait for PowerShell jobs to complete before we continue further execution. However, with the **Wait-Process** cmdlet, we can wait for *any* process running on a system and not just a PowerShell job. This simplified example will wait for the newly created Notepad process to complete before any other commands are executed. We use a PowerShell job to stop the process after a timed interval and the **Get-Date** cmdlet to signify when the process is started and when it is stopped, so we have an indicator that shows us the **Wait-Process** cmdlet is working as intended:

```
"Start $(Get-Date)"

Start-Process Notepad

$Proc = Get-Process Notepad

Start-Job -ScriptBlock{
    param($ProcId)
    Start-Sleep -Seconds 15
    Stop-Process -Id $ProcId
} -ArgumentList $Proc.Id | Out-Null

Wait-Process $Proc.Id

"Stop $(Get-Date)"
```

It will result in an output as shown in *Figure 14.11*:

```
Start 12/19/2023 17:47:03
Stop 12/19/2023 17:47:18
```

Figure 14.11: The output from running the construct that uses the Wait-Process cmdlet

We can see that the **Stop** command was only executed after the Notepad process was stopped 15 seconds later and that the **Wait-Process** command worked as expected by executing the **Stop** command only after the Notepad process was stopped.

- The **Debug-Process** cmdlet is used to attach a debugger to a running process which can be beneficial when we are developing an application or a program and want to inspect or analyze the execution of the code. This feature requires that a debugger is downloaded and correctly configured on the system, then the cmdlet can be used to attach the downloaded debugger to a specific process.

Utilizing PowerShell for managing system processes allows you to automate complex tasks involving processes. You can create scripts that can be used for tasks such as monitoring, starting, and stopping processes based on specific conditions or criteria. As examples you can create scripts that monitors CPU usage and restarts certain processes for releasing resources to the system if the CPU load becomes too high. You can create scripts that stops processes if they are not responding to clean up system resources. You can create scripts that monitors specific processes memory usage and take certain actions if the utilized memory is too high, and so on.

Network settings

Network settings refer to the configuration parameters that define how a computer or device connects too and communicates over a network. These settings control various aspects of network interfaces, such as IP addressing, DNS resolution, the default gateway and more. System administrators must configure various network settings for systems and servers and by utilizing PowerShell and built-in *NetIP* and *DNS* cmdlets, it is easy to manage and configure the different aspects of systems and servers network interface settings and create scripts that can be used for optimizing and automating network tasks.

Recipe 88: Manage and configure network settings for interfaces

To manage network and DNS settings for network interfaces, PowerShell comes with the **NetTCPIP** and **DnsClient** modules. You can use **Get-Command** to list the available cmdlets in these modules:

```
# List commands in the NetTCPIP module
Get-Command -Module "NetTCPIP"
# List commands in the DnsClient module
Get-Command -Module "DnsClient"
```

To view the current network configuration, including IP addresses, default gateway, and DNS servers, we can use the **Get-NetIPConfiguration** cmdlet as shown in *Figure 14.12*. Note that this only shows all non-virtual connected interfaces:

```
PS C:\Temp> Get-NetIPConfiguration

InterfaceAlias       : Ethernet
InterfaceIndex       : 10
InterfaceDescription : Microsoft Hyper-V Network Adapter
NetProfile.Name      : Network
IPv4Address          : 192.168.22.166
IPv6DefaultGateway   :
IPv4DefaultGateway   : 192.168.22.1
DNSServer            : 1.1.1.1
                       192.168.22.1
```

Figure 14.12: Use Get-NetIPConfiguration to view the current network configuration

This cmdlet do not show the subnet mask or any virtual connected interfaces. If we want to get a more detailed list of all the interfaces and their settings, we can use the **Get-NetIPAddress** cmdlet that returns additional network information. These two cmdlets in conjunction will give all relevant information about the connected interfaces, including IP addresses, subnet mask, default gateway and DNS servers. *Figure 14.13* shows an abbreviated output from the **Get-NetIPAddress** cmdlet:

```
IPAddress          : 192.168.22.166
InterfaceIndex     : 10
InterfaceAlias     : Ethernet
AddressFamily      : IPv4
Type               : Unicast
PrefixLength       : 24
PrefixOrigin       : Manual
SuffixOrigin       : Manual
AddressState       : Preferred
ValidLifetime      : Infinite ([TimeSpan]::MaxValue)
PreferredLifetime  : Infinite ([TimeSpan]::MaxValue)
SkipAsSource       : False
PolicyStore        : ActiveStore

IPAddress          : 127.0.0.1
InterfaceIndex     : 1
InterfaceAlias     : Loopback Pseudo-Interface 1
AddressFamily      : IPv4
Type               : Unicast
PrefixLength       : 8
PrefixOrigin       : WellKnown
SuffixOrigin       : WellKnown
AddressState       : Preferred
ValidLifetime      : Infinite ([TimeSpan]::MaxValue)
PreferredLifetime  : Infinite ([TimeSpan]::MaxValue)
SkipAsSource       : False
PolicyStore        : ActiveStore
```

Figure 14.13: Abbreviated output from the Get-NetIPAddress cmdlet

Notice that IPv6 enabled interfaces will result in two interfaces referenced with the same **InterfaceIndex** and **InterfaceAlias** property values. You can use either the **-InterfaceAlias** or the **-InterfaceIndex** together with the **-AddressFamily** parameter to select a specific interface **AddressFamily**, either IPv4 or IPv6. In this example, we are only interested in the IPv4 interface, so we specify this as an argument to the **-AddressFamily** parameter:

```
Get-NetIPAddress -InterfaceAlias "Ethernet" -AddressFamily IPv4
```

If we want to add a new IP address to an interface, we can use the **New-NetIPAddress** cmdlet. Note that the **New-NetIPAddress** cmdlet requires elevated privileges. We need to specify the interface using either the **-IntefaceAlias** or the **-InterfaceIndex** parameter. We also need to specify the subnet mask by its prefix, using the **-PrefixLength** parameter. If not specified, the subnet will be set to the default 255.255.255.255. By default, DHCP is usually enabled on the ethernet interface, and it should be disabled if you need to provide a static IP address or else you might risk that DHCP changes your IP address. We disable this using the **Set-NetIPInterface** cmdlet

```
# Disable DHCP for the interface
Set-NetIPInterface -Dhcp Disabled `
-InterfaceAlias Ethernet
# Create a new IP address using Alias
New-NetIPAddress -InterfaceAlias "Ethernet" `
-IPAddress "192.168.22.222" `
-PrefixLength 24
# Create a new IP address using Index
New-NetIPAddress -InterfaceIndex 10 `
-IPAddress "192.168.22.223" `
-PrefixLength 23
```

We can use the **Get-NetIPAddress** cmdlet to verify that the new IP addresses is added to the specified interface, as shown in *Figure 14.14*. We use **Select-Object** to select certain properties to output:

```
PS C:\Temp> Get-NetIPAddress `
-InterfaceAlias "Ethernet" `
-AddressFamily IPv4 | `
Select-object IPAddress,PrefixLength


IPAddress          PrefixLength
---------          ------------
192.168.22.223               23
192.168.22.222               24
192.168.22.166               24
```

Figure 14.14: Verifying the new interface IP addresses using the Get-NetIPAddress cmdlet

We can also verify the new IP addresses by testing the connection from another host to these addresses. For this we can use the **Test-Connection** cmdlet to ping the IP addresses. We add an array of IP addresses as an argument for the **-TargetName** parameter. This is shown in *Figure 14.15*. Note that for reference we have added an IP address that we know does not exist:

```
PS C:\Temp>
PS C:\Temp> Test-Connection -TargetName @(
    "192.168.22.221",
    "192.168.22.222",
    "192.168.22.223") `
-Count 1 | Select-Object Address,Status


Address                              Status
-------                              ------
                        DestinationHostUnreachable
192.168.22.222                       Success
192.168.22.223                       Success
```

Figure 14.15: *Using the Test-Connection cmdlet, to ping test*
the new IP addresses from another host

We can see that the server is reachable by the new IP addresses that was added to the interface:

> **Note: The Test-Connection cmdlet is not part of either the DnsClient or the NetTCPIP module, but a part of the Microsoft.PowerShell.Management module. It have a few practical use cases for network diagnostics. Besides being able to ping hosts, you can also use it for testing port openings, much like a telnet client, by using the -TcpPort parameter and you can use it for making traceroutes using the -TraceRoute parameter. This is a powerful cmdlet that should be in all administrators toolbox. In earlier versions of PowerShell, the Test-NetConnection is an equivalent cmdlet.**

If we want to remove an IP address from an interface, we use the **Remove-NetIPAddress** cmdlet. It is enough to just specify the IP address or addresses that we want to remove without specifying an interface, the cmdlet will handle this based on the IP address. Since this is a destructive command, we will be prompted for confirmation. We use the **-Confirm:$false** switch parameter to suppress confirmation:

```
# Remove IP addresses from an interface

Remove-NetIPAddress `

-IPAddress "192.168.22.222", "192.168.22.223" `

-Confirm:$false
```

If we want to modify the current IP address for an interface, we have to first remove the current IP using the **Remove-NetIPAddress** cmdlet and then create a new IP address using the **New-NetIPAddress** cmdlet. When we want to create a new IP address, we can also specify a new subnet mask and default gateway for the interface. In the following example we want to only change the IP address but keep the current subnet mask and default gateway. We want the interface to still be on the same network. If we have multiple interfaces, we need to specify the correct one either by its index or by its alias. In this case we want to change the IP address for the *Ethernet* interface, and we use the **InterfaceAlias** to specify this. We could easily just remove the old IP address and then create a new one and specify the correct values for the **-IPAddress** and the **-PrefixLength** (subnet mask) parameters, but since we only want to change the IP address, we will use the **Get-NetIPAddress** cmdlet and get the current values for the subnet mask from the cmdlet output and store this in a variable. We can then use this value to specify the same subnet for the new IP address. We must specify the subnet mask when we create a new IP address, or else it would automatically be assigned the *host-only* subnet (255.255.255.255) which only defines a subnet with a single host. Since we do not want to change the default gateway, we do not need to specify this. The default gateway is bound to the interface and not to the IP address as with the subnet mask. To remove the current IP address, we simply pipe the output object that we have stored in the **$IpConfig** variable from the **Get-NetIPAddress** cmdlet to the **Remove-NetIPAddress** cmdlet. Since this is destructive behavior we need to confirm or suppress the confirmation using the **-Confirm:$false** switch parameter. Once the old IP address (and subnet mask) is removed, we can create a new one using the **New-NetIPAddress** cmdlet with the **-IPAddress** parameter to specify the new IP address, and the **-PrefixLength** parameter to specify the subnet mask. In this case it is the subnet mask that we have stored in the **$SubnetPrefix** variable. This entire construction is shown here:

```
# Store the Interface alias in a variable
$IfAlias = "Ethernet"
# Get and store the Current NetIPAddress object for the interface
$IpConfig = Get-NetIPAddress `
-InterfaceAlias $IfAlias `
-AddressFamily IPv4
# Get the current SubNet (prefix) from the $IpConfig variable
$SubnetPrefix = $IpConfig.PrefixLength
# Remove the current IP address from the interface
$IpConfig | Remove-NetIPAddress -Confirm:$false
# Create a new IP address for the interface
New-NetIPAddress `
-InterfaceAlias $IfAlias `
-IPAddress "192.168.22.250" `
-PrefixLength $SubnetPrefix
```

We can also change the default gateway:

First, we need to remove the current default gateway value from the interface. We can do this by using the **Remove-NetRoute** cmdlet. We need to specify the interface using either the **-InterfaceAlias** or the **-InterfaceIndex** parameter and then use the **-NextHop** parameter to reference the IP address for the current default gateway, the one we want to remove.

Once it is removed, we can specify the new default gateway for the interface when we create the new IP address by adding the new default gateways IP address as an argument to the **New-NetIPAddress** cmdlets **-DefaultGateway** parameter. This is shown in the example below.

We can also note that we use the output from the **Get-NetIPconfiguration** cmdlet, to get the value of the current default gateway IP address, so we do not have to manually specify it for the **Remove-NetRoute** cmdlets **-NextHop** parameter:

```
# Store the Interface alias in a variable
$IfAlias = "Ethernet"
# Get the NetIPConfiguration settings for the Ethernet interface
$NetConfig = Get-NetIPConfiguration -InterfaceAlias $IfAlias
# Get the current Default GateWay from the $NetConfig variable
$Gateway = $NetConfig.IPv4DefaultGateway.NextHop
# Get and store the Current NetIPAddress object for the interface
$IpConfig = Get-NetIPAddress `
-InterfaceAlias $IfAlias `
-AddressFamily IPv4
# Get the current SubNet (prefix) from the $IpConfig variable
$SubnetPrefix = $IpConfig.PrefixLength
# Remove the current IP address from the interface
$IpConfig | Remove-NetIPAddress -Confirm:$false
# Remove the current Default gateway from the interface
Remove-NetRoute `
-InterfaceAlias $IfAlias `
-NextHop $Gateway -Confirm:$false
# Create a new IP address and default gateway for the interface
New-NetIPAddress `
-InterfaceAlias $IfAlias `
-IPAddress "192.168.22.250" `
-PrefixLength $SubnetPrefix `
-DefaultGateway "192.168.23.1"
```

If we also want to change the primary and secondary DNS server address values, we will have to use the **DnsClientServerAddress** cmdlets from the **DnsClient** module. To get the current DNS server values we use the **Get-DnsClientServerAddress** cmdlet. If we do not specify any parameters, we will get a list of all interfaces and their DNS server IP addresses. We can use the **-InterfaceAlias** or the **-InterfaceIndex** parameters to specify the interface, and the **-AddressFamily** to indicate if it should be the IPv4 or the IPv6 family. To change the DNS IP addresses we use the **Set-DnsClientServerAddress** cmdlet. We simply have to specify the interface alias (or interface index) and then use the **-ServerAddress** parameter to specify the new DNS server IP addresses within a string array. In *Figure 14.16* we start by listing the current DNS servers for the *Ethernet* interface using the **Get-DnsClientServerAddress** cmdlet and then we use the **Set-DnsClientServerAddress** cmdlet to change the DNS servers. We list the DNS servers for the interface after the modification, to verify that they have indeed been changed. Note that the **Set-DnsClientServerAddress** cmdlet does not return any output and it does not need confirmation to modify the DNS addresses for the interface:

```
Get-DnsClientServerAddress `
-InterfaceAlias ethernet `
-AddressFamily IPv4

InterfaceAlias                    Interface Address ServerAddresses
                                  Index     Family
--------------                    --------- ------- ---------------
Ethernet                              10 IPv4    {1.1.1.1, 192.168.22.1}

PS C:\Temp>
PS C:\Temp>

Set-DnsClientServerAddress `
-InterfaceAlias ethernet `
-ServerAddresses "8.8.8.8", "8.8.4.4"
PS C:\Temp>
PS C:\Temp>

Get-DnsClientServerAddress `
-InterfaceAlias ethernet `
-AddressFamily IPv4

InterfaceAlias                    Interface Address ServerAddresses
                                  Index     Family
--------------                    --------- ------- ---------------
Ethernet                              10 IPv4    {8.8.8.8, 8.8.4.4}
```

Figure 14.16: Listing and modifying DNS servers using the Get-DnsClientServerAddress and Set-DnsClientServerAddress cmdlets

In these examples we only use a select few of the cmdlets offered by the *DnsClient* and *NetTCPIP* modules for performing some basic network tasks such as configuring IP addresses, subnets, default gateways and DNS servers for network interfaces. These modules also provide cmdlets that can be used for advanced tasks such as configuring advanced TCP/IP settings, manage IP routes, manage DNS cache, resolve DNS queries and configuring DNS client query resolution behavior and much more. These modules provide invaluable tools for an administrator's toolbox when you need to work with and manage all aspects of network interfaces and devices using PowerShell.

Disks and storage

Disks and storage are crucial components in devices where you want to store and retrieve data, such as in workstations and servers. A disk typically refers to a physical device such as a hard drive, SSD or USB disk, or a virtual device such as cloud storage or other kinds of storage that are virtually abstracted from any physical hardware. Workstations and laptops usually have quite few physical disks available for storing both the file system and other kinds of data. Virtualized devices such as servers and cloud systems usually use virtual disks for storage. A virtual disk is a storage resource that is abstracted from a physical storage capacity which could be a **Storage Area Network (SAN)**, a **Network attached storage (NAS)** or other kinds of physical storage device. Virtual storage is presented to an operating system or other application for that matter, as if it were a physical disk. Common types of virtual disks are **Virtual Hard Disks (VHDs)** that are used by Microsoft's Hyper-V and VMDKs that are used by VMware. A disk can be partitioned to make logical segments that work as independent units and partitions are typically created to separate and manage different sections of a disk. A volume is a logical storage unit with a file system on a partition and it represents a formatted area on a disk where data can be stored and retrieved. Volumes are typically associated with drive letters or mount points, and this is what users interact with when storing and retrieving data on a disk. To sum this up: disks are storage devices, partitions are physical divisions of a disk and volumes are the logical storage space with a file system on a partition. A disk may have multiple partitions each containing one or more volumes.

Working with disks and storage using PowerShell involves the usage of various cmdlets that are provided by the built-in *Storage* module.

Recipe 89: Initialize, partition and format disks

The *Storage* module provides cmdlets that can be used for managing physical disks, managing partitions, managing, and formatting volumes, managing disk images, managing storage pools and much more.

To retrieve information about the physical disks on a system we can use the **Get-Disk** and the **Get-PhysicalDisk** cmdlets. The difference between these is that the **Get-PhysicalDisk** cmdlet is designed to provide information about physical disks within storage pools and spaces, and the **Get-Disk** cmdlet is designed to provide information about disks at a higher level, which includes all disks on a system regardless of whether they are part of storage pools etc. The output from the **Get-Disk** cmdlet also includes the partition styles of the disks.

If we use the **Get-Disk** cmdlet to retrieve the disk information on a physical computer, we will get an output as shown in *Figure 14.17*:

```
PS C:\Temp> Get-Disk

Number Friendly Name                            Serial Number                       HealthStatus    OperationalStatus   Total Size Partition
                                                                                                                                   Style
------ -------------                            -------------                       ------------    -----------------   ---------- ---------
1      KINGSTON SNV2S2000G                      0000_0000_0000_0000_0026_B778_5...  Healthy         Online              1.82 TB GPT
0      Samsung SSD 870 EVO 2TB                  S754NS0N701418L                     Healthy         Online              1.82 TB GPT
```

*Figure 14.17: Retrieving disk information from a
physical computer using the Get-Disk cmdlet*

As you can see, we get descriptive valuable information from all the physical disks in the computer such as the disks friendly names, serial numbers, total disk sizes, health statuses, operational statuses, and their partition styles. If we were to execute the cmdlet on a virtual machine, the output will be a little less informative (but still valuable), as shown in *Figure 14.18*:

```
PS C:\Temp> Get-Disk

Number Friendly Name         Serial Number       HealthStatus    OperationalStatus   Total Size Partition
                                                                                                 Style
------ -------------         -------------       ------------    -----------------   ---------- ---------
0      Msft Virtual Disk                         Healthy         Online              40 GB GPT
1      Msft Virtual Disk                         Healthy         Online              30 GB RAW
```

*Figure 14.18: Retrieving disk information from
a virtual machine using the Get-Disk cmdlet*

Since the virtual machine use virtual disks, we are not able to retrieve the information from the underlying physical disk that abstracts the virtual storage from the virtual machine. This disk information is not known to the virtual machine. The virtual disks could be from a SAN storage or from any other kind of disk or storage that could be used for serving the virtual storage to the virtual machine. Some might argue that the virtual disks on the virtual machine are not physical disks, but these are physical disks to the virtual machine from the virtual machines' perspective. If we pipe **Get-Disk** to **Select-Object** and use a wildcard, we can retrieve additional valuable information about the disks, such as their physical location on the motherboard, the bus type, the logical sector size and more. This kind of information is of course most valuable when used to retrieve information from physical disks.

```
# Get disk information (All properties)
Get-Disk | Select-Object *
```

We can select a specific disk using the **-DeviceId** parameter:

```
# Get disk information (All properties) for specific disk
Get-Disk -DeviceId 1 | Select-Object *
```

From the two virtual disks on the virtual machine in *Figure 14.18* we can see that the second disk with disk number (index/id) 1 hasn't been initialized (or formatted with a file system that the operating system recognize), due to its *RAW* partition style. This means that this disk is not usable on the virtual machine yet. We need to first initialize it, then create a partition on the disk and then format this partition with a file system, such as NTFS or FAT32.

We start by initializing the disk using the **Initialize-Disk** cmdlet. We use **Get-Disk** with the **-DeviceId** parameter to specify the disk and then pipe this to **Initialize-Disk**. We also need to specify the partition style using the **-PartitionStyle** parameter. If we omit this, the partition style is set as GPT which is the default:

```
# Initialize a specific (RAW) disk

Get-Disk -DeviceId 1 | Initialize-Disk -PartitionStyle GPT
```

Once initialized we can use **Get-Disk** to check that the partition style has changed from *RAW* to *GPT*. We can then use the **Get-Partition** cmdlet to get an overview of the disks and their partitions. *Figure 14.19* shows the output from both commands:

```
PS C:\Temp> Get-Disk -DeviceId 1

Number Friendly Name        Serial Number        HealthStatus     OperationalStatus     Total Size Partition
                                                                                                     Style
------ -------------        -------------        ------------     -----------------     ---------- ---------
1      Msft Virtual Disk                         Healthy          Online                    30 GB GPT

PS C:\Temp> Get-Partition

   DiskPath: \\?\scsi#disk&ven_msft&prod_virtual_disk#5&ec97dde&0&000000#{53f56307-b6bf-11d0-94f2-00a0c91efb8b}

PartitionNumber  DriveLetter Offset                              Size Type
---------------  ----------- ------                              ---- ----
1                            1048576                           100 MB System
2                            105906176                          16 MB Reserved
3                C           122683392                       39.27 GB Basic
4                            42286972928                      630 MB Recovery

   DiskPath: \\?\scsi#disk&ven_msft&prod_virtual_disk#5&ec97dde&0&000002#{53f56307-b6bf-11d0-94f2-00a0c91efb8b}

PartitionNumber  DriveLetter Offset                              Size Type
---------------  ----------- ------                              ---- ----
1                            17408                            15.98 MB Reserved
```

Figure 14.19: *Using Get-Disk to check the partition style*
and Get-Partition to get an overview of all disks partitions

We can see the partitions for both disks. The disk that was already initialized, the one containing the operating system, have multiple partitions of different types. *System,* *Reserved, Basic* and *Recovery*. All these partitions were created because of the installation of the operating system on that disk. The *Basic* partition with the drive letter *C*, is the partition containing the actual operating system. The other disk, the one that we just initialized, only contains a single system reserved, very small partition. Since we have only initialized it, all the diskspace on the disk is set as unallocated. So, we need to make a new partition and allocate the disk space. We could create a single partition of any size as long as it does not exceed the max. disk size capacity, or we can create multiple smaller partitions as long as their combined size does not exceed the max. disk size. To partition the disk, we use the **New-Partition** cmdlet. We need to specify the disk we want to partition using either the **-DiskId**, **-DiskNumber** or **-DiskPath** parameter. We can manually specify a size for the partition using the **-Size** parameter or we can use the **-UseMaximumSize** parameter to use all unallocated available disk space for the partition. We can also manually assign a drive letter to the partition using the **-DriveLetter** parameter or we can use the **-AssignDriveLetter** parameter to have the cmdlet automatically assign the next available drive letter to the partition. By default, when the disk is of the GPT partition type, the **New-Partition** cmdlet will create a *Basic* data partition. If we wanted to create another type of partition, we would have to use the **-GptType** parameter and specify a unique GUID that uniquely identifies the specific kind of partition type. The valid GUID argument types for this parameter is:

System Partition: "{c12a7328-f81f-11d2-ba4b-00a0c93ec93b}"

Microsoft Reserved: "{e3c9e316-0b5c-4db8-817d-f92df00215ae}"

Basic data: "{ebd0a0a2-b9e5-4433-87c0-68b6b72699c7}"

Microsoft Recovery: "{de94bba4-06d1-4d40-a16a-bfd50179d6ac}"

If we wanted to create a partition of the *MBR* type instead of GPT, we would have to use the **-MbrType** parameter and specify either *FAT12*, *FAT16*, *Extended*, *Huge*, *IFS* or *FAT32* as the argument for the parameter. Since we already specified the partition type when we initialized the disk, we can omit any of these parameters, and the partition will be created as the default *GPT Basic data* type:

```
# Partition a specific disk (Auto assign drive letter and use all available space)
New-Partition -DiskNumber 1 -UseMaximumSize -AssignDriveLetter
```

Once the command is successfully executed, it will output information about the newly created partition. *Figure 14.20* shows the output of this command and the output from the **Get-Partition** command so we can get an overview of all the disks and their partitions:

```
PS C:\Temp> New-Partition -DiskNumber 1 -UseMaximumSize -AssignDriveLetter

   DiskPath: \\?\scsi#disk&ven_msft&prod_virtual_disk#5&ec97dde&0&000002#{53f56307-b6bf-11d0-94f2-00a0c91efb8b}

PartitionNumber  DriveLetter Offset                                        Size Type
---------------  ----------- ------                                        ---- ----
2                E           16777216                                  29.98 GB Basic

PS C:\Temp> Get-Partition

   DiskPath: \\?\scsi#disk&ven_msft&prod_virtual_disk#5&ec97dde&0&000000#{53f56307-b6bf-11d0-94f2-00a0c91efb8b}

PartitionNumber  DriveLetter Offset                                        Size Type
---------------  ----------- ------                                        ---- ----
1                            1048576                                   100 MB System
2                            105906176                                  16 MB Reserved
3                C           122683392                                39.27 GB Basic
4                            42286972928                               630 MB Recovery

   DiskPath: \\?\scsi#disk&ven_msft&prod_virtual_disk#5&ec97dde&0&000002#{53f56307-b6bf-11d0-94f2-00a0c91efb8b}

PartitionNumber  DriveLetter Offset                                        Size Type
---------------  ----------- ------                                        ---- ----
1                            17408                                   15.98 MB Reserved
2                E           16777216                                  29.98 GB Basic
```

Figure 14.20: *Output from the creation of the new disk partition using the New-Partition cmdlet and afterwards the output from Get-Partition to get an overview of all disks and their partitions*

We can see that the disk now contains the new partition with the drive letter *E* of the *Basic* type with a size of (almost) 30GB.

> **Note: The available disk space after partitioning will usually be a little less than advertised. There can be several reasons for this such as file system overhead, binary vs. decimal storage measurements (1GB = 1000MB. 1GiB = 1024MiB), reserved space, partition alignment etc.**

The next step is to format the disk with a file system that the operating system can interpret so that it can become available for that operating system. Essentially, we create a volume which is a formatted accessible space within a partition. For this we use the **Format-Volume** cmdlet. We need to specify the partition we want to format, we can do this using the **-DriveLetter** parameter. We also need to specify the type of file system using the **-FileSystem** parameter:

```
# Format partition as NTFS
Format-Volume -DriveLetter E -FileSystem NTFS
```

> **Note: You can use the -Full switch parameter to perform a full format of the partition. A full format writes to every sector of the disk and takes a long time to complete. If this parameter is omitted the cmdlet defaults to a quick format of the partition.**

Once the partition is successfully formatted the command will output new information about the newly created volume, as shown in *Figure 14.21*:

```
PS C:\Temp> Format-Volume -DriveLetter E -FileSystem NTFS

DriveLetter FriendlyName FileSystemType DriveType HealthStatus OperationalStatus SizeRemaining      Size
----------- ------------ -------------- --------- ------------ ----------------- -------------      ----
E                        NTFS           Fixed     Healthy      OK                    29.91 GB 29.98 GB
```

Figure 14.21: Output from successfully creating a new volume from the partition

The volume is now available to the operating system as any other data drive. In *Figure 14.22* we switch the location into the new volume (*E*) and create a test folder to verify the volume works as expected and is indeed available to the operating system:

```
PS C:\Temp> cd E:
PS E:\> mkdir Test


    Directory: E:\


Mode                 LastWriteTime         Length Name
----                 -------------         ------ ----
d----          22-12-2023     12:28               Test
```

Figure 14.22: Creating a folder in the new volume

All the cmdlets from these examples works with the pipeline and can be combined to perform all the operations as a single command. The following example retrieves all disks that are of the *RAW* partition type, initializes them, creating new partitions using the maximum available size and auto assign the drive letters, and then formats the partitions with the NTFS filesystem all in a single command. This can be quite beneficial if you have many uninitialized disks that you want to manage at once:

```
# Get all RAW disks, initialize the disks, partition, and format them
Get-Disk | Where-Object {$_.PartitionStyle -eq "RAW"} | `
Initialize-Disk -PartitionStyle GPT -PassThru | `
New-Partition -AssignDriveLetter -UseMaximumSize | `
Format-Volume -FileSystem NTFS
```

In this recipe we have shown some of the most basic and common tasks an administrator might encounter when working with disks and storage, especially when managing virtual servers that needs storage assigned from virtual disks. This gives the basic understanding of the usage of the cmdlets within the storage module for managing disks and storage. The module contains a lot more cmdlets that can be used for advanced disk and storage tasks such as creating storage pools, configuring tiered storage spaces, managing disk cache settings, optimizing storage performance (trim and defragmentation operations), retrieving storage health information and much more.

Firewall rules

Firewalls act as a barrier between a trusted internal network and untrusted external networks, such as the internet. Firewall rules are predefined or user-configured settings that dictate how a firewall should handle the network traffic. They play a crucial role in network security by enforcing the rules that are defined to handle the flow of traffic within networks. These rules determine which incoming and outgoing network traffic is allowed or blocked based on specified criteria. All Windows operating systems whether it is a server or client operating system include its own firewall that can be used to govern the inbound and outbound network traffic.

By utilizing cmdlets from the **NetSecurity** module you can manage, create, delete, enable and disable Windows firewall rules using PowerShell.

Recipe 90: Create, configure, and manage firewall rules

The *NetSecurity* module provides cmdlets for managing IPSec, Windows firewall and firewall rules. To list all available cmdlets in the module, use the **Get-Command** cmdlet. If we want to list cmdlets that are specific for managing firewall rules, we can use the **-Name** parameter and specify **"*firewallrule*"** as an argument or specify **"*firewall*"** if we want to list all cmdlets that are specific for managing all aspects of the Windows firewall:

```
# List all module cmdlets
Get-Command -Module NetSecurity
# List cmdlets for managing firewall rules
Get-Command -Module NetSecurity -Name "*firewallrule*"
# List cmdlets for managing all firewall aspects
Get-Command -Module NetSecurity -Name "*firewall*"
```

To list all firewall rules, we use the **Get-NetFirewallRule** cmdlet without any parameters. If we want to list a specific firewall rule, and we know its specific name or display name, we use the **-Name** or **-DisplayName** parameters. *Figure 14.23* shows the output of the cmdlet using the **-DisplayName** parameter to list the specific firewall rule named *RabbitMQ*:

```
PS C:\Temp> Get-NetFirewallRule -DisplayName RabbitMQ

Name                            : {30ED03E4-38D3-486D-BBE3-B01DC356E9D2}
DisplayName                     : RabbitMQ
Description                     :
DisplayGroup                    :
Group                           :
Enabled                         : True
Profile                         : Any
Platform                        : {}
Direction                       : Inbound
Action                          : Allow
EdgeTraversalPolicy             : Block
LooseSourceMapping              : False
LocalOnlyMapping                : False
Owner                           :
PrimaryStatus                   : OK
Status                          : The rule was parsed successfully from the store. (65536)
EnforcementStatus               : NotApplicable
PolicyStoreSource               : PersistentStore
PolicyStoreSourceType           : Local
RemoteDynamicKeywordAddresses   : {}
PolicyAppId                     :
```

Figure 14.23: Listing firewall rule named RabbitMQ using
the Get-NetFirewallRule cmdlet with the -DisplayName parameter

The output gives a lot of information about the specific firewall rule such as its direction, is it an *inbound* or *outbound* rule, the action that applies to the rule, should it *allow* or *block* the traffic and if the rule is *enabled* or *disabled*. One thing this information does not show is the protocol and port(s) that the rule applies to. All firewall rules have a set of associated objects that are individually derived using their own specific cmdlets. These objects contain the specific settings for each firewall rule, such as the network protocol and port(s) that the rule applies to, the local and remote IP addresses that the rule applies to, the application that the rule applies to and so on. The cmdlets for each type of firewall rule associated objects are also referred to as firewall rule filter cmdlets:

```
# Get Firewall rule associated objects

Get-NetFirewallAddressFilter

Get-NetFirewallServiceFilter

Get-NetFirewallApplicationFilter

Get-NetFirewallInterfaceFilter

Get-NetFirewallInterfaceTypeFilter

Get-NetFirewallPortFilter

Get-NetFirewallSecurityFilter
```

If you want to list all firewall rules and all their associated objects you can use the **Show-NetFirewallRule** cmdlet. Notice that this cmdlet returns a formatted list, that is best suitable for printing or storing in a file.

> **Note: For some unknown reason, when executing the Show-NetFirewallRule in the Windows PowerShell ISE, the cmdlet might only return a list with the firewall rule associated objects and not the firewall rule properties themselves. If you experience this try to run the cmdlet in a non-ISE shell to get the full firewall rule list.**

You can pipe the **Get-NetFirewallRule** cmdlet to the specific firewall filter cmdlets and list the relevant firewall rule settings:

```
# List firewall rule protocols and ports

Get-NetFirewallRule -DisplayName RabbitMQ | Get-NetFirewallPortFilter

# List firewall rule scope

Get-NetFirewallRule -DisplayName RabbitMQ | Get-NetFirewallAddressFilter

# List firewall rule programs and services

Get-NetFirewallRule -DisplayName RabbitMQ | Get-
NetFirewallApplicationFilter
```

Figure 14.24 show the output of the *RabbitMQ* firewall rule, with a selective of properties, and the output from the **Port**, **Address** and **Application** filter cmdlets:

```
Get-NetFirewallRule -DisplayName RabbitMQ | `
Select-Object DisplayName,Enabled,Profile,Direction,Action

DisplayName : RabbitMQ
Enabled     : True
Profile     : Any
Direction   : Inbound
Action      : Allow


PS C:\Temp>
PS C:\Temp> Get-NetFirewallRule -DisplayName RabbitMQ | Get-NetFirewallPortFilter

Protocol      : TCP
LocalPort     : 5672
RemotePort    : Any
IcmpType      : Any
DynamicTarget : Any


PS C:\Temp>
PS C:\Temp> Get-NetFirewallRule -DisplayName RabbitMQ | Get-NetFirewallAddressFilter

LocalAddress  : Any
RemoteAddress : Any


PS C:\Temp>
PS C:\Temp> Get-NetFirewallRule -DisplayName RabbitMQ | Get-NetFirewallApplicationFilter

Program : Any
Package :
```

Figure 14.24: *Listing the RabbitMQ firewall rule with selective
properties and some of the firewall rule associated objects*

If we want to Disable an active firewall rule, we can use the **Disable-NetFirewallRule**
cmdlet. This makes the firewall rule inactive but keeps the rule and all it settings in the
Windows firewall. We can enable a disabled firewall rule using the **Enable-NetFirewallRule**
cmdlet. *Figure 14.25* shows the disabling and re-enabling of the *RabbitMQ* firewall rule:

```
PS C:\Temp> Disable-NetFirewallRule -DisplayName RabbitMQ
PS C:\Temp>
PS C:\Temp>
Get-NetFirewallRule -DisplayName RabbitMQ | `
Select-Object DisplayName,Enabled,Profile,Direction,Action

DisplayName : RabbitMQ
Enabled     : False
Profile     : Any
Direction   : Inbound
Action      : Allow


PS C:\Temp> Enable-NetFirewallRule -DisplayName RabbitMQ
PS C:\Temp>
PS C:\Temp>
Get-NetFirewallRule -DisplayName RabbitMQ | `
Select-Object DisplayName,Enabled,Profile,Direction,Action

DisplayName : RabbitMQ
Enabled     : True
Profile     : Any
Direction   : Inbound
Action      : Allow
```

Figure 14.25: *Disabling and re-enabling of the RabbitMQ firewall rule using
the Disable-NetFirewallRule and Enable-NetFirewallRule cmdlets*

If we want to modify the current settings for a firewall rule, we use the **Set-NetFirewallRule** cmdlet. We can use this cmdlet to modify all the settings for the rule such as setting the remote and local addresses, the local and remote ports, the direction, and action of the rule and so on. This cmdlet handles all aspects of re-configuring rules, we do not need a specific filter cmdlet for modifying rule settings:

```
# Modify firewall rule settings

Set-NetFirewallRule -DisplayName RabbitMQ `

-RemoteAddress "192.168.22.0/24" `

-LocalPort "5671","5672"
```

In this command, we modify the settings for the RabbitMQ rule, and we specify that only remote addresses from the 192.168.22.0/24 network (notice the CIDR notation) is allowed, and we add an additional port (5671) to the rule. We need to specify both the current and the new port, or else the current port will be overridden. *Figure 14.26* shows the new firewall rule settings after the execution of this command:

```
Get-NetFirewallRule -DisplayName RabbitMQ |  `
Select-Object DisplayName,Enabled,Profile,Direction,Action

DisplayName : RabbitMQ
Enabled     : True
Profile     : Any
Direction   : Inbound
Action      : Allow


PS C:\Temp>
PS C:\Temp> Get-NetFirewallRule -DisplayName RabbitMQ | Get-NetFirewallPortFilter

Protocol      : TCP
LocalPort     : {5671, 5672}
RemotePort    : Any
IcmpType      : Any
DynamicTarget : Any


PS C:\Temp>
PS C:\Temp> Get-NetFirewallRule -DisplayName RabbitMQ | Get-NetFirewallAddressFilter

LocalAddress  : Any
RemoteAddress : 192.168.22.0/255.255.255.0
```

Figure 14.26: *Modified settings of the RabbitMQ firewall rule*

We can see that the new settings have been applied to the firewall rule. They are instantly in effect and the firewall rule now only allows inbound access on the two specified ports, from IP addresses in the specified subnet.

If we want to delete a firewall rule, we use the **Remove-NetFirewallRule** cmdlet. Notice that we will not be prompted for confirmation and the specified rule will be deleted promptly. We use the **-DisplayName** parameter to specify the rule we want to delete.

Tip: If the Remove-NetFirewallRule cmdlet is executed without using any parameters, the command will remove all firewall rules from your system without confirmation. This is quite destructive and will result in denial of all traffic on all ports. Be cautious when you use this command!

Figure 14.27 shows the successful removal of the RabbitMQ firewall rule using the Remove-NetFirewallRule cmdlet:

```
Get-NetFirewallRule -DisplayName RabbitMQ | `
Select-Object DisplayName,Enabled,Profile,Direction,Action

DisplayName : RabbitMQ
Enabled     : True
Profile     : Any
Direction   : Inbound
Action      : Allow


PS C:\Temp> Remove-NetFirewallRule -DisplayName RabbitMQ
PS C:\Temp>
PS C:\Temp>
Get-NetFirewallRule -DisplayName RabbitMQ | `
Select-Object DisplayName,Enabled,Profile,Direction,Action
Get-NetFirewallRule:
Line |
   2 |   Get-NetFirewallRule -DisplayName RabbitMQ | `
     | ~~~~~~~~~~~~~~~~~~~~~~~~~~~~~~~~~~~~~~~~~~~~~~~
     | No MSFT_NetFirewallRule objects found with property 'DisplayName' equal to 'RabbitMQ'.
 Verify the value of the property and retry.
```

***Figure 14.27:** Removal of the RabbitMQ firewall rule using the Remove-NetFirewallRule cmdlet*

We can create a new firewall rule using the **New-NetFirewallRule** cmdlet. We should specify at least the parameters shown in this example:

```
# Create a new firewall rule
New-NetFirewallRule -Name "RabbitMQ AMQP" `
-DisplayName "RabbitMQ AMQP" `
-Group "Custom Rules" `
-LocalPort "5671", "5672" `
-Protocol TCP `
-Direction Inbound `
-Action Allow `
-LocalAddress "192.168.22.0/24"
```

Once the command is executed and the firewall is successfully created the command will output information about the new firewall rule. You can use the cmdlets and commands from the previous examples in this recipe to manage and retrieve additional information about the new firewall rule. *Figure 14.28* shows the new RabbitMQ AMQP firewall rule in the Windows advanced firewall GUI:

Inbound Rules											
Name	Group	Profile	Enabled	Action	Program	Local Address	Remot...	Protocol	Local Port	Remote Port
Portmap for UNIX-based Softw...	Portmap for UNIX-based So...	All	Yes	Allow	System	Any	Any	UDP	111	Any
RabbitMQ AMQP	Custom Rules	All	Yes	Allow	Any	192.168.22.0/24	Any	TCP	5671, 5672	Any
Remote Desktop - (TCP-WS-In)	Remote Desktop (WebSocket)	All	No	Allow	System	Any	Any	TCP	3387	Any

Figure 14.28: Windows advanced firewall GUI viewing the RabbitMQ AMQP firewall rule

Firewalls and firewall rules are essential security components for managing and limiting access to your systems and servers. By utilizing PowerShell and the cmdlets in the **NetSecurity** module, you can easily manage your systems firewall rules programmatically. However, you should be aware of the **Remove-NetFirewallRule** cmdlets destructive behavior and the missing confirmation for this cmdlet. If this is executed without any parameters and without thought, you might end up limiting your own access to a system. You should always only allow access, especially on inbound connections, from relevant sources and for the relevant ports. If you open up too much access, you must watch out for potential security issues, especially if a server or system is directly accessible through the internet. Make sure such servers and systems at least reside within a DMZ in front of your network.

The task scheduler

The Windows task scheduler is a built-in component in Microsoft Windows operating systems that allow users to automate the execution of tasks at predefined intervals or in response to specific events. The task scheduler consists of a hierarchical structured library that organizes the scheduled tasks, and it includes folders for categorizing the different tasks. Users can create custom folders for their tasks. A scheduled task usually consists of the following, an action that defines what the task should do when triggered. It could be running a script, a program, sending an email etc. A trigger that defines when a task should be executed. Triggers can be time-based and set to execute at specific times, daily, weekly etc. or they can be event-based and set to execute on certain events such as system startup and user login. Conditions specify certain criteria that must be met for the task to execute. For example, tasks can be set to run only if the computer is idle or only when a network connection is available etc. Settings include various options that are related to how a task is executed. It could be that a task should be run with highest privileges or that it should be stopped if it runs longer than a specified duration and so on. Tasks can also be configured to run under specific security contexts such as the user who created the task, in the context of a specific user or service account, or with SYSTEM level privileges. A task can have multiple triggers and actions. This makes the task scheduler a powerful administration tool that enables you to automate tasks from simple scripts execution to perform complex system maintenance and administrative tasks.

Note: It is important to distinguish between the scheduled tasks and scheduled jobs cmdlets. Scheduled jobs are exclusive to PowerShell, and they are essentially PowerShell background jobs that has been configured to run within the task scheduler. Whereas managing scheduled tasks using the scheduled tasks cmdlets directly manages scheduled tasks using the task scheduler interface and is more a general-purpose tool for managing such tasks in general. In this chapter we use the ScheduledTasks module and the cmdlets it provides to manage the Windows Task scheduler.

Recipe 91: Create and manage scheduled tasks

The **ScheduledTasks** module provides cmdlets for managing the task scheduler. We use the **Get-Command** cmdlet to list all available cmdlets in the module:

```
# List all module cmdlets

Get-Command -Module ScheduledTasks
```

To list all scheduled tasks, use the **Get-ScheduledTask** cmdlet. Without any parameters specified, the cmdlet will return all tasks in all library folders, as shown in *Figure 14.29*:

```
PS C:\Temp> Get-ScheduledTask

TaskPath                                        TaskName                           State
--------                                        --------                           -----
\                                               GoogleUpdateTaskMachineCore{3C84... Ready
\                                               GoogleUpdateTaskMachineUA{221F38... Ready
\                                               MicrosoftEdgeUpdateTaskMachineCo... Ready
\                                               MicrosoftEdgeUpdateTaskMachineUA   Ready
\CustomTasks\                                   Advanced Task                      Ready
\CustomTasks\                                   Simple Task                        Ready
\Microsoft\Windows\                             Server Initial Configuration Task  Disabled
\Microsoft\Windows\.NET Framework\              .NET Framework NGEN v4.0.30319     Ready
\Microsoft\Windows\.NET Framework\              .NET Framework NGEN v4.0.30319 64  Ready
\Microsoft\Windows\.NET Framework\              .NET Framework NGEN v4.0.30319 6... Disabled
\Microsoft\Windows\.NET Framework\              .NET Framework NGEN v4.0.30319 C... Disabled
\Microsoft\Windows\Active Directory Rights Ma... AD RMS Rights Policy Template Ma... Disabled
\Microsoft\Windows\Active Directory Rights Ma... AD RMS Rights Policy Template Ma... Ready
```

Figure 14.29: Listing all scheduled tasks

This gives an overview of all the scheduled tasks, their task scheduler library path, and their state. You can use the **-TaskPath** parameter to list all scheduled tasks in a specific library path or use the **-TaskName** parameter to list a specific scheduled task. The output of using the cmdlet with these parameters are shown in *Figure 14.30*:

```
PS C:\Temp> Get-ScheduledTask -TaskPath "\CustomTasks\"

TaskPath                                 TaskName                   State
--------                                 --------                   -----
\CustomTasks\                            Advanced Task              Ready
\CustomTasks\                            Simple Task                Ready

PS C:\Temp>
PS C:\Temp> Get-ScheduledTask -TaskName "Simple Task"

TaskPath                                 TaskName                   State
--------                                 --------                   -----
\CustomTasks\                            Simple Task                Ready
```

Figure 14.30: Listing all tasks in a specific library path and listing a specific task

If we want to get more information about a specific task such as including the actions and triggers for that task, we can pipe the command to **Select-Object**. *Figure 14.31* shows the output when selecting all properties for the specific scheduled task named *Advanced Task*:

```
PS C:\Temp> Get-ScheduledTask -TaskName "Advanced Task" | Select-Object *

State                 : Running
Actions               : {MSFT_TaskExecAction, MSFT_TaskExecAction}
Author                : HOMESERVER3\Administrator
Date                  : 2023-12-25T16:32:32.4893404
Description           :
Documentation         :
Principal             : MSFT_TaskPrincipal2
SecurityDescriptor    :
Settings              : MSFT_TaskSettings3
Source                :
TaskName              : Advanced Task
TaskPath              : \CustomTasks\
Triggers              : {MSFT_TaskLogonTrigger, MSFT_TaskDailyTrigger}
URI                   : \CustomTasks\Advanced Task
Version               :
PSComputerName        :
CimClass              : Root/Microsoft/Windows/TaskScheduler:MSFT_ScheduledTask
CimInstanceProperties : {Actions, Author, Date, Description...}
CimSystemProperties   : Microsoft.Management.Infrastructure.CimSystemProperties
```

Figure 14.31: Selecting all properties for the scheduled task called Advanced Task

In the actions, principal, settings and triggers properties we can see that they are all referencing **MSFT_** objects. Each of these scheduled task objects, or components, have their own object type that define each component individually. Especially notice that the Triggers property contains an **MSFT_TaskLogonTrigger** and an **MSFT_TaskDailyTrigger** object. Each of these defines a specific type of trigger. A logon trigger, and a daily timed trigger. We can list the properties of each of these component's objects for the scheduled tasks, simply by dot sourcing them. The easiest would be to save the task to a variable, and then call each property individually:

```
# Store scheduled task in a variable
$Task = Get-ScheduledTask -TaskName "Advanced Task" | Select-Object *
# View the task actions
$Task.Actions
# View the task Principal
$Task.Principal
# View the task Settings
$Task.Settings
# View the task triggers
$Task.Triggers
```

Figure 14.32 shows the output for the **Actions** and the **Triggers** objects:

```
PS C:\Temp> $Task.Actions

Id                :
Arguments         : -ExecutionPolicy ByPass -NonInteractive -NoProfile -file "C:\Scripts\AdvancedScript.ps1"
Execute           : powershell.exe
WorkingDirectory  : C:\Scripts
PSComputerName    :

Id                :
Arguments         :
Execute           : C:\Windows\System32\cmd.exe
WorkingDirectory  :
PSComputerName    :


PS C:\Temp>
PS C:\Temp> $Task.Triggers

Enabled           : True
EndBoundary       :
ExecutionTimeLimit :
Id                :
Repetition        : MSFT_TaskRepetitionPattern
StartBoundary     :
Delay             :
UserId            :
PSComputerName    :

Enabled           : True
EndBoundary       :
ExecutionTimeLimit :
Id                :
Repetition        : MSFT_TaskRepetitionPattern
StartBoundary     : 2023-12-25T18:00:00
DaysInterval      : 1
RandomDelay       :
PSComputerName    :
```

Figure 14.32: *Listing the Actions and the Triggers objects from the Advanced Task scheduled task*

In these objects we can see that the first action is executing PowerShell.exe with the specified arguments. In this case it runs the script **C:\Scripts\AdvancedScripts.ps1** stated as an argument for the **-file** parameter. It also set the execution policy to **ByPass**, executes as **Non interactive** with no profile loaded as stated by the other arguments. The second action is simply starting **cmd.exe**. The cmd action have no active use in this case though other than opening a cmd shell and this is simply added as an example action. The first trigger is the logon trigger containing very few property values. Simply by having this kind of trigger object, the scheduled task knows it must be triggered at user logon. The second trigger is the daily trigger object type and its **StartBoundry** property has a value. This is the date and time this trigger must be activated for the first time, and then the **DaysInterval** property defines the interval of days when it should re-trigger at that same time. In this case it should trigger each day at the time specified in the **StartBoundry** property. Other available triggers are of a different object type and contains additional and/or different properties that are used to define that specific kind of trigger.

1. When we want to create a new scheduled task, we first need to create the task component objects (triggers, actions, settings and principals) individually and then create a new task and add these components to the task. Lastly, we need to register the task, to add it to the task scheduler library before it is set to execute by the task scheduler. Each of the component objects have their own cmdlets:

```
# Create a Trigger object
New-ScheduledTaskTrigger
# Create an Action object
New-ScheduledTaskAction
# Create a Principal object
New-ScheduledTaskPrincipal
# Create a Settings object
New-ScheduledTaskSettingsSet
```

We want to create a scheduled task that should execute a PowerShell script. It should have two triggers. One that triggers every hour, and one that triggers at logon. We also want to make sure that the script is stopped if it runs for more than an hour and that it can only run a single instance at a time. We also want the task to run as the local SYSTEM account with highest privileges.

2. First, we define the **Action** using the **New-ScheduledTaskAction** cmdlet. We use the **-Execute** parameter to specify that we want to execute PowerShell and we use the **-Argument** parameter to specify that we want to execute the **Update.ps1** script at the specified path, as an argument to the **PowerShell.exe** command:

```
# Define the action
$Action = New-ScheduledTaskAction -Execute "powershell.exe" `
-Argument "-file C:\Scritps\Update.ps1"
```

3. Then we define the **Triggers** using the **New-ScheduledTaskTrigger** cmdlet. For the hourly trigger, we use the **-Once** switch parameter to specify that it should be

executed at least once (this is a kind of activation trigger for the trigger). Then we use the **-At** parameter to specify the time it should be triggered (*hh:mm:ss*) and we use the **-RepetitionInterval** to specify the interval. This parameter takes an argument in the form of a **TimeSpan** object. We can simply specify a timespan as a string with hours, minutes and seconds like this *hh:mm:ss*. To specify one hour, we would use the string *1:00:00* as an argument for the **-RepetitionInterval** parameter. For the login trigger we simply need to create a trigger object by specifying the **-AtLogon** switch parameter:

```
# Define the hourly trigger

$HourlyTrigger = New-ScheduledTaskTrigger `

-Once `

-At "10:00:00" `

-RepetitionInterval "1:00:00"

# Define the login trigger

$LoginTrigger = New-ScheduledTaskTrigger -AtLogon
```

4. Next, we define the **Settings** for the scheduled task, using the **New-ScheduledTaskSettingsSet** cmdlet. We use the **-Priority** parameter to set the priority of the task to **3**. We use the **-ExecutionTimeLimit** parameter to define the maximum run time for the task, for this we also use a **TimeSpan** object in the form of a string "1:00:00", to define the one-hour interval. We use the **-MultipleInstances** parameter with the **IgnoreNew** argument to make sure that only one instance of the task can run at a time:

```
# Define settings

$Settings = New-ScheduledTaskSettingsSet -Priority 3 `

-ExecutionTimeLimit "1:00:00" `

-MultipleInstances IgnoreNew
```

Note: When you create a new scheduled task its priority is by default set to 7 which is very low. If you want to ensure that your actions are executed at a higher priority and that other processes running on your system is not prioritized in favor of your task, it is recommended to set your priority between 2 and 4. On systems where there is a high workload in general, your tasks might take longer to execute if their priority is set too low.

5. Next, we define the **Principal** for which the task much run in the context of, using the **New-ScheduledTaskPrincipal** cmdlet. We use the **-RunLevel** parameter to specify that it must be run with the highest privileges. The **-UserId** parameter is used to specify the user context, in this case we set it to run as the local **SYSTEM** account. For the **-LogonType** parameter we specify that it should run as a **ServiceAccount** type:

```
# Define the principal

$Principal = New-ScheduledTaskPrincipal `

-RunLevel Highest `

-UserId "SYSTEM" `

-LogonType ServiceAccount
```

6. Now that we have defined all the object components for the scheduled task, we can create the scheduled task itself using the **New-ScheduledTask** cmdlet. Each object component has their own parameter in this cmdlet, so we simply need to specify each of them as arguments for their respective parameters. Notice that the **-Trigger** and **-Action** parameters take an array of objects, so that we can specify multiple triggers and actions for each new scheduled task if we want. We can also add a description for the scheduled task using the **-Description** parameter:

```
# Create the scheduled task

$Task = New-ScheduledTask `

-Action $Action `

-Trigger $HourlyTrigger, $LoginTrigger `

-Settings $Settings `

-Principal $Principal `

-Description "Update Task"
```

7. Now, we have created the new scheduled task containing all the object components but this cmdlet does not create the schedule task in the task scheduler library. It only creates an object containing all the settings for the scheduled task. We need to register it using the **Register-ScheduledTask** cmdlet before it is actually created in the task scheduler library. The **-TaskName** parameter is used to set the name for the scheduled task. For the **-InputObject** parameter we specify the scheduled task object that we created using the **New-ScheduledTask** cmdlet. We can use the **-TaskPath** parameter to specify in which folder inside the library the task should be placed within. We also use the **-Force** parameter to register the task without having the cmdlet prompting for confirmation:

```
# Register the task

Register-ScheduledTask -TaskName "UpdateTask" `

-InputObject $Task `

-TaskPath "\CustomTasks\" `

-Force
```

Once executed, the new scheduled task is created in the task scheduler with the settings specified in each object component. The command will output the path, name and state of the newly created scheduled task as shown in *Figure 14.33*:

```
# Register the task
Register-ScheduledTask -TaskName "UpdateTask" `
-InputObject $Task `
-TaskPath "\CustomTasks\" `
-Force

TaskPath                                     TaskName                    State
--------                                     --------                    -----
\CustomTasks\                                UpdateTask                  Ready
```

Figure 14.33: Output for the successful registering of a new scheduled task in the task scheduler library

We can use the **Get-ScheduledTask** cmdlet and **Select-Object** to output our new scheduled task and all its properties, as shown in *Figure 14.34*:

```
PS C:\Temp> Get-ScheduledTask -TaskName "UpdateTask" | Select-Object *

State                 : Ready
Actions               : {MSFT_TaskExecAction}
Author                :
Date                  :
Description           : Update Task
Documentation         :
Principal             : MSFT_TaskPrincipal2
SecurityDescriptor    :
Settings              : MSFT_TaskSettings3
Source                :
TaskName              : UpdateTask
TaskPath              : \CustomTasks\
Triggers              : {MSFT_TaskTimeTrigger, MSFT_TaskLogonTrigger}
URI                   : \CustomTasks\UpdateTask
Version               :
PSComputerName        :
CimClass              : Root/Microsoft/Windows/TaskScheduler:MSFT_ScheduledTask
CimInstanceProperties : {Actions, Author, Date, Description...}
CimSystemProperties   : Microsoft.Management.Infrastructure.CimSystemProperties
```

Figure 14.34: Listing the new UpdateTask scheduled task and all its properties

- If we want to export a scheduled task for backup purposes or if we want to import the same task onto other systems, we can use the **Export-ScheduledTask** cmdlet. we will have to specify the task that we want to export using the **-TaskName** parameter for specifying its name and the **-TaskPath** parameter for specifying its path. The cmdlet returns the scheduled task in XML format, and to save it to a file we must pipe the command to **Out-File**, or else it will just be returned as a string to the console:

```
# Export a scheduled task
Export-ScheduledTask `
-TaskName "UpdateTask" `
-TaskPath "\CustomTasks\" | `
```

```
Out-File C:\Temp\UpdateTask.xml
```

- There are no import scheduled task cmdlet, instead we use the **Register-ScheduledTask** cmdlet for registering a scheduled task that is stored in an exported XML file. We also have to use the **-Xml** parameter and then get the content of the file where the exported task is stored using **Get-Content**. We also need to convert it to a string, since this parameter expects a string object and not an XML object. We pipe the **Get-Content** command to **Out-String**. Then we can register the task as any other by specifying a name using the **-TaskName** parameter and a path in the task scheduler library using the **-TaskPath** parameter:

```
Register-ScheduledTask `
-Xml (Get-Content C:\Temp\UpdateTask.xml | Out-String) `
-TaskName "ImportedTask" `
-TaskPath "\CustomTasks\"
```

Note: Third party scripts and applications that are executed by a scheduled task does not get exported and must be copied or installed individually and placed in the same location on other systems where an exported scheduled task is imported.

- We can enable and disable scheduled tasks using the **Enable-ScheduledTask** and **Disable-ScheduledTask** cmdlets:

```
# Disable Scheduled task
Disable-ScheduledTask -TaskName "UpdateTask" -TaskPath "\
CustomTasks\"
# Enable Scheduled task
Enable-ScheduledTask -TaskName "UpdateTask" -TaskPath "\
CustomTasks\"
```

- We can manually start scheduled tasks if it is allowed to be run on demand (this is default behavior, and you need to specifically configure if a task must not be run on demand). Use the **Start-ScheduledTask** cmdlet:

```
# Start Scheduled task (On demand)
Start-ScheduledTask -TaskName "UpdateTask" -TaskPath "\CustomTasks\"
```

- We can stop an already running scheduled task using the **Stop-ScheduledTask** cmdlet:

```
# Stop Scheduled task (On demand)
Stop-ScheduledTask -TaskName "UpdateTask" -TaskPath "\CustomTasks\"
```

- To delete a scheduled task from the task scheduler library we have to use the **Unregister-ScheduledTask** cmdlet. This is a destructive behavior. We can suppress confirmation using **-Confirm:$false switch** parameter:

```
# Unregister/Remove a scheduled task
Unregister-ScheduledTask `
-TaskName "UpdateTask" `
-TaskPath "\CustomTasks\" `
-Confirm:$false
```

The task scheduler is an invaluable tool in an administrator's toolbox, especially if you want to automate the execution of your scripts and applications on specific timed intervals or upon the occurrence of certain events. Within the task scheduler you can see that several applications including Windows itself, is using scheduled tasks for a multitude of scheduled operations such as updating applications and settings, running maintenance scripts and applications, ensuring that backups are executed at specific intervals and so on.

Conclusion

Within this chapter we have shown basic examples and use cases for some of the more important Windows components that come with PowerShell built-in modules for managing these components. PowerShell comes with a wide range of built-in modules for managing a multitude of Windows components such as the **BitLocker** module used for managing BitLocker, the **PrintManagment** module for managing printers, the **Defender** module for managing Windows Defender, the **Hyper-V** module for managing Hyper-V virtual machines and so on. It is quite powerful for administrators to be able to manage and control all aspects of the different Windows components using PowerShell. This makes it possible to not only programmatically manage these components but also for automating a lot of complex tasks with components. When working on Windows server operating systems there are more components and Windows roles and features that can be managed by PowerShell and respective modules. Whatever Windows component you might need to manage there is most likely a built-in module that is built for that specific purpose. Imagine that with a single script, you can automate almost all aspects of complex system configuration and management for a multitude of servers and systems almost instantaneously. It could be a script that automatically creates a new virtual machine from a predefined image that is fully functional and configured with the correct network settings etc. which are ready for use in your environment a few seconds after you have executed your script. It could be a script that automatically initializes and formats all raw disks on a multitude of virtual servers and so on. The possibilities are almost endless when you know the component your want to manage and the module used for managing it. It is up to you to explore and learn the features and possibilities such modules provide for the components you need to manage.

The next chapter explores the advanced PowerShell IDE created by SAPIEN Technologies. This IDE takes PowerShell scripting to a new level and enables you to not only create advanced scripts from templates but also to easily create and compile sophisticated GUI applications, Windows services, and packaged executables from your PowerShell scripts. This chapter introduces the IDE and demonstrates how to use it to create GUI applications and Windows Services. Furthermore, it depicts how to compile scripts into executables and how to create MSI installers for executables using the packager and installer managers. It also peeks into more applications created by SAPIEN Technologies such as the PowerShell module manager and the VersionRecall versioning and backup tool.

Join our book's Discord space

Join the book's Discord Workspace for Latest updates, Offers, Tech happenings around the world, New Release and Sessions with the Authors:

https://discord.bpbonline.com

CHAPTER 15

SAPIEN PowerShell
Studio IDE

Introduction

When creating and developing scripts and applications it is essential to have the right tools available. An **Integrated Development Environment (IDE)** is essential for developers and administrators as it significantly enhances productivity, and it is used to facilitate the scripting and development process. IDEs provide advanced code editors with features such as syntax highlighting, autocompletion, intellisense and code navigation. This helps writing code more efficiently and reduces the chances of syntax errors. IDEs also typically includes debugging tools that allow you to set breakpoints, inspect variables and step through code which has crucial features that help identifying and fixing bugs and errors. IDEs also often comes with versioning control and can integrate with systems like Git which makes it easier to manage and track changes in codebases, collaborate with team members and maintain a code revision history. Other features that might be offered by IDEs are code analysis and refactoring tools that help identify potential issues, improve code quality, suggests optimizations and help making structural improvements to code without introducing errors. Other features might be code templates and snippets where an IDE comes with pre-built templates and snippets that helps write common pieces of code quickly and reduces the need to type repetitive code manually. While some IDEs are designed to be general purpose and supports multiple languages, others are tailored for a specific language. Such specialization allows language specific features, tools and integrations and optimizes the development experience when working with those specific languages. Throughout this book we have primarily used VS Code with the PowerShell extension. The extension provides some of the most common IDE features for PowerShell when using VS Code. Another IDE for PowerShell is the PowerShell **Integrated Scripting Environment (ISE)** that comes built-in with Windows. It provides a simple yet effective interface for writing, testing, and debugging PowerShell scripts. These PowerShell IDEs are great and work well for creating general purpose scripts and applications and provides you with a lot of the common IDE features that you need. However, there is an IDE specialized for PowerShell that enables you go above and beyond general scripting by providing features and capabilities that allows you build PowerShell GUIs using a visual designer and it provides templates for creating Windows services from your PowerShell scripts. It provides a script packager that not only allows you to compile your scripts into executables but also allows you to compile your PowerShell Windows service scripts into executables. Furthermore, it also comes with an install builder that allows you to create MSI installers for your packaged and compiled executables. These features and capabilities make SAPIEN PowerShell Studio one of the most powerful PowerShell IDEs on the market. By utilizing this IDE, you can elevate your scripting development to new heights and create powerful PowerShell scripts and applications for any purpose whether it being regular PowerShell scripts, GUI form applications or PowerShell Windows Services.

Structure

This chapter covers the following topics:

- Introduction to SAPIEN PowerShell studio

- GUI forms with PowerShell Studio

    o **Recipe 92**: Creating GUI forms

- PowerShell Windows Services

    o **Recipe 93**: Creating Windows services

- The Packager and Installer managers

    o **Recipe 94**: Compiling scripts into executables

    o **Recipe 95**: Creating MSI installers for executables

- More applications from SAPIEN

Objectives

Within this chapter we are going to introduce you to the SAPIEN PowerShell Studio IDE and provide an insight into some of its more powerful features and capabilities such as creating GUI form applications and creating Windows services from PowerShell scripts. How it can be used to compile scripts into executables and how it can be used to create MSI installers from your executables. This chapter will not be used to cover all the features

SAPIEN PowerShell Studio offers in detail but is used to give you an insight into the capabilities and features this powerful IDE offers.

Introduction to SAPIEN PowerShell Studio

SAPIEN, the company behind PowerShell Studio, specializes in creating professional grade tools for Windows PowerShell. PowerShell Studio is the Powerful IDE created by SAPIEN that allows you to take your PowerShell scripting to new heights. PowerShell Studio offers a range of features tailored to enhance your PowerShell development experience. Some of the most notable features include:

- **Visual designer:** PowerShell Studio includes a visual designer that allows you to create **Graphical User Interfaces (GUIs)** from your PowerShell scripts. This feature greatly simplifies the process of building GUI form applications with its intuitive drag-and-drop visual designer and it allows you to easily build interactive and user-friendly applications that includes buttons, text boxes, drop-down boxes, labels, dialogs and much more.

- **Script packaging and compilation:** PowerShell Studio provides capabilities for both packaging scripts and compiling scripts into executables. This makes it easier to distribute and run scripts on systems without the need for the original source code. This also makes it beneficial for creating stand-alone applications and tools and provides obfuscation to your code.

- **Windows service executables:** PowerShell Studio enables the creation of PowerShell scripts that can be compiled as Windows service executables. This allows you to develop scripts that can run as background services on Windows systems and be managed by the Windows Service Manager.

- **Install builder:** PowerShell Studio comes with an install builder that allows you to create MSI installers from your packaged and compiled executables including installers that easily allows you to install your PowerShell Windows service executables on Windows systems. This also makes it easier in general to facilitate the deployment of your scripts and applications.

- **Module creation:** PowerShell Studio enables you to easily create PowerShell modules from your existing functions and enables you to easily create modules and module manifest files from built-in templates.

- **Function builder:** PowerShell Studio comes with an advanced PowerShell function builder that enables you to easily create advanced functions that includes cmdlet and parameter attributes and comment-based help.

Besides these key features PowerShell Studio also includes a robust editor with syntax coloring, reference highlighting, bookmarking, code formatting and code completion. You can create, edit, and manage code snippets. It features a powerful script debugger that allows you to debug scripts and modules both locally and remotely. It comes with a performance monitor and comes with both 32-bit and 64-bit integrated PowerShell consoles for both Windows PowerShell and PowerShell. Furthermore, it integrates with GIT repositories allowing you to backup and version control your script files. It comes with projects that allows you to manage multi-file scripts, create multi-form GUIs and script modules and it can be set to auto-sign your script files using a code signing certificate. It also comes with multiple pre-built templates for both scripts, modules, and GUI form applications.

All these features make PowerShell Studio a very powerful and advanced PowerShell IDE that should meet all your PowerShell scripting requirements combined into a single powerful tool. If you really want to elevate and take your PowerShell scripting to a whole new level, a tool such as this will be invaluable in your toolbox.

The newest version of SAPIEN PowerShell Studio can be purchased and downloaded from the official site here:

https://www.sapien.com/software/powershell_studio

Note: The version of SAPIEN PowerShell Studio used in this chapter is PowerShell Studio 2023 5.8.235.

SAPIEN offers per user annual subscriptions that are either pre-paid for a year or billed monthly. Besides that, you can also buy a perpetual user license. Usually, an annual subscription or a perpetual license comes with 1 year maintenance that allows you to upgrade all minor service builds and major product version releases of the software within that period. Read more about the subscriptions and perpetual licenses here:

https://info.sapien.com/index.php/quickguides/sapien-software-subscriptions

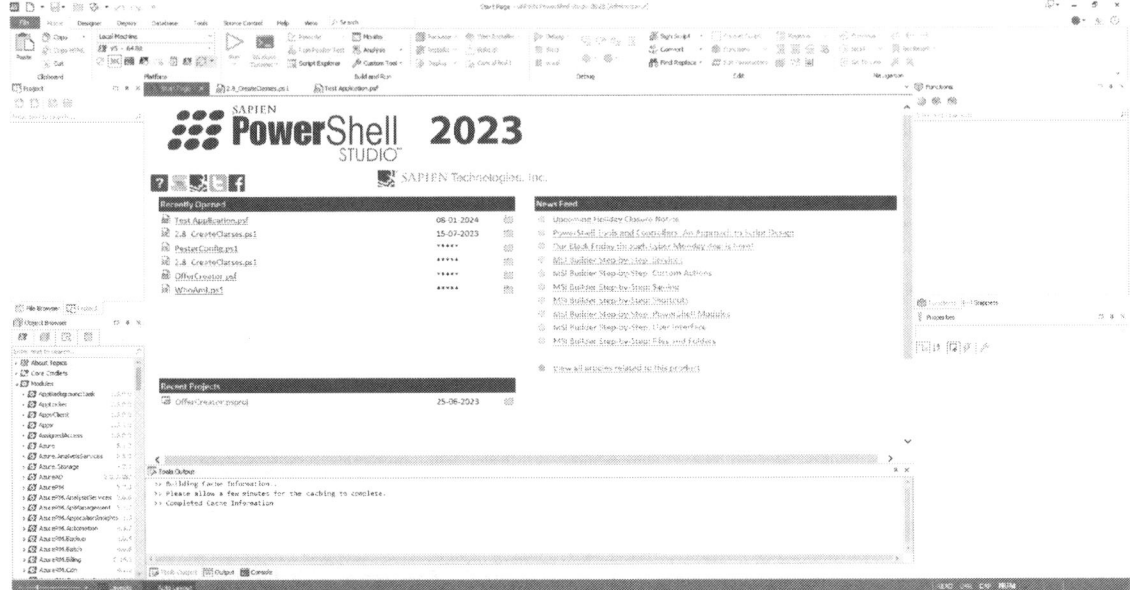

***Figure 15.1:** SAPIEN PowerShell Studio IDE*

If it is the first time you use SAPIEN PowerShell Studio, you can download a free trial before you need to buy a full license.

GUI forms with PowerShell Studio

SAPIEN PowerShell Studio allows you to build PowerShell GUI form applications which enables you to create a wide range of PowerShell applications from simple tools to advanced and complex interfaces. By creating GUI applications instead of regular scripts, you can present information and provide options for users in a visually appealing way. This provides as more intuitive and easy way for users to interact with your scripts and is especially beneficial for users who may not be comfortable or familiar with command-line interfaces. While GUIs offer advantages for users, it's important to consider the trade-offs, such as the potentially increased development effort and the need for additional resources. The decision to use a GUI or a command-line interface depends on factors such as the target audience, the general complexity, and the overall user experience goals. SAPIEN PowerShell Studio significantly simplifies the creation of PowerShell GUI form applications. It is worth mentioning though that GUIs created with SAPIEN PowerShell Studio are using the traditional WinForms class library that is included as a part of the Microsoft .NET framework. Nowadays GUIs usually tend to be created using the more modern XAML-based Microsoft Presentation framework. The main problem with WinForms is that it's pixel-based, so if you have a high-resolution screen, your form may look tiny, while if you have a low-resolution screen then the form can be huge. With the presentation framework the graphical elements can be defined as percentages of the screen size, so they are automatically resized to the correct size. So, the resolution size of your applications and the systems they are going to be used on are something that is worth taking into consideration when building GUIs with PowerShell Studio. It is possible though, to create PowerShell GUIs for high-resolution displays and have PowerShell Studio autoscaling the form controls. For more information refer to the SAPIEN information center under the GUI Design / Best Practice section which can be found here: **https://info.sapien.com/index.php/guis/gui-design-best-practice**.

Recipe 92: Creating GUI forms

When you want to create a GUI form with SAPIEN PowerShell Studio you can choose to create a single form application from a selection of template presets. There are different presets to choose from. You can create an *Empty Form* that provides you with a single empty window, or you can choose from presets such as menu, dialog style, dark and light themed form, wizard style and more. *Figure 15.2* shows the form preset selection window:

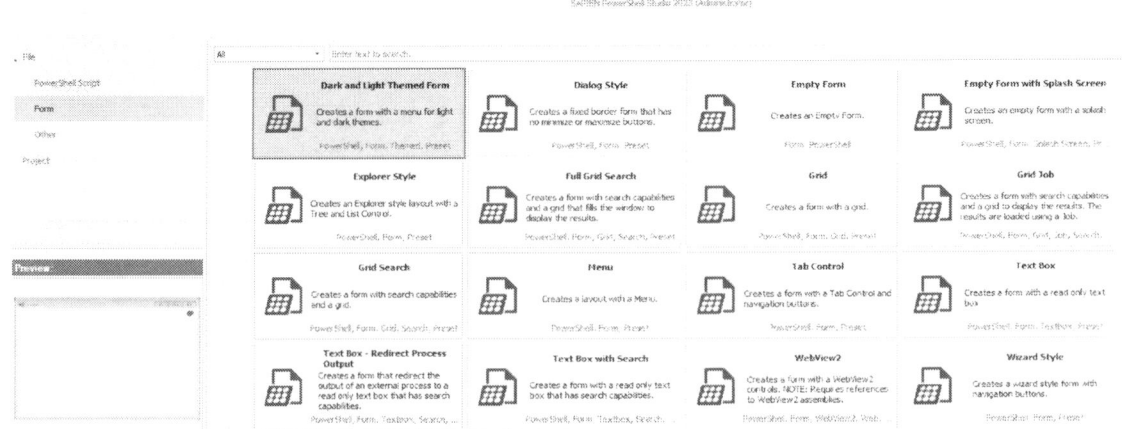

Figure 15.2: Preset selection window when creating a new simple GUI form

You can also choose a project that allows you to create a form project with either a single from or a project containing multiple forms. Such projects are used to create more advanced script applications that use multiple project files. They are also used for separating the code into multiple files. Selecting a form project is shown in *Figure 15.3*:

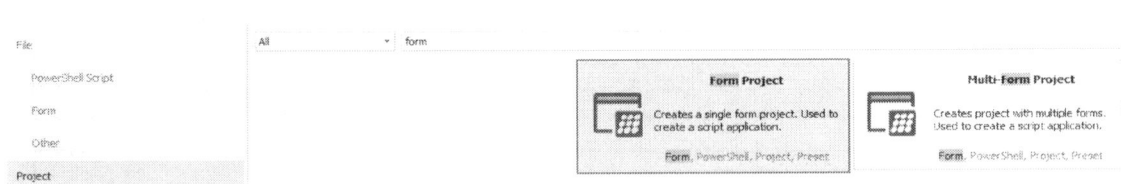

Figure 15.3: Project selection window when creating an advanced application form project

If you select a simple form preset, you will have a single .psf file to work with. This file is divided into two segments. A **Designer** and a **Scripts** segment. The Designer segment is the visual part, and this is where you add the different controls such as buttons, labels, text boxes and so on by simply dragging and dropping them from the control's toolbox onto the form window. Each control has a set of properties that are used to configure the different aspects of the respective control. For a button control, this can be the text inside the button, the size of the button, the alignment of the button in the form window and so on. Each type of control has some specific type control properties and all controls also share a set of common properties. If you select the main form window, you can configure the properties for this such as setting the title and adding an icon and so on. Some controls are passive, meaning that they do not trigger any kind of events.

This could be a label that is simply showing a text, or a text box that are only used for receiving some text but does nothing actively. Other controls are active in the sense that they can trigger events. For a button it could be a click event that would trigger each time the button is clicked, or it could be a text box event that performs a lookup or search each time a character is typed in the text box. Each type of control has a set of events that can be activated and make the control perform certain actions upon the occurrence of the specific event. Even a text box can have a click event and perform a certain action when the text box itself is clicked. There are many types of events, besides the more regular *click* event, such as **MouseOver**, **DragDrop**, **TabIndexChanged** and so on. To add an event to a control, you can right click a control in the visual designer segment and select **Add Events** which gives you a list of events to choose from or you can simply double click a specific control, and it will automatically add the most common event for that control, to your code. In the case of a button, it would be a *click* event which is the most common event for this type of control. *Figure 15.4* shows an application with a few simple labels, a text box and a button control. One of the labels is not visible (it has no text) since this is going to be dynamically updated when the button is clicked. The figure also shows the toolbox where the controls are dragged and dropped from. It shows the properties pane for the *button* control (since this is the control that is currently marked) and it shows a functions pane, that not only shows functions residing in the script segment (notice that there are no functions created for this application, hence no functions are shown in this pane) but also shows all events that are created for the controls that are added to the form application:

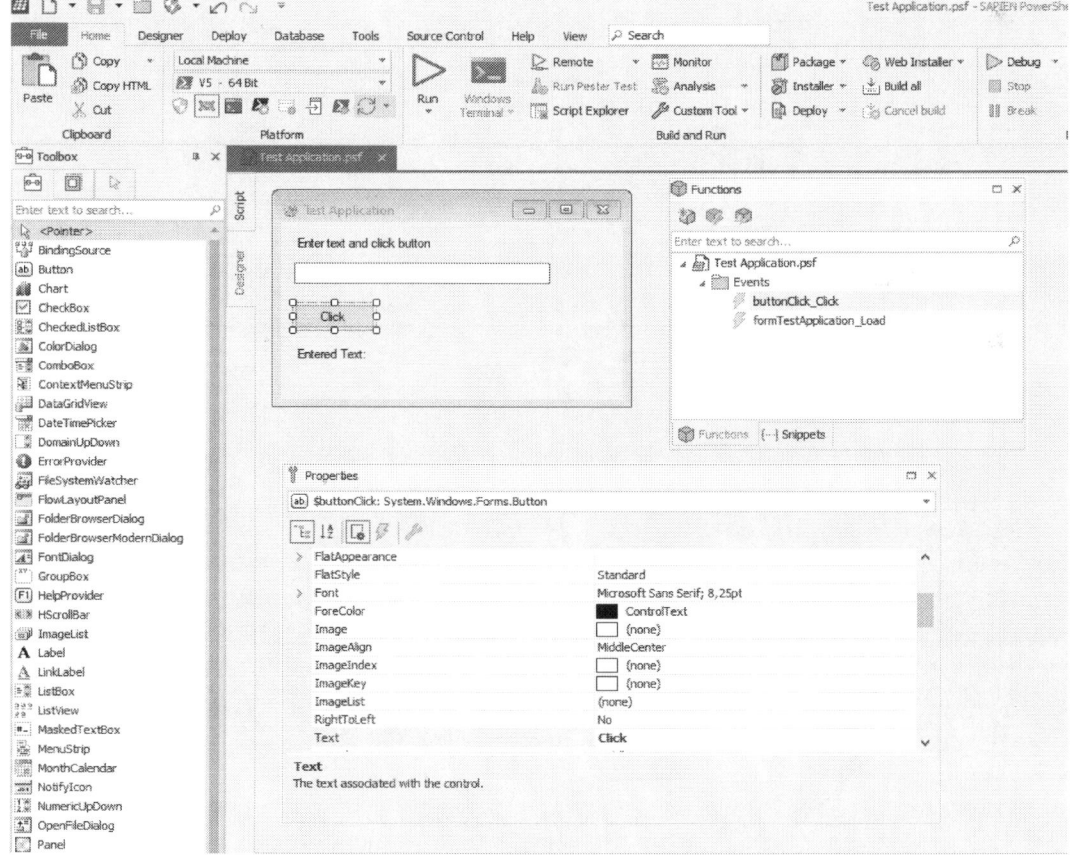

Figure 15.4: *Showing the form Designer segment including the control toolbox, the properties pane and the functions/events pane*

The **Script** segment of the file is where code such as functions, cmdlets and variables are added, but also the controls event code is created in this segment whenever you add an event to a control. *Figure 15.5* shows the Script segment with two events and a custom function:

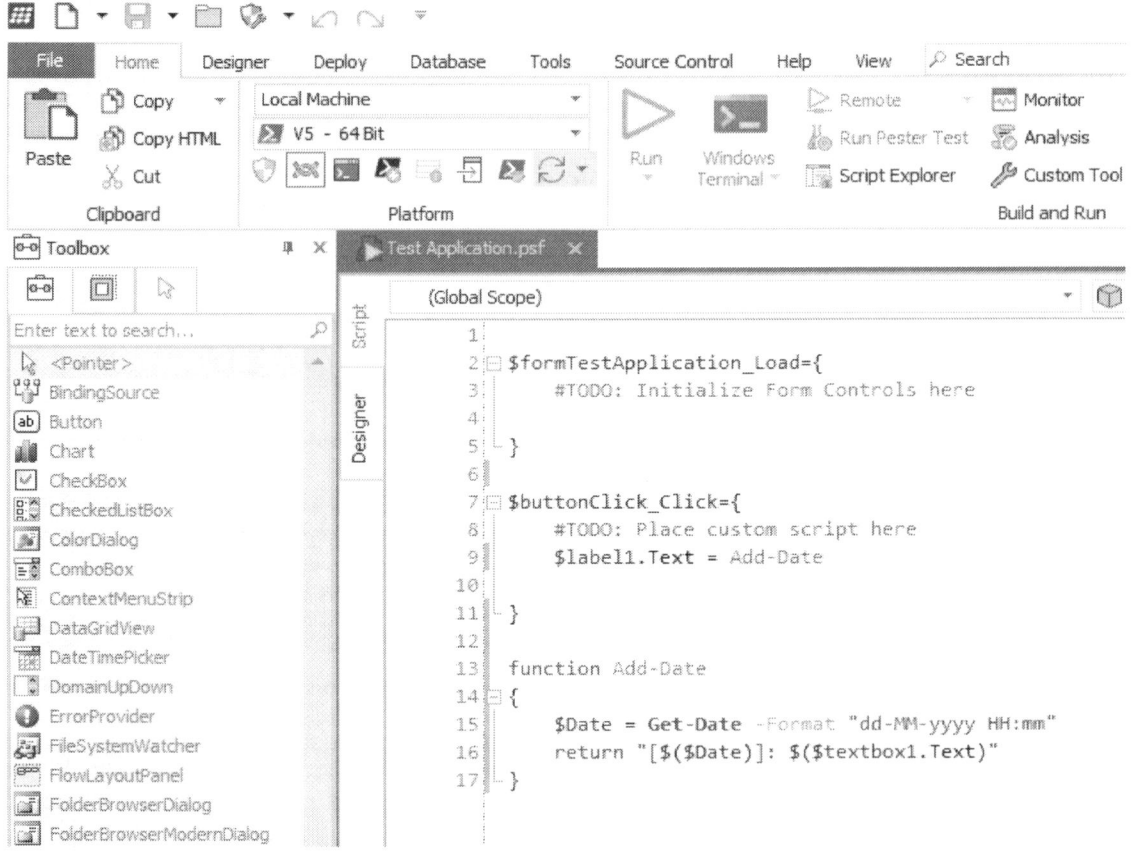

Figure 15.5: *The Script segment of the form file showing two events and a custom function*

The first **$formTestApplication_Load** event is an event that is automatically created when the form application is created. This event occurs when the form is loaded (when the application is started) and can be used for initialization of controls and for loading modules etc. Notice how the events are created and defined much like variables where the name of the variable is a direct reference to the name of the control (the names of controls can be configured in the control properties) and the name after the underscore is the name of the specific type of event (in this case **Click**) and then an equal sign and a script block is used to define an event. The script block contains the code that is executed when the event is triggered. In the **$buttonClick_Click** event we state that the **$label1.text** should be equal to the returned output from the **Add-Date** function. **$label1** is a direct reference to the label control that is created with that name (label1) and **.text** is the property of that label control that holds the text within the label. Controls have both properties and methods. In this case we state that whenever the button click event occurs (when the button called **buttonClick** is clicked) the *text* of the *label* called **label1** should be set as the return output from the **Add-Date** function. Within the **Add-Date** function we return a string that contains the date and time (in the moment when the function is invoked) and the *text* content of the **$textbox1** control (again, the name of each individual control can be changed in the control properties). To sum up, what basically happens is: When the button is clicked (**buttonClick**), the button click event occurs. This event first invokes the **Add-Date** function. This function takes the text in the textbox control (textbox1) and add a formatted date and time to the text string. It then returns this edited text string back to the event, and the event then updates the label (**label1**) text with the output text from the function. *Figure 15.6* shows the running **Test Application** and the button click event occurrence when the button is clicked in the application:

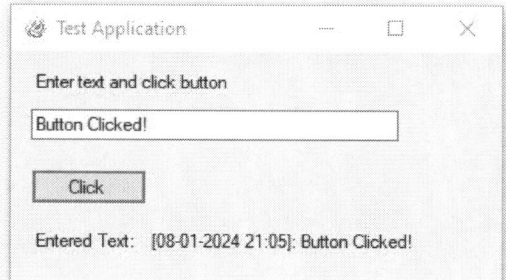

Figure 15.6: Running the Test Application showing the button click event occurrence

This is of course, a very basic example of a PowerShell GUI application created using a simple form preset. If you create a GUI application using a project form template, the principals are the same, but a project divides your code into different files. You will be provided with a **MainForm.psf** file, which is the same type of Designer and Script segmented file you get when using a simple form template. Besides this, you will get a **Startup.pss** file that are used for initializing the GUI. It is also within this file you load modules and add code that should be executed at application initialization (startup) such as opening database connections etc. The third file is a **Globals.ps1** file that you use for declaring global variables, functions and classes and so on. You can add additional script files if needed to a project. Once you package your application, whether it being created from a simple form template or from a project, PowerShell Studio will handle everything that is needed for merging your files and compiling them into a fully functional GUI application.

There is almost no limit to the types of advanced GUI applications you can create with PowerShell Studio. A more advanced GUI application example is the Windows Service Manager application that is shown in *Figure 15.7*:

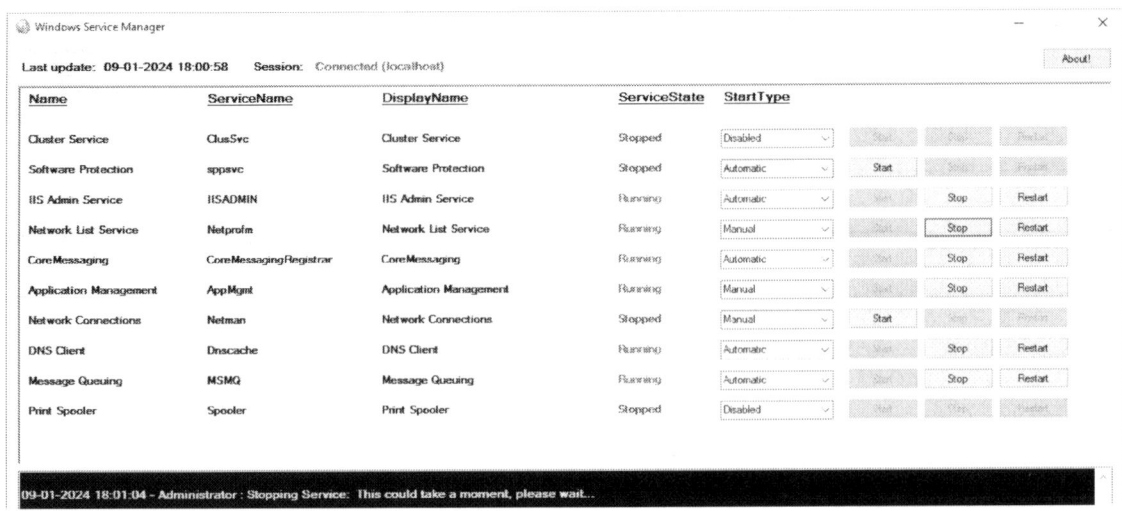

Figure 15.7: Windows Service Manager application created with SAPIEN PowerShell Studio

Not only is this Windows Service Manager used for managing a set of specific Windows services, but it also uses a timed trigger event that runs in the background to keep the services states updated in real-time. So, if you use the Windows built-in service manager or for some other reason a service changes its state or start type, the view in the GUI application will be updated accordingly. Furthermore, it has a text box that is used for as an output for the different actions that has occured, what time they occurred and which user triggered them. Behind the scenes, it also logs these actions to a log file, so it provides traceability and history. It can also connect to and manage services on remote servers. Such a tool could be useful if you have created your own set of application micro services that you (and other users need to) manage. With the correct set of permissions, you can also use this to ensure that specific users can only manage these specific services without having access to all other services on a server or system. This is just another example of a GUI application that is created using SAPIEN PowerShell Studio.

Once you learn how to use the visual designer, the different controls, and the other components, you will be able to create truly powerful GUI form applications using SAPIEN PowerShell Studio for a wide range of purposes and use cases.

PowerShell Windows services

Using a Windows background service provides several benefits in certain scenarios. You might have a script or application with no user interface that needs to run when the system starts. It might be a backup process, a monitoring system or other kind of script or application that needs to be operating continuously and be managed automatically. Services can run under specific user accounts with defined privileges. This allows you to control the security context in which your background tasks operate, enhancing security and access control. Services might also have access to system resources and can perform tasks that require elevated privileges. They can interact with the file system, network, and other resources without the limitations imposed on some standard user applications. These capabilities make Windows services powerful components and with SAPIEN PowerShell Studio you can easily create Windows services from your PowerShell scripts. PowerShell Studio comes with a template preset for creating a PowerShell service script which provides all the necessary functions for creating a Windows service.

Recipe 93: Creating Windows services

In order to create a Windows service script, when you create a new file, select the PowerShell Service Script template preset. This will generate a single file containing the following functions:

- **Start-MyService**: Is used for one time startup code such as initializing global variables and for opening connections such as connections to databases or other systems etc.

- **Invoke-MyService:** Is where you place your service code logic. Note that a service is running in a continuous loop with a timed interval (defaults to 10 seconds) and executes your code logic continuously after execution. It is recommended to create a **Main** function containing your code logic, and then referencing the **Main** function within the **Invoke-MyService** function.

- **Stop-MyService:** This sends a stop signal to the main loop and then waits gracefully for the main loop to exit. You should also place clean-up code here such as closing open connections, terminating jobs, and unloading blocking modules etc.

- **Pause-MyService:** This pauses the service without stopping it. Basically, it skips the execution of the main code logic within the main loop until a continue command is issued. You should save states if needed when pausing a service.

- **Continue-MyService:** This continues the service from a paused state. You should restore any potential saved states if needed.

> **Do not rename the Start-MyService, Invoke-MyService and Stop-MyService functions. These are used by PowerShell Studio to create the Windows service logic behind the scene when you package and compile your service script.**

This is basically everything that is needed in order for you to create a PowerShell Windows service using PowerShell Studio, besides the code logic of course. You will add code as with any other script by creating the functions, variables and other components that will comprise your code logic. As mentioned, it is recommended to create a **Main** function for your code logic that is then invoked within the **Invoke-MyService** function. You should of course make sure that your code logic is not exiting or in any other ways forcibly close the script after execution, or else your Windows service will stop after the first execution iteration. You should also be sure to handle errors. If for example, you open a connection to a database upon service start, and you then continuously execute a query against the database and for a single execution iteration, the query fails and returns an error. If you do not handle such an error gracefully, the service might stop, just like any other script encountering a terminating error that is not properly handled.

> **Note: When you use Write-Host or any other PowerShell output function within a PowerShell Windows service, the output will automatically be written to the systems application event log. Incorporate your own logging function to log output and errors to a log file.**

As an example, we will create a simple Windows service that fetches the weather in Aarhus, Denmark every minute, using the OpenWeatherMap API and then logs the output to a JSON log file within a nicely formatted string.

> **Tip: To use the OpenWeatherMap API you must create a free account at openweathermap.org and create an api key.**

First, we create a function that calls the weather API using the **Invoke-RestMethod** cmdlet. From the response we save the current weather description, the current temperature and the *feels-like* temperature into variables. The API returns the temperatures in Kelvin, so we subtract 273.15 from each temperature to convert them into Celsius degrees. We then return a nicely formatted string message containing the weather information. Notice that we use the string **-f** operator to make sure the temperatures in the string are only using two decimals:

```
function Return-Weather
{
        $ApiKey = "f2d671ac92e02bdd267cd98a1b7d98a3"
        $City = "Aarhus"
        $ApiUrl = "http://api.openweathermap.org/data/2.5/weather?q=$City&appid=$ApiKey"
        $Response = Invoke-RestMethod -Uri $ApiUrl -Method Get
        $Weather = $Response.weather.description
        $Temp = ($Response.main.temp) - 273.15 # From Kelvin to Celcius
        $TempFeels = ($Response.main.feels_like) - 273.15 # From Kelvin to Celcius
        Return "The weather in $City is $Weather with a temperature of{0:F2}
        Celcius that feels like {1:F2} Celcius" -f $Temp, $TempFeels
}
```

For the logging function we use the **Add-LogToJson** function we created in *Recipe 26, Create a custom logging function for structured logging that helps with troubleshooting and debugging errors* in *Chapter 4, Error Handling*. Now we create the **Main** function wherein we invoke the **Return-Weather** function and store the return output message in a variable (we could also invoke this directly in the **-Message** parameter for the **Add-LogToJson** function instead). We then log the returned weather message to a JSON file using the **Add-LogToJson** function. We encase these commands in a **try/catch** block. If for some reason a command should fail in a single iteration, the service will not stop and just try again upon the next iteration. Within the **catch** block, we simply output the error message. Remember that any PowerShell output within the service will be written to the systems application event log. We could also have logged the error to the log file using the **Add-LogToJson** function, but the potential error in this case could be with the logging function itself:

```
function Main
{
        try
        {
                $WeatherMessage = Return-Weather
                Add-LogToJson -LogFilePath C:\Temp\WeatherLog.json -Message
$WeatherMessage
        }
        catch
        {
                $_
        }
}
```

Now the only thing that is left to do is to add the **Main** function to the **Invoke-MyService** function. We also change the service loop sleep timer from the default 10 seconds to 60 seconds. The updated **Invoke-MyService** function is shown in *Figure 15.8*:

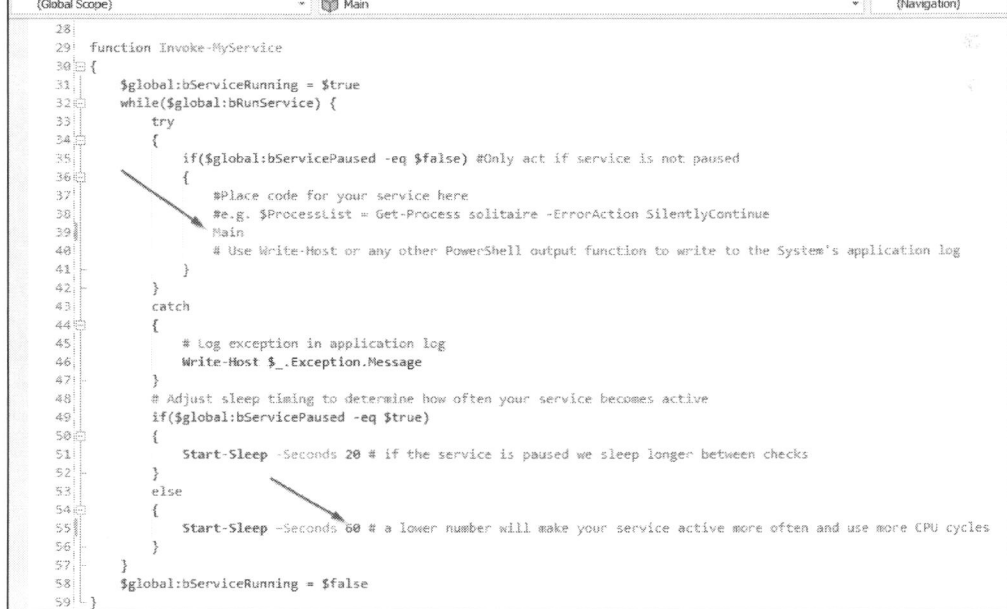

Figure 15.8: *The updated Invoke-MyService function*

Now we have basically created the code logic for a PowerShell Windows service that will call the **Main** function every 60 seconds and execute the code within that function. In this case the **Return-Weather** and the **Add-LogToJson** functions.

> **Note: There will always be some overhead due to the code that is executed. If your Main function takes 2 seconds to execute, the cycle will take 62 seconds in total. If you need more accurate timings in your service, you should accommodate for such overhead.**

Now we would have to first compile the service script into an executable and then register that executable as a Windows service on a server or system. But there is a way for us to test it first. We can simply call the **Start-MyService** and the **Invoke-MyService** functions in the bottom of the script, in that order. This will execute the script and mimic the behavior of the script as a service by first invoking the **Start-MyService** function that initializes the service (by setting the service required global variables etc.) and then invoking the **Invoke-MyService** function that starts the main service loop:

```
Start-MyService

Invoke-MyService
```

In PowerShell Studio, we have several options for running a script as you can see in *Figure 15.9* where we have different *Run* options:

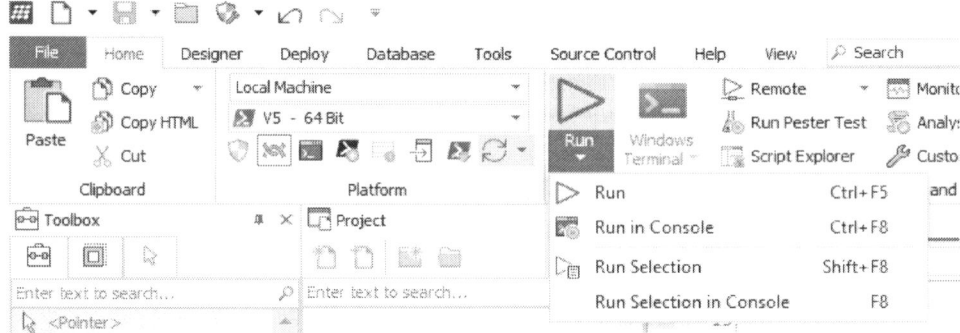

Figure 15.9: *Different Run script options*

Figure 15.10 shows the different **Run with Debugger** options:

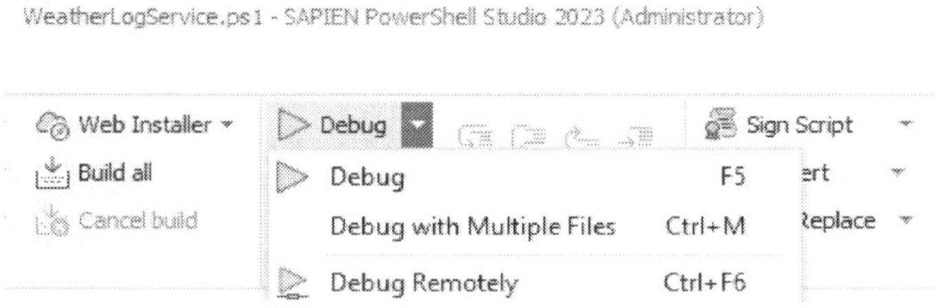

Figure 15.10: *Different Run script with Debugger options*

When we run the script, it should create the `C:\Temp\WeatherLog.json` log file and start adding the weather message data to the file (about) every 60 seconds. To check the content of the file, we can of course simply open it, or use `Get-Content` as shown in *Figure 15.11*:

```
PS C:\Temp> Get-Content .\WeatherLog.json
{"message":"The weather in Aarhus is overcast clouds with a temperature of 0,46 Celcius that feels like 0,46 Celcius
","timestamp":"09-01-2024 22:35:20,619","level":"INFO"}
{"message":"The weather in Aarhus is overcast clouds with a temperature of 0,46 Celcius that feels like 0,46 Celcius
","timestamp":"09-01-2024 22:36:20,669","level":"INFO"}
{"message":"The weather in Aarhus is overcast clouds with a temperature of 0,46 Celcius that feels like 0,46 Celcius
","timestamp":"09-01-2024 22:37:20,698","level":"INFO"}
{"message":"The weather in Aarhus is overcast clouds with a temperature of 0,46 Celcius that feels like 0,46 Celcius
","timestamp":"09-01-2024 22:38:20,744","level":"INFO"}
{"message":"The weather in Aarhus is overcast clouds with a temperature of 0,46 Celcius that feels like 0,46 Celcius
","timestamp":"09-01-2024 22:39:20,776","level":"INFO"}
{"message":"The weather in Aarhus is overcast clouds with a temperature of 0,46 Celcius that feels like 0,46 Celcius
","timestamp":"09-01-2024 22:40:20,818","level":"INFO"}
```

Figure 15.11: Output from the WeatherLog.json file confirming that the PowerShell Windows service work as expected

The log file is created, and the service script works as expected. We can stop the execution of the script in PowerShell Studio using the **Stop** button (or the *Shift + F5* shortcut). Now all we need to do is to compile the script into a service executable using the PowerShell Studio Packager feature and then install the service on a system.

> **Tip: Remember to remove the Start-MyService and Invoke-MyService functions from the bottom of the script before you compile it into a service executable.**

The Packager and Installer managers

Some of the most powerful features that SAPIEN PowerShell Studio offers are the Packager and the Installer managers.

The *Packager* enables you to compile and package not only your *regular* PowerShell scripts but also your GUI application scripts and your PowerShell Windows service scripts into executables. Depending on the type of scripts you want to package, you have the options to create a Command Line executable, a Windows application, a Windows form application, a Windows Tray app, a Windows service and more. You also have the option to select which platform your scripts should be packaged for, 32-bit, 64-bit or even both and there is an option for packaging scripts for the ARM64 platform. You can also choose if your scripts should be packaged with script engines for Windows PowerShell (5.x) or different versions of PowerShell (7.x + PowerShell Core). You have the option to restrict you application executable to different versions of Windows operating systems from Windows 2000 and Windows Server 2003 to Windows 10 and Windows Server 2016 and you can restrict it further to only be allowed to be executed on machines with specific names, MAC addresses and to a specific domain. You can also ensure that only one instance of your application is allowed to be running at once. You can also generate and include a .config file, create and embed a manifest, specify the context and credentials the executable should be executed with, signing the executable with a code signing certificate, specify the icon for the executable, add metadata such as file and product version which can be set to auto-increment and more. The Packager offers a lot of options and possibilities for creating executables from your PowerShell scripts that are suited for your specific requirements. *Figure 15.12* shows the Packager and the Script Engine selection pane:

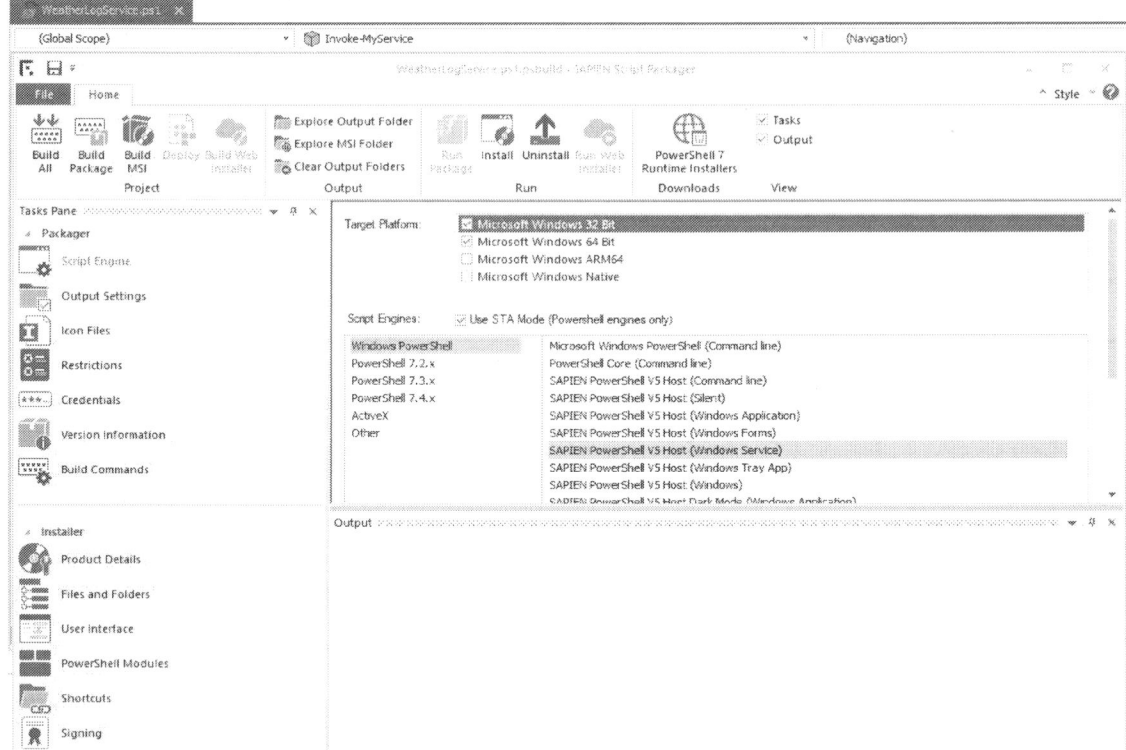

Figure 15.12: The SAPIEN PowerShell Studio Packager and its Script Engine selection pane

> **Note: Not all types of application executables are available for all versions of PowerShell. As an example, only the Windows PowerShell engine enables you to create PowerShell Windows service executables. SAPIEN is constantly developing, updating and adding features to PowerShell Studio expanding its available features. Also note that not all packaged scripts will be packaged as a single executable. Packaging scripts with a PowerShell 7.x engine might add additional dependency files.**

The Installer enables you to create installers from your executables. This allows you to easily distribute and install your scripts and applications executables and their associated files. You can create installers with no user interface or create installers with user interfaces from a selection of different templates such as a minimal interface with a welcome and exit dialogue to a more advanced installer user interface that also includes license agreements, an install folder selection browser, a top banner, and a background image. You can include

PowerShell modules, to ensure that all dependency modules are installed on the targeted system, you can include shortcuts for your executable on the desktop, in the start menu and in the startup folder and you can include custom actions that must occur at both installation and uninstallation of your executable application. It could be a script that must be executed after uninstallation to perform additional system cleanup or the opening of a config file that must be configured directly after installation and so on. You can also sign your installer using a code signing certificate. When you create an installer for a PowerShell Windows service executable you can specify the service details such as the service name, display name and the service description. You can also specify the context and credentials the service should be running as, and you can specify if the service should be started or stopped directly after installation.

Newer versions of PowerShell Studio also include a Web Installer builder, that enables you to create simple web installers for your application executables. This allows you to create installers that provide a more dynamic method of distributing your applications and ensures that users always get the most up-to-date version of the application without having to re-download and re-distribute your installer whenever a new version is required. It is important to note that while web installers offer various benefits, they may not be suitable for all scenarios such as in environments with limited or no internet connectivity. *Figure 15.13* shows the Installer manager and the Production Details pane:

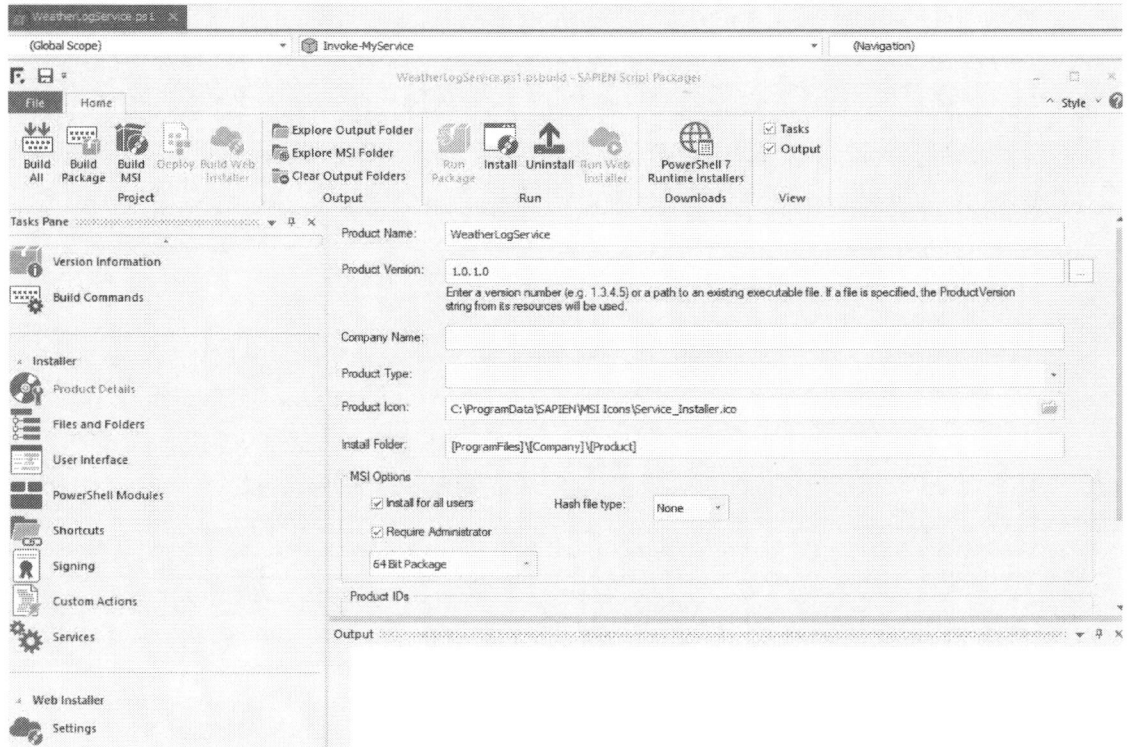

Figure 15.13: The *SAPIEN PowerShell Studio Installer and its Product Details selection pane*

The Packager and the Installer are very powerful tools when you want to compile your scripts into executables and distribute them. Compiling scripts into executables offers several advantages. Executables are often standalone files that consolidates all necessary files and dependencies into a single executable file which can be easily distributed and offers portability and ease of execution for your end users which makes your scripts more user-friendly compared to relying on the opening of a PowerShell console and manually running scripts. Note that packaging some scripts, especially when using the PowerShell 7.x engines for compilation, might add additional dependency files to an executable. It is also easier to integrate executables into other systems or processes that require the execution of external programs. It offers a form of security that helps protect the source code from direct inspection, as an executable is not directly human-readable. While this does not provide absolute security, it adds a layer of obfuscation, making it more challenging for unauthorized users to understand or modify the code. Packaging an executable into an Installer provides several benefits, especially when distributing software to end-users such as providing a user-friendly and standardized way to install your executable applications, providing dependency management that ensures that your application runs correctly on the targeted systems. It also allows the users to customize some aspects of the installation, such as specifying the installation directory and to choose specific features and capabilities, if available and provided by the Installer. It also offers creation of different shortcuts that allows the users to easily access and open your application and it typically includes an uninstaller that cleanly removes the application and all its components from the system.

Recipe 94: Compiling scripts into executables

To create an executable from your script application, select the **Packager Settings** in the **Deploy** pane, shown in *Figure 15.14*. This is also where you start the Installer (and Web Installer) manager:

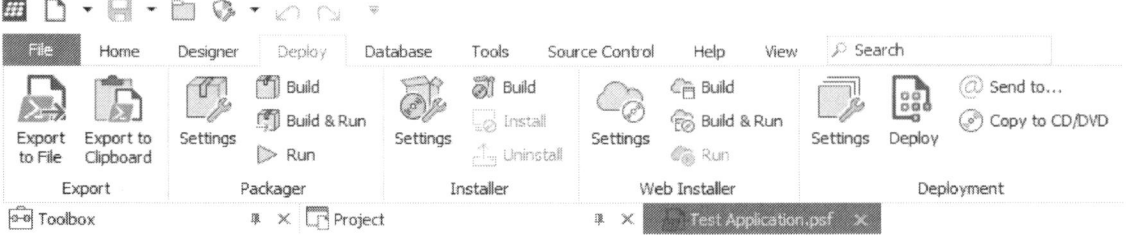

Figure 15.14: The Deploy pane enables you to start the Packager and Installer manager

The Settings button is where you open and configure the Packager (and Installer). If you have already configured these once, you can use the *Build* button to quickly start a build with the last saved configured settings.

When you configure the Packager to create an executable from your scripts, the type of executable and the type of the Packager script engine depends on the type of script application you are creating. For a PowerShell Windows service you would choose the

SAPIEN PowerShell V5 Host (Windows Service) engine and for a GUI application you can choose the SAPIEN PowerShell 7.4.0 Host (Windows Form) engine and so on. The engines are quite self-explanatory and depending on the template preset you have created your script with, the Packager will by default choose the most appropriate engine for your type of script application.

Note: The Windows PowerShell script engines require .NET Framework 4.8 and script engines for PowerShell 7.x requires .NET Core 8.0. If you want to deploy PowerShell 7 packaged executables where the installed PowerShell version does not potentially match the packager target, a runtime for that specific version might be required. You can download such runtimes directly from the Packager manager.

Once you have selected an engine, go through each pane in the Packager section and configure the packaged executable to your requirements. In the *Output Settings* pane, it is enough to just specify the application file name, and the output folder, both of which are pre-filled. The application name is automatically derived from the name of your script file and the output folder defaults to a *bin* directory which will be created as a sub-directory in the root folder where your script file is stored. The output folder is where the Packager saves your compiled file(s). It creates a subfolder in the *bin* directory depending on the target platform. For 32-bit the sub-folder will be called *x86* and for 64-bit the sub-folder will be called *x64*. In the *Output* Settings pane, you also have the option for generating a config file, embedding a manifest, specifying the user context and credentials and for selecting a code signing certificate for signing your compiled packaged executable. In the *Icon Files* pane is where you can select an icon file to use for your packaged executable. In the *Restriction* pane is where you specify the restrictions for your packaged executable. Should it only be able to run on Windows Server 2016 operating systems, does it require the target machine to have a specific MAC address, does it require a specific username (such as Administrator), is it only allowed to run a single instance at a time and so on. In the *Credentials* pane you can add stored credentials to your packaged executable. The Version Information pane is where you specify meta-data such as the product name, description, copyright information and the file and product version of your script application.

Once all the required and the optional Packager settings for your script application have been configured, your start the compilation build using the *Build Package* button in the *Project* menu section. The Packager manager includes an Output pane where you can follow the build process. Once the build has completed, it will also show any potential build errors and warnings. *Figure 15.15* shows the Package manager and the Output pane of a successful build:

Figure 15.15: *The Packager manager showing a successful build in the Output pane*

Also note the **Output** and the **Run** menu sections. These allows you to easily open the packaged executable and the installer output folders, and also easily lets you execute (Run Package) the last build executable and Run the last build MSI installer (Install) including running an uninstallation of the MSI installer afterwards (Uninstall). Exploring the output folder, you can see the newly compiled executable is created as an .exe file as expected. *Figure 15.16* shows the executable in the output folder, the execution of the application and the meta-data details for the executable file:

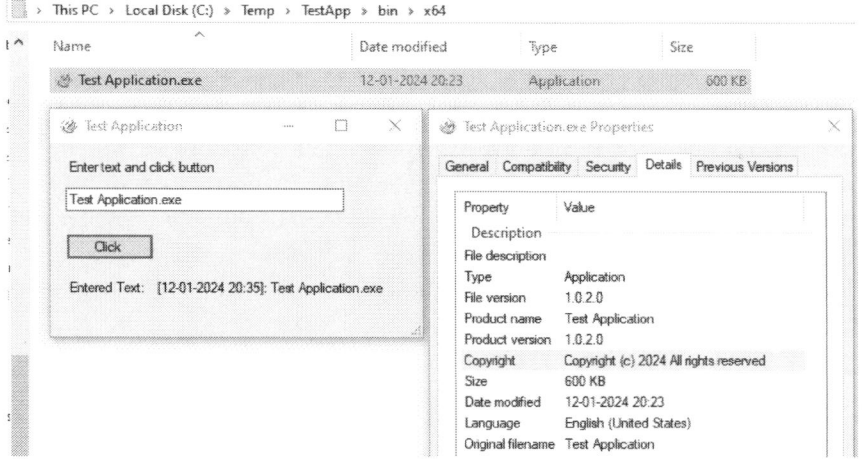

Figure 15.16: *The compiled executable file in the output folder,*
the execution of the application and its details

When you close the Packager (and Installer) manager, you will be prompted to save your build settings. This is preferred and will save the configured manager settings to a SAPIEN Script Packager file in the root directory of your script application. Next time you open your script application for making changes and updates, you simply need to re-build your application using the *Build* button in the Packager section. Unless of course you need to re-configure some Packager settings.

If you compile a PowerShell Windows service executable using the Packager manager, notice that the executable file is not directly executable as shown in *Figure 15.17*:

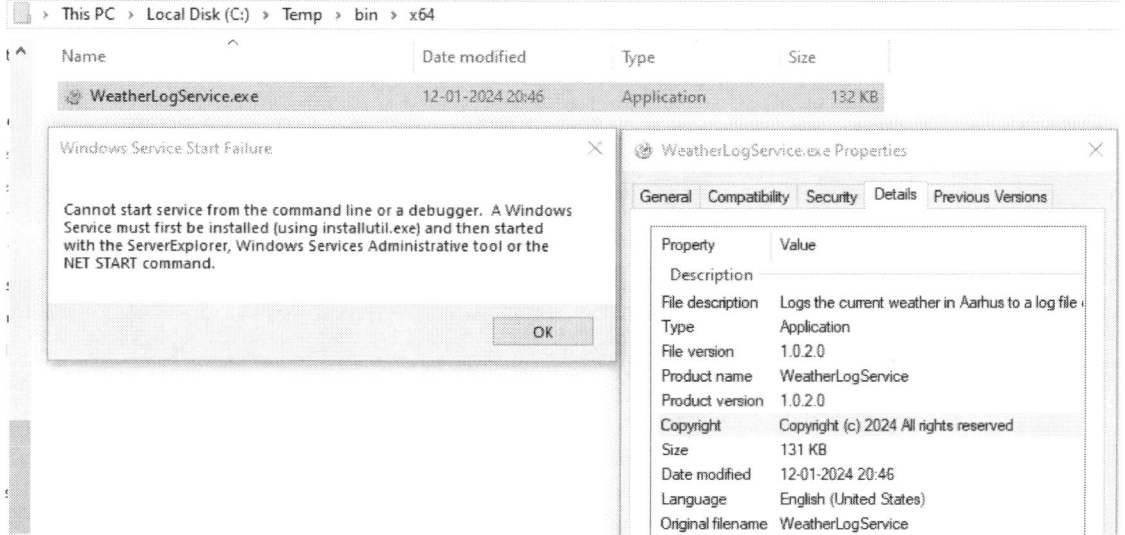

Figure 15.17: *Failed to directly run a PowerShell Windows service executable*

There are several methods for registering a PowerShell Windows service executable as a Windows service, besides using the Install manager to create a Service MSI installer. You can use the **New-Service** cmdlet, to register the service or you can use the *sc.exe* CMD service control manager application. Besides these, the PowerShell Windows service executable comes with its own built-in parameters for installing (registering) and removing (un-registering) the executable as a service. As you can see in *Figure 15.18*, we use the **-install** parameter to register (install) the executable as a service, and we use the **-uninstall** parameter to un-register (removing) it as a service. Note that this will create some install log files which might come in handy if you encounter any errors using this method for registering/un-registering the executable as a service:

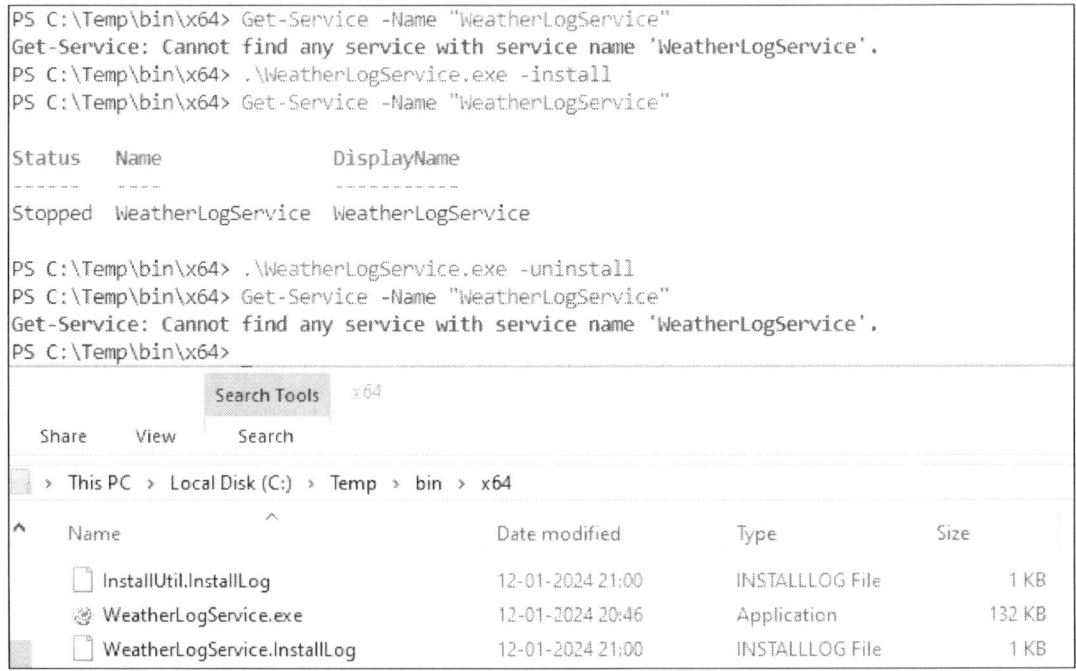

Figure 15.18: Using the PowerShell Windows service executable built-in
parameters for registering/un-registering as a Windows service

Note: For registering and un-registering an executable as a Windows service, you need to run in an elevated shell. If you should encounter any errors or for some reason the executable is not registering as a service as expected, refer to the InstallLog files for more details.

Recipe 95: Creating MSI installers for executables

Once you have an executable (or compiled executable with dependency files) whether it is for a GUI application or a PowerShell Windows service, you can of course just leave it at that and distribute and use it as it is. But why not take it one step further and package your executable into an installer. For GUI application installers you can provide shortcuts to your application, include license agreements, and make sure custom actions are performed after installation and it automatically also includes an uninstaller. For PowerShell Windows service executable installers, you can greatly simplify the service installation process for your Windows service application. To create an MSI installer from your executable, select the **Installer Settings** in the **Deploy** pane (shown previously in *Figure 15.14*). In the Product Details pane, you must fill out the following: The product name (this is derived from the name of the script file). The product version. For this you can point to the existing executable of your application. The product version string from the executable resources is then used. This is particularly handy if you use the auto-increment versioning when compiling your executable, which ensures that the installer use the same version as the executable, even if it auto-increments. You should also specify a company name. This is used as a variable for the install folder property. If your company name is **MyCompany**, the default install folder will be **[ProgramFiles]\MyCompany\[Product]** where product is then the name of the application as in the product name field. You must also specify a product type, which for GUI application executables and PowerShell Windows service executables must be *Windows Application*. Notice that the install folder property use variables as placeholders for referencing other properties. Refer to the official SAPIEN PowerShell Studio documentation for a list of all available variables. You can also change the default icon for the installer with your own custom icon and you can set additional MSI options such as if the installation should be for all users, if it requires administrator privileges and so on. *Figure 15.19* shows the Installer manager and the Product Details pane:

Figure 15.19: *The Installer manager and the Product Details pane*

In the **Files and Folders** pane is where you select all files and folders that should be included in the installer. If you have a single executable, this is of course the only file that you should include. But you can also include dependency files, configuration files and other files and folders that should be installed along with your application. You can also specify the MSI installer name, which defaults to the name of the executable, and you can specify an output folder where the installer should be created. This defaults to the root folder of the selected executable. In the *User Interface* pane is where you configure the user interface for your installer. If you create an installer for a PowerShell Windows service executable you might not require a user interface at all or for an advanced GUI application you might want a user interface with a welcome dialogue, a license agreement, the option of selecting the installation folder and an exit dialogue. You can also add a license agreement and set a top banner and a background for your installer. Within the *PowerShell Modules* pane, you can add dependency modules if required by your application. This helps to ensure that custom modules are installed on the system. In the *Shortcuts* pane, you can choose to add shortcuts to your application in different locations. By default, it will create a shortcut for your application in the **Start Menu | Programs | [Company]** directory. You can add additional shortcuts to the desktop and the startup folders. In the Signing pane, you can sign your installer and the individual files that are added to your installer with a code signing certificate. In the *Custom Actions* pane, you can add actions that must occur upon certain events both when the installer but also when the uninstaller for the application is executed. You might need to perform some specific actions if an installation fails, or you might need to execute an additional clean-up script that removes custom registry keys upon uninstallation and so on. The last pane is the *Services* pane. The setting in this pane is only applicable if you are building an installer for a PowerShell Windows service executable. If you are building an installer for a GUI application executable or other type of executable, you can disregard these settings. In this pane you would have to specify the different service properties and the path to the service file, which is the service executable that was added in the **Files and Folders** pane.

Note: You can add multiple executables and create multiple Windows services in a single installer.

You will also have to specify service parameters, such as the start type of the service and the user context it must run in, which defaults to the **LocalSystem** account. You can also specify if the service should be started immediately after installation. If your service requires additional settings to be configured in a configuration file or you need additional system configuration etc. before your service can run without issues, it is recommended to make sure the service is not started after installation, or else it might fail to start anyways. This all depends on the specific requirements for your Windows service. *Figure 15.20* shows the settings in the *Services* pane when creating an installer for the **WeatherLogService** service executable:

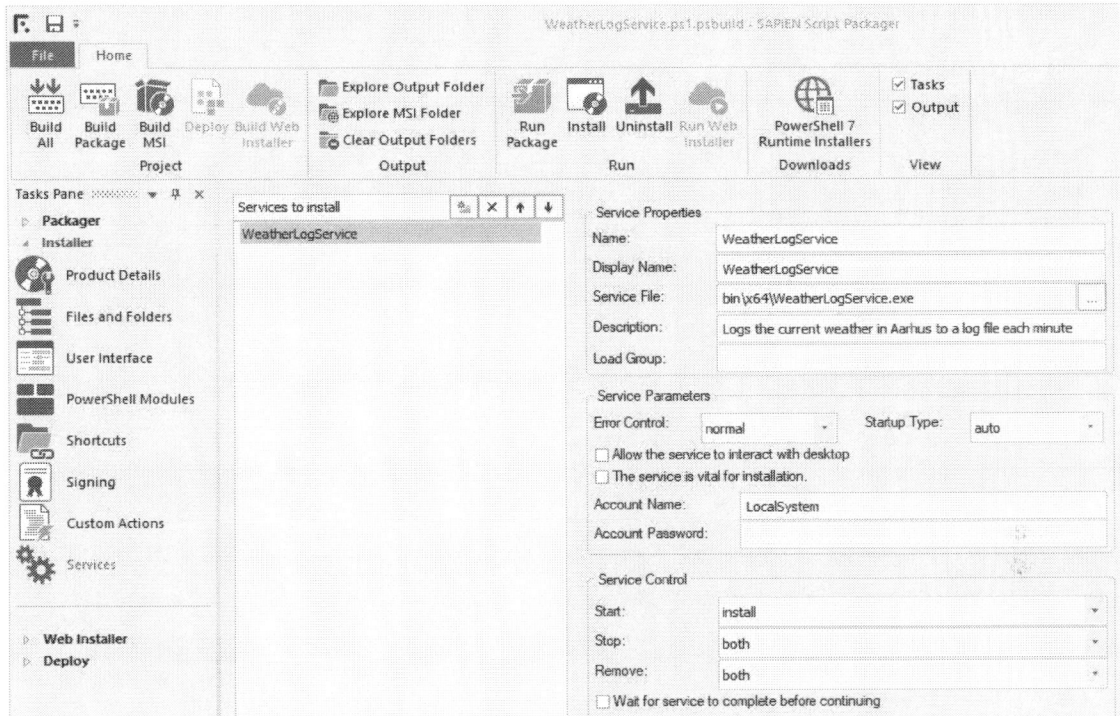

Figure 15.20: *The Installer Services pane when creating an installer*
for the WeatherLogServices service executable

Once all the settings for the Installer are configured, you start the Installer build process using the *Build MSI* button in the *Project* menu pane. The build process will be shown in the Output pane as shown in *Figure 15.21*:

```
Output
  SAPIEN Package and Deploy Tool 4.8 (c) 2005 - 2023 SAPIEN Technologies, Inc.

  Retrieving product version from C:\Temp\bin\x64\WeatherLogService.exe: 1.0.2.0
  Processing input files...
  Processing settings...
  Building MSI file...
  MSI file C:\Temp\WeatherLogService.msi created.

  0 error(s), 0 warning(s)
```

Figure 15.21: *The output from the Installer build process*

In *Figure 15.22* we use the **Get-ChildItem** cmdlet to verify that the **WeatherLogService. msi** file is indeed created and exists. After the execution of the Installer, we can see that the service is installed, registered as a Windows service and is in the running state. The figure also shows the Windows Apps and Features page where the service is also referenced including an uninstaller:

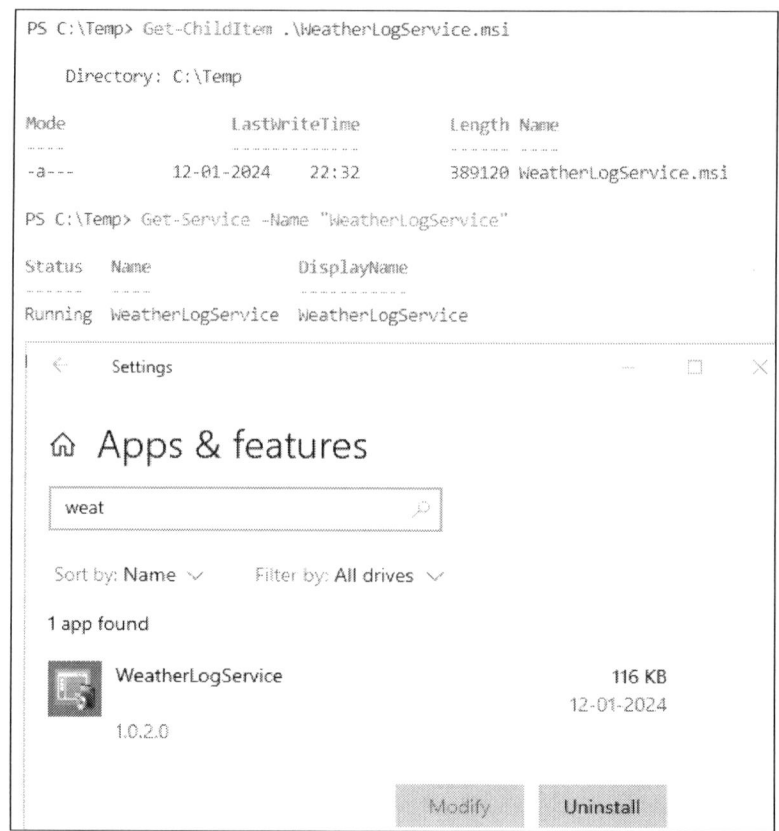

Figure 15.22: The WeatherLogService.msi file, the successful installation and
registration of the service and the Windows Apps & features showing the included uninstaller

Figure 15.23 shows that the PowerShell Windows Service executable is successfully installed
in the folder specified in the *Install Folder* property in the Installer managers *Product
Details* pane. It also shows the Windows service properties for the WeatherLogService,
which confirms that the path to the service executable is indeed the WeatherLogService
executable as expected:

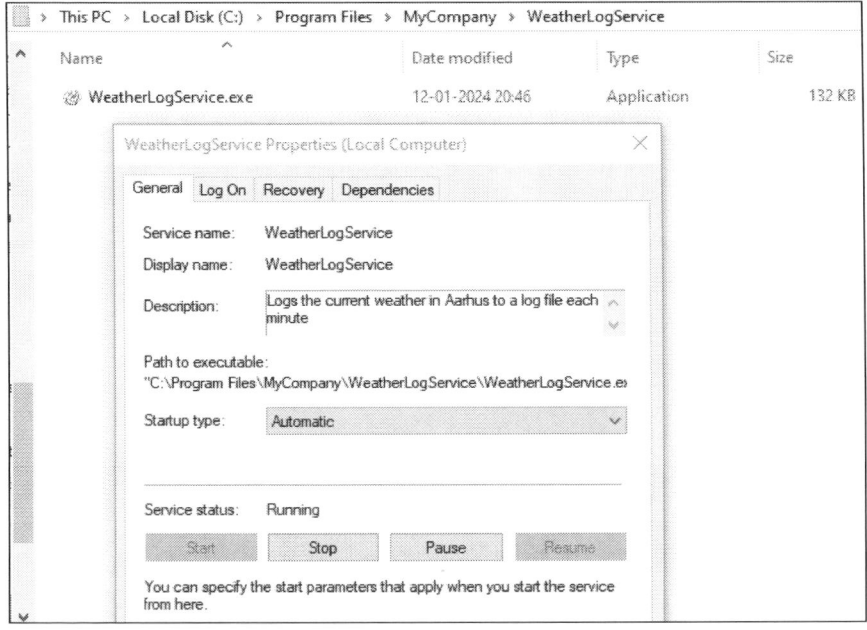

Figure 15.23: *The service executable in the expected install path and the Windows service properties for the WeatherLogService*

More applications from SAPIEN

PowerShell Studio is not the only software for PowerShell that SAPIEN offers, and they also offer a few tools for managing other types of software such as an SQL query development tool and an XML files management tool. Besides the PowerShell Studio IDE that is specialized for PowerShell they also offer a more general IDE for all your administrative and web-development tasks. The following is a list with descriptions about some of the tools offered by SAPIEN:

- **PowerShell Studio:** This is the PowerShell specialized IDE that enables you to create GUI applications and Windows services from your PowerShell scripts. It also offers a package manager that allow you to create executables from your PowerShell scripts and applications, and it offers an installer that allows you to build installers from your executables.

- **PrimalScript:** This is a general scripting IDE for administrative and web-development tasks. This allows you to work with multiple technologies, languages, and file formats at the same time besides PowerShell. It supports more than 50 languages and file types.

- **PowerShell ModuleManager:** The PowerShell `ModuleManager` is a tool that enables you to manage all your PowerShell modules on your machine. It allows you to see module information, release notes, version information and more. You can search repositories such as the PowerShell Gallery or custom repositories, for specific modules and install and manage them directly using this manager.

- **PowerShell HelpWriter:** Is a tool that allows you to professionally write and edit PowerShell help files for all command types including cmdlets, functions, workflows and CIM commands. It also allows you to generate help files from modules by analyzing the module and generating starter help files for the modules code.

- **CIM Explorer:** The CIM explorer is a tool for exploring the Windows Management Instrumentation database. This is used for representing a repository of the CIM classes available to you. It also generates CIM class code that you can easily copy to your scripts or execute directly.

- **VersionRecall:** Is a PowerShell script versioning and backup tool that allows you to save multiple versions of your scripts to remote locations which enables you to restore and go back to previous versions if needed. You can enable PowerShell Studio to automatically submit changes when you save your code and also customize schedules that enables VersionRecall to "check in" you code at pre-determined intervals.

- **PrimalSQL:** Is a tool that allows you to connect to almost any types of database including Microsoft SQL, Oracle, PostgreSQL and more. It allows you to build and test complex database queries and generate code snippets for a variety of languages. It also provides access to shared database connections with PowerShell Studio that can be used in your PowerShell scripts and applications.

- **PrimalXML:** Is a tool that simplifies XML file management, and it is specifically designed to create, edit, and manipulate XML files. It also provides XML syntax coloring, autocompletion and it allows you to validate XML against schema files and more.

Note: SAPIEN also offers a DevOps Suite that includes all these tools in one license.

Besides these advanced and specialized tools, SAPIEN offers a few smaller free tools:

- **PrimalPad:** Is a single file, color coding editor for VBScript, JScript, HTML, C++, C#, SQL and PowerShell.

- **PowerShell Profile Editor:** Is a dedicated tool for managing and editing your PowerShell profiles.

- **PowerShell Help:** Is a repository database that contains all PowerShell help files for your cmdlets, aliases and more.

- **PowerRegEx:** Is a Regular Expression build tool that also easily allows you to export your regular expressions for PowerShell use.

Conclusion

An IDE is the most powerful tool in a developer's toolbox and selecting the right one can sometimes be difficult because some IDEs offers features that others don't and not all are specialized for a particular language. SAPIEN have tried to provide a PowerShell specialized IDE that offers everything you need for working with not only general PowerShell scripts but also by including features that enables you to create powerful GUI applications and Windows services from your PowerShell scripts. It enables you to also compile your scripts and applications into executables and create installers for these executables. SAPIEN PowerShell Studio is more than that, and in this chapter, we have only provided a general introduction to some of its most powerful features and capabilities. The best way to learn how to use this powerful IDE in detail, is to start using it and refer to the official PowerShell Studio documentation and use the concept of **learning by doing**.

Choosing the correct IDE for you is a matter of your personal preferences and requirements. For general scripting purposes an IDE such as VS Code with the PowerShell extension is enough but if you really want to elevate your scipting and development capabilities and create advanced GUI applications, Windows services and executables from your scripts and create installers for your executables, an IDE such as SAPIEN PowerShell Studio might be the right choice for you. Start exploring SAPIEN PowerShell Studio here: **https://www.sapien.com/**.

Join our book's Discord space

Join the book's Discord Workspace for Latest updates, Offers, Tech happenings around the world, New Release and Sessions with the Authors:

https://discord.bpbonline.com

Index

Printed in Great Britain
by Amazon

51901035R00379